MUSICIANS
AND THE LAW
IN CANADA

A Guide to the Law, Contracts and Practice in the Canadian Music Business

Third Revised Edition

Edited by

PAUL SANDERSON, LL.B.
of the Ontario Bar

Research by

RONALD N. HIER, B.A., LL.B., LL.M.
of the Ontario Bar

Contributing Authors:
(listed alphabetically and by chapter)

David L.P. Garson, LL.B., Toby Susan Goldbach, B.A., LL.B., and
Christopher N. Taylor, B.A., LL.B., Chapter 7
Ronald N. Hier, B.A., LL.B., LL.M., Chapters 1, 2, 4, 5, 10, 11, 12
D. Blair Holder, LL.B., Chapters 6, 8
Robert H. Nakano, B.A.Sc., and Frank Farfan, B.Eng., LL.B., Chapter 9
C. Craig Parks, B.A., LL.B., Chapter 3

CARSWELL
Thomson Professional Publishing

Canadian Cataloguing in Publication Data

Sanderson, Paul, 1954-
    Musicians and the law in Canada : a guide to the law, contracts and practice in the Canadian music business

3rd rev. ed.
Previous editions written by Paul Sanderson.
Includes index.
ISBN 0-459-23937-6

1. Musicians - Legal status, laws, etc. - Canada. 2. Music trade - Law and legislation - Canada. 3. Music - Publishing - Law and legislation - Canada. 4. Copyright - Music - Canada. I. Sanderson, Paul 1954-   .
II. Hier, Ronald N. III. Garson, David L.P.

KE3986.M8S22 2000   343.71'07878   C99-932693-7
KF4291.S35 2000

CARSWELL
Thomson Professional Publishing

One Corporate Plaza, 2075 Kennedy Road, Scarborough, Ontario M1T 3V4
Customer Service
Toronto 1-416-609-3800
Elsewhere in Canada/U.S. 1-800-387-5164
Fax 1-416-298-5094

To Cassandra and Jesse

Imagine... always.

ACKNOWLEDGEMENTS

Contributing authors and research

Thanks to all contributing authors, Frank Farfan, David L. P. Garson, Toby Susan Goldbach, Ronald N. Hier, D. Blair Holder, C. Craig Parks, Robert H. Nakano, Christopher N. Taylor, and in particular, Ronald N. Hier, for his contributing author and researching services.

Comments on chapters

David Basskin, Claudette Fortier, Marian Hebb, Ronald N. Hier, Edwin Komen, Len Lytwyn, Heather Ostertag, C. Craig Parks, David Sanderson, Paul Spurgeon, G. Ken Thompson, Michael Wright.

Word processing assistance

Kim Lundrigan-Bettencourt and Karolina Przygocka

Personal

Thanks to the musicians who continue to pour their dreams and lives into music and provide inspiration. I wish you every success.

PREFACE

What is the law that affects musicians in their music business affairs? This third edition, as with the two previous editions, tries to answer that question. In doing so, it presents an overview of the law, contracts, and the legal aspects of musicians' business affairs in the Canadian music business. "Music business affairs" means those activities from which musicians earn income. These activities are specifically outlined in Chapter 12, Tax. The term "musician" includes all types of musicians, composers and recording artists unless the context dictates otherwise. The term "composer" includes writers, songwriters, authors and lyricists of musical compositions unless the context dictates otherwise.

This third edition is the result of substantial revision and updating, by the accredited contributing authors, of my second edition of this book, which was published in 1992. Since that time the *Copyright Act* has been substantially revised and numerous technological and other changes have had an impact on the Canadian music business. Such changes precipitated this third edition and are addressed in the relevant chapters in this text. However, the full impact of digital technology, the Internet and e-commerce on the music business, and the legal and contractual aspects thereof, has yet to be determined.

This book is subdivided into three main sections: 1) the law affecting composers and music publishing, chapters 1-4; 2) the law affecting performers and recording musicians, chapters 5-9; and 3) the legal aspects of musicians' business affairs generally including contracts, business and tax, chapters 10-12. In practice, such areas often intersect and, therefore, the chapters of this book are extensively cross-referenced, through footnotes and in the text, in order to indicate to the reader how the different legal aspects of a musician's business interrelate.

Note that although Chapter 9 has been renamed in the Table of Contents it is still referenced throughout the book, for the sake of simplicity, as Chapter 9, Merchandising.

Since the specific focus of this book is on the law affecting musicians, general Canadian commercial law cases, for example, largely have been excluded. So too have proposed revisions of the law, since they can be highly speculative in nature. However, laws and references from other countries, most notably the United States, are cited for illustrative and comparative purposes, but this is not to imply that they necessarily will be followed in Canada. Quebec law is not referenced in any depth. The emphasis of this book is on common law, not Quebec civil law. However, one should be aware in particular of the distinct laws that affect personal service contracts in Quebec and in particular the effect of the Status of the Artist legislation outlined in Chapter 5.

Specific music business contracts are analyzed paragraph by paragraph and extensive comments regarding negotiation of contract provisions are made. This is done with the knowledge that although every paragraph of an agreement neither can, nor necessarily should be negotiated in practice, one should be aware of the legal implications of each provision in an agreement. Much of the discussion of these agreements is, of course, based on the experience and reflects the opinion of the respective contributing author.

In view of the complexities faced by those dealing with contracts in the music business, it is highly advisable, when negotiating or drafting such agreements, that a detailed checklist be consulted. Sample checklists are included in the appendices. It is hoped that they will assist in the negotiation and drafting of the music business agreements discussed in the text. As well, it is advisable to keep in mind, when drafting or negotiating these agreements, the complex legal doctrines such as restraint of trade, inequality of bargaining power, undue influence and unconscionability which are discussed in Chapter 10, and the tax, business and intellectual property aspects of a musician's business affairs which provide the general legal framework in which a musician's business affairs are situated. These are discussed in Chapters 12, 11, 1 and 9 respectively.

To understand fully the legal problems of musicians in the music business, one needs to understand the music business and its practices. With this in mind, business texts and other source materials are cited in the footnotes and the music business practices in relation to specific legal areas are outlined in the text.

Consistent with the second edition of this book, music business precedents, which can be found in numerous precedent books elsewhere, are not included.

As with the previous editions of this book, the hope is that this third edition will provide a better understanding of the law which affects musicians in their music business affairs. The third edition of this book tries to state the law as of January 1, 2000.

Paul Sanderson, Editor

TABLE OF CONTENTS

CHAPTER 2: THE LICENSING AND ADMINISTRATION OF COPYRIGHT AND THE REGULATION OF MUSIC IN MEDIA

CHAPTER 3: MUSIC PUBLISHING

CHAPTER 4: COPYRIGHT INFRINGEMENT

CHAPTER 6: AGENTS AND MANAGERS

CHAPTER 7: LIVE PERFORMANCE

CHAPTER 8: RECORDING

CHAPTER 9: NAMES, TRADE-MARKS, LICENSING AND MERCHANDISING

CHAPTER 10: PERSONAL SERVICE CONTRACTS

CHAPTER 12: TAX

APPENDICES

TABLE OF CASES

1

COPYRIGHT

Contributing Author: Ronald N. Hier, B.A., LL.B., LL.M.

Introduction

Copyright law is the basis for many of the rights musicians can acquire. It is, therefore, an appropriate beginning to a consideration of the law affecting musicians, particularly if the musician is a composer.[1] Musicians who are composers, by definition, are fundamentally concerned with musical works.[2] Therefore, to discuss the rights subsisting in music and acquired with respect to music is primarily to discuss copyright.

This chapter outlines the Canadian law of copyright, both generally and as it applies in relation to musical works and sound recordings. Also examined are the moral rights of authors and neighbouring rights which, as a result of recent amendments to the *Copyright Act* have now gained statutory recognition in Canada.[3]

---

[1] For the sake of simplicity, 'composer' as used throughout this book includes lyricists, composers, songwriters and writers. These are common terms in the music business. Note that the rights of composers as 'authors' within the *Copyright Act* are analytically distinct from those of "performers" although it is not uncommon for one musician to be both composer and performer.

[2] The term 'musical work' is a term of art defined by s. 2 of the *Copyright Act*; see note 24, infra.

[3] 'Neighbouring rights' include certain rights of performers in their performances, of the makers of sound recordings in their recordings, and of broadcasters in telecommunication signals. Although such rights have been recognized internationally by treaty (see, for example, the 1971 version of the *Berne Convention for the Protection of Literary and Artistic Works* and the 1961 *Rome Convention on the Protection of Performers, Producers of Phonograms and Broadcasting Organisations*), these rights have only recently been incorporated into Canadian law (see *An Act to Amend the Copyright Act*, S.C. 1997, c. 24 assented to April 25, 1997).

1. Basis and Scope

(a) Outlined

Copyright is commonly referred to as a bundle of rights and although this is true, it is a vague description. An examination of the characteristics of this bundle of rights is essential to gain an understanding of copyright.

(i) Major Characteristics

The following are the major characteristics of copyright:

(1) The basis of copyright is statutory. Copyright is the sum total of all the rights conferred by the *Copyright Act* [4] (herein "the Act").

(2) Copyright is an incorporeal form of property, a product of the mind which is recognized as intellectual property.[5]

(3) Copyright is exclusive; it confers the sole right to do or authorize others to do the acts set out in the Act. However, the monopoly granted to the copyright holder is limited[6] and his/her rights are subject to statutory restrictions.

(4) Copyright is divisible; the various rights comprising the bundle of rights that is copyright can be parcelled off and separately dealt with as to time, territory or use.

(5) Copyright is inherent in the work.[7] Thus, no further act on the part of the author is required to secure his/her rights under the Act, for example, registration of the copyright.

---

[4] R.S.C. 1985 c. C-42.

[5] Other forms of intellectual property rights include trademark, patent, industrial design rights and trade secrets. Trademarks are discussed in Chapter 9, "Merchandising". For a discussion of whether Canadian copyright is a monopoly only, or based on a broader concept of property, see R.J. Roberts, "Canadian Copyright: Natural Property or Mere Monopoly" (1979), 40 C.P.R. (2d) 33 and Keyes And Brunet, "A Rejoinder to Canadian Copyright: Natural Property or Mere Monopoly" (1979), 40 C.P.R. (2) 54.

[6] *Hanfstaengl v. Empire Palace*, [1894] 3 Ch. 109 (Eng. C.A.)

[7] The term 'work' is not defined in the Act other than to say that it "includes the title thereof when such title is original and distinctive"; (see definition, s. 2 of the Act). However the Act grants protection, *inter alia*, to "every original literary, dramatic, musical, and artistic work" (s. 5(1)) all of which are defined terms. Notwithstanding the above, judicial opinion has construed the term "work" to include records; *Fly By Nite Music Co. v. Record Wherehouse Ltd.*, [1975] F.C. 386; 20 C.P.R. (2d) 263 (Fed. T.D.). This case is also authority for the proposition (at p. 269) that a work is "everything in which the Act says

(ii) Economic Copyrights

The rights of authors may be considered under two complementary aspects: (1) those rights which allow authors to exploit the economic value of their works; and (2) rights with respect to disclosure, withdrawal, paternity, and integrity of the work.[8] Copyright in the common law world is concerned primarily with the former.

Specifically with respect to music, copyright consists of the following economic rights:

(1) the sole right to produce or reproduce the work or any substantial part of it in any material form or, if unpublished, to publish the work or any substantial part thereof;[9] (2) to produce, reproduce, perform or publish a translation of the work;[10] (3) to convert it into a dramatic work by way of public performance or otherwise;[11] (4) to make any sound recording, cinematographic film or other contrivance by means of which the work may be mechanically reproduced or performed;[12] (5) to reproduce, adapt and publicly present the work as a cinematographic work;[13] (6) to communicate the work to the public by telecommunication;[14] (7) to rent out a sound recording in which the work is embodied;[15] and finally (8) to authorize any such acts.[16]

---

copyright shall subsist be that thing a product of the arts or a product of manufacture and technology."

[8] The rights enumerated under (2) are the moral rights of authors. In Canada, only the paternity and integrity rights have gained statutory protection.

[9] Preamble to s. 3(1) of the Act.

[10] Paragraph 3(1)(a) of the Act.

[11] Paragraph 3(1)(c) of the Act.

[12] Paragraph 3(1)(d) of the Act.

[13] Paragraph 3(1)(e) of the Act.

[14] Paragraph 3(1)(f) of the Act. "Telecommunication" is defined in s. 2 to mean "any transmission of signs, signals, writing, images or sounds or intelligence of any nature by wire, radio, visual, optical or other electromagnetic system". Paragraph 3(1)(f) was implemented by the *Canada-United States Free Trade Implementation Act*, S.C. 1988, c. 65, ss. 61-65; see Ysolde Gendreau, "A Canadian Retransmission Right: A Reality At Last", 4 I.P.J. 397 for a discussion of this right; see also Peter Grant's article in *Entertainment, Advertising and Media Law*, (Toronto: Law Society of Upper Canada, 1989), chapter H. This paragraph has been the source of much confusion in its application to the transmission of musical works by television networks to their affiliates and by cable companies through non-broadcast signals to their subscribers; see the decisions in *CTV Television Network Ltd. v. Canada (Copyright Board)* (1990), 30 C.P.R. (3d) 262 (Fed. T.D.), affirmed (1993), 46 C.P.R. (3d) 343 (Fed. C.A.), leave to appeal to S.C.C. refused (1993), 51 C.P.R. (3d) v (S.C.C.) and *Canadian Cable Television Assn. v. Canada (Copyright Board)* (1991), 34 C.P.R. (3d) 521 (Fed. T.D.), affirmed [1993] 2 F.C. 138 (Fed. C.A.), leave to appeal to S.C.C. refused (1993), 51 C.P.R. (3d) v (S.C.C.) wherein the Federal Court, on a close reading of the Act, determined that musical works were not performed "to the public" because a graphical representation is incapable of performance. The recently amended definition of "musical work" (*An Act to Amend the Copyright Act*, S.C. 1993, c. 23) apparently would now preclude such a result although the matter is not entirely free from doubt; see

(b) Acquiring Copyright

The Act prescribes certain conditions which must be met before copyright can subsist in a work.

(i) Qualified Persons

The author, at the date of the making of the work, must be a citizen, subject of, or a person ordinarily resident in a treaty country.[17] Treaty countries are defined as "a Berne Convention country, UCC country or WTO Member". Additionally, the Act provides that countries which grant by treaty, convention, agreement or law to citizens of Canada the benefit of copyright on substantially the same basis as to its own citizens shall be treated as if they are countries to which the Act extends; therefore citizens of such countries are entitled to copyright protection in Canada.[18] Most countries are signatory to either the Universal Copyright Convention or the Berne Convention, or both, as is the case with Canada.[19]

(ii) Originality

Copyright exists only in original works. To be original a work must be "the result of a substantial degree of skill, industry or experience" and cannot be copied from another.[20] It is not the originality of the idea that is protected in copyright, but the originality of the form of expression.[21]

Ysolde Gendreau , "Recent Developments in Canadian Copyright Law", (1993-94) J. Copyright Society of the U.S.A. 183 at pp. 186-88.

[15] Paragraph 3(1)(i) of the Act.

[16] Post-amble to s. 3(1) of the Act.

[17] Paragraph 5(1)(a). See also paragraphs 5(1)(b)-(c) which provide alternate grounds for cinematographic works and published works, respectively, and ss. 5(1.01) through 5(1.2).

[18] Paragraph 5(2) of the Act.

[19] See below for more on the *Berne Convention for the Protection of Literary and Artistic Works 1886*, as revised Paris 1896, Berlin 1908, Rome 1928, Paris 1971 (herein "Berne Convention") and the *Universal Copyright Convention of 1955* (herein "Universal Copyright Convention") concerning copyright registration. Some countries are also signatory to the *Buenos Aires Convention*.

[20] *L.B. (Plastics) Ltd. v. Swish Products Ltd.*, [1979] R.P.C. 551 (U.K. H.L.); *Ladbroke (Football) Ltd. v. William Hill (Football) Ltd.*, [1964] 1 All E. R. 465 (U.K. H.L.) at p. 478, see also the discussion in Chapter 4, "Copyright Infringement".

[21] *University of London Press v. University Tutorial Press Ltd.*, [1916] 2 Ch. 601 (Eng. Ch. Div.). See discussion below on fixation. It is possible to acquire copyright in an

(iii) Fixation

The term "fixation", common in the music business, appears nowhere in the *Copyright Act*, yet it is clear that a work must be fixed in order to achieve protection. This result follows from the combined action of section 2 and subsection 5(1) of the Act. Section 2 states that "every original, literary, dramatic, musical and artistic work includes every original production in the literary, scientific or artistic domain, whatever may be the mode or form of its expression". By subsection 5(1) it is these works in which copyright subsists. Thus, a work must be in some material form capable of identification, and having a more or less permanent endurance.[22]

Formerly, fixation of a musical work could only be achieved by a graphic reduction to writing.[23] This is no longer the case. Composers can now simply tape-record their music.[24] Of course, transcriptions, which are commonly made by music publishers of the music they own or control, will also qualify as fixations for the purposes of the Act.

(c) Registration

(i) Canada

A. Generally

A copyright owner need not register copyright to acquire copyright protection. However, there are reasons to register copyright: (1) registration is an aid to establishing copyright ownership;[25] (2) it

---

arrangement by arranging a work in the public domain, for example, if the requisite degree of originality is met. Public domain is discussed below section 2(c)(i).

[22]Harold Fox, *The Canadian Law of Copyright and Industrial Designs* 2d ed. (Toronto: Carswell, 1967) (herein "Fox") citing *Canadian Admiral Corp. v. Rediffusion Inc.*, [1954] Ex. C.R. 382, 20 C.P.R. 75 (Can. Ex. Ct.) at 140 (C.P.R.). It should be noted, however, that 'fixation' is not required to gain protection with respect to performer's performances under para. 15(1)(a); additionally, a sound recording first published in a country referred to in para. 18(1)(a) of the Act will gain protection irrespective of where the sound recording was first fixed.

[23] This followed from the definition of "musical work" as "any combination of melody and harmony, or either of them, printed, reduced to writing or otherwise graphically produced or reproduced." This definition was repealed as part of Phase III of copyright reform.

[24] "Musical work" is now defined as "any work of music or musical composition, with or without words, and includes any compilation thereof"; see s. 2 of the Act.

[25] Pursuant to s. 53(1) of the Act, "a copy of an entry in the Register [of Copyrights] is evidence of the particulars of the entry" and by s. 53(2) a certificate of registration "is

constitutes notice to an infringer;[26] and (3) when a work is registered, the certificate of registration can be used as evidence in court.[27]

A certificate of registration is evidence, albeit rebuttable, that copyright subsists in such work and the person who registered is the owner of the copyright.[28]

Any assignment of copyright or grant of an interest by way of licence may be registered.[29]

Registration may be made by the copyright owner or his/her authorized agent or legal representative,[30] and may be effected with respect to either published or unpublished works.

Several compositions may be registered at the same time by registering them as part of a compilation. To register, one must complete an application made in accordance with the relevant section of the Act[31] and send it to the Commissioner of Patents in Hull, Quebec with the current registration fee.

---

evidence that the copyright subsists and that the person registered is the owner of the copyright". See also s. 53(2.1) and s. 53(2.2) for assignees and licensees, respectively, and s-s. 53(3) with respect to the admissibility of certified copies.

[26] Pursuant to s. 39(1) of the Act, a defendant who proves that at the date of the infringement he/she was unaware copyright subsisted in the work can deprive the plaintiff of any remedy other than an injunction. However, s. 39(2) states that s. 39(1) does not apply if the copyright was duly registered at the date of the infringement. Therefore, the plaintiff who registers has all available remedies. See also *Clarke Irwin & Co. v. C. Cole & Co.*, [1960] O.R. 117 (Ont. H.C.).

[27] See note 25 supra. Section 58 prescribes rules for the admissibility of assignments and licences. See also *Anglo-Canadian Music Publishers' Association (Ontario) v. Winnifrith Brothers*, (1885) Vol. XV, The Ontario Reports 165, for a case involving affidavit evidence that was used to establish copyright ownership.

[28] See note 25 supra. See also *Grignon v. Roussel* (1991), 38 C.P.R. (3d) 4, 44 F.T.R. 121. (Fed. T.D.). In this case, where copyright registration occurred after the alleged infringement, the plaintiff had to prove copyright ownership, and was not entitled to the presumptions under the Act that (a) the registrant owned the musical composition; and (b) that copyright subsists in the work. The copyright registration system in this respect favours early registration.

[29] S. 57(1) of the Act.

[30] S. 55(1) of the Act. See also s. 56(1) for copyright in subject matter other than works, i.e., sound recordings, performer's performances and communication signals. Note that where a person purports to have authority to apply on behalf of a third party, any damage caused by a fraudulent or erroneous assumption of such authority is recoverable; see s. 56.1.

[31] The relevant sections are s. 55(2) of the Act for works and s. 56(2) of the Act for subject matter other than works, s. 5(1) of the *Copyright Regulations*, SOR/97-457. The regulation also prescribes the fees applicable and sets out rules, *inter alia*, regarding facsimile transmission, the type of paper to be used in correspondence, and the registration of assignments and licences.

B. Problems with the Registration System

The registration system has deficiencies. The applicant provides only limited information, *viz.*, the name and address of the copyright owner, a declaration of the applicant's status (author/owner/assignee/licensee), the category and title of the work, the name of the author, and if published, the date and place of first publication. There is no public notice of an application for, or the registration of, copyright. Moreover, since the system is voluntary, few copyrights are registered.

Lastly, there is no requirement to deposit the work being registered; in fact, deposit of a work is not permitted. Inaccuracies in the register can be rectified on application to the Federal Court by any interested person.[32]

The U.S. copyright registration system is significantly different from the Canadian system. Below is a brief outline of the U.S. Copyright registration system.

(ii) Note on U.S. Law

Effective March 1, 1989, the *Berne Convention Implementation Act of 1988* (herein "BCIA") came into force.[33] The BCIA amended the U.S. *Copyright Act*[34] to make it compatible with the Berne Convention. The effect of the BCIA was to increase protection available to copyright works, specifically as follows: (1) it eliminated the formality of registering works originating outside of the U.S. prior to bringing an infringement action in the U.S.; (2) it eliminated the requirement of affixing copyright notice from the date of first publication which formerly had been required in order to obtain copyright protection; and (3) it eliminated the requirement to record transfers of ownership of copyright formally, prior to bringing a copyright infringement suit. Copyright registration is now only a condition for bringing suit for copyright infringement for U.S. works, not for works of foreign origin. All works, however, still must be registered in order to be eligible for statutory damages and attorney's fees.[35] Therefore, despite enactment of the BCIA, it is still prudent for Canadians to affix copyright notices

---

[32] S. 57(4) of the Act.

[33] John A. Baumgarten and Christopher A. Meyer, "Effects of U.S. Adherence to the Berne Convention", (1989) Vol. 10, No. 11 E.L.R., p. 3. See also C. Paul Spurgeon, "The United States Adherence to the Berne Convention: A Canadian Perspective", (1990) 31 C.P.R. (3rd) 417, at 422.

[34] Title 17 of the United States Code.

[35] 17 U.S.C. ss. 401-402.

and register their copyrights in the U.S. Copyright Office, Library of Congress[36].

A. Copyright Notices

For works created after January 1, 1978, copyright subsists in the work from the moment of creation, just as is the case under the Canadian system. Although the U.S. Act provides increased protection if a copyright notice is affixed to the work,[37] it is not a prerequisite to copyright protection. It is therefore advisable to use the copyright notice on all works and specifically on all unpublished works if more than a few copies are disseminated.

(1) Generally

Copyright notice consists of: (1) © or the equivalent, such as "copyright" or "copr"; (2) the name of the copyright owner; and (3) the year of the first publication, for example © Jane Musician 1992.[38]

(2) Sound Recordings

The copyright notice for sound recording consists of: (1) a P within a circle; (2) the name of the copyright owner of the sound recording; and (3) the year of first publication.[39] This type of notice may be placed on the surface of the phonorecord of a sound recording or on the phonorecord label or container,[40] and is often placed on both. Although this notice is not required in Canada, these notices are

---

[36] For other changes resulting from the BCIA see Spurgeon, "The U.S. Adherence to the Berne Convention", supra note 33, at pp. 429 - 430.

[37] In the absence of a copyright notice, the defence of innocence infringement is available and damages awarded in an infringement action may be reduced to nothing: Melville B. Nimmer, *Nimmer on Copyright*, (New York: Matthew Bender, 1990), loose-leaf, Vol. 4, Ch. 7, S. 7.02. See Chapter 4 for a discussion of innocent infringement in Canada. See also *Volunteer Lawyers for the Arts Musician's Guide to Copyright*, (New York: Charles Scribner & Sons, 1983), and C. Paul Spurgeon, "Copyright Law in the United States: How Does It Affect Canadian Composers, Lyricists, Publishers", Toronto: C.A.P.A.C., 1980.

[38] 17 U.S.C. s. 401(b).

[39] 17 U.S.C. s. 402(b).

[40] 17 U.S.C. s. 402(c). "Phonorecords" are defined in s. 101 to be material objects in which sounds other than those accompanying a motion picture or other audiovisual work are fixed by any method now known or hereafter developed, and accordingly include CDs and audiocassettes.

often used to give notice to copyright users and it is advisable to use such notices.[41]

B. Registration

Although U.S. registration is not a pre-condition to acquiring copyright protection in the U.S. for Canadian works, registration in the United States is desirable for the following reasons: (1) it is evidence, in the U.S., although rebuttable, of copyright validity; and (2) it is required in an infringement action if one seeks statutory damages or attorney's fees.[42] Copyright can be registered in published or unpublished works and a number of works can be registered at one time under a title that identifies the work as a compilation.[43] The appropriate application form and fee must be filed and a copy of the work may be deposited with the Copyright Office, Library of Congress. For works created on or after January 1, 1978, registration may take place any time during the subsistence of the copyright.[44]

C. Deposit

Subject to certain exemptions, the U.S. *Copyright Act* also requires the deposit within three months of publication in the United States of all published works.[45] The deposit system applies to all types of works; in the case of sound recordings, the phonorecord together with all visually perceptible material (e.g. album cover and liner notes) must be deposited. Records so deposited are available for the use of the Library of Congress. The deposit requirement is for the benefit of the Library of Congress and has no effect on copyright protection. However, failure to deposit such materials within the applicable period can result in a fine.[46]

---

[41] For more on copyright notices on sound recordings, see Chapter 8.

[42] Pursuant to 17 U.S.C. s. 412, no award of statutory damages or attorney's fees shall be made for an infringement commenced prior to the registration of an unpublished work. In the case of a published work, no award will be made for an infringement commenced after publication unless the copyright in the work is registered within three months of publication.

[43] VLA Musician's Guide, note 37 supra, at p. 32. The problem with this type of registration is that the individual works are not indexed and cross-referenced under the owner's name.

[44] 17 U.S.C. s. 408(a).

[45] 17 U.S.C. s. 407(a).

[46] 17 U.S.C. s. 407(d).

(d) Assignments and Licences

Assignments and licences are important because they are the primary means of generating income from copyrights in musical works.

An assignment results in a change of ownership of the copyright whereas a licence gives the right to do something which in the absence of such licence is unlawful.[47] Both an assignment and "a grant of an interest by licence" must be in writing to be valid.[48] It is a question of fact whether a licence or an assignment has been granted.[49]

The owner of the copyright may assign the copyright either wholly or in part and either generally or subject to limitation relating to territory, medium, sector of the market or other limitations relating to the scope of the assignment, and either for the whole term or any part thereof.[50] One may also grant any interest in the right by way of licence. Subsection 13(7) deems the grant of an exclusive licence to be the grant of an interest.

No grant or an interest or assignment is valid unless made in writing and signed by the owner of the right or his/her duly authorized agent.[51] Grants of an interest may be revocable or irrevocable.[52]

Assignments for works not yet created, but which are to be created in the future, create a right enforceable in equity.[53]

(e) Reversion

(i) Under the Act

Where the author of the work is the first owner of the copyright in the work, no assignment of the copyright or grant of an interest therein is operative to vest in the assignee or grantee any rights in the copyright beyond the expiration of twenty-five years from the death of the

---

[47] There are three types of licences: the exclusive licence, the sole licence, and the non-exclusive licence. An exclusive licence precludes the licensor and anyone else from doing any of the acts contemplated in the licence; under a sole licence the licensor is not so precluded; under a non-exclusive licence, the licensor is free to do the acts and free to license third parties to do them as well. For more on the rights of exclusive licensees, see David Vaver "The Exclusive Licence in Copyright", (1995) 9 I.P.J. 163.

[48] Subsection 13(4) of the Act.

[49] Ibid. See Fox, supra note 22 at pp. 290 - 291.

[50] Subsection 13(4) of the Act.

[51] Ibid.

[52] See Fox, cited above, note 22 at pp. 290, 291.

[53] Ward, Lock & Co. v. Long, [1906] 2 Ch. 550. Assignments of this kind are common in music publishing and recording contracts. The rights granted under such contracts are known as copyright in futuro.

author.[54] The purpose of this provision is to protect authors whose works achieve an increase in value not anticipated and bargained for at the time of the original grant. By statute, the reversionary interest in the copyright devolves on the personal representative as part of the author's estate and any agreement made by the author respecting the reversionary interest, except by will, is void. This restriction on the author's right to dispose of his/her interest probably does not apply to sound recordings;[55] nor does it apply to collective works.[56]

(ii) By Contract

Reversionary interests also may be created by contract. The reversion of rights in music publishing agreements and recording agreements is discussed in Chapter 3, "Music Publishing" and Chapter 8, "Recording," respectively.

(f) Minors

Subject to the rules which govern minors' contracts, minors can acquire and sell copyrights.[57]

---

[54] Subsection 14(1) of the Act. See also *Chappell & Co. v. Redwood Music Ltd.*, [1980] 2 All E.R. 817 (U.K. H.L.). Consider also reversion upon bankruptcy, discussed in Chapter 3, "Music Publishing".

[55] There are two questions that must be resolved in order to determine this issue: (1) does the word "work" in s. 14(1) encompass sound recordings; and (2) is the maker of a sound recording its author? As to (1) although the Federal Court, in *Fly by Night Music Co. v. Record Wherehouse Ltd.*, [1975] F.C. 386 (Fed. T.D.) held at p. 393-94 that "the word "work" as used in the *Copyright Act* includes each and every thing in which the Act says copyright shall subsist..." which would seem to include sound recordings, copyright in which subsists by virtue of s. 18(1), this case was decided prior to the Phase II amendments. With regard to (2) if the maker is not the "author", s. 14(1) cannot apply, since s. 24 deems the maker of a sound recording to be first owner of the copyright. In this regard, there is judicial authority for the proposition that the author of a film is its screenwriter/director, who is also first owner of the copyright in the absence of any agreement to the contrary; see *Films Rachel Inc. v. Druker*, infra, note 162. In the recording industry, the directorial ("authorial"?) function is usually fulfilled by the record's producer, although it seems unlikely that a producer would thereby be regarded as "maker" under the Act. English copyright law currently exempts sound recordings from reverter provisions; see *Copinger and Skone-James on Copyright*, (London: Sweet & Maxwell, 1999), vol. 1., p. 277, footnote 59. The question of the authorship of sound recordings is discussed in greater detail below.

[56] Subsection 14(2) of the Act.

[57] *Chaplin v. Leslie Frewin (Publishers) Ltd.*, [1965] 3 All E.R. 764 (Eng. C.A.). See Chapter 10, "Personal Service Contracts" for a discussion of minors' contracts.

(g) Moral Rights

Moral rights are the non-pecuniary rights that an author has in relation to his or her creation. These rights are independent of copyright and may not be assigned by an author notwithstanding any disposition of his/her interest in the copyright.[58] The *Copyright Act* recognizes two specific rights under the rubric of moral rights: (1) the paternity right and (2) the integrity right. These rights are discussed below.

(i) Paternity Right

The paternity right is the right to claim authorship of the work, that is, "where reasonable in the circumstances, to be associated with the work as its author by name or under a pseudonym and the right to remain anonymous."[59]

(ii) Integrity Right

The integrity right is the author's right to the integrity of the work.[60] This right is infringed only if the work, to the prejudice of the honour or reputation of the author is (1) distorted, mutilated or otherwise modified or (2) used in association with a product, service, cause or institution.[61]

(iii) Assignment and Waiver

Moral rights cannot be assigned; however, they can be waived either in whole or in part.[62] An assignment of copyright does not in and

---

[58] See s. 14.1(2) which provides that moral rights "may not be assigned".

[59] Subsection 14.1(1) of the Act.

[60] Ibid.

[61] Subsection 28.2(1) of the Act. The predecessor of this section, s.12(7) of the Act, has been questioned as to its constitutional validity; see *Snow v. Eaton Centre Ltd.* (1982), 70 C.P.R. (2d) 105 (Ont. H.C.). See also David Vaver "Snow v. The Eaton Centre: Wreaths on Sculpture Prove Accolade For Artist's Moral Rights", (1983) 8 Can. B.L.J. 81.

[62] Subsection 14.1(2) of the Act. *Quare* whether there are moral rights in sound recordings, performer's performances or communication signals. The *Fly By Nite* case, supra note 7, is authority for the proposition that a record is a work. Given the recent statutory recognition of neighbouring rights in Part II of the Act, it would seem incongruous to deny the creators of these works moral rights in their creations. The practice in the recording industry is to attempt to obtain waivers from artists (to the

of itself constitute a waiver.[63] Unless there is an indication to the contrary in the waiver, a waiver of moral rights can be invoked by any person authorized by the copyright owner or licensee to use the work.[64]

(iv) Infringement

Any act or omission, contrary to the moral rights of the author, if done without consent, is an infringement of moral rights.[65] The same remedies available for infringement of copyright, namely, an injunction, damages, accounts, and delivery up are available when moral rights are infringed.[66]

(v) Term of Protection

Moral rights exist for the term of copyright, pass on the death of the author to any person to whom they are specifically bequeathed, or in the absence of any bequest to the person to whom copyright is bequeathed and in any other case to the person entitled to any other property in respect of which the author dies intestate.[67]

---

extent that artists may be entitled to such rights) and such clauses are found in most recording agreements. See Chapter 3 for a discussion of moral rights in the context of music publishing.

[63] Subsection 14.1(3) of the Act.

[64] Subsection 14.1(4) of the Act.

[65] Section 28.1 of the Act. In the case of paintings, sculpture or engraving, s. 28.2(2) deems any distortion, mutilation or other modification of the work an infringement under s. 28.2(1); however s. 28.2(3) states that a change in location of the work, the physical means by which the work is exposed or the physical structure containing the work, or steps taken in good faith to restore the work, do not in themselves constitute a distortion, mutilation or modification of the work. In *Patsalas v. National Ballet of Canada* (1986), 13 C.P.R. (3rd) 522 (Ont. S.C.) a slight alteration to a computer work by a competent licensee, who was performing up to a high standard pursuant to the licence, was held not to be an unlawful use or alteration of the work. This case was decided prior to June 8, 1988, the date the Act was significantly amended concerning moral rights. See also *Nintendo of America Inc. v. Camerica Corp.* (1991), 34 C.P.R. (3d) 193 (Fed. T.D.), affirmed (1991), 36 C.P.R. (3d) 352 (Fed. C.A.).

[66] Subsection 34(2) of the Act.

[67] Section 14.2 of the Act.

(h) Other Aspects of Copyright

(i) Droit de Suite

"Droit de suite" is the right to receive compensation after the initial sale of an artistic work on subsequent sales of such works. Such compensation is often referred to as a "resale royalty". Droit de suite is not recognized in Canadian law. It is, however, recognized in some European countries (e.g. France) and in the State of California.[68] This right does not apply to musical works or sound recordings.

(ii) Public Lending Rights

Public lending rights compensate authors for the pecuniary loss arising from the free use of books in public libraries. Canadian authors receive payment for works published in Canada and found in public libraries, with the exception of certain genres, including books consisting mainly of musical scores. Payments to authors are distributed annually by the Public Lending Right Commission, pursuant to a federal government program. The public lending right, however, exists independently of and outside the protection granted authors under the *Copyright Act.*[69]

(iii) Exemption for "Ephemeral" Recordings

"Ephemeral" recordings are recordings made by broadcasters to facilitate the transmission of programs at a later date. In the *Michael Bishop* case,[70] the Supreme Court of Canada held that the making of a videotape on which a vocalist performed a song written by Michael Bishop, intended to be used in a later broadcast and subsequently destroyed, violated the writer's reproduction right notwithstanding that the broadcaster had paid all required performance royalties. Recent amendments to the *Copyright Act* have provided for a limited exception to the holding in the *Bishop* case. Subsection 30.8(1) exempts, *inter alia,*

---

[68] See *California Civil Code,* s. 986 which provides for a minimum 5% royalty on the subsequent sale of works of "fine art". See also S.S. Ashley, "Critical Comment on California Droit de Suite", (1977) 29 Hastings L.J. 249 at pp. 249-260.

[69] For a discussion of public lending rights in the context of the Act, see Keyes and Brunet, *Copyright in Canada: Proposals for a Revision of the Law* (Ottawa: Consumer and Corporate Affairs, 1977) at p. 22.

[70] (1990), 31 C.P.R. (3d) 394 (S.C.C.).

the reproduction by a "programming undertaking"[71] of a performer's performances or works performed live, or a sound recording performed at the same time as the performer's performance if the reproduction is made for the programming undertaking's own use and the broadcaster is authorized to do so. A similar exemption is available for "broadcast undertakings"[72] which reproduce sound recordings or performer's performances solely for the purpose of transferring them to formats appropriate for broadcasting.[73] However, the exemption does not apply if a licence is available from a collective society to make the reproduction.[74]

(iv) Neighbouring Rights

Neighbouring rights are the performance rights performers have in their performances, the makers of sound recordings have in their recordings, and broadcasters have in the communication signals they broadcast.[75] Part II of the Act provides explicit statutory recognition of these rights. Moreover, performers and record producers are given copyright in their performances and sound recordings.[76] These rights will be considered below.

A. Performer's Performances

Part II of the Act extends copyright protection to "performer's performances". Such performances include both the performance of a musical work and the improvisation of a musical work. It is immaterial

---

[71]This term is defined in s. 2(1) of the *Broadcasting Act*, S.C. 1991, c. 11 and refers to television and radio stations.

[72] Subsection 30.9(1) of the Act. The term "broadcast undertakings", also defined in the *Broadcasting Act* include "networks", "distribution undertakings" and "programming undertakings".

[73] The exemption further requires that the reproduction must be destroyed within thirty days of the making thereof unless the copyright owner authorizes retention and receives a royalty; see generally, ss. 30.8 and 30.9 of the Act.

[74] Subsection 30.8(b) of the Act.

[75] These rights form the subject of the 1961 *Rome Convention on the Protection of Performers, Producers of Phonograms and Broadcasting Organisations;* see also the *WIPO Performances and Phonograms Treaty (1996)*.

[76] Although records were formerly given copyright protection by s. 5(3) (repealed by S.C. 1997, c. 24) the rights of record producers have been considerably enhanced under Part II of the Act; see also the *WIPO Performances and Phonograms Treaty (1996)* and in particular, Articles 11-14.

whether copyright in the musical work has expired or the improvisation is based on a pre-existing musical work.[77]

If the performance is live (i.e., it is not yet fixed), performers are given the sole right (1) to communicate it to the public by telecommunication, (2) to perform it in public by telecommunication (otherwise than by communication signal) and (3) to fix it in any material form and to authorize these acts.[78] If the performance is recorded (i.e., fixed), performers are given the sole right (1) to reproduce any fixation made without their consent, (2) if authorized, to reproduce any reproduction of the fixation if the reproduction was made for any purpose other than that for which the authorization was given, and (3) if the fixation was permitted, to reproduce any unauthorized fixation of the permitted fixation.[79] Lastly, performers now have the sole right to rent out sound recordings of their performances.[80]

The above rights are subject to the following conditions: either the performer's performance (1) takes place in Canada or a Rome Convention country; (2) is fixed by a Canadian citizen, permanent resident or corporation headquartered in Canada or a citizen, resident or corporation headquartered in a Rome Convention country; or (3) if live, is transmitted by a broadcast signal from Canada or a Rome Convention country by a broadcaster having its headquarters in the country of broadcast.[81]

---

[77] See definition of "performer's performance" in s. 2 of the Act.

[78] Paragraph 15(1)(a) of the Act. Note that the rights contained within this paragraph cannot be exercised where the performer authorizes the embodiment of his performance in a "prescribed" cinematographic work; see s. 17(1) of the Act; the Cinematographic Works (Right to Remuneration) Regulations, SOR/99-194, prescribe films funded by the CFDC or other government agency, Canadian programs recognized as such by the CRTC, and Canadian film or video productions certified under the *Income Tax Act*. Note further that where there is an agreement providing for "residuals", s. 17(2) gives a right of action against the other party to the agreement, the copyright owner of the film, and their respective assignees.

[79] Paragraph 15(1)(b) of the Act. This provision would appear to outlaw the manufacture of bootleg recordings. Bootlegs come in two forms: (1) the unauthorized recording of live concerts; and (2) the illicit distribution of copies of unreleased studio recordings. The former practice would run afoul of sub-para. 15(1)(b)(i); the latter, of sub-para. 15(1)(b)(iii). For more on bootlegs, generally, see Derrick Oldford, "Out From The Underground: A Survey of "Bootleg" Sound Recordings And Their Status Within Selected Copyright Law Regimes", (1997), 70 C.P.R. (3d) 129; David Schwartz, "Strange Fixation: Bootleg Sound Recordings Enjoy the Benefits of Improving Technology", *1995-96 Entertainment, Publishing and the Arts Handbook*, (New York: Clark, Boardman, Callaghan), p. 351.

[80] Paragraph 15(1)(c) of the Act.

[81] Subsection 15(2) of the Act.

The rights expire fifty years after the end of the calendar year in which the performer's performance was first fixed in a sound recording, or if not so fixed, in which the performance occurred.[82]

B. Sound Recordings

The maker of a sound recording is given copyright in the recording and has the sole right (1) to publish it for the first time; (2) to reproduce it in any material form; and (3) to rent it out.[83] Sound recordings include recordings fixed in any material form exclusive of motion picture soundtracks actually accompanying a film.[84] The maker of a sound recording is the person by whom the arrangements necessary for the first fixation of the sounds are undertaken.[85]

Again, these rights are subject to the condition that either (1) the maker of the recording must be a Canadian citizen, permanent resident, or a corporation headquartered in Canada or a citizen, permanent resident or corporation headquartered in a Berne, Rome, or WTO country at the date of the first fixation,[86] or (2) the first publication of the recording, in sufficient quantity to meets the demands of the public, occurred in any of the above countries.[87]

These rights expire fifty years after the end of the calendar year in which the sound recording's first fixation occurred.[88] Finally, where the sound recording has been published, both performer and maker are entitled to royalties for its public performance.[89] Royalties are payable to the appropriate collective society and are to be divided equally between the performer and maker of the sound recording.[90] This right has the same term — fifty years — as the rights discussed above.[91]

---

[82] Paragraph 23(1)(a) of the Act.

[83] Subsection 18(1) of the Act.

[84] See definition of "sound recording" in s. 2 of the Act.

[85] See definition of "maker" in s. 2 of the Act, paragraph (b). Presumably, this refers to the record company which provides financing for the recording, and not to the producer of the actual record; see infra, note 90.

[86] Paragraph 18(2)(a) of the Act.

[87] Paragraph 18(2)(b) of the Act.

[88] Paragraph 23(1)(b) of the Act.

[89] Subsection 19(1) of the Act.

[90] Subsections 19(2) and 19(3) of the Act. Note that by s. 20(1) royalties are only payable if the maker at the date of first fixation was a *Rome Convention* country or the fixation was made in such a country. The U.S. is not currently a party to this convention. Subsection 20(3) enacts a saving provision whereby a party to NAFTA can request the remuneration right for its nationals — but only in respect of recordings of literary and dramatic works. American performers will, however, obtain protection for musical performances rendered on or after January 1, 1996 pursuant to s. 26(1). This subsection grants to performers whose performances take place in *WTO* countries the sole right to communicate unfixed performances to the public by telecommunication, fix them in

C. Rights of Broadcasters

Broadcasters are now given copyright in their communication signals. This right includes (1) the sole right to fix such signals, (2) reproduce any unauthorized fixation and (3) in the case of television signals, to perform them in a place open to the public on payment of an entrance fee.[92] The broadcaster, at the time of the broadcast, must be headquartered in Canada, a Rome Convention or WTO country and the broadcast signal must originate therefrom.[93] These rights expire fifty years after the end of the calendar year in which the communication signal was broadcast.[94]

D. Generally

As with copyright in musical, dramatic, literary and musical works, the Act provides for reciprocity where a non-Rome Convention country provides substantially equivalent protection to neighbouring rights as are granted under the Act and permits national treatment to the performers, makers of sound recordings and broadcasters of such countries.[95] Moreover, a deeming provision provides protection where the fixation, performance or broadcast took place in a non-treaty country which subsequently becomes a treaty country.[96]

The Act deems the first owner of the copyright in a performer's performances to be the performer, in a sound recording the maker of the sound recording, and in a communication signal, the broadcaster.[97] The rights created in Part II of the Act may be assigned or licensed.[98] Finally, the royalties performers and makers of sound recordings can expect to realize upon the exercise of their Part II rights are in addition to and without prejudice to the rights in works conferred by Part I of the Act.[99]

---

sound recordings, and where a sound recording has been fixed without the performer's consent, to reproduce the fixation. See also s. 26(3) which accords the latter right with respect to performances occurring prior to January 1, 1996.

[91] Subsection 23(2) of the Act.

[92] Subsection 21(1) of the Act.

[93] Subsection 21(2) of the Act.

[94] Paragraph 23(1)(c) of the Act.

[95] Subsection 22(1) of the Act. See also s. 22(2) through (4).

[96] Subsection 23(4) of the Act. The subsection provides protection for any country acceding to either of the *Rome*, *Berne* or *WTO* treaties. See also, s. 23(5).

[97] Section 24 of the Act.

[98] Section 25 of the Act.

[99] Section 90 of the Act. Thus, the writers and publishers of musical works will not be forced to accept a reduction in their royalties to accommodate the new royalties accorded to performers and record companies.

(v) Blank Audiotape and Private Copying

Part VIII of the Act provides for the collection of a blank tape levy from the manufacturers of "blank audio recording medium".[100] The term "audio recording medium" is defined as a "recording medium, regardless of its material form, onto which a sound recording may be reproduced and that is of a kind ordinarily used by individual consumers for that purpose...".[101] The levy, which applies to every manufacturer or importer of blank tape,[102] requires payment of a royalty to the appropriate collecting body for dispersal to authors of musical works embodied in sound recordings[103], "eligible" makers of sound recordings and "eligible" performers.[104] The Act sets out a scheme whereby collective societies may apply to the Copyright Board for approval of a tariff. The board is empowered to set royalty rates and apportion the royalty among rights holders.[105] An exemption is provided for the sale of blank tapes to bodies representing persons with perceptual disabilities.[106] Collecting bodies may sue to recover royalties and the courts are empowered to award an amount up to five times the amount of the levy.[107] Home taping is exempt from claims of copyright infringement,[108] and lastly, the Act makes provision for reciprocal treatment of countries providing rights substantially equivalent to those provided in Part VIII.[109]

---

[100] A "blank audio recording medium" is defined as an audio recording medium on which no sounds have ever been fixed; see s. 79 of the Act.

[101] Ibid.

[102] Subsection 82(1) of the Act.

[103] These authors need not be Canadian. The only requirement is that copyright in their works subsist in Canada; see s. 79 of the Act.

[104] "Eligible" makers and performers are corporations headquartered in Canada, or Canadian citizens or permanent residents whose recordings or performances have copyright protection in Canada; see s. 79 of the Act. The right of remuneration is found in s. 81(1).

[105] See generally, s. 83 of the Act. For a description of the applicable tariff, see "Tariff of Levies to be Collected by CPCC in 1999 and 2000, for the Sale of Blank Audio Recording Media in Canada", a decision of the Copyright Board, released December 17, 1999, found at [1999] C.B.D. No. 8.

[106] Section 86 of the Act.

[107] Section 88 of the Act.

[108] Section 80 of the Act.

[109] Section 85 of the Act.

2. Musical Works

(a) A Discussion

In 1993, Parliament enacted a new definition of "musical work".[110] The former definition defined a musical work as "any combination of melody and harmony, or either of them printed, reduced to writing, or otherwise graphically produced or reproduced". This definition was unsatisfactory in two respects: (1) the requirement that the work be "graphically produced" was in conflict with obligations Canada accepted as a party to the Berne convention;[111] and (2) a literal reading of the definition resulted in judicial decisions which accepted the claim of cable companies and broadcasters that the telecommunication of musical works to the public fell outside the ambit of paragraph 3(1)(f) of the Act.[112]

The current definition defines a musical work to be "any work of music or musical composition, with or without words, and includes a compilation thereof". Notably absent from this definition is the requirement that the work be graphically produced. Therefore, one may argue that the deficiencies discussed above have now been corrected. It may be argued also that the new definition also permits musicians who contribute to the rhythmic aspect of a musical work, and who previously were not considered authors of musical works, to claim copyright with respect to their contribution.

(i) The Status of Songs under the Copyright Act

Both the current and former definitions of "musical work" speak of musical compositions "with or without words". Such language would appear broad enough to encompass songs.[113] Nevertheless, there has been considerable judicial uncertainty as to the exact status of these works perhaps owing to their bipartite nature. Different courts have

---

[110] For the recent legislative history of this provision and the motivation for its amendment, see Norman Tamaro, *The 1998 Annotated Copyright Act* (Toronto: Carswell, 1998), at pp. 93-96.

[111] Article 2(1) of the *Berne Convention* defines "every literary and artistic work" to include "every production in the literary, scientific and artistic domain whatever may be the mode of its expression, such as... musical compositions with or without words...".

[112] See *Canadian Cable Television Assn. v. Canada (Copyright Board)* (1993), 46 C.P.R. (3d) 359 (Fed. C.A.), leave to appeal to S.C.C. refused (1993), 51 C.P.R. (3d) v (S.C.C.); *CTV Television Network Ltd. v. Canada (Copyright Board)* (1993), 46 C.P.R. (3d) 343 (Fed. C.A.), leave to appeal to S.C.C. refused (1993), 51 C.P.R. (3d) v (S.C.C.).

[113] Former s. 2(v) stated that musical works include "musical works or compositions with or without words".

held that (1) a song authored by a single writer would be subject to copyright as a musical work;[114] (2) a song co-authored by two writers whose contributions to the work were indivisible would qualify as a musical work of joint authorship;[115] and (3) a song written by a lyricist and composer might possibly be the subject of two copyrights; one in the lyrics (a literary work), one in the music (a musical work).[116] It has been suggested also that songs might qualify as collective works under the Act, but absent special circumstances, this seems doubtful.[117] Perhaps the best that can be said is that songs are protected, with the form of protection depending on the process leading to their creation.

(ii) Song Titles

The *Copyright Act* provides that a "'work' includes the title thereof when such title is original and distinctive".[118] However, courts have been reluctant to provide more than general formulations as to what this statutory language might mean. In a seminal case, the Privy Council opined that "a title may... be on so extensive a scale and of so important a character as to be a proper subject of protection."[119] However, even if a title fails this test, use by a third party may be restrained under the law of passing-off.[120]

---

[114] *Compo Co. v. Blue Crest Music Inc.* (1979), [1980] 1 S.C.R. 357 (S.C.C.); see also *Fly By Nite Music Co. v. Record Wherehouse Ltd.*, [1975] F.C. 386 (Fed. T.D.).

[115] *ATV Music Publishing of Canada Ltd. v. Rogers Radio Broadcasting Ltd.* (1982), 35 O.R. (2d) 417 (Ont. H.C.); see also *Thibault v. Turcot* (1926), 34 R.L.N.S. 415 (Que. S.C.)

[116] *Ludlow Music Inc. v. Canint Music Corp.* (1967), 51 C.P.R. 278 (Can. Ex. Ct.)

[117] See *ATV Music Publishing*, supra note 115. Section 2 of the Act defines a "collective work" as "any work written in distinct parts by different authors, or in which works or parts of works of different authors are incorporated". However, for a song to qualify as a collective work, an original collocation or arrangement of its parts would have to be made; see *Chappell & Co. v. Redwood Music Ltd.*, [1980] 2 All E.R. 817 (U.K. H.L.) A simple joining of words and music is not an original collocation and it seems that in this case, the composer and lyricist each should be entitled to a separate copyright in respect of their entirely separate contributions to the finished work.

[118] Section 2 of the Act.

[119] *Francis, Day & Hunter Ltd. v. Twentieth Century Fox Corp.*, [1939] 4 D.L.R. 353 (Eng. P.C.); see also *King Features Syndicate Inc. v. Lechter*, [1950] Ex. C.R. 297 (Can. Ex. Ct.) which held the title "Popeye" original and distinctive on the basis that it was a coined term.

[120] See *Flamand v. Societe Radio-Canada* (1967), 53 C.P.R. 217 (Que. S.C.) For more on the protection of titles, see Reuben Stone, "Copyright Protection for Titles, Character Names and Catch-phrases in the Film and Television Industry", [1996] 5 Ent. L.R. 178.

(b) Ownership

(i) Generally

As noted above, a song is the marriage of music and lyrics. Where both are the product of a single imagination, initial ownership of the copyright resides in one author.[121] Many songs, however, are the result of a collaboration, typically between a lyricist and composer. Such works will qualify as works of joint authorship if the contribution of one author is not distinct from that of the other author or authors.[122] Where the contributions are distinct, there will be two separate copyrights; a copyright in the lyrics (a literary work) held by the lyricist, and a copyright in the music (a musical work) held by the composer.[123] Legally, composers of joint works cannot exercise their rights independently of each other[124] although in practice, licences are often granted without the consent of both composers.

---

[121] Subsection 13(1) of the Act provides, subject to certain exceptions, that the author of a work is the first owner of the copyright therein. For a discussion of the term "author", see Barry Torno, *Ownership of Copyright in Canada*, (Ottawa: Minister of Supply and Services, 1981), pp. 1 and 6. It appears that the term "author" was left undefined to allow flexibility in its definition with respect to the domestic, political, social, cultural and economic policies of states signatory to the Berne Convention. Some states define authors only as natural persons, while others define authors to include legal entities such as corporations, which is the case in Canada. See also Barry B. Sookman, "Computer Assisted Creation of Works Protected by Copyright", (1989) 5 I.P.J. 165 at p. 17 for a discussion of this issue in relation to music created in whole or in part with the use of computers. The exceptions to the general principle are discussed as they arise in the text below.

[122] See the definition of "work of joint authorship" in s. 2 of the Act. In *Levy v. Rutley* (1871), 24 L.T. N.S. 621 (Common Pleas), a case decided prior to the enactment of the statutory definition, the court held that joint authorship requires joint labour in carrying out a common design. The court also held that the amount of labour contributed by each author need not be equal. In the recently decided *Neudorf v. Nettwerk Productions*, [1999] B.C.J. No. 2831 (B.C.S.C.), the court stated the test for joint authorship as follows: (1) did the plaintiff contribute significant original expression to the songs? If yes, (2) did each of the plaintiff and defendant intend that their contributions be merged into a unitary whole? If yes, (3) did each of the plaintiff and the defendant intend the other to be a joint author of the songs? The test in *Neudorf*, largely derived from *Childress v. Taylor*, 945 F.2d 500 (2d Cir. 1991), which requires proof of a common intention on the part of songwriters to co-author a work, would appear to depart from previous Anglo-Canadian law in this area. Note that co-owners of copyright in a work of joint authorship hold the copyright as tenants-in-common and not as joint tenants. Thus, either author can bequeath his/her interest in the work to his or her estate.

[123] See *Ludlow*, supra, note 116.

[124] *Cescinsky v. Routledge and Sons Ltd.*, [1916] 2 K.B. 325.

(ii) Compilations

A compilation is a work "resulting from the selection or arrangement of literary ... [or] ... musical ... works or parts thereof".[125] Compilations are entitled to copyright in and of themselves as a species of collective work.[126] The copyright subsisting in such works is independent of the copyrights subsisting in the works that make up the compilation. Moreover, the inclusion in a compilation of works in the public domain will not serve to revive their copyright, for the copyright in the compilation resides in the arrangement of the works contained therein. An example of a compilation is a song folio,[127] which pursuant to section 2 of the Act may be protected as a musical work.

(iii) Contractual Relationships

A. Commissioned Works

When music is commissioned, it can be an issue whether the commissioner of the work or its author is the copyright owner. If the composer is under a "contract of service or apprenticeship and the work was made in the course of his employment by that person, the person by whom the author was employed shall, in the absence of any agreement to the contrary, be the first owner of the copyright."[128] The term "contract of service" as used in the Act must be distinguished from a "contract for services" as these terms are understood at common law.[129] Since it is always advantageous for the author to retain copyright, the composer should strive to ensure that the commission agreement contains an "agreement to the contrary".[130]

---

[125] Section 2 of the Act.

[126] See Tamaro, supra note 110 at p. 43. Of course, this presumes that the author of the compilation has created a work that is in some sense original; see *Slumber-Magic Adjustable Bed Co. v. Sleep-King Adjustable Bed Co.* (1984), 3 C.P.R. (3d) 81 (B.C. S.C.)

[127] Song folios are collections of songs; they may feature the works of an individual composer or be thematically organized collections of the works of various composers.

[128] Subsection 13(3) of the Act.

[129] See Chapter 12 for a discussion of these terms.

[130] See *Copinger and Skone-James on Copyright*, (London: Sweet & Maxwell, 1999), vol. 1, para. 5-24, for a discussion of what is an agreement to the contrary. Generally, an agreement may be written, oral, or implied from the circumstances. See, for example, *University of London Press v. University Tutorial Press*, [1916] 2 Ch. 601, where a contract of service was found to create a master/servant relationship. Commission agreements for motion picture and television scores normally require the composer, an independent contractor, to assign his/her copyright, and/or are structured as "work for hire" agreements. Jingle writers, who are in-house employees of advertising agencies or jingle

B. Crown Works

Where "any work is, or has been, prepared or published by or under the direction or control of Her Majesty or any governmental department, the copyright in the work shall, subject to any agreement with the author, belong to Her Majesty".[131] Composers who have contracted with the Crown often contract to retain their copyright, and license to the Crown only those rights necessary for the Crown's purposes concerning the work involved.

(iv) Derivative and Infringing Works

A. Derivative Works

A derivative work is a work based on a pre-existing work. Although the Act does not define the term "derivative work", it is clear that any such work meeting the standard of originality required by the Act may gain copyright protection.[132] However, because creation of a derivative work necessitates the reproduction of all or a substantial part of a pre-existing work, the author of a derivative work must obtain the consent of the owner of the work from which the subsequent work is derived unless the pre-existing work has fallen into the public domain.[133]

---

production companies, also are required to assign their rights; see Jeffrey Brabec & Todd Brabec, *Music, Money and Success,* (New York: Schirmer Books, 1994), at pp. 211 and 229. For a useful practical article concerning commissioning music, see C. Paul Spurgeon, "Before You Accept A Commission, Read This", *The Canadian Composer,* November, 1986, p. 15. See also Shane Simpson, "The Commission of New Music", in *Music: The Business and the Law,* (Sydney: The Law Book Company Limited, 1986), at pp. 139-148, for an outline of relevant issues involved when commissioning music.

[131] Section 12 of the Act, quoted in part. See also Barry Torno, *Crown Copyright in Canada: A Legacy of Confusion,* (Ottawa: Consumer and Corporate Affairs Canada, 1981). Although there is a presumption that the Crown includes the federal, provincial and municipal governments, the term "Crown" is undefined in the Act. There are other issues concerning Crown copyright: for example, it seems that Crown prerogative is preserved, at least with respect to the federal government, since the federal government has not explicitly stated that it is bound by the Act. The issue is whether the federal government is therefore free to use with impunity works of authors not in its employ. Section 12 of the Act is a troublesome section. These issues are unresolved.

[132] See, generally, William Braithwaite, "Derivative Works in Canada", (1982) 20 Osgoode Hall L.J. 191. Note that copyright in the derivative work is independent of and in addition to any copyright in the pre-existing work.

[133] The issue of copyright arrangements of public domain works is particularly vexatious with regard to folk styles such as the blues. For a discussion of this issue in a U.S. context, see Jennifer L. Hall, "Blues and the Public Domain — No More Dues To Pay?", (1994-95) J. of the Copyright Society of the U.S.A. 215.

Barring such consent, reproduction, publication or performance of the derivative work will constitute an infringement.

Arrangements are perhaps the best example of derivative works in the field of music.[134] Courts have long recognized that they may constitute separate and new works attracting copyright for their authors.[135]

B. Infringing Works

If the degree of labour and skill applied in creating a work is substantial enough to result in a new original work, copyright may subsist in the infringing work even though it simultaneously infringes another protected work.[136]

(v) Legal Entities

Although the Act states that the first owner of a copyright is the author,[137] by reason of certain statutory exceptions, persons other than individuals can become first owners of copyright. In particular, the person who has commissioned and paid for an engraving, photograph or portrait, in the absence of an agreement to the contrary, will be first owner;[138] employers may so qualify,[139] as may the Crown.[140]

Corporations, as first owners or otherwise, can own copyrights. In certain circumstances, unincorporated associations can own copyrights as tenants-in-common and sue as individuals or jointly if there has been copyright infringement.[141]

---

[134] *Quare* whether heavily altered (perhaps unrecognizable) digital samples might qualify as derivative works. Such samples are often utilized by artists working in the rap genre. On arrangements, generally, see Russell G. Benson, "Legal Protection for Arrangements of Musical Works: A Modern Perspective", (1989), 22 C.P.R. (3d) 97.

[135] See Fox, supra note 22 at pp. 148-49 and the cases cited therein.

[136] *Redwood Music Ltd. v. Chappell & Co. Ltd.*, [1982] R.P.C. 109.

[137] Subsection 13(1) of the Act.

[138] Subsection 13(2) of the Act.

[139] Subsection 13(4) of the Act.

[140] Section 12 of the Act.

[141] *Underwriters' Survey Bureau Ltd. v. Massie & Renwick Ltd.*, [1940] S.C.R. 218 (S.C.C.), special leave to appeal to S.C.C. refused [1940] S.C.R. 219 (note) (S.C.C.).

(c) Duration of Ownership

(i) General Rule and Public Domain

The general rule is 'life plus fifty'.[142]. Upon expiration of the fifty year term, the work falls into the public domain. Public domain works can be used freely. There are important exceptions to the general rule. These are outlined below.

(ii) Joint Works

The term for copyright protection of a joint work is fifty years from the date of the death of the last surviving composer.[143]

(iii) Posthumous Works

Under former law, works unpublished as of the date of an author's death were entitled to perpetual copyright. Upon publication or performance, they were limited to a term of fifty years, the term commencing at the end of the calendar year of first publication or performance.[144] However, recent amendments to the Act have abolished the concept of perpetual copyright. Under amended section 7, if a work has not been published as of January 1, 1999 and the author died within the period of fifty years before January 1, 1999, copyright will run for a period of fifty years after 1999 whether or not the work is published after January 1, 1999.[145] If the work has not been published as of January 1, 1999 and the author died more than fifty years before that date, copyright will run for five years after January 1, 1999 whether or not the work is published after January 1, 1999.[146] Unpublished works of authors who die after the amendments come into force will be

---

[142] Section 6 of the Act. Technically, copyright subsists for a term of fifty years, which term commences at the end of the calendar year in which the author dies. However, authors who are nationals of countries not party to NAFTA and whose countries grant a term of protection less than that provided under s. 6 may not claim a longer term of protection in Canada; see s. 9(2) of the Act.

[143] Subsection 9(1) of the Act. The term commences at the end of the calendar year in which the last surviving joint author dies.

[144] Subsection 7(1) of the Act.

[145] Subsection 7(3) of the Act.

[146] Subsection 7(4) of the Act.

protected for fifty years following the end of the calendar year in which the author dies.[147]

(iv) Crown Copyright

The term of copyright for works prepared for the Crown is fifty years from the end of the calendar year of first publication of the work.[148] If the Crown work is unpublished as of the date of the author's death, the rules governing posthumous works will apply.

(v) Anonymous and Pseudonymous Works

Pursuant to section 6.1 of the Act, copyright in the work of an anonymous author subsists for the lesser of: (1) a term consisting of the remainder of the calendar year of first publication plus fifty years; and, (2) a term consisting of the remainder of the calendar year of the making of the work plus seventy-five years. If, during the term, the author's identity becomes known, the term provided in section 6 applies. In the case of works of joint authorship, if the identity of one or more of the authors becomes known during the term, copyright subsists for the life of whichever author dies last, the remainder of the calendar year in which he or she dies and a period of fifty years following the end of that calendar year.[149]

(vi) Term of Copyright in Photographs

Copyright in a photograph, where the owner is a corporation, subsists for a term of fifty years following the end of the calendar year in which the negative or plate was made or, if no negative or plate was made, fifty years from the making of the initial photograph.[150] Where the first owner is an individual, or a corporation controlled by an individual who otherwise would have qualified as the first owner, copyright subsists for the life of the author plus a period of fifty years, from the end of the calendar year in which the author dies. [151]

---

[147] In these cases, the period is determined under s. 6 of the Act. Posthumous works published prior to the coming into force of the section will be governed by the old rule: 50 years from the date of publication; see s. 7(2).

[148] Section 12 of the Act.

[149] Section 6.2 of the Act.

[150] Subsection 10(1) of the Act.

[151] See ss. 10(1); 10(1.1) and 10(2) of the Act; see also ss. 13(2) and 13(3).

3. Sound Recordings

The Act defines a sound recording as any " recording, fixed in any material form, consisting of sounds...".[152] Pursuant to subsection 18(1), the maker of a sound recording has copyright in the recording and by paragraph 24(b) is deemed first owner of the copyright. Copyright in the recording terminates fifty years after the end of the calendar year in which the first fixation occurred.[153]

The maker of the recording is the person by whom the arrangements necessary for the first fixation are undertaken.[154] This definition tracks the language of the *Copyright, Designs and Patents Act, 1988,* c. 48 *(U.K.)* which defines an author of a recording or film as "the person by whom the arrangements necessary for the making of the recording or film are undertaken".[155] British courts, in considering the definition's application to motion pictures, have interpreted it to mean the (corporate) person responsible for production of the work[156], especially in the financial sense, but also generally. Accordingly, where an artist makes a recording under an exclusive long-term recording contract, there seems little doubt that the first owner of copyright and maker of the recording will normally be the record company for which the record is made. However, if the artist is unsigned and, utilizing the services of a producer, makes a recording in the hope of "shopping" it at a later date, it is arguable that the producer is the maker under the Act.[157] Musicians who make their own demos will obtain copyright in their recordings as makers of sound recordings.

Previous Canadian case law offers little guidance with respect to the definition of "maker" as it applies to the makers of sound recordings.

---

[152] Section 2 of the Act. Excluded from the definition are soundtracks synchronized to cinematographic works. This definition replaces the former definition of "mechanical contrivances" found at s. 5(3) and removes any uncertainty that may have existed as to the exact nature of the contrivances qualifying for protection under the Act.

[153] Paragraph 23(1)(b) of the Act. By s. 24(b), the maker is deemed first owner of the copyright.

[154] Section 2 of the Act.

[155] Paragraph 9(2)(a) CDPA

[156] See W.L. Hayhurst, "Audiovisual Productions: Some Copyright Aspects", (1994) 8 I.P.J. p. 321, footnote 9 and the cases cited therein for a discussion of this issue.

[157] In many cases it is the producer who makes the "actual arrangements"; his/her duties might include preparation of the recording budget, hiring of engineers and back-up musicians, choosing and booking the recording studio, supervising the recording and mixing sessions, and in some cases arranging the music as well. Moreover, when the budget is "all in", the producer is given a lump sum from which he/she draws his/her fee and pays all incidental expenses; see Moses Avalon, *Confessions of a Record Producer: How to Survive the Scams and Shams of the Music Business,* (San Francisco: Miller Freeman Books, 1998), for a description of the producer's role.

In *Compo Co. v. Blue Crest Music Inc.*,[158] the Supreme Court stated that the word "make" "may include the general activity of bringing about the production of the record and indirect actions associated therewith."[159] The Court also suggested, without deciding the issue, that the record manufacturer, persons involved in one or more stage in the production chain, and persons co-ordinating but not physically involved in the actual manufacture might be "makers" for the purpose of paragraph 3(1)(d). In *Hyrcyk v. Smichure*[160], an Alberta court found a band leader who ordered the production of a record to be the owner of the original plate, and therefore, owner of the copyright.[161] In *Films Rachel Inc. v. Druker & Associes Inc.*[162], a Quebec court was inclined to regard the writer/director as author of a film in the absence of an agreement to the contrary with its producer.

If one analogizes the arrangements for making a recording to the commissioning of a photograph, it seems that, absent any agreement to the contrary, copyright should reside in the party ordering the sound recording. Doubtless, record companies, at whose behest the rights in Part II were enacted, will include in their contracts language sufficient to negate any inference that the artists or producers involved in the production of masters arranged the first fixation of these sound recordings.

To acquire copyright, the contrivance must be lawfully made.

4. Audio-Visual Recordings

(a) Music Videos

The Act defines a "cinematographic work" to include "any work expressed by a process analogous to cinematography, whether or not accompanied by a soundtrack".[163] This definition is broad enough to encompass works created on videotape; consequently, music videos are

---

[158] (1979), [1980] S.C.R. 357 (S.C.C.). This case was decided under para. 3(1)(d) of the Act which deals with the copyright owner's right to make sound recordings.

[159] Ibid., at p. 378.

[160] (1966), 53 C.P.R. 177 (Alta. T.D.)

[161] See also *Arts Visuels de Lanaudière Inc. c. Perreault* (1987), 18 C.I.P.R. 241 (P.C. Qué.). In this case, the plaintiff and the defendant disagreed on the contractual terms for making a video, but since it was acknowledged that the defendant was to receive no remuneration, the plaintiff was entitled to copyright in the video.

[162] In *Films Rachel Inc., Re* (1995), 34 C.B.R. (3d) 303 (C.S. Qué.), the court held at p. 36 that the producer "did not offer a significant contribution to the intellectual process involved in the creation" which rested with the writer/director; see the citation and translation by Tamaro, supra note 110 at pp. 35-38.

[163] Section 2 of the Act.

"cinematographic works".[164] As in the case of sound recordings, the maker of a cinematographic work is "the person by whom the arrangements necessary to the making of the work are undertaken".[165] However, unlike sound recordings, a film, in addition to having a "maker", will also have an "author". Under the rules in section 5, copyright will subsist in any film if either the author or maker, at the date the film was made, was resident of a treaty country or (in the case of a corporation) headquartered in a treaty country.[166] Duration of copyright is tied to the life of the author under section 6 of the Act.[167] Just who is the author will be decided according to the normal rules governing authorship of a dramatic work. In *Films Rachel Inc. v. Druker & Associes Inc.*[168], the only Canadian case to consider this issue in the context of cinematographic works, a Quebec court was inclined to regard the writer/director as author of a film in the absence of any agreement to the contrary between the writer/director and producer.

Ownership of the video is determined by the rules that apply to dramatic works.[169] If the author creates the video under a contract of service, his/her employer will be deemed first owner; if he/she is an independent contractor, he/she will be first owner.

(b) The Video Soundtrack

As noted above, the definition of "sound recording" contained in the Act specifically excludes any soundtrack of a cinematographic work where it accompanies the work. Moreover, the definition of cinematographic work specifically includes any work accompanied by a soundtrack. From this, it appears that one may reasonably conclude that a single copyright subsists in a film or music video and further, that such a work is not a compilation or collective work.[170]

---

[164] Even under the former definition of "cinematograph" it has been held that videotapes are such works; see *Tom Hopkins International Inc. (Tom Hopkins Champions Unlimited) v. Wall & Redekop Realty Ltd.* (1984), 1 C.P.R. (3d) 348 (B.C. S.C.); *Royalties for Retransmission of Distant Radio & Television Signals, Re* (1994), 32 C.P.R. (3d) 97 (Copyright Bd.), affirmed (1990), 34 C.P.R. (3d) 383n.

[165] Section 2 of the Act.

[166] Paragraphs 5(1)(a),(b) of the Act.

[167] Section 11.1 provides an exception for films not possessing a dramatic character; copyright in such films subsists for fifty years from publication or the date of making if not published. Music videos, however, do possess a dramatic character and are therefore excluded.

[168] Supra, note 162.

[169] Cinematographic works are a species of dramatic works; see definition of "dramatic works" in s. 2 of the Act; see also Hayhurst, supra, note 156.

[170] Prior to the 1997 amendments, a "cinematograph" comprised only the visual elements of a film; the soundtrack was regarded as a separate work having its own

(c) Other Elements

Many videos include choreography. "Choreographic works" are recognized by the Act and protected as a species of dramatic work. Pursuant to paragraph 3(1)(d), the right to make any cinematographic film or contrivance by which the work may be reproduced or performed is reserved to the copyright owner. These rights must be respected; therefore either a licence or assignment of the copyright should be obtained by the producer prior to commencement of pre-production.

(d) Licences Required

Assuming that the video has been scripted and the producer has obtained a suitable grant of rights from the screenwriter, there are two licences required in connection with the music: (1) a licence which permits the musical work to be reproduced and synchronized with the visual images in the music video (the synchronization licence);[171] and (2) a licence from the owner of the master recording permitting its reproduction in the video (the master use licence).[172] If the video reproduces artistic works additional licences may also be required.[173]

(i) The Synchronization Licence

There are a number of issues to be considered when a synchronization licence is granted. These are briefly discussed below.[174]

(1) Duration: Rights can be perpetual, for life of copyright, or for some lesser term.

(2) Rights Granted: In addition to the right to synchronize the work with the video, the rights granted under the licence also include the

---

copyright. Questions then arose as to whether the film could be regarded as a work having its own copyright, either as a compilation or collective work; see Hayhurst, supra note 156 at pp. 336-42. The current definition of a cinematographic work, by including the possibility that it may contain a soundtrack, suggests that this is no longer the case.

[171] Paragraphs 3(1)(d) and (e) of the Act.

[172] Paragraph 18(1)(b) of the Act. Note that music publishers often require their artists to license these rights for free; see Donald Passman, *All You Need To Know About The Music Business*, (New York: Simon & Schuster, 1997), at pp. 229-230.

[173] Paragraph 3(1)(e) of the Act.

[174] For more on synchronization licences, see Brabec & Brabec, supra note 130, at pp. 170-88; see also Jeffrey E. Jacobson & Bruce E. Colfin, "Synchronization Licences in Existing and New Media", *Copyright World*, Issue 63, September 1996, p. 28.

right to distribute the work. The licence will therefore specify the relevant market, for example, theatrical, free TV, cable TV, pay TV, satellite, festival or college run, etc.[175]

(3) Territory: This may be Canada, the U.S.A, the world, the world excluding the U.S.A. or some other territory.

(4) Number of plays: This may be unlimited or limited with respect to different markets.

(5) Blanket Licences: Under U.S anti-trust law, American performing rights societies are prohibited from granting blanket performing right licences to U.S. motion picture theatres. Therefore, in the U.S., producers obtain (and pay for) a synchronization licence which also permits the performance of the licensed work in theatres. This is not the case in Canada, where such blanket licences are available. Canadian producers, therefore, do not have to pay for this right; the cost of such licences falls on exhibitors.

(6) Assignment: Synchronization licences are generally not assignable.

(7) Moral Rights: Synchronization licences may require the consent or waiver of the author concerning moral rights.

(ii) Master Use Licence

A master use licence is necessary when a master recording is used in film. It is acquired from the owner of the sound recording which usually is a record company. Master use licences can be expensive. As a result, music is often re-recorded, and a less costly mechanical licence is obtained from the music publisher. Normally, the owner of the copyright in the new recording will be the film company which paid to have the music re-recorded.

(iii) Other Rights

The producer should consider whether a grant of secondary rights, such as merchandising rights which may attach to the title of the composition, or personality rights which may attach to the performers,

---

[175] Synchronization licences often include a modified mechanical licence type of language granting the right to record the musical work. This does not imply that a synchronization licence is a mechanical licence to make a record into a soundtrack. It is not.

are also required. Additional issues include the payment of union session fees and payments for re-use of existing recordings.[176]

(e) Motion Pictures and Television

The use of music in motion pictures is a complex area of legal practice. Music may be composed specifically for a film; it may be background music or used as a character's signature theme. Quite often, hit songs are licensed; here again, the music may be used as background, it may be performed during a scene or it may be used over the opening or closing credits. Sometimes, the song's title will be used as the title of the film. Sometimes, it will be impossible to secure the rights to the recorded version and the song will have to be re-recorded.[177] Each of these possibilities entails a different form of agreement with different issues and different costs.

However, all issues fall into one of two categories: (1) those relating to acquisition of rights for the film — rights may be held by artists, songwriters, composers, publishers, record producers and/or record companies; and (2) those relating to the exploitation of rights held by the producer; this will include deals for the release of a soundtrack album and single, the licensing of the film for music videos and home video, and the publishing and/or administration of the copyright in the music contained in the film soundtrack.[178]

---

[176] Re-use fees are fees payable to the American Federation of Music when a recording made for a particular use, e.g. a motion picture, is subsequently used in a different manner, e.g. it is later released on a record album. For a discussion of these terms and their applicability, see Chapter 5, "Labour" and Chapter 9, "Recording". For a discussion of music in film and video, see Shane Simpson and Greg Stevens, *Music: The Business and the Law*, (Sydney: The Law Book Company Limited, 1986), at pp. 167, 181, Chapter 13; see also, generally, Thomas D. Selz and Melvin Simensky, *Entertainment Law* (New York: McGraw-Hill, 1991), (annual supplements), f. 225 - f. 286, and Joseph Taubman, *Performing Artist Management and the Law*, (New York: Law-Arts Publishers Inc.), (annual supplements), f. 1B6 to 1B6a; for sample Film Composer Agreements, see Turner Conna Graham, "Video Clips In Popular Music", 1 Australian Journal of Cultural Studies 1983, at pp. 107 - 111. See also Peter E. Steinmetz, "The Video Revolution", in *Entertainment and Sports Law Workshop 1985-86*, (Toronto: Faculty of Law, University of Toronto, 1985-86); for discussion concerning sound-alikes, see Chapter 9, "Merchandising".

[177] Lionel S. Sobel, "A Movie and T.V. Producers Guide to Acquiring and Earning Income from Soundtrack Music", Parts I and II (1985) Vol. 1, E.L.R. Part I p. 2, Part II p. 3.

[178] See Passman, supra note 172 at pp. 384-85. See also Peter E. Steinmetz, "Soundtracks" Chapter I, pp. 1-12 in *Entertainment, Advertising and Media Law*, (Toronto: L.S.U.C., 1991), and citations referred to therein. See also C. Paul Spurgeon, *Musical Scores, Film and Video Media and the Canadian Composer: Facts to Consider*, (Toronto: CAPAC, 1979). See also Garth Drabinsky, *Motion Pictures and the Arts in Canada*, (Toronto: McGraw-Hill Ryerson, 1976), at pp. 113-118.

5. Other Works

(a) Choreography

Choreographed dance steps form part of the presentation of many musicians, both in live performance and music videos. Choreographic works, protected under the Act, are defined as "any work[s] of choreography" whether or not they have a story line.[179] Of major concern, when such works are commissioned, is the nature of the relationship between the choreographer and the other contracting party (musician, record company or music video production company). If the choreographer retains ownership of the work, the musician should seek the broadest grant of rights possible.

(b) Music and Computers

The use of computers in the creation of music is a well-established practice on the part of many composers. This use is of two types: (1) the computer as compositional tool; and (2) the computer as the actual generator of the work.[180] In the first class are those composers who use computers to make digital samples of pre-existing works or to record live instrumental or vocal sounds digitally for use in subsequent recordings.[181] Also included are composers who use computers as electronic keyboards, utilizing a MIDI interface to create digital files which house their compositions. In the second class are composers who write programs containing algorithms capable of generating musical works.

With respect to the first class, it is clear that the composer is an author. With respect to the second class, this seems doubtful. As we have seen, copyright law requires that the author of a work give it its form or expression.[182] This is not the case with respect to computer-generated works which are not emanations of the composer's musical imagination, but rather, the quasi-random output of a computer program. Accordingly, such works could exist only in the public domain.

---

[179] Section 2 of the Act.

[180] See Barry B. Sookman, "Copyright and the Information Superhighway: Some Issues to Think About (Part I)"(1997) 11 I.P.J. 123, at pp. 127-28. See also Barry B. Sookman, "Computer Assisted Creation of Works Protected by Copyright", (1989) 5 I.P.J. 165 at p. 17.

[181] The practice of sampling is considered in Chapter 4.

[182] See Sookman, "Copyright and the Information Superhighway: Some Issues to Think About (Part I)"(1997) 11 I.P.J. 123, supra, note 180, and the cases cited therein.

(c) Music and Multimedia

Multimedia works may be defined as works which combine sound, images and text by means of an interactive computer program that allows for the creation of something new.[183] Despite their novelty, these works are not essentially different from the audiovisual works discussed above.[184] Producers who wish to utilize musical works in their multimedia productions will have to secure licences from the relevant rights holders. Personality rights will have to be considered if use of a musician's likeness is contemplated. A waiver of moral rights may also be required as the digitization of the work may permit its alteration either by the producer or an end-user of the work. If the musical clip encompasses a performance, it may be necessary to obtain a licence from the performer with respect to his/her rights under Part II of the Act. Lastly, if the multimedia work will be placed on the Internet, the producer should obtain a licence from the relevant performing rights society as transmission of the work on a network may constitute either a performance in public or a communication of the work to the public by telecommunication under subsection 3(1) of the Act.

---

[183] See Michael D. Scott & James L. Talbott, "Interactive Multimedia: What Is It, Why Is It Important and What Does One Need to Know About It?"[1993] 8 E.I.P.R. 284. For more on multimedia, see Brian P. Isaac, "Intellectual Property and Multimedia: Problems of Definition and Enforcement"(1995-96) 12 C.I.P.R. 47; Mark Litwak, "Potholes on the Information Superhighway: A Road Map to Legal Issues in Multimedia Productions", in *1995-96 Entertainment, Publishing and the Arts Handbook*, (New York: Clark, Boardman, Callaghan), p. 199; David L. Gersh & Sheri Jeffrey, "Structuring the Multimedia Deal Legal Issues — Part I: Licensing in the Multimedia Arena", [1992] 6 Ent. L.R. 196; and David L. Gersh & Sheri Jeffrey, "Structuring the Multimedia Deal Legal Issues — Part II: Licensing in the Multimedia Arena", [1993] 1 Ent. L. R. 14; Gerald Orakwusi and Martine Alan, "Licensing Music Copyrights in Relation to New Technologies", *Copyright World*, Issue 51, June/July 1995, p. 39; see also "Study on New Media and Copyright", *Final Report*, June 30, 1994, prepared by Nordicity Group for Industry Canada (New Media, Information and Technologies Industry Branch).

[184] Save with respect to their categorization under the Act. While other species of audiovisual works (such as films and music videos) can be categorized as cinematographic works having a single copyright, there will be multiple copyrights in a multimedia work. Copyright will subsist in the sensory output of the work (text, images and sounds), the product as a whole — most likely as a compilation — and in the underlying program comprising its technical base; see Isaac, supra note 183, at pp. 50-51; for a contrary view, see Sookman, supra, note 180, at pp. 134-35, who argues that the interactive nature of multimedia works may preclude their categorization as compilations because, if one of the underlying works is considered a cinematographic work, the non-linear sequencing of images typical of interactive multimedia works may preclude application of this definition.

(d) Music and the Internet

The dissemination of music (and all other forms of data) over the Internet raises numerous difficult questions of copyright law.[185] A detailed exposition of these issues is beyond the scope of this book;[186] nevertheless, some of the more important unresolved issues that affect the on-line transmission of musical works are noted below.

(i) Reproduction

When information travels along a computer network, copies of the data are routed through the network; end-users obtain a reproduction of this data which is temporarily stored in RAM and which may be saved to a permanent storage device such as a hard drive or floppy disk. Reproduction of a work in which copyright subsists is something only the copyright owner may do; since unauthorized copying, if substantial, is an infringement, it would seem that both the uploading and downloading of music will constitute an infringement of the owner's copyright.[187] However, infringement requires reproduction of the work

---

[185] This dissemination is currently taking a variety of forms; among them, the licensed distribution of existing recordings by celestial jukeboxes; the unlicensed distribution of song lyrics and transcriptions of performances available on non-commercial bulletin boards; the promotion of new artist releases by record companies; and the subscription sale of new works by artists directly to the public. For a fuller description of these activities, see Adam P. Segal, "Dissemination of Digitized Music on the Internet: A Challenge to the Copyright Act" (1996) 12 Santa Clara Comp. & Tech. L.J. 97.

[186] One commentator has identified the following issues: (1) questions of authorship when a work is created by several individuals utilizing a network; (2) questions of publication where a work created by a person not resident in a treaty country is first issued by dissemination over the Internet; (3) questions concerning the nature of the infringement, which may occur either by transmission of copies, by browsing, by performance of works or distribution over the Internet; and (4) questions of jurisdiction in infringement suits; see Sookman, supra note 179 for a discussion of these issues. Generally, see G.Gervaise Davis III,"The Digital Dilemma: Coping with Copyright in a Digital World", *Copyright World*, Issue 27, February, 1993, p. 18; Neil J. Rosini, "Copyright Category Confusion and Its Consequences: Online Transmissions and the Right of Exclusive Use under Copyright", *Ent. And Sports Law*, Vol. 16, Spring 1998, p. 11; Steven M. Weinberg, "Charting a Course on the Information Superhighway", *Copyright World*, Issue 54, October, 1995, p. 24.

[187] This was the position taken by the Harry Fox Agency in a class action filed on behalf of its members against Compuserve and subsequently settled; see *Frank Music Corp. v. Compuserve Inc.*, 93 Civ. 8153 (S.D.N.Y. 1993).

"in any material form".[188] *Quare* whether an Internet browser who makes a temporary copy of a musical work in RAM is caught by the Act.[189]

(ii) Performance

As noted above, one of the exclusive rights granted to the copyright owner is the right to perform the work in public and more specifically, to communicate the work to the public by telecommunication. If a musical work is downloaded, is it performed in either of the above senses? What if the download cannot be heard until after the transmission is completed? If a performance licence is required, must the user obtain a mechanical licence as well?[190]

(iii) Derivative Works

To what extent are users of copyright works downloaded from the Internet free to make alterations to those works? What of the author's moral rights?

(iv) Distribution

Paragraph 27(2)(b) of the Act states that it is an infringement of copyright for any person to distribute to such an extent as to affect prejudicially the owner of the copyright material in which copyright subsists. Is the posting of a song on the Internet a distribution?[191] If so, can a user who obtains a copy of a work sell or otherwise permit a third party to make a copy of his/her copy? Under Canadian law, a vendor has no general right to control the resale of works sold by him or her,

---

[188] Preamble to s. 3(1) of the Act.

[189] See Mark S. Torpoco, "Mickey and the Mouse: The Motion Picture and Television Industry's Copyright Concerns on the Internet", (1997) 5 U.C.L.A. Ent. L. Rev. 1, at pp. 37-39 for a discussion of this issue in a U.S. context. Note that the Copyright Board, in "Statement of Royalties to the Collected for the Performance or the Communication by Telecommunication, in Canada, of Musical or Dramatico-Musical Works (Tariff 22)", infra, note 190, has stated that "Internet transmissions remain communications within the meaning of the Act even though they also involve, or result in, one or more transitory or permanent reproductions."

[190] There seems little doubt that the posting of a work on the Internet can result in a communication to the public; see Isaac, supra note 183 at page 53, note 25 and the cases cited therein; see also Barry B. Sookman, "Copyright and the Information Superhighway: Some Issues to Think About (Part II)", (1997), 11 I.P.J. 265 at pp. 266-81. See also the recent decision of the Copyright Board, "Statement of Royalties to be Collected for the Performance or the Communication by Telecommunication, in Canada, of Musical or Dramatico-Musical Works (Tariff 22)", [1999] C.B.D. No. 5.

[191] For a discussion of this issue, see Chapter 4.

but the policy underlying this rule assumes that the purchaser who sells to a third party gives up possession of the work. Here, this is not the case.[192]

(v) Jurisdictional Issues

The international nature of the Internet raises numerous difficult issues with respect to jurisdiction and conflict of laws. These issues include the following: to what extent does a court in Canada have jurisdiction over an act of infringement occurring outside Canada, the effects of which are felt in Canada? Must the act be in breach of Canadian copyright law or is it sufficient that the act breaches the copyright law of the jurisdiction in which it occurs? If the act breaches both the foreign and domestic law, which law is to apply? How does one determine where the infringing act takes place?

It has been argued, although not yet decided, that Canada has jurisdiction to try cases of infringement regardless of where the infringement occurs if there is a "real and substantial connection" between the litigation and the Canadian courts, and further, that the communication of a work to Canadians from outside Canada may constitute an infringement of Canadian copyright law subject to the jurisdiction of Canadian courts.[193]

(vi) Rights Clearance — Current Practice

Because the performance of music on the Internet has been regarded primarily as a promotional vehicle, music publishers are generally willing to license the use of clips less than thirty seconds for free.[194] If the clip is longer, publishers may seek to claim both performance and

---

[192] See Sookman, supra note 190, at pp. 283-84.

[193] Ibid., pp. 291-93. See also, *Braintech, Inc. v. Kostiuk*, [1999] B.C.J. No. 622 (C.A.). Note that in the recent decision of the Copyright Board, "Statement of Royalties to be Collected for the Performance or the Communication by Telecommunication, in Canada, of Musical or Dramatico-Musical Works (Tariff 22)", supra note 190, the Board held that a "communication of a musical work occurs where the transmission originates" subject to the proviso that "the issue of whether an entity that provides content outside Canada with the intention to communicate it specifically to recipients in Canada is communicating it in Canada remains open."

[194] Sales of music over the Internet currently constitute less than 2% of global retail sales. However, major record companies have recently begun to explore the possibility of distributing music over the Internet; the owners of BMG (Bertelsmann AG) and Universal (Seagram Co.) have recently announced plans to develop technology with ATT and Matsushita that will permit users to retrieve and play music accompanied by graphics, videos and lyrics; see "Industry to Target Internet Piracy", The Toronto Star, May 27, 1999. For a general discussion of music piracy on the Internet and methods to avoid it, see Barak D. Jolish, "Scuttling the Music Pirate: Protecting Recordings in the Age of the Internet", 17 Ent. And Sports Lawyer, no. 1, Spring 1999 at p. 9.

mechanical royalties.[195] Both BMI and ASCAP have recently issued blanket licences to web sites in the U.S. with respect to the performance right in musical works.[196] In Canada, SOCAN has applied to the Copyright Board for permission to issue blanket licences to Internet Access Providers.[197] Many copyright owners are currently endeavouring to develop programs that will facilitate online copyright and royalty protection.[198]

---

[195] See Passman, supra note 172, at pp. 375-76. In the U.K., MCPS has licensed the Cerberus digital jukebox and collects on behalf of its members a royalty equal to 10% of the downloading cost; see Segal, supra note 185 at p. 109. However, it is unclear whether this royalty is collected with respect to performance rights, mechanical rights, the right to copy the recording or all three.

[196] BMI has licensed the browsing, listening to, and transmission of musical works to personal computers. ASCAP has licensed an on-line radio service, but its agreement does not permit recording for resale; see Kenneth D. Suzan, "Tapping To The Beat Of A Digital Drummer: Fine Tuning U.S. Copyright Law For Music Distribution On The Internet", (1995-96), Alb. L. R. 789 at pp. 807-8.

[197] For a description of Tariff No. 22, see Supplement to the Canada Gazette, June 13, 1998 at p. 26. SOCAN claims that the transmission of musical works by Internet Access Providers to their subscriber public constitutes a "communication to the public by telecommunication" under para. 3(1)(f) of the *Copyright Act*. Applications have also been made by NRCC and SODRAC. For more on the role of copyright collectives in a digital environment, see C. Paul Spurgeon, "Digital Networks and Copyright: Licensing and Accounting for Use — The Role of Copyright Collectives", (1998), 12 I.P.J. 225.

[198] Thus Sony, Time Warner, Seagram Co. and Bertelsmann AG, together with technology firms including IBM, have begun to develop and test the Secure Music Digital Initiative (SMDI), an encryption technology intended to permit on-line music sales, maintain copyright protection and prevent piracy; see "Music Wars Break Out on Net", The Toronto Star, April 13, 1999.

2

THE LICENSING AND ADMINISTRATION OF COPYRIGHT AND THE REGULATION OF MUSIC IN MEDIA

Contributing Author: Ronald N. Hier, B.A., LL.B., LL.M.

Introduction

This chapter discusses the administration and licensing of copyright in relation to the music business and the regulation of music in the media. Copyright administration is governed by the *Copyright Act*,[1] which provides its statutory basis, and by music business practice as discussed below.

1. Assigning and Licensing Musical Copyright

All income earned from musical works derives from the exploitation of copyright.[2] This exploitation generally takes one of two forms: the licensing or assignment of copyright. Licences and assignments are contracts, governed by the law of contract. However, to operate effectively, assignments and licences must conform to the requirements of the *Copyright Act*. Subject to these considerations, and except as noted in the text below, a copyright owner has the right to negotiate freely the terms of these agreements.

---

[1] R.S.C. 1985, c. C-42, as amended (hereinafter the "Act").

[2] The devise of copyright to an estate is not discussed because even here, any income realized by the estate is earned by means of the licensing or assignment of copyright. See Chapter 1, "Copyright" for a discussion of the copyright basis for assignment and licensing.

(a) Voluntary

(i) Assignments

There are two main assignments with respect to copyright in musical compositions. One is the assignment of the performing right to a performing rights society; the other is the assignment of publication and reproduction rights to a music publisher.[3]

(ii) Performing Rights

Although the terms of the assignment are technically negotiable, SOCAN, Canada's only performing rights society, has a standard form agreement which is seldom amended or negotiated. SOCAN is discussed below in section 3(c).

(iii) Reproduction and Publication Rights

Music publishers normally take an assignment of all rights from writers, except the performing right, which is normally assigned to a performing rights society. The music publisher then licenses specific uses of the copyright, usually through a reproduction rights agency, thereby generating income for itself and the assignor.[4]

(b) Compulsory

Formerly, the Act provided for the granting of a compulsory licence in certain specified situations.[5] These licences have for the most part been abolished.[6] What remains is a system of collective

---

[3] The rights of performers, broadcasters, and the makers of sound recordings under Part II of the Act, which also may be assigned to a collective society, are considered below in part 3(d)(iv). See also SODRAC in note 4 below.

[4] However, see below in the text at 3 b) (iii), with respect to SODRAC. SODRAC's practice differs significantly from the practice outlined in the text.

[5] For example, the Act formerly provided for compulsory licensing of mechanical rights after the making of a first contrivance (s. 19 of the Act); where music had been published or performed in public, then, at any time after the death of the composer, an order could be granted authorizing performance or publication of the work (s. 8(1) of the Act); and finally, 25 years after a composer's death, a work could be reproduced upon payment of a statutory royalty (s. 8(1) of the Act).

[6] Subsection 77(1) provides for the issuance of a licence by the Copyright Board upon application, where the copyright owner cannot be located and a person wishes to

administration, primarily for the administration of performing rights, neighbouring rights, and the blank tape levy. The licensing of these rights, discussed below, can be thought of as compulsory in that rates are fixed pursuant to statutory authority and persons who pay royalties cannot be sued for infringement. For these reasons, statutory licences are sometimes referred to as compulsory licences.[7]

(c) Mechanical Rights

(i) Canadian Industry Standard Rate

Although the fee for a mechanical licence fee is technically negotiable, the general practice is to adhere to an industry standard rate. This rate is set subsequent to negotiations between the Canadian Musical Reproduction Rights Agency ("CMRRA") on behalf of its music publisher principals and the Canadian Recording Industry Association ("CRIA") on behalf of record companies (hereinafter the "contract"). The rate is subject to change from time to time, pursuant to the terms of the contract. The current rate is 7.4 cents per song if the song is less than five minutes; if the song exceeds five minutes, there is an additional charge of 1.48 cents per minute. Royalties are payable under either the "pay as you play"[8] system or the CMRRA's mechanical licensing agreement and are payable with respect to records sold or otherwise distributed. A literal interpretation of the Act, however, could support the view that licence fees should be based on the number of records manufactured without the necessity of distribution or sale.

The impact of the controlled composition rate on the Canadian industry standard rate is discussed in Chapter 8, "Recording".

(ii) Note on U.S. Mechanical Rate

The U.S. mechanical rate is governed by section 115 of the U.S. *Copyright Act.*[9] It is relevant to Canadians for two reasons: (1) although

---

obtain a licence to use a work in which copyright subsists. Apart from licences issued by collective societies, this is the only remaining statutory licence.

[7] See *Performing Rights Organization of Can. Ltd. v. Lion D'Or (1981) Ltée,* (1987) 17 C.P.R. (3d) 542 (Fed. T.D.) at p. 547.

[8] This option is available where a small number of records is manufactured or the licence is granted pursuant to a 'one-shot deal'. The fee is paid at the time the licence is issued and no further royalties are payable.

[9] 17 U.S.C. s. 115; this section provides for the issuance of a compulsory licence upon payment of the statutory fee with respect to the recording of non-dramatic works that have been recorded previously and distributed publicly. The fee, originally set by

the Canadian rate is not tied to a compulsory licence and a statutory rate, it has been and continues to be influenced by the U.S. mechanical rate; and (2) Canadian recordings released in the United States are subject to the U.S. rate structure.

(iii) Sound Recordings

The reproduction of sound recordings should be distinguished from the reproduction of musical works. Whereas the latter requires the issuance of a mechanical licence by the CMRRA, the former requires the issuance of a master use licence. This licence is granted either by the record company on its own behalf or by the Audio Video Licensing Agency ("AVLA"), an organization which administers reproduction rights on behalf of its members. Master use licences are discussed in Chapter 1, "Copyright" and in Chapter 8, "Recording". CMRRA, AVLA and the administration of such licences are discussed in section 3 below.

2. Collective Administration of Copyright

The collective administration of copyright is a major component of the music business both domestically and worldwide.[10] Moreover, it is specifically encouraged by the rules contained in Part VII of the *Copyright Act*.[11]

(a) Collective Societies

The Act employs the term "collective society" to describe any organization engaged in the collective administration of copyright. Such organizations include performing rights societies (those which administer the performing right in musical works), and any society that administers reproduction rights, neighbouring rights, retransmission rights or the rights of broadcasters in their communication signals.

---

statute, is adjusted periodically by the Copyright Royalty Tribunal. Although the fee is seldom used, it provides a benchmark for setting mechanical rates in the U.S. recording industry; see Donald S. Passman, *All You Need To Know About the Music Business*, (New York: Simon & Schuster, 1997), at p. 211. Information concerning the rate can be obtained from the Licensing Division of the U.S. Copyright Office in Washington, D.C.

[10] Performing rights organizations include, *inter alia*, in the United States: BMI, ASCAP and SESAC; in the U.K: PRS; in France: SACEM; in Holland: STEMRA.

[11] As discussed below, in certain cases these rules forbid actions for infringement, if tariffs are not filed, and facilitate collection of royalties when they are filed.

Pursuant to section 2 of the Act, a "collective society" is defined as a "society, association or corporation that carries on the business of collective administration of copyright[12] for the benefit of those who by assignment, grant of licence, appointment of it as their agent or otherwise, authorize it to act on their behalf in relation to collective administration". Collective societies have two statutory functions: (1) the operation of a licensing scheme applicable in relation to a repertoire of works of more than one author,[13] pursuant to which the society sets out classes of use, the royalties, terms and conditions on which it agrees to authorize those classes of use; and (2) the collection and distribution of royalties payable under the Act. Any organization satisfying either of the above criteria will qualify as a "collective society" under the Act.

The Copyright Board has jurisdiction with respect to collective societies: a quasi-judicial body, it has the power to make regulations, conduct hearings, and most importantly, to approve the tariffs proposed by the collective societies.[14]

(i) Performing Rights Societies

Performing rights societies are governed by sections 67 through 68.2 of the Act.[15] The statutory scheme requires that each such society file with the Copyright Board a proposed tariff of fees on or before "the March 31 immediately before the date when its last tariff... expires."[16] Upon receipt of the tariff, the Board publishes it in the Canada Gazette and users are given sixty days to file written objections.[17] The Board

---

[12] Also included within the definition are collective societies that carry on the business of the remuneration right conferred by ss. 19 and 81 of the Act. Section 19 confers a public performance right on performers and makers of sound recordings with respect to the public performance or communication to the public by telecommunication of sound recordings; s. 81 confers a right of remuneration on authors, performers, and the makers of sound recordings realizable through the 'blank tape' levy.

[13] In keeping with the recent amendments to the Act, repertoires of performances, sound recordings or communication signals are also included within the definition.

[14] For the constitution, powers and procedures of the Copyright Board, see ss. 66 - 66.91 of the Act.

[15] This follows from the combined application of s. 67 and s. 67.1(1). Section 67 refers to collective societies that carry on the business of granting licences for the performance in public of musical works or the telecommunication of musical works to the public by telecommunication; these are the societies that are regulated under s. 67.1 of the Act. Section 67 also describes societies that grant licences for the public performance of performer's performances and sound recordings.

[16] Subsection 67.1(1) of the Act.

[17] Subsection 67.1(5) of the Act.

then considers the tariff and any objections thereto.[18] Once the tariff is certified[19], it is published in the Canada Gazette and copies, together with the reasons for the Board's decision, are sent to the collective society and any person who filed an objection.[20] The fixing of royalties entitles the collective society to recover them in any court of competent jurisdiction.[21] If the collective society fails to file a proposed tariff, no action for infringement may be commenced without Ministerial consent.[22]

(ii) Rights Other than Performing Rights

In sections 70.1 and 70.11 to 70.6, the Act sets out a statutory scheme for the collective administration of the rights granted under sections 3, 15, 18 and 21 of the Act.[23] However, the collective administration of these rights is voluntary; collective societies may file a proposal, but are not required to do so.[24] They may also enter into agreements with users.[25] Where a collective society chooses to file a tariff, the procedure is similar to that with respect to the administration of performing rights:[26] interested parties are entitled to notice, and the Board must give reasons for its decisions. Where a tariff is approved, the payment (or offer of payment) of royalties is a bar to proceedings for infringement.[27] However, the tariff will not apply where there is an agreement between the collective society and a user; if an agreement is

---

[18] Subsection 68 (1) of the Act. See also s. 68(2), which sets out criteria and factors the Board must take into account in examining a proposed tariff.

[19] Subsection 68(3) of the Act.

[20] Subsection 68(4) of the Act. Note that under s. 66.52, a decision of the Board may be varied where there has been a material variation in circumstances since the decision was made.

[21] Subsection 68.2(1) of the Act. Courts have ruled that this section has no application in an action for infringement; see *Performing Rights Organization of Can. Ltd. v. Lion D'Or (1981) Ltée*, (1987) 17 C.P.R. (3) 542 (Fed. T.D.).

[22] Subsection 67.1(4) of the Act. Note that where a tariff is filed, no proceedings may be brought for infringement against a person who pays or offers to pay the prescribed royalty; s. 68.2(2) of the Act.

[23] Although section 3 confers a performance right, the collective administration of this right is governed by s. 67.1(1). The rights dealt with, then, under s. 70.1 are the publication and reproduction rights. Sections 15 and 18 enact 'neighbouring' rights for performers and the makers of sound recordings; s. 21 confers on broadcasters copyright in their communication signals. These rights are discussed in Chapter 1.

[24] Section 70.12 of the Act. They are, however, required to answer requests from the public for information about the repertoire under their control; see s. 70.11.

[25] Ibid. However, where there is failure to reach an agreement, either party may apply to the Board to fix the royalty and its related terms and conditions; s. 70.2 of the Act. See also s. 70.3.

[26] Sections 70.14 and 70.15(2) of the Act.

[27] Section 70.17 of the Act.

in force, it will govern.[28] To facilitate the making of agreements, subsection 70.5(3) excludes the application of section 45 of the *Competition Act* in respect of any royalties or related terms and conditions arising under an agreement filed with the Copyright Board.[29]

(b) Retransmission Rights

Collective societies that carry on the business of collecting royalties with respect to the retransmission of distant signals are regulated by sections 71 to 76 of the Act.[30] Filing of tariffs is mandatory[31] and the procedure followed is similar to that discussed above.[32] In determining royalties, the Board is directed to ensure that there is a preferential rate for small retransmission systems,[33] and that royalties are determined and apportioned without discrimination between owners of copyright on the grounds of nationality or residence.[34] The fixing of royalties permits their recovery by the collective society in a court of competent jurisdiction without prejudice to any other available remedies.[35] Copyright owners who are not members of a collective society are entitled to be paid applicable royalties upon application to the Board,[36] but the Act expressly states that an entitlement to royalties is their only remedy.[37]

3. Copyright Administrators

(a) Music Publishers

Music publishers are discussed in detail in Chapter 3, "Music Publishing".

---

[28] Section 70.191 of the Act.

[29] But see ss. 70.5(4) and (5) and s. 70.6 with respect to the examination of agreements by the Director of Investigation and Research appointed under the *Competition Act.*

[30] These provisions also apply to collective societies that license the use of works by educational institutions pursuant to ss. 29.6(2), 29.7(2) and (3). "Distant signals" are defined in the *Local Signal and Distant Signal Regulations,* SOR/89-254.

[31] Subsection 71(1) of the Act.

[32] See ss. 71-73 of the Act.

[33] Subsection 74(1) of the Act. Small retransmission systems are defined in the *Definition of Small Transmission Systems Regulations,* SOR/89-255 am. SOR/94-754.

[34] Subsection 73(2) of the Act.

[35] Section 75 of the Act.

[36] Subsection 76(1) of the Act.

[37] Subsection 76(3) of the Act.

(b) Reproduction Rights

(i) Generally

The *Copyright Act* includes within the reproduction right: (1) the right to make any sound recording by means of which a musical work may be mechanically performed; and (2) the right to reproduce the work as a cinematographic work. For ease of administration, copyright owners often assign these rights to a music publisher or to SODRAC, or appoint a collective rights society to act as their agent in connection with the exploitation thereof. The two main organizations that license reproduction rights in Canada are the CMRRA and SODRAC, both discussed below.

(ii) CMRRA

A. Domestic Role, Purpose and Functions

The Canadian Musical Reproduction Rights Agency Limited ("CMRRA") is a "centralized licensing and collecting agency for the reproduction rights in musical works in Canada and internationally".[38] It is a non-profit, private company owned in trust for the members of the Canadian Music Publishers' Association ("CMPA"). Formed in 1975, it is the largest reproduction rights agency in Canada. It represents over 23,000 Canadian and U.S. publishers and issues licences on behalf of more than 5,000 music users for a total of 50,000 licences issued annually.

CMRRA's purpose is to "administer the reproduction rights of music publishers, ensuring that all reproductions of their clients' music manufactured or sold in Canada are licensed and charged the applicable royalty fees."[39] Any Canadian musical composition may be administered by CMRRA and many music publishers, including the major music publishers, use CMRRA as their agent. CMRRA licenses both mechanical and synchronization rights. Some publishers, however, prefer to negotiate synchronization licences on an individual basis directly with the user.

Unlike SODRAC, CMRRA does not take an assignment of reproduction rights. The agreement between it and its principals is a non-exclusive agency agreement which permits publisher members, as

---

[38] CMRRA Informational Circular (Toronto: CMRRA, 1982).
[39] CMRRA Brochure 1991, p. 3.

well as CMRRA, to grant licences to music users. Licences are granted individually, on a per use basis, with payment calculated on the basis of use. CMRRA charges 5% of gross monies collected for mechanical licences and 10% for synchronization licences with fees being set to cover operating costs. In comparison, the Harry Fox Agency, CMRRA's U.S. equivalent, charges 4.5% of gross monies received for mechanical licences, 10% for motion picture synchronization licences and 5% for all other synchronization licences. CMRRA does not cap the amount it charges for a synchronization licence, but the Harry Fox Agency does. Outside the U.S. and Canada, licensing fees vary between 10% and 15% of gross monies collected.

In addition to licensing rights, CMRRA collects licensing fees for its principals. Fees received are distributed within 30 days of receipt. Where there has been non-payment, or suspected non-payment of fees, CMRRA has the right to audit, and does audit, the books and records of licensees. CMRRA will also assist publishers in infringement actions by providing information and documentation although CMRRA does not generally litigate on its own behalf.[10]

CMRRA also operates a web site accessible through the Internet.[11] Music publishers can use "CMRRA Direct" to communicate with CMRRA, and to address queries regarding copyright registration, licensing and royalties. Synchronization rights users can apply directly for licences over the web and it is CMRRA's intention to extend this service to occasional users of mechanical licences.

B. International Aspects

Because the Canadian mechanical right can be engaged internationally, CMRRA is also active in the international administration of mechanical rights. There are three ways this right can be engaged: (1) by the exportation of a recording that was mastered in Canada; (2) by the exportation to a foreign territory of a record made in Canada; and (3) by the recording of Canadian music in a foreign territory, thereby producing a foreign master recording. Assuming that copyright has not been assigned to a sub-publisher in a foreign territory, each of the above has an effect on CMRRA's administrative role.

---

[10] CMRRA has engaged in test case litigation, e.g. the Michael Bishop case: *Bishop v. Stevens* (1987), 18 C.P.R. (3d) 257 (Fed. C.A.), affirmed (1990), 72 D.L.R. (4th) 97 (S.C.C.); discussion with David Basskin, Barrister & Solicitor, CMRRA, General Manager, February 3, 1992.

[11] CMRRA's site can be found at www.cmrra.ca.

In the first and third cases, the foreign record company must apply to the foreign reproduction rights organization in the applicable territory with which CMRRA has a reciprocal agreement for a mechanical licence. The foreign reproduction rights organization licenses the record company, collects the fee, deducts its administration fee and forwards the balance to CMRRA. CMRRA then distributes this amount, after deducting its administration fee, to the relevant publisher. Royalties payable are based on the royalty rate set in the foreign territory, many of which are higher than Canadian rates.

In the second case, the general rule is that mechanical royalties are payable based on the rate in the country of sale. Royalties are paid and distributed after deducting the applicable administration fee.

In order to facilitate the international administration of reproduction rights, CMRRA has entered into reciprocal agreements with other reproduction rights agencies throughout the world, including, for example, JASRAC (Japan) and MCPS (England). However, the existence of reproduction rights organizations does not replace the need for an effective sub-publisher in a foreign territory.[42]

(iii) SODRAC

A. Generally

The Society for Reproduction Rights of Authors, Composers and Publishers in Canada ("SODRAC") was formed in 1985. It is the successor to S.D.R.M. Canada Ltée. which had operated in Canada since 1970. Unlike CMRRA, SODRAC does not act as agent; it is an authors' society. Authors, composers and publishers are represented directly and royalties are distributed directly to each of the rightful owners in accordance with the contract signed.

Like CMRRA, SODRAC administers the licensing of reproduction rights. For its services, SODRAC charges a commission of 10% on amounts collected in Canada,[43] except that on lump sums which derive from blanket licences, the commission rate is 15%. With respect to amounts received from other countries, SODRAC charges 5%. Royalties are remitted quarterly to its members.[44]

SODRAC has entered into reciprocal agreements with sixty-five sister societies throughout the world to facilitate the administration of

---

[42] See Chapter 3 for a discussion of sub-publishing.

[43] By motion of the Board of Administration, the commission rate was set at 8% for the last three years.

[44] Paragraph 8 of the SODRAC Author-Composer Agreement which is reproduced in full in Appendix 1.

the reproduction right. Applicants for licences can now apply to SODRAC over the Internet at www.sodrac.com.

B. The SODRAC Agreement

Pursuant to the membership agreement, the composer signs exclusively for the world and assigns to SODRAC the right to license and prohibit the reproduction of musical or dramatico-musical works.[45] The rights assigned to SODRAC include the following: (a) to authorize the reproduction of the work and grant licences to that effect; (b) to prohibit the reproduction of the work and take necessary steps in order to do so; (c) to collect and distribute the royalties resulting from the reproduction right, including remuneration for private copying; (d) generally, to monitor the reproduction of the work; (e) to inspect the books and records of users; (f) to institute legal proceedings for the recovery of amounts owing; (g) to negotiate, compromise, and enter into settlements prior to or following the institution of legal proceedings.[46]

Because of this assignment, SODRAC can enter into general agreements with copyright users and negotiate blanket licences.[47] In this way, SODRAC functions more like a performing rights society than CMRRA, which does not take an assignment of rights. As discussed above, CMRRA acts as an agent for its members.

(c) Performing Rights — SOCAN

(i) Generally

The Society of Composers, Authors and Music Publishers of Canada ("SOCAN"), which was formed in 1990, is the result of a merger between Composers, Authors and Publishers Association of Canada ("CAPAC")[48] and the Performing Rights Organization of Canada Ltd. (PRO Canada), also known as "PROCAN".[49] Although

---

[45] Ibid., paras. 1 and 4.

[46] Ibid., para. 4.

[47] As a result thereof, the provisions of the s. 30.8(1) of the Act exempting certain "ephemeral recordings" from infringement claims will not apply since a licence is available from SODRAC to "make the fixation or reproduction of the performer's performance, work or sound recording."

[48] CAPAC was established in 1925 as the Canadian Performing Rights Society and re-named CAPAC in 1945.

[49] PROCAN was formed in Canada in 1976 when it ceased to be a wholly-owned subsidiary of "BMI" (Broadcast Music Inc., U.S.A.) which it had been since 1947.

SOCAN is now Canada's only performing rights society, the U.S. affiliation of SOCAN's predecessor corporations, namely CAPAC with ASCAP, and PROCAN with BMI, is still relevant. SOCAN members must choose which U.S. performing rights society (either ASCAP, BMI or SESAC) will administer their performing rights in the U.S. In the absence of a choice by the member, U.S. performing rights are administered by ASCAP.

Subject to the exceptions contained in the Act,[50] SOCAN's tariffs cover every possible way music is performed in public; fees are set for the use of music in airplanes, elevators, restaurants, theatres and nightclubs, on television and on radio, in motion pictures, and for all other public performances of music.

(ii) The SOCAN Agreement

The SOCAN agreement requires members to assign to SOCAN all "performing rights" in musical works owned or controlled by them for the term of the agreement. The term is two years and is automatically renewable for a period of two years unless terminated by notice given at least three months before the end of any two-year term.[51] The SOCAN writer and publisher agreement defines a musical work as "any musical work... and any words that are associated with the musical work... [including]... the vocal and instrumental music whether live or contained in any reproduction of the musical work on any medium used to reproduce sound..."[52] "Performing" is defined as "performing by any means and in any manner" and includes communication by telecommunication.[53] "Performing right" includes "any right that... exists or may exist in the future... of performance... in public by any means... and in any manner, and of communication by telecommunication..."[54] Excluded from the definition of "performing right" are: (1) the performance of "an opera, operetta, musical play or similar work in its entirety... except in cases where the performance is delivered as part of a pre-recorded audio-visual work..."; [55] and (2) the performance of "a choreographic work in its entirety insofar as it

---

[50] Exceptions include the affirmative defences to copyright infringement discussed in Chapter 4 and the exception with respect to "ephemeral rights" discussed in Chapter 1.

[51] See Appendix 1 for SOCAN agreement.

[52] Ibid., para. 4.1

[53] Ibid., para. 4.2

[54] Ibid., para. 4.3. Also included is the right of "authorizing or prohibiting any public performance or any communication... by means of telecommunication..."

[55] Ibid., para 4.3(i). Thus, authors retain the 'grand rights'; these rights are typically dealt with through a music publisher.

consists of words and or music alone written expressly for it when performed with the live visual representation of... [the]... choreographic work... except in cases where the performance is delivered as part of a pre-recorded audio-visual work..."[56]

Every SOCAN member should insert into any contract for the creation of a musical work a provision making such agreement, whether it be a publishing, film, composer or jingle agreement, subject to the SOCAN Membership and Assignment Agreement.

(iii) SOCAN's Functions

On behalf of its members and its international affiliated societies, SOCAN's primary functions are: (1) the licensing of performing rights; (2) the collection and distribution of licence fees;[57] and (3) the prosecution or defence of infringement actions.[58] Secondarily, SOCAN lobbies the government on copyright matters. Reciprocally, by virtue of bilateral agreements, foreign societies log the use of SOCAN members' performing rights internationally and forward performance royalties to SOCAN. In some cases, SOCAN members can voluntarily file notices of performance to assist the logging of public performances. This may occur, for example, where a member performs music live and in concert.

(iv) Membership Requirements

SOCAN will accept as a member anyone whose music has been: (1) published by a music publisher; (2) performed in some manner either by live performance or broadcast, or in a performance licensed by SOCAN; or (3) recorded by a record company.[59]

(v) Home Taping

SOCAN has recently undertaken to administer, on behalf of its members and affiliated societies, the remuneration right for private copying contained in subsection 81(1) of the Act. Pursuant to the

---

[56] Ibid., para. 4.3(ii).

[57] SOCAN's authority to collect licensing fees is founded in the *Copyright Act*. By virtue of s. 68.2(1), SOCAN cannot collect a fee greater than the fee approved by the Copyright Board. Where necessary, SOCAN can also audit licensees.

[58] The SOCAN agreement., para. 8.

[59] *SOCAN Facts: A Guide for Lyricists, Songwriters and Music Publishers*, (Toronto: SOCAN, 1990), at p. 5.

Agreement to Assign Right of Remuneration for Private Copying, members can assign this right to SOCAN. The agreement also provides that SOCAN will administer its members' right to receive remuneration for home taping under the laws of foreign countries. SOCAN has stated that the cost of administering these rights will be borne only by those receiving royalties for home taping, and not by its membership at large.

(d) Other Relevant Administrators

(i) Audio Video Licensing Agency

The Audio Video Licensing Agency ("AVLA") licenses the exhibition and duplication of music videos and the duplication of master audio recordings. AVLA represents all the major record companies in Canada as well as many independent labels and artists. AVLA members own or control the copyright in over 95% of all sound recordings and music videos produced and/or distributed in Canada. To become a member, one must own or control copyright in at least three music videos and/or sound recordings.[60] AVLA does not take an assignment of rights; like the CMRRA it acts as agent for its principals (record companies).

AVLA has several licensing programs. Its television program licenses the exhibition of music videos on network, regional and local programs, and on pay and cable TV. It also licenses video pools to clubs and dances;[61] video road shows for use by mobile disc jockeys; the use of sound recordings and music videos for in-flight entertainment by Canada's major air lines; and radio stations which use them in television commercials for self-promotion. AVLA also provides independent licences to disc jockeys, restaurants, retail outlets, fitness instructors, dancers, entertainers, or anyone who uses duplicated tapes in the course of their business.[62] Blanket licences available to disk jockey associations permit their members to duplicate tapes for business use. Lastly, licences which permit the duplication and leasing of music to commercial establishments are also available to musical supply services.

Under the Audio Video Licensing Agency Inc. Agent Agreement,[63] AVLA acts as agent "to solicit and negotiate non-exclusive licences for use of music tracks" (as defined in paragraph 1(a) of the agreement)

---

[60] The above (and what follows) is taken largely from an AVLA brochure, undated.

[61] A video pool is a compilation of music videos.

[62] These licences are personal to the licensee and do not permit the duplication of recordings for third parties.

[63] According to AVLA, more agreements will be created in the future.

which includes master records or master videos for the territory of Canada. AVLA deducts an administration fee of 14% from all amounts received and remits the balance to its members. Pursuant to its licences, AVLA is authorized to inspect the books and records of any licensee and does enforce the rights of its members.[64] Part of AVLA's revenue is used to ensure greater compliance by user groups, many of which are unfamiliar with Canadian copyright law.

AVLA is a member of the Canadian Retransmission Collective and the Neighbouring Rights Collective of Canada and has been designated by the latter to collect and distribute neighbouring rights royalties to members of CIRPA.

(ii) Canadian Copyright Licensing Agency

The Canadian Copyright Licensing Agency (herein "CANCOPY") was incorporated in 1988 as a federal non-profit corporation. Its main purpose is the "collective copyright management of the reprographic use of published material" and in this regard it seeks to be "(a) the administrative tool that will provide easy access to copyright material contained within the repertoire and (b) the mechanism that will distribute royalties to the copyright holder".[65]

CANCOPY is relevant to composers whose work is published in print form and can be reproduced reprographically. Composers should consider including a clause in any music publishing agreement permitting the administration of reprographic rights by CANCOPY.

Most of CANCOPY's licences describe authorized copying as visually perceivable facsimile reproduction of all or part of a work made by a reprographic process, including photocopying, xerography, duplication from a stencil, microform (including microfilm and microfiche), typing, transcription by hand or drawing (including tracing) and analogous means; facsimile transmission and transmission by VideoTelecom equipment; a reproduction made by a 'smart copier' such as a Xerox Docutech or Kodak 1500 Series copying machine or by

---

[64] See, for example, *R. v. Miles of Music Ltd.* (1987), 20 C.I.P.R. 157, 18 C.P.R. (3d) 77 (Ont. H.C.), reversed (1989), 74 O.R. (2d) 518 (Ont. C.A.), a case involving compilation tapes made by a disc jockey for a disc jockey franchise. At trial, the issue was whether a search made by the RCMP on behalf of the Canadian Recording Industry Association was an abuse of process under s. 7 of the *Canadian Charter of Rights and Freedoms*. The trial court found that there was an unreasonable abuse of process. However, on appeal, the Ontario Court of Appeal held that the search did not amount to an abuse of process and did not violate s. 7 of the Charter; the case was remitted to the Provincial Court for a new trial on the merits. *R. v. Miles of Music Ltd.* (1989), 24 C.P.R. (3d) 301, 31 O.A.C. 380 (Ont. C.A.).

[65] CANCOPY Fact Sheet, 1991.

input into or output by a computer or word processor, subject to specified restrictions; and digital transmission for the purpose of interlibrary loan. [66]

As is the case with other collectives, CANCOPY acts as a central clearing house for the rights it administers. It engages in reciprocal and bilateral agreements with national and international collectives, thereby greatly enlarging its repertoire beyond the works of its own affiliates. There are two types of licences granted by CANCOPY: (1) the comprehensive licence, intended for frequent users, which permits the copying of any work in the CANCOPY repertoire; and (2) the transactional licence, for infrequent users, which permits the copying of specific works. Comprehensive licences are issued in advance, most often for a fixed fee calculated on a per capita basis, (i.e., with respect to the persons whose copying is covered by the licence), and provide immediate access and reduced administrative costs. Transactional licences must be obtained prior to copying and are priced on a per page basis. Since few licensees wish to keep complete records of their copying, a sampling scheme is used in connection with comprehensive licensing to measure the amount of copying and determine the appropriate royalties. Records are always kept in connection with transactional licences.

(iii) Retransmission Collectives

As noted earlier, the retransmission of distant signals by cable companies, direct broadcast satellites and master antenna systems is governed by the retransmission right contained in section 31 of the *Copyright Act*. Various collectives have been formed to administer this right on behalf of copyright owners. These include SOCAN, the Canadian Retransmission Collective (the CRC, on behalf of non-U.S. independent film and television producers), the Canadian Broadcasters Retransmission Rights Agency (the CBRC, on behalf of private sector Canadian broadcasters), the Canadian Copyright Collective (the CCC, on behalf of U.S. film producers), the Canadian Retransmission Rights Association (the CBRA, on behalf of the CBC/SRC, Radio Quebec, ABC, CBS and NBC), Major League Baseball (MBL) and FWS Sports. The holders of retransmission rights obtain what is in effect a "compulsory" licence.[67]

---

[66] Communication from Marian Hebb, Barrister & Solicitor, counsel for CANCOPY. August 25, 1999.

[67] This is because s. 76(3) of the Act limits the remedy for infringement of the right to the payment of the royalties approved by the Copyright Board. For more on the retransmission right in the context of new media, see "Study on New Media and

(iv) Neighbouring Rights Collective of Canada

The Neighbouring Rights Collective of Canada (the "NRCC"), a non-profit umbrella collective founded in 1997, administers the remuneration right granted to performers and the makers of sound recordings under section 19 of the *Copyright Act*. Its members include: (1) The American Federation of Musicians of the United States and Canada, ACTRA, and ARTISTI (on behalf of the Union des Artistes) as performers' representatives; and (2) AVLA, (on behalf of CRIA, and CIRPA) and SOPROQ (on behalf of ADISQ) as record company representatives. The NRCC has asked the Copyright Board to set tariffs for twenty-eight different types of users, including radio stations, restaurants, theatres, clubs and hotels. Royalties, based on a sliding scale applicable to gross revenues, either as a fixed licence fee or as a percentage of advertising revenue, will be collected and remitted to NRCC members for distribution to recording artists and the makers of sound recordings. As required by subsection 19(3) of the *Copyright Act*, royalties will be divided equally in the aggregate between performers and producers.

(v) Canadian Private Copying Collective

The Canadian Private Copying Collective (the "CPCC") consists of five collectives representing songwriters and music publishers, namely, SOCAN, SODRAC, CMRRA, NRCC, and SOGEDAM. The CPCC will collect and distribute the blank tape levy contained in Part VIII of the Act. The proposed levy applies to the sale of blank audio cassettes and CD-ROM discs, and will be divided among the various interests subject to adjustment when the regulated returns are finally determined.

(vi) Other Collectives

The above collectives are those most relevant to the music business in Canada; other collectives exist and others most certainly will be formed in the future.[68]

Copyright", Final Report, June 30, 1994, prepared for Industry Canada (New Media and Information Technologies Industry Branch) by NGL Nordicity Group Ltd.

[68] Such other collectives include: (1) with respect to neighbouring rights: PUC and SACD; (2) with respect to reproduction rights: CARFAC, UNIQ, and Vis-Art. For the most part, these collectives represent visual artists and writers and have limited relevance for musicians.

4. The Copyright Board

(a) Generally

The Copyright Board's primary function is the setting of royalties, terms and conditions under which collective societies enforce the rights of copyright owners under the Act. A quasi-judicial administrative tribunal, the Board is chaired by a sitting or retired judge of a superior or district court.[69] Its primary duty is the fixing of royalties and their related terms and conditions. In exercising its jurisdiction, the Board has all the rights, powers and privileges as are vested in a superior court of record[70] and its orders may be enforced in the same manner as an order of the Federal Court or any superior court.[71] The Federal Court has held that the Board has the power to make an initial determination on matters incidental to its jurisdiction.[72] Such determinations, however, are subject to judicial review by the Federal Court under section 28 of the *Federal Court Act.*

In setting tariffs, the Copyright Board endeavours to balance the competing interests of music users and copyright owners. This approach is mandated both by statute[73] and case law. The role of the Copyright Board in relation to the collective administration of copyright is discussed below.

(b) Performing Rights

Performing rights fees are one of the most important sources of income generated by the copyright in musical works. The Copyright Board has sole jurisdiction to fix the royalties chargeable for the use of musical works performed in public. Users have sixty days to file written objections to a proposed tariff.[74] If objections are filed, the Board "as soon as practicable" is required to consider the proposed tariff and any objections, and must send to the collective society a copy of the

---

[69] Subsection 63(3) of the Act.

[70] Subsection 66.7(1) of the Act.

[71] Subsection 66.7(2) of the Act.

[72] *CTV Television Network Ltd. v. Canada (Copyright Board)* (1993), 46 C.P.R. (3d) 343 (Fed. C.A.), leave to appeal to S.C.C. refused (1993), 51 C.P.R. (3d) v (S.C.C.), at pp. 348-49; *Canadian Cable Television Assn. v. Canada (Copyright Board)* (1991), 34 C.P.R. (3d) 521 (Fed. T.D.), at pp. 530-33, affirmed 46 C.P.R. (3d) 359 (Fed. C.A.), leave to appeal to S.C.C. refused (1993), 51 C.P.R. (3d) v (S.C.C.).

[73] See, for example, s. 68(1) of the Act; sub-para. 68(2)(a)(ii); and s. 72(2). See also *Canadian Broadcasting Corp. v. Canada (Copyright Appeal Board)* (1986), 8 C.P.R. (3d) 484 (Fed. T.D.).

[74] Subsection 67.1(5) of the Act.

objections. The collective society has a right of reply and the Board must send any reply so given to the person making the objection.[75] Normally, hearings are held and after a consideration of the oral arguments of all interested parties, the Board makes a decision and certifies the tariff as approved.[76] The tariff is published in the Canada Gazette and a copy of it together with reasons for the Board's decision is sent to the collective society and any person who filed an objection.[77] Decisions of the Board are subject to judicial review by the Federal Court of Canada.[78]

(c) Retransmission Rights

The Copyright Board is also authorized to determine tariffs with respect to retransmission royalties[79] and to determine the portion of the royalties that is to be paid to each collective society.[80] In so doing, the Board is enjoined from discriminating between owners of copyright on the ground of nationality or residence,[81] although the Act requires that the Board ensure that there is a preferential rate for small retransmission systems.[82] The approval process is essentially similar to that which governs performing rights societies.[83]

(d) Reproduction Rights, Neighbouring Rights, and the Rights of Broadcasters

If a collective society that administers any of the rights contained in sections 3, 15, 18, or 21 of the Act chooses to file a proposed tariff, the Board is empowered to certify it. The procedure followed is similar to

---

[75] Subsection 68(1) of the Act.

[76] Subsection 68(3). For criteria and factors the Board must consider in examining the proposed tariff, see s. 68(3). See also s. 68.1 which provides for special and transitional royalties with respect to the performance in public or communication to the public by telecommunication of performer's performances and sound recordings. The section provides a cap on the royalties that may be collected by certain transmission systems for the first three years that neighbouring rights are in effect.

[77] Subsection 68(4) of the Act. A decision of the Board may be varied if in the Board's opinion there had been a material change in circumstances since the decision was made; see s. 66.52.

[78] Subsection 28(1) of the *Federal Court Act*.

[79] Sections 71 through 76 of the Act.

[80] Paragraph 72(1)(b) of the Act.

[81] Subsection 73(2) of the Act.

[82] Subsection 74(1) of the Act.

[83] See s. 71-73 of the Act.

that which governs performing rights societies.[84] However, in addition to publicizing the proposed tariff in the Canada Gazette, the Board is required to notify persons affected by the proposed tariff by distributing or publishing a notice in such manner as the Board sees fit.[85]

The Board is also given authority to fix royalties in cases where a collective society and users are unable to agree on the royalties to be paid pursuant to a negotiated agreement.[86] Such royalties are required to be in effect for a period of not less than one year.[87]

As discussed above, section 70.5(3) of the Act exempts any agreement entered into by a collective society and user filed with the Board from the application of section 45 of the *Competition Act*. However, where the Director of Investigation and Research under that act considers that the agreement is contrary to the public interest, he/she may request the Board to examine the agreement. The board may, but is not required to, alter the royalties or any terms or conditions of the agreement after giving all interested parties an opportunity to be heard.[88]

Finally, subsection 77(1) empowers the Board, on application, to issue a licence to do an act mentioned in sections 3, 15, 18, or 21 where the Board is satisfied that the applicant has made reasonable efforts to locate the copyright owner, and the owner cannot be located.[89] The licence must be non-exclusive and is subject to such terms and conditions as the Board may establish.[90]

5. The CRTC

(a) An Overview

The Canadian Radio-television and Telecommunications Commission ("CRTC") is an independent public agency charged, *inter alia*, with the regulation and supervision of the Canadian broadcasting system.[91] The Commission's objects are governed by the broadcasting policy set out in subsection 3(1) of the *Broadcasting Act* and the

---

[84] Sections 70.14 and 70.15 of the Act.

[85] Section 70.16 of the Act.

[86] Section 70.2 of the Act.

[87] Subsection 70.2(2) of the Act.

[88] Subsection 70.6(1) of the Act.

[89] Subsection 77(1) of the Act. The section applies to persons who wish to obtain a licence to use a published work, fixation of a performer's performance, a published sound recording or a fixation of a communication signal.

[90] Subsection 77(2) of the Act.

[91] See s. 5(1) of the *Broadcasting Act*, S.C. 1991, c. 11.

regulatory policy set out in subsection 5(2) thereof. With respect to the former, the *Broadcasting Act* declares that the Canadian broadcasting system should "serve to safeguard, enrich and strengthen the cultural, political, social and economic fabric of Canada"[92] and "encourage the development of Canadian expression by providing a wide range of programming that reflects Canadian... artistic creativity, by displaying Canadian talent in entertainment programming."[93] With respect to the former, the Act avers that "the Canadian broadcasting system should be regulated and supervised in a flexible manner that facilitates the provision of Canadian programs to Canadians...".[94] It is the above objects that provide the statutory basis for the Commission's policies on "Canadian content", discussed below.

Among the powers given the CRTC are the power to: (1) establish classes of licences; (2) issue, amend, renew, suspend, or revoke licences;[95] and (3) make regulations respecting the time devoted to Canadian programming.[96] This regulatory power has been used by the Commission to promulgate regulations concerning Canadian content on AM and FM radio, television, and specialty services. These regulations have the status of law, and the *Broadcasting Act* provides criminal penalties for their violation.[97]

(b) Canadian Content

The Canadian content regulations are found primarily in the *Radio Regulations, 1986.*[98] These regulations require AM and FM radio stations to devote a minimum number of hours per broadcast week "in a reasonable manner throughout each broadcast day"[99] to "Canadian" selections. "Canadian" selections are musical selections written by

---

[92] Ibid., sub-para. 3(1)(d)(i).

[93] Ibid, sub-para. 3(1)(d)(ii).

[94] Ibid., para. 5(2)(e).

[95] Ibid., Subsection 9(1)(a)-(e).

[96] Ibid., paras. 10(1)(a) and (b).

[97] Contravention of the regulations is an offence under s. 32(2) punishable by summary conviction. Individuals are liable to a fine not exceeding $25,000 for a first offence and a fine not exceeding $50,000 for a subsequent offence. Corporations are liable to a fine not exceeding $250,000 for a first offence and a fine not exceeding $500,000 for a subsequent offence.

[98] SOR/86-982 as amended.

[99] Subsections 2.2(3) and 2.2(7) of the Regulations. See footnote 102 infra for special rules applying to commercial licensees.

"Canadian"[100] persons which meet at least two of the following conditions:

(1) the music or lyrics are performed principally by a Canadian;
(2) the music is composed entirely by a Canadian;
(3) the lyrics are written entirely by a Canadian;
(4) the musical selection consists of a live performance wholly recorded in Canada or wholly performed or broadcast live in Canada;
(5) if the performance or recording is made after September 1, 1991, and a Canadian collaborated with a non-Canadian, the Canadian must receive at least 50% of the credit as composer and lyricist according to the records of a recognized performing rights society.[101]

The regulations require commercial licensees to devote 35% or more of the musical selections from Category 2 and 10% from Category 3 to Canadian selections throughout the broadcast week.[102] Categories 2 and 3 are defined in CRTC Public Notice 1991-19.[103] Category 2 covers all the major forms of popular music; Category 3 covers "special interest" genres such as classical, jazz, folk and religious music.[104]

---

[100] "Canadian" persons are persons whose ordinary place of residence was in Canada throughout the six month period immediately preceding that person's contribution to the musical composition or concert: see SOR/91-517, s. 1(3).

[101] Ibid., s. 2.2(2) Also included are instrumental performances the music or lyrics of which are wholly written by a Canadian, performances that a Canadian has composed for instruments only, and musical selections which qualified under the former regulations.

[102] Ibid., s. 2.2(8) and (3) respectively. Pursuant to para. 2.2(6)(a), selections from Category 2 may be reduced to an amount not less than 20% where in any broadcast week, between not less than 35% and not more than 50% of the musical selections are instrumental music; and pursuant to para 2.2 (6)(b) to an amount not less than 15% where at least 50% of the musical selections in any broadcast week are instrumental music. Unless otherwise provided under a licensee's conditions of licence, commercial licensees are required also to devote 35% of music broadcast between 6:00 a.m. and 6:00 p.m., Monday to Friday, to Canadian musical selections from Category 2 (to Canadian selections "broadcast in their entirety"); see s. 2.2(9); see also s. 2.2(11). Non-commercial licensees are required to devote 30% of musical selections from Category 2 to Canadian selections scheduled "in a reasonable manner throughout the broadcast day"; see s. 2.2(7). For French-language broadcasts, see ss. 2.2(5), (10), (12) and (13). Pursuant to SOR/98-597, the above rules came into force January 3, 1999.

[103] The Notice may be found in the Canada Gazette, Part 1, February 23, 1991.

[104] The CRTC's compendious definitions are not without an element of vagueness; compare, for example, Subcategory 24 of Category 2 ("Jazz-oriented") with Subcategory 33 of Category 3 ("Jazz"); or Subcategory 23 of Category 2 ("Folk-oriented") with Subcategory 32 of Category 3 ("Folk").

Canadian content is also regulated on broadcast television and with respect to specialty services.[105]

Although not without controversy, there is little doubt that the CRTC's regulation of Canadian content has been an important factor in ensuring the viability and continued growth of Canadian cultural industries and the Canadian music business in particular.

---

[105] See, for example, the *Television Broadcast Regulations, 1987* and the *Specialty Service Regulations, 1990*; the latter deals with such matters as the broadcast of music videos on cable specialty channels.

3
MUSIC PUBLISHING

Contributing Author: C. Craig Parks, B.A., LL.B.

1. An Overview

(a) Music Publishing Defined

(i) Business Definition

Music publishing is the promotion, exploitation, administration, and protection of musical copyrights which the music publisher owns and controls by virtue of the assignment of rights granted pursuant to a publishing agreement. The music publisher normally controls all the rights associated with copyright, except the performing right, which is normally assigned to a performing rights society (for example, SOCAN in Canada). The music publisher can still exploit and promote the performing right, for example by soliciting radio airplay. Music publishers today mainly exploit musical copyrights by issuing mechanical and synchronization licences, although sheet music (which was the origin of the music publishing industry) is still a small part of the business.

(ii) Legal Definition

However, the *Copyright Act* (herein "the Act"), while updated since the print technology era, is still based on print technology concepts. Under the "Act", publication is defined as "making copies of the work available to the public".[1] The statutory language suggests tangible copies of music (sheet music), not the intangible licensing of rights which forms the mainstay of music publishing today.

---

[1] S. 4 (1)(a) of the *Copyright Act*, R.S.C. 1985, c. C-42, as amended ("the Act"). See also *McFarlane v. Hulton*, [1899] 1 Ch. 884 (Eng. Ch. Div.). The offering of newspapers to the public was held to be a publication.

(b) Music Publishers

(i) Functions

Music publishing is best understood by discussing a music publisher's functions. Music publishers have four broad functions: (a) creative; (b) promotional; (c) business; and (d) administrative.[2] These functions can overlap in practice but they are useful to consider separately here for analytical purposes. Since the music business is international, a music publisher's functions may be carried out internationally either by one large company or by a network of small independent publishers.

A. Creative

The creative function includes assisting in the development of a songwriter's craft, suggesting alterations to music, arranging compatible collaborations between lyricists, composers and co-writers, determining whether translations or adaptations are appropriate, and recording demos which the publisher uses either (i) to shop for a record deal for a singer/songwriter or (ii) to obtain a cover version of a song for a songwriter. A "cover version" of a song is one that is performed by someone other than the original composer.

Where "shopping" for a record deal is the primary objective, the singer/songwriter is often signed to a development deal. If the publisher succeeds in securing a record deal for the singer/songwriter within the agreed time frame, all the songwriter's existing songs and any future songs recorded under the record deal will be published by the publisher.

---

[2] This framework for analysis was adapted from Leonard Feist's *An Introduction to Popular Music Publishing in America* (New York: National Music Publishers Association Inc., 1980) discussed at pp. 72-88. Other analyses can be formulated but this framework is used for convenience. See, for example, David Baskerville, *Music Business Handbook and Career Guide* 4th ed. (Denver: The Sherwood Company, 1985) at pp. 56-63. See also Jeffrey J. Brabec and Todd W. Brabec, "Music Publishing (What Was Once Known as a Business of Pennies, It Sure Has Hit the Big Time)" in *Entertainment, Publishing and the Arts Handbook* (New York: Clark Boardman, 1989) at pp. 96-101 (herein "Brabec"). This article details a publisher's functions. See also Jennifer Wright, Chapter 8, "Music Publishing" in Shane Simpson and Greg Stevens's *Music: The Business and the Law* (Sydney: The Law Book Company Limited, 1986) at pp. 89-107.

B. Promotional

The promotional function consists of approaching producers, managers, agents, musicians, studios, advertising agencies, television and motion picture producers and artists and repertoire ("A&R") staff at record companies, with a view to exploiting the musical copyrights in the publisher's control. These promotional efforts are aimed at other music and entertainment industry professionals, as opposed to a record company's efforts which are more consumer-oriented. Publishers do advertise, but generally in "trade" publications not aimed at the general public. Promotional initiatives include press releases and articles in trade papers about the activities of the music publisher and its composers. This helps build the composers' reputations and promote the composers' music.

Once a song is recorded, the publisher may also promote it by trying to secure other "cover" recordings. A music publisher may also circulate sample recordings of its music to induce those in the music and entertainment industry to use its music in subsequent recordings and in films, television and commercials.

C. Business

Business functions include choosing the music to develop, investing in talent, and determining how much money to spend on projects. The business department (which often includes "legal affairs") drafts and negotiates the contracts on which the publishing industry relies: songwriter agreements, co-publishing agreements, mechanical licences, synchronization licences and so on.

Business functions also include: setting licensing fees in accordance with market demand and industry standards; financial planning which is essential in order to cope with national and international business problems; and instituting and defending copyright infringement actions.

Sometimes a music publisher goes beyond its normal role to create finished product that a record company simply has to distribute.

D. Administrative

The music publisher's administrative functions include registration of copyrights, the assignment of copyrights it secures, and collecting, accounting to and paying royalties to songwriters. Subject to market demand, publishers also arrange for the printing of songs in a folio, the production of lead sheets[3] and arrangements of songs.

(ii) Classes of Music Publishers

A. Legitimate

Generally, music publishers are either subsidiaries of large record companies or independents[4], and may specialize in certain types of music or publish all types of music. In addition to these traditional music publishers, other music industry players sometimes find themselves in the position of a music publisher including: record producers, managers and composers.

Record companies have a subsidiary or affiliate publishing arm to take advantage of the dual role of its singer/songwriter artists whose songs generate a separate stream of income through print, mechanical, performance and synchronization royalties. Such companies use such royalties to offset the financial risks associated with the record business and/or to generate extra income.[5]

In the non-traditional camp, there is the "name" record producer, who, in a speculative venture with a new artist, may take a portion of the copyrights in the artist's songs, thereby effectively becoming a publisher. This can be done in lieu of, or in addition to, payment for his or her services.

Particularly when the sources of commissionable income appear limited, an artist's manager may also insist on a portion of the artist's copyrights, thereby extending the manager's interest in the artist's career well beyond the normal management term.[6]

---

[3] A lead sheet is the musical notation of a composition consisting of chord symbols and a melody line if it is an instrumental, and can also include lyrics if it is a vocal composition. Once a prerequisite of copyright, changes in the Act have removed the technicality.

[4] Paula Dranov, *Inside the Music Publishing Industry* (White Plains, New York: Knowledge Industry Publications, Inc., 1980) at 7.

[5] Controlled compositions pertaining to this practice are discussed in Chapter 8, "Recording" and cross-collateralization is discussed below in the text, section 2(c)(iv).

[6] See *Clifford Davis Management, Gilbert O'Sullivan* and *Elton John* cases and Chapter 10, "Personal Service Contracts". Note the possibility of conflict of interest. In particular, in the *O'Sullivan* case, musical copyrights were re-assigned to O'Sullivan because of the conflict of interest between his manager, Gordon Mills, who also signed him to recording and publishing agreements through a network of companies in which Mills had ownership interest.

Finally, composers can be their own music publishers.[7] First, as original copyright owners, before assigning their copyrights to anyone else, composers are their own publishers. If they are well-connected (and not lured by big publishing advances), they may choose to remain their own publishers and work their songs themselves. In that scenario, they will certainly keep more of the earnings. They must weigh, however, whether 100% of their own pie is better than 50% or 75% of a major publisher's possibly bigger pie.

Indeed, the norm has evolved into a situation where the composer's own publishing company enters into a co-publishing arrangement with a larger publisher who is actually in the publishing business.

B. Song Sharks

There will always be those who seek to take advantage of inexperienced composers by requiring various fees and payments for the privilege of being published and by tying up copyrights without actually exploiting them. These people are known in the music business as "song sharks".[8] Legitimate publishers do not require money from composers to publish their music. Composers and music publishers share in copyright royalties. Song sharks are not as prevalent as they were in the fast-paced song-plugger era of Tin Pan Alley, although they have not totally disappeared. They should be avoided at all costs.

---

[7] The following may be helpful for the composer who wishes to engage in publishing. Leon Kellman, "On Forming a Pop Music Publishing Company" (1971), 2 *Performing Arts Revue* 25; Walter E. Hurst, *How to Be a Music Publisher* (Hollywood: Seven Arts Press, Inc., 1979). See also Jeffrey L. Graubert "Self Publishing and the Songwriter/Music Publisher Agreement" (1986), Vol. 8 No. 4 *E.L.R.* 3 at pp. 3-6 and Don Biederman "Self Publishing, ...: A Rejoinder" (1986), Vol. 8 No. 5 *E.L.R.* 6 at pp. 6-8.

[8] John V. Mills, *You and The Music Business* (Toronto: C.A.P.A.C., 1983) at 31, 32.

(c) Main Copyrights and Revenue Sources[9]

The GST aspects of these revenue sources and the agreements discussed below are outlined in Chapter 12, "Tax".

(i) Performing Rights

Performing rights are generally licensed by performing rights societies, not music publishers. The performing right is the right to perform music in public.[10] Although a separate right under the Act, the right to communicate to the public by telecommunication is treated as a performing right and is licensed by performing rights societies, for example SOCAN in Canada. The key to both rights is the public aspect of the activity.

SOCAN's main licensees are radio and television broadcasting stations. Through recent initiatives taken by SOCAN under broader legislation, cable origination stations and cable operators themselves have started to become significant contributors to SOCAN's income.[11] Other performing rights licensees include concert halls and bars, for example. SOCAN's tariffs for over thirty different types of music use are set out in the Canada Gazette and vary from year to year.[12] Most tariffs take the form of blanket licences for unlimited use of the music in SOCAN's repertoire.

Typically, the music publisher receives half of the performing right income and the composer receives the other half, unless the composer is also a music publisher or a co-publisher, in which case, the discussions in sections 1(d)(ii)C and 3(b)(i) below, concerning the co-publishing agreement, are relevant. Such division of income is referred to in the music business as the so-called "publisher's share" and "writer's share" of public performance income respectively. That is,

---

[9] See Paul Sanderson, "Music Rights and the Music Business in Canada: An Overview" (1980), Vol. 10 No. 4 *P.A.R.* 352. This article is an overview of the copyright basis for the rights inherent in music and the main revenue sources from music. It includes an overview of the Canadian music business, the main licensors and licensees of "music rights", and includes a hypothetical example that illustrates the interrelation between these rights. It also includes an appendix of relevant forms and precedents and was current to 1980. See also Jennifer Wright, "Music Publishing" cited above, note 2, at pp. 105-107.

[10] See 3(1) of the Act and s. 2 of the Act which defines "performance".

[11] As of the date of publication, however, SOCAN has only collected a fraction of the royalties awarded.

[12] The Copyright Board does have the power to set the terms of a licence and users can object to a proposed tariff of fees, for example s. 68(4) of the Act. See discussion in Chapter 2, "The Licensing and Administration of Copyright and the Regulation of Music in Media" regarding the Copyright Board.

50% of net income for performing rights goes to each of the music publisher and the composer.

(ii) Mechanical Rights

This is one of the most important licences. The mechanical royalty rate is discussed in Chapter 2, "The Licensing and Administration of Copyright and the Regulation of Music in Media".[13] The main licensees of mechanical rights are record companies.

(iii) Synchronization Rights

The synchronization right is the right to synchronize music with visual images.[14] It is not defined in the Act. Producers of motion pictures, television programs, television commercials and videos require synchronization licences from music publishers. The following factors are important in determining a synchronization rights fee: (1) the administrative costs of issuing a licence; (2) the popularity of the music; (3) the context of the use; (4) the territory where it will be used; (5) the term of the licence; (6) the media it is used in; (7) the extent of the use, that is, whether the music is used in whole or in part; and (8) whether it is featured on background use.

(iv) Print Rights

A print right is the right to reproduce music in any printed form. The music publisher usually licenses a printing company to print copies of the music and sell it to the public. Educational music, church music, "Top 40" ballads which lend themselves to a piano rendition, and songbook folios of popular rock bands are published regularly in sheet music form, usually by publishers who specialize in this type of music publishing.[15]

---

[13] See also Appendix 1 for a sample mechanical rights licence and Appendix 2 for a sample mechanical rights licence checklist.

[14] See the *Michael Bishop* case discussed in Chapter 1, "Copyright". The synchronization right was recognized as distinct from the performing right in the broadcasting context. See also Appendix 2 for a sample synchronization licence checklist.

[15] Consider the applicability of the Quebec statute, *An Act Respecting the Professional Status of Artists in the Visual Arts, Arts and Crafts and Literature, and their Contracts with Promoters*, R.S.Q., c. S. 32.01. Section 1 of the Act states that it applies to self-employed artists who create works in the fields of visual arts, arts and crafts, and literature. S. 2(3) defines literature as the "creation and translation of original literary works such as novels,

(v) Subsidiary Rights

The term "subsidiary" right is not a strictly legal term and it is not defined in the Act. It is used here to mean any rights not discussed above in sections 1(c)(i)-(iv). Subsidiary rights include, among other rights, the right to adapt, arrange or translate music. Without permission from the music publisher, a substantial re-arrangement, adaptation, or translation of music would be copyright infringement.

There are other rights that can generate revenue from copyrights, for example, the licensing of so-called "grand rights", characterized by the use of music in live stage performances such as opera, ballet, musical comedy and musical revues.[16]

In addition, music is licensed and generates revenue in the following contexts: (1) computer and board games; (2) video jukeboxes; (3) Internet sites; (4) dolls and toys. Each licence is specific to the use being made of the music and the context in which it is used.[17] However, the rights discussed above in sections 1(c)(i-iv) continue to be the main sources of revenue-generating rights in music.

(d) Types of Music Publishing Contracts

The types of agreements outlined immediately below are discussed in more detail in sections 3(b)(i)-(v) inclusive below.

---

short stories, dramatic works, poetry, essays or any other written works of the same nature " — does this cover song lyrics? S. 31 requires a written contract setting forth the nature of the contract, the work forming the object of the contract, any transfer of rights or grant of licence, the purposes, term and mode of determination of the contract, any transfer of title or right of use affecting the work, the (non)transferability to third parties, consideration due, terms of payment, and frequency of reporting by the promoter (publisher). See also s. 33. Chap. III which provides audit rights (s. 39), reporting rights (s. 38) and a right of arbitration (s. 37). There is a right of termination if the promoter (publisher) commits an act of bankruptcy and a receiving order is issued against it under the *Bankruptcy and Insolvency Act,* cited below, in note 62, (Canada), if his/her property is taken possession of according to law or, in the case of a legal person, such person is liquidated. See also Chapter 2, concerning the Canadian Copyright Licensing Agency and reprographic rights which are relevant with respect to sheet music. See also a recent article on print rights: Joseph L. Grier, "Read the Fine Print: It's a Great Tune", in *1991 Entertainment, Publishing and the Arts Handbook* (New York: Clark, Boardman, Callaghan, 1991) at p. 209. The author suggests holding onto the print rights in view of such recent innovations as tableture books, and provides information about royalty structures. See also Peter Muller, *The Music Business* (Westport: Quorum Press, 1994), chap. 12, "The Print Rights Agreement" for a discussion of typical contract clauses.

[16] For a discussion of this issue in the context of the rock opera Jesus Christ Superstar, see John R. Allison, "Protection as Performance Rights to 'Jesus Christ Superstar': The Dramatic-Non Dramatic Dilemma" (1973), Vol. 4 No. 2 *P.A.R.* 13.

[17] See Brabec article cited above, note 2, at pp. 106-115.

(i) Composer-Publisher

The composer-publisher or songwriter-publisher contract is the mainstay of the industry. It not only defines the composer's and the music publisher's rights, but is the legal basis for the music publisher's right to enter into agreements with others. There are two main types of composer-publisher contracts: (a) the single song;[18] or (b) the exclusive term contract. The single song agreement is the assignment of publishing rights for one song, while the exclusive term contract usually assigns publishing rights for a catalogue of songs written during the term of the contract, and often includes previously written songs.[19]

(ii) With Other Publishers

The contractual relationships outlined below are separated for analysis purposes, but often interrelate in practice. A composer who acts as his or her own publisher may, and often does, enter into these agreements and they are therefore relevant to composers. The contractual aspects of these agreements are discussed in more detail in section 3(b)(i-v) below.

A. Co-Publishing

The co-publishing agreement has become standard for deals between songwriters and publishers. One of the music publishers is the active administrator (often a major publishing company) and the other publisher (the songwriter's nominal publishing entity) takes a passive role. It is chiefly a device for splitting income from the exploitation of the songs more favourably toward the songwriter. Twenty years ago, almost every publishing deal split income 50% to the publisher and

---

[18] See J. Stephen Stohn, "Music Publishing Agreements in Canada" in *Copyright Law* (Toronto: L.S.U.C., 1985) (herein "Stohn") at pp. 49-86. This article examines contractual issues concerning music publishing contracts and in particular the single song agreement. In addition, pp. 80-84 outline the various terms and types of agreements discussed below in the text in section 1(d). See also Donald C. Farber, General Editor, *Entertainment Industry Contracts Negotiating and Drafting Guide* (New York: Matthew Bender, 1991) loose-leaf, Part IV: Music, Samuel J. Fox (herein "Fox"), Part I: Songwriters and Music Publishers, Chapter 168, 01-04 inclusive gives detailed descriptions of the music publishing industry with respect to songwriter and publisher agreements. Included are discussions of advances, for example. In addition, in Chapter 169, 101 and in form 169.1, there is a discussion of the single song agreement, and at Chapter 170, the term exclusive writer agreement, form 170.1, is discussed.

[19] The composer-publisher contract is discussed in detail below in the text section 2.

50% to the songwriter. Today, the norm is 25% to the publisher and 75% to the songwriter (i.e. 50% to the songwriter and 25% to the songwriter's nominal publishing entity).

The composer-publisher typically will receive advances from the administrating publisher in return for the right to co-own and administer the composer's copyright.[20] The need for co-publishing also arises when a lyricist and a composer, for example, collaborate and have two different music publishers. There can be any number of co-publishers participating in the ownership and publisher income of a song.

B. Administration

Under an administration agreement, a songwriter or music publisher appoints a full-service music publisher for a limited period of time, normally 3 to 5 years, to administer song copyrights. The main differences between this and other publishing arrangements are that the original owner continues to own the copyrights, and the term is normally less than the life of copyright. The administrative fee, expressed as a percentage of total income generated, is generally less than the 25% normally associated with co-publishing agreements.

C. Sub-Publishing[21]

Sub-publishing involves the granting of certain rights to a foreign publisher for one or more foreign countries for a limited period of time, usually three to five years. While sub-publishers generally take 20 to 25% of publisher income generated in the countries they administer, the benefits to the original publisher can be considerable. First, since the sub-publisher is based in the foreign territory, speaks the language and has the industry contacts, it can solicit local cover versions, synchronization licences and even record licence deals more successfully. Second, as a member of the local performing and mechanical right societies, the sub-publisher receives remittances directly and frequently from those societies and passes through to the original publisher its share without delay. Without a sub-publisher, the

---

[20] Harvey Rachlin, *The Encyclopedia of The Music Business* (Toronto: Fitzhenry and Whiteside, 1981) at 97.

[21] For a more complete discussion of sub-publishing see "Foreign Publishing" in Sidney Shemel and M. William Krasilowsky, *This Business of Music*, Revised 6th ed. (New York: Billboard Publications, 1990) at pp. 217-236. See also Nancy Lathier, "Sub-Publishing: A Key to the International Market", June 1991 *Probe* 4. See Appendix 2 for a sample sub-publishing checklist.

original publisher can wait several years for accountings to find their way from the foreign societies to the publisher's domestic societies and eventually to the publisher. Third, since the sub-publisher is present and has a financial stake, it will ensure that all performances and reproductions are fully accounted for by the local societies.

The term "sub-publishing" is also used to describe the licensing within the publisher's own country of certain rights that the publisher itself is not able to administer efficiently, such as sheet music rights.

D. Participation

Under the participation agreement, one party contracts to share in or "participate" in the publisher's share of net revenue. It is discussed in more detail in section 3(b)(ii) below.

E. Sale of Publisher's Catalogue

The details of this agreement are discussed below in section 3(e).[22]

F. Other Contracts

In addition to the above main agreements, a music publisher may enter into numerous other types of agreements such as: (1) sole selling agent; (2) joint venture arrangements; (3) publication of versions;[23] or a music publisher may arrange a collection contract with another publisher. The sole selling agent agreement is a form of sub-publishing agreement whereby the original publisher prints sheet music and the other music publisher becomes the sole selling agent for the printed music. A joint venture agreement can be arranged in various ways and can include joint ownership of copyright. Publication of versions usually entails a licence granted to another publisher to publish musical arrangements, for example, big band arrangements. These agreements will not be discussed in detail since they are less common than the ones outlined above in sections 1(d)(ii) A-E inclusive.

---

[22] See Brabec article cited above, note 2 at pp. 118-129 and below in text. See also Sidney Shemel "The Acquisition and Sale of Music Copyrights", (1979), Vol. 27 Issue 19 *Bulletin*, and *Copyright Society of the U.S.A.*, 11 at pp. 11-19 and the checklist in Appendix 2.

[23] Joseph Taubman, *In Tune With the Music Business* (New York: Law-Arts Publishers, 1980) at pp. 38-42.

2. Composer-Publisher Single Song and Exclusive Term Contract Discussion

(a) Generally

Bear in mind there is no "standard" publishing contract; every publisher has developed its own documents and, in any event, they are all subject to negotiation.

Nevertheless, there is a high degree of similarity in the subject matter covered in publishing agreements and the following analysis reviews them in detail. This does not, however, imply that each provision of a contract can or should be negotiated. Indeed, the relevance and importance of any provision is often determined by the specific case. [24]

The case law that has interpreted publishing contracts is discussed in detail in Chapter 10, "Personal Service Contracts", and therefore will be footnoted here only to alert the reader to specific issues. As is made clear in Chapter 10, the law in this area indeed can be unclear and uncertain. The English cases discussed in Chapter 10 illustrate that, even with independent legal advice, these agreements may be struck down on the basis of the legal doctrine of restraint of trade. The trend is to make these contracts more fair and reasonable. The analysis below also incorporates suggestions on how to make certain clauses more fair and, as a result, perhaps more enforceable.

(b) Composer's Obligations

(i) Joint and Several

Where there is more than one composer, the obligations under the agreement are usually joint and several. If the several composers part ways, the publisher still owns the songs that they create on their own.

---

[24] For a recent article on long-term exclusive agreements see Don E. Tomlinson, " Everything That Glitters is Not Gold: Songwriter-Music Publisher Agreements and Disagreements", (1995), 18 Hastings Comm/Ent. L. J. 85. The author exhaustively analyzes the provisions of a typically one-sided agreement offered to a novice songwriter and proposes a model agreement that is fair to both sides.

(ii) Assignment of Copyright/Employment/Work-For-Hire

An assignment[25] of copyrights is standard. Without a valid grant of rights, usually by an assignment of rights, the publisher cannot license or effectively deal with these copyrights. Without an express assignment, an assignment will not necessarily be implied. This will be determined by reviewing the terms of the contract.[26] Through the assignment, the publisher becomes the copyright owner, in whole or in part, and has the right to sue for infringement,[27] although this may be contractually altered.

The exclusive term contract normally provides for both an assignment of copyright and an employment relationship. This is intended to protect the music publisher if the agreement is not found to be an employment relationship.[28] If the relationship is not an employment relationship, and there is no assignment, the publisher has not acquired copyright ownership.[29] If it is an employment relationship, there are important tax and labour consequences[30] which are often overlooked in practice. However, publishers do not normally issue T-4's. Canadian contracts often include American terms that attempt to establish an "employment type" relationship. This includes terms such as "employee for hire," "work-made-for-hire," "work for hire".[31] These are included presumably for consistency with the U.S.

---

[25] See discussion of assignments in Chapter 1, "Copyright". See also the leading copyright texts, namely Copinger, Skone-Jones, Laddie, Nimmer and Fox with respect to the issue of assignments in copyright. These texts are cited in Chapter 1, "Copyright". There are detailed discussions in such texts regarding copyright assignments. See however Jane Tatt, "Music Publishing and Recording Contracts in Perspective" in (1987), Vol. 9 No. 5, *E.I.P.R.*, 132 who at pp. 137-138 suggests that the system in the book publishing industry could be a useful model for the music business. Under this system, the writer retains copyright, and licenses the publisher the rights to publish for a specific time, not for life of copyright, in return for specified royalties.

[26] See for example *Jude's Musical Compositions, Re,* [1907] 1 Ch. 651.

[27] See, for example, *Copinger and Skone-Jones On Copyright* (London: Sweet and Maxwell, 1983) at 509 (herein "Copinger").

[28] See s. 13(3) of the Act. See also the discussion in Chapter 12, "Tax", regarding a contract of service, which defines an employment relationship, and Chapter 10, "Personal Service Contracts", regarding whether a music publishing contract is a contract of service.

[29] S. 13 (3) of the Act deems the employer to be the first owner of the copyright.

[30] Employees are entitled to fewer deductions than those who are self-employed and are subject to various provincial and federal laws that protect employees. See Chapter 5, "Labour" and Chapter 12, "Income Tax" for further discussion. The employment language in an exclusive term contract may be an attempt to prevent the copyright from reverting to the composer's estate after the composer's death. See Chapter 1, "Copyright", concerning copyright reversion. See also s. 13(4) of the Act.

[31] 17 U.S.C. paragraph 101. The proper term is "work made for hire". This section is comparable to s. 13(3) of the Act; copyright is owned by the employer, not the employee, unless there is an agreement to the contrary. Under a work-made-for-hire, copyright

Copyright Act, since worldwide publishing contracts are often entered into and may be litigated in the U.S. See the discussion of reversion in section 2(c)(vi) below, and the governing law clause in section 2(d)(i) below.

(iii) Non-assignment of Obligations

Because of the personal nature of songwriting services, the composer must agree not to assign his or her rights or obligations except to a corporation under which he or she carries on business.[32]

The publisher however usually reserves the right to assign its rights and obligations without the composer's consent. Sometimes this assignment is restricted, that is, it is only assignable to a company affiliated with the publisher or a successor company to the publisher, or if the business is sold, amalgamated or merged. The composer should attempt to impose additional restrictions such as limiting assignment to a bona fide publisher of equal or greater stature in the music industry, and obtaining an undertaking that the assignee company will honour all the obligations of the publisher. If the assignee publisher does not work as hard for the composer as the original publisher, the validity of such assignment and indeed the validity of the contract itself may be put into question.[33]

The composer is not likely to secure an unqualified right to approve the assignee publisher, since publishers tend to treat copyrights as business assets to be bought and sold. What can be negotiated are notice rights and consultation rights, and the type or stature of the publisher to whom the copyrights are being sold.

Although not necessarily applicable in Canada, it has been held in the U.S. that if a contract is structured as a personal service contract, neither the composer nor the music publisher can assign the contract without the other's consent.[34] The single-song contract resembles a buy

---

ownership vests in employers under 17 U.S.C. paragraph 201(b). See *Community for Creative Non-Violence v. Reid*, 10 U.S. P.Q. (2d) 1985 (U.S. S.C., 1989). If interpreted by a Canadian court the "work-made-for-hire" type language would probably be considered surplus unless the U.S. *Copyright Act* were incorporated by reference. However, this could be interpreted by a U.S. court, if the U.S. were the jurisdiction where the agreement was litigated and the governing law was that of the U.S.

[32] See Chapter 10, "Personal Service Contracts". See Fox cited above note 18 at 566 and for more information, Copinger cited above in note 27, pp. 513-517 and in particular, p. 513 para 1165.

[33] See Chapter 10, "Personal Service Contracts" for a discussion of the *Holly Johnson* case.

[34] *Biggers v. Vincent Youngman Co.* N.Y. L.J. 7/28/75. For other U.S. publishing cases see Melville Nimmer, *Nimmer On Copyright* (New York: Clark Boardman, 1990, loose-leaf) (herein "Nimmer").

and sell arrangement, and depending on the circumstances, is not usually a contract for personal services.

(iv) Grant of Rights

A. Generally

Generally, the contract provides that "all right, title, and interest" in and to the title, words and music and copyrights are granted by the composer to the music publisher.[35] The grant of rights is usually for compositions written during the term of the agreement, but often includes all the "old repertoire" (i.e. songs written prior to the term of the agreement). This is subject to negotiation.

B. Tied Deals

Sometimes the grant of rights is limited, particularly if it is a "tied deal" with a record company, to only the songs recorded and released on a record recorded pursuant to a recording agreement. A "tied deal" is a situation where a record company signs a recording artist to a record contract, and at the same time, the recording artist, who is also a songwriter, enters into a publishing agreement with the record company's publishing arm.

Even where a publisher is at arm's length with a record company, the term of the publishing deal may be tied to the term of the record deal and the songs covered by the publishing agreement will be those embodied on the master recordings recorded and released under the recording agreement.

C. Territory

The grant of rights is usually for the world. The composer is not likely to be able to negotiate a more localized territory, at least initially. However, the music publisher should be willing to revert certain territories to the composer if it fails to exploit the copyrights in such territories within a specified time period. Most established music

---

[35] Presumably this broad grant would address the situation where a title of a particular piece of music gains a secondary meaning. See Chapter 9, "Merchandising" for a discussion of secondary meaning in the context of trade-mark rights.

publishers have foreign counterparts (sub-publishers) or affiliates to carry out these functions.[36]

D. Controlled Compositions

Under the exclusive term contract, the music publisher, in addition to all original unpublished works written by the composer during the term of such agreement, may seek to obtain all the copyrights in which the composer has ownership, control or interest or has written in whole or part alone, or in collaboration with others, often referred to as "controlled compositions".[37] It is not always possible for the music publisher to obtain the right to publish all the composer's controlled compositions, for several reasons: the rights may have been previously assigned to another publisher, or in the case of collaboration, the composer with whom the composer has collaborated may be bound by an exclusive term publishing contract. Schedules attached to the agreement will specify which works the composer controls or owns and which are subject to the agreement.

The term "controlled composition" is more widely used in the context of reduced mechanical royalty rates, as discussed in Chapter 8, "Recording". Music publishers will resist, if at all possible, licensing mechanical rights at controlled composition rates. In any event, the composer should seek to impose some limitation on a publisher with respect to issuing any mechanical licence at less than "controlled composition" rates.

E. Collaboration[38]

Composers often collaborate with other composers, either on their own initiative or at the music publisher's suggestion. Part of the music publisher's role is to bring together good songwriting teams. While

---

[36] Walter Lorimer and Phalen G. Hurewitz, Editors, *Syllabus on Representing Musical Artists: Legal Business and Practical Aspects* (Los Angeles: Entertainment Law Institute, University of Southern California and Beverly Hills Bar Association, 1975) at 368. See the general discussion of licensing in Chapter 1, "Copyright".

[37] *Ibid.* at 369. See also discussion of the controlled compositions clause in Chapter 8, "Recording". The issues raised by cases such as the *O'Sullivan, Elton John* and *Holly Johnson* cases in Chapter 10, "Personal Service Contracts" call into question an unlimited unqualified grant of such rights which are not exploited adequately or, if not exploited, do not revert to the artist within a reasonable time. This is arguably unenforceable and in restraint of trade.

[38] See also discussion of joint and collective works in Chapter 1, "Copyright". See also Fox, cited at note 18 above, paragraph 171.01. See also Irvin Drake, "The Sub-Lyric Writer" (1972), Vol.3 No. 3, *P.A.R.*, 427.

there is an obvious financial incentive to a publisher to create teams within the publisher's own "stable" of writers, reputable publishers will not block good collaborations between their own songwriters and those signed to other publishers.

Generally, royalties are divided among all collaborators equally in order to avoid future disputes, although particular circumstances will dictate unusual divisions. All collaborators share in the "writer's share" (50%) of net income. Normally, the words are considered worth 50% and the music the other 50% of a song.

When a sub-lyric writer is retained for purposes of translating lyrics into a foreign language, for example, the original composer usually retains an approval right over the new lyrics. This is an important issue to negotiate since, by convention, performing right societies generally allot 25% of the writer share of income to the sub-lyricist, which comes out of the original composer's share.

In some cases a collaboration agreement is in writing, but more commonly there is an agreement between the co-writers on the sharing of income and ownership of specified musical compositions. This is then reflected in the publishing agreement that is entered into by both writers. Parties may also enter into a writing partnership agreement, which is similar to a conventional partnership agreement. Partnership agreements are discussed in Chapter 11, "Business".

F. Renewals and Extensions

The composer generally is asked to grant the right to renew or extend the copyright. This is a carry-over from the pre-1976 U.S. situation in which copyright lasted 28 years but could be renewed for an additional 28 years. However, now the term of copyright in the U.S. has been extended to "life of the author plus seventy years", and in the case of subsisting works, has been extended by an additional 67 years, resulting in a total term of 95 years for such works.[39]

G. Exclusivity

In the single song agreement, the rights are granted exclusively to a particular composition. In the term agreement, rights are granted

---

[39] 17 U.S.C. s. 302(a); also note that with the passage of the *Sonny Bono Copyright Extension Act*, P.L. 105-298 (105th Cong.), which became effective October 27, 1998, for works created after Jan. 1, 1978, in the case of works made for hire, the period is now 95 years from the date of first publication or 120 years from creation, whichever expires first (s-s. 302 (c)). For subsisting works, s. 304 provides for renewal and extension for a second term of 67 years upon expiration of the first 28 year term for a total of 95 years.

exclusively to all musical compositions written during the term, or if tied to a record contract, an album's worth of songs delivered during the contract's term, or perhaps to an entire catalogue of songs. However, this is not to imply that the rights granted are necessarily for the full term of copyright; that is, the composer may contract to have such rights revert within a specified time. See the discussion of reversion in section 2(c)(vi) below. It is less common to have a non-exclusive term contract with a music publisher but it is contractually possible.

H. Alterations/Moral Rights

The publisher usually requests the right to alter and adapt the music and lyrics. This is important in the case of music that may be popular in a foreign market and is often necessary for the purpose of fully exploiting the music. It may also be advisable when a song title is contested.[40] If substantial alterations are requested, the composer should seek some right of approval, for example, if the composer's native language is English, and the lyrics are in English, then the first right to make any English language changes. The right to alter the music should not infringe on the composer's moral right, that is, the right to claim authorship of the music, and should not allow any distortion, mutilation or other modification of the music that is prejudicial to a composer's honour or reputation.[41]

In practice, music publishers often request: (a) a complete waiver of moral rights; or (b) a modified waiver. If songwriters must waive their moral rights at all, they should try to limit the extent of the waiver. Surely they want to retain the right to be credited as authors of their songs (or to remain pseudonymous is they so choose), although the publisher might want to protect itself by providing that any inadvertent failure to afford credit will not be a fundamental breach of the agreement if the publisher makes reasonable efforts to cure such failure. This would leave intact the "paternity" right aspect of moral rights.

The composer may also negotiate to retain the right to approve certain uses of the music, for example, in conjunction with specific advertising purposes. The moral rights issue frequently arises when the publisher wishes to exploit the music in a jingle or advertising

---

[40] See Chapter 1, "Copyright" and Chapter 4, "Copyright Infringement" regarding copyright in a title.

[41] S. 14.1 and s. 28.2(1)(a)(b) of the Act. See Chapter 1, "Copyright" regarding the legal basis for moral rights.

campaign and the composer does not.[42] A standard clause in this regard would prohibit, without the composer's consent, the exploitation of the musical compositions as parodies, in synchronization with films that are unduly exploitative of sex and/or violence, in synchronization with commercials for personal hygiene, alcohol and tobacco products, or in connection with political or institutional causes. These predetermined limitations are usually acceptable to publishers and, from the composer's point of view, are preferable to a blanket waiver of moral rights.

I. Unspecified Uses

An unspecified use, for example, may be the reproduction of lyrics on a greeting card. The composer(s) and publisher(s) typically share equally in any income from unspecified uses and the agreement should be explicit in this respect.

(v) Grant of Other Rights

A. Power of Attorney

Some publishers seek a power of attorney to secure copyright registration throughout the world in the composer's name. From the composer's perspective this provision should be limited to this specific use, or, for example, it may infringe on other powers of attorney granted by the composer under a management agreement.[43] The power of attorney can be contractually limited and it may only be exercised if the composer has refused to do a certain act within a specified time frame, for example, 10 or 30 days.

B. Personality

Publishers need the right to use composers' name, likeness and biographical material to promote their songs.[44] The composer's picture may, for example, be used to promote sales of sheet music. The

---

[42] See Jeffrey J. Brabec, "Music That Sells (A Behind-the-Scenes Look at Advertising, Music and Broadcast Performance Royalties)" (1987) *Entertainment Publishing and the Arts Handbook*, (New York: Clark Boardman, 1987) at p. 341 for a discussion of music in advertising.

[43] Power of attorney is discussed more fully in Chapter 6, "Agents and Managers".

[44] See Chapter 9, "Merchandising" regarding personality rights.

composer should try to restrict the use of his or her personality to promote the music; additional payment should be made for uses of personality rights not strictly promoting the music.[45] In particular, the grant of personality rights should not conflict with a similar grant made in a recording or merchandising agreement, and it should not amount to an endorsement or merchandising scheme without the consent of the composer and further compensation. The grant of personality rights is exclusive during the term of the agreement, that is, no other publisher can exploit the personality rights granted in the same manner as the publisher in connection with the published songs, but after the term of the agreement terminates, such rights become non-exclusive. For songbook folios bearing the likeness and name of the composer, the composer is usually entitled to a higher royalty.[46] An extra 5% of the selling price is typical.

C. Options

The composer often grants the music publisher options to extend the term of the contract. Option periods may be tied to the contract periods set out in a recording agreement or may be for a specific length of time, for example 12 to 18 months. In an ideal world, there would be minimum performance obligations required for the publisher to exercise an option. Such obligations could include: (1) a specified number of demo recordings; (2) a specified number of commercial releases; and/or (3) specified minimum earnings. In practice, these requirements are difficult to extract. Of course, in order to exercise an option, most publishers are required to pay an advance, which has to make financial sense in the context of the music's success to date.

(vi) Representations and Warranties

There are four basic representations and warranties that composers are usually required to give to a music publisher:

(1) that they have the power to grant the exclusive rights being granted in the contract;
(2) that the music assigned or to be assigned to the publisher is original within the meaning of the *Copyright Act*;[47]

---

[45] Lorimer and Hurewitz, Editors, *Syllabus on Representing Musical Artists* ... above note 36 at 373.

[46] See Stohn above note 18 at p.77.

[47] See discussion of originality in Chapter 1, "Copyright".

(3) that they have the full legal right and capacity to enter into the contract and fulfill its terms and conditions;[18] and

(4) that there are no liens, encumbrances or claims outstanding with respect to the rights assigned under the agreement.

From the composer's perspective, it is preferable to qualify representations and warranties by saying that they are made to the best of the composer's knowledge, in order to limit damages that may result from the inadvertent breach by the composer of any representation or warranty.

In addition, publishing contracts often require a representation and warranty that the performing rights have not been subject of a performing right society advance.

(vii) Indemnity

The composer is asked to indemnify the music publisher if it satisfies a judgment or settles a claim and incurs expenses arising out of breach of the composer's representations and warranties. The music publisher is usually entitled to withhold the composer's royalties. The amount of royalties withheld should be reasonably related to the claim, particularly if it is the music publisher's actions that resulted in a lawsuit.[49] In addition, the composer should try to require that such funds be held in an interest-bearing trust account pending resolution of the claim and be released within one or two years if an action is not pursued.

(c) Music Publisher's Obligations

(i) Advances

Advances paid pursuant to an exclusive term agreement are usually paid on signing and upon the exercise of options. Advances levels reflect the track record and bargaining power of the composer. Ideally, they should escalate over time or be tied to an objective level of performance (e.g., income generated in the preceding contract period). The industry norm for escalations is currently two-thirds of the mechanical royalty income earned in the preceding period, measured

---

[48] See discussion on minors' contracts, for example, in Chapter 10, "Personal Service Contracts", which can affect this representation and warranty.

[49] Victor D. Rappaport, *Making It In Music* (Englewood Cliffs, N.J.: Prentice-Hall, Inc., 1979) at 66.

at the time of exercise of an option, with guaranteed minimums in the order of magnitude of the initial advance. In some instances, a composer can negotiate a higher percentage and/or include performing rights income in the calculation. Such advances may be subject to a "Min/Max" formula similar to those discussed in Chapter 8, "Recording" in section 2 (b) (ii) B II.

An advance paid to the composer pursuant to a single song agreement may be nominal. Advances are "non-returnable but recoupable." This means that if there are no earnings from the musical copyrights assigned to the music publisher, the composer is not liable to reimburse the publisher for these advances. However, the publisher does recoup advances paid to the co-publisher and the composer out of their respective royalties, as and when such royalties are earned. As composers receive their performing rights royalties directly from their society, however, that portion of earnings generally is not applied toward recoupment.

Whether the composer is entitled to a share of third party advances is a negotiable issue in any music publishing agreement. It is rare that a composer shares in a catalogue sale advance since it is difficult to attribute a precise portion of such advance to the composer's share of the catalogue. However, there should always be a clause that provides for advance sharing where a portion of it is earmarked or easily attributed to the composer's songs.

Although more easy to attribute in theory, the receipt by a publisher of an advance from a foreign sub-publisher raises other issues.[50] It is difficult to determine in advance how income will be earned. For example, where there is an "airplay hit" that generates performing rights income and no record sales, a music publisher risks over-paying the composer if the advance is simply paid out on a proportionate basis. More specifically, if a $1,000 advance is received from a foreign sub-publisher and if the composer/publisher share 50/50 in the advance, then $500 is paid to the composer and $500 is paid to the publisher. If only airplay royalties are earned, in the amount of $2,000, the result would be as follows: assuming that 25% is deducted from the publisher's performing rights share by a foreign sub-publisher, then $750 remains. An amount of $750 would not recoup the initial advance of $1,000 and the original advance to the publisher is still unrecouped by $250. However, in this case, the composer has received $1,000 of performing rights royalties directly from the performing rights society of which he/she is a member and has received a $500 advance from the publisher for a total of $1,500. Bear

---

[50] See Stohn cited above at note 18, pp. 80-81. This problem is compounded when there are several songs in a catalogue because all songs do not necessarily earn income; therefore, an advance must be apportioned between them.

in mind that the performing rights societies collect their administration fee prior to paying performing rights royalties to the publisher and composer. The publisher has received only $500 (i.e.: its share of the original advance from the sub-publisher), since the original advance of $1,000 is not yet recouped. For this reason, it is unusual for a composer to successfully negotiate entitlement to a share of foreign advances.

However, in a participation or co-publishing deal, these arguments are not as valid. In such agreements, composers (in their capacity as co-publishers) should be entitled to a share of such advances reasonably related to the composer's entitlement to publishing income. The issue of foreign advances does not arise when the deal is with a major publisher, since advances are not normally paid between affiliates. The issue is important, however, when the deal is with an independent publisher.

Since advances are "credited" and not considered "earned" or "actually received", this type of language in a publishing agreement implies that a composer is not to share in advances. If the agreement does not stipulate that there will be a sharing in advances, then presumably the composer will be paid based on earnings only, that is, based on the actual income actually earned and received. If the composer does not participate in advances, the advance paid to the publisher may be treated in one of two ways: (a) the composer receives net income when earned, irrespective of publisher's recoupment of such advances; (b) the composer receives net income after the advance is fully recouped. In scenario (a) above, if the advance is never recouped, the publisher keeps the portion of the advance that did not recoup and the composer obtains no parallel windfall. The publisher's argument is that since it is an advance to the publisher only, the publisher should be entitled to such sum; the advance is to be retained to be used for publishing expenses and to pay the writer when income is earned. In scenario (b) above, if the advance is not recouped, the composer might receive no income at all other than performing rights income, if any, which the composer receives directly from his or her performing rights society. It is also an issue whether the publisher's obligation to pay the composer occurs when the publisher recoups the entire advance or as income is actually earned. Preferably the proper interpretation would be the latter, not the former, if the agreement does not address this issue. For these reasons, the advance issue is one that should be addressed carefully in negotiations. One should also consider the GST and income tax implications of advances and royalties. These are outlined in Chapter 12, "Tax".

(ii) Royalties/Net Income

Royalties under publishing contracts are fairly standard. (Royalties are the main method of compensating the composer.) Unless the composer is successful and in a good negotiating position, he/she will be entitled to 50% of most sources of net income. However, if there is a co-publishing agreement, the combined co-publisher/composer receives 75% of the net income and the publisher receives 25%. In Europe, by comparison, a 75/25 or 80/20 division in favour of the composer is not uncommon; however, under such agreements, unlike the co-publishing agreement, the publisher acquires 100% of the copyright. See the discussion below in section 3(b) regarding co-publishing and participation agreements.

The definition of gross and net income should be examined carefully. Do gross receipts include monies earned and actually received or do they also include advances? Obviously, the composer should try to negotiate the inclusion of the latter.

Most agreements define net income as "gross sums less all direct out-of-pocket costs of collection and any sums actually paid to third parties."[51] However, the more comprehensive and detailed the list of deductions, the more potential for negotiating some of the deductions out, for example, if the definition of net income is:

* All costs incurred by the publisher in realizing or collecting revenue from a musical composition or exploiting in any manner the musical composition, including without limitation:

    (a) costs of copyright registration of the musical composition;
    (b) fees of a collecting agent for licensing of rights in the musical composition;
    (c) legal fees including fees arising out of or relating to any claim of copyright infringement brought by or against the publisher relating to the musical composition;
    (d) accounting fees;
    (e) costs of any recordings of the musical composition distributed for promotional purposes, including "demos" and the out-of-pocket costs of such distribution;
    (f) the costs of translation;
    (g) agents fees;
    (h) transcribing, preparing lead sheets and arranging; and
    (i) travel costs.

The composer should attempt to limit legal and accounting fees that are incurred by the music publisher in the ordinary course of

---

[51] *Ibid.* at p. 61.

business and are not specifically expended to secure a third party agreement. It is not unusual to negotiate on the composer's behalf that only half of the costs of demonstration records and promotional records be charged against the composer's share of net income. Travel costs may sometimes be justifiable in specific situations; however, even if they are, some limitation should be placed on these expenses, especially if the music publisher is working more than one song catalogue. Travel expenses should be apportioned *pro rata* among the composers who are being promoted and on whose behalf costs are being expended. There should be no expenses deducted twice.

Finally, it is still not unusual for a publisher to ask for a 10% to 15% administration fee of gross income received. This practice is basically a "double-dip" and should be resisted.

A. Piano or Vocal Copies

Composer royalties fall within the range of 10 to 15 cents per copy sold and paid for in Canada and the United States. Royalties may be expressed also as a percentage of either the wholesale or retail selling price of such copies. Arguably the composer should receive 50% of net income received by the publisher, as is the case with mechanical, synchronization and performing rights revenue.

B. Folio and Print Income

A folio is a book of songs. It consists of numerous songs by one or more composers; some may be hits, others lesser known or even public domain material. Folio and printed royalty rates are applicable to band and orchestral arrangements. It is common practice to pay $12^1/_2$ % to $17^1/_2$ % of the wholesale or retail selling price of folios sold and paid for. When there is more than one composer these royalties are prorated and shared between them. This can create problems where one composer's material is hit material and is being used as a selling point for the folio or where the folio includes public domain material. Reasonably speaking, the "hit" composer should be compensated more favourably by providing for a proportionately higher percentage of the total royalty. Public domain music should be omitted from the *pro rata* formula because the publisher pays no royalties for use of public domain copyright.[52] The above royalty formula should be based on royalty-bearing musical compositions. Print income is one of the few sources where the music publisher may be justified in holding a

---

[52] See Chapter 1, "Copyright" for more detail concerning public domain.

reserve. A reserve protects a music publisher against returns of printed music which, like records, are sold at retail on a consignment basis. Any reserve should be specified and preferably equally liquidated over a given number of accounting periods. Reserves are discussed in more detail in Chapter 8, "Recording".

C. Mechanical and Performing Rights

The composer and music publisher share 50-50 in net income from mechanical royalties. The publisher and composer also divide performing rights income 50-50 and this amount is paid directly from the performing rights society. From the composer's point of view, mechanical royalties granted at less than the Canadian industry-negotiated rate or U.S. statutory rate should be avoided. See discussion of controlled compositions in Chapter 8, "Recording".

One should keep in mind that if a co-publishing agreement is in place, the end result is a 75/25 division of income in favour of the composer/co-publisher.

D. Foreign Income/"At Source"

Foreign income can be generated through sub-publishers.[53] Assuming a standard publishing agreement is in place, it is common that 50% of the net mechanical income from sub-publishing territories goes to the publisher and 50% goes to the composer after the sub-publisher takes its 20%-30% share. (If a co-publishing agreement is in place, a 75/25 division of net income in favour of the composer/co-publisher is typical). The composer receives foreign performing rights income through remittance by the foreign performing rights society to the composer's home society.

The above scenario normally results in the composer and publisher sharing equally somewhere between 70% and 80% of the income from the foreign territory. The trend today, however, is for composers to demand that foreign income be paid "at source." In its pure form, "at source" means that the composer's share is always 50%, while the sub-publisher's commission comes entirely out of the publisher's share. An "at source deal" ensures that the writer's share (that is, 50% of income) is not diluted by the intervention of the sub-publisher. For example, if the sub-publishing agreement provides for a 75/25 division of royalties between publisher and sub-publisher, under an "at source deal", the

---

[53] See sub-publishing discussion above in section 1(d)(ii)C and below in the text in section 3(d) and sources cited in note 21 above.

composer would be entitled to 50% of the net income "at source" and the publisher and sub-publisher would divide the remaining 50% equally, that is 25% each. The effect of an "at source" agreement is that the publisher's share of net income is reduced by the difference between half of 75% and 25%, which equals $12^1/_2$%. "At source" agreements are most commonly entered into with major music publishers, whose affiliates are the sub-publishers.

A fallback alternative to the "at source" deal is to limit (or cap) the sub-publisher retention at, say, 20%. This trims 5% off the 25% norm, but since the sub-publisher is not party to the agreement, it is still entitled to 25% and the difference must be absorbed by the original publisher.

Foreign income is subject to additional dilution by translation fees and percentages, withholding taxes and collecting society fees. The sub-publisher's share is often increased if a cover version or synchronization licence is obtained and, while the standard is 60/40, it is negotiable.

E. Synchronization Licensing Income

Because of the high transactional costs associated with soliciting and licensing synchronizations of music in films, television programs, commercials, CD-ROMs, the Internet and other media, publishers are increasingly unwilling to pay out the normal 75% of net receipts from such licences. As the industry settles upon the co-publishing model as the norm, the reduced payments are usually drafted into the co-publishing agreement. The composer/co-publisher is normally offered between 20% and 40% of the publisher share of income from such licences. The rates themselves are negotiable and, since transactional costs are similar for large and small licence fees, the composer might also propose a higher share of fees for licences in excess of a determined amount, e.g. $1,000.

F. Professional Copies

A professional copy may be a lead sheet, a demo or even a master recording. No royalties are paid on professional copies because they are used for promotional purposes. Costs for professional copies are paid for by the publisher but are recouped at either 100% or 50% of a composer's royalties. Some assessment must be made of the costs of producing professional copies and their potential for reducing royalties. There should be some limitation on free copies or promotional goods. It can also be stipulated that there be no commercial release of demo recordings without the consent of the composer.

G. Unspecified Uses

The composer normally receives 50% (75% if a co-publishing agreement) of the net royalties from other copyright uses, with the exception of synchronization licensing income which is normally skewed more favourably toward the publisher.

H. Collaboration

A typical structure for the payment of collaborative royalties is 50% to the publisher, 25% to the composer and 25% to the lyricist. Other structures can be mutually agreed upon having due regard to the relative creative input of the composers. The composer may contract to restrict the payment of collaboration royalties to prevent a non-collaborating lyricist who translates lyrics from sharing equally with the composer of the original music.

I. Reserves

Reserves should not be provided for in a publishing agreement, except perhaps in connection with print income. (See section 2(c)(ii)B. Reserves protect a publisher from overpaying the composer if print copies are returned without being sold. However, most publishers today out-source their printing functions and the printers take their own reserves before remitting payment to the publishers.

There is certainly no justification for taking reserves on synchronization or mechanical royalties. (Performing rights income flows directly from the society to the composer). Synchronization licences are generally paid on a flat fee basis for film and television, although some synchronization licences for home video sales entail the payment of royalties on an ongoing basis. With respect to mechanical royalties, most record companies pay mechanical royalties based on records sold and not returned, so there is already a reserve applied by the record company with respect to such royalties. Some publishing contracts stipulate that the reserve for mechanicals is contingent upon a reserve being taken by the record company, that is, the publisher's reserve is one and the same as the record company's reserve and not in addition to the record company's reserve.

(iii) Accounting and Audit

A publishing contract typically offers semi-annual accounting, but usually can be negotiated upward to quarterly. If a publisher fails to render royalty statements or allow an audit, the contract may provide for termination on notice to the publisher by the composer and a reversion of all rights to the composer should this occur, subject to the default and cure clause, if applicable. See the discussion of such clause in section 2(d)(v) below.[54] Where there is a profit-sharing relationship (that is, the right to share in royalties), there may be a fiduciary relationship between publisher and composer and even without an accounting clause the composer may be entitled to an accounting.[55] The preferable solution is to contract expressly for regular accountings and for the right to audit the publisher to verify accuracy.[56] The composer should have the right to engage a representative (usually a chartered accountant) to audit the publisher's books on reasonable notice, and it is typical to specify that objections to royalty statements should be within a specified time, anywhere from six months to three years (two years, however, appears to be the standard). After this stipulated contractual time frame, composers loses their right to object.

The accounting and audit provision should give the composer the right to:

(1) examine the publisher's books and records; and

(2) take excerpts of these books and records insofar as they pertain to the composer's songs.

---

[54] See J. P. Shedd, "A Composer/Songwriter's Unilateral Termination of An Exclusive Term Agreement" in *Entertainment, Publishing and the Arts Handbook* (New York: Clark Boardman, 1986) 199 and specifically 221-224. See cases cited at note 94 in the above-noted article and in particular: *Gumm v. Jerry Vogal Music Co. Ltd.*, 158 F.(2d) 516 (1946); *Nolan v. Sam Fox Publishing Co. Inc.*, 499 F.(2d) 1397 (1974); *Karma Rippa v. Melanie Schkeryk*, 510 F.(2d) 837 (1975); *Chase v. Shelby Singleton Corp.* N.Y.L.J. 7/18/74 (Sup. N.Y. Co.), p. 2. See also *Waterson Berlin & Snyder Co. Fain v. Irving Trust Co.*, 48 F.(2d) 704 (1931), where it was held that substantial frustration must be the result of a default which is "fundamental and pervasive" before rescission is allowed. For more detail concerning U.S. cases see also Nimmer cited above at note 34. This is not to imply this necessarily will be followed in Canada. It is used here as an illustration. In the U.S., default in payment or rendering royalty statements may be a basis for an accounting, or in some instances a rescission of the contract.

[55] *Barry v. Stevens* (1862), 31 Beav. 258. This case involved a book publishing contract. For a U.S. case involving royalty overpayments to the Kingston Trio, see *Hansen Publications Inc. v. Atzal Music Inc.*, 30 N.Y. (2d) 564. See the *O'Sullivan* and *Elton John* cases discussed in Chapter 10, "Personal Service Contracts" which support the argument that there is a fiduciary duty and therefore a duty to account, however, the publisher is not to be deprived of a reasonable profit for exploiting copyrights.

[56] Canadian lawyers should take note that in the U.S. if the lawyer neglects to have an audit clause in the contract, a malpractice suit can arise.

The accounting period should be for money earned, not received. The composer should not have to finance the publisher's debt collection. It is not unusual to restrict the audit right to once every calendar year and to restrict the right to examine any given statement only once. There is often a stipulation that an audit cannot be carried out by an accountant currently auditing the publisher. Statements may be deemed to be binding after two years if there has been no objection, in the absence of fraud or negligence. An objection in writing is typically required for there to be a valid challenge to accountings and statements.

(iv) Cross Collateralization

Cross collateralization is the practice of applying advances and other sums, which would be otherwise payable to the composer, to recoup expenses incurred under any agreement between the composer and publisher. This is particularly relevant if the composer is also a recording musician, and has a recording agreement with the record company who is also the music publisher. If this clause applies, recording and other costs can be recouped from the composer's royalties and the music publisher has the right and obligation to do so. The practice has virtually disappeared at the multi-national/major publisher level. However, certain smaller record companies may insist on it as a means of reducing their financial risk. Cross collateralization is also discussed in Chapter 8, "Recording".

(v) Ownership of Professional Copies

The contract should specify who owns the professional copies, that is, the lead sheets, demos and master recordings produced under such an agreement. It should also state the restrictions to be placed upon such copies. Under the *Copyright Act*, the maker of a sound recording (a demo recording for example) is the owner of the sound recording.[57] This would normally be the music publisher under the publishing contract. The publisher would have the right to make reproductions of the sound recording, subject to any limitations set out in the contract.[58]

---

[57] S. 2 of the Act. See also Chapter 1, "Copyright" for a discussion of sound recordings.
[58] *Joan Baez v. Fantasy Records*, 144 U.S.P.Q. 537 (1964). It has been held in the U.S., although this may not be the case in Canada, that the release of recordings commercially is within the scope of a recording agreement, not a publishing agreement. Such a release probably would put the composer in breach of the recording contract if the composer is also a recording musician.

The agreement should clearly stipulate that no commercial release of demo recordings will be made without the consent of and compensation to the composer. In an ideal world, the composer would be compensated for the sessions worked on to produce demo recordings or lead sheets as is any other session player or arranger. However, the practice is to pay the composer a recoupable advance as opposed to a non-recoupable fee.

(vi) Reversion

A. Failure to Account or Allow an Audit

As previously discussed, failure to account or allow an audit may be legal grounds for having the copyright (which was granted pursuant to the agreement) revert to the composer. However, the publisher may be granted a specified margin of error in accounting (for example, 10% to 20%). Such a clause is usually subject to a default and cure clause. See section 2(d)(v) below.

B. Failure to Exploit

Although it should be a fundamental term of the contract that the publisher exploit the copyright, most standard form publishing contracts still do not obligate the publisher to do anything. Such agreements give rise to the issues discussed in Chapter 10, concerning restraint of trade and unconscionability. In the alternative, single song contracts, in particular, often state that a commercial record release must be secured within one year or the copyright reverts to the composer. Other performance obligations can be negotiated and specified in the agreement.

It can be argued that if the publisher fails to exploit the rights granted, then the exclusive term agreement (but not necessarily the single song agreement) is void as being in restraint of trade.[59] Damages may be recovered against a music publisher for royalties, which are reasonable in the circumstances, and based on an estimate of royalties that would have accrued if the publisher actually did exploit the copyright.[60] The composer may also be entitled to damages for loss of

---

[59] See *A. Schroeder* and *Clifford Davis Management* cases as discussed in Chapter 10, "Personal Service Contracts". In the U.S. cases, as discussed above in the Shedd article cited above, note 54, there is an implied obligation to exploit if such term is not expressly set out in the agreement.

[60] *Abrahams v. Herbert Reiach Ltd.*, [1922] 1 K.B. 477 (Eng. K.B.).

publicity.[61] In the alternative, rather than contract to have copyrights revert or institute a lawsuit for damages based on failure to exploit copyright, the agreement could provide that it is a condition precedent to the agreement coming into force that a recording of the musical composition be made and released within a specified time and territory.

C. Bankruptcy

The parties should stipulate that upon bankruptcy, the term of the agreement terminates. A deemed assignment of copyrights could occur, subject to payment of any unrecouped advances, or the transfer to the composer of such copyrights at their fair market value. Care should be taken to structure such a provision in view of bankruptcy legislation and in such a way that, if a preference is created, it will be enforceable legally. The agreement itself could stipulate that the composer shall have a power of attorney to reassign copyright and make all recording arrangements based on the happening of certain events including bankruptcy. In such a case, a music publisher's dealings with all copyrights which are the subject matter of the agreement should cease, and all professional and other copies should be returned to the composer.[62] A bankruptcy clause is advisable particularly in the case of small independent music publishers.

D. By Contract and Under the Act

A reversion of copyright prior to the full term of copyright protection can be negotiated and set out in the agreement, and

---

[61] *Goffin v. Staples and Staples Ltd.* (1946-47), Macg. Cop. Cas. 1.

[62] See Mills, *You and the Music Business*, above note 8 at 37. See also, generally, s. 83(1)(2)(3) of the *Bankruptcy and Insolvency Act*, R.S.C. 1985, c. B-3, as amended. The effectiveness of this clause is questionable. However, a right of first or last refusal to purchase such rights at fair market value could be enforced. Consider also the reversion which is statutory under s. 14(1) of the *Copyright Act.* See also Jonathan E. Fleisher, "Intellectual Property Rights and Bankruptcy" (1990), Vol. 7 No. 7 *Business and the Law* pp. 50-52. The author suggests a number of clauses could be added to a licence agreement in order to protect the licensor if the licensee becomes bankrupt: (1) the assignment rights to a third party should be limited; (2) the licence itself should be terminated in the event of insolvency or bankruptcy; (3) the right to receive royalty payments in the event of insolvency or bankruptcy; and (4) triggering events such as the assignment and termination may enforce the purchaser to pay an additional fee for purchase of the bankrupt's assets. Consider whether it would be appropriate for the writer to take a security interest in the copyrights enforceable in the event of bankruptcy, or other default under the agreement, under the *Personal Property Security Act*, R.S.O. 1990, c. P.10, for example.

preferably, from the composer's view point, should be. Also, in certain limited circumstances, the *Copyright Act* stipulates that there is to be a reversion of copyright. These types of statutory reversions were discussed in Chapter 1, "Copyright".

(vii) Infringement Actions

Infringement actions arise two ways: (1) the music publisher sues to protect the copyright it owns and controls; and (2) the music publisher and the composer are sued. If the music publisher's suit against an infringer is successful, the publisher and the composer typically share equally in the award (75/25 if a co-publishing agreement) less reasonable expenses incurred. If the publisher is sued, it may be stipulated that the composer's royalties be held in trust pending the outcome of the claim, or alternatively, paid to the composer upon his/her posting of a bond reasonably related to the amount of the claim.[63] However, bonds are expensive to secure and not within the financial means of most composers. Concerning infringement actions, the composer's approval rights with respect to any settlement may be negotiated and contractually stipulated.

(d) General Provisions

As in other contracts, certain general provisions should be set out. The main ones are discussed below. See also Appendix 2 for a checklist for such provisions.

(i) Governing Law

The "governing law" clause is particularly important since many Canadian songwriters enter publishing agreements with foreign publishers and both parties wish to avoid conflict of law situations.[64]

(ii) Prior Contracts

The publishing agreement should acknowledge the precedence of the songwriter's agreement with SOCAN, or other applicable

---

[63] *Ibid.*, Mills at pp. 36, 37.
[64] See discussion in Chapter 10, "Personal Service Contracts" regarding conflict of laws.

performing rights society. Also, if the composer entered into a previous publishing agreement for earlier compositions and the rights to them have not reverted, the current agreement should specify that only new compositions are covered.

(iii) Term and Options/Reversion

Most long-term contracts with composers who perform their own material and are signed to a recording deal provide for initial and option periods that are in lock-step with the recording deal. If the recording deal ends, there is usually an additional period in which a certain number of songs must be delivered. Publishers will ask for a long enough period to allow a replacement recording deal with another label to be secured.

The contract periods in long-term contracts with non-performing songwriters are usually annual, with typical minimum delivery commitments of ten (10) to fifteen (15) songs written 100% by the writer or, if co-written with other composers, song portions that aggregate to the equivalent.

In either case, the term of the publishing agreement will continue until all advances have been recouped. It is important to stipulate that recoupment be calculated with reference to "pipeline income"[65] (income that has accrued but is not yet payable), because an accounting may not be required until six months after income is accrued.

The issue of term raises restraint of trade issues and should be negotiated and drafted carefully. At the very least, no option period should be exercisable by a publisher unless further advances are paid.

There is a growing trend toward negotiated reversion of copyrights after a certain number of years and/or inactivity of a song. The best that most new writers can expect to achieve is reversion of songs that are not "exploited" three to five years after termination. (Exploitation includes earning synchronization, and mechanical, print, or performing rights income, for example). Established writers, however, often can negotiate much earlier reversion, in the range of 7 to 15 years, without a non-exploitation proviso. These concessions depend heavily on the composer's bargaining position. See also the case law discussion in Chapter 10.

---

[65] See Shane Simpson, *Music: The Business* ..., cited above, note 2, at p. 102.

(iv) Termination

Most agreements terminate automatically when the publisher does not exercise an option. If the publishing agreement is tied to a recording agreement which stipulates that the agreements are "co-terminous", then the publishing agreement will terminate when the recording agreement does. Otherwise, the composer generally has no right to terminate the contract, except if the publisher is in breach of the agreement.

(v) Default and Cure

If the publisher is in breach, there is normally a clause in the contract that allows a time period for the breach to be corrected. The composer must give the publisher written notice of the alleged breach. Then, within the time period provided in the contract, the publisher must cure the breach (or deny its validity). If the breach is not cured, the term of the agreement terminates. The cure period provides some flexibility to correct an oversight. However, its abuse should be avoided by providing that sequential breaches of a similar nature (e.g. late royalty remittance) should not be subject to cure or at least to a shorter cure period.

(vi) Independent Legal Advice

The case law is very clear that independent legal advice should be obtained prior to entering into any music publishing agreement. See Chapter 10, "Personal Service Contracts", for more detail.

(vii) Miscellaneous

There are of course endless varieties and permutations of negotiations and terms in any agreement; publishing agreements are no exception. Some of the above noted provisions are the most common; however, other important issues can arise that are negotiable:

(1) Occasionally it is specified in an agreement that royalties are payable only if the composer is not in breach of the agreement. The composer should try to insert the word "material" before the word "breach" or have the clause removed altogether.
(2) Sometimes there will be a suspension clause. This clause is discussed in more detail in Chapter 8, "Recording".

(3) The following clause may be added to clearly address GST obligations:

At the same time as the Publisher accounts to the Composer for any royalties or other revenues, the Publisher shall also prepare an invoice in respect to the Goods and Services Tax (GST) payable on such revenues and forward the invoice to the Composer, together with payment of such revenues and related GST, unless otherwise directed by the Composer (if Composer earns $30,000.00 or less annually from his or her business and has not registered for GST).[66]

3. Music Publishing Contracts: The Major Types

This section will not revisit the detailed terms found in every variety of music publishing contract. See section 2 above. Detailed checklists are also found in Appendix 2. Keep in mind that in any royalty based agreement, a number of general issues must be addressed, as discussed in Chapter 1, "Copyright".

(a) Co-Publishing

(i) Generally

As discussed above, most publishers have rolled into a single document a comprehensive co-publishing agreement which comprises a songwriter agreement and co-publisher agreement. In such a co-publishing agreement, the composer is a nominal co-publisher but is not, in fact, active. Sometimes, the non-active co-publisher is an entity who previously acquired the composer's publishing rights, such as the publishing arm of an independent record label. In either case, the copyrights are owned by the nominal co-publisher and the active publisher, and net publishing income is typically shared on a 50/50 basis, although any variation is possible. Income division can be subject to predetermined variation based on income levels achieved and/or the exercise of successive options. In any event, net income is determined <u>after</u> payment to the writer of the writer share (normally 50%) of net income. The net effect is that the composer who is also a co-publisher earns 75% of the income and the other co-publisher earns 25%.

---

[66] This clause is adapted from the Canadian Reprography Collective agreement. This collective is discussed in Chapter 2, "The Licensing and Administration of Copyright and the Regulation of Music in Media".

(ii) Negotiable Elements

Term is negotiable, as discussed in section 2 d) (iii), above. The compositions covered by the agreement can be defined in a number of ways, for example: (a) songs written during the term with or without songs written before the term; and (b) songs written during the term and recorded and released pursuant to a record agreement. It is also negotiable whether or not there will be reversion, that is, a period of time after which the rights to such songs revert to the co-publisher.

The definition of net income is important and the costs to be deducted in order to determine net income are subject to negotiation (see section 2 c) (iii) above for a more comprehensive discussion). Generally, there should be some reasonable limit on such costs. Such costs could include, for example: the cost of registering copyright in the songs; demo recordings; travel; promotion; transcribing the lead sheets; legal fees; and accounting fees. In some instances, subject to negotiation, the cost of demo recordings is only half recoupable.

Direct payment of the publisher share performing rights to the co-publisher may sometimes be negotiated, although if there is any advance, the main publisher will want to apply such income toward its recoupment.

Other elements that are relevant:

(1) To what extent should the co-publisher retain approval rights over certain uses, particularly: synchronization rights (see moral rights issues under section 2 b) (iv) H); translation rights; grand rights; and mechanical rights licensed at lower than industry standard rates?

(2) Should the major publisher have an obligation to secure cover versions, or to make print copies of songs that are administered pursuant to this agreement?[67]

(3) Amount of timing of advances: are they payable upon signing the agreement and upon exercising various options? Will the co-publisher share in advances from foreign territories (see section 2 c) (ii) D in this regard)?

(4) Are royalties to be calculated "at source" (see section 2 c) (ii) D)?

(5) Consider also the effect of the controlled composition clause in the recording agreement, if applicable. Does the composer who is also a recording musician have the first right to record

---

[67] See Form 173-1, "Co-Publishing Agreement", in *Entertainment Industry Contracts* ... cited above in note 18. See also Chapter 23, "Co-ownership and Joint Administration of Copyrights" in *This Business of Music* ... cited above in note 21 at pp. 259-264, and the co-publishing agreement checklist in this book, Appendix 3.

such compositions governed by this agreement? A hybrid form of this agreement is the joint publishing agreement or joint co-publishing agreement. [68] This is not common and will not be discussed in detail here.

(b) Participation Agreement

(i) Co-Publishing and Participation Agreement Compared

The participation agreement is sometimes referred to as a co-publishing agreement and many of the same concerns that arise in a co-publishing agreement arise in a participation agreement. Both afford the songwriter/participant a contractual right to participate in the net income of the publisher. The main difference is that the income participation agreement allows the active publisher to maintain an ownership of all right, title and interest in the copyright of the musical compositions that are the subject matter of the agreement. [69]

(ii) Generally

Typically the publisher administers all rights and merely permits participation of the specified party in net income, not gross income from the musical compositions. For this reason, the accounting and audit clauses are particularly relevant. They are discussed above in section 2 c) (iii) in the context of the exclusive term publishing agreement. The obligation to account to the participant should survive any assignment of the publisher's rights to the musical compositions.

A participation agreement may be appropriate for a number of business relationships. If the songwriter is in a "tied deal" with a record label, the participation level may escalate in lock-step with the record royalties, based on successive albums and/or sales levels, and it also may be tied to recoupment of recording costs. For example, the participation percentage may start at 20% and escalate to over 50% of the publisher's share of net income with successive albums or gold or platinum sales levels.

A participation agreement is sometimes a means by which persons who invest in the songwriter's career secure a return on their investment.

---

[68] *Ibid.*, Form 173-4.
[69] *Ibid.*, Form 173-5, "Income Participation Agreement".

It is also sometimes used to induce a successful artist to record a songwriter's song. The recording artist participates in the income that the song generates because he/she has brought the song to market. Participation should be contingent upon commercial release of a particular song through normal retail channels in specific countries. One should bear in mind that SOCAN presently cannot attribute income to a particular recording of a song. Accordingly, if subsequent recordings of the song are released, the original participating artist will participate in all such recordings as well. One way around this is to limit the participation to a number of years, or to mechanical royalties on the original recording only. See also the discussion below in section 3(c) for various formulas.

The definitions of gross income and net income are significant. See the discussion above in section 3(a), 'Co-Publishing' in this regard.

(c) Administration

(i) Generally

Under this agreement, the songwriter/publisher assigns the administration rights in the compositions to an administrator for a period of time, usually three or five years. In this way, an administration agreement is like a sub-publishing agreement for a foreign territory, but is in force either domestically, or often on a worldwide basis.[70] If it is a worldwide administration agreement, and foreign sub-publishers are not excluded from gross income, there is the risk of two administration fees being deducted.[71] Generally, as is the case in most publishing agreements, the rights granted to the administrator will not revert until advances have been fully recouped or, if so agreed, have been repaid in full.

Advances are usually substantially lower than those payable under a co-publishing agreement. The administration agreement may require that if the administrator secures a recording agreement for the songwriter/publisher, then the latter must enter into a full co-publishing agreement with the administrator.

---

[70] *Ibid.*, p. 173-46.
[71] *Ibid.*, at p. 173-51.

(ii) Negotiable Elements

As distinguished from the negotiable elements of a co-publishing agreement, the following elements are negotiable in an administration agreement:

(1) With lower advances and a lower level of income participation for the administrator, performing rights should be paid directly to the original publisher by its performing rights society.

(2) Is it an exclusive or non-exclusive right of administration?

(3) The general administration fee charged can vary between 10% and 25% of gross receipts (or net receipts), depending on the bargaining strengths of the parties. High earning songwriter/publishers have been known to negotiate fees down to 5% of net receipts;[72]

(4) Also negotiable are the (justifiably higher) fees to be charged for cover versions and synchronization uses, typically 40% but ranging up to 50% of either gross or net income. However, as noted above, performing rights societies have no way of distinguishing airplay of particular recordings of a song. Accordingly, a formula should be imposed to avoid overcompensation, since the cover version will not account for all the performing rights income from a particular country. One reasonable method is to multiply total performing rights income from the territory by the fraction of total mechanical income from that territory attributable to the cover version. One drawback to this method, however, is that it assumes that mechanical and public performance royalties can be equated, which is not always the case. The cover version may get substantial airplay because of domestic content regulations (e.g.: a French language version in Quebec) but sell relatively few records compared to the original English language version.

(5) The cost of demos, lead sheets, copyright registration and their deductibility is negotiable;

(6) Any promotional or exploitation costs should be subject to joint approval;

(7) Should the administrator have a right of first refusal if the owner-publisher wishes to sell its copyrights? (This right is virtually standard in co-publishing agreements);

(8) To what extent should the administrator have the right to initiate and defend copyright infringement actions?

---

[72] *Ibid.*, Form 173-6, "Administration Agreement". See also administration agreement checklist in Appendix 3.

(9) Maximum sub-publisher fees may be negotiated. The administrator is already taking its administration fee; added to that will be any sub-publishing fees that its sub-publishers take. However, as a second-best alternative to "at source", one can negotiate "caps" to sub-publishing fees. Any coverage effectively comes out of the administrator's share. Normally the sub-publisher's fees can be capped as follows: 25% of the original version's mechanical royalties; 50% to 75% of any cover version mechanical royalties; 50% for synchronization fees; and 50% of public performance royalties.

(d) Sub-publishing

(i) Generally

The sub-publishing agreement is an agreement that is in place for a specific period of time, in a specific territory, usually for specified musical compositions, such as a catalogue, compositions on one or more albums, or one song. The sub-publishing agreement is similar to an administration agreement but is applicable in a particular territory. See the discussion above in section 3 (c) on administration agreements.

Sub-publishers can be more effective than original publishers because they are more familiar with the music infrastructure of their own territory. They are better situated to promote song catalogues, collect mechanical royalties, obtain cover versions and synchronization licences.

The fee charged by a sub-publisher is typically 15% to 25% of the gross income from the songs in its territory. The territory may be a single country, a grouping of smaller countries (e.g. Scandinavia) or a number of large countries (e.g. Western Europe). The same royalty division discussed above in section 3 (c) for the administration agreement also applies to the foreign sub-publishing agreement.

A typical sub-publishing agreement would be for a specific territory, for example G.S.A. (Germany, Switzerland, Austria) for a three-year period, with a specified grant of rights including the following: (a) print, publish and licence specific rights both on an exclusive basis (for example, mechanical royalties), and on a non-exclusive basis (for example, synchronization rights); (b) the non-exclusive right to adapt, translate, and arrange the musical composition with consent of the original publisher; (c) the right to register copyright to music which is being sub-published in the name of the publisher; and (d) the obligation to place proper copyright notices for the musical compositions that are sub-published.

An independent publisher is more likely to obtain and share with its writers an advance received from a clearly identifiable sub-publishing source. Major publishers already have their affiliates in place worldwide who do not pay each other advances.

The sub-publisher normally acquires the rights to grant a non-exclusive synchronization licence for films or television produced in the territory for the territory. However, the original publisher typically reserves the right to issue worldwide synchronization licences, irrespective of the origin of the production. The original publisher normally will retain other basic rights, such as dramatization rights, conversion rights and, of course, any other rights requiring songwriter or co-publisher approval.

"Governing law" is once again an important issue, as described above in section 2(d)(i). The sub-publishers may require the songwriters in question to sign an inducement letter agreeing to the grant of sub-publishing rights.

(ii) Negotiable Elements

The following elements of a sub-publishing agreement are negotiable:

(1) The extent of rights granted. Does the sub-publisher have the right to make translations and versions with different lyrics and different arrangements? If so, the total payable to the sub-lyric writer for translations is usually specified as 25% of the songwriter's share, as automatically applied by most performing rights societies. The ownership of translations and adaptations should be specified in the agreement. Normally, the original publisher would retain such ownership.

(2) Term. As discussed above, a three to five-year term is typical but the sub-publishers may want (and the original publisher may resist) an extension of the term for any song for which a cover version is obtained.

(3) Advance. The size depends on the territory, financial clout of the sub-publishers and income earning potential of the repertoire. The foreign sub-publisher will want to receive public performing rights directly, prior to remitting them to the original publisher, to recoup its advance. However, the process will speed royalties to the original publisher faster than if they had to pass through performing rights societies.

(4) The issue of copyright infringement actions should be addressed. Typically the sub-publisher has a non-exclusive right to pursue copyright infringement claims. Amounts recovered

from such claims are typically divided 50/50 after the deduction of costs, and specifically legal costs. Some type of formula to distinguish original and cover versions of a song and to allocate royalties should be included in the agreement. (See section 3 c) (ii) above in this regard.)

(5) Other key issues discussed in section 2 are also relevant in any publishing agreement, e.g.: reversion of copyright for failure to exploit, account or allow an audit, and on bankruptcy. The costs of translating, adapting and arrangement should be borne by the sub-publisher.

(iii) Specific Problems with Sub-publishing Agreements

There are certain problems that are often associated with sub-publishing agreements:

(1) The rights that sub-publishers acquire are often restricted to a specific territory, particularly in Europe. This prevents the problem of one mechanical royalty being paid in a country with a low mechanical rate, but a record embodying the song sub-published being sold in a country with a high mechanical rate.[73] If there is an administration agreement in place, the sub-publishing fees should be restricted to the pre-negotiated amounts that the sub-publisher can reasonably deduct.[74] If the sub-publishing agreement is for more than one country, it is preferable that the earnings be paid "at source" in order to prevent further dilution by collecting bodies or sub-publishers within the territory.[75]

(2) Copyright should continue to be registered in the original publisher's name, otherwise copyright registration may dilute the original composer's share of income of a foreign version even if there has been no release of that version.[76]

(3) The rights of the sub-publisher concerning cover versions should be specified. Typically, they would be retained up to five years, but could be for the life of the copyright depending on the negotiating strengths of the parties and other factors,

---

[73] *Ibid.*, Form 176-1, "Sub-Publishing Agreement", pp. 176-1 to 176-33. See also generally Chapter 20, "Foreign Publishing", in *This Business of Music* ... cited above in note 21 at pp. 217-236, and Form 11, "Foreign Sub-Publishing Agreement" at pp. 648-65. See also the sub-publishing agreement checklist in Appendix 3.

[74] *Ibid.*, *This Business of Music* ..., p. 251.

[75] *Ibid.*, p. 226-228.

[76] *Ibid.*, p. 222.

for example, the chart positions reached by the cover version in the sub-publishing territories.

(4) Ordinarily there is a period after the term, during which the sub-publisher continues to collect "pipeline income" as discussed above in paragraph 2 d) (iii). This is particularly important if there are unrecouped advances.

(5) There is often a legal liability on the part of the sub-publisher to withhold taxes.

(6) There are potential problems of conflicting laws. For example, under European Union laws, certain territorial restrictions are not valid.[77] Obtaining the advice of local counsel would be prudent.

(7) The original publisher should be entitled also to any so-called "black box" monies, that is, monies for songs not identified by a performing rights or mechanical rights society, and that may be paid out *pro rata* in the relevant accounting period according to a formula such as: total distribution of black box monies multiplied by (assuming a 25% sub-publishers fee) 75% of distribution of black box money by the society to the publisher regarding the musical composition, divided by the total distributed from the society for all musical compositions regarding black box monies.[78]

(8) Conflicts of law and suing foreign companies who have little or no assets are part of the complexities involved when entering into sub-publishing arrangements. See discussion in Chapter 10, "Personal Service Contracts" in this regard.

(e) Sale of Music Publisher's Catalogue

(i) *Generally*

All the legalities surrounding the purchase of a business apply to the sale of a publisher's catalogue. The usual way to structure this agreement is as an asset purchase, but it also may be structured as a share purchase agreement. The way in which the transaction is structured will be significant for tax purposes. Skilled tax advice should be sought. The publishing company's name may be part of the assets that are being sold. Inquiries should be made about the financial status of the publisher, including an audit of the vendor's books, royalty

---

[77] *This Business of Music ...* cited above in note 21, p. 228.

[78] Adapted from Form 176-1, p. 176-19, "Sub-Publishing Agreement", in *Entertainment Industry Contracts* cited above in note 18. See also "Foreign Publishing" in *This Business of Music ...* cited above at note 21.

statements, any exchange rate conversions, taxes paid, unrecouped advances, future contingent liabilities and any applicable audit recoveries. The purchase and sale documents should include the following: (1) a business summary of the publisher; (2) recent financial statements; (3) a list of all songs being purchased and the related songwriter agreements; and (4) any relevant commitments of the publisher.[79] A search of all relevant copyrights should be conducted.

It may be advisable to have key employees of the publisher enter into employment agreements in order to maintain continuity of the music publishing catalogue as a business.

From a legal perspective, the following should be completed: (1) a review and analysis of the accuracy of the copyright registrations; (2) a review of any agreements under which rights were transferred to the publisher; (3) an examination of the chain of title of copyrights; (4) an examination of relevant liens, encumbrances and mortgages; (5) an examination of pending or actual litigation; (6) a review of licensing agreements including sub-publishing arrangements and all songwriter agreements and reversions under these agreements; (7) a determination whether there is a key person clause in any agreement (see Chapter 6 for a discussion of the key person clause); (8) an examination of other contractual commitments including advances and guaranteed income commitments; (9) the actual term or expiration of the songwriter agreements; (10) the existence of any unpaid taxes;[80] and (11) the extent of the grant of rights under the agreement.

(ii) Evaluation

An assessment of the catalogue is done either on a cash basis, that is "gross royalty income received by the selling company less all royalties payable to the songwriters and other third parties"[81] or the accrual method: "... under this method the buyer takes the gross earnings received during the year and deducts the income actually paid to songwriters and other third party royalty participants from that year plus royalties which will be paid out in future from that income."[82] The accrual method is the method most often used. Information such as synchronization licence fees for television and movies is also relevant. Sub-publishing, administration and co-publishing agreements clearly affect the value of the publisher's catalogue. Other relevant factors include:

---

[79] *Ibid.*, pp. 120-123.

[80] *Ibid.*, adapted from p. 123.

[81] Brabec cited above in note 2 at p. 118.

[82] *Ibid.*, p. 119.

1. The remaining life of key copyrights (will there be early reversion; when did the composer die?)[83] It is important to bear in mind that while most catalogues have many songs, it is only a few of those songs that actually produce a majority of the earnings.

2. Whether there are significant liens or encumbrances on the catalogue (any arrears of royalties, copyright infringement claims, collateral mortgages?);

3. The extent of unrecouped advances; and

4. Purchaser-related factors (e.g. is the purchaser a record company that plans a major reissue?).

A typical history of earnings, including performance and mechanical licence fees which account for the bulk of a song's earnings, should be compiled for analysis purposes.

(iii) Purchase Price

The purchase price of a catalogue is normally a ratio that can be expressed as follows: the average of net earnings annually, based on the last three to five years of annual earnings, multiplied by three to ten times this amount. Whether the multiple is closer to three or to ten depends on the risk involved in the catalogue, such as the presence of lawsuits and the term of the copyrights being purchased. Net income consists of the gross royalty income, minus royalties paid to songwriters and direct costs to third parties, and is usually calculated on an accrual (as opposed to cash) basis.[84] The overhead costs, including costs of demonstration recordings and copyright registration, leases and employees' salaries, are not normally included in determining what the buyer would offer as a purchase price for a publisher's catalogue. A number of representations and warranties are relevant to the status of

---

[83] *Ibid.*, p. 13. See also Paul Edward Geller, "Worldwide Chain of Title to Copyright" (1989), Vol. 11 No. 5 *E.L.R.* 3. A number of questions are raised in this article that should be considered when one acquires copyright: (1) the extent of the rights granted; (2) if the title to copyrights being acquired is clear; (3) who held the original rights and in whom did they originally vest; (4) any contracts which exist which transferred title; and (5) has there been any transfer by law. Clearly the rights in effect, and where they are vested, will significantly affect the evaluation of a copyright catalogue.

[84] For a useful checklist concerning this issue see Sidney Schemel, "The Acquisition and Sale of Music ..." cited above in note 22. See also "Buying and Selling Copyrights", Chapter 30, in *This Business of Music* ... cited above in note 22. See also Brabec cited above in note 2 at pp. 118-129. Two recent articles on the valuation of catalogues are Mark Bezant & Kevin Brown, "The Valuation of Copyright", *Copyright World*, Issue 70, May 1997, p. 17; Geraint Howells, "The Valuation of and Accounting for Catalogues of Recorded Music", *Copyright World*, Issue 37, February 1994, p. 39.

the titles to musical compositions, including liens and encumbrances, the originality of the compositions, and the effect of the agreement on writers, co-publishers and other rights of third parties. These are important in determining the purchase price.

(iv) After Sale

Subsequent to the sale, appropriate documents, such as assignment of copyright, should be registered. Appropriate notices should be sent to all relevant parties, including writers, performing rights societies and mechanical reproduction rights agencies.

4

COPYRIGHT INFRINGEMENT

Contributing Author: Ronald N. Hier, B.A., LL.B., LL.M.

1. Two Main Types

There are two types of copyright infringement: direct and secondary. Direct infringement occurs when any person, without the consent of the copyright owner, does anything that only the owner of the copyright has the right to do.[1] Consent may take the form of a licence, express or implied, or of an assignment of all or part of the copyright.[2] Neither good faith nor ignorance provides a complete defence to the innocent infringer. Nor does it matter that the infringer's use is without any element of financial gain.

Secondary infringement occurs when a person: (1) sells or rents out; (2) distributes to such an extent as to affect prejudicially the rights of the owner; (3) by way of trade, distributes, exposes or offers for sale or rental or exhibits in public; (4) possesses for the purpose of doing anything referred to in (1) to (3); or (5) imports for the purpose of doing anything referred to in (1) to (3), a copy of a work, a sound recording, a fixation of a performer's performance or a communication signal that the person knows or should have known

---

[1] Subsection 27(1) of the Act. The rights of owners are found in s. 3(1). They include, *inter alia*, the rights of reproduction, performance and publication. The copyright owner is also granted the right to authorize any of the acts which are reserved to the copyright owner. Thus, authorization of infringement would constitute a direct infringement of copyright.

[2] Subsection 13(4) of the Act states that no assignment or grant of an interest in a copyright is valid unless made in writing. Failure to comply with the subsection will result in the invalidity of the transfer; see Normand Tamaro, *The 1998 Annotated Copyright Act*, (Toronto: Carswell, 1998), at p. 270. It would appear, then, that a transferee who takes under an oral agreement and who then attempts to exercise his/her rights is technically an infringer. However, courts will, in certain circumstances, recognize the existence of an implied licence, either on the basis of an incomplete written agreement or resulting from trade practices; see Tamaro, at pp. 274-77.

infringes copyright or would infringe copyright if it had been made in Canada.[3] Knowledge can be imputed if the work contains a copyright notice or the infringer receives written notification.

Additional acts of infringement set out in the Act include the manufacture or possession of plates designed to make infringing copies of a work,[4] permitting the public performance of a work for profit in a theatre or place of public entertainment without the consent of the copyright owner,[5] and, subject to certain exceptions, importing books without the consent of the copyright owner.[6]

2. Direct Infringement of Copyright

There are three elements which must be present before an unauthorized reproduction can be said to constitute an infringement: (1) copyright must subsist in the work copied; (2) the infringer must be shown to have had access to the infringing work and to have copied a substantial portion of it; and (3) the infringing work must not be a work of independent creation.[7] Of particular importance is item (2) which is discussed below.

(a) Substantial Reproduction

Although the Act gives the sole right to reproduce a work to the copyright owner, not every unauthorized reproduction is an infringement. The copying must be substantial.[8] What constitutes substantial copying is a question of fact. Generally, courts will give greater weight to the 'quality' of what is taken than to the 'quantity' taken. Other factors that have been considered include: (1) the extent to which the defendant's use adversely affects the copyright owner; (2) whether the material copied is the proper subject matter of copyright; (3) whether there was an intentional taking by the defendant; and (4) whether the material taken is used in the same or a similar fashion as the plaintiff's use.[9]

---

[3] Subsection 27(2) of the Act.

[4] Subsection 27(4) of the Act.

[5] Subsection 27(5) of the Act.

[6] Section 27.1 of the Act. Infringement under this section is secondary infringement requiring actual or implied knowledge on the part of the importer.

[7] *Productions Avanti Cine-Video Inc. c. Favreau* (1997), 79 C.P.R. (3d) 385 (C.S. Qué.) at p. 389.

[8] Subsection 3(1) of the Act.

[9] See *U & R Tax Services Ltd. v. H & R Block Canada Inc.* (1995), 62 C.P.R. (3d) 257 (Fed. T.D.) at p. 268. See also *Ladbroke (Football) Ltd. v. William Hill (Football) Ltd.*, [1964]

(i) Digital Sampling

The issue of substantial reproduction is raised most sharply in connection with digital sampling.[10] This practice, now widespread, has created much uncertainty in the music industry. Some have argued that the use of any sample, recognizable or not, constitutes an infringement of copyright while others assert that the practice of sampling, as seen, for example, in the genre known as 'rap', comprises a kind of post-modern musical collage which should be immune from the copyright laws.[11]

The practice of sampling has yet to be considered by a Canadian court, but three recent decisions of the U.S. and British courts suggest, albeit without deciding the issue, that the unauthorized sampling of sound recordings can, in the right circumstances, amount to copyright infringement. In *Grand Upright Music Ltd. v. Warner Brothers Records Inc.*[12] a U.S. District Court granted a preliminary injunction to the copyright owner of Gilbert O'Sullivan's 1972 hit "Alone Again (Naturally)" preventing the distribution of an album by rapper Biz Markie containing his new composition "Alone Again". Markie had sampled a twenty second passage from Sullivan's work using three words and eight

---

1 All E.R. 465 (U.K. H.L.) wherein the House of Lords outlined the following test: (1) whether the copying is done directly; (2) the qualitative nature of the part reproduced; (3) whether the part copied is original, i.e., does it exhibit a substantial degree of labour and skill; and (4) whether it forms an essential part of the work. In *Preston v. 20th Century Fox Canada Ltd.* (1991), 33 C.P.R. (3d) 242 (Fed. T.D.), affirmed (1993), 53 C.P.R. (3d) 407 (Fed. C.A.), a case involving a literary work, the court, adopting a U.S approach, held the test is whether an average lay observer would recognize the copy as having been appropriated from the copyrighted work. The U.K. Court of Appeal has held that even one frame of a film could be a substantial part of a film; see *Spelling Goldberg Productions Inc. v. B.B.C. Publishing*, [1979] F.S.R. 474 as cited in Michael F. Flint, "Opinion: Scratch Videos" (1986), Vol. 4 No. 2, I.M.L. 10 at p. 10.

[10] Sampling has been defined by BMI as the process whereby "sound bytes are removed electronically from a master recording and through technological imitation placed within the context of another composition"; Broadcast Music Inc., *A Guide to Music Publishing Terminology* (1990) cited in Jeffrey H. Brown, "They Don't Make Music The Way They Used To: The Legal Implications of "Sampling" In Contemporary Music" (1992) Wisconsin L.R. 1941 at p. 1942, footnote 7. Most samples are no more than several seconds in length. For a discussion of the technique of sampling, see Mark G. Quail, "Digital Samplers: Can Copyright Protect Music from the Numbers Game? (1991) 7 I.P.J. 39 at pp. 42-43.

[11] See for example, Jason H. Marcus, "Don't Stop That Funky Beat: The Essentiality of Digital Sampling to Rap Music", in *1992-93 Entertainment, Publishing and the Arts Handbook*, (New York: Clark, Boardman, Callaghan), p. 247; see also Robert M. Syzmanski, "Audio Pastiche: Digital Sampling, Intermediate Copying, Fair Use" (1996), 3 U.C.L.A. Ent. L. Rev. 271.

[12] 780 F. Supp. 182 (S.D.N.Y. 1991). For a discussion of this case, see Carl A. Falstrom, "Thou Shalt Not Steal: *Grand Upright Music Ltd. v. Warner Bros. Records Inc.* and the Future of Digital Sound Sampling in Popular Music" (1994), 45 Hastings L.J. 359.

bars of music. However, in granting the injunction, the court did not consider the issue of substantial similarity.[13] In a second case, *Jarvis v. A & M Records*,[14] the court held that the sampling of a bridge and keyboard riff might infringe if what is sampled is "sufficiently distinctive".[15] In reaching this conclusion, the court applied the 'fragmented similarity test' espoused by Nimmer.[16] In the third case, *BBC v. Precord Ltd.*,[17] the plaintiffs obtained an interlocutory injunction to prevent the release of a record which used 63 sampled words taken from an interview given by Neil Kinnock, the former leader of Britain's Labour Party. The words were combined with additional words and music to be released as a Christmas novelty record. The injunction was granted on the basis of the plaintiff's property right in the sound recording of the interview, but this case, too, failed to consider the issue of substantial similarity.

Should a sampling case ever be litigated in Canada, it seems clear that the court will have to consider the following issues: (1) if the sample merely reproduces a drum beat or other instrumental or vocal sound, does copyright subsist in the sampled material[18]; (2) is there scope for a *de minimis* defence[19]; (3) does use of the sample constitute "fair dealing" with the copied work[20]; (4) if the sample is uncredited, is

---

[13] The Court was content to rely on the defendant's "callous disregard for the law and the rights of others" and cited the Seventh Commandment, "Thou shalt not steal"; see p. 185 of the judgment. The case was settled several days after the court issued its ruling; see Brown, supra note 10 at p. 1968.

[14] 27 U.S.P.Q. (2d) 1812 (D.N.J. 1993). In this case, the court refused to grant the defendant's motion for summary judgment. As in the Biz Markie case, there was no final resolution of the issue. See also *Tuff 'N' Rumble Management Inc. v. Profile Records Inc.*, 42 U.S.P.Q. (2d) 1398 (S.D.N.Y., 1997) and *Tin Pan Apple Inc. v. Miller Brewing Co.*, 30 U.S.P.Q. (2d) 1791 (S.D.N.Y., 1994); all three cases are discussed in Susan Upton Douglass & Craig S. Mende, "Music Sampling: More than Digital Theft?", *Copyright World*, Issue 82, August 1998 at p. 23.

[15] *Ibid.*, p. 1818.

[16] This test looks at whether the value of the original work is substantially diminished; this will be the case where what is sampled is of great qualitative significance to the work as a whole; see Syzsmanski, supra note 11 at p. 302.

[17] SRIS C/89/91 Harman J., November 11, 1991, Ch. D.; for a discussion of this case, see Lionel Bentley and Brad Sherman, "Culture of Copying: Digital Sampling and Copyright Law", [1992] 5 Ent. L.R. 158.

[18] Often, what is sampled is a bass line or drum beat idiomatic of a particular style of popular music. In *Tin Pan Apple*, supra note 14, in refusing to grant summary judgment in favour of the defendants, the Court held that the unique vocal sounds "Hugga Hugga" and "Brrr" of the rap group, The Fat Boys, might possibly qualify for copyright protection.

[19] See Bentley and Sherman, supra note 17 at p. 159 who argue that British law, which is not essentially different from Canadian law, leaves room for such an exception.

[20] In *Campbell v. Acuff-Rose Music Inc.*, infra note 170, the U.S. Supreme Court suggested that the sampled bass line of Roy Orbison's "Oh, Pretty Woman" might not infringe where it was part of a song parody.

the defendant liable for passing off under the *Trade-Marks Act* or at common law; and (5) does the digital alteration of the sample and/or any failure to credit the creator of the sample violate the moral rights of the author?[21] Plaintiffs in such cases may also claim that the unauthorized sampling of their compositions or performances violates their right of publicity.

Because of the uncertainty surrounding these issues, many samples are currently being licensed by music publishers and record companies. With respect to the former, licenses may provide for a flat fee (a "buy out") or a continuing royalty based on exploitation of the copyright and/or the number of records sold. Sometimes, publishers will insist on a share of performance royalties or a co-ownership interest in the new composition. In the extreme, they even may seek an assignment of the copyright in the new composition. With respect to the latter, the sampler will need to obtain a master use licence from the record company. Such licences are generally negotiated on terms similar to mechanical licences.[22]

(b) Access

Because it is possible that two authors working independently may create works of striking similarity, the law requires that the original work must be the source from which the copy derives. There must be a "causal connection" between the two works. This connection may be established by showing that the infringer had access to the original work. However, access need not be direct; it may be gained through an intermediary and further, it may be demonstrated by circumstantial evidence.[23]

(i) Subconscious Copying

U.S. courts have held that copying need not be intentional so long as access is shown, and have founded liability on the basis of

---

[21] See, for example *Morrison Leahy Music Limited and Another v. Lightbond Limited*, [1993] E.M.L.R. 144 in which George Michael argued that a licensed remix of one of his compositions was "derogatory". While the court did not decide the point, it accepted that a derogatory remix could be actionable. For a discussion of this case, see Stephen Bate and Lawrence Abramson, "To Sample or Not to Sample?", [1997] 6 Ent. L.R. 193.

[22] For a discussion of licensing practices, see Al Kohn & Bob Kohn, *The Art of Music Licensing*, (Inglewood: Aspen Law & Business, 1996) at pp. 803-27; see also Brown, supra note 10 at pp. 1956-1961.

[23] *Grignon v. Roussel* (1991), 38 C.P.R. (3d) 4 (Fed. T.D.); see also *Francis Day & Hunter Ltd. v. Bron*, [1963] 2 All E.R. 16 (Eng. C.A.).

subconscious copying.[24] However, Canadian and British courts have yet to embrace fully the concept of unconscious copying.[25]

(ii) Plagiarism and Music

A. Authorship and Ownership

As noted above, the plaintiff in a plagiarism suit must prove copyright in the work that is copied. Copyright presumes originality; it is therefore open to the defendant to argue that the part of the work allegedly copied is not original to the plaintiff. This will be the case if it can be shown to be part of the public domain or to have originated with some other composer. Often, the defendant will argue that the musical phrase allegedly copied can be found in the pre-existing musical literature or forms part of the common language of a particular genre or style.

Subsection 53(2) of the Act provides a rebuttable presumption that a certificate of registration of copyright is evidence that copyright subsists and that the person registered is the owner of the copyright.[26] However, registration will not assist the plaintiff if copyright is registered after distribution by the defendant of the allegedly copied work.[27]

B. Substantial Copying

Because direct infringement requires proof that a substantial part of the work has been copied by the defendant, musical analysis by a qualified expert is invariably required. The expert will consider such factors as: (1) any musical similarities between the two works; (2) any

---

[24] See for example, *Bright Tunes Music Corp. v. Harrisongs Music Ltd.* 420 F.Supp. 177 (S.D.N.Y., 1976) in which the court concluded that George Harrison in writing "My Sweet Lord" unintentionally but subconsciously copied the Chiffons' hit record, "He's So Fine".

[25] In *Gondos v. Hardy* (1982), 64 C.P.R. (2d) 145 (Ont. H.C.) the concept was argued, but the court declined to pronounce on the matter; see also *Drynan v. Rostad* (1994), 59 C.P.R. (3d) 8 (Ont. Small C. Ct.) and *Francis Day & Hunter*, supra note 23. Some authorities, however, believe that infringement may result from unconscious copying; see Huges G. Richard, "Concept of Infringement in the *Copyright Act*", in *Copyright and Confidential Information Law of Canada*, G.F. Henderson, ed., (Toronto: Carswell, 1994), p. 208 at pp. 209-10.

[26] There are other statutory presumptions as well. These include the presumption of copyright under para. 34.1(1)(a); and the presumption that the author is the owner under para. 34.1(1)(b). See also s. 34.1(2) for the presumptions that arise in the absence of registration of an assignment or grant of an interest.

[27] *Grignon v. Roussel*, supra note 23, at pp. 7-8.

differences between the two works; (3) similarities of melody, harmony, key signature, rhythm, structure, tempo, timbre, structure, and where relevant, lyrics; (4) the likelihood that any such similarities are indicative of copying; (5) the fact that any similarities are dictated by the genre of composition; (6) the percentage of each work that is similar; and (7) the qualitative importance of the similarities to each work.[28]

If it can be shown that there is a "striking similarity", a "sufficient objective similarity" between the works or that the "substance of the original work" has been taken, a court will find for the plaintiff.[29]

C. Access

Access may be shown where there is direct contact between the plaintiff and defendant[30] or where the defendant receives a copy of the copied work through an intermediary.[31] If the plaintiff's work is disseminated to the public, for example, through radio airplay or public performance, access may be inferred.[32]

---

[28] Adapted from Christine Lepera & Michael Manuelian, "Music Plagiarism: A Framework for Litigation", Ent. & Sports Law., Vol. 15, No. 2, Summer 1997, p. 3 at p.4. Inquiry often focuses on the "hook", that part of the tune (usually the chorus or a clever lyric) which renders it memorable and gives it commercial appeal. For judicial recognition of the importance of hooks, see *Grignon v. Roussel*, supra, note 23 at p. 16 and *Drynan v. Rostad*, supra, at p.18. For more on the use of experts in a U.S. context, see Alice J. Kim, "Expert Testimony and Substantial Similarity: Facing the Music in (Music) Copyright Infringement Cases" (1994-95), 19 Col.-VLA J. of Law & The Arts 109 and Judith Greenberg Finell, "Using an Expert Witness in a Music Copyright Case"(1990), Ent. L. Reporter, Vol. 12., No. 3., p.3.

[29] See *Grignon v. Roussel*, supra note 23, at pp. 13-17 and the cases and authorities cited therein. See also Preston, supra note 9; which applied the 'unlawful appropriation' test developed by the U.S. courts. This test was first applied in *Arnstein v. Porter*, 154 F.2d 476 (2d Cir., 1946) and subsequently refined in *Sid & Marty Krofft Television Productions Inc. v. McDonald's Corp.*, 562 F.2d 1157 (9th Cir., 1977). Under *Arnstein*, the plaintiff must first prove an objective copying of the plaintiff's work. If successful, the plaintiff must then show unlawful appropriation. Although the first factor may be established by expert testimony, the court held that the second could be established only by the response of the ordinary lay hearer; i.e., not on the basis of expert testimony. For more on the U.S. approach, see Kim, supra note 28.

[30] *Drynan v. Rostad*, supra note 25.

[31] *Grignon v. Roussel*, supra, note 23.

[32] *Bright Tunes Music Corp. v. Harrisongs Music Ltd.*, supra note 24. See also *Gondos v. Hardy*, supra note 25; the plaintiff alleged that the defendant heard him perform the work in a hotel bar.

D. Independent Creation

The defendant will escape liability if he or she can establish that his/her work is a work of independent creation. Evidence that the impugned phrase also can be found in other works of the defendant, especially if written prior to access to or creation of the plaintiff's work, should meet the evidentiary burden.

(c) "Common Law" Copyright and Evidence of Ownership

Many composers try to prove ownership of copyright in their works by mailing a lead sheet or a cassette recording of the work to themselves by registered mail.[33] Musicians sometimes refer to this practice as a "common law copyright" although technically, in Canada, copyright is solely a creature of statute. However, it is preferable to mail such a letter with the tape enclosed to an independent witness; if necessary, the witness can be called to testify in court. Of course, any such letter should not be opened prior to its being used as evidence. An alternative practice is for the composer to swear an affidavit at the time the music is created stating the date of composition. Such an affidavit could also be used in court.

The registration of a certificate under section 55 of the Act is better evidence than either a registered letter or an affidavit. If the composer is a member of the Canadian Songwriters' Association, the title may be registered and a copy of it may be deposited with the association. If the composer is a member of SOCAN it is also advisable that he/she register the title of the composition with SOCAN. Such registrations and deposits are business records admissible under a hearsay exception and may help to establish important dates at trial.

(d) By Recording Music

(i) Sound Recordings

Pursuant to paragraph 3(1)(d) of the Act, the copyright owner has the sole right to make a sound recording of a work in which copyright subsists. Consequently, the unauthorized recording of a musical work is an infringement of copyright. This type of infringement can be avoided easily by obtaining the consent of the copyright owner, usually in the

---

[33] For an example of this, see *Grignon v. Roussel,* supra, note 23.

form of a mechanical licence.[34] If the words and music are owned by different composers or publishers, a licence should be obtained from all rights holders prior to making the recording.[35]

The failure to obtain a licence may result in a finding of liability on the part of the artist, producer, record company and even the manufacturer of the records.[36] To safeguard against this possibility, manufacturers should obtain an indemnity from makers of record masters or failing that, ascertain whether all necessary licences have been granted.[37]

The digital sampling of recordings also has given rise to issues of copyright infringement. These are discussed in Part 2 (a)(i) above.

(ii) Videotapes

Pursuant to paragraph 3(1)(d) of the Act, the copyright owner has the sole right to make a cinematograph film or other contrivance by which the work may be performed mechanically. This language is broad enough to encompass film, video[38] and any storage medium hereafter known. Therefore, it is an infringement of copyright to place a musical work on the soundtrack of a video or motion picture without the copyright owner's consent. Consent normally takes the form of a synchronization licence, so called because it permits the synchronization of music with the visual images that make up the film.

(e) Performing in Public

Among the rights reserved to the copyright owner is the right to perform the work in public.[39]

The Act defines a 'performance' to mean "any acoustic... representation of a work... including a representation made by means of any mechanical instrument or radio... or television receiving set".[40]

Courts have held that any acoustic representation of a work (regardless of the mode of transmission) is a performance,[41] and that a

---

[34] See Appendix 2 (II) 1for a mechanical rights licence checklist.

[35] *Rubens v. Pathe-Freres Ltd.*, [1911-16] Macg. Cop. Cas. 58.

[36] *Compo Co. v. Blue Crest Music Inc.*, [1980] 1 S.C.R. 357.

[37] See case comment, W.L. Hayhurst, "*Compo Co. v. Blue Crest Music Inc.* (1979), [1980] 1 S.C.R. 357 (S.C.C.)", in *Chronique de Jurisprudence* 242 at p. 248.

[38] *Warner Brothers - Seven Arts Inc. v. CESM-T.V. Ltd.*, (1971), 65 C.P.R. 215 (Can. Ex. Ct.).

[39] Subsection 3(1) of the Act.

[40] Section 2 of the Act.

performance takes place whenever steps are taken causing the work to be heard.[42] Moreover, one presentation of a work may give rise to several distinct performances.[43]

A performance takes place 'in public' whenever it is made available to members of the public; it is immaterial whether the listeners attend to the performance collectively in a public place or individually in the privacy of their own homes.[44] Thus, the following have all been held to be performances 'in public' under the Act: live performance on stage,[45] live performance in a hotel,[46] radio broadcast of recorded music,[47] communication of music through telephone lines,[48] radio broadcast to patrons individually in their hotel rooms,[49] and music performed by juke box in a restaurant.[50] This type of infringement can be avoided by obtaining a performing rights licence from SOCAN.

(f) Communication by Telecommunication

In addition to performances given 'in public' works may be communicated 'to the public' by telecommunication.[51] When this is done without authorization, the result is an infringement of copyright. Although the performance right is separate from the right to communicate to the public by telecommunication described in

---

[41] See *Canadian Cable Television Assn. v. Canada (Copyright Board)* infra note 53 at p. 369.

[42] *Performing Rights Society Ltd. v. Hammond's Bradford Brewery Co.*, [1934] 1 Ch. 121 (C.A.) at p. 137.

[43] For example, a live recital broadcast on radio and received by the owner of a bar gives rise to three distinct performances, all of which would infringe the performing right in the absence of a licence; see Tamaro, supra note 2 pp. 105-106.

[44] An early case, *Canadian Admiral Corp. v. Rediffusion Inc.* (1954), 20 C.P.R. 75 (Can. Ex. Ct.), following a line of British cases, had held that the issue should be determined from the point of view of the listener. However, this view was rejected in *Canadian Cable Television Assn. v. Canada (Copyright Board)* infra note 53 at pp. 369-71. This case is authority for the proposition that whether a performance takes place 'in public' must be determined from the point of view of the broadcaster. For a discussion of the issue, see Tamaro, supra note 2 at pp. 174-83.

[45] *C.A.P.A.C. v. Western Fair Assn.*, [1951] S.C.R. 596 (S.C.C.).

[46] *Composers, Authors & Publishers Association of Canada Ltd. v. Kiwanis Club of West Toronto*, [1953] 2 S.C.R. 111 (S.C.C.).

[47] *C.A.P.A.C. v. Maple Leaf Broadcasting Co.*, [1954] S.C.R. 624 (S.C.C.); *Durand & Cie. v. La Patrie Publishing Co.* [1960] S.C.R. 649 (S.C.C.).

[48] *Associated Broadcasting Co. v. C.A.P.A.C.*, [1954] 3 All E.R. 708 (Canada P.C.).

[49] *Canadian Performing Rights Society Ltd. v. Ford Hotel* (1935), 73 Que. S.C. 18.

[50] *Vigneux v. Canadian Performing Rights Society* (1945), 4 Fox Pat. C. 183 (Canada P.C.); *C.A.P.A.C. v. Siegel Distributing Co.*, [1959] S.C.R. 488 (S.C.C.).

[51] Paragraph 3(1)(f) of the Act. 'Telecommunication' is defined as "any transmission of... signals... or sounds...by wire, radio, visual, optical, or other electromagnetic system"; see s. 2 of the Act, and includes any broadcast or cable transmission of a musical work.

paragraph 3(1)(f), it is clear that the prohibition is concerned with the unauthorized performance of works by the telecommunications industry.[52] Nevertheless, in several cases involving the transmission of music, the courts have essentially severed the two concepts.[53] However, recent amendments to the definition of 'musical work' ensure that if a musical work is communicated to the public, the copyright owner will be protected, if not under the rules governing a performance in public, then pursuant to those governing telecommunication to the public.

(g) The Retransmission Right

Not all unauthorized telecommunications constitute an infringement. Subsection 31(2) provides an exemption for the simultaneous retransmission of an entire signal comprising a (musical) work. If the signal is a local signal, the exemption is absolute; if it is a distant signal, applicable retransmission royalties must be paid in accordance with a separate regime under the Act to secure the benefit of the exemption.[54]

---

[52] Paragraph 3(1)(f) was originally enacted to satisfy Canada's obligations under art. 11 *bis* of the *Berne Copyright Convention (Rome Revision)* which gave authors the exclusive right of authorizing the communication of their works to the public by radiocommunication. This right may be viewed as a performance right and is licensed as such by performing rights societies.

[53] In *CTV Television Network Ltd. v. Canada (Copyright Board)* (1993), 46 C.P.R. (3d) 343 (Fed. C.A.), leave to appeal to S.C.C. refused (1993), 51 C.P.R. (3d) v (S.C.C.), the court held that a network which transmitted musical works to its affiliated stations was not engaging in a telecommunication to the public. In *Canadian Cable Television Assn. v. Canada (Copyright Board)* (1993), 46 C.P.R. (3d) 359 (Fed. C.A.), leave to appeal to S.C.C. refused (1993), 51 C.P.R. (3d) v (S.C.C.), the court held that the provision of specialty cable channels did not constitute a telecommunication to the public but was a performance in public under the preamble to s. 3(1). These cases turned in part on the former definition of 'musical work' which required a graphical representation of the composition; under this definition the transmission was held to be a performance of a work and not a transmission of the work itself. Although musical works no longer need be fixed in written form, the courts are still reluctant to assimilate the two concepts. Thus, following the decision in *Canadian Assn. of Broadcasters v. SOCAN* (1994), 58 C.P.R. (3d) 190 (Fed. C.A.), the Canadian Copyright Board has held that "the transmission of music by cable operators... was transformed from a public performance to a public telecommunication"; see Tamaro, supra note 2 at pp. 202-3. See also s. 2.3 of the Act.

[54] See ss. 71-76 of the Act for the rules governing the applicable tariff.

(h) Publication

(i) Publishing Unpublished Music

The Act defines 'publication' to mean the making of copies of a work or sound recording available to the public.[55] The 'public' is that group of individuals outside the author's family and circle of friends.[56] However, the mere making of the work available to the public is insufficient to constitute publication; the author must intend to issue copies of the work.[57] Although the unauthorized publication of an unpublished work is an infringement, once the work is published, others are free to offer the published work for resale without violating the publication right.[58]

Paragraph 3(1)(a) of the Act reserves to the copyright owner the right to publish a translation of the work. This right is independent of the right of first publication. Accordingly, any unauthorized publication of a translation of a published or unpublished work is an infringement of the owner's copyright. Finally, the act of publishing can involve the unauthorized reproduction of the work and may also involve an act of authorizing an infringement.

(i) Authorizing Acts of Infringement

Copyright includes the right to authorize any of the acts reserved to the owner of copyright.[59] It is therefore an infringement to authorize any such acts without the consent of the copyright owner. The term "authorize" is used in its ordinary sense, that is, "to sanction, approve and countenance."[60] A performance is sanctioned, approved or countenanced if it is done under the control of the defendant.[61] In a

---

[55] Subsection 2.2(1) of the Act. However, paras. 2.2(1)(c) and (d) specifically exclude from the definition of 'publication' the performance in public or the communication to the public by telecommunication of a work or sound recording. Therefore, the public performance of a musical work will not violate the composer's publication right.

[56] *Prince Albert v. Strange* (1849), 41 E.R. 1171 (Eng. Ch. Div.), affirmed (1849), 64 E.R. 293 (Eng. C.A.).

[57] *Underwriters' Survey Bureau Ltd. v. Massie & Renwick Ltd.*, [1940] S.C.R. 218 (S.C.C.), special leave to appeal to S.C.C. refused [1940] S.C.R. 219 (note) (S.C.C.).

[58] See Tamaro, supra note 2 at p. 189. Of, course such publication may violate the author's reproduction rights.

[59] Post-amble to s. 3(1) of the Act.

[60] *Muzak Corporation v. Composers, Authors & Publishers Assn. (Canada)*, [1953] 2 S.C.R. 182 (S.C.C.) at p. 193.

[61] *de Tervagne v. Beloeil (Town)*, [1993] 3 F.C. 227 (Fed. T.D.), at pp. 248-49.

series of cases largely decided in the 1930s, courts have found the requisite degree of control where the defendant and a performer stood in the relationship of principal and agent,[62] master and servant,[63] and engager and independent contractor.[64] These cases gave an expansive reading to the meaning of 'control', finding liability even in the absence of any controlling act on the part of the defendant. However, in *Vigneux v. Canadian Performing Right Society*, the Privy Council decided that the mere provision of the means by which an infringing performance might take place could not be construed as an authorization under the Act[65], so that the status of these cases is today somewhat doubtful. Recent English cases have also taken this view.[66]

Sometimes, defendants seek to escape liability by arguing that they have acted with the implied consent of the copyright owner. However, courts are reluctant to accede to such arguments and jealously guard

---

[62] For example, in *Canadian Performing Rights Society Ltd. v. Yee*, [1943] D.L.R. 732 (Alta. Dist. Ct.), the owner of a restaurant who hired an orchestra was held to authorize an infringement where although he lacked 'practical control' over the orchestra, the leader acted in the scope of his employment for the benefit of the defendant.

[63] *Canadian Performing Right Society Ltd. v. Canadian National Exhibition Assn.*, [1934] O.R. 610 (Ont. H.C.); here, the defendant hired an orchestra to play copyright works during concerts organized by the defendant. The court held that because of the master/servant relationship between the defendant and the bandleader, the defendant could dictate the conduct of the band.

[64] *Canadian Performing Right Society Ltd. v. Canadian National Exhibition Assn.*, [1938] O.R. 476 (Ont. H.C.); here, the defendant hired Rudy Vallee to perform at the CNE and although Vallee had the contractual right to select the works to be performed and the time of the performance, the court found liability as the defendant had made no effort to ensure that only public domain works were performed. Following *Muzak Corp. v. Composers, Authors & Publishers Assn. (Canada)*, [1953] 2 S.C.R. 182 (S.C.C.); *de Tervagne v. Beloeil (Town)*, supra note 61; and *Vigneux v. Canadian Performing Right Society* (1943), 4 Fox Pat. C. 183 (Canada P.C.), it is doubtful whether this case would be so decided today.

[65] *Vigneux v. Canadian Performing Right Society* (1943), 4 Fox Pat. C. 183 (Canada P.C.). In *Vigneux*, the defendants leased record players and records to restaurants for use on the premises. However, the defendants did not control the time or manner of performance, and on this basis the Privy Council held that there had not been an authorization. *Vigneux* was approved by the Supreme Court of Canada in *Muzak*, supra note 64.

[66] See *C.B.S. Songs Ltd. v. Amstrad Consumer Electronics plc*, [1988] 2 All E.R. 484 (U.K. H.L.), in which the House of Lords rejected the claim that the sale of cassette decks with tape duplication facilities constituted an authorization; see also *C.B.S. Inc. v. Ames Records & Tapes*, [1981] 2 All E.R. 812 (Eng. Ch. Div.) wherein a record library which leased out records and sold blank tapes at a discount at the point of sale did not authorize an infringement. For a contrary view, see *Moorehouse v. University of New South Wales*, [1976] R.P.C. 151 (H.C.) in which the High Court of Australia held there was a sufficient degree of control where a university provided photocopiers and took no steps to limit their use to legitimate purposes; see also *RCA Corp. v. John Fairfax & Sons Ltd.*, [1982] R.P.C. 91 (S.C. N.S.W.). Note that these cases were decided prior to the *Copyright Amendment Act, 1986*.

the rights of copyright owners.[67] Both corporations and trade unions may be found liable for acts authorizing infringement, as may be directors, officers and union officials.[68]

(j) Neighbouring Rights

(i) Performers' Performances

As noted in Chapter 1, performers have copyright in their performances pursuant to subsection 15(1) of the Act. Accordingly, the unauthorized commission of any of the acts specified therein is an infringement of the performer's copyright in his or her performance. Performers of musical works also have the right to collect royalties through the relevant collective society for the performance of published sound recordings which embody their musical performances.[69] Although failure to pay such royalties would not constitute infringement of copyright, failure to pay is actionable and proceedings may be brought by the performer's collective society.[70]

(ii) Sound Recordings

Pursuant to subsection 18(1) of the Act, and as outlined in Chapter 1, the makers of sound recordings have copyright in their recordings. Accordingly, the unauthorized commission of any of the acts specified in subsection 18(1) is an infringement of copyright. Like performers, the makers of sound recordings have the right to collect royalties for the performance of their recordings.[71] Such royalties are payable with respect to any performance in public or telecommunication to the public of a published sound recording. Failure to pay is actionable and proceedings may be brought by the relevant collective society.[72]

---

[67] Thus, licences are strictly construed against licensees; see *Warner Brothers-Seven Arts*, supra note 38; and *Bishop v. Stevens*, [1990] 2 S.C.R. 467 (S.C.C.).

[68] See Tamaro, supra note 2 at p. 305 and the cases cited therein.

[69] Paragraph 19(2)(a) of the Act.

[70] Section 70.4 of the Act, but see para. 68.2(2)(b). Performers of literary or dramatic works may sue personally if no royalties are paid for the performance of their recordings; para. 19(2)(b) of the Act.

[71] Paragraph 19(2)(a) of the Act.

[72] See note 70 supra for the applicable provisions.

(k) Other Types of Direct Infringement

The other types of direct infringement include the unauthorized doing of any of the acts that only the copyright owner can do. These acts are outlined below.

(i) Arranging and Adapting Music

The making of an arrangement or adaptation of a musical work without the consent of the copyright owner is copyright infringement. Also actionable are the making of arrangements or adaptations which alter the melodic, harmonic or lyrical content of the work.[73] The author of an arrangement can restrain a third party from copying his or her arrangement irrespective of whether the arrangement itself infringes copyright.[74]

(ii) Converting Music into a Dramatic Work or Converting a Dramatico-Musical Work into a Non-Dramatic Work

It is an infringement of copyright to convert a musical work into a dramatic work by way of public performance or otherwise.[75] Such prohibition would extend to the lyrics, if they alone were used, for whether characterized as part of a musical work or as a separate literary work, lyrics are not "dramatic" works as that term is defined in section 2 of the Act.

If music is contained in a film, the soundtrack will form part of a cinematographic work and hence a dramatic work protected by copyright. Therefore, to the extent that music embodied in the soundtrack is converted to a novel or other non-dramatic work, there will be infringement of copyright in the motion picture.[76] Curiously, nothing in the Act explicitly forbids the novelization of a song or other musical work.[77]

---

[73] *Austin v. Columbia Gramophone Co. Ltd.*, [1923] Mac. & G. 398.

[74] *Zyx Music v. Pinnacle*, [1995] F.S.R. 567. Here, the plaintiff producer mixed two compositions to produce a disco dance version of "Please Don't Go", first recorded by KC and the Sunshine Band. The court held that (1) copyright subsisted in the new work and (2) the plaintiff was obligated to account to the original author for his share of the recovery; for a discussion of this case, see Bate and Abramson, supra, note 21 at pp. 194-95.

[75] Paragraph 3(1)(c) of the Act.

[76] Paragraph 3(1)(b) of the Act.

[77] Any such prohibition would have to be found in the pre-amble to s-s.3(1) of the Act which reserves the right to reproduce the work in any material form to the copyright

(iii) Translating Lyrics

It is copyright infringement to "produce, reproduce, perform or publish any translation of the work" without authorization.[78]

(l) Films

It is copyright infringement to reproduce, adapt or publicly present a musical work as a cinematographic work without the copyright owner's consent.[79]. However, music is not publicly presented as a cinematographic work merely by using the title of the work in a film.[80]

3. Secondary Infringement

(a) Generally

(i) Knowledge

Unlike direct infringement, which may be regarded as a matter of absolute liability, secondary infringement requires consideration of knowledge on behalf of the defendant. In particular, it must be shown that the defendant knows or ought to have known that the copy of the work with which he or she deals infringes copyright.[81] Knowledge has been held to mean "notice of facts such as would suggest to a reasonable man that a breach of the copyright law was being committed".[82] Knowledge need not be specific. It is sufficient if there is a reasonable ground for suspicion that copyright is being infringed.[83] Reasonable grounds will exist where the work carries a copyright

---

owner. Protection should also extend to dramatico-musical works, such as opera, which can be regarded as musical works under the Act. Operettas and Broadway musicals, which possess a 'book', are hybrid works; they, too, should be protected under the pre-amble, or if the 'book' were hived off from the songs and score, under the pre-amble and para. 3(1)(b).

[78] Paragraph 3(1)(a) of the Act.

[79] Paragraph 3(1)(d) of the Act.

[80] *Francis, Day & Hunter v. 20th Century Fox Corporation*, supra note 23.

[81] Subsection 27(2) of the Act. But see s. 27(3) for a limitation with respect to the knowledge of importers.

[82] Spence, J. in *Clarke, Irwin & Co. v. C. Cole & Co.*, [1960] O.R. 117, 19 Fox Pat. C. 143 (Ont. H. Ct.) at p. 150, citing *Albert v. Hoffnung & Co.* (1921), 22 S.R.N.S.W. 79 per Harvey, J. at p. 81.

[83] *955105 Ontario Ltd. v. Video 99* (1993), 48 C.P.R. (3d) 204 (Ont. Gen. Div.).

notice[84] or the defendant has been notified of his or her infringement.[85] The courts have also held that a defendant has an obligation to make "positive inquiries" to ascertain the copyright status of works with which he or she deals[86].

(ii) Onus of Proof

Because the plaintiff bears the burden of proof in an action for infringement, it is always prudent to obtain a certificate of registration. Registration is evidence that copyright subsists, and where a work is registered, the defendant must prove that he or she was unaware that the work was subject to copyright to defeat the statutory presumption.[87] However, late registration will not benefit the plaintiff.[88]

(b) Sell or Rent Out, Expose or Offer for Sale

Paragraph 27(2)(a) of the Act makes it an infringement for any person to sell or rent out a copy of a work that infringes copyright. For there to be a sale, there must be more than an attempt to sell or the mere showing of a sample.[89] However, paragraph 27(2)(c) makes it an infringement for any person, by way of trade, to distribute, expose or offer for sale or rental or exhibit in public a copy of a work that infringes copyright. Although it has been suggested that the exposure for sale or hire by way of trade is not an act that amounts to an offer for sale,[90] such exposure should constitute an infringement under paragraph 27(2)(c). The sale in Canada of albums imported from the U.S., which are legally made there, can be an indirect infringement if

---

[84] *Simon & Schuster Inc. v. Coles Book Stores Ltd.* (1975), 9 O.R. (2d) 718 (Ont. H.C.) at p. 720.

[85] *Profekta International Inc. v. Lee* (1995), 105 F.T.R. 155 (Fed. T.D.), varied (1997), 129 F.T.R. 320 (note) (Fed. C.A.).

[86] *Columbia Pictures Industries Inc. v. Robinson*, [1986] 3 All E.R. 338 (Eng. Ch. D.) at 363.

[87] *Dictionnaires Robert Canada SCC v. Librairie du Nomade Inc.* (1987), 16 C.P.R. (3d) 319 (Fed. T.D.) at p. 329, affirmed (1990), 37 F.T.R. 240 (note) (Fed. C.A.).

[88] *Grignon v. Roussel*, supra note 23.

[89] *Britain v. Kennedy* (1902) 19 T.L.R. 122.

[90] See Hugh Laddie et al., *The Modern Law of Copyright and Designs*, (London: Butterworths, 1995), vol. 1, p. 534, which suggests that an " 'offer for sale' would be interpreted in accordance with the general law of contract so that exposure of goods in a shop window... would be regarded as an invitation to treat".

the party selling or offering them for sale in Canada does so without a licence.[91]

(c) Distribution

Paragraph 27(2)(b) of the Act makes it an infringement for any person to distribute a copy of a work that infringes copyright, to such an extent as to affect prejudicially the owner of the copyright. Paragraph 27(2)(c) makes it an infringement for any person by way of trade to distribute a copy of a work that infringes copyright. With respect to the latter, it has been held in the U.K. and may be the case in Canada that for a distributor to indirectly infringe he or she must (1) be a trader (and not merely a carrier or warehouse), and (2) have the requisite knowledge that the works infringe copyright.[92] With respect to the former, it has been held that the distribution by a union of leaflets to union members (as opposed to members of the general public) that depicted the plaintiff's logo in an unflattering light did not prejudicially affect the copyright owner.[93] Moreover, the absence of a profit motive is not a defence.

(d) Importation

Paragraph 27(2)(e) makes it an infringement for any person to import into Canada for the purpose of sale, rental, distribution or exhibition a copy of a work that infringes copyright. Therefore, importation for private and/or non-commercial use, unless caught by paragraph 27(2)(b), is not in direct copyright infringement. However, paragraph 45(1)(a) of the Act, which permits the importation for personal use of not more than two copies of a work or other subject matter, probably has the effect of restricting the personal importation to two copies of a sound recording.

Sometimes records legally manufactured in one jurisdiction are imported into and sold in a second jurisdiction.[94] This practice is

---

[91] *Fly By Nite Music Co. v. Record Wherehouse Ltd.*, [1975] F.C. 386, 20 C.P.R. (2d) 263 (Fed. T.D.). Because the U.S. manufacturer would have infringed copyright if it had manufactured its records in Canada, being licensed to manufacture in the U.S. for the U.S. market only, pursuant to s. 27(2), the persons selling the imported records in Canada infringed the plaintiffs' copyrights.

[92] *Smith Kline and French Laboratories Ltd. v. R. D. Harbottle (Mercantile) Ltd.*, [1979] F.S.R. 555.

[93] *Cie. Générale des Etablissements Michelin-Michelin & Cie. v. C.A.W.-Canada* (1996), 71 C.P.R. (3d) 348 (Fed. T.D.) at p. 386.

[94] Typically, they are cut-outs obtained at a deep discount.

known as parallel importation. Although British courts have held that parallel importation is not copyright infringement,[95] this is not the case in Canada. In *Fly By Nite Music*, it was held that parallel imports, even though lawfully made in the U.S., infringed the copyright owner's rights when they were imported into and sold in Canada.[96]

(e) Public Performance for Profit

Subsection 27(5) of the Act makes it an infringement of copyright for any person, for profit, to permit a theatre or other place of public entertainment to be used for the performance in public of a work without the consent of the copyright owner unless the person was not aware, and had no reasonable grounds for suspecting, that the performance would be an infringement of copyright. Courts have held that the director of a company who controlled the music played in a cabaret owned by a corporation was a 'person' within the meaning of this section;[97] however, the performance must be for the private profit of the person who gave permission.[98]

The words 'theatre or other place of entertainment' are broadly construed. Thus, dance pavilions, open-air bandstands, and hotel restaurants are all places of entertainment under subsection 27(5).[99] The word 'permit' has been interpreted to mean 'authorize', and permission has been inferred where the defendant was indifferent to the performance of the work.[100]

[95] *Polydor Ltd. v. Harlequin Record Shops Ltd.*, [1980] F.S.R. 194, [1980] 2 C.M.L.R. 413 (C.A.), first instance at [1980] F.S.R. 193; *The Who Group Ltd. v. Stage One (Records) Ltd.*, [1980] F.S.R. 268; *C.B.S. United Kingdom Ltd. v. Charmdale Records Distributors Ltd.*, [1980] F.S.R. 289. See also Case Comment, Michael Hicks "The Harlequin, Who and Charmdale Cases: Parallel Imports, UK and EEC Law" (1980), Vol. 2 E.I.P.R. 337. However, pursuant to s. 27(3) of the *Copyright Design and Patents Act, 1988* there is a breach of the *Copyright Act* if the imported or manufactured material is in breach of the exclusive licence provisions of the Act. Remedies in Canada available to deal with parallel importation include injunctions and Anton Pillar orders. See discussion in s. 4(a)(ii), and the text below, regarding injunctions and Anton Piller orders, and the discussion in note 145 infra. Consider also the applicability of s. 44.1 of the Act.

[96] See note 91 supra. See also s. 27.1 of the Act which makes the parallel importation of books an infringement in certain circumstances.

[97] *Performing Rights Organization of Can. Ltd. v. Lion D'Or (1981) Ltée.* (1987), 17 C.P.R. (3d) 542 (Fed. T.D.)

[98] *Canadian Performing Right Society Ltd. v. Canadian National Exhibition Assn.*, [1934] O.R. 610 (Ont. H.C.) at p 616.

[99] *Canadian Performing Right Society Ltd. v. Ford Hotel*, [1935] 2 D.L.R. 391 at 400.

[100] *Performing Right Society Ltd. v. Ciryl Theatrical Syndicate Ltd.*, [1924] 1 K.B. 1 (Eng. C.A.); see also *Moorehouse v. University of New South Wales*, supra note 66.

4. Remedies

(a) Civil Remedies

(i) *Generally*

The remedies available in all civil actions are available in copyright infringement actions.[101] The composer or other person who has a "right, title or interest by assignment or grant in writing" may sue to enforce such rights.[102] An action may be brought in the Federal Court of Canada or any provincial court.[103] Costs are in the absolute discretion of the court.[104] Proceedings for infringement of copyright or moral rights or for detention of works imported in violation of copyright may be taken by way of summary application.[105] Venue is determined on the basis of the balance of convenience. If the action is commenced in Federal Court, this is done by way of motion; if in a provincial court, the provincial Rules of Practice governing venue will apply. The limitation period is three years from the date of the infringement where the plaintiff knew or could reasonably be expected to know of the infringement at the time that it occurred, and in any other case, three years after the time when the plaintiff first knew or could reasonably have been expected to know of the infringement.[106] Where there are multiple infringements, the time begins to run from the date of the last infringement. If the infringement has been concealed or in the case of fraud, the limitation period may be extended.[107]

---

[101] Subsection 34(1) of the Act. For an overview of copyright remedies see L. Lambert, "Enforcement of Copyright" in *Protecting Creative Effort Through Copyright*, (Mississauga: Insight Press, 1989).

[102] Subsection 36(1) of the Act. Note that a distributor of a copyrighted work, by reason only of being a distributor, does not have an interest sufficient to sue under this subsection; *Mobilevision Technology Inc. v. Rushing Water Products Ltd.* (1984), 1 C.P.R. (3d) 385 (Fed. T.D.) at p. 386; see also *955105 Ontario Inc. v. Video 99* (1993), 48 C.P.R. (3d) 204 (Ont. Gen. Div.) at p. 208.

[103] Section 37 of the Act. Provincial small claims courts have claimed jurisdiction under this section; see for example *Belanger v. AT & T Canada Inc.* (July 4, 1994), Doc. C94-2481; *Drynan v. Rostad*, supra note 25.

[104] Subsection 34(3) of the Act.

[105] Subsection 34(4) of the Act.

[106] Subsection 41(1) of the Act.

[107] *Warner Brothers-Seven Arts Inc. v. C.E.S.M.-T.V. Ltd.*, supra note 38.

(ii) Injunctions

A. Interlocutory Injunctions

Injunctions are the most common type of remedy sought in copyright cases because they can be granted quickly and because there is often a need for immediate relief.[108] The test applied in granting an interlocutory injunction is the test laid down in *American Cyanamid Co. v. Ethicon Ltd.*[109] Under this test the plaintiff must establish that there is a serious issue to be tried. Assuming this threshold test is satisfied, the court will then ask the following questions: (1) will the plaintiff suffer irreparable harm if the injunction is not granted; (2) does the balance of convenience favour the plaintiff or the defendant; and (3) if the balance of convenience favours neither party, should the status quo be maintained? If the answers to questions (1) and (2) favour the plaintiff, then an injunction will be granted.

Some courts have held that it is unnecessary for the plaintiff to establish irreparable harm or a favourable balance of convenience in

---

[108] The importance of injunctive relief is recognized by the Act; subsection 39(1) provides that in any proceeding, the plaintiff is always entitled to an injunction. Other remedies require that the defendant have knowledge of the plaintiff's copyright.

[109] [1975] 1 All E.R. 504 (U.K. H.L.). The test was adopted by the Federal Court of Canada in *Turbo Resources Ltd. v. Petro-Canada Inc.* (1989), 24 C.P.R. (3d) 1 (Fed. C.A.), and is now routinely applied by the Court in copyright cases; see for example, *Somerville House Books v. Tormont Publications* (1993), 50 C.P.R. (3d) 390 (Fed. T.D.), affirmed (1993) 53 C.P.R. (3d) 77 (Fed. C.A.); *Titan Linkabit Corp. v. S.E.E.* (1993), 48 C.P.R. (3d) 62 (Fed. T.D.). In *Turbo Resources*, the court alluded to the following factors gleaned from the judgment of Lord Diplock in *American Cyanamid*: (1) whether damages would be an adequate remedy that the defendant would be able to pay; (2) whether the defendant can be compensated financially for the restriction on his/her activities where damages are not an adequate remedy; (3) where there is doubt with respect to items (1) and (2) as to which party is favoured by the balance of convenience; (4) where other factors are balanced evenly, whether it is desirable to preserve the status quo; (5) where the evidence on the application shows one party's case to be proportionately stronger than the other's, the balance of convenience may tip in his/her direction provided the uncompensable disadvantages to either party do not differ widely; and (6) unspecified factors specific to the case. With respect to interim injunctions and quia timet injunctions, the test is essentially the same; see *Succession Picasso v. PRC Inc.* (1996), 70 C.P.R. (3d) 313 (Fed. T.D.); see also *RJR-MacDonald Inc. v. Canada (Attorney General)*, [1994] 1 S.C.R. 31 (S.C.C.); for quia timet injunctions, see *Taco Time Canada Inc. v. John Doe*, 1 to 50 (1996), 64 C.P.R. (3d) 495 (Fed. T.D.). For more on interlocutory injunctions, see Brian MacLeod Rogers and George W. Hately, "Getting the Pre Trial Injunction" Vol. 60 C.B.R. 1. See also L. David Roebuck, Allan M. Rock, Q.C., Co-Chairman, *The Law of Injunctions*, (Toronto: CBAO/CLE, 1989), and particularly, R. Scott Joliffe, "Interlocutory Injunctions In Intellectual Property Cases" in *When, Where and Why to Seek Injunctions*, (Mississauga: Insight Press, 1990).

cases of blatant copying.[110] Irreparable harm may be presumed where there is unauthorized use of a musical work.[111]

B. Permanent Injunctions

It is unnecessary for the plaintiff to prove damages to obtain a permanent injunction.[112] The injunction is granted to restrain the unauthorized use of the plaintiff's property.[113] Further, the injunction can prohibit future infringements[114] or infringements of the copyright in any other works owned by the plaintiff where the court is satisfied that the defendant likely will infringe the copyright in those other works.[115]

C. Anton Piller Orders

In appropriate circumstances, plaintiffs may avail themselves of an Anton Piller order. The order is an ex parte injunction that functions essentially as a civil search warrant. First developed in the U.K.,[116] Anton Piller orders have been used in Canada, particularly in intellectual property cases[117]. They have proven an ideal way for copyright owners to surmount the problems of record piracy, bootlegging and counterfeiting.

---

[110] *Overseas Enterprises v. Feathers Publishing & Marketing Inc.* (1990), 34 C.P.R. (3d) 78 (Fed. T.D.); *I.B.M. Corp. v. Ordinateurs Spirales Inc./Spirales Computers Inc.* (1984), [1985] 1 F.C. 190 (Fed. T.D.); *Jeffrey Rogers Knitwear Productions Ltd. v. R.D. International Style Collection, Ltd.* (1985), 6 C.I.P.R. 263 (Fed. T.D.); *Universal City Studios Inc. v. Zellers Inc.*, [1984] 1 F.C. 49 (Fed. T.D.); *Selection Testing Consultants International Ltd. v. Humanex International Inc.* (1987), 13 C.I.P.R. 27 (Fed. T.D.).

[111] *ATV Music Publishing of Canada Ltd. v. Rogers Radio Broadcasting Ltd.* (1982), 35 O.R. (2d) 417 (Ont. H.C.)

[112] *R. v. James Lorimer & Co.*, [1984] 1 F.C. 1065 (Fed. C.A.)

[113] *Groller v. Wolofsky* (1934), 72 Que. S.C. 419

[114] *R. v. James Lorimer & Co.*, supra note 112.

[115] See s. 39.1 of the Act. Wide injunctions may be either permanent or interlocutory.

[116] *Anton Piller KG v. Manufacturing Processes Ltd.*, [1976] 1 Ch. 55 (Eng. Ch. Div.). For more on Anton Piller orders, see Allan M. Rock and Anil Varna, "Anton Piller Order: Practical Considerations", in *The Law of Injunctions*, (Toronto, CBAO/CLE, 1989); Jeffrey Berryman, "Anton Piller Injunctions: An Update" (1986) 2 I.P.J. 49. Also, Jeffrey Berryman, "Anton Piller Orders: A Canadian Common-Law Approach" (1984) 34 U. of T.L.J. 1. See also Norman R. Shapiro, Q.C., "The Anton Piller Order in Canada" (1983) 6 E.I.P.R. 164.

[117] *Michael Jackson v. Bi-Way Stores Limited*, (July 6, 1984), Doc. 19564/84 (Ont. S.C.). See also *Nintendo of America Inc. v. Coinex Video Games Inc.* (1982), 69 C.P.R. (2d) 122 (Fed. C.A.).

Anton Piller orders grant relief in three ways: (1) by permitting access to premises to search for infringing copies; (2) by requiring disclosure of information, for example, the names and addresses of suppliers of infringing material and the location of infringing material; and (3) by requiring the production of documents relating to activities concerning infringing material. Plaintiffs may also seize and retain infringing copies of works found on the premises.

To obtain an Anton Piller order, there must be an extremely strong prima facie case. Further, the potential or actual damage must be very serious. There must be clear evidence that the defendants have in their possession incriminating documents or materials and that there is a real possibility that such material will be destroyed before an application inter partes can be made.[118] Lastly, the plaintiff must give an undertaking as to damages intended to indemnify the defendant for any losses he or she may suffer should the plaintiff ultimately prove unsuccessful in his/her claim.

There can be problems with the order. In particular, following the decision in *Rank Film Distributors Ltd. v. Video Information Centre,*[119] it is unclear to what extent a defendant may resist the obligation to disclose on the basis that such disclosure violates a common law privilege against self-incrimination.[120] There are problems of costs if the order is granted against an innocent infringer[121], and incomplete disclosure by the plaintiff may leave him/her open to an action in damages. As well, the plaintiff is not entitled to force entry so that if the defendant refuses to allow access, the plaintiff's only remedy is to seek an order for contempt.

---

[118] Anton Piller, supra note 116 at p. 62. For a recent Canadian case discussing Anton Piller orders and the possibility of discharge where the plaintiff failed to disclose material facts, see *Pulse Microsystems Ltd. v. SafeSoft Systems Inc.* (1996), 67 C.P.R. (3d) 202 (Man. C.A.).

[119] [1981] 2 All E.R. 76 (U.K. H.L.)

[120] Although *Rank* has been overruled in the U.K. by statute with respect to passing off and intellectual property cases, the principles expressed therein are apparently still applicable in Canada; for a discussion of this issue, see Robert J. Sharpe, *Injunctions and Specific Performance,* (Aurora: Canada Law Book, 1998), at pp. 2-72 to 2-75. See also, D. M. Paciocco, "Anton Piller Orders: Facing the Threat of Privilege Against Self Incrimination" (1984) 34 U. of T. L.J. 26. For more on the *Rank* case, see Gerald Dworkin, "Case Comment, The Rank Film Case, Has Anton Piller Been Emasculated?" (1981), 6 E.I.P.R. 180.

[121] See Michael Hicks, "Opinion: Anton Piller Orders, Let the Punishment Fit the Crime" (1982), 10 E.I.P.R. 267.

D. Mareva Injunctions

A third type of injunction, the Mareva injunction, permits a plaintiff to restrain the defendant from disposing of his/her assets prior to judgment. To obtain the injunction, the plaintiff must establish a strong prima facie case that the defendant has assets in the jurisdiction and that there is a real risk of the assets being removed before judgment, and must give an undertaking as to damages.[122]

(iii) Damages

A. Generally

Assuming the defendant had knowledge of the infringement on the date he or she infringed, the copyright owner is entitled to a remedy in damages.[123] Damages for copyright infringement are compensatory in nature and are paid to recompense the owner for the infringement of a right. It is therefore immaterial that the infringer has made no profit from the infringement.[124] However, where the defendant has profited, the copyright owner may claim and is entitled to the infringer's profits.[125] Damages are "at large"[126] and are awarded regardless of whether the plaintiff has proven or suffered loss.[127] Courts assess the quantum broadly "as a matter of common sense".[128] Among the factors considered are: (1) the profit made from the infringement; (2) the loss of professional recognition or damage to reputation of the author; (3) the loss of profits to the owner resulting from the infringement; and (4) the cost of a licence to use the copyright work.[129]

---

[122] See, for example, *Jelin Investments Ltd. v. Signtech Inc.* (1990), [1991] 1 F.C. 365 (Fed. T.D.), affirmed (1991), 34 C.P.R. (3d) 176 (Fed. T.D.) for application of the concept in the context of copyright infringement.

[123] Subsection 39(1) of the Act.

[124] *Therrien v. Schola* (March 2, 1981), Doc. T-84-80 (Fed. T.D.).

[125] Subsection 35(1) of the Act. The right to the defendant's profits is discussed infra in notes 137-144.

[126] *Joseph v. National Magazine Co. Ltd.*, [1959] Ch. 14 at 21; *Massie & Renwick Ltd. v. Underwriters Survey Bureau Ltd.*, [1937] S.C.R. 263 (S.C.C.), varied [1940] S.C.R. 218 (S.C.C.).

[127] *Durand & Cie. v. La Patrie Publishing Co.*, [1960] S.C.R. 649 (S.C.C.). However, where there is no proof of loss, damages may be nominal: *Canadian Performing Right Society Ltd. v. Canadian National Exhibition Assn.*, [1934] O.R. 610 (Ont. H.C.).

[128] *C.P. Koch Ltd. v. Continental Steel Ltd.* (1984), 82 C.P.R. (2d) 156 (B.S. S.C.), affirmed (1985), 4 C.P.R. (3d) 395 (B.C. C.A.)

[129] *Bishop v. Stevens* (1985), 4 C.P.R. (3d) 349 (Fed. T.D.), reversed (1987), 18 C.P.R. (3d) 257 (Fed. C.A.), affirmed 31 C.P.R. (3d) 394 (S.C.C.). The Copyright Board's tariff

This latter factor seems to have particular relevance with respect to musical works.[130]

A plaintiff's conduct, however, may result in it being disentitled to damages.[131]

B. Exemplary Damages

Although the Act does not expressly provide for the awarding of exemplary damages, courts have ruled that they may be awarded in an appropriate case.[132] In particular, where the infringement was 'flagrant, fraudulent or malicious'[133] or where the defendant's conduct has been calculated to make a profit at the expense of the plaintiff, such damages will be awarded.[134]

Exemplary damages have been awarded in several cases involving the infringement of musical works. In *Joubert v. Géracimo*[135] the plaintiff recovered exemplary damages from a defendant who had performed musical works without authorization, retitled them and deleted the author's name from posters advertising the performance. In *MCA Canada Ltd. (Ltée.) v. Gilberry & Hawke Advertising Agency Ltd.*[136], $5,000 was awarded against the defendant which had brazenly commissioned a jingle parodying "Downtown", a song made popular by Petula Clark.

---

may be used to establish the quantum of damage; see for example *Performing Rights Organization of Canada Ltd. v. Patrick Holdings Ltd.* (1987), 13 C.P.R. (3d) 177 (Fed. T.D.).

[130] See for example, *MCA Canada Ltd. (Ltée.) v. Gilberry & Hawke Advertising Agency Ltd.* (1976), 28 C.P.R. (2d) 52 (Fed. T.D.); *Sedgewick v. Atlantic Media Works Ltd.* (1991), 38 C.P.R. (3d) 526 (N.B. Q.B.), affirmed (September 25, 1991), Doc. 108/91/CA (N.B. C.A.). However, one of the problems in seeking damages is that often legal costs are greater than the amount recovered by the plaintiff.

[131] *Aldrich v. One Stop Video Ltd.* (1987), 17 C.P.R. (3d) 27 (B.C. S.C.). Here, the plaintiff was distributing obscene works.

[132] *Pro Arts Inc. v. Campus Crafts Holdings Ltd.* (1980), 50 C.P.R. (2d) 230 (Ont. H.C.); see also *R. v. James Lorimer & Co.*, [1984] 1 F.C. 1065 (Fed. C.A.) For a discussion of exemplary damages, see Gordon Zimmerman, "Exemplary Damages and Copyright in Canada" (1981), Vol. 57 C.P.R. (2d) 65.

[133] See *Prise de parole Inc. v. Guérin, Editeur Ltée* (1995), 66 C.P.R. (3d) 257 (Fed. T.D.) at p. 267, affirmed (1996), 73 C.P.R. (3d) 557 (Fed. C.A.) for this typical description of the defendant's conduct. In general, the plaintiff's conduct must be deliberate; see *Allen v. Toronto Star Newspapers Ltd.* (1995), 63 C.P.R. (3d) 517 (Ont. Gen Div.), reversed (1997), 78 C.P.R. (3d) 557 (Fed. C.A.); some courts have alluded to a standard of recklessness; see *Bishop v. Stevens* (1985), 4 C.P.R. (3d) 349 (Fed. T.D.) at p. 366, reversed (1987), 18 C.P.R. (3d) 257 (Fed. C.A.), affirmed 31 C.P.R. (3d) 394 (S.C.C.).

[134] *Rookes v. Barnard*, [1964] A.C. 1129 (U.K. H.L.) at p. 1226 as cited in *Jelin Investments Ltd. v. Signtech Inc.*, supra note 122.

[135] (1916), 26 Que K.B. 97.

[136] (1976), 28 C.P.R. (2d) 52 (Fed. T.D.).

However, the court absolved the writer hired to compose the jingle due to his co-operation at trial and his naivete.

C. Defendant's Profits

In addition to damages, the copyright owner is entitled to any profits the infringer has made from the infringement.[137] However, to prevent double recovery, the defendant's profits are reduced to the extent that they have been included in any amount awarded to the copyright owner as damages.[138] The remedy is cumulative[139] and courts are given wide discretion in applying it.[140] Because of the difficulty in proving profits, the plaintiff is only required to prove receipts derived from the infringement; however, the Act requires that the defendant prove every element of cost that the defendant claims.[141] The term 'profit' is given its ordinary meaning[142] and defendants are entitled to deduct reasonable expenses but not 'overhead'.[143] The court can take notice of the infringer's skill and labour in exploiting the copyright, and the party who has suffered an infringement is entitled to the benefit accruing from such infringer's labour and skill.[144]

(iv) Other Remedies

Plaintiffs in copyright cases are also entitled to delivery up of infringing articles under subsection 34(1) and recovery of infringing copies and plates under subsection 38(1) of the Act. Where works that would infringe copyright if made in Canada are imported or about to be imported into Canada, plaintiffs may invoke section 44.1 of the Act. This section allows a copyright owner to obtain a court order directing the Minister of National Revenue to detain the infringing works.[145] The

---

[137] Subsection 35(1) of the Act. Section 35 implements the right to an accounting given in s. 34(1), removing much of the difficulty inherent in this form of remedy.

[138] *Ibid.*

[139] *Aldrich v. One Stop Video Ltd.*, supra note 131; *Performing Rights Organization of Canada Ltd. v. Manoir Mercier Inc.* (1985), 3 C.P.R. (3d) 90 (Fed. T.D.).

[140] *Slumber-Magic Adjustable Bed Co. v. Sleep-King Adjustable Bed Co.* (1984), 3 C.P.R. (3d) 81 (B.C. S.C.).

[141] Subsection 35(2) of the Act.

[142] *Pro Arts Inc. v. Campus Crafts Holdings Ltd.*, supra note 132.

[143] *Ibid.*

[144] *Redwood Music Ltd. v. Chappell & Co.*, [1982] R.P.C. 109, citing *Phipps v. Boardman*, [1964] 1 W.L.R. 993 (Eng. Ch. Div.) at 1018, affirmed [1965] Ch. 992 (Eng. C.A.), affirmed [1967] 2 A.C. 46 (U.K. H.L.).

[145] Subparagraph 44.1(3)(a)(i) of the Act; see s. 44.2 for the importation of books, and s. 44.4 for the importation of sound recordings, performer's performances and

application may be made on an ex parte basis.[146] Additional remedies outside the *Copyright Act* include actions for breach of confidence, unfair competition, false attribution of authorship and malicious falsehood.

(v) *Statutory Damages*

Section 38.1 enacts a right of statutory damages intended to assist plaintiffs who are unable to establish their damages or the defendant's profits.[147] Pursuant to subsection 38.1(1), plaintiffs may elect, with respect to all infringements involved in the proceedings concerning any one work, an amount of not less than $500 or more than $20,000 as the court considers just. The election may be made any time before final judgment. If the defendant establishes that he/she was not aware and had no reasonable grounds to believe that he/she had infringed copyright, the court may reduce the amount of the award to less than $500, but not less than $200.[148] In exercising its discretion, the court is directed to consider all relevant factors, including the good or bad faith of the defendant, the conduct of the parties before and during the proceedings, and the need to deter other infringements of the copyright in question.[149] Any amount so awarded is in lieu of the damages and profits recoverable under subsection 35(1). Finally, an election by the plaintiff does not affect any right he or she may have to exemplary or punitive damages.[150]

---

communication signals. Prior to the enactment of this section, there have been attempts to rely on s. 44 of the *Customs Act* and Sch. VII to the *Customs Tariff*, R.S.C. 1985, c. C-54, but in the absence of a court order, the Minister was reluctant to act. In *Takara Co. v. Gamex International Inc.* (1989), 28 C.P.R. (3d) 575 (Fed. T.D.), the court refused to grant an order of mandamus to compel the Minister to act, on the basis that "there is no clear duty on the part of the Minister owing to the plaintiffs". The new s. 44.1 creates such a duty.

[146] Subsection 44.1(4) of the Act.

[147] See Gail Henley, "A Case For Statutory Damages In Canadian Copyright Law" (1995-96), 12 C.I.P.R. 81 for a discussion of the usefulness of this remedy.

[148] Subsection 38.1(2) of the Act. See also s. 38.1(3) which permits the court to reduce further the amount of the award where more than one work is infringed in a single medium. See s. 38.1(4) for elections by collective societies.

[149] Subsection 38.1(5) of the Act.

[150] Subsection 38.1(7) of the Act.

(b) Criminal Remedies

(i) *Under the* Copyright Act

In addition to the civil remedies discussed above, the Act sets out certain criminal offences. Pursuant to subsection 42(1) it is an offence to: (1) make for sale or rental an infringing copy of a work; (2) sell or rent out or by way of trade, expose, or offer for sale or rental an infringing copy of a work; (3) distribute infringing copies of a work whether for the purpose of trade or to such an extent as to affect prejudicially the copyright owner; (4) by way of trade exhibit in public an infringing copy of a work; or (5) import for sale or rental in Canada any infringing copy of a work.[151] Pursuant to subsection 42(2), it is an offence to make or possess any plate specifically designed or adapted for the purpose of making infringing copies, or, for private profit, to cause to be performed in public a work in which copyright subsists, without the consent of the copyright owner.[152] Pursuant to subsection 43(1), it is an offence to perform knowingly or cause to be performed in public and for private profit without the written consent of the copyright owner any part of a dramatic or operatic work or musical composition.[153] Pursuant to subsection 43(2), it is an offence to make or cause to be made without the author's consent any change in or suppression of the title or author's name, or to make or cause to be made any change in a dramatic or operatic work or musical composition in order that it may be performed in public for private profit.[154] Offences under section 43 are summary conviction offences. The offender is liable to a fine not exceeding $500, and in the case of a second offence is liable either to that fine or to imprisonment for a term not exceeding four months, or to both.[155]

With respect to offences under subsections 42(1) and (2), the Crown can elect to proceed either by summary conviction or by indictment. Proceedings by summary conviction must be instituted

---

[151] The term "infringing", defined in s. 2, includes any copy or colourable imitation of a work, a fixation or copy of a fixation of a performer's performance, a copy of a sound recording or fixation or a copy of a fixation of a communication signal. For a discussion of colourable imitations, see Tamaro, supra note 2 at pp. 69-73.

[152] Note that under s. 42(3) in any proceedings under s. 42, on conviction, the court has the power to order the destruction or delivery up of all infringing copies of the work and plates which are in the possession of the offender and are predominantly used for making infringing copies.

[153] Subsection 43(1) of the Act.

[154] Subsection 43(2) of the Act.

[155] Offences under section 43 are governed by the six month limitation period applicable to summary conviction offences contained in s. 786(1) of the *Criminal Code*.

within two years after the time the offence was committed[156] and the trial takes place before a provincial court judge. On conviction, an infringer is liable to a fine not exceeding $25,000, or imprisonment for a term not exceeding six months, or both.[157] Where the Crown elects to proceed by indictment, the accused will have the option of trial before a provincial court judge, a superior court judge sitting alone, or before a judge sitting with a jury. On conviction, an infringer is liable to a fine not exceeding $1,000,000, or imprisonment for a term not exceeding five years, or both.[158]

There are three essential elements the Crown must prove with respect to all copyright offences: (1) that the accused "knowingly" dealt with (2) "infringing copies" of (3) "a work in which copyright subsists". [159] Specifically, the Crown is required to prove the infringement, chain of title, lack of authorization and the non-applicability of any copyright exemption. Offences are full mens rea offences.[160] The standard of proof, as in other criminal cases, is "beyond a reasonable doubt".[161]

(ii) Under the Criminal Code

Copyright infringement can also be the subject of proceedings under the *Criminal Code.* Cases have been brought with mixed results under the fraud provisions[162], although it is clear that copyright infringement does not amount to theft.[163]

---

[156] Subsection 42(4) of the Act.

[157] Paragraphs 42(1)(f) and 42(2)(c) of the Act.

[158] Paragraphs 42(1)(g) and 42(2)(d) of the Act. See *R. v. Miles of Music Ltd.* (1989), 24 C.P.R. (3d) 301 (Ont. C.A.).

[159] See Scott & Collins, infra note 161.

[160] *R. v. Laurier Office Mart Inc.* (1994), 58 C.P.R. (3d) 403 (Ont. Prov. Div.), affirmed (1995), 63 C.P.R. (3d) 229 (Ont. Gen. Div.).

[161] Ibid. For a discussion of the issues involved in criminal prosecutions of copyright offences, see David W. Scott & Timothy Collins, "Criminal Copyright Offences: The Defence Perspective", Parts I and II at (1995), 38 Crim. L Q. 104 and 158.

[162] See Scott & Collins, supra note 161 at pp. 120-22 and footnote 35.

[163] *R. v. Stewart* (1988), 41 C.C.C. (3d) 481 (S.C.C.).

5. Civil Defences and Acts Not Constituting Infringement

(a) Civil Defences

(i) Generally

There are several defences which may be raised in copyright infringement actions: (1) there is no copyright in the work, (for example, the music is part of the public domain or is, along with the infringing work, derived from a common source and therefore not capable of meeting the originality criterion for acquiring copyright); (2) there has been no infringement (for example, the copying is not substantial); or (3) where the two works are similar, it may be shown that the 'infringing' work was created independently, and therefore was not derived directly or indirectly from any other work.

(ii) Innocence

There are two situations where innocence may be raised as a defence to copyright infringement: (1) where there is secondary infringement and the requisite knowledge is not present (if successful, this is a complete defence); and (2) in a case of direct infringement where the alleged infringer proves that he or she "was not aware and had no reasonable grounds for suspecting that copyright subsisted in the work". However, this is only a partial defence; pursuant to subsection 39(1) of the Act, the plaintiff still can obtain an injunction to stop the infringement. However, if the copyright is registered, the defence is not available.

(b) Acts Not Constituting Infringement

Not all unauthorized dealings with substantial parts of works in which copyright subsists constitute infringements. The Act contains a number of exceptions which permit users to deal with copyrighted works for certain specified purposes. These exemptions are narrowly interpreted by the courts. The most important of these are discussed below.

(i) Fair Dealing

The fair dealing sections of the Act are intended to balance the economic rights of copyright owners with the societal interest in encouraging the widest possible dissemination of knowledge and culture. 'Fair dealing' is not defined in the Act. However, courts employ a general test of fairness.[164] In Canada, it has been held that 'fair dealing' requires that use of the copyright must be 'fair', and further, that the copyright must be treated in a good faith manner.[165] The following acts are permitted to users of copyrighted works:

A. Fair Dealing for the Purpose of Research or Private Study[166]

This exception permits the reproduction of copyrighted works for private study, but it does not sanction publication of substantial reproductions of copyrighted works in the researcher's own publications. Doubts as to whether home taping for private study purposes constitutes infringement have been removed by reason of the enactment of subsection 80(1) which provides a specific exception with regard to private copying.

It should be noted that the U.S. legal concept of "fair use", discussed below, is not a Canadian legal concept and currently has no application under the Canadian *Copyright Act.*

B. Fair Dealing for the Purpose of Criticism

This exception permits fair dealing for the purpose of criticism or review provided that the user credits the source, and the name of the author, performer, maker of the sound recording or broadcaster of the communication signal.[167] Thus, one may partially quote the lyrics of a

---

[164] See Harold G. Fox, *The Canadian Law of Copyright and Industrial Design,* (Toronto: Carswell, 1967) at pp. 419-425 for a list of relevant factors. For the British approach to 'fairness', see *Hubbard v. Vosper,* [1972] 2 Q.B. 84 (Eng. C.A.); *Sillitoe v. McGraw-Hill Book Co.,* [1983] F.S.R. 545 (Eng. Ch. Div.).

[165] *Cie. Générale des Etablissements Michelin-Michelin & Cie. v. C.A.W.-Canada* (1996), 71 C.P.R. (3d) 348 (Fed. T.D.) at p. 384.

[166] Section 29 of the Act. For a recent case discussing the meaning of "research or private study", see *Hager v. ECW Press Ltd.,* [1998] F.C.J. No. 1830 (Fed. T.D.), in which the court refused to accept the defence of fair dealing under ss. 29 and 29.1 of the Act. In this case, the defendant had authored a book about country singer Shania Twain, making liberal use of an interview conducted by the plaintiff reproduced in her own book, and had produced a "colourable imitation" of the plaintiff's prose as well.

[167] Section 29.1 of the Act. For a recent case discussing the meaning of "criticism or review", see *Hager v. ECW Press Ltd.,* supra note 166.

song for the purpose of criticism, but it is not fair dealing to reproduce a work in full without the copyright owner's consent.[168]

The defence of fair dealing for the purpose of criticism is also relevant to works of parody.[169] In the U.S., the Supreme Court has recognized that parody may constitute 'fair use' if the parody can be characterized as a 'transformative work'.[170] Although invited to do so, at least one Canadian court has refused to extend the defence of fair dealing into parody.[171] This judicial reluctance seems unwarranted,

---

[168] *Zamacois v. Douville*, [1943] 2 D.L.R. 257 (Can. Ex. Ct.).

[169] A parody is a work which ridicules another work by mimicry of its language or style. Parody, therefore, requires the copying of a substantial part of the parodied work and is copyright infringement in the absence of an affirmative defence or consent of the copyright owner. In the case of song parodies, typically, the parodist grafts a new and original set of lyrics onto the melody of the parodied work.

[170] 17 U.S. Code s. 107 exempts the 'fair use' use of copyrighted works from claims of copyright infringement. In *Campbell v. Acuff-Rose Music Inc.*, 114 S. Ct. 1164 (1994), the appellant, Luther Campbell, and his band, 2 Live Crew, used Orbison and Dees' "Oh, Pretty Woman" as the basis for their composition "Pretty Woman". The court, in considering the four factors laid out in s. 107, insisted that the central question was "whether the new work merely 'supersede[s]' the objects of the original creation' or instead adds something new, with a further purpose, meaning or message", calling such works 'transformative' and holding that "the goal of copyright... is generally furthered by transformative works." See Campbell at p.1171. For a discussion of this case, see Judith B. Prowda, "Parody and Fair Use in Copyright Law: Setting a Fairer Standard in Campbell v. Acuff-Rose Music, Inc." (1995) 17 Comm. And the Law 53; see also, Shira Perlmutter, "The United States Supreme Court Reviews Parody Under the Fair Use Doctrine", *Copyright World*, Issue 40, May 1994, p. 17. For a discussion of cases pre- and post-*Acuff-Rose*, see Michael J. Bazzi & Martha J. Widdows, "Parody and the Fair Use Doctrine Revisited", *Ent. & Sports Lawyer*, Fall 1998, Vol. 4., No. 1 at p. 41.

[171] *Cie. Générale des Etablissements Michelin-Michelin & Cie. v. C.A.W.-Canada* (1996), 71 C.P.R. (3d) 348 (Fed. T.D.). In this case, the defendant CAW used depictions of the Michelin tire man on handouts in an organizing drive; a grinning "Bibendum" was shown about to stomp two workers with his boots. The Court refused to analogize between the U.S. and Canadian legislation, stating that a long line of cases have held that parody is not an exception to copyright infringement in Canada; see pp. 377-86. The cases cited include *Ludlow Music Inc. v. Canint Music Corp.* (1967), 62 D.L.R. (2d) 200 (Can. Ex. Ct.); *MCA Canada Ltd. v. Gillberry & Hawke Advertising Agency Ltd.* (1976), 28 C.P.R. (2d) 52 (Fed. T.D.); and *ATV Music Publishing of Canada Ltd. v. Rogers Radio Broadcasting Ltd.* (1982), 65 C.P.R. (2d) 109 (Ont. H.C.). In fact, it is submitted that there is nothing in Canadian copyright law to prevent acceptance of U.S. doctrine in this area; see James Zegers, "Parody and Fair Use in Canada After Campbell v. Acuff-Rose" (1994-95), 11 C.I.P.R. 205; see also Catherine Ng, "When Imitation Is Not the Sincerest Form of Flattery, Fair Dealing and Fair Use for the Purpose of Criticism in Canada and the United States" (1997), 12 I.P.J. 183. See also *Productions Avanti Ciné-Vidéo Inc. c. Favreau* (1997), 79 C.P.R. (3d) 385 (S.C. Qué.), reversed at [1999] J.Q., No. 2725 (Que. C.A.). The trial court, which appeared receptive to the arguments in favour of the parody defence reached its decision on the basis that there was no substantial similarity between the plaintiff's and defendant's works. In reversing, the Quebec Court of Appeal suggested that a parody, the aim of which is a critique of an existing work, could claim the protection of s. 29.1 so long as the exigencies of the section are satisfied; however the court went on, at para. 68, to suggest, without deciding the issue, that an authentic

given that song parodies are unlikely to affect materially the economic rights of the copyright owner and, as original works of criticism in their own right, they are capable of furthering the ends that copyright law is designed to promote.[172]

C. Fair Dealing for the Purpose of News Reporting

This exception permits fair dealing for the purpose of news reporting provided that the user credits the source, and name of the author, performer, maker of the sound recording or broadcaster of the communication signal.[173] One English court has held that the making of a newsreel film in which a band played two bars of the "Colonel Bogey March" was not fair dealing within the English Act.[174]

(ii) Other Exemptions

A. Agricultural Exhibitions, Religious, Fraternal and Educational Institutions

Subsection 32.2(2) of the Act permits the live performance of musical works and sound recordings embodying musical works where the performances are given without motive of gain at agricultural or agricultural-industrial exhibitions or fairs that receive grants from or

---

parody may be protected even if it fails to comply with the section so long as it is an original work which mocks or ridicules another work or criticizes social or political events.

[172] Note that song parodies must be distinguished from songs which use the melody of a pre-existing copyright work in conjunction with a new non-parodic set of lyrics. Such was the case in *ATV Music Publishing of Canada Ltd. v. Rogers Radio Broadcasting* (1982), 35 O.R. (2d) 417 (Ont. H.C.); here the defendants used the musical component of The Beatles' "Revolution" in connection with a new set of lyrics under the title "Constitution". Although the new lyrics commented on the proclamation of the *Constitution Act* of 1982, they did not parody the Beatles' lyrics, and consequently the new work was not a parody within the definition set out supra in footnote 169.

[173] Section 29.2 of the Act. For a case involving the unauthorized reproduction of a photograph on a magazine cover in which fair dealing was not established, see *Allen v. Toronto Star Newspapers Ltd.* (1995), 63 C.P.R. (3d) 517 (Ont. Gen Div.), reversed (1997), 78 C.P.R. (3d) 115 (Ont. Div. Ct.).

[174] *Hawkes & Son (London) Ltd. v. Paramount Film Service Ltd.*, [1934] Ch. 593 (Eng. C.A.); the court held that the reproduction violated the copyright owner's synchronization right. New section 30.7 which, inter alia, permits the incidental and non-deliberate inclusion of a work or other subject-matter in another work or subject-matter, would appear to provide a defence on the facts of this case. Note that the section is not limited to news reporting, but applies to all works and subject-matters.

are held under federal, provincial or municipal authority.[175] The Supreme Court of Canada has interpreted subsection 32.2(2) to forbid the making of a profit by anyone involved in the performance. Thus, it is not enough that the event is non-profit; neither must the performers make a profit.[176]

A similar exception exists with respect to performances authorized by religious organizations, educational institutions, and charitable or fraternal organizations,[177] provided that the performance is given "in furtherance of a religious, charitable or educational object." The Supreme Court of Canada has interpreted this phrase narrowly to mean that the performance must be a "participating factor in the charitable object". Thus, in one case, the Court ruled that performances paid for and given at a dance organized by a fraternal organization (with the profits going to charity) are not exempt from the payment of royalties.[178]

B. Radio Performances in Places Other than Theatres

Subsection 69(2) of the Act exempts from the payment of royalties the owner or user of a radio receiving set where the radio is used to give public performances in any place other than a theatre regularly used for entertainment to which an admission charge is made. The section further requires the Copyright Board to provide "in so far as possible" for the collection of royalties from radio broadcasting stations in respect thereto.[179]

This subsection was originally enacted to facilitate the collection of performance royalties with respect to the performance of works by means of gramophones and radios found in restaurants, hotels and other public places. In theory, royalties were to be collected in advance from radio broadcasters and manufacturers of gramophones. The recent amendment has limited its application to "radio receiving sets".

---

[175] Included in the exception are: (1) the live performance in public of a musical work; (2) the performance in public of a sound recording embodying a musical work or a performer's performance of a musical work; and (3) the performance in public of a communication signal carrying a musical work or sound recording described in (2).

[176] *C.A.P.A.C. v. Western Fair Assn.*, [1951] S.C.R. 596 (S.C.C.).

[177] See subsection 32.2(3) of the Act which permits the kinds of performances discussed in footnote 175 supra.

[178] *Composers, Authors & Publishers Association Canada Ltd. v. Kiwanis Club of West Toronto*, [1953] 2 S.C.R. 111 (S.C.C.) at p. 115.

[179] Pursuant to s. 69(3), in fixing royalties, the Board must take into account any expenses saved by copyright owners in consequence of s. 69(2).

C. Other Exceptions

There are numerous other exceptions contained in the Act not directly related to music or musical works. These include certain reproductions and performances of works by educational institutions,[180] reproductions and photocopying by libraries, archives and museums,[181] reproductions by the National Archives of Canada,[182] certain reproductions of computer programs,[183] the incidental non-deliberate inclusion of a work in another work,[184] the making of ephemeral recordings,[185] the retransmission of local signals,[186] the disclosure of governmental records,[187] and any of the uses found in subsection 32.2(1) of the Act.[188]

(iii) No Copyright Protection

The following are not protected by copyright: (a) ideas; and (b) titles. Although a work is defined to include its title, the copying of a title, unless such copying amounts to a substantial reproduction, is not copyright infringement.[189] There may be other bases for protecting a title, such as passing off, which is discussed in Chapter 9, "Merchandising", but an action for copyright infringement is not normally the remedy.

---

[180] Sections 29.4 to 29.9 of the Act; see also s. 30.

[181] Sections 30.1 to 30.3 of the Act.

[182] Section 30.5 of the Act.

[183] Section 30.6 of the Act.

[184] Section 30.7 of the Act.

[185] Sections 30.8 to 30.9 of the Act; see Chapter 1 for a discussion of 'ephemeral rights'.

[186] Subsection 31(2) of the Act. See also para. 2.4(1)(b) and s. 2.4(3).

[187] Section 32.1 of the Act.

[188] These include: (1) use by an author of an artistic work of materials used by him or her in the creation of a copyrighted work owned by another; (2) certain reproductions of architectural works; (3) the permitted publication of a news report of a lecture; (4) the recitation in public of a reasonable extract of a published work; and (5) the report of a political address given at a public meeting.

[189] *King Features Syndicate Inc. v. Lechter*, [1950] Ex. C.R. 297 (Can. Ex. Ct.). In contrast it has been held in the U.S. that a single, wholly original title could acquire copyright, but this is an exceptional situation; see *Life Music Inc. v. Wonderland Music Inc.*, 241 F. Supp. 653 (1965) in which the song title "Supercalifragilisticexpialidocius" was in issue. Consistent with Anglo-Canadian doctrine is the holding in *Neudorf v. Nettwerk Productions*, [1999] B.C.J. No. 2831 (B.C.S.C.) that the contribution of a title to a musical work does not give rise to a claim of joint authorship.

6. Infringement of Moral Rights

Any act or omission that is contrary to the moral rights of an author is, in the absence of consent or a waiver of such rights, an infringement of the author's moral rights.[190] A single act can give rise to both an infringement of copyright and an infringement of moral rights.[191] The remedies for infringement are the same as those for infringement of copyright,[192] and in an appropriate case, punitive damages[193] and interlocutory injunctions will lie.[194]

Subsection 28.2(2) provides that the author's integrity right is infringed only if the work is, to the prejudice of the honour or reputation of the author, distorted, mutilated or otherwise modified, or used in association with a product, service, cause or institution. Courts have held that there is a certain subjective element or judgment on the part of the author in determining whether the modification of a work is to the prejudice of the author's reputation.[195]

7. Other Issues

Perhaps the greatest threat of copyright infringement today lies in the uncontrolled distribution of copyright works over the Internet. Although the issue of infringement has yet to be litigated in the context of a civil action, there has been one case establishing liability under the Act's criminal provisions. In *R. v. M.(J.P.)*,[196] the court held that a young offender who operated a computer bulletin board which contained copyright computer programs, accessible to a restricted class of users,

---

[190] Section 28.1 of the Act. See s. 14.1(1) for a definition of moral rights. See also s. 28.2 for a deeming rule with respect to the prejudicial modification of certain artistic works.

[191] See Tamaro, supra note 2 at p. 346. The omission of an author's name from a work violates both rights. The violation of moral rights can also give rise to a copyright offence; see s. 43(2) of the Act.

[192] Subsection 34(2) of the Act. The remedies for infringement of a moral right include all remedies by way of injunction damages, accounts, and delivery up that are or may be conferred by law for the infringement of a right.

[193] *Guillemette c. Centre cooperatif de loisirs & de sports du Mont Original* (1986), 15 C.P.R. (3d) 409 (Fed. T.D.); *Joubert v. Géracimo* (1916), 26 Que. K.B. 97.

[194] *Pollock v. CFCN Productions Ltd.* (1983), 73 C.P.R. (2d) 204 (Alta. Q.B.).

[195] *Snow v. Eaton Centre Ltd.* (1982), 70 C.P.R. (2d) 105 (Ont. H.C.) at p. 106. The court further stated that the author's judgment must be "reasonably arrived at." Note, however, that this case was decided prior to the 1988 amendments. See also *Prise de parole Inc. v. Guérin, Editeur Ltée* (1995), 66 C.P.R. (3d) 257 (Fed. T.D.), affirmed (1996), 73 C.P.R. (3d) 557 (Fed. C.A.), wherein the court held that there must be an objective valuation of the plaintiff's claim based on public or expert opinion.

[196] (1996), 67 C.P.R. (3d) 152 (N.S. C.A.).

distributed the works in contravention of the Act.[197] Doubtless, the development of new technologies such as digital watermarks and digital object identifiers will go far in standardizing the collection of royalties with respect to the on-line distribution of copyrighted works.

---

[197] The court also held that he distributed the works when he accessed his computer by modem from the homes of friends and downloaded the works onto their computers. Several U.S. cases have found infringement in a civil context; see *Playboy Enterprises v. Frena*, 839 F. Supp. 1552 (M.D. Florida, 1995); *Sega v. Maphia*, 857 F. Supp. 679 (N.D. Cal., 1994); see also *Frank Music Corp. v. Compuserve Inc.*, 93 Civ. 8153 (S.D. N.Y., 1993); *Religious Technology Center v. Lerma*, 897 F. Supp. 260, 908 F. Supp. 1353 (E.D. Va., 1995); *Religious Technology Center v. Netcom Online Communication Services, Inc.*, 923 F. Supp. 1231, 907 F. Supp. 1361 (N.D. Cal., 1995); for a discussion of these cases and others, see Mark S. Torpoco, "Mickey and the Mouse: The Motion Picture and Television Industry's Copyright Concerns on the Internet", (1997), 5 U.C.L.A. Ent. L. Rev. 1 at pp. 23-29; Clark B. Siegel, "Copyright Infringement on the Internet", in *1996-97 Entertainment, Publishing and the Arts Handbook*, (New York: Clark, Boardman, Callaghan), p. 133; and Jason K. Axe, "Computer Bulletin Boards and Software Piracy: Are System Operators to Blame for the Acts of Copyright Infringement by Their Users?", in *1996-97 Entertainment, Publishing and the Arts Handbook*, (New York: Clark, Boardman, Callaghan), p. 141.

5

LABOUR

Contributing Author: Ronald N. Hier, B.A., LL.B., LL.M.

1. The American Federation of Musicians in the United States and Canada

(a) Objects

As stated in the Bylaws of the American Federation of Musicians of the United States and Canada ("AFM"), the AFM's objects are, *inter alia*, (1) to better the economic status, social position and general welfare of its members, (2) to negotiate collective bargaining agreements on behalf of its members, (3) to provide assistance in contract administration and enforcement, (4) to resolve grievances and disputes, (5) to advocate the interests of members to the public and governments, (6) to encourage and promote audiences for the enjoyment of performances by professional musicians, (7) to advocate the rights of musicians in their live and recorded performances, and (8) to collect and distribute compulsory royalties subject to collective administration.[1]

(b) Membership

The AFM's membership consists of instrumental musicians, vocalists, instrumental musicians who are librarians, arrangers and

---

[1] Article 2, Section 1 of the Bylaws of the American Federation of Musicians of the United States and Canada, Revised September 15, 1997 (the "International Bylaws").

copyists, or any person who performs musical services for a fee.[2] The latter may include composers.[3]

(c) Structure and Jurisdiction

The AFM's Bylaws determine the structure of the organization and how it is governed. The AFM has a two-tier structure: (1) international; and (2) local. However, matters involving purely Canadian issues, Canadian locals and Canadian members are addressed by a Canadian conference of musicians and are administered through the office of the Vice President from Canada, referred to as the AFM's Canadian office.[4] The AFM's structure is discussed below.

(i) International

The AFM is governed by an elected executive committee called the International Executive Board (the "IEB") which consists of an International President, two vice-presidents (an International Vice President and a Vice President from Canada), an International Secretary-Treasurer, and a five member executive committee elected from the members-at-large.[5] The International Executive Board has general supervision of all AFM matters; it has the power and jurisdiction to dispose of all matters relating to the AFM, its locals and membership. It negotiates travelling and national scales, grants local charters and adjudicates disputes and claims.

The Vice President from Canada is required to maintain a full-time office in Canada and is responsible for the administration of AFM affairs throughout Canada. In an emergency, he/she has authority to make decisions affecting solely Canadian members.[6]

The AFM holds a convention in every odd-numbered year. The convention elects all officers and IEB members and deals with

---

[2] Subsection 4 (1) of the Constitution and Bylaws of the Toronto Musicians Association, local 149 AFM, January 1, 1998 (the "Local Bylaws"); note that subject to the International Bylaws, each local has its own set of bylaws which may differ; see Article 5, s. 1(a) of the International Bylaws; see also Article 11, s. 1(a) of the International Bylaws for membership eligibility.

[3] Composers are mainly represented by SOCAN and the Canadian Songwriters Association. SOCAN is discussed in Chapter 2.

[4] Article 3, ss. 6(a)-(d) of the International Bylaws.

[5] Article 3, s. 1 of the International Bylaws; see generally Articles 3-8 for the rights and duties of these officers.

[6] Article 3, s. 6(b) of the International Bylaws.

resolutions and recommendations submitted by the delegates and IEB.[7] Amendments to the Bylaws are normally made by a majority vote of delegates present.[8]

(ii) Locals

To obtain a charter, a local must consist of a minimum of fifty members.[9] Each local operates in a specific geographic area and has autonomy over its local affairs, electing its own governing board from the local's membership. Locals are required to adopt as part of their local constitutions and bylaws a provision stating that the local constitution and bylaws are subordinate to the International Bylaws. The local bylaws must also contain provisions permitting, at a minimum, the annual amendment of the bylaws and requiring, at a maximum, a two-thirds majority vote to amend the local bylaws.[10]

(d) Functions

The functions of the AFM can be classified broadly as follows: (1) provision of member services; (2) resolution of disputes; (3) regulation of local fees and working conditions; and (4) lobbying on behalf of its membership. These functions can and do overlap. The AFM also acts as the exclusive bargaining representative for agreements covering the services of its members.[11]

(i) Member Services[12]

A. Insurance

Life insurance is arranged and paid for automatically upon initiation into some locals of the AFM. The AFM also endorses all risk,

---

[7] However, pursuant to Article 3, s. 1 of the International Bylaws, only Canadian delegates may elect the Vice President from Canada.

[8] See generally, Articles 23 and 24 of the International Bylaws.

[9] Article 4, s. 1(a) of the International Bylaws. However, the International Executive Board may grant a charter to a local consisting of less than 50 members if the board finds it in the best interest of the AFM and the musicians involved.

[10] Article 5, s. 1(a) of the International Bylaws.

[11] Article 12, s. 20(a) of the International Bylaws.

[12] For a general description of member services, see "Jammin', Perks and Union Privileges", *International Musician*, Official Journal of the American Federation of Musicians of the United States and Canada, December 1998, pp. 4-5.

musical instrument and equipment insurance. Such insurance is advisable, particularly for travelling musicians who are vulnerable to equipment theft and breakage while travelling. The AFM-endorsed plan generally offers lower rates and deductibles than are available on homeowners' policies, and in Canada such insurance is available to members through their locals.

Also available in Canada via the same insurance carrier is commercial general liability insurance. The plan provides up to $1 million coverage for bodily injury and property damage.[13]

B. Trust Funds

The AFM has negotiated with employers and has established trust funds administered by independent trustees for the benefit of its members. Two of the most important are the AFM-Employers' Pension Fund operating in the U.S. and AFM Employers' Pension and Welfare Fund (Canada) operating in Canada. Subject to age and vesting requirements, members engaged under AFM contracts in both countries are entitled to a pension that provides death and disability benefits. The Fund is financed exclusively by participating employers.

The Lester Petrillo Memorial Fund for Disabled Musicians is a charitable trust providing financial aid to disabled, injured or seriously ill members. At the discretion of the trustees, the International Vice-President and the Secretary-Treasurer, modest assistance may be granted on an emergency basis to members in good standing who suffer either permanent or temporary physical or mental disabilities.

The Recording Industry Music Performance Trust Fund (commonly known as the "MPTF") and the Phonograph Record Manufacturers Special Payments Fund ("MSPF") are two other important trust funds. The MPTF is funded by royalties received from record companies which are signatories to the Phonograph Record Labor Agreement. The MPTF is used to underwrite live public performances given free-of-charge by AFM members. AFM members are paid by the MPTF for performances which are co-sponsored by community organizations that have agreed to pay at least half of the performers' fees.

The MPTF represents an attempt by the AFM to cope with the loss of engagements resulting from the displacement of live performance

---

[13] *International Musician*, supra note 12 at p. 4. Note that because performers can be found liable if a member of the audience sustains an injury during a performance, some venues require that musicians carry such insurance.

caused by the emergence of recording technology.[14] The fund also provided a contractual solution to the problem of the lack of recognition of neighbouring rights under copyright law which existed prior to the *Copyright Act* amendments of 1997,[15] and helps to promote live popular music by providing engagements for performing musicians.

The MSPF benefits musicians who perform on recordings in proportion to the number of sessions on which they have performed. Record companies which are signatories to the AFM Phonograph Record Agreement pay into the fund an amount based on the number of records sold in the year. This money is then allocated and distributed to session musicians on the basis of an established formula.

C. Other Services

Other member services include: (1) the distribution of publications containing information of use to members; (2) the provision of AFM standard form engagement contracts; (3) assistance with debt collection when musicians are not paid by engagers; (4) the Emergency Travel Assistance Program which provides emergency funding to AFM members on the road when contracts are not honoured;[16] (5) the establishment of credit unions by some of the larger locals for the benefit of their members; (6) the support by some locals of the National Youth Orchestra and the co-sponsorship of AFM student members;[17] (7) the establishment by some locals of contract guarantee programs and contract defence funds for the purpose of guaranteeing local scale amounts on engagements for which contracts have not been honoured;[18] (8) the provision of active referral services; for example,

[14] See Robert Gorman, "The Recording Musician and Union Power: A Case Study of the American Federation of Musicians", (1983), 57 Southwestern L.J. 697 at pp. 749-60 and pp. 780-83 for a description of the labour struggles predating the creation of the fund; see also Christopher Milazzo, "A Swan Song for Live Music?: Problems Facing the American Federation of Musicians in the Technological Age", (1995-96), 13 Hofstra Labor L.J. 557.

[15] For more on neighbouring rights and their recent recognition in the *Copyright Act*, see Chapter 1. The AFM is a member of the Neighbouring Rights Collective of Canada and intends, as part of that collective, to collect and distribute royalty payments under Part II of the *Copyright Act* to those of its members who, pursuant to Article 12, s. 20(c) of the International Bylaws, have authorized it to do so.

[16] The AFM maintains 1-800 numbers in Canada and the U.S. to provide assistance at all times in such an event.

[17] The National Youth Orchestra serves as an apprenticeship for aspiring symphonic musicians.

[18] See for example, s. 94(1) of the Local Bylaws. Members who wish to take advantage of the program must be prepared to assist the local in enforcing claims should this occur; see generally ss. 94-95 of the Local Bylaws.

some locals provide services similar to those provided by booking agencies to promote live engagements for their members; (9) the provision of collective bargaining with such engagers as the CBC or local symphony boards; and (11) the resolution of disputes. The AFM has also been certified by the Canadian Artists and Producers Professional Relations Tribunal established under the *Status of Artist Act*, and has entered into agreements with the CBC pursuant thereto.[19]

(ii) Dispute Resolution

A. Members versus Members

Procedures have been implemented to facilitate the resolution of disputes between members at the local level. The system functions as follows: (1) a member submits a written and signed report to the local's secretary outlining the particulars of the claim;[20] (2) the Board of Directors reviews the claim and at its discretion deals with the matter or refers it to a Board of Arbitration;[21] (3) if authorized by the Board of Directors, the President appoints a Board of Arbitrators;[22] (4) the matter is heard and adjudicated by the Board of Arbitrators.[23] A decision of a Board of Arbitrators may be appealed to the Board of Directors of the local within 30 days.[24] Members may request, for appeals only, that proceedings be transcribed,[25] and proceedings are secret unless publication is ordered by the Board of Directors.[26] Findings and decisions of the Board are published in the local's next succeeding publication.[27] A decision of the local may be appealed to the Canadian Office of the AFM within 30 days of the receipt of the decision.[28] Any decision of this body is final and binding on the parties.[29]

---

[19] The *Status of Artist Act* is discussed below in Part 1(k)(i).

[20] Subsection 96(1) of the Local Bylaws. The claim also must be filed with the Vice President from Canada within one year after the claim arises or it is barred; see Article III, s. 2(a) of the Rules of Practice and Procedure of the Canadian Office of the American Federation of Musicians for Matters of Solely Canadian Appeals, Claims and Charges (revised Sept. 15, 1997) (the "Rules").

[21] Subsection 96(2) of the Local Bylaws.

[22] Subsection 97(1) of the Local Bylaws.

[23] Subsection 97(2) of the Local Bylaws.

[24] Subsection 99(2) of the Local Bylaws.

[25] Section 100 of the Local Bylaws.

[26] Section 101 of the Local Bylaws.

[27] Section 104 of the Local Bylaws.

[28] Article III, s. 1(a) of the Rules.

[29] Article I, s. 3 of the Rules.

B. Members versus Engagers

AFM standard form Canadian live performance contracts contain language requiring the parties to submit claims arising out of the contract to the relevant local or the Canadian Office of the AFM for settlement. If the submission does not result in a mutually agreeable settlement, the contract permits the parties to initiate court proceedings.[30]

Pursuant to the AFM's International Bylaws, where a collective bargaining agreement or engagement contract does not contain grievance or arbitration provisions, a member may make a claim against an engager through his or her local if the contract is dishonoured.[31] The local will act as agent if the rules of court so permit. Where the claim is made pursuant to a Contract Defence Fund, the local will be entitled to deduct any advance or court costs awarded from amounts collected in respect of the claim.[32]

Travelling members can seek assistance under the Travelling Claims Program. Under this program, in case of emergency, the Federation will provide cash advances if the member authorizes the AFM to retain a collection agency or sue on his or her behalf. In the event of recovery, the AFM is authorized to deduct any cash advances.[33]

(iii) Regulation of Members

A. Tariff of Fees

AFM Local members unilaterally determine a tariff of fees at a general meeting. The tariff sets out the minimum fee ("scale") a member is to be paid for an engagement. Scale depends on the type and length of the engagement. A major function of the local executive is to maintain and enforce scale. Thus, a member who works for less than scale may be charged for infractions of Local Bylaws and upon being found guilty, may be fined, suspended or expelled.[34]

---

[30] See, for example, AFM "Live Performance Contract for Canada", reproduced in Appendix 4.

[31] Article 9, section 2 of the International Bylaws. In some cases, the claim can be made through the Federation.

[32] Subsections 94(3)(a) and (b) Local Bylaws.

[33] Ibid., p . 15.

[34] See sub-para. 15(1)(j)(i), ss. 44 and 48 of the Local Bylaws.

B. Licensed Booking Agents

The AFM franchises booking agents. The franchise program is an attempt to assist AFM members in securing the services of fair, honest and scrupulous booking agents and to protect members against unfair dealing in order to enhance employment opportunities and wage scales of AFM members.[35] The franchise agreement sets out limits on commissions and provides for the resolution of disputes. AFM members are forbidden to accept or play an engagement for a booking agent who is not licensed by the AFM.[36] Under the International Bylaws, a member may act as a booking agent without becoming a party to the Booking Agency Agreement where he/she acts (1) in connection with engagements to be performed within the jurisdiction of his/her local; and (2) if the activity is incidental, for engagements to be performed outside the local's jurisdiction, provided that the rates of commission and other terms conform to those prescribed with respect to 'licensed' or franchised booking agents.[37]

C. Field Services Representatives

Pursuant to the International Bylaws, each local is required to have at least one field service representative.[38] The duties of these representatives include visiting locations where musicians perform in the local's jurisdiction and assisting members with respect to any problems arising on-site in the course of an engagement.

D. Unfair Lists

The AFM maintains an "unfair list" at both the local and international level. The International Unfair List designates engagers with whom the AFM has "a primary labor dispute".[39] Pursuant to the International Bylaws, members are forbidden from rendering musical services for organizations, establishments or people who have been placed on the International Unfair List.[40] Members are also forbidden

---

[35] Article 22, Section 1 of the International Bylaws.
[36] Para. 15(1)(e) of the Local Bylaws.
[37] Article 22, section 5 of the International Bylaws.
[38] *Ibid.*, Article 5, section 22.
[39] *Ibid.*, Article 10, section 1.
[40] *Ibid.*, Article 10, section 3.

from accepting engagements from parties whose names appear on the local unfair list.[41]

A member who performs for an employer on the International Unfair List is subject to a fine of not more than $10,000, or expulsion.[42] A member who performs for an engager on the local unfair list is subject to a fine of not more than $1,000, suspension or expulsion.[43] Violators are subject to a hearing and there is a procedure for appeals.[44]

E. Travelling Musicians

Musicians who travel between Canada and the U.S. are subject to the immigration laws of both countries. The AFM Canadian Office processes requests by all AFM members crossing the Canada/U.S. border. The office will assist Canadian members with applications for P-2 permits for entry into the United States and provides to the INS all supporting documentation, including a copy of the INS-approved reciprocal exchange agreement, statements from sponsoring organizations describing the exchange, evidence that the appropriate U.S. labour organization (i.e., the AFM) was involved in negotiating the exchange program and the AFM's written advisory opinion.[45] Similar services are available with respect to American members working in Canada.

The Federation also maintains a toll-free number to assist travelling members who are in need of the Emergency Travelling Assistance Program.

F. Relocating Members

The AFM International Bylaws require members to join the local having jurisdiction over the area in which they reside.[46] However, members who are part of a self-contained travelling group may apply for membership in any local in which they perform an engagement.[47] Members are required to maintain membership in the local so long as

---

[41] Subparagraph 15 (1)(n)(i) of the Local Bylaws. Also forbidden is the acceptance of an engagement with a person, firm or corporation directly or indirectly connected with a person whose name appears on the local or International Unfair List; sub-para. 15(1)(n)(ii).

[42] Article 13, section 13 of the International Bylaws.

[43] Section 48, Local Bylaws.

[44] See supra under "Dispute Resolution" and infra under "Review by the Court".

[45] "Crossing the U.S./Canada Border", *International Musician*, supra note 12 at p. 7.

[46] Article 11, s. 2 of the International Bylaws.

[47] Article 11, s. 2 of the International Bylaws.

they reside in the local's jurisdiction and are engaged in performing musical services in the jurisdiction.[48] However, if there is compliance with the AFM International Bylaws, a local cannot prevent a member from relocating.[49] A local generally tries to protect its members from potentially harmful competition from members of other locals.

(iv) Lobbying

The AFM pursues its members' interests by lobbying government and other organizations. Specifically, the AFM lobbies in support of legislation beneficial to musicians, and against the passage of legislation detrimental to them.[50]

(e) AFM Agreements

The terms and conditions of all AFM agreements should be considered carefully since they define a musician's rights in a specific contractual situation. Often the agreements interrelate. For example, an individual agreement signed at the local level may incorporate terms found in national or international agreements. The most important agreements are described briefly below.

(i) International

A. Generally

The AFM administers international "agreements" [51] in four main categories:

(1) recording; (2) film; (3) radio; and (4) television. Although commonly referred to as "collective agreements", these agreements are not the result of negotiations between a recognized employer and a certified bargaining unit, and therefore are not collective bargaining

---

[48] Article 11., s. 2(a) of the International Bylaws.

[49] An individual also may be a member of more than one local; see Article 11, s. 11 of the International Bylaws.

[50] Ken Foeller, "What Does the Union Do For Me?", *International Musician*, June 1976, p. 4.

[51] AFM agreements also are discussed in Chapter 7, "Live Performance" and in lesser detail, infra.

agreements in the sense understood in labour relations law.[52] Nevertheless, because this usage is prevalent in the music business, they will be referred to as agreements for purposes of this chapter. Moreover, such contracts are generally treated as agreements by the AFM and the signatories thereto.

The agreements generally take the form of "scale" agreements. They establish the minimum fees and conditions applicable to the musical services and the product being recorded, and also govern the commercial distribution and/or broadcast use of the products and services of AFM members. In particular, the agreements set out minimum fees, conditions of work and hours of engagement, residual payments, credit requirements, pension contributions, and dispute resolution procedures. AFM bylaws are generally incorporated by reference. Payment for "doubling" is dealt with.[53] The terms of the international agreements, with variations, apply to Canadian musicians if a Canadian agreement does not suffice.[54]

B. Recording

Because AFM bylaws prevent members from recording unless the person employing or engaging the member has entered into an agreement with the AFM,[55] record companies who wish to procure the services of AFM members for the purpose of producing commercial CDs, tapes, etc. must be signatories to the relevant agreements. There are two basic agreements: (1) the Phonograph Record Labor Agreement for distribution in Canada and/or the world; and (2) the Limited Pressing Agreement.

The Phonograph Record Labor Agreement governs the terms and conditions under which AFM members perform services in the recording of phonograph records in the U.S. and Canada. The Phonograph Record Labor Agreement, in Part I of Exhibit "A", specifies minimum wages and working conditions for instrumentalists, leaders and contractors. The Exhibit also provides pay scales for arrangers, orchestrators and copyists. Executed simultaneously with the Labor Agreement are the Phonograph Record Manufacturers' Special

---

[52] Unlike collective bargaining agreements which cover contracts made between the members of a collective bargaining unit and their employer, the agreements negotiated by the AFM cover all its members irrespective of their employers and/or engagers.

[53] "Doubling" is the playing by a musician of more than one instrument when required by the musical director or the musical score performed by the musician.

[54] In certain cases, producer-engagers of Canadian musicians have the option of contracting under U.S agreements if the production is being made solely for the U.S. market.

[55] Article 21, section 1 of the International Bylaws.

Payments Fund Agreement and the Phonograph Record Trust Agreement, which are discussed above.

The Limited Pressing Agreement governs recordings where less than 2,000 copies are pressed. The agreement is between a local and a 'producer', who may be a member of the local who wishes to produce and have available his or her own recordings for sale at concerts, clubs or other performances. While pension payments must be made, there is no provision under this agreement for the payment of royalties.

A third agreement of lesser importance, the Electrical Transcription Agreement, contains terms and conditions applicable to the recording of background music by companies such as Muzak. The recordings subject to this agreement are not intended for sale in retail outlets.

C. Broadcasting Agreements

The AFM has entered into two agreements with the CBC: (1) the CBC/AFM Radio Agreement; and (2) the CBC/AFM Television Agreement.[56] Both agreements cover all members of the AFM who are independent contractors engaged by the CBC to perform the function of instrumental musician, conductor, vocalist or arranger. The agreements cover such matters as auditions, recordings, minimum basic fees, and payments for commercial use of the recorded product. Both agreements permit the CBC to engage the services of non-members under certain stipulated conditions.[57] If a non-member is engaged, the relevant AFM Local is entitled to receive a work permit fee in an amount deducted from the fees established under these agreements. The CBC is also required to pay penalties to the local with respect to non-member musicians who are ineligible for work permits and who are engaged in an instrumental performance on a broadcast or recording.[58] The above provisions constitute a limited exception to AFM rules which prohibit members from performing with non-members.

---

[56] CBC/AFM Television Agreement, April 1, 1997 to March 31, 2001; CBC/AFM Radio Agreement, April 1, 1997 to March 31, 2001. In addition, each local can negotiate its own local agreements with local radio stations.

[57] See Article 16 of the Television Agreement and Article 16 of the Radio Agreement.

[58] Excepted, however, are certain performances by elementary school teachers and students, participants in a regular form of religious service, performers in ethnic groups, amateur groups, participants in bona fide talent opportunity programs, and certain musicians who play instruments not played by any members of the local having jurisdiction; see Articles 16.2.1 through 16.2.7.

The Television and Radio Commercial Announcements Agreement for Canada[59] applies to television commercial announcements and/or radio jingles produced and recorded in Canada which consist of "words accompanying music or of words under or over the music, or music intended to be performed without words (not including theme music for a program)".[60] This agreement covers persons engaged as musicians, orchestrators, music proofreaders and librarians and sets out, *inter alia*, minimum fees, local fees, rules relating to doubling, dubbing, new-use,[61] and re-use of musical sound tracks.

The Radio Non-Commercial Identification Announcement Agreement[62] covers the employment of instrumentalists, leaders, contractors, arrangers, orchestrators and copyists who are employed in the making of non-commercial identification announcements for broadcast by radio stations. Identification announcements are tapes, transcriptions and recordings "which contain vocal and instrumental musical performances relating specifically to some facet or aspect of radio station programming, excluding any and all revenue-producing entities (for example, radio station call letters, weather breaks, and similar identification material and no other advertising material)".[63]

There are two international agreements covering television: (1) the Basic Television Film Agreement applicable to Independent Producers[64]; and (2) The Television Videotape Agreement.[65] The AFM also has contracted with the Ontario Educational Communications Authority with respect to the production, broadcast and distribution of videotape, film and radio programs.[66]

---

[59] Television and Radio Commercial Announcements Agreement for Canada, June 15, 1996 to June 14, 1998.

[60] *Ibid.*, Article 1.

[61] New use is defined as the transfer of a music track into one or more different commercials and/or when broadcast in a different broadcast medium; *Ibid.*, article 9, section D.

[62] Radio Non-Commercial Identification Announcement Agreement, December 1, 1995 to October 16, 1998.

[63] *Ibid.*, section 1.

[64] Basic Television Film Agreement, February 16, 1996 to February 15, 1999. This agreement applies to "television motion pictures" which by s. 1 thereof are defined to mean "motion pictures initially released in free TV whether made on or by film, tape or otherwise...".

[65] The Television Videotape Agreement, September 6, 1996 to May 31, 1999. This agreement covers music used in connection with variety shows, talk shows and the like.

[66] Agreement Between The Ontario Educational Communications Authority and the AFM, May 1, 1998 to April 30, 2000. Of limited relevance to Canada is another international agreement, the National Public Television Agreement.

D. Film

There are two international film agreements: (1) The Basic Theatrical Motion Picture Agreement for independent producers;[67] and (2) the Industrial Films Agreement.[68] The agreements apply with respect to employees, conductors, featured instrumentalists and orchestras employed by producers in the United States or Canada whose services are rendered in connection with the production of theatrical or industrial films. Under the former agreement, theatrical motion pictures are defined as "motion pictures initially released in theatrical exhibition, whether made on film, tape or otherwise"; under the latter agreement, an industrial film is defined as a non-theatrical, non-television film "not to be exhibited in theatres where admission is charged or on television."[69] Also pending is a third agreement, a Canadian Film Agreement, for films produced in Canada by Canadian producers.

A soundtrack recorded under either agreement may not be used for any purpose except to accompany the picture for which the music soundtrack was originally prepared, subject to certain stipulated exceptions. These include, *inter alia*, use in trailers advertising the picture, and use to "stock" subsequent pictures for sneak previews.[70]

Both television and theatrical films which require specific music ("scoring") obligate producers to score and record the music in the U.S. or Canada.[71]

The AFM also has entered into an agreement with The National Film Board of Canada (the "NFB").[72] This agreement applies to any engagement of members of the AFM by the NFB. Excluded from the agreement are films produced by the NFB for the Department of National Defence which do not go the public and have no commercial content. Also excluded are full-time salaried employees of the NFB whose duties include composing, music editing and arranging, unless

---

[67] Basic Theatrical Motion Picture Agreement, February 16, 1996 to February 15, 1999. See also the Basic Television Film Agreement, discussed supra, note 64.

[68] Industrial Films Agreement, February 16, 1996 to February 15, 1999.

[69] Section 1 of each relevant agreement.

[70] See the Sound Track Regulations; para. 8 of the Theatrical Agreement, para. 12 of the Industrial Agreement.

[71] Basic Theatrical Motion Picture Agreement, s. 2; see also s. 3 of the Basic Television Film Agreement. Scoring consists of the particular combination of instruments specified in the score of a composition. A score is a notation showing all the parts of an ensemble arranged one underneath the other on different staves; see Don Michael Randal, *Harvard Concise Dictionary of Music*, (Cambridge: The Belknap Press of Harvard University Press, 1978), p. 454.

[72] Agreement between The National Film Board of Canada and the AFM, September 16, 1996 to August 31, 1998.

their services are required as conductors, copyists, contractors or instrumentalists.[73]

E. Legitimate Theatre

The AFM also has concluded agreements with respect to the employment of instrumental musicians, conductors, assistant conductors, arrangers, orchestrators, copyists and librarians by producers engaged in the production of "legitimate first class commercial theatrical production[s]". One such agreement is the Touring Theatrical Musicals Agreement.[74] This agreement, made with the League of American Theatres and Producers, Inc., provides *inter alia* for minimum weekly salaries, out of town living expenses, and rehearsal rates, and contains rules for travel and performance conditions applicable to bus, truck and national tours. This international agreement is utilized in both Canada and the United States.

(ii) National

National agreements are negotiated by the AFM Vice President from Canada and not by the International Executive. The purpose of this practice is to assure that the agreements conform with Canadian laws and music business practices. The agreements, discussed above, include: (1) the CBC/AFM Radio and Television Agreements; (2) the Television and Radio Commercial Announcements Agreement for Canada; (3) the Booking Agent Agreement;[75] (4) the National Film Board Agreement; (5) the OECA Agreement; and (6) the pending Canadian Film Agreement.

(iii) Local and Individual

A. Generally

Local executive boards are empowered to negotiate with engagers situated within a local's geographical jurisdiction.[76] However, individual

---

[73] *Ibid.*, paras. 2-3.

[74] Touring Theatrical Musicals Agreement, April 1, 1995 to March 31, 1999.

[75] As to which, see Chapter 6.

[76] In negotiating with symphony orchestras, locals are required to provide *inter alia*: (1) competent representation as reasonably requested by orchestra members; (2)

musicians or groups also can negotiate and contract with engagers subject to the minimum tariffs established by the local. Such negotiations often are carried out by the musician's agent or manager. Depending on the popularity and status of the musician, the fee negotiated can be well above scale.

This characteristic of individual bargaining in the performing arts distinguishes it from labour relations in other industries. Under the regime of collective bargaining applicable to other industries, bargaining agents, who represent the union, negotiate with employers on behalf of a group of employees who comprise a certified bargaining unit. Once an agreement is ratified, employees who are members of the bargaining unit are bound by the results of the negotiation. There is therefore no opportunity for such employee-members of the bargaining unit to bargain separately, nor can they obtain more favourable terms than are contained in the collective agreement.

B. Types of Contracts

The casual and steady engagement contracts[77] are two of the most important contracts made by musicians. Casual engagements are engagements for single performances and are generally referred to in the business as "one-nighters". Steady engagements are normally weekly engagements.

Other contracts correspond to specific situations outlined in the international agreements. These include contracts to: (1) make phonograph recordings; (2) record music for television and radio commercial announcements and electrical transcription; (3) record music for motion picture films, television films, industrial, documentary, and educational films; (4) make appearances on local or national television or radio programs; and (5) make demonstration recordings. Unlike the above agreements, which incorporate the AFM's Bylaws and the terms of international agreements, the casual and steady engagement contracts do not. However, the casual and steady engagement contracts do contain language whereby it is acknowledged that the musician is a member of the AFM who is obligated to adhere to the professional standards (code of ethics) established by the AFM and to conform to the rules, regulations and bylaws of the local and the AFM.[78]

---

continuing contract administration; and (3) all reasonable and necessary out-of-pocket expenses incurred by the orchestra committee; see Article 5, section 24 of the International Bylaws.

[77] See Chapter 7 for a discussion of these contracts.

[78] For such language see also the AFM Live Performance Contract for Canada, reproduced in full in Appendix 4.

(f) Legal Status

(i) Canada

Although the AFM is an organization formed for the purpose of regulating relations between its members and engagers, the AFM has not, for the most part, been certified as a bargaining agent under provincial or federal labour statutes. These statutes regulate the relations between employers and employees and do not apply to the relations between independent contractors, such as musicians, and the parties who engage their services.[79] However, to the extent that members of the AFM are employees or 'dependent contractors'[80], the statutes do apply and the AFM is entitled to seek certification.[81] The AFM is also competent to and has obtained certification as a certified artists' association under the federal *Status of the Artist Act*[82].

Because trade unions are exempt from the application of competition laws, and are in some respects treated more favourably than other unincorporated associations under the rules of civil procedure, it can be an issue whether the AFM is a trade union where such rules and laws apply. These issues are discussed below.

---

[79] For a list of factors to be taken into account in determining whether a performer is an employee or independent contractor in the labour context, see *Algonquin Tavern v. Canadian Labour Congress*, [1981] 3 Can. L.R.B. 337 (Ont. L.R.B.).

[80] Dependent contractors are persons who perform work for others on terms and conditions such that the contractor is in a position of economic dependence upon the other and in a relationship more closely resembling that of employee than independent contractor. Such persons are often deemed to be employees under labour relations statutes; see for example, the *Labour Relations Act, 1995*, S.O. 1995, c. 1, Sched. A, s. 1(1).

[81] With respect to dependent contractors, see *Re Société Radio-Canada/Canadian Broadcasting Corporation and Union des Artistes* (1982), 1 C.L.R.B.R (N.S.) 129 (Can. L.R.B.). As for employees, symphony musicians have been recognized as such both in the context of income tax, unemployment insurance and pension legislation; with respect to the latter, see for example, *Vancouver Symphony Society v. M.N.R.*, a decision of the Pension Appeals Board, Jan. 11, 1974, found at (1974), C.B. & P.G.R., 6179. The VSO, AFM and orchestra members have also participated in proceedings under British Columbia labour statutes in connection with both unfair labour practices and the union's duty of fair representation; see for example *Adams v. Vancouver Symphony Society & Musicians Assn., Local 145*, [1976] 1 Can. L.R.B.R. 192 (Can. L.R.B.); *Stafford v. Vancouver Symphony Society & Musicians Assn., Local 145*, C223/91 (B.C. I.R.C.); and *Adams v. Vancouver Symphony Society & Musicians Assn.*, [1987] B.C.L.R.B. 136-17 (B.C. L.R.B.).

[82] Thus, both the CBC and NFB agreements discussed above are subject to the jurisdiction of the Act.

(ii) U.S.

Whereas in Canada the AFM is an unincorporated association (or union) of largely self-employed musicians not generally governed by labour statutes, in the U.S. disputes between musicians and engagers are decided by the National Labour Relations Board. The AFM in the U.S. has a long and distinct history of labour struggles which differentiates it significantly from its Canadian counterpart.[83]

(g) Legal Capacity

(i) To Sue or Be Sued in its Name

At common law, an unincorporated association of individuals, having no existence apart from its members, can neither sue nor be sued in its own name.[84] However, a trade union, in certain circumstances, does have the right to sue and can be sued in its own name.[85] This right possibly may extend to conduct outside the discharge of a union's obligations or the exercise of rights under a collective bargaining agreement.[86] If the AFM is regarded as a trade union, it may in an appropriate case avail itself of this right. If it is not regarded as a trade union, it may be possible for the AFM or a local to sue or be sued in a representative or class action.[87] However, numerous

---

[83] See Gorman, supra note 14; see also Robert S. Lecter, *The Musicians*, (New York: Bookman Associates, 1953).

[84] See generally, Arthur J. Meagher and Ronald A. Meagher, *Parties to an Action*, (Toronto: Butterworths, 1988), chapter 7. For a useful general reference, see John P. Hamilton and Hugh McD.Kelly, *The Law of Groups*, (Toronto: CBAO, 1985).

[85] Several provinces have legislated that unions can sue or be sued in their own name; these include Newfoundland, New Brunswick, Prince Edward Island and Quebec. In Alberta, British Columbia, Manitoba and Saskatchewan, unions have a limited right to sue; the action must relate to the purposes of labour relations statutes. In Ontario and Nova Scotia, the right is even narrower. Thus, in Ontario, unions may be parties to prosecutions only under the *Labour Relations Act* and with respect to orders of the Labour Relations Board and decisions of arbitrators; see *Labour Relations Act, 1995*, S.O. 1995, c. 1, ss. 106-108. See generally Michael MacNeil, Michael Lynk & Peter Engelmann, *Trade Union Law in Canada*, (Aurora: Canada Law Book, 1998), at p. 1-4 to 1-6.

[86] *Maritime Employers' Association v. I.L.A., Local 273* (1978), 89 D.L.R. (3d) 289 (S.C.C.). According to MacNeil et al. supra note 85 at p. 1-9, cases have established that "in the absence of an explicit statement, the granting of quasi-corporate powers leads to the trade union having a generally wide ranging capacity to sue and be sued."

[87] See, for example, the *Class Proceedings Act, 1992*, S.O. 1992, c. 6. Under this Act, which replaces former Rule 12 (which itself replaces former Rule 75), a union may bring a class action under s. 2(1); see Watson & McGowan, *Ontario Civil Practice, 1999*,

courts have held that before a representation order may be granted, the plaintiff must demonstrate: (1) the existence of a trust fund to which he or she can look for payment of damages; and (2) that the persons sought to be named in the order are the trustees of, or in control of the fund.[88]

The difficulty of establishing the existence of trust funds is illustrated by *Body v. Murdoch*,[89] a case involving a jurisdictional dispute between Local 149 of the AFM and the American Guild of Variety Artists (the "AGVA"), a rival union. Murdoch, President of Local 149 of the AFM issued a direction to a member of the local not to accompany certain dancers who were members of AGVA and who had contracted to perform on certain programs produced by the CBC. As a result of union pressure, the CBC cancelled the plaintiff's contract. Local 149 had a general fund for current expenses and a welfare fund, but the general fund was not a trust fund and the welfare fund was not available to pay damages. The court therefore refused to grant a representation order.

In cases where a representation order is unavailable, an action may be brought against officers or executives of the union in their personal capacity.[90]

(ii) Collective Agreements Unenforceable at Common Law

The AFM signatory agreements as well as the international and local bylaws, to the extent that they are in restraint of trade, are unenforceable at common law. In practice, however, the CBC,[91] symphony societies and other signatories to AFM collective agreements voluntarily accede to their terms. This is a matter of practical reality. It

---

(Toronto: Carswell, 1999), at vol. 2, p. 460. The authors point out that a union also may be sued under new Rule 12.07 which reproduces the text of former Rule 75.

[88] See for example under former Rule 75 of the Ontario Rules of Practice; *Harrison v. Sinclair*, [1945] O.W.N. 399 (Ont. H.C.); *Body v. Murdoch*, [1954] O.W.N. 658 (Ont. H.C.); *Smith Transport Ltd. v. Baird*, [1957] O.W.N. 405 (Ont. H.C.); *Anderson Block & Tile Ltd. v. Mior*, [1961] O.W.N. 292 (Ont. H.C.). Note that civil practice in some provinces does not require the plaintiff to establish the existence of a trust fund; see *Wytosky v. C.J.A., Prince Albert Local 1990* (1986), 44 Sask. R. 122 (Sask. Q.B.).

[89] *Body v. Murdoch*, [1954] O.W.N. 658 (Ont. H.C.).

[90] In *Body v. Murdoch*, supra note 88, the plaintiff was able to obtain an interlocutory injunction personally restraining the defendant president of the local; see *Body v. Murdoch*, [1954] O.W.N. 515 (Ont. C.A.).

[91] Relations between the CBC and the AFM are now governed by the *Status of the Artist Act*, discussed below. This act provides a regime of collective bargaining for artists who contract with the CBC; these contracts are subject to the enforcement mechanisms contained in the Act. Note that s. 9(2) of the Act specifically exempts the AFM from the application of s. 4(1) of the *Competition Act*.

is in the interests of the parties, for the sake of administrative expediency, to negotiate and enter into collective agreements rather than contracting individually with every musician in their employ.

Unlike the AFM collective agreements, contracts entered into by individual AFM members and engagers (for example, the casual or steady engagement contracts) are generally enforceable at common law.

(h) Common Law Actions

The activities of the AFM and its locals are vulnerable to the application of various common law doctrines developed by the courts to regulate what they regarded as the anti-competitive behaviour of unions. These doctrines and some of the cases in which they have been applied are discussed below.

(i) Restraint of Trade

To protect the economic interests of its members, the AFM's international bylaws and those of its locals typically enact compulsory minimum wage scales, provide for closed shops, and restrict the freedom of members to work for non-signatory parties and with non-members. At common law, provisions such as these are in restraint of trade and courts have not hesitated to declare them illegal and unenforceable.

Thus, in *Parker v. Toronto Musical Protective Assn.*,[92] the Ontario High Court struck down a bylaw enacted by the defendant (the "TMPA") which provided that "No member of this association shall play on any engagement with any person who is playing an instrument, unless such person can shew the card of this association in good standing."[93] The bylaw had been challenged by a musician who had been fined for performing with non-union members of a military band and expelled when he refused to pay the fine in a timely manner. The court held that the bylaw was an unreasonable restraint of trade and that the plaintiff had been invalidly expelled from the union.

Although left unstated by the court, the finding in *Parker* presupposed that the TMPA was not a trade union. Trade unions are

---

[92] (1901) 32 O.R. 305 (Ont. H.C.). See also *GKO Associates Ltd. v. Parrish* (1977), 35 C.P.R. (2d) 22 (Ont. H.C.), wherein it was held that a provision of ACTRA's constitution preventing ACTRA members from contracting with non-franchised talent agents and personal managers was *prima facie* in restraint of trade.

[93] *Ibid.*, p. 307.

exempt from the doctrine of restraint of trade[94] and if the court had found that the TMPA was indeed a union, it would have been compelled to find for the defendant.

So long as the AFM's status is uncertain, other bylaws, if challenged in court, may be considered in restraint of trade on similar grounds.[95]

(ii) Conspiracy

The classic definition of conspiracy states that a conspiracy is "the agreement of two or more to do an unlawful act, or to do a lawful act by unlawful means".[96] Under modern Canadian law, there will be an actionable conspiracy if: (1) whether the means used by the defendant are lawful or unlawful, the predominant purpose of the defendant's conduct is to injure the plaintiff; or (2) where the conduct of the defendants is unlawful, the conduct is directed toward the plaintiff and the defendants should know in the circumstances that injury to the plaintiff is likely and does result.[97] Liability requires proof of damage; where an injunction is sought, proof of a threat of damage is required.[98]

The above formulation recognizes the possibility that the defendant may have a legitimate purpose to advance which has the secondary effect of injuring the plaintiff; in such cases, the defendants will not be liable. Thus, in *Scala Ballroom (Wolverhampton) Ltd. v. Ratcliffe,* [99] the English Musician's Union was absolved from liability when it advised the owner of a ballroom who proposed to refuse entry to blacks that the union would not allow its members to play so long as the ban

---

[94] See, for example, s. 2 of the *Rights of Labour Act*, R.S.O. 1990, c. R.33. Pursuant to this Act, a trade union and the acts thereof will not be deemed unlawful by reason only that one or more of the union's objects are in restraint of trade. Similar legislation exists in B.C. and Saskatchewan: *British Columbia Labour Code*, R.S.B.C. 1996, c. 244; *Trade Unions Act*, R.S.S. 1978, c. T-17, s. 28. If the AFM and its locals are regarded as a trade union under these statutes, the common law doctrine of restraint of trade will not apply to their activities. See also s. 29 of the *Trade Unions Act*, R.S.C. 1985, c. T-14 which exempts union members from criminal prosecution and prevents union agreements from being deemed void or voidable because the "purposes of any trade union... are in restraint of trade..." Trade union activities are also exempted from the provisions of the *Criminal Code* dealing with conspiracies in restraint of trade; see *Criminal Code*, R.S.C. 1985, c. C-46, ss. 466-67.

[95] Note that in the context of labour law, at least one provincial labour board has found the AFM and one of its locals to be a trade union, despite the fact that the members of the proposed bargaining unit were held to be independent contractors; see *Saskatchewan Gaming Corp., Re*, [1997] Sask. L.R.B.D. No. 25.

[96] *Mulcahy v. R.* (1868), L.R. 3 H.L. 306 (U.K. H.L.) at 317.

[97] *Canada Cement LaFarge Ltd. v. British Columbia Lightweight Aggregate Ltd.* (1983), 145 D.L.R. (3d) 385 (S.C.C.).

[98] G.H.L. Fridman, *The Law of Torts in Canada* (Toronto: Carswell, 1990), vol. 2 at p.263.

[99] [1958] 3 All E.R. 220 (Eng. C.A.).

was in effect. The plaintiff claimed that the union was attempting to induce a breach of contracts it had made with union members, and sought damages for conspiracy and an injunction. The court, following an earlier case,[100] held that where the predominant purpose of the defendants was the lawful protection or promotion of a lawful interest, there could be no tortious conspiracy even if the agreement resulted in damage to others. Here, the union had an interest in protecting itself and its members, many of whom were black, from the strife that would result if the union did not take steps to oppose the ban.

Unions also may be protected if the conspiracy has, as its purpose, actions done in furtherance of a trade dispute.[101] However, where no such defences exist, the AFM's executive committee and the general membership can be held liable for the expressed or implied authorization of unlawful acts.[102]

(iii) Intimidation

The tort of intimidation consists of causing harm to the plaintiff by means of a threat to commit an unlawful act.[103] The threat may be directed at the plaintiff or at a third party whose subsequent actions cause harm to the plaintiff. The harm suffered is normally an economic loss. Cases have held that the unlawful act includes acts which are criminal, tortious, or in breach of contract.[104] To succeed, the plaintiff

---

[100] *Crofter Hand Woven Harris Tweed Co. v. Veitch*, [1942] A.C. 435 (U.K. H.L.).

[101] *Canadian Training & Development Group Inc. v. Air Canada* (1986), 39 C.C.L.T. 72 (Ont. Div. Ct.), applying s. 3(1) of the Ontario Rights of Labour Act to an illegal strike of air traffic controllers which had the foreseeable effect of injuring the plaintiff. But cf. *Jose v. Metallic Roofing Co.* (1905), 12 O.L.R. 200 (Ont. Div. Ct.), affirmed (1907), 14 O.L.R. 156 (Ont. C.A.), reversed [1908] A.C. 514 (Ont. P.C.), wherein the court held that an action in conspiracy would lie where the union had as its immediate purpose "the hurt of another". In this case, as part of its attempt to obtain a closed shop on the plaintiff's premises, the union announced that it would call out the workers of any business that dealt with the plaintiff.

[102] Douglas J. Sherbaniuk, "Actions by and against Trade Unions in Contract and Tort", (1957-58) Vol.12 University of Toronto L.J. 151 at 178.

[103] *Rookes v. Barnard*, [1964] A.C. 1129 (U.K. H.L.). In *GKO Associates Ltd. v Parrish*, supra note 92, the court granted an interlocutory injunction to a personal manager and talent agent who refused to participate in ACTRA's franchising program on the basis that: (1) a provision of ACTRA's constitution forbidding members from contracting with non-franchised agents was *prima facie* in restraint of trade; and (2) fines threatened or levied against members in consequence thereof constituted an illegal act within the meaning of *Rookes v. Barnard.*

[104] *Morgan v. Fry*, [1968] 2 Q.B. 710 (Eng. C.A.). For a description of the tort, see Fridman, supra note 98, at pp. 279-89. See also *I.B.T., Local 213 v. Therrien*, [1960] S.C.R. 265 (S.C.C.); in this case the Supreme Court of Canada also held, following *Taff Vale Railway v. Amalgamated Society of Railway Servants*, [1901] A.C. 426 (U.K. H.L.), that the union could be sued in its own name because it was a union recognized by labour statutes

must establish the threat, and further, that he/she (or the third party to whom the threat was made) acted in such a way as to cause injury to the plaintiff.

(iv) Inducing Breach of Contract

A person commits the tort of inducing breach of contract when, having knowledge of a contract and sustaining an intention to bring about its breach, he or she engages in conduct which results in the breach, damage is suffered by the plaintiff, and the defendant cannot justify his/her conduct.[105]

Body v. Murdoch,[106] discussed above, provides an example of the tort. Murdoch, then president of Local 149 of the AFM, directed a member of the local not to accompany members of the American Guild of Variety Artists ("AGVA") on a CBC program on which they had contracted to appear. As a result of this pressure, the CBC cancelled its contract with the guild members. In granting an injunction to restrain the defendant from causing a breach of the CBC contract, the court held that the defendant had committed a wrongful act by interfering without just cause or excuse with the contractual rights of the plaintiff, and had done so by the employment of unlawful means (the calling out of the accompanist on an "illegal strike").[107]

(v) Breach of Contract and Ultra Vires

The members of a trade union, or any unincorporated association, are bound to each other by the terms of the union's or association's constitution and bylaws. Thus, in case of a dispute between the association and a member, where the aggrieved party alleges a breach of the constitution or bylaws, the normal remedy is an action for breach of contract.

In *Bonsor v. Musicians' Union*,[108] the plaintiff, a member of the Liverpool branch of the Musicians' Union who had been expelled, sought a declaration that his expulsion was null and void, an injunction

---

and not just an unincorporated association of working men; see also *Central Canada Potash Co. v. Saskatchewan, (Attorney General)* (1978), 88 D.L.R. (3d) 609 (S.C.C.).

[105] Fridman, supra note 98 at p. 293; see generally pp. 291-312.

[106] *Body v. Murdoch*, [1954] O.W.N. 515 (Ont. C.A.).

[107] For a case in which the actions of the defendant were justified, see *Brimelow v. Casson*, [1924] 1 Ch. 302 (Eng. Ch. Div.), a case involving underpaid chorus girls and attempts to stop the underpayment which had led to prostitution.

[108] [1955] 3 All E.R. 518 (U.K. H.L.). A breach of contract action also may be available for wrongful suspension.

and damages. The court held that the expulsion was a breach of contract liable in damages on the grounds that there had been either: (1) breach of contract between the union as an entity and the plaintiff;[109] or (2) breach of the union's rules, which constituted a binding contract between the plaintiff and other members of the union. The court also held that the plaintiff only could have recourse to the union's fund to satisfy any judgment in his favour.

When the AFM acts beyond the powers contained in its constitution and bylaws, an action may be brought on the basis that its acts are *ultra vires*.[110] Thus far, cases have been restricted to situations where there has been unlawful expulsion of a member or misapplication of union funds.[111]

(i) Competition Act

(i) *Possible Offences*

At first glance, it appears that many of the AFM's efforts to regulate the terms under which its members provide services to engagers may be a conspiracy, combination, agreement or arrangement to restrain or injure competition unduly,[112] or an agreement influencing upward or discouraging the reduction of the price of services.[113] For example, the AFM International Bylaws provide for minimum fees which members may not undercut either in accepting engagements from engagers or in paying members when they act as leaders. Other practices may be considered to be exclusive dealing[114] (the AFM requires engagers who are signatories to its agreements to deal exclusively with AFM members

---

[109] This followed from the court's finding that the union, because it was a registered trade union, could be sued for breach of contract as a legal entity. The authority for this proposition was the *Taff Vale* case, discussed supra at note 104.

[110] See *Orchard v. Tunney*, [1957] S.C.R. 436 (S.C.C.), wherein the Supreme Court of Canada held that the expulsion of a union member, not in accordance with the rules, constituted a tort not binding the members of the union because it was *ultra vires* the powers of the union's executive board.

[111] Sherbaniuk, "Actions by and against Trade Unions", supra note 102 at p.177. Sherbaniuk argues that the doctrine, which denotes a limitation on the legal personality of corporations, should not apply to trade unions which have no legal personality, and further, that the actions of trade unions are effected by individuals whose powers are unlimited, so that the only question is whether union officials, when acting as agents of the union, have exceeded their authority.

[112] Paragraph 45(1)(d) of the *Competition Act*, R.S.C. 1985, c. C-34.

[113] *Ibid.*, para. 61(1)(a).

[114] *Ibid.*, sub-paras. 77(1)(a)(i) and (ii).

when fulfilling engagements) or refusal to deal[115] (the AFM forbids its members from accepting engagements with engagers on the unfair list or working with members on the defaulters' list).

(ii) Defences

The *Competition Act* expressly exempts from its application any combination or activities of workmen or employees for their own reasonable protection as workmen or employees.[116] The exemption does not grant blanket protection to trade unions, but may protect them if they engage in anti-competitive behaviour directly in their self-interest.[117] Historically, unions have not been prosecuted under the *Competition Act*.[118]

To avail itself of the exemption, the AFM would need to establish that it is a combination of "workmen or employees". While the issue has not been adjudicated under the *Competition Act*, federal and provincial labour boards have ruled that dependent contractors are "employees" under labour codes, and in one case, the AFM has been held to be a trade union.[119] One might expect, therefore, that if the AFM's agreements and activities are directly in its self-interest and do not depart from the practices of other unions, they will be 'reasonable' and the AFM will not be subject to the provisions of the Act.[120]

---

[115] *Ibid.*, s. 75. See also generally, A. McNiece Auston, "Groups and Competition Law", in *The Law of Groups*, supra note 84. See also C. Backhouse, "Labour Unions and Anti-Combines Policy", (1976), 14 Osgoode Hall L.J. 113.

[116] *Ibid.*, para. 4(1)(a).

[117] See R.J. Roberts, *Roberts on Competition/Antitrust: Canada and the United States*, (Toronto: Butterworths, 1992) at pp. 397-404 for a discussion of this issue and union activities which may or may not constitute protected anti-competitive behaviour.

[118] MacNeil et al., supra note 85 at p. 1-25, but see the cases cited in footnote 128 thereof for cases dealing with union immunity.

[119] The Canada Labour Board has decided that dependent contractors are employees for purposes of the *Canada Labour Code*; see *Re Société Radio Canada*, supra note 81. Many musicians are dependent contractors. As well, the Saskatchewan Labour Board has held that the AFM and its locals form a trade union; see *Sask. Gaming Corp., Re*, supra note 95.

[120] With regard to some of its agreements, the AFM also will be able to rely on subsection 9(2) of the *Status of the Artist Act*, discussed infra, which deems certified artists associations to be combinations of employees for purposes of s. 4(1) of the *Competition Act*; the AFM has been so certified with respect to independent contractors engaged by the CBC.

(j) Review by the Court

Where the constitution and/or bylaws of an unincorporated association provide for the adjudication of disputes, the courts are generally reluctant to review until all remedies provided by the domestic constitution have been exhausted fully.[121] However, if the domestic tribunal acts without jurisdiction or in breach of the rules of natural justice, the court may interfere to help an aggrieved party.[122] The courts require that the domestic tribunal act in good faith;[123] and where it is shown that the association has acted unlawfully in suspending or expelling a member, the plaintiff may claim, in addition to an injunction or declaration, damages for breach of contract.[124] However, although the courts will review the wrongful expulsion of a member, they will not intervene to review the refusal of an applicant for membership even where the prohibitions against entry are unreasonable.[125]

(k) Other Relevant Legislation

As discussed above, artists and musicians, unless they are dependent contractors, have not been able to secure the benefits of collective bargaining available to employees under labour relations statutes. In recognition of this fact, the federal government and the province of Quebec have enacted legislation to promote the collective

---

[121] *Kuzych v. White (No. 3)*, [1951] A.C. 585 (B.C. P.C.), reversing [1950] 2 W.W.R. 193 (B.C.C.A.), affirmed [1949] 2 W.W.R. 558 (B.C. S.C.). See also *Zilliax v. Independent Order of Foresters* (1906), 13 O.L.R. 155 (Ont. H.C.), and Robert L. Fulby, "Court Actions by and against Groups", in *The Law of Groups*, supra note 84.

[122] *Lawson v. Atlantic Federation of Musicians, Local 571* (1986), 74 N.S.R. (2d) 131 (N.S. T.D.). In *Lawson*, the plaintiff was tried in absentia for violations of the local's bylaws. The court held that the domestic tribunal had a judicial or quasi-judicial function, and in granting an injunction to prevent it from conducting a re-hearing or appeal, further noted that it had failed to act in accordance with prescribed procedure and the rules of natural justice. The actions of the local's president also created a reasonable apprehension of bias in the plaintiff. For an older case in which the court refused to remedy a breach of natural justice until all domestic remedies were exhausted, see *Kemerer v. Standard Stock & Mining Exchange* (1927), 32 O.W.N. 295 (Ont. C.A.).

[123] *Patillo v. Cummings* (1915), 24 D.L.R. 775 (N.S. T.D.).

[124] *Leblanc v. Winters* (1986), 53 Sask. R. 22 (Sask. C.A.). However, the court distinguished between acts beyond the jurisdiction of the association and acts constituting an improper exercise of authority; it is the latter that bring about a breach of contract giving rise to damages. Damages are assessed in accordance with the principle laid down in *Hadley v. Baxendale* (1854), 9 Exch. 341 (Eng. Ex. Div.). See also *Bonsor v. Musicians' Union*, supra note 108, wherein the court held that wrongful expulsion was a breach of contract giving rise to liability in damages.

[125] *Faramus v. Film Artists' Assn.*, [1964] 1 All E.R. 25 (U.K. H.L.).

organization of business affairs by artists who are independent contractors. This legislation is discussed below.

(i) Federal

The *Status of the Artist Act*[126] imposes a system of labour relations on artists and producers. It applies to certain federal government institutions,[127] broadcast undertakings under CRTC jurisdiction,[128] and to independent contractors[129] who are, *inter alia*, authors of musical works within the *Copyright Act*[130] or performers or singers in musical works.[131]

In order to qualify as an artist under the Act, the independent contractor must be a 'professional'. Factors to be taken into account in deciding whether an artist so qualifies include: (1) whether the artist is paid for the presentation of his or her work; (2) whether the artist is recognized by other artists; (3) whether the artist is in the process of becoming an artist according to the practice of the artistic community; and (4) whether the artist is a member of an artists' association.[132]

Professional artists have the right to organize themselves into artists' associations.[133] Once certified, such associations have exclusive authority to bargain on behalf of artists in the relevant sector,[134] and the artists' association may require a producer or producers' association to bargain for the purpose of entering into a scale agreement.[135] Scale agreements provide minimum terms and must contain provisions for

---

[126] S.C. 1992, c. 33.

[127] By sub-para. 6(2)(a)(i) of the Act, it applies to the government institutions listed in Schedule I to the *Access to Information Act*, the schedule to the *Privacy Act*, and to such institutions as are prescribed by regulation.

[128] *Ibid.*, sub-para 6(2)(a)(ii).

[129] *Ibid.*, para. 6(2)(b). Such independent contractors must be professional artists who satisfy the criteria of para. 18(b) of the Act.

[130] *Ibid.*, sub-para. 6(2)(b)(i).

[131] *Ibid.*, sub-para. 6(2)(b)(ii). See also sub-para. 6(2)(b)(iii) for other persons who contribute to the creation of, *inter alia*, music and sound recordings.

[132] *Ibid.*, s. 18(b).

[133] *Ibid.*, s. 25. Certification is granted by the Canadian Artists and Producers Professional Relations Tribunal, a quasi-judicial body set up to administer the Act. The Tribunal has powers and duties analogous to those of administrative tribunals constituted under labour relations statutes; see generally ss. 10-22 of the Act. There is a limited right of appeal to the Federal Court under grounds contained in paras. 18.1(4)(a)(b)(e) of the *Federal Court Act* of determinations or orders of the Tribunal. For more on artists' associations, see s. 8, s. 23, and ss. 25-30.

[134] *Ibid.*, para. 28(5)(a). Pursuant to s. 24 of the Act, producers may form associations for the purpose of collective bargaining.

[135] *Ibid.*, s. 31(1).

the final settlement of all disputes, by arbitration or otherwise.[136] The determination of an arbitrator is final and not reviewable by any court.[137]

The statute also governs unfair practices, sets out a system of fines and penalties and allows a strike thirty days after the expiry date of an agreement or six months after certification of an artists' association.[138]

(ii) Provincial

Statutes similar to the federal statute have also been enacted or proposed at the provincial level. The Quebec legislation, *An Act respecting the professional status and conditions of engagement of performing, recording and film artists,* [139] is a useful example. The Act sets out a collective bargaining regime which applies to artists and to producers who retain their professional services in the following fields of artistic endeavour:

...theatre, the opera, music, dance and variety entertainment, the making of films, the recording of discs and other modes of sound recording, dubbing, and the recording of commercial advertisements.[140]

An artist for the purposes of the Act is defined as:

any natural person who practises an art on his own account and who offers his services for remuneration, as a creator or performer in any field of artistic endeavour referred to in Section 1.

The Act permits professional artists to establish and join artists' associations[141] which are empowered by the statute to defend and promote the economic, social, moral and professional interests of artists,[142] and in particular, to establish model contracts, make agreements with producers as to the use of such contracts, and to

---

[136] *Ibid.*, s. 36(1). If the agreement fails to provide for arbitration, there is a statutory right to arbitration; see s. 36(2). For more on arbitration, see ss. 36-43 of the Act.

[137] *Ibid.*, s. 37(1). To this end, s. 37(3) provides that an arbitrator is not a federal board within the meaning of the *Federal Court Act.*

[138] As to which, see ss. 46-49 for pressure tactics; s. 50 for unfair practices, and s. 57 for offences and penalties. Note that with respect to prosecution of offences under the Act, artists' and producers' associations are persons who may sue and be sued in their own name; see s. 58.

[139] *An Act respecting the professional status and conditions of engagement of performing, recording and film artists,* R.S.Q., c. S-32.1. The Act is administered by the Commission des Reconnaissances des Associations D'Artistes; see ss. 43 - 46 of the Act. The Commission's duties are set out in Section 56. Section 69 sets out offences.

[140] *Ibid.*, s. 1. Note that unlike the federal legislation, the Act covers the private sector and, pursuant to s. 4, is binding on the Crown.

[141] *Ibid.*, s. 7. See s. 5 for limits on the applicability of the Act.

[142] *Ibid.*, s. 24(1).

negotiate group agreements for the performance of services by artists.[143] Artists and producers bound by a group agreement cannot stipulate for conditions of engagement less advantageous than those contained in the group agreement.[144] The Act further provides a set of rules under which the parties may resort to "concerted action" and regulates the use of boycotts and pressure tactics.

2. Other Labour Organizations

(a) ACTRA

Instrumental musicians who appear on radio or television as actors or performers (but not in their capacity as musicians) are subject to the jurisdiction of the Alliance of Canadian Cinema Television and Radio Artists ("ACTRA"). ACTRA also has jurisdiction over vocalists who do not perform on musical instruments. This jurisdiction appears to overlap that of the AFM which also claims jurisdiction over singers. To resolve this conflict, it has been the practice, in the case of joint membership, for one association to acquiesce to the other if a member would receive more favourable treatment under the other association's agreement than under its own.

(b) Actors' Equity

The definition of an actor in the constitution and bylaws of the Canadian Actors' Equity Association includes singers but excludes instrumental musicians.[145] Canadian Actors' Equity's jurisdiction is restricted to live theatre. Its agreements provide, *inter alia*, for the payment of royalties upon the recording of cast albums of theatrical productions, recording for radio, and recordings in general.

It is possible for a vocalist to be a member simultaneously of the AFM and Actors' Equity (and even ACTRA), although this rarely occurs in practice.

---

[143] *Ibid.*, ss. 24(6) and (7).

[144] *Ibid.*, s. 8. For more on group agreements, see ss. 27 - 42 of the Act. Such agreements potentially include recording contracts and record producer agreements.

[145] Canadian Actors' Equity Association Canadian Theatre Agreement, June 19, 1989 to June 15, 1992 at p. 18.

6

AGENTS AND MANAGERS

Contributing Author: D. Blair Holder, LL.B.

1. Overview

(a) Agents and Managers Distinguished

In the general business sense, the role of agents and managers is clearly understood. The agent — or more precisely, the booking (or talent) agent — arranges personal appearances and live performances for musicians. Typically, these are referred to as engagements. The manager, who is most typically the personal manager, but often is also business manager and sometimes road manager, assists in the development of the musician's career by giving artistic and business advice and by using personal contacts. However, in the legal sense, the relationship between agents, managers and musicians is not as well understood. Both agents and managers are, in law, "agents" of the musician, and the musician is the "principal" who engages the "agent" to perform various functions.

(b) Role of Personal Representatives

The types and roles of the various personal representatives of musicians are outlined below.[1]

---

[1] For a general discussion, see Chapter 9, "Agents and Managers", in Sidney Shemel & M. William Krasilovsky, *This Business of Music*, Sixth Ed., (New York: Billboard Books, 1990), at pp. 90-100. "Personal representatives" is used generally to mean all types of personal representatives of musicians in their music business affairs. See also Luane L. Quast, "Musicians, Their Representatives and Agreements between Them", in *Entertainment, Publishing, and the Arts Handbook*, (New York: Clark Boardman Company Ltd., 1990), at 191 (herein "Quast"). See also Michael I. Yanover and Harvey G. Kotler, "Artist/Management Agreements and the English Music Trilogy: Another British

(i) Booking Agents

The booking agent's role is to obtain engagements, negotiate and prepare contracts, see that the contracts are distributed properly, and ideally, deal with any problems that might come up between the employers and the musicians.[2] Some musicians act as booking agents for other musicians and, until there is a significant demand for their services, many musicians act as their own booking agent.

(ii) Lawyers

A. Generally

The roles of a lawyer in the music business are to negotiate and draft contracts that are specific to the music business, to provide advice to his or her clients with respect to the business and legal aspects of a client's music business affairs, to structure agreements between musicians and third parties, and to resolve and/or litigate disputes between music industry clients and third parties. In private practice, most typical contracts will include: (1) publishing agreements; (2) recording agreements; (3) the personal management agreement; and (4) producer and production agreements. Because a lawyer in the music industry is involved in a large volume of agreements between musicians, songwriters, record companies, and music publishers, he or she often will have extensive music industry contacts which may be beneficial to developing artists. As a result, a music lawyer also may act as a "deal shopper" for his or her musician client. In addition, legal advice is given on corporate, commercial, copyright, tax and litigious matters, although not all lawyers do all of these types of legal work. A sound knowledge of copyright law is essential to the music business lawyer, because many of the agreements that musicians enter into involve not only services but also the exploitation of copyrights.

B. Conflict of Interest

A lawyer or other person in a fiduciary relationship to the musician should exercise extreme caution when acting in another capacity in

---

Invasion?", in *Entertainment, Publishing, and the Arts Handbook*, (New York: Clark Boardman Company Ltd., 1989), at 181 (herein "Yanover").

[2] Mona Coxson, *Some Straight Talk About the Music Business*, (Toronto: CM Books, 1989), at p. 86.

addition to that of a lawyer or the other primary role (manager, for example). A breach of fiduciary duty and conflicts of interest can result. Conflicts of interest can arise: (1) when the lawyer is performing the role of both lawyer and another role; and (2) because of the relatively small size of the music business and the limited number of lawyers who do most of the work; as a result, a lawyer may represent the same clients in a number of different capacities.[3]

(iii) Accountants

The role of an accountant may include servicing the bookkeeping, accounting, and tax planning needs of a musician and in order to do so, he or she should be familiar with the specific tax and accounting

---

[3] For a discussion of these issues, see, for example, Jerry S. Grafstein, "Ethical Constraints, Conflicts of Interest, Applicable Regulations of the Law Society of Upper Canada", in *Supporting the Star (or the Prospect?)*, (Toronto: Canadian Bar Association, Continuing Legal Education, 1978), at pp. 101-106. See also the case of *McCauley Music Ltd. v. Solomon*, [1982] O.J. No. 997 (Ont. H.C.), appeal dismissed (June 7, 1984), (Ont. C.A.), which discusses at length the conflicts of interest arising between Bernard Solomon who acted as lawyer for McCauley Music Ltd. and Dan Hill, and Finkelstein and Fiedler, who were managers of Hill. The case was ultimately decided upon a question of Solomon's negligence in that he failed to advise McCauley Music of the notice required to exercise the option to keep contracts with Hill from expiring. This case stated it is the duty of the lawyer to advise the client of such conflicts or potential conflicts. See also The Law Society of Upper Canada's *Rules of Professional Conduct*, in particular, Rule 5, *Conflicts of Interest*, and associated commentary which makes it clear that a conflict exists where the lawyer has a financial interest in the transaction. There are numerous articles and cases concerning conflicts of interest outside the context of the music industry; the leading case is *Martin v. Gray* indexed as *MacDonald Estate v. Martin*, [1990] 3 S.C.R. 1235 (S.C.C.). See also, B.G. Smith, *Professional Conduct for Canadian Lawyers*, (Toronto: Butterworths, 1989), pp. 27-31. For a discussion in the U.S. context, see S.L. Kadison and Norman L. Wilky, "Attorney and Client", in Walter Lorimer and Phalen Hurewitz, Eds., *Syllabus on Representing Musical Artists: Legal Business and Practical Aspects*, (Beverly Hills Bar Association and the University of Southern California Law Center, 1975), at pp. 2-50. Some recent U.S. articles are: "Crossing the Thin Line Between Manager and Attorney in the Entertainment Industry", Gary Greenberg, 14 Ent. & Sports Law., Fall 1996, at p. 7; "Agents, Managers, and Lawyers: A Roadmap for the Entertainment Attorney", Kenneth J. Abdo, 14 Ent. & Sports Law., Fall 1996, at p. 7; "Conflict of Interest in Entertainment Law Practice, Revisited", Richard E. Flamm and Joseph B. Anderson, 14 Ent. & Sports Law., Spring 1996, at p. 3; "Conflicts in the Entertainment Industry?...Not!", E. McPherson, 10 Ent. & Sports Law., Winter, 1993, at p. 5; and "A Response to Conflicts in the Entertainment Industry?... Not!", 11 Ent. & Sports Law., Summer 1993, at p. 8. See also *Croce v. Kurnit* (1982), 565 F. Supp. 884, which held that a lawyer who was a partner in a publishing company had a fiduciary duty to Jim Croce when Croce signed a publishing agreement even though he had not been retained by him. However, although the lawyer/publisher was found to have such a fiduciary duty to Croce, the court ultimately refused to nullify the recording and publishing contracts as Croce had requested, finding that the contracts did not differ substantially from standard industry practices. See also *Croce v. Kurnit* (1984), 737 F. 2d 229.

issues that arise in the music business, including GST returns, in some instances. The accountant also gives advice as to the choice of business entity, bookkeeping systems, and the need to "interpret and verify royalty statements".[4]   More specifically, an accountant prepares financial statements, files income tax returns, and occasionally conducts audits of music publishing and record companies in order to verify royalty statements.

(iv) Business Advisers

As discussed, in Canada the personal manager is usually the musician's business manager also. It is more common in the United States for an artist to have separate personal and business managers, particularly for the more established, commercially successful acts. If the business manager is separate from the personal manager, the business adviser may be an accountant, lawyer, or a person who advises only on estate, insurance, banking, or investment matters.[5]   The business advisor is retained on a fee basis, or sometimes on a commission basis, for example, 2% - 6% of the musician's gross income.[6]

(v) Publicists

The publicist or "PR" person is retained either independently by the musician, or by the record company or manager to promote the musician to and in the media. A publicist also may be an employee of a record company. Sometimes musicians will engage the publicist on a general retainer, on an hourly rate, or on a "per contract" basis. Publicists are also discussed in Chapter 7, "Live Performance", concerning their role in media relations and publicity relating to live performances.

---

[4] Lee Frascogna, *Successful Artist Management*, (New York: Watson-Guptill, 1978), at 81. See also, generally, Joseph Taubman, *In Tune With the Music Business*, (New York: Law-Arts Publishers, 1980), at pp. 90-91. See Chapter 148, pp. 148.1-148.8 of Fox, cited below, note 23, for a discussion of a business advisor agreement.

[5] *Ibid.*, Frascogna at 82 and Taubman at pp. 88-89.

[6] See Quast, cited above, note 1 at p. 201, and various Bar Association and Law Society materials.

(vi) Managers

A. Personal

The personal manager's role is "planning, organizing, and attending to all details that will help further the [musician's] career."[7] This includes: (1) creative guidance; (2) marketing the talent; (3) using industry contacts to create new opportunities for the artist; (4) advising, guiding, and counselling the artist on all key career decisions; (5) taking a lead role in finding and negotiating agreements on behalf of the artist, often through a lawyer; (6) assisting the musician in building the best "team" possible, including selecting an agent, lawyer, publicist, and if applicable, a business manager; and (7) if total management - as opposed to personal management only - is involved, a manager will usually assume the administrative duties, which might include legal work, accounting, overseeing business investments, and secretarial work.[8] The personal manager may function also as a business manager or road manager. In short, the personal manager of a musician does anything from "negotiating million-dollar contracts to picking up the star's laundry".[9] The personal manager is integral to a musician's success.

B. Business

The business manager may function as a business adviser but primarily is concerned with managing (rather than advising) the musician in business dealings. This includes bookkeeping and accounting on a day-to-day basis, and collecting monies owing to the musician. The business manager may be an assistant or employee of the musician's personal manager. As discussed above, a business manager who is separate from a personal manager is more common in the U.S. than in Canada.

C. Road

The road manager oversees the details of live performances. Such details include supervising the transportation, maintenance, and repair

---

[7] Coxson, *Some Straight Talk* ... cited above, note 2 at 132.

[8] *Ibid.*, at 133.

[9] David Baskerville, *Music Business Handbook and Career Guide*, Third Ed., (Denver, Co.: The Sherwood Company, 1982), at 154.

of musical equipment, travel and accommodation arrangements, administering travel and tour budgets, overseeing any border-crossing, customs, and immigration matters that may arise, stage, sound, and light production at the show(s) and any other details of life on the road. The road manager may be either an assistant to the personal manager, or in the case of personal managers or musicians not yet well established in the industry, the personal manager may be the business and/or road manager also.

(vii) Summary

The various responsibilities of the personal representatives outlined above are often borne by the same person. For example, a manager who is also the musician's booking agent is not unusual.

The two main entities that represent musicians are: (1) booking agents; and (2) personal managers. At various stages, lawyers and accountants play important roles in the musician's career, but generally, booking agents (engagements) and personal managers (career development assistance) are the most important persons representing a musician on a daily basis. The purpose of hiring personal representatives is to free the musician to be a musician; that is, to record, write and perform songs. There is a necessity to work with trustworthy representatives, as trust is fundamental to any "agency" relationship, such as that between the artist and manager, or between the artist and other personal representatives. This should be kept in mind when a musician is considering forming any of these relationships.

Not all musicians require every personal representative referred to above. A musician's needs depend upon many factors: their particular goals and future career plans; whatever stage of their career in which they presently find themselves; and the fans' and the music industry's general demands for their services. For example, some artists handle their own personal management and booking, and feel that they cannot afford the services of personal representatives. However, a successful recording musician usually requires a team of representatives, which may consist of all or any combination of the representatives discussed above.

2. Booking Agents and the AFM

AFM-licensed agents do not have to book exclusively either AFM members or non-members. However, they cannot: (a) book non-union musicians using AFM form agreements; or (b) book AFM member musicians using agreements which are not AFM-approved agreements. These are founding tenets of the Agreement between AFM-licensed agents and the AFM.

(a) AFM Exclusive Agent-Musician Agreement

At the point when the musician is established and in demand, he or she may enter into the AFM Exclusive Agent-Musician Agreement.[10] Although available at each 'local', the AFM Exclusive Agent-Musician Agreement is a contract created and approved by the International AFM. The term of this agreement usually will not exceed three years, although in some cases this agreement can be for a term of up to five years. The term is negotiable. It is an exclusive, worldwide agreement with respect to the agent's services, meaning only that particular agent is permitted to book the act throughout the world, unless the parties agree that it will be otherwise.[11] The agent, on the other hand, may book as many other acts as he or she wishes, unless otherwise stated in the agreement. It is not unusual, for example, to have one exclusive agent for Canada and another for the U.S. or the rest of the world.

The agent's primary role is to assist in obtaining and negotiating fees and other terms for engagements between the musician and the purchaser of the musician's services. The musician must approve all engagements. The agent may advise the musician regarding the live performance aspect of his or her musical career, and promote and publicize the musician's name and likeness. In this regard, however, the agent usually does not obtain agreements concerning the musician's merchandising rights. This is part of the responsibility of the musician's personal manager. The agent is not prevented from entering into business ventures, nor is the musician prevented from employing a personal manager. The agent has the right to publicize the fact that the agent is the exclusive booking agent and representative for the musician.

The agent is entitled to a percentage of the musician's gross receipts for services rendered. These percentages are up to 15% on steady engagements, or for engagements which are three days or less, the agent's fee may be up to 20%. When two agents book the same engagement, the combined maximum commission chargeable by the two agents is still 20% and the total commission is divided between the

---

[10] Reproduced in full in Appendix 3. See also Fox, cited below, note 23 at chapter 149 for a detailed discussion of the manager/artist agreement.

[11] This is often done by an addendum. See Fox, cited below, note 23, for comments useful in drafting this addendum. See Quast, above, note 1, at pp. 202-206 for a general discussion of the agent agreement.

two agents. Where the musician has terminated the term of one agency agreement and hired another agent, a reduced commission may be negotiated for either or both the current and former agents, or the musician's fee may be commissioned by two agents at full commission rates. The agent agreement should not conflict with the rights granted by the musician to a manager, nor apply to other than personal appearances or live performances of the musician. Payments to the musician for performances booked by an AFM-licensed agent cannot be less than scale. Additionally, the agent is required to negotiate his or her fee exclusive of and in addition to these minimum scale payments to the musician. The result is that payments to AFM member musicians are not affected negatively by the agent's commission. Further, agents' commissions are not payable unless and until the musician receives his or her full contracted fee.

The exclusive agreement may be terminated by the musician if the agent does not obtain engagements for the musician for: (a) any four consecutive weeks; (b) 20 cumulative weeks during a six-month period; or (c) if there is not a total of 40 cumulative weeks of engagements within a year. Other terms may be negotiated and if the agent fails to meet them, the musician should be able to terminate the term of the agreement, for example, for the agent's failure to obtain minimum fees or obtain a minimum gross income for the musician. The agent should have the right to terminate the term of the agreement if the musician becomes disabled, or if the musician unreasonably refuses to accept engagements.

This agreement is governed by the terms of the AFM's Booking Agent Agreement for use in Canada. The AFM's constitution and by-laws are incorporated as part of the agreement. The agent must maintain its status as an AFM booking agent. The agreement cannot be assigned by either party without consent of the AFM. The agreement must be filed with the AFM local within 30 days of its execution and be approved by the AFM in writing for it to become effective. A key person clause or leaving member clause can be negotiated and set out in the agreement. These clauses are discussed below in the context of the management agreement.

(b) Non-Union Agent Agreements

Non-union agent agreements are contracts created and used by booking agents who are not licensed by the AFM. These agreements are not AFM created or approved; however, they may be similar to the

AFM Booking Agreement.[12] Typical clauses for negotiation in a non-union agreement include: (1) the territory, that is whether it is to be worldwide or for the territory of Canada only; (2) the scope of the agent's authority to obtain engagements - for example, film engagements may not be included; (3) the term of this agreement - typically one to five years, perhaps with some performance obligations to be met, such as the obligation to obtain a certain level of gross revenue in a specific time frame; (4) whether there is a leaving member clause and a key person clause (these clauses are discussed below in the context of the personal management agreement in sections 3(g)(ii) and 3(h) respectively); (5) the commission fee, which is usually in the range of 10% to 15% and is sometimes 20% depending on the type of engagement; (6) the obligation to collect money for unpaid commissions (it is negotiable whether the obligation would be the agent's or the musician's); (7) any right beyond the right to obtain live performance engagements or personal appearances is negotiable, for example, the right to a percentage of merchandising revenue such as T-shirt sales at live performances (generally, it is preferable for the musician that such a clause not be included, but this is negotiable); and (8) often, an arbitration clause. The arbitration clause is discussed below in the context of the personal management agreement in section 3(k)(ii).

(c) National: Booking Agent Agreement for Use in Canada

The aim of this national agreement is: (a) to ensure that "competent, fair, honest and scrupulous booking agents" provide services to musicians; (b) to "prevent unfair dealing"; and (c) to "maintain minimum fees" for AFM members.[13] Under this agreement, the AFM approves and licenses an agent to act as an agent for AFM members.[14]

The agent is responsible for any "sub-agents" which may be employed or engaged by the agent. The agent does not act as an engager, but as an agent to secure engagements for musicians. Any deposit for payment of a musician's services is held in escrow for the musician. All contracts for bookings are to be filed with the AFM. No

---

[12] See Fox, cited below, note 23, chapter 149 at pp. 149-159 for a discussion of non-union agreements, sometimes referred to as a general services agreement. See also form 149-5 for a sample non-union agent agreement. The AFM booking agreement is a model for such agreements.

[13] Booking Agent Agreement for Use in Canada, Para. A, p. 1.

[14] See Article 22, Sect. 4, 5 of By-laws of AFM Revised, September 15, 1997, which prohibits AFM members from engaging booking agents that are not licensed by the AFM.

agent can knowingly solicit engagers who are on the AFM's unfair list. This agreement cannot be assigned without the AFM's approval.

Any disputes arising from this agreement are to be submitted to the vice-president of the Canadian AFM. If disputes are not resolved at this stage, some are submitted to the secretary-treasurer of the AFM for a decision by the AFM's International Executive Board. If the dispute is still not resolved, it is settled in court.[15] When there is a claim against an AFM member for commissions, either the local association or the Canadian vice-president's office may deal with the matter at first instance, or if it is not resolved at this stage, then it is submitted to the secretary-treasurer of the AFM for a decision by the AFM's International Executive Board, as outlined above.

Statements of account are to be rendered by the agent for the musician. There is a one-year limitation on claims arising from such statements of account. A percentage on the amount of unpaid commissions is allowed. The agent is paid directly by the engager or the musician.

The AFM has the power to cancel the agent's licence. The agent is entitled to a hearing by the vice-president from Canada and may be represented by legal counsel prior to such cancellation.

Schedule 1 to this agreement sets out the maximum commissions which an agent may charge. These are 15%, if the engagement is two or more days per week, and 20% for single miscellaneous engagements of one day. If the agent is also acting as manager, the agent/manager may charge, as a management fee, 5% in addition to the commission charged as agent.

(d) AFM By-laws

If there is a conflict between the by-laws of the AFM (international) and those of the local, the AFM (international) by-laws govern.[16] No AFM member is to retain a booking agent unless such agent is a party to the booking agent agreement with the AFM.[17] A member musician may act as a booking agent without becoming licensed as such, but only with respect to engagements performed within the jurisdiction of the local in which they are a member, and only if they do so on a casual basis.[18] In these instances where a member acts as a booking agent, the commissions and other terms and conditions are the same as those

---

[15] Booking Agent Agreement ... above, note 13, p. 3, Para. 9(a).

[16] See discussion of local, national and international aspects of the AFM in Chapter 5, "Labour".

[17] *Ibid.*, Sect. 4. See also Sect. 6.

[18] *Ibid.*, Sect. 5. The AFM must approve exclusive agreements with AFM members and booking agents.

prescribed under the national agreement.[19] Musicians sometimes act as booking agents to supplement their income from live performances, recording or producing. The by-laws state that no exclusive agreement with any musician shall exceed five years, but the AFM recommends a term of no more than three years.[20] The agreement is to be terminated if the terms (as discussed under the AFM's local agreement for providing engagements) are not met. A booking agent is not entitled to demand that an engager give them booking privileges to the exclusion of other agents.[21]

(e) Booking Agents as Personal Managers: The AFM Personal Management Agreement

AFM booking agents are not prevented from acting as personal managers. However, they are required to sign a personal management agreement which provides, among other things, that

"the personal manager agrees to advise and counsel the artist with respect to the following: (a) the selection of literary, artistic and musical materials; (b) any and all matters relating to publicity, public relations and advertising; (c) the adoption of the proper format for the best presentation of the artist's talents; (d) the selection of booking agents to procure maximum employment for the artist; (e) the types of employment which the artist should accept and which would prove most beneficial to their career; (f) any and all other duties customarily performed by personal managers in the entertainment field."[22]

The percentage of gross monies to which the manager is entitled for the services listed above is set out in the agreement. Schedule 1 of the booking agent agreement for Canada states that personal managers who are also AFM booking agents are allowed a management commission of 5% of monies received by the member for each engagement, in addition to their agent commission. This agreement incorporates by reference the constitution, by-laws and regulations of the AFM and is not assignable.

---

[19] *Ibid.*, Sect. 5.

[20] *Ibid.*, Sect. 7.

[21] *Ibid.*, Sect. 8. Other details concerning reports for all engagements, and the requirement to list AFM members on all contracts, for example, are set out in these by-laws.

[22] Quoted from the AFM Personal Management Agreement, which is reproduced in Appendix 3.

3. The Personal Management Agreement[23]

(a) General Comments

(i) Legal Relationship

The legal relationship between the personal manager (the manager) and a musician is that of "agent and principal". That is, the musician is the principal and the manager acts as the agent of and is engaged by the musician. It is a fiduciary relationship and a fiduciary relationship imposes a duty of utmost loyalty.[24] The manager, when carrying out fiduciary duties, must ensure there is: (1) no conflict of interest; (2) no secret profit; and (3) no appropriation of "corporate opportunities or opportunities in favour of the beneficiary of the trust".[25] In addition, "a fiduciary is not allowed to profit by direct dealing with a principal and his property; and a fiduciary must not use his position to appropriate for himself benefits which he ought to have acquired, if at all, for the principal".[26]

A clearly worded contract which sets out the scope of and limitations on the authority of the personal manager is essential, because the "agency" relationship can arise expressly, impliedly, or

---

[23] For a detailed discussion on personal management agreements, on a clause-by-clause basis, other than this text, see also Donald C. Farber, General Editor, *Entertainment Industry Contracts Negotiating and Drafting Guide*, Part IV Music, Samuel J. Fox, Ed., (New York: Matthew Bender, 1990), subpart C, Chapter 147 (herein Fox). See also Cynthia Pinkos and Allan H. Bombser, "The Musician's Personal Management Contract: Sample Contracts and Comments", (1985-1986), Vol. 10, Columbia V.L.A. Journal of Law and the Arts 245 (herein "Pinkos"); and Greg Stevens, Chapter 3, "Management", in Shane Simpson and Greg Stevens, *Music: The Business & the Law*, (Sydney: The Law Book Company Limited, 1986), at pp. 20-29 (herein "Simpson"). See also *Counselling Clients in the Entertainment Industry*, (New York: Practising Law Institute, 1988), at pp. 131-155 for a useful discussion and pp. 155-220 for sample management agreements.

[24] The fiduciary obligations between manager and musician also have been applied to publishing and record agreements to which a musician is a signatory, and where the manager has an interest in such company. See the *O'Sullivan* case, note 30, below. See also the recent British case of *Nelson v. Rye and another*, [1996] 2 All E.R. 186 (Eng. Ch. Div.), in which the plaintiff, formerly a member of the group Bebop Deluxe, sued his former manager for an accounting. Although the defendant manager was under a fiduciary duty to the plaintiff artist, the plaintiff's delay in bringing suit precluded him from obtaining an accounting for the several years in question.

[25] *Keech v. Sandford* (1976), 25 E.R. 223, as summarized by Stephen Selznick in "Legal Aspects of Entertainment and the Arts", Sect. B, *The Business Entity*, at pp. 9-10 (herein "Selznick"). See also Sanford Jossen, "Fiduciary Aspects of The Personal Manager's Relationship with a Performing Artist" (1981), Vol. 11 P.A.R. 108 for the U.S. perspective.

[26] *Ibid.* See also *Boardman v. Phipps*, [1967] 2 A.C. 46, affirming (sub nom. *Phipps v. Boardman*), [1965] Ch. 992. This case generally has been applied in Canada.

"even ostensibly" by the conduct of the parties,[27] and the personal manager can have the authority to bind the musician to third parties even in the absence of the musician's knowledge or consent.

Sometimes in practice a manager may be a record producer and music publisher also, although this is not advisable since conflicts of interest can result. Generally, the manager has a duty to disclose material facts in relation to his or her position as "agent" and fiduciary of the musician, and care should be taken to avoid conflicts of interest and a breach of fiduciary duties.[28] Conflicts of interest were discussed above in section 1(b)(ii) B.

(ii) Business Relationship

To be successful, managers require "money, patience, promotional abilities, basic business and baby-sitting skills, some legal knowledge, and above all credibility and a phone book full of numbers and contacts. They also need to be hardnosed."[29] A successful business relationship between a musician and a manager requires mutual trust. The manager must be able to provide sound advice and the musician must be willing to follow it.

(iii) Trial Basis

It is often advisable for the manager and the musician to work together on a trial basis, that is, for a limited period of time (e.g., six months), in order to determine whether they can work together on a more long-term basis. A trial arrangement of this sort may be on the

[27] *Ibid.*, Selznick at pp. 9-10. A detailed discussion of agency law is beyond the scope of this book. These legal issues are only highlighted here. For a general discussion of agency law, see, for example: G.H.L. Fridman, *The Law of Agency*, Fourth Ed., (London: Butterworths, 1976), (herein "Fridman").

[28] *Syllabus on Representing Musical Artists* ... cited above, note 3, at pp. 85-86. See also Chapter 10, "Personal Service Contracts" for a discussion of the *Clifford Davis Management* case. Clifford Davis managed Fleetwood Mac and also acted as their music publisher. The agreement was not enforced, on the basis of inequality of bargaining power, undue influence, and inadequate consideration because the contract did not obligate the manager to do anything. Conflict of interest was mentioned. See also below, note 30, and the cases cited therein. Another relevant discussion of the types of conflicts that arise between artist and manager, with numerous examples and a discussion of various approaches by U.S. and English courts, can be found in Hal I. Gilenson, "Badlands: Artist-Personal Manager Conflicts of Interest In The Music Industry", in (1991), Cardozo Arts & Ent. L. J. 501.

[29] Richard Flohil, "The Biz", Chapter 10, in Peter Goddard, Phillip Kamin, Eds., *Shakin All Over The Rock `N' Roll Years in Canada*, (Toronto: McGraw-Hill Ryerson Limited, 1989), at p. 190.

basis of a "handshake", that is, an oral agreement, or may be a written agreement. A written agreement is preferable even in the trial period since it can avoid the legal uncertainties present in an oral arrangement. A trial agreement, which is in writing, may be for a short initial period (six months, for example), but can include all of the terms of the long-term management agreement which are discussed below, and it can be drafted in either a short or long-form agreement format. It is also common that if, during the trial period, a specified performance obligation which was imposed on the manager is not met (for example, the obligation to obtain a record agreement), then the term of the agreement would terminate, ending the artist-manager relationship.

(iv) Definitions

It is advisable to define the following in the agreement: (1) the parties to the agreement, including both the musician and manager - sometimes the manager will be an individual, and sometimes a partnership or a corporation. It is always important to clarify which individuals or business entities will be bound by the terms of the agreement, and who is "on the hook" in the event of a law suit; (2) the scope within the entertainment field that the manager has to bind the musician - in other words, (i) will the manager be overseeing the music career only or all of the artist's endeavours throughout the entertainment industry; and (ii) what powers will the manager have to bind the artist to various agreements or commitments; (3) gross earnings / net earnings - will the manager be paid before or after making payments to third parties or paying expenses; which monies or income sources will be commissionable and which will not; and exactly what costs, expenses or third party payments will be deducted before calculating the "net" income, if a "net" calculation is chosen; and (4) commissions after the expiration of the term of the contract - also called the "Sunset Clause". These terms are discussed in the relevant sections below. Other terms may require specific definition in a specific contractual situation, or else ambiguity and legal disputes can result.

(v) Independent Legal Advice

Without independent legal advice, a management agreement may not be upheld by a court of law. More specifically, if there is an inequality of bargaining power between two parties (the manager is typically the established party in the music business and in a superior bargaining position), then the agreement may not be upheld if independent legal advice has not been obtained.[30] It should be noted that a provision is often inserted in the contract stating that the musician has been advised to seek independent legal advice. However, if independent legal advice was not obtained, and even more particularly, if the bargain struck was unconscionable or in restraint of trade, then such a provision would not result in the court upholding the contract.[31]

(vi) No Partnership

The management agreement is usually structured as an agreement between two independent contractors (artist and manager), not as a partnership between them.

(vii) Compensation

The commission (i.e. percentage-based) agreement, rather than a salary arrangement, is by far the most common form of management compensation. However, either a salary-based or a commission agreement is preferable to a situation where the manager is also a shareholder or partner of the musician or his/her corporation, because the musician is better protected against conflicts of interest that may arise.[32]

(b) Exclusivity

(i) Musician

The musician typically contracts with the manager on an exclusive basis throughout the world.[33] This means that the musician is

---

[30] See the *Clifford Davis Management* case discussed in Chapter 10, "Personal Service Contracts". Note, however, that even when independent legal advice was obtained, recording and publishing agreements were not upheld in the *Holly Johnson* case because they were found to be in restraint of trade.

[31] See the *Holly Johnson* case discussed in Chapter 10, "Personal Service Contracts".

[32] See Simpson cited above, note 23, at p. 30 and Gilenson, above at note 28 for a discussion of the problems involved in this regard.

[33] See Fox 14-1, cited above, note 23. However, Pinkos, cited above, note 23, argues at p. 261 that there is no reason why the territory of the agreement should not be limited to the territory in which the manager is most effective, for example Canada or the U.S. The territory could be extended when the manager becomes more effective in those territories. Sometimes a co-management agreement is entered into, whereby one

prohibited from retaining the services of any other person, firm or corporation for the purposes of managing the musician. This exclusivity provides incentive to the manager to exploit the musician's career to the fullest and prevents two or more managers from competing with each other. However, the parties may enter into a co-management agreement, as discussed below in section 3(1).

(ii) Manager

The manager does not typically contract with the musician on an exclusive basis, and is therefore free to manage other artists. However, the musician may try to restrict the manager to a specific number of acts that the manager is allowed to manage. This may be justified in some circumstances - for example, where due to the small size or inexperience of the management company, it may be difficult for the manager to manage more than three or four acts competently, and conflicts of interest could arise.[34] However, the manager typically will manage two, three or more acts in order to earn a living exclusively from management in the music business, and may be reluctant to agree to such a restriction.

(c) Manager's Services

The manager's services clause either will be broadly and vaguely worded, or may state specifically the types of services to be rendered, for example: "Manager shall exert all reasonable efforts to further artist's career as well as to co-operate with artist in the interests of promoting artist's career during the term of this agreement".[35] Alternatively, the manager's services may be set out more specifically as follows: (1) to act as musician's negotiator in all contracts; (2) to be available and confer with the musician in all matters concerning the musician's career; (3) to exploit the musician's personality in all media; (4) to engage and direct all other agents including booking agents; and

---

manager (not the musician) hires another manager in another territory. This is discussed in the text in section 3(l) below.

[34] The possibility of conflicts of interest is present. For example, the manager may be representing both the headlining and support acts, particularly where the manager is also a booking agent representing several competing acts. See also Fridman, cited above, note 27 at p. 138. In this situation, the agent (manager) must disclose his or her interest and act with the utmost good faith.

[35] Peter E. Steinmetz, "Commentary on Negotiation Points: The Manager's Perspective", in *Syllabus on Music Industry: Contract Negotiations and the Law*, (Toronto: York University, 1980), at 191.

(5) to represent the musician in all dealings with labour organizations.[36] When the management agreement is worded too broadly or vaguely, the contract may be unenforceable.[37]

The management agreement usually states that the manager is not responsible for obtaining employment (i.e. live performances) for the musician, and although there is no obligation to do so, the manager often is either instrumental in obtaining employment or actually does obtain employment for the musician, particularly in the early stages of the musician's career and until there is enough demand to attract a professional booking agent to handle live performances. A manager is not legally prohibited from obtaining engagements for musicians in Canada.[38]

---

[36] *Ibid.*, at 219, adapted from the musician-oriented precedent supplied by Peter M. Thall. *Quaere*, however, whether R.S.O. 1990, c. E.13, for example, and particularly s. 1(b), acting in conjunction with and at request of talent agency are applicable.

[37] This has been the case in the U.S. and may be the case in Canada. See, however, *Meyers v. Nolan*, 18 Cal. App. 2d 319, where the contract was upheld on the basis of the reasonable intentions of the parties, and *Burgermeisters Etc. Corporation v. Bowman*, 277 Cal. App. 2d 274, where the contract was upheld (though its terms were uncertain) on the basis of partial performance. Both cases are cited in *Syllabus on Music Industry* above, note 35 at 193.

[38] See, however, the U.S. position, particularly developed in California where personal managers are prohibited from soliciting employment; *Buchwald v. Superior Court* (1967), 254 Cal. App. 2d 347 (the *Jefferson Airplane* case) or the recent cases of *Wachs v. Curry*, 16 Cal. Rptr. 2d 496, *Waisbren v. Peppercorn*, 48 Cal. Rptr. 2d 437, and *Hall v. X Management*, T.A.C. No. 19-90, at 37 (California Labor Commissioner, 1992). See also Erik B. Atzbach, "Drawing the Line Between Personal Managers and Talent Agents: Waisbren v. Peppercorn", (1996), 4 U.C.L.A. Ent. L. Rev. 81. Talent agents must be licensed by the California Labor Commissioner. See, however, Paul L. Brindze, "California Assembly Bill 997: The Personal Manager's Relief Act", in *Entertainment, Publishing and the Arts Handbook*, (New York: Clark Boardman, 1983), at 247, which surveys legislation affecting personal managers in California. Talent agencies are dealt with in Division 2, Part 6, Chapter 4 of the *California Labor Code* at ss. 1700-1700.47. See also Quast, cited above, note 1, at p. 195. An exemption from a manager's prohibition against procuring employment is, for example, a manager's right to obtain recording contracts, found at s. 1700.44(a) of the *California Labor Code*. The *California Labor Code*, s. 1700.4, amended 1988, would apply. Note the restrictions regarding commission for talent agents; unlike the *New York General Business Law*, there is no exemption for managers. Under the New York statute, procuring a record contract is deemed to be procuring an agreement for employment; however, personal managers will be exempt where procuring a recording contract is only incidental to other management duties. See, for example, *Pine v. Laine*, 36 A.D. 2d 924, 321 N.Y.S. 2d 303 (1st Dept. 1971), where the plaintiff was denied recovery for services rendered in negotiating a recording contract because he was not licensed as an employment agent, and did not come within the incidental procurement exemption for personal managers. For a further discussion, see also "How New York and Tennessee Regulate Talent Agencies", Paul Karl Lukacs, 14 Ent. & Sports Law, Fall 1996, at p. 15. For the history of California's legislation in this area, see "Agents and Managers: California's Split Personality", Bruce C. Fishelman, (1991), 11 Loyola Ent. L. J. 401. Recent amendments to the *Employment Standards Act*, R.S.B.C. 1996, c. 113, in force July 19, 1999, now require talent agencies to obtain a licence under that act. A

(d) Manager's Authority

(i) Scope

The scope of the manager's authority should be specified clearly. Generally, the manager's authority should be to deal with the day-to-day business aspects of the musician's career and to render advice concerning the musician's career. The musician should have primary control over and be concerned with the creative aspects of being a musician,[39] however, there should be some checks and balances on the manager's authority and the musician is well advised to stay informed as to all business dealings over which the manager has responsibility. The suggested limitations are discussed below.

(ii) Limitations

It is suggested that the musician have some approval, subject to the manager's input, concerning the following: (1) the use of the musician's personality (i.e. his/her name, likeness, photograph, biographical material, facsimile signature, sobriquet, etc.) in merchandising and endorsements; (2) the appointment of other personal representatives; and (3) the scheduling of live performances, including tour schedules, venues, and personal appearances for promotion purposes.[40] Other limitations may be desirable depending on the situation.

---

talent agency is defined as "a person that for a fee engages in the occupation of offering to procure, promising to procure or procuring employment for... performers." The amendments give rights to employees where wages are received by the agency and not paid to the employees in a timely fashion; they are entitled to interest on delinquent payments after a "determination" (s. 80(2)). Also, if a determination or order is made by the Director under the Act, the Director is entitled to a lien on the property of the agency. (s. 87 (1.1)). Directors and officers of corporations that are talent agencies are personally liable for unpaid wages (s. 96(2.1)). Pursuant to the Ontario *Employment Agencies Act*, R.S.O 1990, c. E.13, s. 1, an employment agency is defined as "a business of procuring for a fee, reward or other remuneration persons for employment or employment for persons ...". *Quaere* whether in Ontario, for example, talent agencies would fall under s. 2(b) of the *Employment Agencies Act Regulations*, R.R.O. 1990, Reg. 320, as Class B agencies (i.e., agencies that procure employment for persons other than sitters or homemakers). S. 12(2) of the Regulation sets out applicable rates of commission. Under s. 2 of the Act, a licence is required, or one is liable for a fine under s. 13. Note, however, that generally the manager and musician are self-employed, independent contractors, and therefore it could be argued that they are not seeking employment.

[39] Quast, cited above, note 1, at p. 193.

[40] *Ibid.*, at p. 193.

(iii) Power of Attorney

A. General

A manager often tries to gain a broad power of attorney, that is the right to make decisions and commitments and sign documents on behalf of the musician. This may be for a number of reasons, including the efficient execution of managerial functions, in order to take advantage of opportunities for the musician as they become available, and to administer the business of the artist with a minimum amount of disruption or lost time. A broad power of attorney may include the manager's right: (1) to control the musician's finances (i.e., collecting monies owed to the musician by third parties; making bill payments; conducting audits; and controlling payments to the musicians themselves); (2) to negotiate and sign all contracts, which may include record or publishing contracts, or contracts to borrow money or purchase equipment; (3) to hire all representatives and personnel; and (4) to exploit the musician's personality.[11] The musician should try to limit this power of attorney and, for various legal reasons, the manager should too.[12]

Limitations on the power of attorney are determined by the negotiating strengths of the parties and the parties' personal strengths and weaknesses. Typically, a manager's authority to make commitments and sign contracts on behalf of the musician should be limited by requiring some prior approval by the artist, sometimes in writing, and often with the stipulation that such approval is not to be "unreasonably withheld (by the musician)". It is reasonable for a manager to have the power to sign most live performance contracts, since, due to tour commitments, the musician may be travelling and therefore unavailable to sign agreements personally when such opportunities present themselves. Even though the manager may have a broad power of attorney, third parties such as merchandising companies, record companies and music publishers often will insist on the musician signing such agreements personally. This protects the manager from a claim by the musician that the power of attorney was breached, and ensures the third party that the musician is personally bound to such an agreement.

Occasionally, U.S. language is used in the agreement and the manager is referred to as an "attorney-in-fact" - i.e., a legal agent.

---

[11] Baskerville, *Music Business Handbook* ... cited above, note 9 at 185. See pp. 181-189 generally, for an analysis of a Personal Management Agreement. See Chapter 9, "Merchandising" regarding personality rights.

[12] See, for example, the *Powers of Attorney Act*, R.S.O. 1990, c. P.20.

Presumably it is included to ensure clarity and enforceability if the contract is litigated in a U.S. court, but it is probably unnecessary when the governing law is that of a Canadian province.

B. Coupled with an Interest

Many agreements use the term "power of attorney coupled with an interest". This tries to extend the power of attorney by granting to the manager an ownership interest in the monies to be collected by the manager. Some agreements go even further and stipulate that the power of attorney is "coupled with an interest" and "irrevocable". This power of attorney will be ineffective and unenforceable unless "the agency (i.e., the management relationship) is for the benefit of the agent (manager), and is to secure the performance of a pre-existing duty or to protect a title", and "the power must be given with consideration"[43] (i.e., with the exchange of money or something else of value). This may only arise, for example, "in the case where a manager makes a loan to the [musician] and simultaneously, the [musician] gives the manager the authority to collect the amount of the loan from third parties and to apply this to the [musician's] loan account".[44]

(e) Manager's Compensation

(i) Commission

Managers are compensated most typically by means of commission payments, because it is difficult to assess the specific value of a manager's contribution to a musician's career. There are other means of compensation such as a flat fee or salary, but commission compensation is standard.

---

[43] Peter Steinmetz, *Syllabus on Music Industry*...cited above, note 35 at pp. 195-196, referring to Restatement Agency Section 138. U.S. and Canadian law appear to be the same in this regard. See *Jay v. Dollarhide*, 3 Cal. App. 3d 1001, 84 Cal. Rptr. 538 (1970), and Phalen G. Hurewitz, "Personal Managers", in *Syllabus on Representing Musical Artists*, cited above in note 3 at pp. 73-74. See also *Black's Law Dictionary*, Rev. 4th Ed., (St. Paul, Minn.: West Publishing Co., 1968), at p.1334 for a definition.

[44] *Ibid.* The effect, if granted, is to require a release from the manager upon termination of the agreement.

A. Gross

In Canada, the commission payable to the manager on gross earnings of the musician is typically in the range of 20% to 25%, depending on the experience and bargaining power of the respective parties. The manager and musician may agree to have the manager's percentage commission escalate based on the triggering of certain events. For example, the commission may increase from 20% to 25% following the second option period or the second album released pursuant to a recording contract, or after the attaining of a specific minimum level of gross earnings. This is sometimes referred to as a "sliding scale" or escalating commission, and could be specified also by providing that the manager will receive 10% in the first year, 15% in the second year, and 20% in the third year of the management agreement. It also may vary with respect to a specific source of income, for example, 10% of music publishing income, 15% of recording income, and 20% of live performance and merchandising income. This percentage is based on the negotiating strengths of the parties, including the experience and relative "clout" that the musician and manager have in the music business. A manager might agree also to a reduced income for the first year or two under the agreement, where the musician is obliged to pay continuing commissions from the same income source (e.g. a record deal) to a former manager.

A commission rate that is too high can cause bitter feelings, financial difficulties for the musician, and a breakdown of the artist-manager relationship. Indeed, combined management and agent commissions are often in the range of 30% to 45% of the musician's gross income, which can prove to be a tremendous burden on artists before they have established their place in the industry and a solid financial base. Conversely, a commission that is too low will not provide adequate incentive for the manager to work hard to generate income for the musician, where the manager also manages one or more other musicians who pay much higher commissions. In some cases, the courts have found management commissions to be excessive and they have been reduced.[45]

Gross earnings typically include all earnings from the "entertainment field".[46] The term entertainment field usually is broadly defined to include income from all sources in the broader entertainment industry, including income as an actor, screenwriter, or

---

[45] See the Australian cases in this regard: *Terzian v. Gattelari*, [1972] A.R. (N.S.W.), reduced from 25% to 10%, 591; and *Layton v. VandVision Promotions*, (Unreptd.), Industrial Commission of New South Wales, (October 11, 1983), No. 354 of 1989, reduced from 40% to 17%.

[46] See Baskerville cited above, note 9 at p. 186.

film producer, but may be limited by exceptions, for example, excluding income from acting or literary pursuits. However, not all earnings may be part of gross earnings, as they also may be limited by excluding specific sources, such as a prior record deal, or by defining "gross income" as only that income above certain pre-established income levels.

Alternatively, commissions may be payable on net earnings or on a combination of gross earnings and net earnings, depending on the income source that is being commissioned - i.e., using a "gross income" basis for recording and publishing income, and a "net income" basis for merchandising and live performance income. Note that commissions should be on those receipts earned and received, not just credited or accruing, otherwise a musician may owe a manager commission on income that is never received.

B. Net

A net income base means gross earnings minus specified expenses such as travel, or agent's commissions. Most managers reject a net earnings commission basis for payment because of the difficulty of controlling "expenses" (which could be anything from payments to background vocalists or sound and light technicians to the musicians' travel and party expenses), all of which can significantly erode the income base upon which a manager's commission is calculated. In some agreements, however, record royalties are commissioned on a net basis, and live performance and publishing income are commissioned on a gross basis.

C. Reduction

The agreement may provide for a reduced percentage commission: (a) until the musician is earning a sufficient amount to justify the full commission - for example, no commissions may be payable until a base amount of $100,000 gross annual income is received; or alternatively (b) only with respect to certain income sources. Care should be taken to avoid exorbitant commissions which try to make up for lost time when no commissions were payable, since they can make it difficult for the musician to earn a living.[47]

---

[47] As discussed above, note 45, the commission may be reduced by the courts.

D. Exclusion

Some exclusions from gross earnings can be negotiated, including earnings from contracts entered into before the current management contract, or earnings from specific sources (such as acting income) where the musician is already established at the time the management agreement is signed. Some other sources of income which may be excluded from the commission base include: (1) performing rights payments; (2) advances from record companies which actually are used for video, record production, tour support or independent radio or television promotion; or (3) payments at less than AFM scale.

E. Continuing Commissions

The continuing commission clause specifies those commissions which will continue after the termination of or expiration of the term of the agreement, and is sometimes referred to as the "sunset clause".[48] The principle behind a sunset or continuing commission clause is that the manager should be compensated for his/her efforts which benefited the musician during the term of the agreement. The musician may argue that a reduced rate of commission to the manager after termination or expiration of the term of the agreement is fair, since the manager is not providing full management services to justify a full commission. The manager, on the other hand, will contend that he/she facilitated or secured the agreement and therefore should benefit from it fully, for as long as the musician benefits from it. A difficult point of negotiation is always how to structure the "sunset" or "wind-down" formula for continuing commissions. A relevant factor to be considered in arriving at this formula is the number of years the agreement was in effect, and whether or not the musician is obliged to pay commissions to a new manager. A formula preferably would be specified so that the musician is not unduly financially burdened when engaging a new manager at a full management percentage. A reduced but increasing or "phased-in" commission also may be negotiated with the new manager, in order to ease the financial burden of payments to two managers (one current, one former) and to facilitate the transition.

The former manager may be entitled to a percentage of continuing earnings from specified sources only. The following are some examples:

---

[48] See Peter Steinmetz, *Syllabus on Music Industry* ... cited above, note 35 at pp. 201-202 for a detailed discussion of a continuing commission formula.

Scenario One   (1) full management commission on recording and publishing agreements, but only on such copyrights and recording masters created during the term of the agreement;
(2) a declining scale on all other income.

Scenario Two   A declining scale on all income sources after the term as follows:

Year One	20%
Year Two	15%
Year Three	10%
Year Four	5%
Year Five	0%

Each sunset clause is unique to the parties and should be negotiated and drafted carefully.

(ii) Time of Payment

Payments are usually on a weekly, monthly, or even a quarterly basis, and should be stated clearly.

(f) Finances

(i) Expenses

The manager is normally reimbursed for expenses incurred to further the musician's career, but limitations may be placed on the "money, area, time and type" so that the musician has the control over the manager's spending in this regard.[49] There are numerous ways to structure an expense provision, and because it can be a source for disagreements, thought is required in drafting it. Typically, expenses over a specific amount (for example, $500 or $1,000) require approval of the musician. Expenses should not include the manager's office overhead, but all other expenses typically are charged to the musician and are deducted prior to paying the musician's share of net or gross income, as the case may be.

---

[49] Frascogna cited above, note 4, at p. 58; *Ibid.*, Chapter 5, "The Management Contract" also contains a useful general discussion of the personal management agreement.

(ii) Loans

A manager often is called on to lend money to a musician for career development, because musicians find it difficult to borrow money from a bank or find private investors for their career. Preferably this should not be done, but if it is, independent legal advice concerning this loan agreement is advisable. A repayment plan with specified interest can prevent disputes when the debtor/creditor relationship impinges on the existing agent/principal relationship.[50] Less typically, a manager may require a collateral mortgage or promissory note in order to secure the loan.

(g) Group Provisions

(i) Name

Typically in this clause, a musician's professional name or the group's name is subject to a representation and warranty as to the musician's ownership of such name, and the manager is usually indemnified from any claims which arise concerning the name. If the group disbands, the manager may seek to continue managing a group consisting of former members, or perhaps consisting entirely of new members under the group name. Preferably the manager would not have an interest in the group name except in very specific circumstances.

(ii) Leaving or Joining Members

The manager may justifiably seek to have some control over group members who are leaving or joining. However, since it is the musician who must be able to work with a new group member for long periods on various personal and professional levels, the musician's consent also should be required. The manager may have the right to terminate the agreement if the progress of the group is seriously impeded by a member who is not contributing to the group. Consider the situation where there is a group partnership or a shareholders agreement and

---

[50] See Simpson cited above, note 23, at p. 37 for a discussion. See also the *Interest Act*, R.S.C. 1985, c. I-15, and in particular s. 4. The agreement must state a yearly rate pursuant to a written agreement, otherwise no interest greater than 5% per annum will be allowed. See the case of *Niagara Air Bus Inc. v. Camerman Alexander Coach Lines Inc.*, and see also *4500 Taxi Ltd. v. Camerman* (1991), 3 O.R. (3d) (Ont. C.A.), at 108, which interprets s. 4 of this statute.

no provision for buy-out; the manager who insists on expelling a member may be committing a tort (i.e., a civil wrong giving rise to a law suit) for interfering with contractual relations, or may be committing a breach of contract which has the effect of disrupting the group.[51]   In groups, personal alliances can have as much importance as the musical talent within the group. The group provision requires serious thought; its impact is great. Careers can be made or broken when a leaving or new member clause is invoked.

(iii) Joint and Several Obligations

When group members sign a management contract, a provision is usually inserted making the members both jointly and severally liable. The result is that one musician may be liable for the other musicians' contractual obligations, such as loan repayments to the manager. This in turn may result in the salary or other income of one member being garnished to re-pay group debts. Whether or not all provisions will be interpreted to be joint and several is determined by the courts in a given fact situation.[52]

(h) Key Person and Assignment

In keeping with the importance of personal relationships involved in this agreement, if the key person in a management company or agency is no longer there, then the musician may wish to terminate the agreement upon giving notice after a specified period of time. Similarly, the manager may want to terminate the term of the agreement if the key person in the group leaves. In addition, the musician may wish to stipulate that the contract cannot be assigned by the manager to a third party, at least not without the musician's consent or a guarantee that the key management person remains involved as the group's day-to-day manager following the assignment. Typically, a musician will have the right to assign the agreement to a corporation under which he or she carries on business, provided documents of personal adherence are entered into which are acceptable to the manager.

---

[51] Hurewitz, *Syllabus on Representing Musical Artists* ...cited above, note 3 at p. 102. See also Pinkos cited above, note 23 at p. 274.

[52] See, for a U.S. example, *Williams v. Mercury Record Corporation* (1961), 295 F. 2d 284, where it was held on the specific facts of this case that the liability of the members was joint only; group members could contract individually with other record companies.

(i) Representations, Warranties and Indemnity

A representation and warranty is a statement by one party to an agreement effectively insuring that certain factual assumptions can be made and relied on by the other party. Both the manager and the musician often are asked to make certain representations and warranties upon which the agreement is based. For instance, the musician usually represents and warrants that the musician is not bound by any other management contract, and is therefore free to enter into a management contract with the manger. The manager may represent and warrant that the manager is not representing any other musician who is providing services similar to or competitive with the musician, although most managers will be reluctant to restrict themselves in that way. Other representations and warranties may be present and are usually coupled with an indemnity which provides for full compensation to the party who has suffered loss or damage due to a breach of a representation and warranty.

(j) Term and Options/Performance Obligations

Management agreements typically last from three to seven years. A common term is five years. A minimum five year term ensures that some benefit flows to the manager since it often takes two or three years to see results from the efforts of the manager, and to see the overall development of the musician, particularly when the musician's career has begun only recently. The term of the agreement (for example, the five year period referred to above) usually is structured in terms of an initial period, plus option periods. For example, in an agreement with a five year term, the initial period would often be twelve months, after which typically it would be the manager who has four option periods, each of one year duration. Each option period might be triggered automatically upon the expiration of the previous period or, in some cases, only after certain obligations evidencing a musician's success are met. Alternatively, the term of the agreement may be structured to become "co-terminous" (i.e., running and ending simultaneously) with the term of a recording agreement, if one is secured.

To protect the musician, some levels of performance often are set out in the agreement, as described briefly above. For example, the manager may be required to ensure a level of gross earnings or perhaps to obtain a major recording contract within a specified time frame. If these performance obligations are not met, then the term of the agreement may be terminated. However, it is also common that once a recording agreement is obtained, the term of the management agreement extends to become co-terminus with the recording agreement (which typically lasts longer than the five years), thus extending the management term beyond the five year period which was initially agreed upon. Consider the issue of restraint of trade if the term of the management agreement is too long.[53]

(k) Important General Provisions

(i) Accounting and Audit

This is a particularly important clause. The manager should account for expenses incurred and monies paid and collected on behalf of the musician, and the musician should have the right to audit the manager's books and records. This is particularly important when the personal manager is also a business manager. If the musician is accounting to the manager, the manager should have the right to a similar accounting and audit. If the manager and musician can afford it, a useful solution to the problem of accounting is to retain an independent third party who performs the task of money management and record keeping. The accounting and audit provision is essential but is often overlooked or trivialized in the early stages of the musician/manager relationship or before there are substantial monies for which to account. Typically, the right to an accounting under the management agreement may be monthly, quarterly or sometimes semi-annually. An audit right is typically exercisable once per calendar year upon reasonable notice. A standard notice period in which to exercise an audit right is ten days.

(ii) Arbitration

Some management contracts contain an arbitration provision. This provision attempts to avoid the bitterness and expense of litigation when disputes arise. However, the manager/artist relationship may have terminated or should terminate when it has reached the stage of requiring arbitration. An arbitration provision should be considered carefully.[54]

---

[53] See the *Gilbert O'Sullivan* case, discussed in Chapter 10. Here a five-year contract with a two-year extension was considered to be too long.

[54] See for example the *Arbitrations Act*, R.S.O. 1990, c. A.24.

(iii) Termination

A clear notice and termination clause should be set out because of the problems with actual, implied or ostensible authority of agents, and the potential of liability of a musician to third parties.[55] Both parties should know clearly when a contract has ended and another can be entered into. Numerous situations may warrant termination of the manager and could be specified in the agreement, for example: (a) bankruptcy of either party; (b) failure to account or allow an audit; (c) mental incapacity; (d) death; (e) failure of the manager to meet performance criteria; and (f) either manager or musician discontinuing their career.

Other general provisions such as the default and cure clause (which is discussed in Chapter 8, "Recording") may be part of the agreement as required. See also the General Provisions Checklist in Appendix 2 for a list of other general provisions which may be relevant.

(l) Note on Co-Management Agreements

It is not unusual for musicians to be managed by more than one manager, for example, a road manager or a business manager, or in a "co-management" situation. The situation discussed here is not that of two persons carrying on business in partnership, or the case of two or more managers who are shareholders in a corporation,[56] although a co-management agreement also can be structured in either of these two ways. This discussion assumes that the co-management agreement is a contract between two independent contractors (i.e., a contract between the two separate managers).

A co-management agreement, as discussed here, usually involves two managers in different territories, for example one in Canada and one in the U.S., who obtain exclusive but potentially conflicting, overlapping or competing interests with respect to a musician. Issues such as the scope of each manager's authority, limitations on their ability to act, the powers of attorney granted to them, the territorial definitions, and the issue of how to allocate commissions on advances and earnings generated from each territory, must be scrutinized carefully when considering a co-management agreement. Each and every aspect of the above-noted personal management agreement should be reviewed in order to structure the co-management

---

[55] See for example G.H.L. Fridman, "Self-Authoring Agent" (1983), Vol. 2 Man. L.J. 1.

[56] See Chapter 11, "Business" for a discussion of partnership and shareholder agreement issues.

agreement properly. In view of the international nature of the music business, the need for standard worldwide management and co-management agreements is becoming more common.

7

LIVE PERFORMANCE*

Contributing Authors: Christopher N. Taylor, B.A., LL.B.,
Toby Susan Goldbach, B.A., LL.B. and
David L.P. Garson, LL.B.

1. Outlined

(a) A Definition

Live performances are often the single most important form of income for musicians. Many musicians never compose music or record[1] but still earn their living from performing. In this chapter, live performance means a performance before a live audience, where the main purpose is to entertain and not to record the performance. This definition is used to distinguish live performance from a performance where the purpose is to reproduce the performance, which itself is "live", for example, a recording before a studio audience.[2] Note also that this definition does not include a performer's copyright in a recorded performance on a sound recording, as set out in section 3(a)(i) below.

---

* Part of this chapter is adapted from an article authored by Paul Sanderson and Christopher N. Taylor, which was published previously as Chapter IV, "Live Performance Contracts Between Promoters and Artists", in *Business and Legal Aspects of Live Concerts and Touring*, Arend Jan van der Marel and Louise Nemschoff, eds., (Apeldoorn, Netherlands & Antwerp, Belgium: MAKLU Publishers, 1998), and was published in association with the reports presented at the meeting of the International Association of Entertainment Lawyers, Midem 1998, Cannes, France.
[1] See also the discussion in Chapter 3, "Music Publishing" and Chapter 8, "Recording", concerning the difficulties in earning income from these sources.
[2] See Chapter 1, "Copyright" and Chapter 8, "Recording", for a discussion of a musician's rights in a recorded performance.

The rights that a musician has under a live performance contract differ from the rights that are acquired in a musician's performance. These two should be distinguished[3] and are discussed separately below.

(b) Types

There are two main types of live performances: one-night engagements (one-nighters) which are also known as "miscellaneous" or "casual engagements", such as weddings, bar mitzvahs or concerts, and "steady engagements" (one week or more) at a hotel, bar, or lounge, for example. Other types of steady engagements include symphony players who contract for a concert season, for instance. Musicians often perform in a combination of several live performance engagements in a year, month, week, or even a single day.[4] Another factor which distinguishes one live performance from another is the presence of a promoter, which is common in concert performances, but largely absent in other types of live performances.

Live performance as discussed in this chapter is focused mainly on the concert-type performance.

(c) Occupational Characteristics

Occupational characteristics of performing musicians can be broadly summarized:[5]

1)   the work is often "part-time" in the sense that it is contractual in nature and there is time in between engagements;
2)   the musicians provide their own equipment, such as musical instruments;
3)   they must constantly seek new contracts for employment and incur significant expenses doing so, for example: (a) agent's and manager's fees; (b) lessons and training; (c) audition expenses; and (d) travel and accompanist expenses;
4)   they constantly travel, often to other cities and countries;
5)   their work is mostly at night;

---

[3] Contractual rights govern the relationship between the performer and the other parties effecting the performance. The musician's rights in the performance exist independently of a contract, and include rights in the live performance itself.

[4] Adopted from Russell Disney, *Federal Tax Issues of Concern to the Arts Community in Canada: An Analysis*, (Ottawa: Department of the Secretary of State; 1977), Appendix B, pp. 1-6.

[5] *Ibid.*, at pp. 13-15. See Chapter 12 for a discussion of the impact of these factors concerning whether a musician is an employee or is self-employed for tax purposes.

6)   there sometimes is a fixed fee as a basis for pay or sometimes it is
      a percentage of gross receipts with a minimum guarantee; and
7)   expenses are often half or more of gross earnings.

(d) Entities Involved

In addition to musicians, there are numerous entities involved in
live performances depending upon the type of engagement. Any, but
not necessarily all of the entities discussed below may be involved.

(i)   The American Federation of Musicians of the United States and Canada

The American Federation of Musicians of the United States and
Canada (herein the "AFM") is a significant presence in the live
performance field. The AFM establishes minimum fees for its
musicians' members. In addition, the internal rules of the AFM and/or
its locals require members to sign a standard AFM live performance
contract whenever they provide their professional services. Additions to
the contract may be made by riders or addendums. AFM contracts must
be filed with the relevant AFM local in advance of a performance. If
there is a dispute involving the performance or the contract, then the
musicians and the engager of the musicians must attempt first to reach
a settlement through the AFM or the local having jurisdiction over the
live performance. If such settlement process fails, either party to an
AFM Live Performance Contract may initiate litigation by a court of
competent jurisdiction.[6]

(ii)   Booking Agent

As discussed in Chapter 6, the agent's role is mainly to engage
musicians for live performances but the agent also may provide advice
and help negotiate contracts with the promoter or engager. All
booking agents which book AFM members are to be licensed by the
AFM[7] under the Booking Agents Agreement for Canada as discussed in
Chapter 6, "Agents and Managers".

---

[6] See Chapter 5, "Labour" for more detail concerning the AFM and its role in such
dispute resolution. For a general discussion of the AFM, see Janice Papolos, *Performing
Artist Handbook*, (Cincinnati, OH: Writer's Digest Books, 1984), at page 49 and Dick
Weissman, *The Music Business*, (New York: Three Rivers Press, 1997), at page 116.

[7] See Chapter 6, "Agents and Managers", for more detail on an agent's functions and
Chapter 5, "Labour", for a discussion of the AFM's purpose and functions.

(iii) Personal Manager

Generally, the personal manager's main function is to advise the musician on various aspects of his or her career,[8] but the personal manager also may assist in negotiating live performance contracts, may oversee the staging of the live performances and, especially in the case of new musical groups, may act as road manager too.

(iv) Promoter

A promoter engages in concert promotion and may be involved in promoting performances in high-profile bars as well. The promoter contracts through the booking agency for the musician's services, books the hall, and takes care of all details of the performance including security, insurance, and many other details.[9] The promoter is a key entity in concert performances, but, in other types of live performances which are not concerts, there often is no promoter.

(v) Engager

An engager is the party who contracts for the live performance services of a musician. An engager may be a bar owner, or the father of the bride, for example, depending on the type of engagement. If it is a bar owner, he or she may contract directly with the musician or through a booking agent.

(vi) Publicist

The role of the publicist is to assist the musician in creating and enhancing a marketable image and to work with persons in the music business and the media in order to promote the musician. A publicist must be well informed about the music business, have good media contacts in order to obtain print, radio and television coverage, and be

---

[8] See Chapter 6, "Agents and Managers", for more detail on a personal manager's functions.

[9] See, generally, Howard Stein and Ronald Zalkind, *Promoting Rock Concerts*, (New York: Schirmer Books; 1979), and especially Appendix B, Production Cost Analysis Form, pp. 133-138 for a checklist. See also David Baskerville, *Music Business Handbook and Career Guide*, 6th ed. (Thousand Oaks, Cal.: Sage Publications Inc., 1995), and Chapter 6, "The Promoter", by Martin Cooper, at pp. 55-65, in Shane Simpson and Greg Stevens, *Music: The Business and the Law*, (Sydney: The Law Book Company Limited; 1986), for discussion of the role of the promoter.

able to orchestrate the marketing and promotion of the musician at press conferences, record launches, live performances and personal appearances.[10] The publicist is sometimes an employee of a record company or an independent contractor, hired by either the musician or the record company or both. In fact, there may be more than one publicist for different assignments.

(vii) Sponsor

Concert performances are often sponsored, sometimes by local radio stations or community groups. Sponsors may assist in financing the performance and providing media coverage to advertise, promote and publicize the performance. Sponsors are often major corporations seeking to benefit from the publicity generated by a tour and from association with the musician's goodwill.[11] Corporate sponsorship, most notably by beer companies, has a significant role in the business of live musical performances.[12] A recent amendment to the *Tobacco Act*, however, essentially prohibits sponsorship by tobacco companies.[13] The record company with which the musician has an exclusive record agreement may also have an interest in the tour and provide tour support funding. This, however, is not sponsorship.

(viii) Merchandiser

On larger tours, a musician might grant merchandising and licensing rights for the manufacture, distribution and sale of souvenir merchandise at concert venues.[14] The musician likely would be compensated in the form of a one-time fee or on a royalty basis reflected in proceeds of sale. Any contract with a merchandiser should be careful not to conflict with the rights granted to a sponsor, which also may include the right to promote and distribute tour merchandise.

---

[10] *Ibid.*, *Music: The Business and the Law*, above in note 9, "Marketing, Promotion & the Publicist", by Pam Saunderson at pp. 49-54.

[11] The intricacies of tour sponsorship agreements are dealt with in Chapter 20 of Peter Muller, *The Music Business*, (Westport: Quorum Books, 1994).

[12] See Form 156-1, "Tour Sponsorship Agreement with Commentary", in *Entertainment Industry Contracts* cited below, note 47, at p. 156-4.

[13] The new s. 24 of the *Tobacco Act* (s. 1 of *An Act to Amend the Tobacco Act*, S.C. 1998, c. 38) received Royal Assent on December 10, 1998. Events that received sponsorship from tobacco companies between January 25, 1996 and April 25, 1997 will be able to continue to receive sponsorship until October 1, 2000, s. 4(3) of *An Act to Amend the Tobacco Act*.

[14] See Chapter 9, "Merchandising" for more discussion on this issue.

2. Contracts

Unlike other agreements that musicians enter into, the contract for live performance, particularly in a concert situation where the musician is a star, can be worded in favour of the musician and it is the concert promoter who bears most of the risks. As in most other negotiating scenarios, the musician's ability to obtain concessions from the promoter will be determined largely by the musician's bargaining power. In the live performance context, this will be contingent on: (1) whether the musician has a history of success in selling out venues in the marketplace; (2) the musician's exposure in the period prior to the performance – this will be high if the artist is releasing a new recording backed by a large marketing/promotion campaign; (3) whether the musician has performed recently in that location or whether there is otherwise a demand for the artist;[15] and (4) whether there are a number of promoters bidding competitively for the musician's services.

(a) AFM

The standard form contract of the AFM,[16] or applicable AFM local, is the basic contract for live performances, which include, for example, bar engagements, weddings, concerts, musical festivals, etc. There are standard terms and conditions contained in the contract that are not subject to negotiation. The terms which are negotiable are usually dealt with by filling in the blanks on the form contract. Such terms include, for example, the dates, hours, fees payable and services required. Other specific details may be dealt with by the addition of a rider, or an appendix. The standard terms of the AFM agreement, and the specific terms set out in applicable riders, together constitute the terms agreed to by the parties. Riders are discussed in the text below.

(b) Riders

"Riders" is the term used by those in the music business when referring to memoranda, addenda, schedules or amendments to the live performance agreement. Written collateral agreements which add

---

[15] The enthusiastic response to the Eagles "Reunion Tour" in the early 90's likely was partially due to the band's absence from the marketplace for over a decade. It will be interesting to note whether or not subsequent tours, in closer proximity to previous tours, will meet with as much public enthusiasm.

[16] See Chapter 5,"Labour" for discussion of AFM contracts, and Appendix 4 for AFM Live Performance Contracts for Canada.

to, or alter, the terms of this contract, such as riders, generally will bind the parties, whereas collateral oral arrangements between the parties are not necessarily enforceable.

Riders set out the specific details and requirements that either the musician or the promoter requires with respect to the live performance. Either the musician or the promoter may have a rider. The musician's rider covers two basic areas: (1) the technical specifications required for the performance, including lighting, sound equipment, etc.; and (2) the additional incentives to enter into the contract, such as specific food and hotel requirements. These latter specifications are sometimes called "perks" by those in the music business. Often restrictive covenants are added in a rider to a live performance agreement. For example, a musician often agrees not to perform in a specified geographic area for a period of time before or after the engagement. Such restrictive covenants will be upheld if they are fair, reasonable and justified in the circumstances.[17]

(c) Provisions of a Non-AFM Contract

(i) Parties

The parties include the musician and the promoter. The booking agent negotiates contracts for the musician but is not a party to this agreement. The promoter books the venue, usually by obtaining a licence to do so with a particular concert venue.[18] This is a separate contract and the owner of the venue usually would not be a party to the live performance contract unless the owner were otherwise involved in the live performance - as promoter, for example.

---

[17] See restraint of trade discussion in Chapter 10, "Personal Service Contracts".

[18] See Stein and Zalkind, *Promoting Rock Concerts*, above note 9, Appendix C, for a sample Major Facility Licence Agreement. The case of *Mills v. Triple Five Corp.* (1992), 6 Alta. L.R. (3d) 105 (Master) discusses the issue of proper parties and liability in the context of live performance contracts. In this case a band had contracted with what was apparently a nightclub. The contract was executed in the name of the club by the club's manager. The club was operated by the defendant corporation. Shortly after the contract was made, the defendant leased the club to a third party which agreed under the lease to take on the liabilities of the defendant. The court held that because the club manager was an employee of the defendant, the defendant was liable for breach of contract, and further, that it could not rely on the doctrine of novation to escape liability.

(ii) Basic Terms

The basic terms of this agreement include: 1) the time of the performance; 2) the venue; 3) the duration of the performance, or the number of sets or shows per engagement; 4) the musician's control over production and presentation of the performance; 5) the seating capacity of the venue; and 6) the terms of payment.

(iii) Payment

Payment may consist of a guaranteed "flat fee", a combination of a guaranteed "flat fee" and percentage of net or gross receipts from ticket sales, or solely a percentage of gross receipts.[19]

A. Generally

Payment terms are specified, for example, 1/2 of the flat fee paid either on signing, or before the performance, by certified cheque, or its equivalent; the remainder would be payable on completion of the performance or prior to the musician going on stage. In some instances, the initial payment may be made "in trust". Alternative payment schemes are possible. For example, 100% of the agreed upon amount is paid prior to the performance.

Payment may be either on a gross or a net receipts basis. When payment is made on a net receipts basis, expenses are subtracted from the gross ticket sales, and the musician and promoter share an agreed upon percentage of the remaining (net) receipts. In this situation, it is not unusual to stipulate that the musician will be paid a guaranteed minimum fee and also share in the promoter's profit on an 80/20, 85/15 or, in the case of musicians with significant bargaining power, a 90/10 ratio of the promoter's profit. These percentages are in favour of the musician. A musician's percentage can range from 60 to 90 percent of gross receipts.[20]

On the biggest shows, in order to avoid the necessity of counting expense receipts, the artist may, for example, merely divide gross receipts on a 65/35 basis, in favour of the artist, after deduction of

---

[19] However, artists who have a "steady engagement", for example a "house band", usually would be paid by way of salary. For a more detailed discussion of extended engagement contracts, see Chapter 18, "The Lounge Act" in Muller, *The Music Business*, above note 11.

[20] Harvey Rachlin, *The Encyclopedia of the Music Business*, (Toronto: Fitzhenry and Whiteside; 1980), at p. 90.

taxes and SOCAN fees. Promoters of shows with audience attendance over 3,200, or of shows where alcohol is served, will pay two taxes: GST (7% of gross receipts) and amusement taxes (10% of gross receipts), unless certain exemptions apply, such as the exemption for the Canadian National Exhibition with respect to the amusement tax.[21] SOCAN generally collects 2.5% of gross receipts less taxes with respect to performing rights fees pertaining to "Popular Music Concerts".[22]

B. Specific Example

The following is a specific example of how payment may be made concerning a live performance: 1) $1,000 received by way of deposit in advance; 2) $1,000 received at the time of the performance; and 3) 60 % of the gross greater than $5,000, with a gross of $8,000 after the performance. The total of $8,000 less $5,000 equals $3,000, which multiplied by 60 % equals $1,800. The result is: $1,000 deposit, plus $1,000 received at time of performance, plus $1,800, for a total of $3,800.[23]

New major label recording groups performing on the bar circuit may be paid in the above manner.[24] Mid-level groups with a significant following performing in venues with capacity of 1,000-5,000 may expect a 70/30 share of net receipts with a 15% promoter profit built into expenses.[25] Successful international touring acts may demand a 85/15 share of net receipts with no promoter profit built into expenses, or may require a 65/35 share in reference to the above.[26]

(iv) General Provisions

Other provisions may be added to the live performance contract or may be included in either the promoter's or the musician's rider. For example:

---

[21] See Chapter 12, "Tax", for a more detailed outline of amusement tax.

[22] For a full review of SOCAN fees with respect to live performances, see Tariff No. 4 and No. 5 in the Canada Gazette, Part I, Supplement, May 24, 1997.

[23] Example adopted from Gary Burton, A Musician's Guide to the Road, (New York: Billboard Books; 1981), at p. 80.

[24] Young groups with moderate followings who sell in the range of 5,000-15,000 records per release in Canada with moderate radio and video airplay.

[25] This would include groups that achieve near gold sales status (50,000 records sold) in Canada with above average radio and video airplay.

[26] Artists that routinely draw crowds of at least 10,000 per show and are regularly achieving platinum selling status (100,000 records sold) in Canada.

1) As is consistent with the legal nature of a personal services agreement, musicians cannot assign their obligations under the agreement, although the promoter may be able to do so.

2) In order to limit liability and avoid an agency relationship, it is usually stated that the promoter and the musician recognize that they are independent contractors,[27] acting neither as agents of the other, nor as a partnership, joint venture or under any other similar arrangement.

3) The musician is not usually liable for the failure of the promoter to fulfil its obligations under the live performance agreement. The musician should be indemnified by the promoter so that if the promoter is sued, the musician will not bear any financial or other risk.

4) The contract is the entire agreement, there are no additional oral terms which vary the agreement, and there will be no variation of the agreement unless in writing, signed by the parties to the agreement.

5) A provision with respect to GST, amusement and withholding tax; usually the promoter is liable to pay amusement taxes, although in some provinces, the ticket price includes amusement taxes.[28]

6) There may be a requirement that: (a) the performance not include any illegal act;[29] (b) the performance not be contrary to the AFM's by-laws and constitution, which may be incorporated by reference; and (c) the live performance contract is to comply with the AFM's by-laws and constitution.

7) The governing law clause is important in order to resolve the conflict of laws issue, as discussed in Chapter 10, "Personal Service Contracts".[30]

8) The riders are incorporated as part of the live performance agreement.

9) Approval of the musician is often required before interviews are granted and appearances or sponsoring or co-promotion of the performance are permitted.

---

[27] See discussion of this issue in Chapter 12, "Tax".

[28] See Chapter 12, "Tax", for a discussion of withholding tax, GST and amusement tax.

[29] The defendant could be liable in the case of an indecent performance contrary to s. 167 of the *Criminal Code*, R.S.C. 1985, c. C-46 (herein the "*Criminal Code*").

[30] An example of conflict of laws in live performance contract disputes is *T.D.I. Hospitality Management Consultants Inc. v. Browne* (1994), 117 D.L.R. (4th) 289, 28 C.P.C. (3d) 232 (Man. C.A.). In this case, the defendant, an agent of the band who lived in Manitoba, arranged for them to play in a hotel in Alberta. The band reneged. The hotel sued the band and the agent, got a judgement in Alberta and sought to enforce it in Manitoba. The Manitoba court held that because the defendant had not attorned to the court in Alberta, the plaintiff could not rely on Manitoba legislation permitting the registration of foreign judgements.

10) Ancillary rights may be included, for example, the right to record the performance and the specific terms in relation thereto, including merchandising or bar profits.

11) Other general provisions may be added. Consult the general provisions checklist in Appendix 2 for a list of other general provisions which may be relevant.

(d) Musician's Rider Provisions

(i) Billing

"Billing" is the way the musician is referred to in all advertising and publicity. It may be set out precisely as to: 1) the obligation, if any, to advertise; 2) who bears the expense; 3) the creative approval and quality control over advertising; 4) the supply of information to the media such as a press kit and promotional recordings; and 5) the size and type of lettering which is to be used in all promotion. At other times, the language is imprecise and merely states that the headliner, that is, the "star act", receives 100 percent "exclusive billing" in any and all advertising.[31] The promoter also may be given a billing, which may be in the range of 10% of 100% of the star's billing, meaning that the billing for the promoter is no more or less than one-tenth of the size of the star's billing on all advertising and promotion.

(ii) Advertising and Promotion/Merchandising

The promoter contracts to use the name and the likeness of the musician in advertising and promotion. This use should be limited strictly to the advertising and promotion in connection with the performance. Ideally, the musician should have as much input as possible into the advertising of the performance including print, radio and television, and the access of the press and other interviewers prior to and after the performance. The merchandising in connection with the performance, such as the sale of souvenir programs, posters and T-shirts, may be granted to the promoter, or shared with the booking agent or may be reserved by the musician. The right to sell recordings at the venue, so called "off stage" sales, subject to any obligations the musician has with respect to the record company, may be stipulated.

---

[31] Rachlin, The *Encyclopedia*, above, note 20 at 91. See Appendix 4 for musician's rider checklist.

Alternatively, the promoter may contract to participate in a percentage of the merchandising, for example, up to 20% of the merchandising.

Care should be taken when the promoter seeks to use the musician's name and likeness in merchandising products. This raises the issue of products liability. The musician should have some right to approve merchandising on a case by case basis. Merchandising is discussed in Chapter 9.

(iii) Tickets

A. Manifest

To prevent disputes concerning gross receipts, a "ticket manifest" is often required. The ticket manifest outlines the specifications, including the number, colour and price of all tickets. It may be printed by a bonded printer and notarized.[32]

B. Complimentary

Complimentary tickets are often supplied to the media, or other special guests, and limited to a specific number.

C. Discounts

Discounts on the ticket price may be subject to approval by the musician.

D. Scale

The scale for all tickets should be set out in order to determine the gross receipts with accuracy. For example, box seats may be more expensive and balcony seats less expensive. The ticket scale may be on a general admission basis where every ticket costs the same, or may be directed specifically to reserved seats. The scale for ticket prices is to be distinguished from union scale payments which, as discussed in Chapter 5, "Labour", are minimum fees to be paid to AFM musicians.

---

[32] *Ibid.* See also Form 151-4, Ticket Sale Information [Exhibit "A" to Personal Appearance Rider] with commentary, in *Entertainment Industry Contracts,* cited below, note 47.

E. Time and Place

Specifications as to the time and place for ticket sales may be outlined in the rider.

F. Other Specifications

Other specifications may include: 1) the right to designate a representative to enter the box office to examine ticket sales records; 2) the right to examine ticket stubs and unsold tickets for a specified period after the date of the performance; 3) an obligation by the promoter to compensate the musician for every seat sold for the performance; and 4) the right to approve changes in the ticket price.

(iv) Production Equipment

There are two basic types of production equipment required: sound equipment and lighting equipment. Either of these types of equipment may or may not be supplied by the promoter. Again, the musician's ability to say which equipment and which companies will be used for the performance will depend on the musician's bargaining power relative to the promoter.

Production equipment can include: 1) a stage of specific dimensions; 2) an intercom system; 3) adequate electrical power; 4) a loading ramp; 5) spotlights, including colour gels and other specified lighting equipment; and 6) a piano.

Each situation is specific to the musician. The above examples are not exhaustive; however, they constitute some common examples.[33]

(v) Production Personnel

Production personnel may include: 1) a piano tuner; 2) a sound technician and assistant which may or may not be supplied by the musician; 3) an electrician; 4) stage hands; 5) ushers; 6) a stage manager; and 7) back-up musicians or other musicians as required by labour agreements and other such personnel as required.

Each live performance situation is specific. The above list is provided as an example only; it is not exhaustive.

---

[33] *Ibid.* See also "Artist Performance Contract with Technical Rider" in *Entertainment Industry Contracts,* cited below, note 47 at p. 397. Form 151-5, Technical Rider [Exhibit B to Personal Appearance Rider] with commentary.

(vi) Security

Adequate security is essential, to protect the musicians, persons in the audience, and others connected with the show. It is the promoter's obligation to supply and pay for both security guards and police, when required.

(vii) Rehearsal and Sound Check

Before the performance, the promoter often is asked to allow the musician to do a "sound check". A sound check allows the musician to perform several numbers to ensure the sound system is working properly, to set sound levels, and to mix and balance the sound properly for a specific venue. During the sound check, the audience should not be allowed to enter the venue. If the public were allowed to enter, this would be unprofessional and might impede the progress of the sound check. In some situations there also may be a request to have rehearsal time, which is important, particularly for travelling musicians who do not have the time or a venue in which to rehearse.

(viii) Cancellation

In addition to the *force majeure* provision, the contract may stipulate certain events that entitle the musician to cancel the performance. Examples are: 1) the occurrence of specified events; 2) the promoter's failure to perform material obligations; 3) events such as illness of musicians which may or may not entail arrangements for a new concert date; and 4) the right of the musician to cancel if ticket sales are less than necessary to ensure the live performance is successful and profitable. Such events may or may not require the musician to return a deposit.[34]

In most cases, the artist will attempt to re-book a cancelled show. Nevertheless, the promoter typically will lose all the money spent on advertising for the cancelled performance. Informal procedures develop between promoters and artists to minimize damages in such circumstances. For example, the artist may accept a reduced fee upon his or her return performance, to compensate the promoter for the

---

[34] One court has held that the "loss of publicity" was "not too remote" and was compensable in general damages where the defendant cancelled the performance. See *Robertson v. Judd,* [1984] B.C.J. No. 721. Presumably in such cases, the right to retain the deposit would be part of the damage award. With respect to cancellation and liability see, for example, *Mills,* supra note 18.

loss incurred from a prior cancellation. In some cases the artist may have purchased cancellation insurance to alleviate some of the financial problems associated with cancelled performances.

(ix) Note on U.S. Law

In the U.S., there have been many illustrative cases which discuss liabilities for performances which were cancelled. It has been held that damages for cancellation of a performance could include lost profits.[35] Upon breach of a contract, whereby a wedding band failed to show up for a performance, damages were awarded in excess of the contract amount.[36] Numerous other contractual issues have arisen, for example, where a live performance was cancelled because of the controversial and political nature of the concert.[37]

(x) Insurance

The promoter must be adequately insured. Adequate insurance includes insurance for personal injury and cancellation insurance. It is the promoter, and not the musician, who is normally sued, although it is possible that musicians may be added as parties to a lawsuit. Adequate insurance for musicians is therefore advisable. Such insurance should include personal liability, equipment and disability insurance. In some cases where a major tour is involved, it is also advisable for musicians to obtain cancellation insurance. Although liability is sometimes apportioned contractually in the rider, more typically, musicians are completely indemnified by the promoter from any liability, either in the rider or the main contract. Consider whether

---

[35] *Kerner v. Hughes Tool Company* (1976), 128 Cal. Rptr. 839 (Cal. App.). Here, the plaintiff promoter recovered damages for loss of profits. See, however, *Zaycielz v. The State of New York* (1976), 382 N.Y.S. 2d 867, where the opposite was held, that damages to the promoter did not include loss of profits where the concert was cancelled by the hall.

[36] *Dietsch v. The Music Company,* 453 N.E. 2d 1302 (Ohio Mun. 1983). The plaintiffs were compensated for "distress, inconvenience and diminution of value of their reception" which were the "natural and probable consequences of the breach" of contract.

[37] *East Meadow Community Concerts Association v. Board of Education of Union Free School District No. 3, County of Nassau* (1966), 273 N.Y.S. 2d 736. Here, the court found the cancellation of a Pete Seeger concert was an unlawful restriction of freedom of speech and assembly and the court ordered that a permit be issued allowing the concert. See, however, *Contemporary Music Group Inc. v. Chicago Park District* (1978), 372 N.E. 2d 982 where the cancellation of a permit for a concert was held to be a valid exercise of police power when a similar concert by Sly and the Family Stone caused a riot.

the promoter actually has the funds to ensure that this indemnity is viable.

(xi) Recordings

Often it is stipulated in the musician's rider that no recordings, broadcastings, photographs or videos are to be made of the performance. This is also stipulated in the AFM Live Performance Contract for Canada. Alternatively, there may be provision for such recordings either by the promoter, or by the venue, or even the record company, and in some instances the venue may take a percentage of the proceeds from the concert, or even contract to receive record royalties.

(xii) Supporting Act

The headline (or the star) act may contract to have control over the choice of the supporting act which plays before it. The supporting act's billing is often limited, for example, to either 50% or 75% of 100% of the headliner's billing. The supporting act may be restricted in terms of sound check time, rehearsal time and the use of the stage and lighting. Typically the supporting act also gets less perks. Perks are discussed above in section 2(b) "Riders" and in section 2(d)(xiii) "Benefits" below. The headliner may have the right to prohibit substitution of one supporting act for another if the supporting act cancels.

(xiii) Benefits

Much media attention has been paid to the benefits which make the musician's touring life more comfortable. Any number of "perks" may be contracted for, including: 1) food requirements for both the road crew and the musicians; 2) the number and size of dressing rooms and the specification of sanitation and convenience standards; 3) limousine service to and from the hotel before and after the performance; and 4) any number of other requests depending on the negotiating strengths and peculiarities of the musicians, including a case of Dom Perignon, Perrier, or other more bizarre requests. The artist should be aware that normally, perks are expenses deducted from the gross revenues in a "net revenue" calculation for the purpose of net profit division.

(xiv) Permits

Performing right licences from SOCAN and other documents, licences, permit authorizations, visas and certificates are usually entirely the responsibility of the promoter.

(xv) Miscellaneous

Other miscellaneous specifications may be added in a rider,[38] such as the payment of travel costs, an option for further performances, or a specification that the contract does not infringe any statute, by-law or regulation of any common law, or any federal, municipal or provincial governments.

(e) Promoter's Rider

(i) Restrictive Covenants

Restrictive covenants are often added to riders both at the bar circuit and the concert level.[39] A typical example is to restrict performances within a geographical area or within a specific time, for example, performances may be restricted within a 100-mile radius two weeks before the performance, or within a given radius for a matter of time after the performance. There also may be some contractual provision as to the musicians' behaviour, for example, in the case of schools or religious institutions, there may be a request not to smoke or consume alcohol on the premises.

(ii) Control of Production

The promoter may have the sole control over the presentation of the production, including the right to control the volume of the sound system and the duration of the sound check and rehearsal time. This

---

[38] See sample riders in "Business Rider to Performance Agreement" in *Counselling Clients*, 1988, cited below, note 47, at 387 and Form 151-3, "Personal Appearance Rider to Artist Agent Agreement with Commentary", in *Entertainment Industry Contracts*, cited below, note 47.

[39] See Chapter 10, "Personal Service Contracts", regarding restrictive covenants and restraint of trade.

may be as a result of noise or other restrictions placed on the venue in city or town by-laws.[40]

(iii) Injunctions and Nuisance

Noise levels or sanitation facilities either may breach existing by-laws or may amount to a civil or criminal nuisance.[41] If not specified in the musician's rider, promoters should direct their minds to the possibility of an injunction based on breach of by-laws and, in particular, with respect to outdoor concerts, the possibility of an injunction based on nuisance.[42]

(iv) Miscellaneous

Other terms may be added, including a limitation of expenses for hotel and travel, or limitations on the right to cancel the performance. It may be stated in the contract that all terms in the rider are of the essence and a breach of any of its terms constitutes a material breach of the agreement. Whether or not the term is a material term will be

---

[40] Often the city or local fire department imposes restrictions on the hall capacity and "standing room only" areas. Also, a city by-law or the venue's management may require the promoter to hire security. For a general discussion of the promoter's concerns in promoting a concert or performance, see *Music Business Handbook*, cited above, note 9.

[41] S. 180 of the *Criminal Code*. An interlocutory injunction was refused in *Toronto (City) v. Exhibition Place*, [1983] O.J. No. 420 (Ont. S.C.). For cases concerning nuisance as a tort, see *Ontario (Attorney General) v. Orange Productions Ltd.* (1972), 21 D.L.R. (3d) 257 (Ont. H.C.) (injunction issued to prevent a rock festival on the basis of sanitation problems), and *Johnson v. Clinton (Town)*, [1943] O.W.N. 480 (H.C.) (damages awarded for "loud, vulgar and profane language...and the use of the lane as a urinal"...in connection with property adjacent to a public dance hall). For a general source on the law of nuisance, see Beth Bilson, *The Canadian Law of Nuisance*, (Toronto: Butterworths, 1991) and R.A. Buckley, *The Law of Nuisance*, (London, Ont.: Butterworths, 1996).

[42] See above, note 41, for a discussion of injunctions and nuisance. See also Chapter 10, "Personal Service Contracts". For U.S. material concerning nuisance, see Daniel D. Gilson, "Nuisance: Rock Concert Injunction Unconstitutional", (1984), 4 Loyola Entertainment Law Journal 168; Mead Woodstock, "Rights and Remedies in Rock Festival Litigation and Legislation", (1971), Vol. 7 Issue 14, Columbia Journal of Law and Social Problems 141; and Byron L. Freeland, "Nuisance - Rock Festivals and Nuisance: Case Notes", (1971), 25 Arkansas Law Rev. 362. "Nuisance: Rock Concert Injunction Unconstitutional" concerns an Ohio promoter, against whom a temporary and permanent injunction was sought on the basis of illegal drug activity that occurred on the site in previous years. The court held that the concert was a protected form of expression and that such expression could not be completely prohibited simply because some patrons acted illegally. The court was swayed by the fact that the promoter had taken steps to minimize the illegal activity - for example, by hiring security guards.

decided by the courts. Other specific terms and conditions may be added in addition to the above provisions relating to the musician and promoter.[43]

(v) Ticket Scalping

Although not usually discussed in the contract or riders, ticket scalping is an issue for the promoter and there is legislation dealing with this issue.[44] The promoter should address the issue before the concert and perhaps preventative measures, such as an injunction, should be considered.[45] This problem is prevalent in the U.S. as well, and it may be helpful to examine the legal methods that have been used there to deal with scalping.[46]

(f) Overview of Other Relevant Agreements

The purpose of this section is to provide an overview of other relevant agreements in a live performance area in addition to ones discussed in paragraph 2 (a-e) above. Many of these agreements are relevant only to a specific fact situation and will not be discussed in detail here. The intent is to alert the reader to the plethora of agreements that can be entered into with respect to live performances. Keep in mind that depending on the stature of the musician, other agreements may not be entered into at all, or may be entered into on an oral basis. Whenever possible, however, it is advisable to have such agreements in writing.

---

[43] For additional promoter provisions see Burton, *A Musician's Guide* ... above, note 23, Appendix D, at pp. 150-152.

[44] See, for example, *Ticket Speculation Act*, R.S.O. 1990, c. T-7, and other applicable laws in each province. In *Toronto Blue Jays Baseball Club v. Tri-Tickets Inc.* (1991), 6 O.R. (3d) 15 (Ont. Gen. Div.), the court found that reselling tickets at a substantial premium violated s. 2 of the *Ticket Speculation Act*, but on its own, would not entitle the Blue Jays to an injunction. In a second case, *Toronto Blue Jays Baseball Club v. John Doe* (1992), 9 O.R. (3d) 622 (Ont. Gen. Div.), the Blue Jays brought an action against unnamed ticket scalpers. They were unsuccessful in arguing that they could refuse admission to anyone by relying on conditions printed on the reverse of each ticket, that the ticket was a "personal, common, revocable, license."

[45] See discussion of injunctions in Chapter 9, "Merchandising", and Chapter 4, "Copyright Infringement".

[46] See, for example, Quentin Kiegal and Dwight Duncan, "Producers' Rights to Limit Ticket Scalping", (1978), Vol. 8 No. 2 P.A.R. 155.

(i) Agreements with Other Musicians

It is common practice to hire additional musicians either on a permanent basis or for a specific purpose, for example, a specific tour.[47] The tax aspects of whether the musician is hired on an employed or self-employed basis are discussed in Chapter 12, "Tax".

(ii) Transportation Agreement

Various transportation agreements may be entered into including, for example, an aircraft charter agreement or an agreement for transportation equipment and staging.[48] The latter agreement is usually entered into with a trucking company and deals with the transporting of necessary musical, sound and lighting production equipment.

(iii) Sound and Lighting Agreement

This agreement may specify, among other things, the type of lighting system, crew, production manager, stage manager, technical personnel such as stage carpenters, security, parking and transportation crew to be supplied.[49] In addition, a specific stage lighting agreement or stage lighting designer agreement may be entered into.[50]

---

[47] For sample agreements, see Chapter 4, "Touring", in Martin E. Silfen, Chairman, *Counselling Clients in The Entertainment Industry*, (New York: Practising Law Institute, 1988), (herein "*Counselling Clients*"). See also Donald C. Farber, General Ed., and Samuel J. Fox, Ed., Vol. 4 Part V, "Music", in *Entertainment Industry Contracts Negotiating and Drafting Guide*, (New York: Matthew Bender; 1990), (herein "*Entertainment Industry Contracts*"), Chapter 146, "Employment of Band Members"; Form 146-1, "Employment of Band Member with Commentary"; Chapter 152, "Concert and Tour Related Services and Equipment"; and Form 152-1, "Musician Employment Agreement: Live Performances with Commentary".

[48] *Ibid.*, *Counselling Clients*, 1988, "C: Aircraft Charter Agreement", at p. 347; Form 152-4, "Transportation Agreement for Equipment and Staging with Commentary", in *Entertainment Industry Contracts*, cited above, note 47.

[49] "Sound and Lighting Agreement", cited above, note 47, *Counselling Clients*, 1988, p. 335. See also *Entertainment Industry Contracts*, cited above, note 47, Chapter 152-2, Form 152-2, "Lighting Production Services Agreement with Commentary".

[50] *Ibid.*, *Counselling Clients*, 1988, "D: Stage Lighting Agreement", at p. 357; and "E: Stage Lighting Designer Agreement", at p. 365.

(iv) Other Agreements

Other relevant agreements may include: 1) tour merchandising agreement;[51] 2) tour support agreement;[52] 3) tour photographer agreement;[53] 4) radio broadcast agreement;[54] and 5) other services agreements, such as a personal assistant to the musician or a publicist agreement.

3. Legal Issues

(a) Rights Concerning Live Performances

(i) Copyright

A performer has a right against unauthorized recordings and broadcasts of his or her performance.[55] The *Copyright Act* gives a performer the sole right to fix, perform, record and communicate his or her performance to the public by telecommunication, as well as to authorize such acts.[56] A performance is defined as "any acoustic or visual representation of a work, performer's performance, sound recording or communication signal",[57] and includes both live and recorded performances and representations made by mechanical instruments, such as radio, television sets or other audio or video players. Performances of musical works, regardless of whether they were previously fixed in a material form,[58] and improvisations of

---

[51] *Ibid.*, Form 155-1 in *Entertainment Industry Contracts*. This agreement is discussed in Chapter 9, "Merchandising".

[52] Tour support is often arranged with the musician's record company on the belief that adequate financial support is necessary in order to allow the musician to tour to support a record release and to promote record sales. Tour support is discussed in Chapter 8, "Recording". See also *Counselling Clients*, 1988, "F: Tour Support Agreement", at p. 367.

[53] *Ibid.*, "J: Tour Photographer Agreement", at p. 383. A key term in this agreement is to stipulate who owns the photographs and negatives of photographs taken on the tour by the tour photographer. In many ways this agreement has elements of both a services agreement and a copyright assignment. Copyright assignments are discussed in this book in Chapters 1, 2 and 3.

[54] *Ibid.*, at p. 369. See, for example, "Agreement between Contract Musician and Band for Tour Performing Services", p. 373.

[55] S. 15 (1)(a) of the *Copyright Act*, R.S.C. 1985, c. C-42 (herein the *"Copyright Act"*).

[56] *Ibid.*, s. 15(1).

[57] *Ibid.*, s. 2.

[58] *Ibid*, definition of "performer's performance".

musical works, regardless of whether they were based on a pre-existing work,[59] are also afforded copyright protection.

A performer's performance is subject to copyright[60] and the duration of this copyright is fifty years from the date when the performance first took place.[61] Also under the *Copyright Act*, it is a copyright infringement for a person to permit, for profit, an unauthorized performance in a theatre or other place of entertainment.[62]

(ii) Contracts

If possible, the musician should contract to prevent the unauthorized use of a live performance, including unauthorized recordings or broadcasts of a live performance, or the unauthorized use of the musician's performance in a recording. Problems of enforcement arise when the unauthorized use is committed by a third party. If the contract does not cover third party uses, the musician will have to rely on copyright, personality rights and other connected rights. For example, a musician may have an action in libel, where his or her performance does not receive proper billing, on the basis that the musician's stature was undermined in the eyes of a specific community.[63]

(iii) Postering

In order to promote live performances, many musicians engage in postering. Postering consists of placing posters, usually in public places, for purposes of advertising a performance. Postering has been held to be a protected form of expression within the meaning of the Canadian *Charter of Rights and Freedoms*,[64] regardless of whether the posters are for advertising, political or artistic purposes. By-laws that restrict postering on all public property are overly broad and are constitutionally invalid.[65] Regulations regarding the location and size of posters, the

---

[59] *Ibid.*

[60] S. 15 (1) of the *Copyright Act*. This principle was articulated in *C.A.P.A.C. v. CTV Television Network*, [1968] S.C.R. 676 (S.C.C.).

[61] *Ibid.*, s. 23(1).

[62] *Ibid.*, s. 27(5).

[63] See *Rusell v. Notcutt* (1896), T.L.R. 195. See also *Elen v. London Music Hall Ltd.*, The Times, Jan. 1, 1906. British libel law has been applied in Canada. See also generally, the *Libel and Slander Act*, R.S.O. 1990, c. L.12, for example.

[64] Part I of the *Constitution Act, 1982*, herein "the Charter."

[65] *Ramsden v. Peterborough* (1993), 106 D.L.R. (4th) 233 (S.C.C.).

length of time they stay up, and the type of substance used to affix posters may be reasonable limits on the freedom of expression,[66] but are, practically speaking, difficult to enforce. By-laws that put unattainable conditions on postering are unconstitutional.[67]

(b) The Audience's Rights

An audience may have an action in negligence or breach of duty under an *Occupier's Liability Act*[68] against a promoter who does not take adequate precautions to protect the audience.[69] There also could be criminal sanctions for police brutality if the audience is mistreated by the police when attempting to maintain crowd control.[70] The audience has other rights, for example, the right to express an opinion about the performance.[71]

(c) "Immoral Theatrical Performances"

(i) *Charter of Rights and Freedoms*

Performance of live music in public will almost always be protected under the section governing freedom of expression, s. 2(b) of the

---

[66] *City of Edmonton v. Orchard et al.* (1990), 74 D.L.R. (4th) 547 (Alta. C.A.).

[67] *City of Toronto v. Quickfall* (1994), 111 D.L.R. (4th) 687 (Ont. C.A.).

[68] An occupier is defined in, for example, s. 1 of Ontario's *Occupiers' Liability Act*, R.S.O. 1990, c. O.2 as a person in physical possession or a person who has control over (i) the condition of the premises, (ii) the activities carried on, or (iii) which persons are allowed to enter the premises. British Columbia, Alberta and Ontario all have acts replacing the common law duty of care and establishing a statutory duty for occupiers to take reasonable care to ensure that persons or their property are reasonably safe while on the premises.

[69] *Greenville Memorial Auditorium v. Martin*, 291 S.E.2d 546 (S.C. 1990). In this case a patron at a Loverboy concert was struck by a glass bottle thrown from the balcony and successfully argued that the city was negligent in providing adequate security. Claims for negligence have been successful in the U.S.; see Jim Lewis, "Crowd Control at Concerts: Hazards of Festival Seating", (1992), 28 No. 6 *Trial* 71.

[70] S. 29 of the *Criminal Code*.

[71] See Harold Fox, *The Law of Copyright and Industrial Designs*, 2d Ed., (Toronto: Carswell, 1967), at p. 611, citing *Clifford v. Brandon* (1810), 2 Comp. 358 at 369. While it is industry practice to refund a ticket or reschedule if a performance is cancelled, it is not clear that ticket holders have a legal right to a refund. In an action against Livent Inc. for proceeds of ticket sales for performances at the Ford Theatre, an Ontario judge held that there was no right to a refund under the *Consumer Protection Act*, R.S.O. 1990, c. C.31, or under the common law of trusts, *Re Livent Inc.* (1998), 42 O.R. (3d) 501 (Ont. Gen. Div.). A class action suit is currently pending in Quebec against Universal Concerts Canada and Admission Inc. with respect to the refund of service fees charged on Edgefest 99 tickets.

Charter, because a live artistic performance is by its nature an expressive activity, the form of which is not inherently violent.[72] Nonetheless, as discussed below, some limits on freedom of expression have been held to be justifiable pursuant to s. 1 of the *Charter*.[73]

(ii) Prohibition of "Immoral Theatrical Performances"

The focus here is on immoral live performances, as delineated in section 167 of the *Criminal Code*, rather than obscenity in recordings, which is discussed in Chapter 8.

Occasionally, in the interests of artistic expression or provocativeness for its own sake, a musician's live performance may include swearing, partial nudity and lewd gestures. Normally, such behaviour would not attract criminal charges. However, the issue arose in a case involving the MacLean Brothers, whose performance, billed as "Toilet Rock", was interspersed with profane language and sexually suggestive references.[74]

It is a criminal offence for an actor, performer or assistant to take part in an immoral, indecent or obscene performance.[75] It is also an offence under the *Criminal Code* to present or allow to be presented a

---

[72] The first step in determining whether an activity is *prima facie* protected by s. 2(b) is to ask whether the activity conveys or attempts to convey a meaning: *Irwin Toy v. Quebec (Attorney General)* (1989), 58 D.L.R. (4th) 577 (S.C.C.) at 606-607. A performance that is a purely physical activity, such as purely sexual activity, does not convey or attempt to convey a meaning, and it will not be an "expression" protected under s. 2(b), *R. v. Ludacka* (1996), 105 C.C.C. (3d) 565 (Ont. C.A.) at 572, appeal quashed at show cause hearing, [1997] S.C.J. No. 28. If the essence of the form of the expression is violent, it will not be protected, *Dolphin Delivery Ltd. v. R.W.D.S.U., Local 580* (1986), 33 D.L.R. (4th) 174 (S.C.C.) at 187; *R. v. Keegstra*, [1990] 3 S.C.R. 697 at 729 (S.C.C.).

[73] See, for example, *R. v. Butler* (1992), 70 C.C.C. (3d) 129 which upheld the definition of obscenity in s. 163(8) of the *Criminal Code* as being a justifiable infringement of the freedom of expression. It will not be enough to argue that the limit on expression denies one's rights under s. 7 of the Charter, *R. v. Red Hot Video Ltd.* (1985), 18 C.C.C. (3d) 1, 45 C.P.R. (3d) 36 (B.C. C.A.).

[74] *R. v. MacLean* (No. 1) (1980), 49 C.C.C. (2d) 399, *R. v. Hilsinger* (1981), 58 C.C.C. (2d) 318 (Ont. C.A.), *R. v. MacLean* (No. 2) (1982), 1 C.C.C. (3d) 412 (Ont. C.A.), leave to appeal to S.C.C. refused (1982), 1 C.C.C. (3d) 412n. Shocking behaviour in music performances has traditionally garnished attention. In a recent example, 10 U.S. senators sent a letter to Seagrams, owner of Interscope Records, asking it to stop distributing Marilyn Manson's music, on the basis that that it glorifies violence; see *Music, Violence, and the RIAA* (May 3, 1999), at www.wired.com/news/news/culture/story/-19464.html.

[75] S. 167(2) of the *Criminal Code*. It is also an offence to do an indecent act and publicly expose or exhibit an indecent exhibition, s. 173 and s. 175(1)(b) respectively. Under s. 174, public nudity is an offence. In *R. v. Yorke* (1997), 186 N.B.R. (2d) 89, the accused was found guilty under s. 167 and s. 173 after participating in a public performance, which consisted of an act of fellatio to live guitar.

performance that is immoral, indecent or obscene.[76] An owner or promoter of a venue could be found guilty for allowing an immoral, indecent or obscene performance where there was "concerted acquiescence" or the owner or promoter was wilfully blind to the nature of the performance.[77]

A. Community Standard Test

Whether a performance is immoral, indecent or obscene is determined by the "community standard of tolerance" test. The community standards test is an objective test which looks at the community as a whole to determine what Canadians would tolerate other Canadians being exposed to.[78] The level of tolerance is determined on the basis of the degree of harm that may flow from such exposure. If there is a greater risk of harm, there will be less tolerance.[79] The consent of the parties likely to be harmed is irrelevant.[80]

B. Immoral or Indecent Distinguished from Obscene

The surrounding circumstances and the context in which the performance occurs are important in determining whether a performance is indecent or immoral.[81] Conduct not immoral or indecent in some circumstances may become immoral or indecent by reason of the context in which the conduct takes place.[82] On the other hand, a performance is obscene irrespective of the person to whom it is shown or the place or manner in which it is shown. According to its definition in the *Criminal Code*, obscenity is the undue exploitation of sex, or of sex and crime, horror, cruelty and violence.[83] Indecent and

---

[76] S. 167(1) of the *Criminal Code*. This section was held to be constitutionally valid in *R. v. Mara* (1996), 105 C.C.C. (3d) 147 (C.A.), reversed in part, [1997] 2 S.C.R. 630 (S.C.C.), and *R. v. Ludacka*, above note 72.

[77] *R. v. Mara*, [1997] 2 S.C.R. 630 (S.C.C.). The court equated "allow" in s. 167(1) with "knowingly" in s. 163(2), discussed by the Supreme Court in *R. v. Jorgensen* (1995), 129 D.L.R. (4th) 510 at 543-544 (S.C.C.).

[78] *R. v. Butler*, above note 73 at 145, following *Towne Cinema Theatres Ltd. v. R.* (1985), 18 C.C.C. (3d) 193 (S.C.C.) at 205.

[79] *R. v. Butler*, above note 73 at 150; *R. v. Mara*, above note 76 at 154. Harm may be evidenced by an act that predisposes a person to act in an antisocial manner. An example would be the physical or mental mistreatment or the degradation or dehumanization of persons protected under s. 15 of the Charter.

[80] *R. v. Butler*, above note 73 at 147; *R. v. Mara*, above note 76 at 156.

[81] *R. v. Ludacka*, above note 72 at 572.

[82] *Ibid.* at 574.

[83] S. 163(8) of the *Criminal Code*.

immoral are not defined. The constitutionality of the *Criminal Code* definition of obscenity and the prohibition against immoral, indecent, or obscene performances have been upheld.[84]

(iii) Nudity

Few musicians perform nude in a public place. Even if there were complete nudity of a performer, cases involving nudity have acquitted strippers in a bar,[85] for example, and therefore musicians may be afforded similar protection.

(iv) Simulating Sex

Even if the live performance involves simulating the act of having sex, a criminal charge may not result in a conviction because of the difficulty of proving that simulated sexual acts are indecent, immoral or obscene.[86] This is not to suggest that one should proceed without caution; criminal charges can result.

(d) Travelling Musicians

(i) AFM By-laws

The AFM by-laws which affect travelling musicians and transfer membership of the AFM are discussed in Chapter 5, "Labour".

---

[84] See generally *R. v. Butler*, above note 73; *R. v. Mara*, above note 76; *R. v. Ludacka*, above note 72.

[85] *R. v. Depoma*, 49 C.C.C. (2d) 472 (Ont. Prov. Ct.), and *R. v. Campbell* (1974), 17 C.C.C. (2d) 130 (Ont. Co. Ct.). Section 174 of the *Criminal Code* sets out this offence. Proceedings require consent of the Attorney General. Under s. 174(2), nudity would include a person "so clad as to offend against public decency or order". However, in certain cases, strippers who are partially clothed have been acquitted. See *R. v. Gray* (1982), 65 C.C.C. (2d) 353 (Ont. H.C.). In addition to these sections of the *Criminal Code*, there may be municipal regulations in force concerning nudity in a public place which should be considered in the relevant fact situation.

[86] See *R. v. Kleppe* (1977), 35 C.C.C. (2d) 168 (Ont. Prov. Ct.), regarding amateur strippers and *R. v. Campbell* above note 85; but see *R. v. Yorke*, above note 75 for an example where a conviction was entered. Section 173 of the *Criminal Code* prohibits indecent acts in a public place, which could include a bar or concert venue. See Alan Young, "From Elvis's Pelvis to As Nasty As They Wanna Be: Freedom of Expression and Contemporary Popular Music", (1991), 1 M.C.L.R. 155.

(ii) Customs Issues

The musician who is leaving Canada with musical instruments and other types of musical goods must comply with customs and excise laws. There are two legal problems the musician faces: 1) proof that while outside of Canada, the goods were bought and owned by the musician in Canada; and 2) upon returning to Canada, proof that the goods were bought and owned by the musician in Canada and therefore no customs and excise duty is owing.[87]

A. Leaving Canada

The Canadian musician who is leaving Canada for a live performance should complete a "manifest", which is a form listing all the equipment which is being taken out of the country.[88] The equipment may be inspected and the form will be stamped by Canadian Customs. Upon return, the form will act as proof that the musical instruments are not being imported.[89]

When travelling internationally, a carnet is advisable because it will effectively reduce delays in travelling. A "carnet" is a customs document which allows persons to bring "professional equipment, and other goods into specified countries for a temporary period".[90] With respect to musicians, such professional equipment may include: 1) musical instruments; 2) amplifiers and other sound equipment; 3) lighting; 4) special effects and stage props; 5) video recording equipment; 6) sound recording equipment; and 7) other equipment related to their live performances. A carnet acts as a guarantee that the duties and taxes

---

[87] S. 12(1) and s. 12(3.1) of the *Customs Act*, R.S.C. 1985, c. 1 (2nd Supp.) (herein the *"Customs Act"*), require a person to report all goods, including goods that are returned to Canada, at the nearest customs office. A person so reporting may be required to open or unpack any container that a customs officer wishes to inspect.

[88] A "certificate of origin" may be required in order to obtain a preferential duty. There are two types of certificates of origin: one under the North American Free Trade Agreement (form B-232E) and the other for those countries with whom Canada has signed a tariff agreement (Form A); see Ann Curran and Gerhard Kautz, *Exporting from Canada: a practical guide to finding and developing export markets for your product or service*, 3rd ed. (Vancouver: Self Counsel Press; 1994), at page 58.

[89] For further information, see Customs and Excise Departmental Memorandum D8-1-7; Returning Canadian Persons; D2-3-1 Returning Persons' Exemption Regulations; D2-3-2 Former Residents of Canada — Tariff Item 9805.00.00; D2-6-5 Documentation of Goods for Temporary Exportation. Goods bought in Canada can be sent abroad for repairs or alterations, D8-2-1 Canadian Goods Abroad.

[90] Jeremiah J. Spires, *Doing Business in the United States*, (New York: Mathew Bender & Co., Inc.), at s. 33.02[9]. See Thomas Lindsay and Bruce Lindsay, *Outline of Customs in Canada*, (Vancouver: Erin Publications; 1989), at 128-130.

owing will be paid should the goods not be re-exported. A carnet is issued by the Canadian Chamber of Commerce and is valid for one year from the date of issue. No extensions are possible. The cost of the carnet varies with the value of the equipment. A Canadian bank or bonding company guarantees the amount involved and charges a fee for this service.

Non-resident musicians entering Canada are allowed to pay a refundable deposit for the excise tax, sales tax, and duty which otherwise would be payable on imported goods, thereby avoiding problems with customs.[91] Musical equipment and other goods temporarily imported by non-resident musicians are an exception under the temporary importation for special use category which can be obtained by: 1) posting a bond; or 2) the use of a carnet.[92]

B. Returning to Canada

Three important issues arise upon returning to Canada. First, the musician and his or her property may lawfully be the subject of a search at the Canadian border.[93] Consequently, the musician should not be importing any illicit goods, as the goods may be confiscated, and the musician may face criminal charges.[94] Second, where goods are purchased abroad, customs and excise duties are payable for goods which are intended to be consumed in Canada. Payment is based on the fair market value of the goods at the date the goods were brought

---

[91] See also Memoranda D8-1-7 above, note 89.

[92] A U.S. musician probably will not use the carnet unless other countries besides Canada are part of the tour.

[93] S. 11 of the *Controlled Drugs and Substances Act*, S.C. 1996, c. 19, authorizes a peace officer to execute a warrantless search for controlled substances if exigent circumstances make it impracticable to obtain a warrant. A peace officer also can obtain a search warrant by telephone. Under s. 98 of the *Customs Act*, an officer can search any person who has arrived or is about to leave Canada if the officer reasonably suspects that prohibited goods – under the *Customs Act* or any other statute – are being hidden on or about a person. On request, the person to be searched must be taken before the senior officer present and the search must be executed by a person of the same sex. Section 99(1) permits the examination of any package or container of imported goods. The sections authorizing personal searches are constitutional, but a "strip search" at a customs office triggers the right to retain and instruct counsel; *R. v. Simmons*, [1988] 2 S.C.R. 495 (S.C.C.).

[94] For example, the *Criminal Code* prohibits the unauthorized importing of a firearm or restricted weapon (s. 103 and s. 104); it also prohibits the importing of instruments or literature for illicit drug use, which includes importing a controlled substance contrary to the *Controlled Drugs and Substances Act* (s. 462.2). The case of *R. v. Richards* (1979), 11 C.R. (3d) 193 (Ont. C.A.), which involved the Rolling Stones lead guitarist Keith Richards, is an example of some musicians' penchant for illicit substances. The decision discusses the principles of sentencing, particularly with regard to possession of heroin.

into Canada. The "transaction value" method generally is used to determine the value of the goods; ordinarily it will be the price paid by the importer for the goods being imported.[95] Thirdly, any applicable G.S.T. must be paid.[96]

C. Note on U.S. Customs

Musicians travelling to the U.S. require a temporary importation bond which lists the equipment being imported and its value. No duty is payable. Forms are available at an airport, or if the musician is crossing the border by car, at the point where the musician is crossing the border.

(iii) Immigration

Canadian immigration laws will not be discussed here because they are relevant to foreign musicians, not Canadian musicians. U.S. immigration laws are important because many Canadian musicians travel to the U.S. for engagements. Other immigration laws for other countries are also relevant, and advice should be obtained concerning them before travelling to a specific country.

(iv) Note on U.S. Immigration Law

Contributing Author: David L.P. Garson, LL.B.

This note is not intended as a detailed analysis of U.S. immigration laws. For the complexities and intricacies of these laws, further sources should be consulted.

---

[95] S. 17 of the *Customs Act*, above in note 87, states that imported goods are charged with duties from the time of importation until the duties are paid or the charge is otherwise removed. The duty is applied to the goods' values determined in accordance with ss. 45-55. Usually, the goods' values are determined according to their "transaction value", pursuant to s. 47(1). Ordinarily this will be the price paid for the goods, s. 48(4), subject to the adjustments prescribed by s. 48(5). However, there are other methods of appraisal. Under s. 143, any amount owing pursuant to the *Customs Act* constitutes a debt to Her Majesty in right of Canada. For more information, see H. Stikeman and R. Elliott, eds., *Doing Business in Canada*, (New York: Matthew Bender & Co., Inc.), at s. 6.03[4]. Also see Memorandum D8-1-7, cited above in note 89 at 10; the *Customs Act, Customs Tariff*, S.C. 1997, c. 36; and the *Excise Tax Act*, R.S.C. 1985, c. E-15.

[96] GST is payable on goods imported when the duty is payable under the *Customs Act*, above in note 87. See s. 212 of the *Excise Tax Act*, above in note 95.

Canadian musicians performing in the United States may require a temporary work visa for non-immigrants under U.S. immigration law.[97] The United States Immigration and Naturalization Service has a myriad of non-immigrant visas available; those most applicable to Canadian musicians are the "O" visa and the "P" visa.[98] Both O-visas and P-visas require the approval, concurrence or recognition from the appropriate U.S. labour organization. Musicians entering the U.S. and working without obtaining the appropriate work visa may be subject to expedited removal and barred from the U.S. for 5 years, on the basis of a material misrepresentation of fact. There is no reviewable recourse once the bar has been issued.

When petitions for an "O" or "P" visa are submitted, the petitioner will be the party proposing to engage the musician. As well, the musician's skills, talents and extra-ordinary abilities must be demonstrated, and consultations with labour unions or peer group support documentation should be included in the application. Applicants applying for certain O and P categories also may be required to demonstrate that they maintain a foreign residence which they have no intention of abandoning. All other grounds of inadmissibility to the U.S. apply to those who are seeking non-immigrant visas.[99]

The "O" visa applies to individual musicians, groups and their accompanying performers and essential support personnel. An individual applying for an "O" visa should meet the criteria set out in the following definition:

> an alien who has extraordinary ability in the sciences, arts, education, business or athletics which has been demonstrated by sustained national or international acclaim...and whose achievements have been recognized in the field through extensive documentation, and seeks to enter the United States to continue work in the area of extraordinary ability...or seeks to enter the United States temporarily and solely for the purpose of accompanying and assisting in the artistic or athletic performance by an alien [who is admitted pursuant to an "O" visa].[100]

In order to qualify for an O-1 visa, various documentary evidence is required in support of an application. Musicians who have received awards or nominations, such as a Grammy or Juno, should note this in their application, as well as including any documents evidencing their

---

[97] *The Immigration and Nationality Act*, 1952, Pub. L. 101-649, 104 Stat. 4978, (codified as amended at 8 USC ss. 1101-1524) (hereinafter "*INA*"), s. 212(a)(6)(C)(i).

[98] *INA*, s. 101(a)(15)(O) and (P) respectively.

[99] Among the various grounds of inadmissibility are exclusions for health reasons, criminality, security issues, labour certification, illegal entrance, immigration violations, and false documents.

[100] 8 Code of Federal Regulations (hereinafter CFR), s. 214.2(o)(ii)(A)(i).

extraordinary ability.[101] Musicians applying for an O-1 visa should have performed at events with distinguished reputations, should have achieved national or international recognition, should maintain commercial or critical success and command a high salary or other substantial remuneration.[102] O-1 visas are approved for a maximum of 3 years for a specific tour. Formal requests for extensions may be made, and possibly may be approved in one-year increments.

O-2 visas are available to musicians or essential support personnel accompanying the O-1 musician. O-2 applicants must be petitioned for in conjunction with the O-1 alien.[103] O-2 visas may be granted to individuals who are an integral part of the O-1 alien's entourage and who are required to accompany or assist and have "...critical skills and experience with such alien which are not of a general nature and which cannot be performed by other individuals".[104] This must be demonstrated through documentary evidence. O-2 applicants often will include backstage assistants or stage technicians. An O-3 visa is available to the alien spouse or child of an O-1 or an O-2 applicant, should the spouse or child be either accompanying or joining the O-1 or O-2 visa holder.[105] Documentary evidence providing proof of the relationship will be required.

A "P" visa is available to those who are performing "...as an artist or entertainer, individually or as part of a group", or to those who are "...an integral part of the performance of such a group...."[106] "P" visa applicants must be entertainers or part of a group "...recognized internationally as being outstanding for a sustained and substantial period of time."[107] As in the "O" visa category, the "P" visa has a series of sub-classes. A P-1 visa applicant must have been involved with the group for a period of more than one year and, as a general rule, 75 percent of the group members must have been with the group for one year.[108]

A P-2 visa is available to musicians participating in a reciprocal exchange program between a Canadian and U.S. organization "...which provides for the temporary exchange of artists and entertainers."[109] P-3 visas are for performers, performing groups, teachers or coaches and

---

[101] *Ibid.*, s. 214.2(o)(3)(iv).

[102] *Ibid.*, s. 214.2(o)(3)(iii).

[103] *Ibid.*, s. 214.2(o)(4)(i).

[104] *INA*, s. 101(a)(15)(O)(ii)(III)(a).

[105] *Ibid.*, s. 101(a)(15)(O)(iii).

[106] *Ibid.*, s. 101(a)(15)(P).

[107] *Ibid.*, s. 101(a)(15)(P)(ii)(I).

[108] This provision of the *Immigration and Naturalization Act* is also available to athletes. Note that there are exceptions to this rule. This rule will be waived if a member replaces an essential member of the group on account of illness or other unusual circumstances, or if the new member augments the group by performing a critical role. 8 CFR s. 214.2(p)(4)(iii)(B).

[109] *INA*, s. 101(a)(15)(P)(ii)(II).

essential support personnel who seek to enter the U.S. for the purpose of performing, teaching or coaching a non-commercial program that is culturally unique.[110] An application for a P-3 visa will include evidence of authentic skills in the unique or traditional art form, as identified by testimony from experts recognized in the field and published reviews.[111] A P-4 visa will allow for the spouse or child of a P-1, P-2 or P-3 visa holder to accompany or join the alien.[112]

The O and P categories are specifically geared to established and successful performers. New or moderately successful artists will have difficulty qualifying for any visa category, without labour organization agreement or overwhelming documentary evidence in support of their application.[113] Musicians who do not qualify for O or P status can apply for an H-2B visa, which is provided to aliens coming temporarily to the U.S. to perform non-agricultural services which cannot be performed by a person already in the United States. The petitioner would have to prove that the employment of the musician will not adversely affect the wages and working conditions of workers in similar situations in the U.S.[114]

---

[110] 8 CFR s. 214.22 (p)(ii)(c).

[111] See www.dfait-maeci.gc.ca/english/culture/guidecul/visa.htm.

[112] *INA*, s. 101(a)(15)(P)(II)(iv).

[113] For further discussion on this issue, see Peter H. Loewy, "Dramatic Changes in the Immigration Law and How They Affect the Entertainment Industry", in *Entertainment, Publishing and the Arts Handbook*, (New York: Clark, Boardman, Callaghan, 1992-93), at page 465, and Lea Greenberger, "Temporary U.S. Work Visas for Foreign Performers", in Arend Jan van Marel and Louise Nemschoff, eds., *Business and Legal Aspects of Live Concerts and Touring*, (Apeldorn: Maklu Publishers, 1998).

[114] 8 CFR s. 214.2(h)(5)(i). A petitioner also could apply for a Q class visa, which includes: "participants in international cultural exchange programs".

8

RECORDING

Contributing Author: D. Blair Holder, LL.B.

The copyright aspects of audio and audio-visual recordings relevant to this chapter are discussed in Chapter 1, "Copyright" and will not be discussed again here. The GST aspects of the agreements discussed in this chapter are set out in Chapter 12, "Tax".

1. Record Companies

(a) Role and Object

The main object of a record company is to sell units of "recorded product". With this in mind, record companies contract with recording artists (musicians and/or vocalists with commercial potential), develop their recording career and sell recorded product featuring their performances. Recorded product includes both analog and digital reproductions of master recordings, including compact discs, vinyl records, cassettes and videos, for example. The terms "records" or "recordings", when used in this chapter, will mean any and all such "recorded product".

(b) Functions and Structure

(i) Outlined

In addition to finding and developing talent, the primary functions of a record company are to: (1) produce; (2) manufacture; (3) distribute; and (4) market and promote the sales of records. Not all record companies, however, perform all of these functions directly; third party companies may be engaged to assist the record company in fulfilling any of these functions. For example, many independent record companies have the ability to produce master recordings but must engage the services of both a record manufacturer and a distributor to duplicate the master recordings and get the product into retail outlets for sale. Additional functions of a record company may include merchandising, not only recordings, but also the musician's name, likeness, and/or trademark(s) on items such as t-shirts, hats, posters, dolls, etc., as discussed in Chapter 9, "Merchandising", and publicizing the musician's live performances in order to promote record sales.

Although no two record companies are necessarily structured in exactly the same way, the following departments normally exist in one form or another within most record companies: (1) artists and repertoire (A&R); (2) business and legal affairs; (3) marketing and promotion; and (4) distribution and sales.[1] These are outlined below.

(ii) Artists and Repertoire ("A&R")

The main roles of the A&R department of a record company are to find and sign musicians (i.e., "artists") and to record repertoire (i.e., songs and music). Recording musicians are commonly referred to in the business as "recording artists" but the term recording musician is also used here for the sake of consistency with the other chapters of this book. More specifically, A&R functions include: (1) discovering and nurturing talent; (2) discovering music with commercial potential; (3) overseeing the recording of music by overseeing the recording process and providing creative input relevant to all phases of production, including pre- and post-production of the recordings; (4) supervising the quality control of the final recording; and (5) evaluating other master recordings in order to test their commercial potential in the record company's territory.[2]

A&R personnel are also concerned with touring. They provide direction as to appropriate locations, territory and the timing of the tour and deciding whether the recording musician tours as a solo or supporting act.[3] A&R also shapes the musician's media image and gains media exposure for the musician in order to promote record sales. Here, a musician's manager and publicist often are also involved. A record company's A&R department may also assist a musician in obtaining representation by managers, booking agents and lawyers if the musician is not already represented, although many musicians

---

[1] For more detail, see Harvey Rachlin, *The Music Business Encyclopedia* (Toronto: Fitzhenry and Whiteside, 1979) at 317.

[2] *Ibid.*, at 317, 318.

[3] *Ibid.*, at 321.

already have such representation before signing with a record company.[4]

(iii) Business Affairs

The legal and business affairs department of a record company (which is often referred to simply as business affairs) is responsible for various legal, business and administrative matters within the record company. Lawyers, accountants and others with a legal background or experience in bookkeeping, copyright administration and/or licensing make up the business affairs departments in most record companies. Their tasks include: establishing recording budgets; overseeing financial matters such as payments to musicians and producers; registering the various copyrights involved in a recording (including the sound recording itself, accompanying artwork, liner notes, and photographs); and securing mechanical licences. As well, business affairs is responsible for drafting and negotiating agreements with artists and producers, and other relevant parties.

(iv) Marketing, Promotion and Publicity

Most of the efforts of the promotion department are directed at obtaining radio and video airplay. While it is well established that radio airplay has a significant impact on record sales, the impact of promotional music videos on record sales seems less direct. Music videos, however, are still generally believed to be an important aspect of the promotion of record sales and can be very effective with respect to promoting certain artists' recordings. Promotional records and other promotional material such as photographs, biographies, merchandise, and press releases highlighting the creative and business team of the artist are often sent to the media generally, including radio stations, in order to generate awareness of an upcoming release. Promotions may be carried out either by in-house staff of the record company or by independently contracted promotion companies who are engaged to further the record company's efforts. Smaller independent record companies often hire independent radio and T.V. promoters who may be entirely responsible for the promotion of a record to radio and video broadcasters.

A publicist focuses on obtaining media exposure for the musician. This helps sell recordings. Most publicity campaigns involve the use of a complete press kit including biographical material, photographs or

---

[4] See Chapter 6, "Agents and Managers".

other visual representations, press clippings, and a promotional CD of the musician. Sales angles or a media "hook" consistent with the music, the musician's image and his/her career direction are also important parts of creating interest and excitement in the media and with a musician's current and potential audience. Other publicity efforts include arranging interviews, album signing sessions in retail stores and other public appearances. The independent publicist is also discussed in Chapter 6, "Agents and Managers" and in Chapter 7, "Live Performance".

Major record companies have more recently adopted street teams as an essential part of a promotion and publicity campaign, and as a way of building a "grass-roots" awareness of the product and the artist. Street teams originally developed as the "grass-roots" marketing approach of predominantly young, urban, music entrepreneurs who did not have large marketing budgets available to them for expensive television and radio commercials and billboard advertisements. Typically, street teams consist of groups of young people who carry out a campaign 'blitz' which may include: heavy postering of the street; give-aways of stickers, buttons, and other merchandise; and the spray-painting of sidewalks and construction-site barricades with a name, logo, and/or campaign "hook" of an upcoming album release.

Finally, the Internet (in particular, the "World Wide Web") is fast becoming an essential new medium through which record companies' marketing and promotional efforts are being carried out. Banner advertisements, artist web-pages and web-sites, digitally downloadable or play-only "streaming" audio and video music samples of upcoming releases and live performances via "web-casting" comprise some of the marketing and promotions applications of the Internet. The Internet's promotional and sales potential cannot be overlooked by artists, their representatives, or record companies which produce and market their music product.

(v) Sales and Distribution

The sales department "develops sales campaigns, determines policies for discounts, special deals and returns, takes orders for recordings, oversees sales activities on local levels, provides financial assistance to accounts for advertising and oversees billings".[5] Record sales can be either national, regional, or local.[6]

Record distributors deal with sub-distributors, including "rack jobbers" and "one-stops" whose job it is to sell wholesale records to

---

[5] Rachlin, above, note 1 at 327.
[6] *Ibid.*, at 327.

retail outlets. Rack jobbers are sub-distributors who supply music product (i.e., CDs, cassettes, etc.) by leasing floor space in large department store chains such as Wal-Mart and Zellers. One-stops distribute a wide range of music product, from both major and independent record companies, to the smaller "mom and pop" type record stores. In addition, independent record production companies often contract with major record companies to distribute recordings either by a licence agreement or by a distribution agreement or a combination licence/production agreement. These agreements are outlined below in sections 1(d)(i-iv).

The Internet has emerged not only as a medium of advertising music product, but also as a means of delivering music to the audience of the artist and other music consumers. The combination of digital technology and data compression software such as MP3 technology makes this digital medium a distribution force to be utilized in addition to traditional 'bricks and mortar' retail distribution. Significantly expanding network bandwidth, and developing a universal, secure digital delivery technology that protects copyright creators, owners, and performers, are the last two major hurdles record companies have to overcome prior to fully embracing the Internet as a standard method of music distribution, and an alternative to traditional 'plastic and cardboard' manufacturing. All five major multinational record distributors are participating in the "Secure Digital Music Initiative" (the "SDMI") which seeks to overcome the latter of these two obstacles.

(vi) Production

Record production is the creation of a master recording. Some of the largest ("major") record companies have in-house producers and their own recording studios. However, most record companies, including the "majors", contract with independent record producers, on an album-by-album, or song-by-song basis.

The creative producer works with the engineer, vocalists and musicians in the recording studio to shape and define the finished recorded sound of the master in order to create an artistic product that will be commercially successful. See also the discussion of the record producer in section 1(d)(vi)A, for more detail.

There also may be a production co-ordinator who acts as an "executive producer", administering the creative and non-creative business aspects of the recording. An executive producer may be, and often is, the person who finances the recording. Alternatively, the executive producer may be an influential producer, manager, or record company executive who made production of the record possible and who lends his or her name and reputation to the recording. Sometimes an executive producer also is actually the creative producer, who engages in creative decisions and who, as executive producer, co-ordinates the overall production. Alternatively, the role of executive producer may be fulfilled by the record company's A&R personnel.

(vii) Manufacturing

Conventional album manufacturing consists of three main processes: (1) mastering; (2) lacquering and plating; and (3) pressing.[7] Mastering involves the manufacturing of the master disc from which the records are cut; the master is then plated and recordings are pressed. Compact disc and cassette mastering consists of equalizing the final mixes of the record master, and technically perfecting the sound of the master by removing distortion and other engineering imperfections which may arise throughout the recording process.

See also the discussion above in 1(b)(v) concerning digital delivery of music as an alternative to conventional manufacturing and distribution.

(c) Two Main Types

There are two main types of record companies: major record companies ("majors") and the independent record companies ("independents" or "indies"). Record companies tend to be referred to simply as "majors" or "indies". Majors typically have all of the departments described above and fulfill all of those functions discussed, while independents tend to have more limited human and financial resources. Out of economic necessity, therefore, independents may have one person fulfilling several or all of the above functions. In Canada, with the notable exception of Universal Music, the majors are subsidiaries of foreign-owned multinational corporations. The majority of independents are Canadian-owned and the larger independents are most often distributed by the majors.

There are various other specialized or hybrid record companies such as: (1) true independents - those with no affiliation or involvement whatsoever with a major record company; (2) major-distributed independents - independent record companies whose records are distributed by a major; (3) major-owned independents - independents wholly or partially owned by a major; (4) "boutique" labels often owned or co-owned by an influential, established manager,

---

[7] *Ibid.*, at 333. Note that traditional phonograph records sales have dwindled and CD's and cassettes account for the majority of record sales.

artist, or producer, which are financed, marketed, promoted and distributed by a major, and usually have a clear "identity" in the marketplace such as Maverick, Bad Boy, and Dreamworks; and (5) "specialty" labels, that is, labels that only produce music in one, limited-market genre (e.g., Baby Einstein Records for children's music) or who only market their music in very specialized ways (CDnow, for example, only distributes music via the Internet).

A distinction also should be made between independent record companies which are musician-owned and actually function as a true record company (finding, signing, and developing new talent, and financing and producing master recordings), and a so-called artist "loan-out" company. A loan-out company is wholly owned by the musician or band under which the musician or band carries on business, and is incorporated primarily as a tax-planning vehicle for musicians earning significant income from their careers in the music business. These "loan-outs" often do not function as true record companies but are essentially a legal way to reduce the artist's tax burden at higher income levels.

The independents are an important link between recording musicians and major record companies. The independents often finance recordings in whole or in part, and present finished masters to major companies for licence, lease, sale or distribution by the majors. They fulfill the important role of investing in new recordings, and contribute to the viability and variety of recordings in the marketplace.[8] Independents often can respond more quickly than a major record company to new music trends.[9]

(d) Types of Agreements

(i) Generally

The main types of contracts related to recording are: (1) the exclusive long term recording contract; (2) the record production agreement; (3) the pressing and distribution agreement (the "distribution agreement"); (4) the licence or lease of record masters

---

[8] Peter Steinmetz, "The Recording Industry", in *Copyright For The General Practitioner* (Toronto: C.B.A.O., 1978) (herein "Steinmetz") at p. 53. The Canadian Independent Record Producers Association ("CIRPA") is a useful source for information concerning independent Canadian record production and the legalities and practicalities of the record business in Canada.

[9] See David E. Kronemeyer and J. Gregory Sidak, "The Structure and Performance of the U.S. Record Industry" in *Entertainment, Publishing and the Arts Handbook*, above, note 8, at pp. 263-282, which discusses these issues in the U.S. context.

agreement; (5) the producer agreement; and (6) the music video production agreement.[10] Also relevant are the master use agreement and the sale of master recordings agreement. Each of the above-noted agreements is a distinct, complex, commercial agreement; however, there are terms common to each contract.

The musician who operates an independent record production company, either by choice, for reasons of artistic control, or if he or she is unable to secure a recording contract, may enter into any or all of the above agreements. Any of the above contracts may be entered into separately or there may be a mixing and matching of the above relationships in one agreement. The exclusive long term recording contract between an artist and record company is generally the most comprehensive agreement and its terms are relevant to the other agreements. A recording agreement is usually entered into before the other agreements referred to above are secured.

(ii) Production

The contractual terms and conditions of a record production agreement can be very similar to the exclusive term recording agreement discussed below. However, a production agreement and a long term recording agreement do differ, mainly in their financial terms and in the way in which records are to be marketed and distributed. A record production company (the "production company"), which is not a major record company, is not expected to function (nor can it) on the same level as a major in terms of resources - i.e., staff and money - or in its ability to market, promote, and distribute records. In the past, production companies often did not engage in national record distribution without the assistance of a major. However, in the face of consolidation of major record companies, and with the emergence of new technologies such as the Internet, production companies are increasingly employing new and creative ways of distributing and marketing their music without the assistance of the majors.

However, production companies still commonly seek to obtain licences or a licence/production/distribution agreement with other larger independents or major record companies. In this sense, the

---

[10] Other agreements such as soundtrack albums also may be entered into, but the agreements outlined in the text are the most common. See Clive Fisher, PromoVideos, "Record Company Agreements" (1984) Vol. 2 No. 6 I.M.L. 42 (herein "Fisher"). See also Ronald H. Gertz and Gary D. Culpepper, "Music Video: Realities of the Business", in *Entertainment, Publishing and the Arts Handbook* (New York: Clark, Boardman, 1986) at pp. 283-299 for a discussion of the video production business and video production agreement (herein "Gertz/Culpepper").

production company acts as a broker between itself, the musician, and third parties. It is not unusual for a musician who is negotiating a production agreement to require in a contract that the company obtain, within a specified time after the commencement of the agreement, a licensing or distribution commitment from a third party major record company or national distributor, if the production company does not already have national or international distribution in place. If successful in obtaining a third party recording or licensing agreement within the time specified, then the term of the agreement between the production company and the musician often becomes co-terminous and co-extensive with the terms of the third party agreement.[11]

Under a production agreement, a musician signs exclusively to the production company to record one, two, or more albums' worth of masters. Once the production company has acquired these exclusive rights, it often then contracts with a larger record company: (1) to provide to such company the services of the musician and the master recordings which are the products of the musician's services; and (2) to have such company distribute, market and promote the album(s) delivered by the production company.

Royalties are paid to the musician as follows: the record company distributes and sells records and pays a royalty to the production company, which in turn pays a percentage of these "net" proceeds (i.e., the production company's receipts minus its costs) to the musician (and any independent record producer(s) who produced the masters). The difference between the royalty (or share of net receipts) which the production company receives from the record company and the royalties paid by it to the musician and the respective record producer, is its net revenue, or profit, from such recordings. The production company's recording costs, which are often paid for by the record company, are typically the main cost deducted from the gross proceeds to arrive at the "net" sum.

Typically, recording budgets provided by the independents are smaller than those available from major record companies. Other issues — for example, tour support, video commitment and the royalty rate, all of which are negotiable — are often dealt with differently in a production agreement than in a record agreement. Other terms, however, which are fundamental to all recording and production agreements, such as royalties, reserves, packaging deductions, controlled composition clauses, re-recording restrictions, and accounting and audit clauses, are often addressed in detail in this agreement, just as they are in a recording agreement.

---

[11] See the *Holly Johnson* case discussed in Chapter 10, "Personal Service Contracts" which discusses the restraint of trade issues raised by this practice.

(iii) Distribution

In order to obtain greater access to larger markets and ensure the security of payment from established retail accounts, record production companies often seek distribution agreements with major distributors who distribute recordings nationally, or internationally, through normal commercial retail channels. When licensing and/or distribution agreements are not available through major record companies and/or distributors, production companies may contract with smaller independent distributors to release their records commercially. The distribution agreement can be a combination of pressing-distribution or production-distribution, or perhaps even a combination licence/pressing-distribution agreement. The terms of the distribution agreement are discussed in detail below in section 3(e).

(iv) Licence of Record Masters

The record licence (or lease) agreement can be thought of as a form of franchise agreement.[12] The record production company (which in some cases may be the musician who has paid for, produced, and owns the masters) licenses the rights to use such masters to other record companies under the licence agreement. Under this agreement, the record production company (the "licensor") maintains ownership over all of the masters and supplies the record company (the "licensee") with labelling information concerning reproduction and packaging, and the licensee reproduces the labelling. The licence agreement is discussed in detail below in section 3(d)(iii).

(v) Producer Agreement

A. The Producer's Role

The producer plays a key creative, technical, and administrative role in the recording process. The producer oversees all of the record production, from pre-production to recording and mixing of the final

---

[12] See, generally, Joseph Taubman, *In Tune With The Music Business* (New York: Law Arts Publishers, 1980) at p. 70 for a discussion of lease agreements, pp. 70-75 for licence agreements, and pp. 65-70 for purchase and sale agreements. See also Sidney Shemel and M. William Krasilovsky, *This Business of Music*, Rev. 6th Ed. (New York: Billboard Books, 1990), chapter 2, "Foreign Record Deals" at pp. 24-38. Granting a licence essentially means granting permission to use and/or exploit commercially (but not own) property. Record masters are licensed property relevant to this part of this chapter.

master. The main creative role of the record producer is to record the musician's performances and produce artistically, commercially and technically viable record masters. Together with recording musicians, producers are often active in the selection of material they will record, and they often co-write with the musician and help shape the musical and/or vocal arrangements of the material to be recorded.

Producers must be aware of both new and developing trends and established recording techniques and technology. They also attempt to maximize the commercial potential of a record and ensure that it is compatible with its intended market (for example, commercial radio markets or other niche markets such as instrumental or heavy metal music). The sound of the record is integral to the sales and marketing of a recording, and the producer is integral both to producing that sound and to the entire recording process. This is why record producers, if they are successful, are often as well known within the music business as successful recording artists.

The producer is also ultimately responsible for overseeing the recording budget, ensuring that the anticipated and approved recording costs are not exceeded, and that the masters are completed and delivered to the record company on time. Over time, as musicians gain experience, they may produce or co-produce their own recordings for the record company, but usually, a recording musician will work in close conjunction with the producer to produce finished masters.

B. The Agreement

The producer agreement may be either between a musician and an independent record producer or between a record company (or a production company) and the independent record producer. When the agreement is between a musician and a producer, often the producer will also seek to obtain a licence agreement or record production agreement with a third party record company on the artist's and producer's behalf. Alternatively, the producer is hired either by an independent or major record company when a recording agreement is already in place with the recording artist/musician. Producer agreements are discussed below in section 3(c)(iii).

(vi) Video Production Agreement

The video production agreement is an agreement related to the video production commitment under a production agreement or an exclusive recording artist agreement. Video production is distinct from record production. A video is produced by a director, with or without the assistance of a separate video producer, or video production company. However, the definition of a "master" and a "record" under a recording agreement and record production agreement usually includes audio-visual recordings, such as promotional and commercial music videos, therefore the terms of the production and record agreement are relevant to the production of music videos.

Music video production is where the film and video business and the music industry most clearly intersect because music video production has aspects that are similar to production of television movies and feature films.

The specific terms of this agreement are discussed in detail below in section 3(b)(i-iv).

(vii) Master Use Licence

A master use licence usually occurs when a single master is licensed for use in a television program, commercial, or feature film, for example. The master use licence is similar to the licence agreement for master recordings and contains many of the same terms and provisions. What distinguishes it is that, under a master use licence, the master recording is generally not used for the commercial sale of recordings to the public, but rather is a licence to incorporate a recording into the on-screen soundtrack of a film, television show or commercial, for example. Details of the master use licence are discussed below in section 3(d)(i).

(viii) Master Purchase/Sale Agreement

Record companies may engage in the purchase and sale of masters for a number of reasons, namely: if the record company's assets are being sold as part of an overall sale of the company; if a record production agreement provides that a musician would sign to the production company for a fixed term, and would be entitled to purchase the masters if a third party agreement were not obtained in a specific period of time; or if the purchase of an independent recording artist's independent recording is part of the long term recording agreement. The sale of a catalogue in music publishing was discussed in Chapter 3, "Music Publishing" and many issues relevant to that agreement are relevant to this one. The master purchase/sale agreement may be either an asset purchase by way of an assignment of all right, title and interest in and to the masters, or may be effected by a purchase of shares in the production company itself. The terms of this agreement are discussed below in section 3(d)(ii).

2. Exclusive Term Record Contract

Although all agreements discussed in this text have their complexities, the long term exclusive record agreement, in particular, is a complex commercial document. The discussion below is general in nature. It does not attempt to address every contingency or clause in such agreements. Every recording agreement is unique and each varies from company to company. In addition, the full impact of digital technology, the Internet and e-commerce on this agreement (and the recording industry generally) has yet to be determined.[12a] In any given contractual situation, skilled legal advice should be sought. The discussion below takes into account a number of variables under the following agreements: (a) the exclusive term agreement with a record production company; (b) the exclusive term record agreement with a major record company; and (c) a net receipts and "off-the-top" agreement.

(a) Musician's Rights and Obligations

(i) Generally

The law in relation to exclusive term recording contracts is complex and evolving as is discussed in Chapter 10, "Personal Service Contracts". The relevant legal doctrines which discuss the musician's rights and obligations under such agreements are discussed there and will not be discussed in detail below, but some of the specific legal concerns related to these agreements, which have been discussed in the case law, will be footnoted here.

(ii) Exclusive Personal Services

The recording agreement is a personal service agreement[13] whereby the musician is engaged,[14] on an exclusive basis, to provide

---

[12a] See Bobby Rosenblum's "Sorting Through the Confusion: Interpreting Standard Recording Agreement Provisions in the Digital Era", Vol. 21, No. 6 E.L.R. 1999 for a U.S. perspective in this regard.

[13] See Chapter 10, "Personal Service Contracts" for a discussion of personal service contracts. Note that exclusive contracts can give rise to the issue of restraint of trade as is discussed in Chapter 10. Also, for U.S. recording contracts governed by California law, *California Labor Code* s. 3351.5 provides that persons engaged to create specially commissioned works who agree in their contracts that works are "works for hire" as defined in the U.S. copyright law are "employees" for the purposes of the Code. In Joseph B.

recording services that are of a "unique, intellectual and extraordinary character" to a record company.

The main service that the musician provides is that of personal recording services for the purpose of recording master recordings, but numerous other obligations are also specified in the agreement. They typically include making audio-visual recordings (i.e., music videos) to promote recordings produced under the agreement; the recording musician is also expected to attend interviews for promotional purposes and make personal appearances on radio and T.V. and in the media to promote and publicize recordings. Generally, aside from the expenses incurred which are directly related to such activities, no additional payment is paid to the recording musician for these promotional services; however, the musician is usually paid advances, session fees and record royalties.

The musician is also generally expected to maintain a live performing act, because live performances promote record sales. It is possible to have a provision in the agreement stipulating that the musician must provide a live act for a specified number of appearances per year; however, this would not be advisable since it is difficult to predict in advance how many live performances a musician can reasonably perform in a year. Musicians also usually agree to maintain membership in good standing in the applicable union or guilds (the AFM or ACTRA, for example) if requested by the company. Record companies often include this clause because they are, or may in the future become, signatory to the AFM phonograph labour agreement.[15]

It is possible for a recording agreement to be non-exclusive, but this would be unusual except in a few very limited situations, such as in the jazz recording field or when a musician has contracted for a single album or series of albums. Care should be taken to ensure that the exclusive nature of this agreement does not prevent the musician from: appearing as a side person on the records of other artists; recording commercial jingles; or appearing in films. Many recording musicians require income from such sources in order to make a living. Additional "carve-out" clauses are usually provided in the agreement.

Anderson, "The Work for Hire Doctrine and California Recording Contracts: A Recipe for Disaster", (1995), 17 Hastings Comm./Ent. L.J. 587, the author argues that the effect of this definition and the terms of a typical recording contract are such as to render virtually all California record companies in breach of their obligations to pay unemployment insurance and workers' compensation premiums as well as minimum wages to their artists, thus making it possible for their artists to overturn these contracts, obtain the return of their recordings and sue for lost wages.

[14] See Chapter 12, "Tax" for a discussion of the musician as self-employed or employed individual for income tax purposes.

[15] See Chapter 5, "Labour" for a discussion of this agreement and other aspects of the AFM and a musician's membership in this union.

(iii) Representations, Warranties, Indemnity

Representations and warranties are assurances and statements of fact made by one party to another in a contract, which are intended to induce that party to enter into the agreement and upon which the relevant party relies. For example, musicians may be required to represent and warrant to the record company that: (1) they are free and clear to perform and execute the contract; (2) they are under no disability or restriction and have the capacity to grant all rights under the agreement; (3) they are over the age of eighteen years, unless clearly they are being signed as minors;[16] (4) they will do no acts inconsistent with the company's rights under the agreement, either before or after the term of the contract; (5) none of the services to be rendered under the agreement will violate common law or statutory rights, including copyright law;[17] (6) there are no prior unreleased recordings; (7) they are not bound by a previous recording contract; and (8) they are or will become members in good standing of the AFM.

If any of these representations and warranties are breached, the record company is typically to be fully indemnified, that is, compensated by the musician, if damages result. In addition, not unlike a music publisher in an exclusive term publishing contract, the record company may, at its election, either demand immediate payment, or withhold the musician's royalties, usually up to the amount of the actual claim. Alternatively, the company may agree to allow royalties to be paid if the musician posts a suitable bond.

A more equitable indemnification clause would provide for mutual indemnification by the parties. This means that the musician would also be indemnified by the record company in situations where the company is also responsible, in whole or in part, for any claims or damages that arise.[18]

---

[16] See Chapter 10, "Personal Service Contracts" for a discussion of contracts with minors.

[17] See, for example, *Allan v. Bushnell T.V. Co.*,[1968] 1 O.R. 720 where it was held that there is an implied fundamental condition in a contract between a broadcasting company and a news service to provide news to the broadcasting company that the news was not defamatory. By analogy, in a recording contract there may be an implied condition that the songs supplied to the record company were not obscene, for example, which is a breach of common and statutory law. Obscenity is discussed in Chapter 7, "Live Performance" and below in the text, section 4.

[18] See the indemnification discussion in Chapter 3, "Music Publishing".

(iv) Definitions

The exclusive term recording contract, like other contracts that a musician may enter into, should contain precise definitions. One should pay particular attention to certain definitions, for example, the definitions of "royalties", "net receipts", "master" and "record", because they can affect other provisions of the agreement and determine rights under the agreement - for example, the artist's right to receive certain monies, and to appear on television or in movies. In fact, anything that seeks to reduce royalties or extend standard rights, or that reduces or delays payments to a musician, is financially important, should be carefully reviewed, and should be negotiable.

Since recording agreements typically do not state royalties as a penny rate, the actual "dollars and cents value" of the royalty provisions of such agreements should be calculated, insofar as possible.[19] In this regard, it is much more useful to know that a CD sale in Canada will yield a royalty of $1.50 for the artist - commonly referred to as the "penny rate" - than to know only that the artist is entitled to a royalty of "14% of the suggested retail list price of 90% of net sales, minus packaging, free goods, reasonable reserves, and other standard deductions".

Provisions that are typically defined and negotiated are discussed in the text below.

A. Record

The term "record" should be clearly defined. It is usually defined to include all types of analog and digital records including compact discs (CD's), DAT's, cassettes, computer discs, and phonograph records in any combination or configuration now in use or which may be invented in the future. The term record may be distinguished from audio-visual recordings (i.e., videos), but more commonly the definition of a record also includes all forms of audio-visual recordings. This has relevance concerning royalties payable for records and therefore videos, as is discussed in section 2(b)(v)K below. It also means, in most cases, that the recording artist /musician must obtain the consent of the record company to appear in a TV series or film, particularly where a recording of the musician's performance is to be made in conjunction therewith.

---

[19] See Neil Roberts, David Matheson, cited below at note 20, *Syllabus on Music Industry* ... at pp. 37.

B. Master/Outtakes

The term "master" usually means original recordings of the musician's performances either in the form of a fully mixed $^1/_4$" tape, DAT (digital audio tape) or 1630 videotape equivalent form, from which records are to be manufactured. The master recording also may be stored only in the form of a computer hard disc or may be "burned" directly to CD-R (recordable compact disc). The term "masters" also usually includes both audio recordings and audio-visual recordings. This has relevance concerning royalties payable to the musician (and perhaps the individual record producer) with respect to videos, which are discussed below in section 2(b)(v)K.

Numerous recordings may be recorded for the purposes of completing an album. The tracks not included on the album are often referred to as "outtakes". In negotiating the recording or production agreement, the musician may be successful in stipulating that no outtakes are to be released without the musician's consent.

C. Recording

The definition of a "recording" will usually mean an original sound recording or a sound-and-visual recording "whether on magnetic recording tape or wire, lacquer or wax disc, film or any other substance or material now known or unknown".[20]

---

[20] Neil Roberts, David Matheson, Eds., *Syllabus on Music Industry: Contract Negotiations and the Law* (Toronto: York University, 1980) at p. 85. This list of definitions is adapted in part from the long form recording contract in these materials. At pp. 37-60, there is a useful discussion on negotiating the recording agreement from the Canadian perspective. For a general discussion of recording agreements, see Greg Stevens and Nina Stevenson, Chapter 9, "Recording and the Recording Contract" in Shane Simpson and Greg Stevens, *Music: The Business and the Law* (Sydney: The Law Book Co. Ltd., 1986), pp. 108-130. See also *This Business of Music...* cited above in note 12, Chapter 1, "Recording Artist Contracts", at pp. 3-23, Chapter 4, "Independent Record Producers", at pp. 49-59, Chapter 5, "Record Clubs and Premiums", at pp. 60-62, Chapter 6, "Labour Agreements", at pp. 63-75, for a general discussion of the record business and recording agreements in the U.S. music business context. For an in-depth look at of the inner workings of the record industry in the U.S., see Fredric Dannen Hitman, *Power Brokers and Fast Money Inside the Music Business* (New York: Times Books/Random House, Inc., 1990). See also as a general source, *Sound Investments: The Recording Industry* (Toronto: CIRPA, 1987). An in-depth discussion is also found in Donald C. Farber, *Entertainment Industry Contracts Negotiating and Drafting Guide* (New York: Matthew Bender, 1990), Vol. 4 Music, Samuel Fox, Ed. (herein Fox), specifically Chapter 159, a discussion of the recording contract, and in particular Chapters 160 and 161, which discuss in detail and comment on the exclusive long term recording agreement.

D. Album

The term "album" still may be defined as follows: "a sufficient number of masters to have a playing time equivalent to one 12-inch, 33-1/3 rpm long-playing record, that is not less than 40 minutes nor more than 50 minutes in playing time provided that where the company shall sell as one package unit the masters for two or more long-playing records (or their tape equivalents) such masters shall be considered hereunder for all purposes as one album only".[21] It is not uncommon to require that an album be 45-50 minutes in playing time, though it is unusual to specify a maximum time.

E. Territory

The territory in which the record company owns rights to the musician's services (and in which the company may exploit the musician's recordings) must be specified. In theory, the territory may be for Canada only, Canada and the U.S., or may be for "the world" or "the universe". However, unlike licence or distribution agreements which typically are territorially specific, it is unusual for the territory in a recording contract to be anything other than the world, or the universe.

F. Term

The "term" of the contract refers to the duration of the agreement, and should be specifically set out as well. It may be stated as either: (a) a fixed initial period of time, plus options; (b) the time it takes for a specified number of recordings to be recorded and delivered; (c) in the case of a record production agreement, the contract may be co-terminous with a third party record agreement, management agreement, or publishing agreement; or (d) the term could be a fixed number of records with a "rolling option" period. A rolling option is where the contract states that the option period will expire, for example, either in (a) 12 months from the beginning of the applicable contract period; or (b) six months from the date that the album is completed and delivered to the record company, whichever is later. Currently, the "rolling option" is the most typical way the term is defined. See also section 2(b)(x)D below.

---

[21] *Ibid., Syllabus on Music Industry...*

G. Recording Costs

Recording costs are payments made by the record company to create masters. They include costs for studio time, engineering fees, equipment rental, sample clearances, payments to all accompanying "session" performers and all those persons or other entities who have provided services or goods including producer's fees, union or guild payments, default and cancellation of session expenses, and any reasonable costs incurred up to the point of manufacture of records, excluding artwork and (arguably) mastering costs. Costs incurred beyond post-production, including manufacturing, shipping and promotion costs, should be the record company's responsibility.

H. Royalty Rates

Royalty rates should be defined and specified. These rates are discussed below under the record company obligations in section 2(b)(v).

I. Other

Other terms also may be defined for greater certainty, including: (1) merchandising rights; (2) controlled compositions; (3) the company's licensees or distributors; (4) recording sessions; (5) options; (6) recording obligations, such as minimum and additional recording obligations; and (7) net receipts. The above list and discussion are not exhaustive. Bear in mind that each agreement is distinct and other definitions may be relevant in any given case.

(v) Contracting Entity/Personal Liability/Joint and Several Obligations

The contracting entity of the musician may be a sole proprietorship, partnership, corporation or a joint venture,[22] each of which has different business and tax considerations as discussed in Chapters 11 and 12, respectively.

Part of the essential element of personal service contracts (as discussed in Chapter 10) is the obligation to provide the personal services of the musician. Where the musician contracts as a sole

---

[22] See Chapter 11, "Business" for a discussion of business entities.

proprietorship or partnership, the musician is personally liable under this agreement. In the case when a musician enters into this agreement through a corporation that is not yet formed, there can also be personal liability.[23]

Even when a musician seeks to limit personal liability, by signing through a corporate entity that is properly constituted (which would be either a personal "loan out" company of the musician, or a production company which owns exclusive rights to the musician), the musician typically is personally bound by this agreement. The most common way to bind the musician to provide personal services is by an inducement letter.[24]

Even if a contract is not signed, whenever there are obligations and consideration (i.e., things of value) flowing between the parties, or as a result of incomplete negotiations, there may be liability incurred by one or both parties. Pre-contract expenditures, for example, may be recoverable if the parties to the contract anticipated those expenditures before signing the contract.[25]

It is also important to ascertain which entity a musician is contracting with: for instance, the parent record company, an affiliate, or a subsidiary of the parent company. Smaller subsidiary and affiliate companies are generally less stable in terms of financing, structure, and personnel. However, recent mergers and rumoured mergers demonstrate that even life at a major record company can be volatile and unpredictable. Parent, affiliate or subsidiary companies also may have different policies and practices regarding the computation of royalties.[26] If the musician is a minor, this has important legal consequences as to the enforceability of the agreement.[27]

Obligations of musicians under a recording contract are often stated to be joint and several, that is, they apply to the individual

---

[23] *Phonogram Ltd. v. Lane*, [1981] 3 All E.R. 182. This case involved a management company, not yet formed, which was to contract with the record company to provide the musician's services. This case was decided under the *European Communities Act 1972*, which found the defendant Lane personally liable for £600 advanced in consideration of completion of the contract as "an agent for a company not yet formed". A similar result could be reached in Canada. For a recent Ontario case, not in the record industry, see *Szecket et al. v. Huang et al.* (1998), 42 O.R. (3d) 400.

[24] *Ibid.*, see below section 3(c) - producer agreements for a discussion of the inducement letter.

[25] *Anglia Television v. Reed*, [1971] 3 All E.R. 690 (Eng. C.A.). This case involved the repudiation of a contract by an actor, Reed. Claims for pre-contract expenditures were allowed instead of loss of profits. See also note 23 above.

[26] Walter Lorimer and Phalen Hurewitz, *Syllabus on Representing Musical Artists: Legal Business and Practical Aspects* (Los Angeles: Entertainment Law Institute and the Beverly Hills Bar Association, 1975) at p. 283.

[27] See Chapter 10, "Personal Service Contracts" for a discussion of agreements with minors.

musicians and other parties to the contract (for example, the musician's corporation) separately and collectively. From the company's perspective, this is important because, for example, if a group disbands, the company still will have contractual commitments from and obligations to each individual musician and the group jointly, regardless of who remains in or has left the group. From the musician's viewpoint, the contract should not permit the company to recover damages against any musician or other contracting party, such as the musician's corporation, which has not breached obligations under the contract.

(vi) Personality Rights/Merchandising Rights

In order for record companies to release recordings, and promote and advertise records to the public, the record company must acquire by contract the right to use the musician's name, likeness, biographical material and other attributes of the musician's personality. This right usually will be exclusive during the term of the agreement and non-exclusive thereafter. The record company will also contract to have the right to publicize the musician as the exclusive recording artist of the company.

Significant monies can be generated from the manufacture and sale of commercial merchandise such as t-shirts, hats, dolls, and knapsacks at concerts and/or in retail outlets. Sometimes the record company will attempt to acquire these merchandising rights as part of the recording contract. Preferably it will not, unless it is a well-established merchandising operation (selling more than records), with a track record of successfully moving significant amounts of high quality commercial merchandise. Also, the record company should be willing to pay the musician a substantial amount from the sale of merchandise, in addition to the personal and production advances payable under the contract. But the record company should focus its efforts on selling records, not merchandise.

If the record company does obtain 100% of merchandising rights, it might agree to share net revenue 75/25 (in favour of the musician), or an even 50/50 split. The key issue here is which party will administer the merchandising rights - the company itself, or will it try simply to secure a licensing arrangement with a third party merchandise company? If so, what will that third party's share of income be? The definition of "net revenue" is significant. See Chapter 9, "Merchandising" for further discussion of merchandising rights and agreements.

(vii) Artistic/Creative Control

Artistic or creative control is also an important point for negotiation.[28] The beginning recording musician typically has less contractual control over artistic decisions than more established musicians. However, in practice, most creative decisions usually involve the musician, the record company and often the musician's management as well. The choice of studio, producer, material to be recorded, and the recording location are artistic issues that ideally should be mutually agreed upon, since all of these issues can have an important impact on the final recording. The musician at least should be consulted, and ideally would have approval rights with respect to certain key creative decisions. Some of these decisions are discussed below.

A. Producer

The record producer's primary objective is to deliver a recording that is acceptable to the record company and the musician, and that is interesting and exciting to the consumer. To be able to do this, the producer must create or facilitate a productive and creative environment. The record producer and the recording musicians must be compatible both personally and artistically, otherwise an inferior recording may result.

B. Material

The "material" or music to be recorded is often mutually chosen by the company's A & R department, the producer, and the musician, sometimes with the assistance of the musician's personal manager. Normally, until the musician has a successful history of record sales, artistic control regarding selection of material is not placed solely in the hands of the musician; it is subject to the record company's final decision.

---

[28] See Chapter 10, "Personal Service Contracts" and in particular the *Holly Johnson* case which suggests that the absence of a musician's right to control, including control over recording budgets, raises restraint of trade issues.

C. Quality

The quality of recordings has three aspects: (1) technical; (2) commercial; and (3) artistic. The first two aspects are usually fully within the purview of the recording company. U.S. case law has outlined the extent and limits of a musician's rights with respect to artistic quality under standard recording agreements. Whether these principles would be applied in the Canadian courts is not known, but they are useful to consider here. For example, where a musician was dissatisfied with the quality of recordings and the company exercised its contractual rights to associate the name and likeness of the musician with the recordings made under the recording agreement, the musician was not successful in suing on the basis of a right of privacy, or unfair competition, simply because the albums were not up to the quality expected or desired by the musician.[29] Where there was a partly oral and partly written contract granting Roberta Flack the right of approval over the quality of her recordings, an injunction request by her, which would have prevented the showing or distribution of a motion picture and a soundtrack album including a Roberta Flack recording, was not awarded[30] because there was no evidence that there would be "irreparable damage" to her career.

D. Merchandising and Artwork

Musicians should seek to have some control over how their records and related artwork are merchandised, since this is integral to the musician's image, career development and record sales.

(viii) Assignment

Typically, the contract allows only the record company and not the recording musician to assign its rights under the agreement.[31] The case law suggests that restraint of trade issues are present and that there should be some restriction on the record company's assignment of rights. Perhaps a fair restriction would be to restrict such assignment only to a successor or affiliated company, or a mutually acceptable third

---

[29] *Johnny Desmond v. 20th Century Fox Record Corporation and ABC Paramount Records, Inc.*, 321 N.Y.S.2d 45 (S.C. App. Div. 1971).

[30] *Flack v. United Artists Corporation*, 378 F.Supp. 637 (1974).

[31] See Chapter 3, "Music Publishing" for a discussion concerning assignment. It may be an issue whether either party can assign its rights without consent of the other if it is a personal service agreement.

party record company which will be bound by the terms of the agreement. Pursuant to an assignment of rights under a recording agreement whereby the company seeks to assign a contract option, notice must be given to the musician who is contractually bound by the assignment, in order for the assignment to be validly exercised.[32] This was the holding in a case where Rod Stewart, through his corporation, Rollgreen Ltd., granted an assignment to Mercury Records and Mercury assigned its rights to Phonogram, a related company. When Phonogram tried to exercise this option, the court held it could not be exercised without notice to Rod Stewart as grantor.

A musician who is unincorporated should have the right to assign the agreement to a corporation under which he or she carries on business, provided documents of personal adherence are entered into which are satisfactory to the record company. Musicians should also have the right to assign monies owing to them under the agreement to third parties, if they so choose and the need arises.

(b) Record Company's Rights and Obligations

(i) Generally

As discussed in sections 1(b)(i)–(vii) above, generally a record company's role is to produce, manufacture, promote and sell records. However, some recording agreements require that the record company do little more than finance the recordings and pay royalties if a record recoups, but, the trend is to more reasonable agreements.[33]

---

[32] *Warner Bros. Records Inc. v. Rollgreen Ltd.*, [1976] Q.B. 430 (Eng. C.A.). English contract law is generally applicable in Canada in the common law provinces, that is, other than Quebec. The issue of the assignability of the contract also gives rise to the issue of restraint of trade as indicated in the English cases discussed in Chapter 10, "Personal Services Contracts", and in particular the *Holly Johnson* case. Other cases in the commercial law context have also considered the assignability of contracts. See, for example, *Positive Seal Dampers Inc. v. M & I Heat Transfer Products Ltd.* (1991), 2 O.R. (3d) 225 (Ont. Gen. Div.), affirmed (1997), 73 C.P.R. (3d) 319 (Ont. C.A.). See also *Steinberg Inc. v. Tilak Corp.* (1991), 2 O.R. (3d) 165 (Ont. Gen. Div.) per Potts, J.

[33] As discussed in the *Holly Johnson* case, this raises the issue of restraint of trade. See Chapter 10, "Personal Service Contracts" for a discussion of this case and the issues of restraint of trade and other legal issues that affect recording agreements.

(ii) Payment

A. Generally

The main types of payment under a recording contract include: (1) advances; (2) fees and per diems for recording sessions or other contracted promotional appearances, at union scale, or otherwise; (3) record sale royalties; (4) union payments other than session fees, such as pension and trust fund payments; and (5) copyright royalties, including mechanical and synchronization royalties, and royalties from the "new income streams", in particular so-called "neighbouring rights" and blank tape/CD-R levies.

It is expected that the performer's 50% of the neighbouring rights payments and the artist/songwriter's share of income from the blank tape/CD-R levy will be paid directly to the artist from the NRCC (the Neighbouring Rights Collective of Canada) and the CPCC (the Canadian Private Copying Collective) respectively, rather than through the record company. However, attention should be paid to contractual provisions that may direct or suggest otherwise. These payments are discussed below in more detail.

B. Advances

(1) Generally

An advance is usually a non-returnable, but fully recoupable, prepayment against a musician's royalty account. This means that before receiving any royalty payments, advances must be repaid from royalties or net receipts otherwise payable to the musician; however, advances are not otherwise repayable. This is the same as publishing contract advances. Advances can be one of five types: (1) an advance on signing; (2) an advance on exercising an option period; (3) advances payable with respect to recording costs; (4) tour support and other miscellaneous advances; and (5) label advances. An advance on signing can range from a nominal advance to an advance in the tens of thousands of dollars and more, depending on the factors in a given case. These factors include: the stature of the musician in the music business; the size of the record company; and whether there are other record companies also interested in signing the artist. The size of option advances is also greatly influenced by the stature of the artist, the bargaining power of the parties, and the degree of success in previous contract periods. Recording costs are advances to the musician to make recordings. Recording costs are discussed in section 2(b)(iv)A below, and in section 2(a)(iv)G above.

(2) Minimum/Maximum Formula

Sometimes the agreement stipulates that both artist advances and recording advances are subject to a minimum/maximum formula. That is, such advances would not be less than, or more than, the specified minimum or maximum amounts. Typically, this clause stipulates that the size of the advance is determined as either a minimum or maximum amount, or somewhere in between, by calculating all or a percentage, for example 2/3 – 3/4 of the record sales royalties from the previous album, or the average of the last two albums, whichever is lower. In this regard, the "pipeline income", that is record sales royalties accrued, but which have not yet been accounted for, should be factored into the minimum/maximum formula in order to ascertain the amount of an advance payable.

(3) Label Advances/Licence Advances

Label advances are similar to publishing catalogue advances, in that they are monies paid by third party companies who, by licence, acquire the right to exploit a catalogue of certain property rights (in this case, rights in the master recordings), typically in foreign territories. The advance is paid prior to actually exploiting the masters or earning any income from such exploitation.

Musicians do not typically receive an advance when the record company receives a label advance from a third party licensee (usually in a foreign territory), unless such advance is specifically tied to a particular record, or that specific artist, not the record company's catalogue generally.[34]

---

[34] The following clause addresses a sharing of advance monies under a label catalogue advance and was worked out by Graham Henderson, Barrister & Solicitor, and Steven Ehrlick, Barrister & Solicitor: Artist shall receive a portion of an advance of royalties paid to Company for Masters licensed with other masters including a label licence of Masters of more than one of Company's artists, payable in the following manner: fifty percent (50%) of any such "label" advance (the "artist share") shall be paid to Artist and all other artists who form the subject matter of such third party agreement (the "Label Artist") on a *pro rata* percentage basis determined by totalling Company's record sales for all Label Artists for the six months preceding the payment of the label advance and assigning a *pro rata* percentage to each of the Label Artists based on their respective sales then remitting to the Artist the applicable percentage amount of the "artist share". For the sake of clarity and by way of example only, in the case where Company receives a "label" advance of $100,000 and the Artist is responsible for thirty

Record companies are reluctant to share such advances with musicians signed to them, because it is difficult to ascertain which of several records to which the advance is tied will actually generate income and because such monies are used to finance the record label. It is more typical and easier to negotiate a share of a specific advance when one is dealing with an independent record company which licenses one single act, or one set of masters only.

Advances that are not advances to pay for recording costs and not label advances for a label's entire catalogue are usually treated in one of four ways: (1) no share of such advances is payable to the musician; (2) a percentage of the advance is paid to the musician - for example, 10% of the gross advance; (3) the artist's share of the advance - for example, 50% of the net advance under a production agreement - is applied to the artist's recoupment account (that is, if there is an unrecouped balance outstanding from a previous recording budget, the artist's percentage of the advance would be applied against the artist's recoupment account, and only if recouped would the artist actually receive payment of a share of such advance); and (4) the musician and production company share the advance 50/50 "off-the-top", that is, after recoupment of outstanding recoupable costs. How such advances are treated is a key point in negotiation, particularly with respect to record production agreements, and should be considered carefully in each instance. Foreign advances can be a significant income source for the company and a loss of income for the musician, if the musician is not entitled to such advances.

The "no share of advances" option above in (1) is typical in either a tough bargaining situation, or in the case where a major record company, like a major publisher, does not actually receive advances in foreign territories. In cases where the company uses advances to finance recordings, it will be difficult to share in such advances unless the agreement is an "off-the-top" agreement. This is because advances to be used for recording are considered to be part of the "gross" receipts, and typically the company and artist share only in specified net earned royalties or receipts for records sold and not returned, after the recoupment of specific recoupable costs. Advances are considered to be credited, not actually earned. If the artist and company share in any net advances, the definition of "net" is important. Usually a net receipts definition includes deduction for reasonable legal and accounting fees, withholding tax, the costs of securing the third party agreement, and any and all reasonable travel and related costs. Also "net" typically is determined after deduction of any and all copyright licence fees payable.

---

percent (30%) of Company's sales for the previous six month period, the Artist shall receive $100,000/2 x 30% = $15,000.

(4) Miscellaneous/Tour Support

Miscellaneous and tour support advances are paid periodically and only as needed, to cover ongoing tour shortfall, or in the case of miscellaneous advances, other unforeseen personal expenses of the musician. Record companies will rarely commit contractually to a pre-set amount for miscellaneous types of advances, and may refuse to make reference to them in the agreement at all. However, record companies are called on from time to time to assist the artist financially with travel, accommodation, clothing, or other personal expenses and may agree to advance amounts to the artist as needed, particularly when the costs are tied in some way to the artist's image and/or reputation in the eyes of the public, or to a tour. It is not in the interests of a musician or the record company for the artist to appear to the fans to be unhappy or suffering. Tour support advances are usually tied to specific tours. See also the discussion of tour support in section 2(b)(iii)D below.

C. Recoupment

Recoupment is the repayment of recording costs and other recoupable costs to the company out of royalties and other monies otherwise payable to the musician. By way of example, if $50,000 was spent to record an album, and the production company is to pay the musician a royalty, expressed in dollars-and-cents terms, of $1.00 per CD or cassette sold, then in order for the musician to be in a "recouped" position, the company must have sold 50,000 CDs or cassettes ($1.00 X 50,000 CDs = $50,000). This example assumes, for the sake of simplicity, that there are no other complicating or delaying factors such as reserves, or a prior advance to the label, that first must be re-paid. In many cases, the production company already will have received revenue exceeding recording costs, from its gross proceeds, by the time the musician recoups all recoupable costs.

Recoupment, therefore, is a concept that usually has nothing to do with the company's profit or its actual earn-out of recording costs, unless it is an "off-the-top" agreement; that is, unless it is agreed between the production company and artist that all of the income received from the exploitation of the masters (and not just the artist's portion of that income) will be used to re-pay the costs incurred to produce the masters. If recoupment does occur at the company's "gross income" rate in an "off-the-top" deal, with recoupment being based on the record company's royalty rate, using the example of $50,000 in recording costs, and if the record company receives a royalty rate of

12% on a licence agreement, for example (which has an equivalent "penny rate" of $2.00), then there would have to be sales of only 25,000 CDs or cassettes for the recording costs to be "recouped" ($2.00 X 25,000 = $50,000). This could occur in an "off-the-top" agreement. However, consider that in some agreements, typically production agreements, all costs including video production and promotion costs are recouped "off-the-top".

The effect of the typical recoupment scenario is to shift the high financial risk of producing and selling records onto the musician as much as possible. By doing so, the record company is able to maximize its profits and offset its losses from the commercial failure of other recordings, which can be significant. Also, by delaying the payment of royalties until the point of recoupment, the company ensures that the actual profit from a record can be re-directed to finance the record company's roster, pay overhead and spread the financial risk amongst its other recording musicians.

If at all possible, recoupment should be done on an album-by-album or contract-by-contract period basis. However, this is a difficult point of negotiation and is not often achieved. Accordingly, for most artists, advances and other recoupable costs and royalties usually are fully cross-collateralized over all of the albums under a contract.

Sometimes, through negotiation, a recording artist will be successful in having the record company create several separate "territory" accounts for royalties, the key one being the domestic account, with perhaps several additional or secondary foreign accounts. That could mean that even if the artist has not recouped in the domestic territory, the artist has negotiated and would share in advances (as discussed above) on a territory-by-territory basis - outside of Canada, for example.

Note that with FACTOR funded recordings, or VideoFact funded videos, it is common practice that the forgivable portion of a loan, or a grant, is not recoupable. FACTOR and VideoFact are discussed in Chapter 11, "Business".

(iii) Commitment

There are various commitments, that is, contractual obligations, that the company should be willing to give and these should be set out in the agreement. The term "commitment" is used in the music business, but it is also occasionally referred to as a performance obligation and these terms are used interchangeably. Common contractual commitments are outlined below.

A. Product

The types of recordings that the company is willing to produce should be specified. These different "configurations" can include albums, EPs, cassettes, minidiscs, CDs, Enhanced-CDs, DVDs and video cassettes, for example.

B. Release

The number and timing for release of recordings also should be specified.[35] Sometimes the number and the timing of the release of records are linked to the right of the musician to terminate the term of the agreement. For example, a negotiated contractual provision might provide that failure to release an album commercially in a specified territory, within four to nine months following its delivery, provided that album is "technically satisfactory" for the production of recordings, gives rise to the musician's right to terminate the term of the agreement. Usually, there is an obligation that the musician notify the record company of its failure to release recordings, as required, under the agreement. If the company then fails to cure this default by carrying out the required commercial release of records within either 30, 60 or 90 days (depending on the wording of the contract), then the musician is able to terminate the term of the agreement and seek out a new agreement with a different record company. See discussion of default and cure in section 2(b)(xi)G below.

Case law has implied that a record company's failure to record and release at least an album's worth of masters in a contract period may render the agreement unenforceable as being in restraint of trade.[36] However, in certain situations, decisions by a record company that may appear at first to be in restraint of trade might actually be found by a court to be the exercise of a bona fide business judgement. For example, in dance music, it is not unusual to have agreements signed guaranteeing only one 12" single in a specific contract period, or a 12" and an EP (an EP being four masters), or two 12" singles, and be signed for only one or two singles.

Also, for valid business reasons, not all companies commercially release all of the recordings that are produced. For example, a recording may not be "technically", "artistically" or "commercially" satisfactory and the record company may determine that releasing the record would damage the reputation and/or integrity of the label, the

---

[35] See the *Holly Johnson* (1990) case discussed in Chapter 10, "Personal Service Contracts".
[36] *Ibid.*

artist, or both. The determination by a record company as to whether or not a master is "satisfactory" for release is a highly subjective decision, and for that reason could be subject to interpretation by the courts. Other reasons for not releasing a record may be a lack of sufficient funds to promote it adequately or the loss of a national distribution agreement. From the musician's view, there should be a firm commitment in writing to release the musician's records within a specified time after recording is completed. A period of four to six months following the date of delivery, but in no event later than the end of the then-current contract period, would be in the range of acceptability. Musicians should not rely on legal doctrines and court proceedings, as the costs and delays of litigation can be significant. Rather, they are well advised to have the contractual right to terminate the term of the contract if the company fails to release records.

The definition of "commercial release" also should be made clear in the agreement. For example, the territory in which records are to be released may be stipulated: either nationally (for example, throughout Canada), or worldwide; with a specific type of distributor (for example, a major record company). In the absence of a clear definition in the agreement, a release commitment may be worded quite vaguely to the detriment of the musician.[37] As is discussed in Chapter 10, "Personal Service Contracts", without a commercial release obligation, the issue of restraint of trade is raised. It is not unusual to negotiate certain foreign territory release commitments as well. See also the discussion below in section 2(b)(xi)C concerning release in foreign territories.

C. Promotion, Advertising and Publicity

It is unusual, in the absence of a bidding 'war', for a record company to specify in the agreement either the money that will be committed, or the strategies that will be pursued with respect to promotion, advertising, or publicity.

Care must be taken that the advertising undertaken by the record company to promote albums using the name and likeness of the performer is not misleading. Music recorded earlier, but released on a later album, where a current picture of the artist was used to promote record sales based on the artist's current popularity has been found to be misleading in the U.S.[38]

---

[37] Ordinarily, a release is defined as follows: "nationally through ordinary commercial retail channels throughout the territory", preferably through a recognized national record company distributor.

[38] An injunction was granted preventing sale of the album. Although this was decided under the U.S. *Trade Marks Act* cited below in note 80 which deals with false description of goods, applicable business practice statutes in Canada might lead to a

D. Tour Support

Even established musicians may require tour support, since many tours are known to be loss-leaders. It is difficult but advantageous to obtain tour support commitment in a record contract, because touring can promote record sales. Tour support is usually considered a recoupable advance to pay for rehearsal space, equipment, travel costs, hotel and other types of expenses to cover some of the costs of a tour. It is negotiable whether or not the musician is able to commit the record company to fixed amounts for these expenses and whether 100% of tour support advances would be recoupable. Again, the outcome depends on the bargaining power of the parties.

E. Recording and Video Budgets

Recording budgets in Canada can vary on average anywhere from $30,000 to $150,000 per album for beginning recording musicians and can be up to $1,000,000 or more for "superstars". Video budgets can range from $50,000 to $75,000 for new artists and can be much higher, depending on the facts of each case. By way of comparison, recording and video budgets at major labels in the U.S. can be five to ten times these amounts or more. The amount of such budgets is determined by the size and stature of the label, the artist's commercial track record, the genre of music, the perceived potential of the musician to recoup such budgets, the record company's business experience and the artist's bargaining power.

Recording and video budgets should be planned carefully since the musician must, in addition to all other advances, recoup these costs from the musician's share of royalties.[39] In addition, there is usually a penalty if costs exceed budgeted amounts. The record company may attempt to make such cost "overruns" re-payable to the company on demand. However, in practice, in most cases the record company recognizes the inability of most artists to repay such monies on demand, and will in fact treat them as further recoupable but non-returnable advances.

Some record contracts specify that monies advanced are a recording fund to cover recording costs and, if the musician completes the record under budget, the musician is entitled to keep the

---

similar result. Whether or not this U.S. case is followed in Canada, the principle is worth considering.

[39] The artist should have consultation and some control over recording costs or the validity of the agreement may be called into question. See the *Holly Johnson* case discussed in Chapter 10, "Personal Service Contracts".

difference; however, such amounts are still recoupable. Other times, recording budgets are structured as recording costs whereby the record company commits to pay up to the amount of an approved budget and, in addition, pays an amount for the musician as a personal advance (i.e., an artist advance). If the musician stays on budget, such advance is paid to the musician in full, either upon or shortly after delivery of the masters. On the other hand, if the recording goes over budget, the personal advance portion will be reduced by an amount equal to the overage. For example, if the approved recording budget is $150,000 and the allocated personal advance is $50,000, then as long as the band stays on budget, they receive $50,000 after the record company has received the masters which are satisfactory for release. However, if due to delays, tardiness, or a lack of productivity in the studio, the record costs $175,000 to complete, the artist would be entitled to only $25,000 as an artist advance.

(iv) Recordings

A. Costs

In addition to recording costs discussed above in section 2(a)(iv)G, recording costs include payments in excess of union scale which may be payable, either because one or more high-profile session musicians are hired as players on the record, or because overtime costs are incurred due to failure to complete recording sessions on a timely basis. If the recording is done in the record company's studio, the musician should try to obtain the recording at a preferred rate, that is, one which is less than the standard rate. As discussed above in section 2(b)(ii), recording costs are fully recoupable, but the contract stipulates that the company is responsible for paying for such costs.

B. Number/Overcalls

The number of recordings is important.[40] The record company usually specifies a minimum number, usually one album's worth of recordings per contract period (each one usually being 12 to 18 months). It is typical to commit to record from five to eight albums under this agreement. This is a point for negotiation. Although the practice is declining, the company also may try to obtain up to one

---

[40] The number of recordings has been subject to case law interpretation. See the cases discussed in Chapter 10 in this regard.

album's worth of additional recordings - known as "overcall" recordings - during each contract period.

Overcalls can prove to be onerous for musicians who have live performance and other promotional commitments which can prohibit them from completing such additional recordings on a timely basis. Therefore, overcall recording commitments in a given contract period should be reasonable and flexible primarily because of the requirement that the musician perform live. If attention is not paid to negotiating these "overcall" provisions in the agreement, the musician's failure to deliver overcall recordings could allow the record company to withhold advances and other payments owed to the musician under the agreement, or suspend or extend the term of the agreement.

It is not unusual to have an overcall restricted as follows: (a) no overcalls in the first contract period; and (b) overcalls cannot be required more frequently than every other contract period - not in each and every contract period. An overcall should not be used to put the term of the agreement in suspension, if the musician is unable to fulfill such commitment, due to touring schedules or other bona fide professional reasons. Suspending the agreement has the effect of extending the contract period and the overall time for which the artist is bound to the record company; this is not generally in the musician's interests. See the suspension clause discussion below in section 2(b)(xi)H. Default on an overcall can have the effect also of keeping the musician at a lower royalty rate during the next contract period, when the musician's royalty rate would otherwise have been raised.

C. Location

The location of recording is important for several reasons: 1) there are cost factors such as travel and hotel expenses; 2) possible tax consequences for recording in different locations; and 3) the studio environment, equipment and its personnel can affect the artistic and creative output of musicians and ultimately the final recording. Therefore, mutual consultation as to the location for recordings is important, although the record company usually will have the final say over the location, at least until the artist attains a certain level of experience and success.

D. Sessions

The record company typically requires the musician to attend at times and dates designated by it to record and to use best efforts to rehearse and follow the company's instructions. If the company has a studio and it is not available, the musician should be able to record at another suitable studio.

The timing of recording sessions is particularly important for live performing musicians. In view of the musician's contractual commitments for personal appearances or other reasonable professional engagements, the musician may not be able to record. Consider, however, that technology has made it possible in some cases to build entire "state of the art" recording studios into the tour buses of some major acts. As a result, recording, or at least the pre-production of music tracks, is now possible while the musician is on the road. All decisions concerning the scheduling of recordings should be made mutually between the company, the musician and his/her management team to avoid the contractual problems that can arise if the musician cannot record on a timely basis.

If there are delays in recording due to some act or omission of the musician, the record company may contract to be reimbursed for costs occasioned by such a delay. Musicians should contract to avoid paying costs for delays that are not within their control or costs which are attributed to delay by the record company.

E. Pay or Play

The "pay or play" provision in the contract gives the company the right to pay the musician session payments only, or sometimes all or a portion of the applicable advance for that contract period, and by doing so, the company has the right to exercise a contract option without recording the stipulated masters for that period. Its effect is to bind the musician contractually without the company actually recording or releasing recordings.[41] If the "pay or play" provision is

---

[41] *Syllabus on Representing Musical Artists...* above, note 26 at 296. In a long term exclusive recording agreement, with no other justification, such language raises restraint of trade issues. See the *Holly Johnson* case discussed in Chapter 10, "Personal Service Contracts" in this regard. The state of California has two laws that endeavour to protect recording artists who have signed long-term exclusive recording contracts. One is s. 3423 of the *California Civil Code*, which provides that a record company in California may seek injunctive relief for a breach of a personal service contract if and only if it guarantees certain minimum payments to the artist contractually, and actually makes the payments prior to seeking the injunction; see "A Guide to the "9000 Plus" Law: California's Statutory Insurance Policy Against Artists Defecting from Record Companies", William I. Hochberg, *1995-96 Entertainment, Publishing and the Arts Handbook* (New York: Clark, Boardman, Callaghan), p. 325. The second is s. 2855 of the *California Labor Code* which provides that an employee may not be bound to an exclusive employment contract beyond seven years; see Gary A. Greenberg, "Seven Years to Life: the Fight for Free Agency in the Record Business", *1995-96 Entertainment, Publishing, and the Arts Handbook* (New York: Clark, Boardman, Callaghan), p. 337. Often, the record company seeks to include 'choice of law' and 'choice

exercised, the musician usually has some right to terminate the term of the contract and seek out a new label that is more able or willing to produce and release the band's music.

F. Special

In addition to "standard" recordings embodying only the musician's newly recorded studio performances, the company may contract for the right to issue "special" recordings. Special recordings might include: (1) "best of" albums - including both current and past hit recordings; (2) compilations - albums which include recordings of several musicians "coupled" on the same album; (3) joint performances, which include two or more different royalty artists performing on the same recording; and (4) "live" albums - recorded during a club or concert performance. Special recordings may be viewed as diverse and interesting because they depart in presentation and content from the standard studio recordings and can increase record sales because of their particular appeal to a certain cross-section of the musician's fan base. However, depending on the circumstances, there can be disadvantages associated with such recordings including: (1) unfavourable comparisons between other musicians; (2) an emphasis on the record label and not the musician; (3) identification with sometimes unfavourable publicity; (4) the loss of control of image and marketing; and (5) a lower selling price than a regular album by the same musician.[42] The musician should be consulted about the type and timing of marketing these special recordings, and ideally the final decision concerning all such recordings should be made mutually. It is important to note also that special recordings may not count towards the musician's album delivery commitment under the agreement.

G. Re-recording Restriction

The record company often requires that the musician not re-record the same musical compositions that were recorded under the agreement for a certain period of time, typically: (a) five years after the time that the master was initially recorded; or (b) two years after the expiration of the agreement, whichever is later.[43] This clause serves to

---

of forum' clauses for jurisdictions outside of California (usually New York or Tennessee, if it has offices in those states) to attempt to escape liability under these sections.

[42] *Ibid., Syllabus on Representing Musical Artists* ...cited above, at 292.

[43] As discussed in Chapter 10, "Personal Service Contracts" and specifically the *Holly Johnson* case, this provision may be upheld by the courts as reasonable, provided the time restriction is not undue.

reduce competition in the marketplace and protects the company's exclusive interest in that musician's recordings produced under the recording agreement.

H. Masters

The ownership of both audio and audio-visual masters is an important provision in the contract. The company generally owns 100% of all masters; however, if possible, the musician should try to obtain ownership, after a period of time, if those masters have not been exploited (i.e., distributed, sold or licensed).[44] U.S. case law also has discussed the situation where companies who have access to a recording artist's or composer's demonstration recording may try to release it commercially.[45]

Bear in mind that the record company will continue to own the masters almost always, despite the fact that, while the record company initially pays for all recordings, the musician subsequently may fully recoup these recording costs. Record companies are very reluctant to provide a buy-back provision with respect to masters. However, in some

---

[44] Various U.S. cases have dealt with legal issues raised by a company re-issuing recordings after a number of years, when the musician has changed record companies and often at that point has become more popular than when signed to the previous record label. A case involving Jimi Hendrix and Curtis Knight illustrates one such example: *Yameta Co. Ltd. and Jimi Hendrix v. Capitol Records Inc., PPX Enterprises Inc., Edward Chalpin and Curtis Knight* (1968), 279 F.Supp. 582, 393 F.2d 91 (1975). On appeal from the injunction granted, the order was reversed on other grounds. Jimi Hendrix signed a contract with Sioux Records. The contract was then assigned to Yameta Records. He also signed a contract after the Sioux contract with PPX Records, who in turn licensed to Capitol Records the rights to release the album *Get That Feeling: Jimi Hendrix Plays and Curtis Knight Sings*. Upon application to the court by Yameta Records, a temporary injunction was granted preventing Capitol from using Jimi Hendrix's name and picture on the album on the basis that it was misleading, because it implied Hendrix was the principal performer on the record when in fact he was a session player. They are included here not to suggest that such cases necessarily will be followed by Canadian courts, but to show how the question of ownership of masters and the manner in which they are exploited can arise and is important.

[45] This happened in a case involving Joan Baez: *Baez v. Fantasy Records, Inc.*, 144 U.S.P.Q. 537 (1964). It was held in that case that the defendant music publisher had no right to the tapes, and a permanent injunction was granted against the record company that released the tapes. This was decided on the basis of a violation of a common law copyright in the recordings owned by Baez and on the basis of unfair competition. The court found that the recordings unfairly competed with valid recordings which were produced after these demonstration recordings. Common law copyright since has been abolished in the U.S. and as discussed in Chapter 1, "Copyright", all copyright in Canada is statutory. See also *Squire Records Inc. v. Vanguard Recording Society Inc., Maynard Solomon and Herb Korsak*, 268 N.Y.S.2d 251 (1966) for another case involving early Joan Baez recordings.

cases (for example, a small independent company run by an individual producer), the masters may be bought out for the then unrecouped recording costs, for the amount of the recording costs plus a percentage override, or for a bonus or other negotiated sum. Sometimes even major record companies might negotiate such terms.

Due to current radio and video airplay policies, the average duration of a commercial recording is approximately four minutes or less. Therefore, under the recording agreement, a record company may attempt to restrict the length of recorded time of each master.

Consider the potential moral rights aspects concerning masters. In most cases, the record company will request the waiver of whatever moral rights the musician has in the masters and in the compositions and recorded performances embodied on the masters. See the discussion in Chapter 1, "Copyright" regarding moral rights.

(v) Royalties

A. Domestic and Foreign Base

Record royalties may be based on a percentage of the suggested retail list price (SRLP), or wholesale price, and in many European territories in particular, royalties are based on PPD (the published price to the dealer). This is commonly referred to as the "royalty base price".

Assuming it is not a net receipts type production agreement and the musician is not responsible for paying the producer from his or her share of record sales royalties, royalties for new artists range from 10% to14% of the SRLP on Canadian and U.S. sales for top-of-the-line (top line) records. This is called a "producer out" agreement. Where there is an "all-in" or "producer-in" agreement, which is common, these percentages would be increased by the amount that would be paid to a producer (the "producer royalty") - commonly between 1% and 3% of SRLP. In a typical "producer in" agreement for a new artist, the range would be 12% to 16% of SRLP,[46] for example. Such royalties depend on

---

[46] See Christian L. Castle and James L. Swanson, "Practical and Ethical Issues in Negotiating the Leaving Member Procedure", *Entertainment Publishing and the Arts Handbook* (New York: Clark Boardman, 1989). This article states that the U.S. "all-in" royalty rate for new artists is "typically in the 10%-13% range". In the U.K., see Clive Fisher, "Record Royalties - Precedents" (1982) Vol. 1, No. 2, I.M.L. 18. It is suggested in this article that in England, the royalties are based not on a retail price but on an actual selling price on a category-by-category basis. See also Lionel S. Soble, "Recording Artist Royalty Calculations: Why Gold Records Don't Always Yield Fortunes", 2nd Ed. (1990) Vol. 12, No. 5, E.L.R. 3. In this article, the author discusses in detail the effect of royalties,

the size and type of record company, the music genre, and the number of record companies interested in signing the artist. The above royalties are commonly referred to as the "basic royalty rate" or the "base rate royalty". If the musician is a superstar, such royalties may be as high as 20% or more of the SRLP.[17]

Royalties also will vary depending on the type of sales format or configuration, whether they are from domestic or foreign record sales, and whether they are subject to container and other deductions. Foreign sales royalties can range anywhere from 50% to 90% of the base rate or, alternatively, in the case of production agreements, might be specified as a percentage of the company's net receipts from that foreign territory. Royalties also may be negotiated on a territory-by-territory basis, although this is unusual, unless the musician is more established and successful. For example, a higher royalty may be negotiated, usually based on the level of sales success in particular territories (such as Germany or England).

The base rate may escalate based on sales under the contract. For example, typical escalation points would be after sales of 50,000 (gold, in Canada) and 100,000 (platinum, in Canada),[18] or any other agreed upon sales plateaux, or after achieving the #1 chart position in a major trade publication such as Billboard in the U.S. or The Record in Canada. Royalty escalations are also negotiable depending on the musical genre. For example, if it is a pop, rock or urban record, the above sales plateaux are probably applicable; however, it would not be unreasonable for an artist to request a lower sales escalation point for smaller, specialty or niche market albums in the jazz or children's music genres, for example.

It is also possible to negotiate an escalation in royalty rates based on subsequent albums - for example, 13% on album 1, 14% on album 2, and 15% on albums 3 and 4 under the agreement.

If record sales are significant and the artist has attained star status, the musician and record company may, during the term of the agreement, re-negotiate royalties, despite any legal or contractual obligation to do so. This is usually a decision based on good business practice rather than legal or contractual requirements, since the musician is presumed to be contractually bound by the recording contract as it was signed. A record company can justify this kind of 'concession' as the prudent exercise of business discretion: it is better to

---

reserves and packaging deductions, and why certain clauses can have a substantial impact on the actual question of whether or not recordings will earn money.

[17] Donald S. Passman, *All You Need To Know About the Music Business* (New York: Simon & Schuster, 1997) at p. 109.

[18] See the *Holly Johnson* case in Chapter 10, "Personal Service Contracts", which discusses the contractual need to have the artist participate in further advances and escalations based on sales success, in order to avoid restraint of trade.

co-operate and pay more to placate a musician who is capable of significant record sales, than to be inflexible at the expense of the artist-label relationship.

Royalties may be based on either 85%, 90% or 100% of records sold and not returned,[49] depending on the company. In this regard, the figure of 90% was originally rationalized on the basis of an expected 10% allowance for losses due to vinyl record breakage. This is no longer justifiable, because CDs (the record industry's main sales configuration) are relatively indestructible (as opposed to vinyl records), and in any case, the record company is protected against such risk by withholding a reserve against returns to cover any defects. Ideally, the musician would negotiate to have royalties paid on 100% of records sold and not returned, or alternatively, the penny rate the musician believes he or she is entitled to, accounting for the record company's breakage reduction and returns.

The basis upon which royalties are paid, that is, upon records "sold and not returned", reflects the established industry practice of allowing retailers to return 100% of unsold music product to the distributing record company. Reserves, which are relevant to this practice, are discussed below in section 2(x)B.

The above base rate royalties are based on top-of-the-line records, but as discussed further below, such rates are reduced based on the various configurations (e.g., albums, EPs, etc.) and types of recordings (for example, budget and premium records).

B. Records/Sales Configurations

As discussed above, the royalty rate for top-of-the-line albums is referred to as the royalty base rate. Variations in the base rate apply to EP's (extended plays), singles, and maxi-singles and other sales configurations, as indicated below. These are often expressed as a fraction of the base rate. For singles, particularly, the base rate may be reduced to a percentage of the royalty base rate (60% to 75%, for example) because singles are generally thought of as loss-leaders which promote album sales.

C. Cassettes

The cassette royalty should be the full base rate royalty, subject to standard and applicable deductions.

---

[49] See the *Soble* article, cited above in note 46, for a discussion of the effect on royalty calculations when the musician is paid based on 90%, not 100% of records sold.

D. Compact Discs/New Technologies

The royalty rate for albums formatted in CD or other new and digital technologies such as minidisc, digital compact cassette, or audiophile recordings is usually a fraction of the base rate. Record companies attempt to justify this reduction based upon the research and development costs associated with these emerging formats and the higher manufacturing costs. Both reasons may be justifiable for a period of time, while the technology is still in its infancy. However, once the new format is fully developed and widely used, manufacturing the new formats almost always becomes more efficient and therefore cheaper, and any royalty rate reduction becomes less easily justified. However, "industry practices" often crystallize around the original pricing and royalty structure. As a result, the current royalty rates for CDs and other new technologies are often based on 75% to 85% of the base rate, although some companies pay 100% of the base rate for CDs and 75% of such rate on new technologies such as DVD, CD and CD-ROM enhanced CDs, CD-I and direct transmission such as downloading via the Internet. However, in some contracts, digital downloading will be paid on the basis of a percentage of net receipts. While it is still common practice to reduce the royalty payable on CDs in this way, the suggested retail list price of the CD, like other new and digital technology configurations, is higher than analog cassette, and therefore the penny rate royalty that actually goes into the musician's pocket is higher than it is for cassettes. As new technologies develop, record contracts are amended, and the above practices concerning such royalties can change. Each agreement should be reviewed thoroughly with this in mind.

E. Record Club

Record club sales are still important for some large record companies. With respect to musicians such as hard rock or heavy metal acts that receive little or no airplay, retail sales can be undermined by a fanatical following that will purchase from the company through record club subscriptions. Because the dollars-and-cents return to the record company is less than on retail sales due to the "buy-one-get-ten-free" marketing approach to record club sales, artist royalties may be only 50% of net receipts, or sometimes no royalty, where the sale is stated as a 'freebie' to the club subscriber. With this in mind, the agreement should limit or prevent record club sales.

F. Promotional

No royalties are paid on promotional albums (referred to in the business as 'freebies') which are given away to radio stations, DJs and other industry taste-makers and media. The standard record company practice is to provide retail accounts with free goods as an incentive for them to purchase larger volumes of the product. Again, in order to avoid a substantial loss of royalties payable to the musician, it is important to place some restriction on the number of promotional and other free goods permitted under the agreement. Typically, this would be in the range of 10% to 20% of the total number of records shipped.[50] Limits on free goods may differ depending on the format or configuration - for example, 40% for singles and 15% for albums; it may be higher for record clubs.

G. Special

The type of special royalties will vary depending on the type of recording and the specific record company's policies. Each agreement should be reviewed carefully with this in mind.

H. Budget/Premium/Mid-Price

Major companies often have subsidiary or "imprint" labels that release budget recordings, which may be of inferior quality and are priced lower than recordings on the main label. Budget recordings are sold at lower prices to stimulate sales - for example, 60% to $66^2/_3$% of the SRLP for top-of-the-line product. The musician's royalties also are reduced proportionately, i.e., to 60% to $66^2/_3$% of the base rate. Note that a reduction of $^2/_3$ of full royalty rate on $^2/_3$ of SRLP translates into $^4/_9$ or only 44% of the premium that would be earned on a top line product. Premiums may be priced as the actual sales price and the base rate may be reduced by 50%. Mid-price recordings typically are priced between 60% to 80% of the SRLP and the royalties often are reduced to 80% of the base rate. The above pro-rations are fairly typical, but may be negotiable, as is the timing whereby the company may engage in such price reductions (for example, not before 18 to 24 months after the first release of the album).

---

[50] David E. Kronemeyer and J. Gregory Sidak, "Two Factors That Reduce Record Company Profitability", in *Entertainment, Publishing and the Arts Handbook* (New York: Clark Boardman, 1987) at pp. 372-374. This article discusses the rationale for free goods and return policies of record companies in some detail.

I. Institutional

Institutional sales could include sales to educational, military, or other government institutions and royalties typically would be 50-75% of the base rate. A reasonable limit should be placed on the number of these types of sales.

J. Deletes

Deleted recordings are those that have not sold well enough to justify their continued sale and are identified often by a hole punched through the album cover, cassette J-Card or CD "jewel box". Some albums are deleted very quickly, for example, within 120 days from the date of initial distribution. No royalties are paid on deletes, and therefore some time limitation should be stipulated before which the product may not be deleted. This may not be possible due to a lack of bargaining power on the part of the musician.

K. Videos

The trend has been for record companies to reduce and even remove any commitment to do music videos. Whereas previously, record contracts might have obligated the company to produce two or three videos per album, currently it is not unusual to acquire only a minimal commitment of perhaps one video per album. In some cases, the record company will not even guarantee one video due to the costs involved, and depending on musical format (i.e., country, rap, adult-contemporary, for example). This is due to uncertainty about the effect that airing such videos has on record sales, and because there are a limited number of national video programs available to acquire airplay. With the exception of MuchMoreMusic for adult-oriented music, and Bravo for a limited amount of classical music and jazz, there is an almost complete absence of video broadcast outlets, especially for "non-commercial" music such as jazz and certain types of hard or heavy metal music. Regardless of the record company's willingness to guarantee the production of music videos, the company will always contract for the right to do so, when and if they deem it beneficial and in the interests of selling more records.

With the exception of long-form, commercially sold videos (which often are a compilation of an established artist's hit videos, or sometimes a behind-the-scenes "making-of" type of documentary or live concert type video), videos are still used primarily as promotional vehicles to sell records. The musician's right to income from the exploitation of "sell-through" music videos may be treated in one of two ways. In some agreements, because audio-visual recordings fall within the definition of "records", record sale royalties, or a lower specified record type royalty, also apply to videos which are actually sold and not returned. Other agreements stipulate that the record company and recording musician share 50/50 in net receipts generated from video sales, as is discussed below.[51]

A musician's arguments about the recoupability of video costs can be summarized as follows: since music videos are still largely promotional vehicles, they should be the company's responsibility, since it is historically the company's responsibility to pay for all promotional costs. In practice, usually no more than 50% of all video costs will be recoupable from and therefore cross-collateralized with record royalties; however, the other 50% of the video budget also may be typically recoupable from any commercial exploitation of the video (for example, from the sale of the single-song or long-form video through video retail outlets). Each record company may have a different contractual obligation in this regard. Small independent record production companies in particular still may seek to have 100% of video costs recoupable. See also the discussion in section 2(b)(iii)C above regarding recoupment.

Also pursuant to the controlled composition clause, the musician usually will be asked to provide a royalty-free synchronization licence for any song which is written by the musician and used in the promotional video.

L. Other

In the case of off-stage sales, for example, the right to engage in such sales can often be negotiated. Typically in such cases, preferential rates are negotiated to allow the musician to purchase product and sell it at concerts.

In many agreements, a 50/50 net receipts sharing is stipulated in the event of certain licences - for example, master use licences in films. See the discussion in section 1(d)(ii) above regarding net receipts.

---

[51] See the AFM Video Agreement. Videos that generate sales or are licensed to T.V. should yield royalties. For example, pursuant to the terms of its current broadcast licence and a licence agreement with AVLA (the Audio Visual Licensing Agency), CMT (Country Music Television) pays $150 per play (up to a maximum of $18,000) to the owners of music videos which are shown on CMT. See p. 297 of Gertz-Culpepper, cited above in note 8, for a discussion of the video royalty structure. Note as well that videos may be subject to residuals payable to the respective unions. See p. 289 of Gertz-Culpepper in this regard.

(vi) Packaging Deductions

In addition to the bonus, freebies, deletes and promotional recordings that reduce the royalties paid to the musician, the company also makes various other deductions from the royalties before the final tally of the amount owed to the artist is made. The practice is that royalties are paid on a net basis, that is, the artist's gross royalty is subject to all applicable deductions. These include packaging deductions (also called "container charges") which are usually in the range of 10% to 25% of SRLP, depending on the type of configuration (that is, whether it is an analog tape, vinyl record, CD, minidisc, or other new technology). Typical deductions are 20% for cassettes and 25% for CDs. The container deduction theoretically accounts for the cost of packaging the recording, although it has been suggested that it is merely a disguised way of compensating the company for its manufacturing costs.[52] In addition to these deductions, taxes are also normal deductions.

(vii) Computation of Record Royalties

Record royalties are the recording artist's share of income from record sales, not copyright royalties. Sample computations of such royalties are set out below.

A. Generally

For example, if the musician is getting a 10% "producer-out" royalty for CD albums sold in Canada on a SRLP which hypothetically is $22.98, and if there is a container charge of 25% (i.e., a further reduction of $5.75), the computation of the artist's net Canadian royalty would be as follows:

SRLP		$22.98
minus the container charge		$ 5.75
	=	$17.23
x 85% (CD Reduction)	=	$14.65
x a 10% artist royalty	=	$ 1.47 per CD sold in Canada

The above example does not take into account the applicable free goods before the royalties are payable. Therefore, if the recording costs were $75,000 and there are a total of 15% of records shipped that are

---

[52] See Roberts and Matheson above, note 20 at p. 53.

given away as free goods, then the company must ship and sell 68,028 copies in order for the musician to be "recouped" and to begin receiving royalties.[53] This is how the accounting would look:

records shipped and sold   = 68,028
x 85 %   = 51,021 royalty-bearing copies sold
51,021 copies x $1.47   = $75,000.87
minus $75,000 in recording costs   = 87¢ in total royalties payable to
                                     artist

The above hypothetical example is oversimplified in that it does not take into account taxes, reserves, deletes or pro-rations based on other configurations (for example, budget recordings, EPs, etc.). In reality, recoupment likely would be further delayed because: 1) musicians must produce music videos at a cost often ranging between $25,000 to $85,000 or more per video – which costs are recoupable, at least in part; 2) recording budgets, even for new artists, often exceed the $75,000 provided for in the example above; and 3) typically, recoupable tour support costs are also incurred. However, the above example illustrates that even a record which sells between 'gold' and 'platinum' sales levels in Canada may not find the artist in a "recouped" position. The need for Canadian musicians to be able to compete and sell records internationally is clear.[54] Domestic record sales alone generally cannot recoup the cost of "world-class" recordings and videos. When a net receipts formula is used rather than a royalty base, see the discussion above in section 1(d)(ii).

B. Coupling

Royalties for "coupled" records (for example, a compilation CD released by the artist's label) usually are calculated as follows: a fraction, with the numerator being the number of masters in the coupled recording featuring the musician (often "1"), and the denominator being the total number of masters included in the coupled recording (often "10"); this fraction, 1/10th, is then multiplied by the applicable royalty rate to arrive at the musician's royalty for sales of the coupled record. For example: a base royalty of 12% x $^1/_{10}$ = 1.2% of the suggested retail list price for sales of the compilation. Although this is the standard way to compute coupling royalties, sometimes it is

---

[53] These figures and the hypothetical example are adapted from Statistics Canada, *Culture Statistics Recording Industry 1978* (Ottawa: Minister of Supply and Services, 1980) at p. 3 and note 2. For more detail see Soble cited above in note 46.

[54] See *Sound Investments...* cited above in note 20. According to this source, approximately nine out of ten Canadian albums do not recoup their costs and few albums which are released reach gold or platinum status in Canada.

expressed as a fraction with the numerator being the playing time of the master or masters and the denominator being the total playing time of all the masters on the release. This fraction is then multiplied by the otherwise applicable royalty rate of the artist.

C. Joint Performances

A joint performance is a single master or record on which an artist performs together with one or more other artists. Sometimes the artists are from the same label and, other times, the contributing performers are artists signed to different labels. An example would be the recent Jive Records recording of "I'm Your Angel", a ballad jointly featuring R. Kelly (signed to Jive) and Celine Dion (a Sony/550 artist). Typically, the royalty payable to each artist for joint performances is calculated by multiplying a fraction, the numerator being one and the denominator being the total number of musicians to whom royalties are payable (in the above example, $^1/_2$), which is then multiplied by the applicable royalty rate to determine the royalty payable to the artist. There may be other methods of calculating this type of royalty, particularly in a situation such as the Kelly/Dion collaboration above, where the artists have attained "superstar" status; however, this is the most common method.

(viii) Cross-collateralization

Cross-collateralization is the practice of using revenue from one or more royalty accounts of the musician to recoup unrecouped costs (i.e., usually advances), regardless of where such costs were incurred. For example, when a musician receives money as a recording advance, one would expect that this advance would be recouped only from the musician's record royalty account. One would not automatically expect (nor would the musician desire) that a recording advance would be recouped from music publishing income, such as mechanical royalties. If it is, then such income is "cross-collateralized" against, in this case, unrecouped recording costs.

For example, under a record agreement, where mechanicals are cross-collateralized, and there is a publishing advance to be earned out, then there would be no mechanical royalty income payable to the musician (until recoupment) from which the publisher can recoup publishing advances paid to the musician. Further provisions and penalties may be set out in the publishing agreement in order to compensate for such a clause.

Cross-collateralization may occur within one agreement, or between one or more agreements and royalty sources - for example, recording, publishing or merchandising royalties. It is an established practice for record companies to cross-collateralize record royalties from all albums; however, the musician should try to avoid the cross-collateralization of certain other types of income and advances - for example, between recording and merchandising, publishing, or other income. Cross-collateralization delays the actual payment of royalties, and may mean that the musician receives no royalties whatsoever; the fact is that recording and other recoupable costs may not ever be recouped, despite cross-collateralization.

As a general rule, as is clear from the above discussion, the goal of counsel for the musician, when negotiating recording agreements, is to create certain income streams that are not cross-collateralized, and which therefore flow through freely to the musician.

(ix) Controlled Compositions

Controlled compositions, as defined in most recording agreements, are songs that one either: (1) owns; (2) has written; or (3) controls wholly or in part. The owner may be the musician or the record production company who is a party to the record agreement. The typical controlled composition clause requires that controlled compositions be licensed to the record company at a controlled composition rate. At present, the most commonly applied controlled composition rate is $^3/_4$ of the industry standard rate which is set by CRIA and CMRRA, as discussed in Chapter 2. Currently, the applicable industry standard rate, which is the result of the *Mechanical Licence Agreement* (the "MLA"), a negotiated agreement between the CMRRA and record company signators, is 7.4¢ for songs of 5 minutes or less in duration.[55] Pursuant to the current MLA, signatory companies cannot set the initial rate at less than $^3/_4$ of that "industry standard" rate (7.4¢) and can pay no less than 50% of the full rate, or 3.7¢ per song, of which the publisher collects 100% and remits the writer's share - typically 50% - to the songwriter/recording artist. By comparison, there is no agreement in place in the U.S. to provide an absolute minimum such as

---

[55] See David A. Basskin, "Controlled Composition Clauses and Systematic Inequality of Bargaining Power", (1999) unpublished (CMRRA). This article outlines the history and development of the controlled composition clause in Canada and the positive effects of the MLA for songwriter recording artists and music publishers. Also see David Moser, "The Controlled Composition Clause: Is It out of Control?" Ent. & Sports Lawyer, Vol.14, No. 4, Winter 1997, at p. 3 for a discussion of the rationale and pitfalls of the controlled composition clause in the American context, and ways in which the artist's representative can ameliorate its effects.

the 3.7¢ set in Canada. As a result, it is possible in the U.S. for the recording musician who is bound by the controlled composition clause (depending on the number of non-controlled or partially controlled compositions recorded on an album) to end up owing the record company money because of the "excesses" which must be paid to the company to compensate for full mechanical royalties paid to non-controlled songwriters. Such excesses are usually charged against artist royalties.

In addition, a controlled composition clause usually will place an aggregate limit on the number of songs for which the record company is liable to pay mechanical royalties. Pursuant to the most recent MLA, signatory record companies cannot "cap" the aggregate amount at less than 12 compositions per album. Under this clause, the aggregate amount in dollars and cents that the record company pays is "capped" at 12 times the minimum controlled composition "rate" [i.e., 12 x (7.4¢ x $^3/_4$), or 66.6¢]. This clause is problematic for a number of reasons: (1) it reduces mechanical royalties otherwise payable to both the publisher and the musician/songwriter; and (2) it is usually coupled with a penalty if, in the case of a co-written composition, one composer is subject to a controlled composition clause, namely the recording musician, and the other is not. The penalty is the difference between the full industry standard or statutory rate (currently 7.4¢) and the controlled rate (5.55¢) pro-rated for the portion of the song not written by the recording musician. The difference will be set off against the royalties which otherwise would be payable.

In certain instances, depending on the number of non-controlled or partially controlled compositions recorded, the musician will receive a substantially reduced mechanical rate. Fortunately, however, due to the provisions of the MLA, to which most record companies are signatories, not less than 50% of the full rate (or 3.7¢) is payable for mechanicals. This would not be the case, for example, if the writer/artist was signed to a smaller independent record company which was not a signatory to the MLA.[56]

To soften the effect of a controlled composition clause, one may negotiate an increase of such rate over time to the full applicable industry or statutory rate, or after recoupment of recoupable costs, for example. This is a negotiable issue.

Although, pursuant to the U.S. *Copyright Act* regulations, the rate increases over time, whether the initial rate "floats" with the increases is still negotiable in the U.S. By contrast, in Canada, the MLA rate is now set as "a percentage of the royalty rate which is otherwise in effect at the time a record is sold or otherwise distributed by the licensee".[57]

---

[56] *Ibid.*, "Controlled Composition Clauses..." at 19.
[57] *Ibid.*

Accordingly, unless the record label is a small independent company, and not a MLA signatory, the rate "floats" and need not be negotiated.

(x) Important General Provisions

A. Accounting, Payment

Accounting generally occurs by way of written royalty statements provided to the musician on a semi-annual, or perhaps, quarterly basis. With a successful negotiation, mechanical royalties, for example, may be paid quarterly. If royalties are owed to the musician, a cheque will be included with the statement or may follow shortly thereafter. However, no royalties will be payable until all recoupable costs are fully recouped. Such payment will generally consist of "net" royalties, that is, gross royalties minus unrecouped advances, recoupable costs and chargeable costs, including packaging deductions, the cost of changing foreign royalties into Canadian currency and deductions for union and guild payments and reserves. The company typically will specify that the royalty statement is binding unless it is objected to within a fixed time period, usually two years. In the case of groups, there should be a designated recipient for all payments, which may be a manager or business manager, or a member of the group. For further discussion concerning accounting, see Chapter 3, "Music Publishing". Merchandising and video sales may be paid on a different basis, particularly if there is a separate agreement in place concerning such sales - for example, within thirty days of the receipt of monies by the merchandising or video production company, or "upon receipt" of accounting from a third party.

B. Reserves

Record companies have developed a standard practice of withholding a percentage of royalties payable to the musician known as a "reserve", to protect against overshipping, returns and breakage. Since the musician is paid on the basis of records "sold and not returned" rather than on records "shipped", the contract will stipulate a reasonable reserve, or a specified maximum reserve rate (up to 50%) of royalties payable for each particular accounting period. Some limit should be placed on these reserves, and they should be liquidated, that is, released and credited to the musician's account, preferably equally, over a specified number of accounting periods. For example, it may be specified that "amounts reserved on each accounting date will be liquidated evenly over the course of the next one, two or perhaps three semi-annual accounting periods".[58]

C. Audit

It should be specified contractually that an accountant or other authorized representative of the musician is entitled to audit, examine and take photocopies of the record company's relevant books and records periodically. This is an important clause from the musician's view, because, depending on its accounting practices, the volume of musician accounts, and the experience and number of staff at the record company, errors and/or omissions in the calculation of royalties owing to the musician are possible.[59] The extent of the right to audit is negotiable. Relevant to such negotiation is the timing of an audit - for example, not more than once per calendar year, upon ten days notice - and the right to take extracts, and/or to photocopy books, records and perhaps the company's underlying manufacturing records.

D. Term and Options

The term, or duration, of an exclusive term recording contract usually consists of an initial period of 12 to 18 months, plus a number of irrevocable options each of which may be one year or longer. Sometimes, in the case of independent record production companies, the initial period is two years, during which time the company might be contractually obligated to meet a foreign release commitment, obtain another defined agreement with a third party, or lose the rights to the artist's services. Alternatively, the term may be: (a) based on a number of albums to be delivered; or (b) a period of time which is co-terminous with a publishing or management agreement.

The term is usually a "floating term". That is, it is defined as a recording period - 6 to 9 months, for example, which ends with the delivery of the masters - and a release period, another 9 to 12 months following the recording period and during which the album is to be distributed, marketed, and promoted. A "contract period" is the

---

[58] Peter Steinmetz, "The Recording Industry" in *Copyright for the General Practitioner*, cited above in note 9, at p. 50. See Fisher, "Record Royalties...", cited above in note 26. See Kronemeyer and Sidak, "The Structure and Performance...", cited above in note 10. See also Gertz-Culpepper, cited above in note 8.

[59] See the discussion in Chapter 3, "Music Publishing" for more detail and Leonard M. Marx, "A Practitioner's Guide on How to Avoid or Pursue Suits", in *Counselling Clients in the Entertainment Business* (1988), (New York: Practising Law Institute, 1988) at pp. 329-331.

generic way of referring to either the initial period or an option period and is determined by reference to the delivery date, the release date, and/or a specific period of time following either of these dates.

Certain performance levels may have to be met before an option can be exercised, for instance: (1) advances paid; (2) complete fulfilment of a domestic or foreign[60] territory release commitment; (3) payment of a minimum amount of royalties during the previous contract period; or (4) sometimes the operation of a "pay or play" provision, which allows the record company to make only minimum union scale payments. See the "pay or play" discussion in section 2(b)(iv)E below.

(xi) Other Considerations

A. Leaving Members

A leaving members provision addresses the basic rights and obligations of the artist and the label when a group breaks up, or when one or more members leave the group. This clause can affect the fundamental freedom to decide the make-up of a band, and makes it clear that a group break-up is not an automatic way to terminate a record contract. Under this clause, the company may contract for the right to determine who will replace the leaving member, and for the right to terminate the term of the agreement if a key member in the group (for example, the lead singer) leaves the group or the music business altogether. Members of the group may contract for mutual approval of any replacement member. Some record companies try to bind the leaving member(s) to the contract, but at reduced royalties.[61] The company also may contract to have the right to approve new members before they can join the group. As discussed in Chapter 6, "Agents and Managers", the management agreement may deal with group break-ups or leaving member situations also. Care should be taken to ensure that the leaving member clauses in the management agreement and recording agreement do not conflict.

As discussed in section 2(a)(v) above, "joint and several" obligations mean that the members of a group are liable, both

---

[60] Steinmetz, cited above in note 9, p. 41.

[61] See the *Holly Johnson* case discussed in Chapter 10, "Personal Service Contracts" which in particular found that the leaving member clause typical to many recording agreements was in restraint of trade. See also the Castle article, cited above in note 46 which discusses in detail the ethical and legal issues which a lawyer faces when acting for all members of the band who have signed an agreement which contains a leaving members clause.

collectively and/or individually, to fulfill their obligations under the agreement which would include being legally responsible for recoupable amounts advanced to the group. It also means that even after the group has disbanded, the individuals comprising the group are bound to the agreement. The result may be that the remaining members or a solo artist, who was formerly a group member, may end up paying off an old group debt (including unrecouped recording costs) out of royalties or advances which would otherwise be payable to him or her as part of a new act.

It is preferable, from the musician's view, to negotiate a new contract with the company when a group disbands or a musician goes solo, or a proper release of contractual obligations should be obtained when a member leaves or the group disbands. If the leaving member clause is invoked, that leaving member: (a) normally would be required to deliver new demo recordings; (b) should be entitled to a "formerly of..." type of credit; and (c) should be entitled to a *pro rata* share of advances and royalties pertaining to recordings which were completed while still a member of the group. Consider also the effect of the key person clause as discussed in Chapter 6, "Agents and Managers", and the cross-collateralization clause as discussed in section 2(b)(viii) above in a leaving member situation.

B. Credits

Although album credit is customarily afforded to recording musicians, recording contracts typically do not specify the type of credit to be given. Record companies usually will resist attempts to specify credits in any detail.[62] Third party credits such as engineering and producer credits may be specified in other agreements - for example, the producer contract discussed above in section 1(d)(v).

C. Foreign Release

The need to break markets in foreign territories and to compete internationally is significant to most Canadian musicians and was previously discussed in section 2(b)(iii)B above. A U.S. release is particularly desirable because the U.S. is the single largest record-buying nation in the world, and constitutes a market ten times the size of the Canadian market. The United Kingdom, Germany and Japan are also important territories. Ideally, from the musician's viewpoint, the

---

[62] For the importance of credit in the U.S. see, generally, Selz and Simensky, *Entertainment Law* (New York: McGraw-Hill Inc., 1983) at Chapter 16.

record company would be contractually required to release recordings in foreign territories. If such obligations are set out in the agreement, the musician may contract also for the right to terminate the term of the agreement, have the rights to the recordings revert to him or her after a given period of time[63] - perhaps one or two option periods - or have the right to seek a release of the subject recordings in the applicable territories, if the required foreign release has not occurred. The provision guaranteeing a foreign release might include any of the following: (a) a release in a specified territory or territories such as the U.S.A, Germany, the United Kingdom, and Japan or any combination of those; or (b) the requirement that a specified label carry out the release - for example, a third party major record company based in the U.S. or any other "major" territory.

D. Distribution

The recording contract does not often deal with distribution in any depth and the company probably would resist attempts to detail its distribution practices. However, inadequate distribution is extremely detrimental to record sales and, therefore, to the musician's recording career. The ideal contract would require distribution to be carried out in good faith, with all reasonable efforts, in the manner in which the company is accustomed through normal commercial retail channels, nationally and in any territory in which releases are secured. This arguably would set an objective standard for distribution and release in the event of a dispute or lawsuit. However, without a specific and detailed outline of how, when, and where recordings are to be distributed, this clause still may be of minimal benefit.

E. Copyright Revision

All provisions in a recording contract and any other long term agreement that are affected by or based on the *Copyright Act* or "standard industry practices" should be reviewed carefully. These provisions must take into account the possibility of copyright revision and changes in industry standards concerning payments such as mechanical, synchronization, and neighbouring rights royalties, blank tape levies and future copyright royalties.

---

[63] Steinmetz, "The Recording Industry"... cited above in note 9, p. 43.

F. Force Majeure

A force majeure provision is often included in a recording contract. This is the so-called "act of God" clause which protects the company should it be unable to fulfill its obligations under the agreement for reasons beyond its control such as wars, floods or labour unrest in the record industry. There should be some negotiation as to whether this clause should apply mutually. Preferably, the force majeure clause should place an absolute limit on the period of time that a record company is allowed to default on its obligations to the musician. For example, if the company still has not fulfilled its commitment to make a record after 180 days, the musician may contract to have the right to terminate the term of the agreement. Additionally, this clause can act as a type of suspension mechanism, wherein the term of the agreement is suspended for a period equal to the 'down time' caused by that particular labour dispute or natural disaster. In this regard, the clause should be worded carefully so that it is actually a true force majeure clause rather than a suspension clause. The suspension clause is discussed below. Sometimes the force majeure provision is worded broadly enough that the issue of restraint of trade might be raised by the musician. See Chapter 10 for a discussion of restraint of trade.

G. Default and Cure

This clause was discussed in the context of publishing agreements in Chapter 3, "Music Publishing" and will not be discussed again in detail here. However, one should be aware that the default and cure clause found in most music industry agreements has the effect of creating a fixed period of time during which, depending on the wording in the agreement, one or both of the parties to the contract has the right to cure its default or breach, before the agreement may be terminated by the other party. The cure period typically will be between 30 and 60 days. Careful attention at the drafting stage of this agreement is necessary to ensure, for example, that this default and cure clause is not used routinely to account to or pay royalties to the musician late. To avoid this type of delay, the period of time to cure could be shortened, for example, to five or ten days to cure such default. In some instances, for example, where the musician wishes to change labels, it may be in the musician's favour not to have a default and cure clause at all, but merely have the right to terminate the term of the agreement if there is a material breach of the agreement. What constitutes a material breach of the agreement is discussed below in section 2(b)(xi)I. In addition to a default and cure clause, a suspension clause, which is discussed below, may be invoked if the musician is in breach of the agreement.

H. Suspension

In the event of a breach or threatened breach of the agreement by the musician, the effect of a suspension clause is to halt temporarily the running of time (i.e., the term) under the agreement. The suspension clause raises the issue of restraint of trade, which is discussed in Chapter 10, "Personal Service Contracts". Ideally, from the musician's perspective, the suspension clause should be omitted from the agreement altogether, although many record companies are reluctant to do so. In any event, the suspension clause preferably should be worded as an extension clause, the effect of which would be to extend the term of the agreement in order to facilitate compliance with the agreement. The extension then would be limited to a set period of time, for example, 120 or 180 days and thereafter, the record company would be forced to decide whether or not to terminate the term of the agreement. In the case of a group, it is important to bear in mind that, since the provisions of the agreement are applied both jointly and severally, it is possible for the term to be extended unilaterally against any one member of the group ("severally") or all of the group ("jointly").

I. Termination

The contract may contain performance criteria which, if unfulfilled, would allow the artist to terminate the term of the agreement. These may include: (1) failure by the company to permit the artist to meet a minimum recording commitment; (2) failure to release a musician's recordings within a specified time or territory; (3) failure to meet foreign release commitments, if applicable; (4) failure to account, and pay advances, or royalties to the artist; (5) failure to allow an audit; and (6) insolvency or bankruptcy on the part of the record company.[64] There are also a number of criteria whereby, in the event of a default by the artist, the company may have the right to terminate the term of the agreement, such as: (a) the musician's

---

[64] See, for example, in the U.S. context, Ronald S. Orr and Shelly Rothschild, "Entertainment Contracts: Creative Bankruptcy" (1986) Vol. 4 No. 5, I.M.L. 26. See also M.R. Julius and R.A. Batz, "Bankruptcy: The Death of Recording Contracts" (1983) 2 Cardozo Arts and Entertainment Law Review 189.

inability to perform adequately - for example, in the case of a loss of the lead singer's voice; or (b) a musician's refusal to fulfill the minimum recording commitment.

3. Other Contracts

The other agreements that are relevant in the recording context are outlined above in section 1(d). The purpose of the discussion below is to highlight what contractual aspects make these agreements distinct and what terms can be negotiated. General aspects of these agreements will not be discussed again in detail here. Checklists for these agreements are included in Appendix 5. Bear in mind that in any royalty-based agreement, a number of general issues must be addressed: (1) the territory; (2) the grant of rights; (3) the term of the agreement and whether or not there are to be any options, extensions, or renewals of such term; (4) payment and compensation structure; (5) whether it is an exclusive or non-exclusive agreement; (6) whether or not aspects of the agreement are irrevocable; and (7) general contractual issues such as proper parties, accounting and audit rights, representations, warranties and indemnifications, and other general provisions, such as the governing law and assignment clauses.

(a) Production Agreement

This agreement was discussed in detail in the context of the exclusive term record production agreement and in section 1 (d)(ii) above, and will not be discussed again here.

(b) Video Production Agreement

(i) Generally

Even though the music video production agreement can be a detailed, complicated agreement, in practice, the video production agreement, particularly when musicians are acting as their own independent record production company and production budgets are small, is often an oral agreement. Major record companies, on the other hand, usually insist that video production agreements be detailed and in writing.

The copyright basis for the visual components of a music video are discussed at length in Chapter 1, "Copyright" and should be consulted in relation to the discussion below. As well, the discussion in Chapter 12, "Tax", of the certification of film and video masters, is also relevant here, as is the definition of a Canadian music video for purposes of Canadian content regulations.

Bear in mind that the myriad legal complexities which characterize a film or television production - including insurance, union requirements, copyright clearances, model releases and the administration of production budgets - also can be present in the production of a music video.[65] The threat or initiation of a lawsuit based on the "appropriation of personality" by individuals appearing in the video (other than musicians who have already granted such rights to the record production company) exists if no model releases are obtained. For a detailed discussion of the legal basis for a claim arising out of the authorized use of one's name and likeness, see Chapter 9, "Merchandising" in this regard.

What also may be overlooked in this agreement is the necessity of clearing certain subsidiary rights - for example, the right to reproduce works of art in footage that is part of the music video. This might occur, for example, when a musician's performance is filmed for the video in front of a large mural which forms the backdrop. To avoid potential liability for copyright infringement, these rights should be cleared by obtaining the necessary licence from the owner(s) of such works. If the record company is not also the music publisher, or if the musical copyright is not owned or controlled by the musician (who typically agrees in the record agreement to grant a synchronization licence for nominal consideration for the purposes of producing a music video), then a synchronization licence will be required from the music publisher. The video is usually done by a freelance independent video production company. The discussion below outlines terms of the agreement for the production of a music video between a video production company and a record company.

(ii) Key Points to Consider

Key provisions in this agreement include the following: (1) the supply of the musician's services, customarily without charge; (2) the compensation to the director, usually a flat fee, although in some cases the director may contract to be paid royalties (for example, if the video is sold commercially); (3) compliance with union requirements; (4) the clearance of any and all rights and licences, and any releases to be obtained by the video director; (5) an assignment by the video production company of all right, title and interest, including the

---

[65] Gertz-Culpepper, cited above in note 8, p. 283.

copyright, in and to the video production to the record company or record production entity; (6) the date for completion and delivery of the video; (7) a commitment that the video will be marketable and suitable for television broadcast; and (8) a stipulation as to who bears the costs if the video needs to be re-edited or re-shot.[66]

If the music video director is participating in royalties, the provisions are similar to any record agreement, including provisions dealing with recoupment, accounting, free goods, reserves and packaging deductions, for example.

(iii) Underlying Rights

The underlying creative rights in a music video can include: (a) the underlying musical compositions including both the music and the lyrics; (b) screenplay or teleplay describing the visual imagery and any other dialogue over and above the lyrics embodied in the underlying musical composition; (c) choreography that is performed visually and captured in the music video; (d) paintings, photographs, statues or other graphic works protected by copyrights that are reproduced in film or video tape and captured in the music video; (e) the musical (vocal, instrumental) and dance or dramatic performances of the performing artists which are embodied in the music video.[67]

With respect to the above-noted underlying components, the video producer must obtain consents and clearances, and meet union requirements (where applicable). Union requirements apply to AFM and ACTRA members - for example, the screenplay writer, who may be a member of ACTRA.

The rights necessary to perform publicly the song, the performer's performances therein and the master recording used in the video are often covered by blanket licences from SOCAN and the NRCC, respectively. However, if the grand rights and so-called "dramatic rights" in the musical composition have been reserved to the composer, the composer's consent must be obtained.[68] The moral rights aspects to the music - which were discussed in Chapter 1, "Copyright" and in the context of music publishing agreements in Chapter 3, "Music Publishing" - also should be kept in mind. These sections should be consulted for clarity as needed. Moral rights also apply in relation to

[66] These points are distilled from the Fisher article cited above in note 8 at p. 43. This article contains a sample short form video agreement. See also pp. 292-293 of Gertz-Culpepper cited above in note 8 for a discussion of the video production agreement.

[67] Peter E. Steinmetz, "The Video Revolution" in Gordon I. Kirke, Moderator, and Michael I. Yanover, *Entertainment and Sports Law Workshop 1985-1986*, (Toronto: U.T. Faculty of Law), at p. 4.

[68] Gertz-Culpepper, cited above in note 8, p. 294.

the master. See also above in sections 2(b)(iv)H, 2(b)(v)K and 2(b)(viii) for the discussion of other issues involved in the production and release of music videos. These include concerns such as cross-collateralizing video costs against record royalties, and what royalties will be payable with respect to the commercial exploitation of the video. See also the discussion in Chapter 1, "Copyright" as well as Appendix 2, the "Synchronization Licence Checklist", regarding the particularities of synchronization licences. Bear in mind that it may be extremely difficult to clear all synchronization licences necessary for a non-controlled composition with multiple owners or writers. See the AFM Phonograph Record Labour Agreement for payments concerning union aspects of this agreement and the discussion of the AFM found in Chapter 5, "Labour". Many videos, however, are often produced on a non-union basis. The discussion of the Audio Video Licensing Agency concerning the administration and licensing of music videos (found in Chapter 2) is also relevant.

(iv) Provisions of the Agreement

Several specifics of this agreement should be stipulated, including: (1) the length of the final edit of the video; (2) the song performed and the particular version or mix of the song, that is, whether it is the "radio edit", a "re-mix", or a long form version; (3) the name of the artist and any featured performer(s); (4) the video producer; (5) the director; (6) the date photography is to start and be completed; (7) the video format, that is, whether it is on beta, 16mm or 35mm film, for example; (8) the location of the shoot; (9) the definition of "the video", which usually includes all elements of the finished product, including answer prints, and optical elements; (10) the party responsible for obtaining all rights, clearances and consents; and (11) a detailed definition of what constitutes delivery of the master, including the kind and 'specs' of the tape, such as 1", $^3/_4$ " or $^1/_2$ " tape, and where, when, and to whom the video master must be delivered. Typically, the record company, sometimes in consultation with the artist, maintains the right to alter or edit the video. It is negotiable whether responsibility for the costs of doing so should be borne by the record company or the video production company. Preferably it should be the record company's cost if the record company has already approved certain elements of the production, including the story board and script. The producer may have contracted to have the first right to make any changes to it. To the extent that this is not a "work-made-for-hire", then there generally should be an assignment to the record company of all right, title and interest, including the copyright, in and to the video masters. Compliance with applicable union agreements should be a material term of the agreement.

A. Producer's Services

The video producer (or production company) is to deliver: (1) a script and storyboard prior to the commencement of the shoot; and (2) a finished video master of quality suitable for broadcast television. The record company and/or the musician may have the right to approve the script and storyboard and in the absence of such approval right, if there are costs incurred to re-edit or re-shoot the video, these may have to be borne by the video production company.

B. Producer's Compensation

The compensation payable to the video production company is usually a flat fee payable, for example, as follows: half on signing the agreement, or upon the approval of the production budget; and half on the completion of photography, receiving a rough edit, or on delivery of the final edited video. The payment schedule is negotiable. Proof of payment of applicable union payments also may be a prerequisite for final payment. It is usually the responsibility of the video director to obtain all clearances, releases and licences, with the exception of the following record company-owned rights: (1) the rights of the recording musician(s) to appear in the video; and (2) rights in the master audio recording. See the discussion of master use licences below in section 3(d)(i).

C. Costs

Costs are payable by the video producer according to the approved production budget and include: errors and omissions insurance, any production equipment rental, taxes, personnel and when applicable, workers' compensation and other standard employee deductions. Requisite insurance coverage usually includes public liability in general, for not less than one million dollars.

D. Failure to Deliver

Video production is often a very time-sensitive endeavour, since a music video is often created after a single has been released, hence time is always "of the essence" (that is, it is always a material condition of the agreement, the breach of which can give rise to a lawsuit). The failure to deliver a finished video in a timely manner will, in most cases, prejudice the record company's rights and affect record sales negatively. The record company may try to negotiate the right to be reimbursed for all production costs, if the production company fails to deliver on time. However, consider that if the video production company has complied materially at all times with the record company's requests and the record company delayed in exercising its approval rights, the wording of this clause becomes very important, and is a reasonable point for negotiation.[69]

E. General Provisions

Standard clauses including an independent contractor clause, indemnity clause and injunctive relief clause may be, and often are, part of the agreement. If the video production company is participating in royalties, the royalty provisions of the record agreement which apply to audio-visual "masters" and "sight and sound" devices are applicable and should be incorporated into the agreement. The video production company must represent and warrant that it is free and clear to enter into the agreement and will comply with all material terms of the agreement including the obligation to obtain all requisite rights, clearances and licences. The company also may obtain the right to use the name, likeness and biographical material of the video producer or director for the purposes of promoting the video. The record company generally will be given the right to attend at all post-production locations until delivery of the final edit.

In some instances, where a major record company has signed a licensing/production agreement with an independent record production company for masters embodying the artist's performances, or for the artist's services respectively, the major record company may ask the artist to sign an inducement letter. Inducement letters are discussed below in section 3(c)(iv).

---

[69] See Form 163-1, "Music Video Production Agreement" in Fox cited above in note 20 for a detailed discussion of this agreement and a sample video production agreement. See also chapter 7, "Music Videos" in *This Business of Music...*, cited above in note 12 at pp. 76-82 for a general business discussion of music videos.

(c) Producer Agreement

(i) Generally

There are many different types of agreements under which record producers provide their services. The discussion below focusses on two distinct types of record producer agreements: (1) where a recording contract is in place and the producer is hired by a record company; and (2) where a producer records masters embodying an artist's performances and "shops" for a recording agreement, also known as a "development agreement" or a "shopping deal". (This is to be distinguished, however, from the "deal shopper" agreement with a lawyer, manager, or other music industry 'insider' which usually consists mainly of sending out press kits and solicitation letters, and/or arranging special meetings to present an artist's material to selected record executives. This "deal shopper" agreement may involve a percentage-based commission (usually 10% to 15%) or a flat fee to obtain a record agreement and is not discussed in detail herein.)

Most of the discussion below is relevant to both producer agreements described in (1) and (2) above. However, the main focus in this section will be on the record producer agreement where a recording contract is in place.

Some of the provisions which are applicable to both agreements include: (1) the producer's compensation, including advances and royalty payments; (2) the ownership of masters; (3) credit requirements; (4) the definition of a master and when it is to be completed; (5) whether or not the producer is exclusively or non-exclusively providing services; and (6) accounting and audit rights.

(ii) The "Development" or "Shopping" Agreement

This agreement is necessarily speculative in nature. The producer typically provides or secures studio time and producer services, usually at a reduced fee or for no up-front fee, with the expectation that the producer and the musician will be successful in securing a third party recording or licensing agreement for the musician's services or the products thereof. For this reason, this type of arrangement with a producer and/or studio owner is often referred to as a "spec" deal. The producer may or may not be paid studio time or producer fees, and the producer royalty may be delayed or deferred until there is interest from a third party record company.

This agreement is often entered into by a producer who owns a studio and/or a record production company and who acts as record producer and/or independent record production company in completing the masters. The producer's services ordinarily include pre-production of demo recordings (if demos are to be recorded), arranging and overseeing recording and studio time and the creation of "demo quality" or "commercial quality" masters - from pre-production through to the final mix. This agreement may require, as a fundamental condition to the benefit of the musician, that a recording agreement be obtained within a specified period of time, failing which the agreement would be terminated.

Sometimes the producer's fees are deferred until the recoupment of all costs from the proceeds under a licensing or sale of the masters or the receipt of advances pursuant to a 'flow-through' production agreement with a third party record company. Alternatively, a reduced fee is negotiated, subject perhaps to the musician's obligation to pay the producer a bonus or advance upon securing a third party record or licence agreement. A producer also may have contracted not only for record sale royalties, a share of advances and a producer's fee, but also to a share in the ownership or income from music publishing and/or sound recording copyrights. For example, assuming the songwriter and recording musician is the same person, as is often the case, there may be a participation by the producer in the musician's public performance royalties, mechanical licence income, or neighbouring rights royalties, for example. This is a point for negotiation. A *pro rata* share of advances under the record deal, based on the number of tracks that the producer has produced, also may be warranted. For example, if the musician has secured a record agreement, and negotiated to have four of the masters which were produced by the producer included on the final album (which consists of twelve masters), the producer may be entitled, subject to the recoupment of any outstanding producer fees, to one third of such album's advances.

There may be a "best efforts" obligation on the part of the musician to use the producer's services in connection with another album. However, if a recording musician is successful in obtaining a third party agreement, but the producer's services are not used for such album, one of two scenarios may apply: (1) a percentage override of the musician's royalties may be paid to the producer if the record company selects a new producer; or (2) a "buy-out" at a flat fee per master may be negotiated.

The producer's credit usually is negotiated also. See the discussion below in section 3(c)(iii)E. There also may be a provision for direct payment to the producer by the third party record company, which is usually done by a letter of direction. It is unusual to have a producer contracted on an exclusive basis, although in some cases it may be warranted in both the shopping agreement and in the situation where the record company has signed an artist, and a record agreement is in force.[70] The number of recordings to be produced should be set out clearly in this agreement, as well as whether there are to be demonstration recordings or commercial quality masters. Since recording ventures can be expensive, and because the quality and quantity of studio facilities and equipment vary tremendously, a recording budget is critical. Both the producer and the musician should have a clear idea as to what is being spent. A recording budget should be approved mutually by the musician and the producer.

The producer may insist on final approval over all production matters, thus preventing the musician from making any changes or re-mixing the masters. He/she may also insist on a re-recording restriction which would prevent the artist from re-recording the same songs with another producer for a specified period of time. In addition to the producer's fee, there may be an additional fee for securing an agreement - for instance, a finder's fee of 10% of net royalties, although preferably the producer's incentive would be limited to receiving a share of advances and a producer's royalty, without the added finder's fee.

In a shopping agreement, a producer may be entitled to receive a higher producer royalty for having speculated time on the project in the beginning. It is negotiable whether or not the producer's override royalty would apply to any particular set of recordings or whether it would apply generally to a specific record agreement. If the masters have been re-worked or re-mixed by another producer, other than the original producer, arguably that producer should be entitled to co-producer credit and co-producer royalties and the original producer's royalties may be reduced accordingly. Other aspects which may be relevant with respect to this agreement are discussed below in the context of the producer agreement with a record company.

(iii) The Producer's Agreement with a Record Company

A. Generally

The producer's services usually are provided on a non-exclusive basis, although in certain situations, this agreement could be exclusive for a term. For example, a major record company may contract with a major recording act to have the producer deliver the masters within three months of the date of the commencement of the agreement and

---

[70] See Christian L. Castle, "An Introduction to Negotiating Record Producers Agreements", in *Entertainment Publishing and the Arts Handbook* (New York: Clark, Boardman, 1988) at pp. 149-153. See also chapter 4, *This Business of Music...*, cited above note 12 at pp. 49-59 for a discussion of this agreement.

require that the producer render services exclusively for the purposes of fulfilling the terms of the agreement in the time specified. More typically, the producer may be producing a number of musicians at one time and the producer's services are rendered on a non-exclusive basis.

The producer is usually an independent contractor who provides services through a production company; therefore, the inducement letter discussed below in section 3(c)(iv) is relevant. The producer's services are often subject to approval by the record company and the producer may be removed during the term of the agreement if the record company is not satisfied with the producer's work.

Key provisions from the record agreement normally are incorporated by reference into the producer agreement. These include the definition of recording costs, record masters and videos. Normally the record company obtains all right, title and interest in and to the products of the producer's services, but not the rights to the musical compositions embodied in the masters. The record company, not the record producer, is responsible for paying mechanical royalties. The producer ordinarily will make representations and warranties similar to those made by the musician in the exclusive recording agreement. These are coupled with an obligation to indemnify the company with respect to any loss, damage or lawsuit arising from a breach of such representations and warranties. A producer agreement that guarantees the use of the producer's services beyond recording one album, or a number of masters on one album, may tie such a guarantee to sales performance. For example, the album which the producer produced must sell 50,000 units or more (i.e., a minimum of certified "gold" sales in Canada), or some other objective test. Such an agreement is not common. It is more common to have a one album commitment agreement only.

B. Producer's Services

The producer usually provides the following services: (a) selecting personnel for recording sessions; (b) selecting, in conjunction with the musician and record company, the music to be recorded - in many cases it will be songs that have been written by the recording musician; (c) supervising recording sessions; (d) assisting in the preparation of the recording budget; (e) preparing the paperwork, including union contracts; (f) overseeing the technical, commercial and artistic aspects of the recording; (g) overseeing the final mix and perhaps editing, re-mixing and/or mastering the recordings until the record company and the musician are satisfied that the masters are satisfactory for commercial release; and (h) ensuring that all union session payments, taxes, studio fees, engineering equipment rental, and mastering costs from the approved budget are paid. All of the above services are subject to the final approval of the record company or, if hired by the musician, the musician.

Attention should be paid to the criteria of acceptability contracted for in the agreement regarding the masters produced. One should be concerned with the words "commercially" or "artistically" satisfactory, as it is difficult to define these two concepts. In the interests of the producer, these words should be deleted from the agreement in favour of a "technically satisfactory" standard of quality for delivered masters. Arguably, the record company should be satisfied with the words "technically satisfactory" for the production of records as defined in the recording agreement, or perhaps the producer should not have been hired. Often, however, a producer does not enjoy this kind of absolute creative freedom until he/she is well established and has a string of commercially successful recordings to his/her credit. The time frame for providing services is subject to the musician's reasonable availability and must be agreed upon with the record company, the artist and the producer.

C. Over-budget

If the producer is over-budget, the producer may be liable to pay costs, either on demand, or out of his or her royalties, particularly if these overages are the result of the producer's direct acts or omissions. This clause covering budget excesses often is included in the recording agreement with the musician also. The producer's liability is usually contingent upon the recording costs being over-budget by a minimum of 10% to 15% of the total budget. Although this clause is rarely enforced, it constitutes a significant legal liability for the producer. It is included in order to allow the record company to impose a penalty, if the producer is significantly over-budget. Recording costs are the responsibility of the producer, but the producer should not be responsible for costs outside the producer's control, such as the musician's failure to be ready, willing and able to perform and record, or other unforeseen events.

D. Payment

The initial payment is usually a fee which is paid as a non-returnable (but recoupable) advance against future producer royalties. Payment of producer royalties is typically contingent upon recoupment of recording costs and recoupment of any advance paid to the producer. Some payments to the producer may not be recoupable out of the producer's royalties, such as a fee payable to the producer as engineer or session player. The recoupability of such costs can depend on the producer's bargaining power in the music industry. The producer also typically receives a royalty in the range of 1% to 3% of the suggested retail list price of the records sold; it is calculated in much the same manner as the musician's royalties. Depending on the stature of the producer in the music business, this percentage may be 4%, 5%, or more.

If the company is accounted to on a wholesale or net receipts basis, the producer's royalties usually would be converted to the equivalent royalties expressed as a percentage of net receipts or wholesale receipts. In this regard, the producer is typically very much subject to the terms of the musician's record agreement, including deductions, prorations, reserves and free goods which are usually incorporated into the producer agreement by reference. For example, prorations for foreign royalties may be one-half to two-thirds of the applicable domestic producer royalty rate, or the same prorations that apply to the artist's royalties under the recording agreement. However, a producer of some stature in the record industry may not agree to these types of royalty reductions. For example, if a producer is entitled to 2% of the suggested retail list price, the producer may continue to receive such royalties without being prorated, even in a foreign territory. When the musician is wholly or partly responsible for paying the producer's royalties out of royalties due or payable to the musician, this will reduce the musician's royalties accordingly. Normally the producer is subject to the same accounting and audit rights as the musician under the recording agreement. Once recording costs are recouped, the producer is often entitled to be paid directly from the record company, pursuant to a letter of direction signed by the musician.

If the producer has not produced all of the masters that are contained on a record, the producer's royalty typically is prorated further, according to the following formula: the number of masters produced by the producer divided by the number of masters contained on the record. However, to prevent this formula being applied to singles, a producer may be successful in obtaining "A-side protection".[71]

"A-side protection" means that the producer can retain full producer royalties on any particular track he or she produced, if released as a single, regardless of the fact that a different producer may have produced the other cut(s) on the single. It also may apply to "B-sides" - that is, if applicable, producer royalties for the "B-side" of a single also would not be prorated or reduced in any way by other

---

[71] Robert Horsfall, "UK Records", "Record Producer Agreements" (1986) Vol. 4 No. 6, I.M.L. 37 and "UK Records", "Record Producer Agreements(2)" (1986) I.M.L. 44 at p. 45.

producer royalty-bearing masters on the same commercial single. This is relevant when there are two or more different producers for the A and B sides of a single.

Sometimes the producer is also successful in obtaining "re-mix protection". Practically, this means that the producer has the first right to re-mix any masters recorded pursuant to the producer's agreement, and may not have his/her producer royalty reduced by any payments or royalties that must be paid to a third party re-mix producer. In some cases, specialized dance re-mixers could be engaged, and the record company may resist granting re-mix protection to the producer. In such cases, the producer may be and perhaps should be entitled to a co-producer credit and a prorated royalty. Subject to the discussion above regarding "A" and "B" side protection, if there is more than one individual producer producing a track, the royalties typically are prorated and the liability is joint and several. However, in some instances, depending on the producer's concern for his or her reputation, the producer may not want such credit.

At the time of writing, it remains unclear whether producers will be entitled to payment for so-called "neighbouring rights" uses. It is unlikely, based on current discussions amongst neighbouring rights stakeholders. The producer's contractual right to receive "neighbouring rights" payments could be addressed in the net receipts clause, or in separate negotiated contractual provisions. See Chapter 1, "Copyright" for a discussion of the copyright basis of neighbouring rights.

Typical advances to producers are in the range of $1,000 to $5,000 per master, depending on the status of the producer (and whether the recording is a demo or a commercial master) and can be much higher, particularly in the U.S. where producer advances can range from $25,000 USD to $100,000 USD or more, per track. The producer advance typically is paid one-half on commencement of recording, and the other half on delivery of the masters, subject to any penalty for being over-budget. If the recording is completed under budget, the amount by which the recording is under budget may be considered a further advance to be divided between the musician and producer. This is a point for negotiation.

Although most videos are used solely as promotional vehicles, the definition of a master will often take into account video sales. In addition to customary record royalties, the producer may be entitled to a specific share of the artist net receipts from the sale of videos. For example, if the musician is entitled to 50% of such net receipts, the ratio that the producer's royalty bears to the musician's royalty would be the appropriate *pro rata* share to which the producer is entitled. For example, in a recording agreement where the musician is getting 10% of the suggested retail list price, inclusive of producer royalties, and the producer is getting 3% of the suggested retail list price, the producer royalty is 3/10ths of the musician's total royalty. Accordingly, the producer and musician would share 3/10ths and 7/10ths respectively in the musician's 50% share of net receipts. This same ratio typically would apply to other net receipts under the record agreement.

Payment to the producer typically occurs at one of three different points: (1) either after recoupment - but only recoupment of the producer's advance; (2) after recoupment of all recording costs, including any producer advances paid, but excluding video costs and artist's tour support; or (3) the producer is paid "off the top" prior to the production company and artist sharing in net receipts. The most typical scenario is the second one, but other scenarios can be negotiated. When recording costs are recouped, producers may be paid retroactively from the first record sold, that is, from "record one", subject to recoupment of any advances paid to the producer. This is a point for negotiation.

The royalty figure used to determine the point of recoupment may be either: (1) at a rate which is the combined artist/producer gross royalty rate (i.e., the "all-in" rate); or (2) at a rate which is the artist's "net" rate (i.e., excluding the producer royalty). Since the "all-in" rate is a larger figure, the recording and other recoupable costs will be "recouped" at an earlier point in time using the "all-in" rate than if the artist's "net" rate were used. Unless the producer has significant clout in the music industry and therefore leverage in the negotiation, recoupment typically will take place at the artist's "net" rate. Bear in mind that the record producer may be recouped prior to recoupment by the musician of recoupable costs and usually will receive royalties prior to the musician, particularly since the musician must recoup video and tour support advances in addition to recording costs.

An escalation in producer royalties based on specific sales plateaux may be negotiated - for example, a further 0.5% at 'gold' (50,000) and another 0.5% again at 'platinum' (100,000) sales, based on SRLP, or otherwise, on a national, territory-by-territory, or worldwide basis. Alternatively, if certain sales plateaux or figures are achieved, a non-returnable and possibly non-recoupable bonus could be paid. Such amounts are negotiable depending on the bargaining strengths of the parties.

The producer normally will be paid travel and accommodation costs and per diems which form part of the musician's recording costs and are recoupable from the musician's royalties, and sometimes the producer's royalties. However, there should not be any double recoupment of the same costs or expenses.

Also consider the effect of cross-collateralization and the controlled composition clause with respect to mechanical royalties and producer royalties if the producer is also a songwriter, particularly if there are two or more producers on one album. If the producer is a songwriter and has written a song that is released commercially on an album, the producer's advances should not be recouped from mechanical royalties.[72]

E. Credit

As discussed below in section 4, the issue of credit is significant and lawsuits can arise. The credit clause can be detailed and specific regarding re-mixing, co-producer, assistant producer and engineer credits, and trade advertisements. It also can be substantially negotiated. However, ordinarily, and where applicable, the record company will abide by the credit-related contractual obligations that bind the production company or the musician.

It is negotiable where credit will be affixed, but typically it is found on inserts, labels and liner notes and in all trade ads greater than half a page. A typical producer's credit clause would read: "Producer shall be accorded credit on all single and album covers, liners, and labels, as follows: "Produced by J. Smith for Smith-Platinum Productions". Failure to give proper credit is usually subject to a default and cure clause. Such clause gives the record company a period of time to cure the breach, following receipt of the appropriate written notice from the producer advising the record company of its error. There also may be a contractual and moral right not to be credited in cases where the recording has been edited or re-mixed by a different producer.

The contract should stipulate a non-exclusive right to use the producer's name, approved likeness and biographical material in connection with the exploitation of the recordings produced pursuant to the agreement.

F. Acceptance of Masters

The term of this agreement is usually tied to completion of the masters, which usually means delivery of a fully edited and mixed master tape to the record company. If only "acceptance by the record company" constitutes delivery, and the masters are never accepted (because of technical or artistic flaws, for example), then the term of this agreement can be indeterminate and the producer may be liable to edit or re-mix masters indefinitely, without further pay. Therefore, it is important to set a deadline for acceptance. There should be either

---

[72] Fox cited above in note 20. See Form 165-1, "Producer - Record Company Agreement".

acceptance within a specified period of time of delivery to the record company, or a deemed acceptance, unless the record company notifies the producer, in writing, to the contrary.

(iv) Inducement Letter

The inducement letter, which sometimes is referred to as a declaration, occurs in a number of situations, for example: (1) when a musician signs to a record agreement, but carries on business under a corporation; (2) where a producer is carrying on business as a corporation and provides services to the record company through such corporation; (3) where the record production company has signed a musician and the record production company licenses rights to videos and record masters to a third party record company who pays significant advances to the record production company; and (4) as part of a personal guarantee under a distribution agreement as discussed below in section 3(f). The effect of an inducement letter is: (1) to bind the signing party personally to a third party, particularly if there is a breach of the agreement; and (2) to provide assurance that a corporation has the right to provide an individual's personal services.[73]

The following provisions typically are included in a producer's inducement letter: (1) a representation and warranty that the producer has the right to enter into the agreement free and clear of any and all claims whatsoever; (2) that the materials delivered pursuant to the agreement are free and clear of any and all claims; (3) that the producer, in certain instances, will perform services personally for the record company; (4) that the producer has the right to grant the right to use his or her name, likeness and biographical material to the record company in connection with exploitation of records; (5) that the producer will comply with any re-recording restriction (there often will be a re-recording restriction either in the production agreement or the inducement letter, or both); under such a restriction, the producer would not have the right to re-record songs recorded on the masters for a specified period after they are recorded, delivered or released under the record agreement; (6) an injunctive relief clause, which is tied to a breach of the producer's representations and warranties; (7) that the producer is liable for damages and recoupment from sums otherwise payable to the producer, if there is an authorized settlement, or a judgement, against the producer; and (8) that the producer personally will look to his or her corporation for payment of royalties. That is: (a) there is not to be direct payment to the producer, unless

---

[73] *Ibid.* See Form 165-2, "Inducement Letter" and Forms 165-3, 165-4, "Producer Royalty Authorization".

otherwise advised; (b) the producer will look solely to the corporation for payment; and (c) payments to the producer will be to the corporation only.

Preferably any representations and warranties given pursuant to the inducement letter would be qualified by the words "to the best of the producer's knowledge", in order to mitigate damages and the extent of personal liability of the producer in the event of a breach of such representations and warranties.

(d) Record Master Agreements

(i) Master Use Licence

A. Generally

A master use licence typically is granted by a record company for use of a specific master in a specific situation, such as in synchronization with a film. (Reference to a film or other production that incorporates and uses the master audio recording will be referred to as the "Production"). Typically, the grant of such master use rights includes the right to exhibit, distribute, exploit, sell, lease and license the Production embodying the master worldwide. Rights are usually granted on a non-exclusive basis, but may be licensed exclusively for a very specific use and period of time. A specific use - for example, in a (film) Production - typically would include the right to use the master in trailers, advertising and promotion of such Production, and also could include the right to broadcast the Production on free television, cable television, pay television, include it on home use video cassettes or other specified and agreed upon uses of the master. The master use licence may or may not include the right to use the name and likeness of the recording musician. The agreement usually stipulates a specific time and territory and other rights-limiting terms of the agreement.

B. Points to Consider

In the recording agreement pursuant to which the master was produced, any non-phonographic uses may require approval of the recording musician. Therefore, an examination of the recording contract may be necessary in order to ascertain the extent of the musician's rights with respect to the master to be used in films or other similar productions. Since it is the record company which owns the master, the record company is free (subject to any approval right on the part of the musician in the recording agreement) to negotiate payment from the third party licensee.

Payment to the musician will be either on a flat-fee basis or expressed as a royalty. If a royalty is the basis of payment, typically such royalties would be subject to the same deductions and prorations that are specified under the recording agreement. Where payment is made as a one-time flat fee for a certain use (such as video), the artist typically would share the master use licence fee with the record company, often on a 50/50 basis. Careful attention should be paid to the definition of "master" and "net receipts" under the record agreement, to ensure the musician is entitled to share in such payments.

There should be some credit given in conjunction with the specific use - in film credits, for example. Credits in such a film production could include: the recording musician; the record company; the author; and the owner of the copyrights in the musical composition embodied in the master. The right to use the musician's name, likeness and biographical material should be secured, if relevant.

Standard representations and warranties included in this licence would be: (1) that the licensor record company is the exclusive owner of the entire right, title and interest in and to the masters that are the subject matter of the licence; (2) that the licensor has complied with the rules and regulations of the AFM or other applicable unions and has paid the applicable union fees; and (3) that the licensee would have the right to enter into and perform the agreement free and clear of any and all claims.

In certain situations, union re-use fees are applicable[74] - for example, when a recording intended for a phonograph record is used in a different medium such as film or television. Re-use fees can be as much as the original union scale session payments. Bear in mind that this is a master use licence only, therefore a synchronization licence for the musical composition embodied in the master still must be obtained from the music publisher when that master is used in synchronization with visual images. Synchronization licences are discussed in Chapter 1, "Copyright". See also the synchronization licence checklist in Appendix 2. Typically, the licence would not be assignable to a third party without the consent of the licensor.

---

[74] Chapter 10, "Licensing of Recording for Motion Pictures", *This Business of Music...*, cited above in note 12, at p. 103. See also Chapter 5, "Labour" for a discussion of applicable AFM agreements.

(ii) Master Purchase/Sale Agreement

A. Generally

The master purchase/sale agreement has terms that are similar to the terms discussed above in section 3(d)(i), regarding the master use licence agreement. However, the master purchase/sale agreement is not a licence. It may be structured either as: (1) an assignment of copyright in the master; (2) an asset purchase agreement, particularly where the entire catalogue of masters is purchased; or (3) as a purchase and sale of shares of a corporation which owns the masters, such as a record production company. See the discussion, "Sale of Music Publisher's Catalogue", in Chapter 3, "Music Publishing"; the general considerations in such a sale agreement are relevant to this agreement.

B. Points to Consider

The grant of rights typically would include all right, title and interest in and to the masters and would require the delivery to the purchaser of the original masters. A review of the contract with the recording artist may be necessary in order to determine whether or not the assignment of the rights to the masters requires the consent of the recording artist. Payment for the masters could be either a flat fee, a royalty percentage or a combination of the two. Standard representations and warranties include: (1) that the seller is the exclusive owner of the entire right, title and interest in and to all of the masters that are the subject matter of the agreement; (2) that the seller has complied with all rules and regulations of applicable unions, including all AFM producer and musician payments; (3) that there are no liens or encumbrances on the masters (an encumbrance can be any right or interest that a third party, other than the seller, has in the masters, such as a security interest, collateral mortgage, a lien, or contractual rights that require the payment to and/or permission from another person before or after the rights in the masters are transferred; it may exist for various reasons, including unpaid record royalties, advances, or studio fees or other recording artist and/or producer rights); (4) that the seller and purchaser respectively have the right to contract, authorize and enter into and perform the terms of the contract free and clear of any and all claims; and (5) that there is no litigation outstanding with respect to the masters.[75] The provisions in

---

[75] See Joseph Taubman, *In Tune With the Music Business...*, p. 65-70 cited above in note 12.

the relevant record and producer agreements can be relevant to this agreement and should be reviewed.

(iii) Licence of Record Masters Agreement

A. Grant of Rights

This type of licence agreement occurs most often between an independent label or production company and a domestic or foreign based record company. Typically, it is a licence of either a single master that will be included on a compilation, or an album's worth of masters that will be re-packaged (and sometimes re-mixed and/or mastered) and released as an entire album by the third party record company which acquires such rights. The grant of rights made pursuant to this agreement is usually exclusive, for a defined territory, and includes the right to manufacture, distribute, sell, advertise and perform publicly and broadcast the specific record masters. However, certain rights may be reserved to the licensor, including rights to sell records off-stage and over the Internet, for example.

With respect to neighbouring rights, the licensee typically would have the right to collect fees accruing under this agreement with respect to such rights in the masters, and may contract to share in the proceeds therefrom, if the licensee of record masters is a foreign record company, and if that foreign country's copyright or related laws provide for reciprocal neighbouring rights payments to Canadians. See Chapter 1, "Copyright", for the copyright basis of such rights.

The licensee should have the right to use the musician's name and likeness in connection with the sale of the licensed recordings. Typically, there would be no right to edit or alter the masters in any way without consent from the licensor record company, and in some instances, the consent of the musician also. Bear in mind that the definition of record masters includes video masters as well, and the licensee usually has the right to use such videos in the licensed territory. However, it is negotiable whether such use requires an additional payment, such as an additional advance or a higher licence fee, and whether such uses would be promotional only, or for purposes of sales. The licensee may or may not have the right to couple masters with other masters. If the licensee's intention is to couple or combine the licensed masters with masters from various record companies (for example, on a compilation), the right to "couple" is essential to the licensee. Otherwise, this is a point for negotiation. The licence may be for specific masters - for example, a single, or alternatively, one, two or three albums. In some cases, the licence may be for the entire catalogue of the record company. Copyright clearances (in this case, mechanical licences, and when applicable, synchronization licences) are the responsibility of the licensee.

The licensor supplies labelling information to the licensee. With respect to labelling and trade-mark issues, quality control should remain with the licensor and a certain quantity of sample pressings should be supplied free of charge to the licensor prior to the release of the licensed recordings, in order to maintain quality control. The licensor continues to retain ownership of the masters. The licensee obtains no ownership rights in the masters by virtue of this licence arrangement and the contract is not usually assignable. For most compilations, the licence is non-exclusive. Similarly, where there is a film release and potentially both a soundtrack recording in a specific territory and the release of the same master(s) on the recording artist's album, the licence is non-exclusive. However, for most full-album deals, the licence is exclusive to the licensee.

B. Payment

Compensation normally consists of an advance against royalties, plus royalties when the advance is earned out. An advance is sometimes structured as a "rolling" advance, that is, the advance payable subsequent to the initial advance is based on earning out the first advance and is reduced proportionately (if the earlier advance is only partially earned out), or it is paid according to a formula based on record sales, with minimum and maximum amounts. Alternatively, the advance could be a lump sum on signing and a further lump sum on exercising an option.

A typical royalty range is 12% to 20% of the suggested retail list price (prorated based on the percentage of the licensor's master on the licensee's album) based on either 90%, but preferably 100%, of records sold and not returned, through normal commercial retail channels, in such territory. Royalties payable are all-inclusive - that is, they include any royalties that the licensor is required to pay to the recording musician(s) and producer(s). The licensee, not the licensor, is generally responsible for paying any applicable union fees to funds such as the Music Performance Trust Fund and the Phonographic Record Manufacturers Special Payments Fund.

C. Term/Termination/Options

The term is usually a minimum of three years but a five-year, seven-year or longer term is not unusual depending on the particular label and territory, and the amount of the advance paid to the licensor. The term itself should be subject to release commitments - that is, the album or master must be commercially released in the specified territory, typically within four to six months of delivery. After the first album, or after the "initial period", depending on how the term is defined in the licence agreement, there may be an option period for a further record album of a specified artist, or for all or part of the licensor's catalogue. This option should be exercisable only if the licensee fulfills the previous contract period release commitment and other contractual obligations. An option also may be subject to meeting a certain performance obligation - for example, achieving a specific record sales figure or a particular position on a foreign record chart. Failure to meet such obligation would mean that the licensee is prevented from exercising the next option under the licence agreement, thereby ending the term of the licence.

The licensee has the obligation to provide statements of account detailing record sales, typically at semi-annual periods, and to permit an audit by the licensor. The licence agreement should specify events of default that would allow termination of such agreement as follows: (1) failure to pay advances and royalties; (2) failure to account or allow an audit; (3) failure to meet release commitments; and (4) bankruptcy.

D. General Provisions

A sell-off period after the term of the agreement is usually granted which allows the continued sale of records, but only those that were manufactured prior to the end of the term. This sell-off period typically lasts for up to six months. This enables the licensee to sell all recordings on hand and after such period, to destroy such inventory, or depending on the terms of the agreement, have them purchased by and shipped back to the licensor. Alternatively, if unrecouped, the licensee may have the right to extend the term of the agreement until recouped. Normally, following termination of the agreement, the licensee would have simply the "sell-off" rights outlined above.

In the case of a licence agreement with a foreign licensee, the governing law clause is particularly important. It determines which country's laws and legal system (the licensor's or the licensee's) will govern if the contract is breached. See Chapter 10, "Personal Service Contracts" regarding conflict of laws and Chapter 3, "Music Publishing" for more discussion of the governing law clause. It can be extremely expensive to litigate in foreign countries and the amount of money in dispute may not justify a lawsuit. Therefore it is advisable to have a contractual relationship with a licensee who is reputable. In any event, the governing law clause should be stipulated.

The royalties payable may be subject to taxes, duties and withholding tax obligations, in addition to standard packaging deductions and reserves, as is typical in any recording agreement.[76] The currency in which payments will be made should be specified, as should the method of payment - for example, through international bank transfer. In certain situations, due to the national laws of the foreign territory, payments cannot be withdrawn from a country immediately, and a "blocked currency" clause is relevant. In many instances, foreign licensees pay in U.S. dollars, in part as a way to avoid the ambiguities of dealing in other foreign currencies.

(e) Distribution Agreement

(i) Generally

The distribution agreement that is discussed below is not the type of relationship that generally exists between an independent recording musician and a retail record store. That relationship normally would be structured as a simple consignment agreement entered into on an individual basis with each retail outlet.[77] The distribution agreement discussed below is typically made between either a musician, record production company, or a smaller independent label which has produced an independent record, and an independent distributor, or a third party major distributor.

The distribution agreement is substantially different from a licence agreement. The distributor pays the production company a set price on a "dollars and cents" basis, for CD's and cassettes sold. In return, a distributor distributes records through normal commercial retail channels (i.e., retail stores), often nationally, and accounts to the production company either monthly, or sometimes on a quarterly basis, with respect to records sold. The rate of return on a distribution agreement is substantially higher than from a licence agreement and is an alternative to such agreement. However, because all other costs such as manufacturing, marketing and promotion expenses and mechanical licence fees are the responsibility of the production company or label (whereas under the licence agreement these costs would be the licensee's responsibility), the distribution agreement tends to require

---

[76] *Ibid.* For more information, consult Taubman, pp. 65-70 in *This Business of Music...*, and Chapter 2, "Foreign Record Deals" cited above in note 20 at pp. 24-38. See Form 15 for a sample Foreign Record Licensing Agreement at pp. 665-668.

[77] See Diane Sward Rappaport, *How to Make and Sell Your Record: The Complete Guide to Independent Records* (San Francisco: Headlands Press, 1981), at pp. 25-27 for a sample consignment agreement.

substantial independent financing and therefore is a riskier venture for the owner of the masters than a licence.

For example, in a licence agreement, approximately $1.00 to $1.50 may be payable for cassettes and $1.40 to $1.80 or more for CD's, whereas under the distribution agreement, it may be in the range of $4.00 to $5.00 for cassettes and $6.00 to $8.00 for CD's, or sometimes higher. However, in a pure distribution deal, the production company has the responsibility to promote the sales of recordings - for example, through trade ads, music videos, posters and independently contracted radio promoters. In such a distribution agreement, known as a pressing and distribution agreement (a "P&D deal"), typically no advances are payable. However, as is discussed below, in some P&D deals, particularly deals for an entire label, substantial advances to cover manufacturing costs and to pay mechanical royalties, for example, might be included.

The distributor typically provides the following services: (1) distribution of recordings to retail outlets or in other specified ways - for example, television sales; (2) possibly advertising or promoting records distributed depending on the terms of the agreement; (3) providing sales information regarding distributed product; and (4) manufacturing, if it is a P&D agreement. There should be some commitment on the part of the distributor to distribute to particular accounts, such as the large chain retailers like HMV, Tower Records, and Sam's, and to meet specified shipping dates, with a stipulation regarding what happens if these dates are not met. Bear in mind that the production company may be under an obligation to release within a specific time period, pursuant to its recording agreement with the musician. Typical production company obligations and restrictions may be as follows: (1) it must not release the same record with any other distributor in any other territory before releasing the record in the specific territory covered by the distribution agreement; or (2) it must not release the record as a budget record in other territories before release in the specific territory; (3) it must accept and be responsible for returns of records, possibly including records released before the distribution agreement is signed; and (4) it must provide a schedule of releases and product commitment.

(ii) Points to Consider

(1) The definitions contained in this agreement are similar to those found in the exclusive term recording agreement, and should be reviewed carefully and negotiated, when warranted.

(2) The term of the agreement is negotiable. It typically is a minimum of two or three years and may include an option to extend the term for a further year or two. Some smaller distributors allow termination on three to six months' notice.

(3) Most distribution agreements are for a specified territory only, and there is no right to export outside of such territory. Alternatively, there may be an option to distribute recordings outside the territory of Canada, which may be exercised upon specified notice - for example, 30 to 60 days. This is a point for negotiation.

(4) The distributor should be insured for unforeseen events that can prevent distribution.

(5) The numbers and names of specific recordings to be distributed may be set out in the agreement, or it may be an agreement for all rights acquired by the record production company during the term of the distribution agreement.

(6) Upon notice to the distributor, the production company should have the right to alter the labelling information or artwork in the product and the recording itself.

(7) There should be a notice and termination provision. The agreement may be terminable on notice by either party, subject to repayment of unrecouped advances or manufacturing costs. If there are unrecouped advances after the term, the distributor will want to (and may contract to) extend the term of the agreement until such advances are earned out, through the sales of such recordings. In this event, the record production company should contract to have the option to 'buy out' any unrecouped advances and terminate the term of the agreement.

(8) There should be a clause governing breakage of recordings and an indemnification of the production company from claims arising from distribution.

(9) Whether or not the record company receives an advance depends on the following: (a) prior contractual dealings between the distributor and record company; (b) the earnings potential of the records being distributed, as demonstrated by past commercial success or a current or recent radio hit; and (c) the number and quality of distributors competing for rights to the same product. Where there is an advance, the distribution fee usually will be increased to allow for more prompt recoupment of such advance. There may be a non-returnable advance paid to the production company by the distributor upon signing, but in a conventional distribution agreement this would be unusual.

Significant advances may be secured as loans, and the distributor may insist on securing these against the production company's assets.

(10) Typically, the distributor will have at a minimum the right to distribute through normal commercial retail channels. Some rights that may be reserved to the record production company in a particular territory are: (a) the right to sell off-stage, particularly if the recording artist is also a performing group; and (b) the right to sell recordings - for example, through a direct television campaign, via the Internet or through other "non-normal" commercial retail channels (the so-called "alternative" market).

(11) The production company retains exclusive ownership of all of the recordings and the related creative elements including album covers, jackets, artwork and all major advertising and promotional material including photographs.

(12) The distributor should not have the right to sell "cut-outs" nor should it share in the proceeds of "cut-outs". "Cut-outs" are deleted recordings. However, the distributor will contract for the right to scrap records upon notice to the production company. In this regard, the production company should have a specified time to elect to pay merchandising, warehousing and other costs and to purchase from the distributor the remaining stock on hand.

(13) The distributor typically will not have the right to distribute audio-visual products that are promotional music videos. However, it may be necessary for the distributor to acquire rights to distribute audio-visual product, which is in the form of a multimedia or "enhanced" CD which has been augmented with audio-visual elements and computer graphics. Traditionally, the distribution agreement covers only audio recordings sold through normal commercial retail channels.

(14) The distributor typically will have the right to decline to distribute the following types of recordings: (a) libellous, slanderous or obscene recordings; (b) recordings that infringe copyright; and (c) recordings not delivered within the agreed upon release schedule.

(15) The distributor typically would have no right to re-compile, re-master, edit or alter recordings in any way. Bear in mind that any such alteration may infringe the musician's rights under the recording agreement, and accordingly would require approval of the musician and perhaps the record production company, if the distributor intends to do so.

(16) For purposes of promotion, the distributor would have the rights to publicize, advertise and exploit masters, permit public performances, to use the name and likeness of the recording artists and producers of

the recordings for the purposes of promoting record sales, and to use the trade-mark of the artist and record production company in promotional advertisements. See the discussion in Chapter 9, "Merchandising" regarding trade-marks.

(17) The distributor also may contract to have the right to terminate the term of the agreement if the record production company fails to pay amounts owing to the artist, or if there is a breach by such company of a warranty contained in the distribution agreement.

(18) The distributor may require a letter of credit to cover potential losses from over-manufacturing that the distributor may incur. Alternatively, the principal(s) or owner(s) of the production company may be required to sign a personal guarantee to protect the distributor against such losses. This is a point for negotiation. Clearly, from the record production company's perspective, personal liability should be avoided if at all possible.

(19) Other general provisions are advisable, including: accounting and audit; waiver; entirety clause; and the governing law clause.[78]

(iii) Payment/Accounting/Reserves

Distributors normally account monthly within fifteen days after the month's end. The distributor subtracts a distribution fee, typically 15% to 40% of gross billings (which are based on the distributor's 'dealer' price), depending on the type of agreement and whether or not there are manufacturing, promotion, marketing, artwork and labelling charges and mechanical fees payable by the distributor. Co-operative advertising costs, reductions for cash discounts and an allowance for bad debts may be included in the distributor's fee or may be charged in addition to such fee. If there is an unutilized allowance for co-operative advertising, this should be credited to the production company. The distributor also deducts credits for returns and is allowed to deduct returns that exceed the reserve, which legally may become a demand debt of the production company to the distributor.

A reserve may be 25% of the amount invoiced, or higher. Reserves should be liquidated over a reasonable time period, and should be subject to periodic review (for example, annually) to determine if the reserves are excessive and can be reduced reasonably without risk to the distributor. Reserves may be extended for a period of time after expiration of the term of the agreement, if there is an unrecouped account between the record production company and the distributor.

---

[78] See Fox, cited above, Form 167-7 for a sample distribution agreement.

The opposite should apply if the account is recouped; that is, the reserve should be limited.

Bad debts and free goods are deducted. However, there should be a limit put on free goods - for example, 25% of singles shipped, and 15% on all other configurations such as albums in the cassette, CD, or minidisc format. A typical period to object to accounting statements would be two years, and as always the company being distributed should have the right to audit the distributor.

(iv) Security Interest/Letters of Credit

Letters of credit often are required to secure the financial obligations of the company being distributed. A personal guarantee also may be in place concerning lawsuits arising with respect to libel, obscenity or copyright infringement. In some cases a security interest is taken by the distributor in the masters. If so, it should only extend to the amount actually owing under the distribution agreement. When acting on a security interest, notice should be given to the record production company and the security interest should terminate within a specified time period: for example, one year after termination of the agreement, or when all sums owing to the distribution company are repaid. Security interests, other than in the record masters which are being distributed, may be granted as collateral security subject to the approval of the distributor.

4. Labelling, Credit and Notices on Recordings

There are three basic surface areas that are involved in labelling, credit and notices with respect to recordings: (1) the outside cover; (2) the inside cover; and (3) the record label. There are numerous ways in which labelling, credit and notice requirements for recordings arise: (a) by statute; (b) by case law; (c) by agreement; and (d) by industry custom and practice. Each of these is discussed below. Except for the requirements set out in sections 4(a)(iii) and 4(b) below, the labelling, credit and notice requirements in any given situation are governed by a combination of all of the above, as well as cost factors and aesthetic preferences.

(a) Statute

(i) Copyright Notices

Copyright notices are relevant with respect to: both the lyrics and music comprising each song; photographs, artwork, and graphics which are part of the record cover and liner notes; and, of course, the sound recordings. The copyright notice should identify all of these works.

The applicable international treaties and conventions stipulate as follows: (a) Berne Convention - no notice is required; (b) Universal Copyright Convention - notice is advisable, but not required; and (c) Buenos Aires Convention - "all rights reserved" notice is advisable.[79]

For copyright in a sound recording, the notice consists of the following: (1) the letter "P" contained within a circle; plus (2) the name of the copyright owner; and (3) the year of publication. With respect to literary, artistic and musical works the symbol is: (1) © or the word "Copyright" or "Copyr."; plus (2) the name of the copyright owner; and (3) the year of publication. Note that it is advisable, but not mandatory in Canada, to affix such copyright notices and it is common practice to do so.

(ii) Trade-marks

A. Generally

There are numerous trade-marks and trade names that are placed on a recording and/or its packaging, including: (a) the group name or name of an individual if it is a trade name (the professional name of an individual may be a trade name also); (b) the title of the recording if, for example, it is a group name, but generally album titles do not acquire protection as a trade-mark; (c) the name of the record company, particularly if it is also a trade-mark; (d) the name of the publishing company, if it is also a trade name or trade-mark; and (e) the names of other companies - for example, the musician's and/or the producer's corporation which also may be trade names or trade-marks.

---

[79] *Ibid.* See generally Chapter 8, "Record Covers, Labels and Liner Notes". See also Chapter 15, "The Nature of Copyright in the United States", Chapter 35, "Names and Trademarks" and Chapter 36, "Protection of Ideas and Titles" in *This Business of Music* ..., cited above in note 20 at pp. 83-89, pp. 133-160, pp. 352-366 and pp. 367-370 respectively.

B. Notices

Canadian trade-mark law does not require that a trade-mark notice be affixed in order to claim protection. However, trade-mark notices are customarily used and are relevant. See Chapter 9, "Merchandising", for a discussion of trade-mark notices and the legal basis of trade-marks.[80]

(iii) Consumer Packaging and Labelling Act

Under this statute,[81] which applies to pre-packaged products (a recording is a pre-packaged product), no dealer (which includes a retailer, manufacturer, processor, producer, importer or packager) shall "sell, import...or advertise any pre-packaged product" unless the product is labelled.[82]

Although not all aspects of this statute are applicable to all products in all cases, this statute sets out a number of specific requirements for labels on pre-packaged products. More specifically, the product label is to contain a "declaration of net quantity" and "shall be clearly and prominently displayed, easily legible ... and located on the principal display panel" of the package.[83]

For recordings, this is often on the jacket, sleeve, J-card, or other insert material. The main requirement of this statute is that the label must show the "identity and principal place of business of the person by or for whom the pre-packaged product was manufactured..."[84]

Generally, all information which is required on product labels by statute must be in English and French. However, the information relating to the identity of the person for whom the product was manufactured, and such person's principal place of business, may be in one official language only.[85] In addition to the requirements for labels under this statute, one also should consider the use of the French language for recordings which are distributed in Quebec.[86]

---

[80] *Ibid.* Chapter 8, p. 86; this notice is suggested here but is not required under the U.S. *Trade Marks Law Revision Act, 1988*, c. 22 15 U.S.C 180. See also Chapter 9, "Merchandising" for a discussion of such notices.

[81] R.S.C. 1985, c. C-38 (herein "CPLA").

[82] *Ibid.*, s. 4(1).

[83] *Ibid.*, s. 4(2).

[84] *Ibid.*, s. 10(b)(i), but also see s. 13 of the Regulations.

[85] S. 6(2) *Consumer Packaging and Labelling Regulations*, C.R.C. 1978, c. 417 (herein the "CPLA Regulations").

[86] Quebec *Charter of the French Language*, R.S.Q., c. 11. See in particular Chapter VII, "The Language of Commerce and Business", and s. 51 thereof which deals with labels.

If the record is imported into Canada, the label must show the place of business and identity of the person in Canada for whom it was made[87] and this must be preceded by the words "imported by" unless the geographical origins of the recording are stated on the label.[88] Any reference on the label pertaining to the place of manufacture of the label or container must be stated only on the label or container.[89]

The minimum height for the type size of letters indicating the net quantity is set out in the Regulations to the Act.[90] Information shown on a label, other than the declaration of net quantity, must be shown in a manner that is easily legible to the consumer in letters at least 1/16th of an inch, or 1.6 mm in height.[91]

The *Consumer Packaging and Labelling Act* also prescribes limitations concerning the other information that appears on the label, namely: (a) that there should be no false or misleading representations that reasonably may be regarded as relating to the product, nor can the label imply that the product contains "any matter not contained in it" or that "it does not contain any matter...contained in it";[92] (b) that the dealer may not sell or import pre-packaged products, the packaging for which does not comply with the regulations;[93] and (c) nor shall a dealer sell, import or advertise any pre-packaged product in a container that has been manufactured in such a manner that the consumer reasonably might be misled with respect to the quantity and quality of the product.[94]

Contravention of this statute can lead to criminal proceedings and result in a fine, imprisonment or both. Musicians who produce independent recordings would be wise to comply with this statute in view of the above, and if they are in doubt, should contact Industry Canada to ensure compliance with this law.

---

[87] S. 31(2) CPLA Regulations.

[88] *Ibid.*

[89] *Ibid.*, s. 31(1).

[90] *Ibid.*, s. 14.

[91] *Ibid.*, s. 15.

[92] See generally s. 7(1) and s. 7(2) of the Act for a definition of "false and misleading", and in particular s. 7(2)(b) regarding requirements pertaining to matter contained in a product.

[93] *Ibid.*, s. 6.

[94] *Ibid.*, s. 9.

(b) Agreement

(i) Credit

The obligation to give credit on recordings arises in a number of ways: (a) by contract; (b) by implied contractual rights; (c) by statute; (d) by case law; and (e) by custom. The list of credits on recordings can be extensive, for example: (a) producer and distributor; (b) production company; (c) record company; (d) artist names and instruments; (e) publishing companies, composers, and lyricists; (f) song titles; (g) back-up session musicians and singers; (h) additional musicians; (i) artwork and photographs; (j) technicians; and (k) "thanks to" credits including: (i) lawyer; (ii) manager and/or business manager; (iii) equipment supplier; (iv) studio; (v) engineer; (vi) fans; (vii) road crew; (viii) personal assistant; (ix) make-up artist and/or stylist; and (x) other miscellaneous credits. Credits also may be required if the musician has an endorsement or merchandising agreement with an equipment supplier or sponsor. The credit afforded to musicians, which arises by contract under the record agreement, is often an implied contractual term rather than an explicit term. Other contractual obligations to accord proper credit may arise with respect to producers, engineers and co-producers. For a more detailed discussion, see section 3(c)(iii)E above regarding producer credits.

(ii) False Accreditation

False accreditation can arise in several ways. For example, a musician may have recorded previously as a session musician only, and such recordings are then re-released, subsequent to their initial release, after the musician has become successful as a solo artist. For marketing purposes, the musician is given inappropriately prominent credit. In such case, the public can be deceived, since the musician is actually a side musician only. In numerous instances in the United States, U.S. musicians have been successful in obtaining injunctions if the accreditation on a recording is substantially misleading.[95] The issue can

---

[95] For a discussion of the misattribution of vocal/instrumental performances, see Robert Clarida, "Did Milli Vanilli Do the Mashed Potato? Lanham Act Responses to Misattribution in the Music Industry", (1992) 16 Col.-VLA J. of Law & The Arts 327. The author examines the issue of uncredited performers whose performances are attributed to the artists on whose albums they perform. He considers whether such action would attract liability under s. 43(a) of the *Lanham Act* (potential plaintiffs include "any person who believes that he or she is likely to be damaged by such act" and could include record companies in competition with the defendant, the miscredited performer and/or misled

arise also when there is a change in the popularity of a co-artist on a recording, which necessitates a change in credit. The right to use a group name after a group has disbanded or changed membership may involve such legal issues also.

False attribution or false accreditation may give rise to various lawsuits - for example, misappropriation of personality, which is discussed in Chapter 9, "Merchandising". Issues of moral rights in the sound recordings, the crediting of recording musicians, and composers' moral rights are also relevant. Moral rights were discussed in Chapter 1, "Copyright" regarding composers' rights in music, and in this chapter in section 3(c)(iii) regarding sound recordings.

(c) Industry Custom and Practice

(i) Industry Notices

There are various other notices and labels that are included on recordings: (a) a Juno award sticker or other stickers which include notice of a hit single or featured artist; (b) the "MAPL" logo, created by Stan Klees for RPM Magazine, which consists of a circle with the letters "MAPL" in four sectors indicating the following: "M", music composed by a Canadian; "A", the music or lyrics are performed principally by a Canadian artist; "P", the production consists of a live performance of music that is: (i) recorded wholly in Canada; or (ii) performed wholly in Canada and broadcast live in Canada; and "L", the lyrics were written by a Canadian.[96]

---

consumers). He concludes that the law as currently interpreted by the courts most likely would not support such a claim. Nothing comparable to s. 43(a) exists in Canada. In *Masdeva v. Scholz*, 742 F.Supp. 713 (D. Mass. 1990), the former drummer for the group Boston brought suit alleging violation of s. 43(a) of the *Lanham Act* when the drummer that replaced him copied his drumming on a demo track when recording the same tune on the group's first album. The court held, following earlier authority, that mere imitation of a performance was not actionable under the section and noted that Masdeva had been given credit for the one tune on the album on which he had actually played. See also *Yameta Co. v. Capitol Records, Inc.*, cited above in note 44, and *Sims v. Blanchris, Inc.*, 648 F.Supp. 480 (S.D.N.Y. 1968). In the Yameta case, Jimi Hendrix sought a preliminary injunction to prevent Capitol from selling a Curtis Knight album - on which Hendrix was a session player - as a "Hendrix" album; in the Sims case, a drummer who led a session on which Chick Corea played as a sideman prior to stardom objected to the album (released after Corea became a star) which gave the impression that it was a "Chick Corea" album. Both these cases recognized the statutory tort of reverse passing off under s. 43(a). For a detailed discussion of the legal issues involving credit in the U.S., see Selz and Simensky cited above in note 62, Chapter 13. See also notes 44 and 45 above.

[96] "CRTC Clarifies Ownership of MAPL Logo and System", March 7, 1992, RPM Magazine, p. 2.

This logo often is used in conjunction with records released in Canada. It often is included on Canadian recordings and in Canadian record sales charts to identify the fact that the recording is Canadian. The "MAPL" logo also is used to identify the Canadian content of records for purposes of compliance with the CRTC broadcast regulations. These were discussed in Chapter 2, "The Licensing and Administration of Copyright and the Regulation of Music and Media".

Finally, a notice of membership with SOCAN and the NRCC is advisable, where applicable, so that they can track public performances of SOCAN repertoire more accurately.

(ii) Industry Codes

Industry codes contained in a recording could include the following: (a) digital coding;[97] (b) other designations, such as whether or not the record was recorded originally in mono or simulated stereo; and (c) the International Standard Recording Code (IRSC) for each master. Bar coding also is included on the record, in order to facilitate inventory controls and sales tracking with respect to recordings, and may be included on either the actual recording or affixed as a sticker.[98]

(iii) Warning Stickers

A. Generally

Notices may consist of warning stickers - for example, CRIA's "guideline" on explicit lyrics which consists of the following: "Explicit Lyrics - Parental Advisory".[99] More explicit warning stickers may be used - for example, one which was used on a Geffen Records release: "This album contains language which some listeners may find objectionable. They can "F?!* OFF" and buy something from the New Age section".

B. U.S.

The Recording Industry Association of America also has adopted a warning similar to that of CRIA: "Parental Advisory - Explicit Lyrics". This guideline is used: (1) where contractually permissible; and (2)

---

[97] See Chapter 8 in *This Business of Music...*, cited above in note 20 at p. 85 for more discussion concerning digital coding.

[98] *This Business of Music..*, cited above in note 20 at Chapter 8, p. 87.

[99] CRIA Press Release, December 1988.

where it is warranted in the opinion of the record company and at the record company's discretion. It is to be placed on the cover of the album and in addition to the warning, the record company may, at its option, print the lyrics on the back of the album cover or on a "displayed lyric sheet under the plastic wrap".[100]

C. Negligence and Obscenity

Issues concerning recordings that may be potentially obscene have arisen numerous times both in the U.S. and in Canada.[101] The content of recordings also has resulted in high profile litigation concerning subliminal messages, such as the "death by suicide" cases. The issue of negligence on the part of record companies and distributors concerning their recordings has been litigated also. Presumably, explicit lyrics warning stickers are an attempt to lessen liability should a musical group or a record company be found negligent or contributorily negligent in this regard. Cases that have been litigated in the United States have not yet found musicians or their record companies liable for negligence concerning the content of such recordings.[102]

---

[100] For a detailed discussion of this warning sticker, see Paul Sanderson, "The Canadian Recording Industry Association's Guidelines on Explicit Lyrics", (1987), Vol. 8 No. 2 Journal of Media Law and Practice 42a.

[101] See, for example, *R. v. Emery* (1991), 4 O.R. (3d) 344 (Ont. Prov. Div.), affirmed (1992), 8 O.R. (3d) 60 (Ont. Gen. Div.), for a case involving the recording by 2 Live Crew "As Nasty As They Wanna Be" and an accused retail operator charged with selling such recording contrary to s. 163(2)(a) of the *Criminal Code*, R.S.C. 1985, c. C-46. The accused was found guilty. This case was appealed unsuccessfully by the accused: *R. v. Emery* (1992), 8 O.R. (3d) 60 (Ont. Prov. Div.). The court relied on *R. v. Butler* (1992), 70 C.C.C. (3d) 129 (S.C.C) in rejecting the accused's argument that s. 163(8) of the *Criminal Code* was so vague as to violate the Canadian *Charter of Rights*. Also of interest in relation to the 2 Live Crew case is the case of *Skywalker Records Inc. v. Navarro*, 739 F.Supp. 578 (S.D. Florida 1990) in which 2 Live Crew's record company successfully sued the sheriff of Broward County, Florida after he succeeded in having a Florida Circuit Court Judge issue an order finding probable cause that the album, "As Nasty As They Wanna Be" was obscene under s. 847.011 of the Florida Statutes and used the order to induce more than 40 record stores to remove the album from the racks. This was held to be a violation of the plaintiff's rights under the First and Fourteenth Amendments. See Vivian R. King, "Anything Goes, or Enough Already? Sexually Explicit Lyrics: Florida and Texas Perspectives on *Skywalker Records, Inc. v. Navarro*", (1991), 17 Thurgood Marshall L.J. 113.

[102] See, for example, "Judas Priest Musical Group Found Not Liable in 'Suicide-by-Subliminal-Message' Case", (1990), Vol. 12 No. 7, E.L.R. 3 at pp. 3-5. For an analogous situation, see "Distributor of 'Dungeons & Dragons' Games Not Liable in Wrongful Death Action Arising from Players Suicide", (1990), Vol. 12 No. 6, E.L.R. 12. See also "Ozzy Osbourne and CBS Records Are Not Liable for Damages Sought by Parents of Teenage Suicide Victim, Rules California Appellate Court", (1988), Vol. 10, No. 3, E.L.R. p. 8. See also *This Business of Music...*, cited above in note 20, at pp. 88-89. See also a recent article

5. Other Legal Aspects Concerning Recordings

(a) Model Releases

When artwork is used on an album cover that includes a photograph or other image or likeness of an individual or group of models or musicians, it is necessary to obtain the proper consent or release in writing from the appropriate individual or group. A written consent for the use of someone's name, likeness, and other "personality rights" is referred to commonly as a "model release" and is necessary in order to avoid being sued for name and likeness misappropriation. See Chapter 9, "Merchandising" for a discussion in this regard. In order to protect the record company and perhaps the musician who is carrying on business as an independent record production company, adequate releases must be obtained. This includes the consent of all persons whose name, likeness, and/or other identifiable elements of his/her personality are being depicted on the record cover, label or liner notes. If the depicted image is a photograph or other likeness of musicians who have signed a recording agreement with the record company, it is likely that the company already has acquired the necessary name and likeness rights through that recording contract.

(b) *National Library Act*

This statute is relevant to musicians who produce and sell independent recordings. Musicians can be considered to be "publishers" for the purposes of this statute.[103]

Similarly, the definition of a "book", pursuant to this Act, includes any "record, tape or other thing published by a publisher, on or in which information is written, recorded, stored or reproduced".[104]

This applies to CD's and presumably other digital devices. According to this statute, two copies of any "book" published in Canada must be sent to the national librarian at the publisher's expense within one week of publication.[105] However, the regulations require that only one copy of sound recordings and certain multi-media publications be deposited.[106]

---

on this phenomenon: Juliet Dee, "Subliminal Lyrics in Heavy Metal: More Litigation Anyone?", (1994), 16 Communications and the Law 3.

[103] R.S.C. 1985, c. N-12.

[104] *Ibid.*, s. 2.

[105] S. 13(1).

[106] *National Library Book Deposit Regulations*, SOR/95-199. S. 3(a) of the Regulations provides this stipulation regarding sound recordings; s. 3(b) of the Regulations describes

Sound recordings that are only manufactured and distributed in Canada and that do not have any Canadian content or any major Canadian contributor such as a composer, artist, narrator, orchestra, performer, writer, or producer are exempt from the deposit requirement.[107] In this case, publication in Canada means a sound recording released in Canada.[108]

---

the exemption for multi-media publications consisting of two or more parts in different formats.

[107] *Ibid.*, s. 4(j).
[108] S. 2 of the Act.

9

NAMES, TRADE-MARKS, LICENSING AND MERCHANDISING

Contributing Authors: Robert H. Nakano, B.A.Sc., LL.B.
and Frank Farfan, B. Eng., LL.B.

1. Overview

(a) Names, Trade-marks and Other Identifying Attributes

In selling, providing, distributing and promoting his/her musical products and services,[1] the musician will develop a reputation. That reputation, another word for which is goodwill, can have a substantial commercial value to the musician[2] and can be exploited in various ways, as described below in this chapter and elsewhere in this book.

All of that reputation is signified by the musician's name, logo, words and other symbols or identifying attributes associated with the musician. Thus, any or all of these indicators can develop tremendous value, but the name is usually the first and most important. For example, the mere mention of the phrase ROLLING STONES instantly brings to mind the tremendous renown, reputation, history and success of the famous group. The name thus represents a short hand for referring to that reputation. Likewise, a logo or symbol, such as the famous Lips and Tongue logo used by the Rolling Stones, can bring to mind instantly the identity of a musician and his/her reputation. Other identifying attributes of a musician's business or personality also can act as short-hand references to the musician's reputation.

---

[1] For example, through live performances, personal appearances, radio or TV airplay, media exposure, sale of recordings and other products, and promotion and advertisement of all of these.

[2] Goodwill has been described as "the friendly attitude and patronage of customers", that is, the measure of one's reputation; although intangible, substantial value flows from goodwill. See, for example, Daniel R. Bereskin, "Trade Marks" Bar Admission Course Corporate and Commercial Law Lectures Notes, (Toronto: L.S.U.C. 1980), at p. 10-3.

Names, phrases, logos and other symbols can function as trade-marks, and when a name, phrase, logo or other symbol is used to associate a musician with a particular product or service at the time of sale, it is a trade-mark. [Note: for ease of reference in this chapter, the word "trade-mark" is sometimes informally shortened just to "mark".]

If a musician's well known name or mark is associated with any products or services, whether musical or not, there is an instant connection in the minds of viewers or potential customers between such products or services and the musician. It is hoped that such a connection will translate into ready acceptance of, and a willingness to purchase, the particular products or services. More products and services can be sold with less effort and advertising and promotion cost, which would be extremely desirable for any business selling those products or services, whether it be a record company, a publishing company, or some other business. Thus, the instant recognizability of a name and marks associated with a musician potentially gives them tremendous commercial value to the musician. The more distinctive the name and marks, the more uniquely they will identify the musician and his/her reputation and the more valuable those names and marks become, especially as the musician's own musical reputation and musical career grow.

In light of this potential value, it is crucial from the beginning of a musician's career that he/she be aware of that potential value and, as much as possible, take steps to protect and enhance that potential value. If the right steps are not taken, it is possible that the reputation or uniqueness of the names and symbols will be diluted or in the worst case destroyed, with attendant loss in value or potential value to the musician. As set out below in further detail, the right steps include taking care: (1) in the initial name/mark selection process; (2) to secure protection for the name/marks; (3) that appropriate legal agreements are in place to protect the uniqueness and ownership of the name/marks; and (4) to allow and control the use of the name/marks on only the products and services that are right for the musician and his/her objectives.

(b) Name Selection

The name selection process is thus crucial. The purpose is to identify a name which will have the long term potential to identify the musician uniquely, at least in the markets (i.e., countries) which are likely to be important to the musician. Whatever name is selected will become associated with all of the musician's products (for example, recordings and publications) as well as any services supplied by the musician (for example, performances). Having committed to a name, and possibly having launched a career under a particular name, it would be a major set-back for a musician to be required by another person or the court to change his/her name. In addition, if a weak name is selected (for example, one which is simply a variation of several other similar names used by others), then all of the investment that the musician and his/her various business associates will make in the musician's reputation and name will be less valuable than might have been the case otherwise. Put another way, it is more difficult and expensive to promote a weak name rather than a strong, distinctive name.

(c) Licensing and Merchandising

Any situation in which the musician wishes to allow another person to manufacture, sell or offer products or services in association with the musician's name, trade-marks or other identifying attributes requires a licence.

Any name, mark or any other identifying attributes associated with a musician can have licensing and merchandising value because they are all short-hand references to the musician and his/her reputation. The right to control the association of a name, mark or any other identifying attribute with any products or services can be considered to be the musician's "merchandising rights".

As already noted, the musician's usual products are recordings, publications, and other musical products. The musician's name and marks are licensed to the record company or the publishing company to be associated with the musical products at the time they are sold. The necessary licensing terms are included in the typical record agreements and publishing agreements.

Merchandising is the licensing, marketing and selling of other, usually non-musical, products that are directly associated with the musician. The products become associated with the musician by displaying the musician's name, marks or other identifying attributes - in short, by directly referring to the musician or his/her business, reputation or personality. Potential products for merchandising range from T-shirts and other clothing to posters and other souvenirs and novelties to lunch-boxes, toys, food and personal toiletries. In fact, any conceivable product can be merchandised. The only limits are dictated by the hard business consideration as to whether there are likely to be sufficient customers who would purchase a particular product at a particular price (because it has been associated with the musician), all so as to allow a sufficient profit to be made.

Whether a particular musician should choose to allow merchandising of certain products is a different, but nevertheless very important, question. The musician must decide whether having his/her name associated with particular products would reflect the kind of image, reputation and market segments that the musician wishes to develop.

A merchandising arrangement should be reflected in a proper licence or merchandising agreement.

(d) Importance of Merchandising

For musicians, merchandising can provide an important additional revenue source in addition to performing, recording and publishing revenue streams. For example, concert tours may lose money because of substantial touring costs. This loss can be offset by the presumed indirect effects of touring, including increased record sales, publishing incomes and merchandising sales. In fact, some musicians make most of their touring income from the sale of merchandise. It has been estimated that an average of 20% of the gross income from a tour comes from the sale of merchandising products.[3] Of course, this figure can be higher or lower in a specific situation.[4] Merchandising is an important way to market a musician to persons in the music business, to consumers and to the media generally. Conversely, a musician's image and career can be damaged by incompatible merchandising schemes; therefore, the commercial and career potential of such schemes should be considered carefully.

(e) Endorsements

Endorsements can be considered to be a type of merchandising right. Endorsements involve an association between a musician and the products, services, business or causes of others, even if the products (if any) involved do not refer specifically to the musician or his/her rights. For example, Band X may promote the sale of Brand Y cars; the association between the musician and the product is made simply through advertising; the words Band X do not appear on the actual car.

---

[3] Allen Arrow, "Packaging and Merchandising the Artist", in *Supporting the Star (or the Prospect?): Representation of Professional Athletes and Entertainers*, (Toronto: Canadian Bar Association, 1978), at p. 88.

[4] For example, as of January 1991, the musical group New Kids on the Block generated some $1 billion in revenues: 80% from merchandising, 15% from concert revenues and only 5% from record sales. See Randy S. Frisch, "New Kids on the Block: New Kids on the Block v. News America Publishing, Inc.", in *1992-93 Entertainment, Publishing and the Arts Handbook*, (New York: Clark, Boardman, Callaghan), at p. 193 in note 5.

The association of the musician with the endorsed product or service generally implies that the musician approves or endorses the product or service.

Endorsements can include agreements to act as corporate spokespersons or any means of advertising products or services. Such schemes may involve use of various media, including television and radio, or use of a musician's personality on products, indicating approval of that product.

(f) Commercial Tie-Ins

A "commercial tie-in" or "commercial tie-up" is the use of a musician's rights "in the context of an advertisement without necessarily indicating that the celebrity endorses the product or services advertised."[5] It will be dealt with here as part of merchandising.

2. Name Selection Process

One of the most important assets of any musician or musical group may be his/her/its name. The name will not only be the key symbol of a musician's reputation and goodwill, but it will also promote and enhance the musician's image and identity. It will also be suggestive of marketing and merchandising strategies and will be associated visually and aurally with the musician. A poorly chosen name may hinder the musician's career and business development.

The name therefore should be chosen very carefully so as to ensure that:

1. the name will suit the musician's professional and artistic purposes and objectives going forward into the foreseeable future. That is, will the image of the proposed name suit the image the musician wishes to present publicly?
2. the name is available to be used by the musician. That is, would use of the proposed name in the geographic markets of interest to the musician infringe the already established rights of some other musician or other person?
3. the name preferably will be as unique and as distinctive as possible, so that it will stand out from other names. That is, will the

---

[5] Thomas D. Selz and Melvin Simensky, *Entertainment Law: Legal Concepts and Business Procedures*, (New York: Sheppards/McGraw Hill Inc., 1990), (herein "*Entertainment Law*"), at para. 18-51, pp. 18-107, 18-108. This three volume set (plus forms) details the laws of credit, contract law, unfair competition, right of privacy, right of publicity, libel, moral rights and remedies in the U.S. entertainment law context.

musician's investment in his/her career result in a truly distinctive reputation?

4. the criteria for trade-mark registrability[6] are met, if the musician wishes to secure the advantages of registering the name as a trade-mark (highly recommended; see at section 4(a)(ii)E below).

The musician should start by identifying, on a preliminary basis, a potential name that he/she believes satisfies all the above objectives, especially objective #1.

Next, as thorough a name search as a musician's budget will allow should be performed to assess the availability of the name, ideally covering at least all important jurisdictions (i.e., usually each important country) in which the musician expects to be significantly active. Unfortunately, the international nature of the music business compounds the difficulties and costs of effective searching. It should be appreciated also that no searching, even the most extensive, can guarantee freedom from problems. As much as possible though, the musician will wish to avoid walking into problems which, with reasonable diligence, could have been avoided. Trade-mark lawyers or trade-mark agents should be consulted and retained to advise and assist with proper name searching.

General trade-mark and business name searches may access trade-mark records, business record computer databases, the Internet and telephone and trade directories. For a Canadian musician just starting out, at minimum, a Canadian trade-mark search should be conducted, but more extensive searching is usually highly advisable. Such general searches may disclose that names or trade-marks, either identical to or confusingly similar to the musician's proposed name, are already in use by other persons or businesses. The rights of such other persons in their names or trade-marks may be infringed by a musician's use — sometimes even if the products and services of the other person are quite different from those the musician will offer. In particular, if the other person's name or trade-mark is sufficiently well known, they might be able to prevent the use by the musician of the proposed name in connection with some or all of the wares and services a musician might foreseeably wish to offer. It is important to get proper legal or trade-mark advice on these points.

As an example of the problems that might be encountered, consider the following. If a clothing manufacturer has registered Band X as a trade-mark for T-shirts and if the mark is not known in any significant way outside that field, then Band X may be available for use on musical products or services. However, looking down the road, it may not be safely available to be used with a full range of typical

---

[6] See Section 4(a)(ii) D below.

merchandise. This fact may affect the musician's decision in selecting the name in the first place.

Additional specific searches relating to musical group names should be performed. Given the international nature of the music business, both Canadian and international directories[7] should be searched. Even musicians who are known only locally should conduct such searches, because if they are successful, their name can become known internationally and their chances of being able to engage in international activities without having to change their name would be improved. The Internet is helpful in this regard; there are numerous websites which list directories of band names.

The AFM also has records of musical group names. Files at the head office in New York or the local AFM office may be searched.[8]

When selecting a name for a music publishing company, it is also advisable to search music publishing company names with SOCAN, because SOCAN administers international performing rights for foreign societies with which it is affiliated, and has a database of international music publishers.

The above suggestions are not exhaustive; it is advisable to consult all relevant sources.

It is important to realize that searching provides a snapshot at one particular time only and that circumstances can change subsequently. Assume, for example, that a Canadian musician selects a name for use in Canada which seems available internationally. The musician proceeds to use that name locally in Canada for 5 years and then an opportunity arises in the U.S. It is possible that during the 5 years someone else, either innocently or intentionally, may have started using that same or a similar name in the U.S. Unless the Canadian musician had developed some rights in the U.S., he/she may not be able to operate under the same name in the U.S. Names and trade-marks operate on a territorial basis. The protection coverage provided by a trade-mark registration in a country goes no wider than that particular country; in short, registration protection is on a country-by-country basis.[9] Outside of trade-mark registrations, a musician's rights will only extend to the geographic zones in which the musician can prove

---

[7] Examples of such sources are the Billboard International Talent Directory or Phonolog Experts. In Canada, search Robert Lyttle's "A Chartology of Pop Music", (Toronto: RPM Magazine, 1977); and in the U.S., Joel Hitburn's "The Billboard Book of Top 40 Hits 1955-1985", (New York: Billboard Publications Inc., 1985), and other music business trade publications.

[8] Mona Coxson, "Taking Care of Business: Naming Your Band - Part I", (1983), *Canadian Musician*, Vol. V. No. 6, p. 71.

[9] Wider regional rights can be developed in some parts of the world (e.g., the European Community), but not in North America.

his/her reputation actually exists.[10] The general rule is that whoever develops rights first in a particular country or place will be able to keep those rights, at least for as long as they are being exercised.

Substantial legal and other out-of-pocket costs, threatened and actual lawsuits, loss of name rights and career setback can result if a musician uses a name in which another person may prove, or even just claim, rights. Thus it must be emphasized that a carefully selected name is very important. The selection should be made with the assistance of proper legal or trade-mark advice.

3. Basics of Protection of Names and Trade-marks

Once an appropriate name has been selected, there are several steps a musician can take immediately (or, at least, soon) to maximize the protection for it and thus to maximize the value of the musician's investment in it. These steps are discussed in section 3 a) – d) inclusive, below.

(a) Trade-mark Applications and Registrations

First, the musician should consider filing applications to register that name as a trade-mark in Canada and in each other country where the musician expects to be significantly active in the foreseeable future. Typically, the major music business countries such as the United States and the United Kingdom should be considered.

Trade-mark registrations will provide national protection, not restricted only to such local areas inside a country where the musician's reputation can be proved to exist. Registrations make it easier to prevent or stop infringements, both preventatively[11] and also legally in court. In the event of a claim against the musician by another person, having a registration will also provide an improved bargaining position to the musician and thus some defensive measure of comfort (although

---

[10] That is, if a musician's name is not registered as a national trade-mark, the geographic scope of his/her protection likely will be restricted to the geographical zone where the musician can show that in fact he/she has a reputation. For example, if a musician only performs in a local area around a particular city (and has not had any wider exposure), the musician's rights to the name may be restricted to that local area. As another example, if a musician has had significant airplay on a nationally broadcast service (e.g., national radio or a nationally available specialty cable channel, such as MuchMusic), then the musician may enjoy nationally protectable rights. Of course, reputation may subsist geographically beyond or between such extremes, according to the facts of the particular situation.

[11] Anyone who performs a trade-mark search seeking their own identical or similar name will locate the musician's registration and thus be forewarned to avoid such name.

not necessarily a legal defence) that the claim can be disposed of in a favourable manner. Some other advantages of trade-mark registration are set out in section 4(a)(ii)E below.

Trade-mark lawyers or trade-mark agents should be consulted and retained to advise and assist with trade-mark applications in each relevant country. The musician's Canadian trade-mark lawyer or trade-mark agent will have a network of international associates to assist with all necessary searches, applications and advice in each foreign country of interest.

(b) Confirm Ownership

Second, the musician should ensure that all proper paperwork is in place regarding ownership of the name. Valid names/marks can only be owned by one legal entity. In the case of a musical group, this frequently leads to problems when the group splits up and there is a dispute as to who can continue using the name/mark. Some or all of the members of a group often make up a legal partnership. The partnership is the entity that would own the name/mark. It also would be possible to have the band members be shareholders in a corporation which in turn could own the name/mark. In either case, it is crucial that there be an agreement amongst the members specifying what happens to the name if the group splits up. Who can use it and on what terms (if any)? In the case of a partnership, these provisions could be included in the partnership agreement (frequently called a band members' agreement) which should be in place. In the case of a corporation, the provisions could be included in the unanimous shareholders agreement which should be in place.

An important note: if the entity using the mark is different from the intended trade-mark owner, a licence agreement is likely necessary (see section 5(a) below).

The employment or contracting terms of any person associated with the musician or group who is not intended to have any ownership interest (for example, a back-up musician) should be made clear in writing as well. The musician or group will certainly not wish to have a non-member claiming partnership or ownership rights to the name through a lax arrangement respecting that non-member.

As an important aside, ownership considerations also should be given to all works created by others which the musician intends to use, particularly if those works may become an important part of the musician's business or persona. For example, if a freelancer or consultant is retained to develop or create an artistic work (for example, a graphic artist to develop a logo or other artwork, or a photographer to take a photograph of the musician), then ideally, the musician wishes to have ownership of all rights relating to that artistic work. The general rule is that an independent contractor (i.e., someone who is not an employee, such as an outside consultant or freelancer) would own any rights associated with their creations, such as copyrights, unless there is an agreement to the contrary.[12] If the musician does not obtain clear ownership of all such rights, then his/her ability to exploit that work fully as part of the musician's business may be restricted or hindered. There should be agreements in writing with any such independent contractors making it clear that any and all rights to the contractor's work/product will be transferred to the musician. Such agreements should contain waivers of moral rights also; see Chapters 3 and 8 regarding same in the context of music publishing and record agreements respectively.

(c) Proper Trade-mark Use

Third, when a musician starts using the selected name/mark, it should be used in a manner which will enhance the protection afforded to the name/mark. For example:

1. Names/marks should be made to stand out from any surrounding text. This may be done in any number of ways — such as by using a special logo format, by using trade-mark designations (see item #2 below), or simply by using a different style of text (for example, upper case lettering when surrounding text is lower case, or a different size of lettering, or bold face compared to the surrounding text).

2. At least on the most prominent uses of a name/mark on any printed material (for example, posters, advertisements, flyers, album artwork), a discrete but legible trade-mark designation should be used if possible. A trade-mark designation is a superscript or subscript reference appearing next to the name/mark to indicate to the public that trade-mark rights are being claimed in it.

    Commonly, if a name/mark is registered, the symbol "TM" would be used, for example Band X™. This designation commonly would be used in conjunction with a footnote trade-mark notice, also printed in the same material; see item #3 below. Alternatively, if a

---

[12] Note: one important exception to this rule is photographs, where the reverse applies — namely, the person commissioning the photograph is the owner of the copyrights, unless there is an agreement to the contrary; *Copyright Act*, s. 13(2). See also s. 4(b) below.

name/mark is registered in Canada, many people would use the symbol ®, for example Band X®.

The ® symbol is actually an American symbol mandated by United States legislation.[13] It indicates that the mark has been registered in the U.S. The ® symbol has no authority under Canadian legislation, but it is nevertheless generally used and recognized in Canada as indicating a registered trade-mark. It is for this reason that it is popular to use the ® symbol in Canada. However, technically, it is prohibited in the U.S. to use the symbol ® unless the trade-mark is registered there. Thus, if goods from Canada are likely to be sold in the U.S. and there is no U.S. registration, problems may be encountered. In such circumstances, out of an abundance of caution, some people would avoid the use of the ® symbol. It is recommended that a musician discuss these points with his/her trade-mark lawyer or trade-mark agent at the appropriate time. If a name/mark is registered in the United States, then the symbol ® should be used in the United States as additional substantive advantages accrue to the trade-mark owner.

If a name/mark is not registered, then one of the common designations "TM" or "*" would be used, for example, Band X™ or Band X*. These latter two (but especially the "*" symbol) are commonly used in conjunction with a footnote trade-mark notice also printed in the same material; see item #3 below.

3.   Use trade-mark notices as footnotes in any printed materials (for example, tags, packaging, graphic reproductions, cover artwork, promotional materials, advertisements) referring to the name/mark. For example,

Band X is a reg'd TM of Band X,

or TM of Band X,

or * TM of Band X

Note: if a mark is licensed, for example in a merchandising or other licence arrangement, these notices may be somewhat different; see section 5(a) below.

These various notices are also discussed in Chapter 8, "Recording", regarding labelling and notices for recordings.

4.   Finally, although not usually applicable to the typical activities of musicians, no name or trade-mark should be used in a generic or

---

[13] See the U.S. *Lanham Act*, s. 29 (15 U.S.C. 1111).

purely descriptive manner to identify the physical products or the services provided. For example, it is "a Ford car", not "a Ford".

(d) Use It or Possibly Lose It

Trade-marks cannot be reserved indefinitely if they are not being used in the normal course of trade. Once a trade-mark registration is in place, the trade-mark should continue to be used in the marketplace if the musician wishes to be guaranteed of keeping the registration. If the registered mark falls into disuse in connection with some or all products or services, then all or a portion of the registration may be expunged for lack of use. In addition, if there is any argument or chance that a musician has abandoned a name or mark, it may be considered to have reverted to the public domain and thus be available to others. The governing principle is, in essence, "use it or possibly lose it".

In this context, it is also worth knowing that if a mark is registered in a particular format, it should be used in that identical format. If a mark as used is different from the mark as registered, the registration may be attacked for lack of use. If the variations are not too extensive, such attack is not likely to succeed.[14] However, it is preferable not to have to rely on the vagaries of the findings that might be made by the Trade-marks Office or the courts. In short, one of two things should be done to be guaranteed of maintaining a trade-mark registration: (1) use the mark that is registered; or, (2) register the mark that is being used.

(e) Principles Are Also Applicable to Other Trade-marks

The discussion in sections 2 and 3 above has focused on the protection of names and on names as trade-marks. However, it is important to appreciate that all of the principles described in those sections are equally applicable to any other trade-marks that a musician may care to select and use, such as logos, words, slogans or any other symbols associated, or to be associated, with the musician.

---

[14] See *Promafil Canada Ltee. v. Munsingwear Inc.* (1992), 44 C.P.R. (3d) 59 (F.C.A.).

4. Detailed Basis and Scope of Licensing and Merchandising Rights

A musician will be well placed to consider exploiting his/her rights to a name and other trade-marks beyond the musical field, after first selecting and starting to use a name and other trade-marks in connection with his/her musical endeavours, or maybe after filing for or obtaining trade-mark registrations. A musician also might want to consider exploiting these rights after writing various musical works and having ownership of the rights in various artistic works (for example, logos and photographs). In addition, if there are other identifiable aspects of a musician's business or personality, then the defining attributes thereof may also be available for exploitation beyond the musical field.

Thus, there are four main legal bases for licensing and merchandising rights: (1) musician's name; (2) other trade-marks; (3) copyrights; and (4) personality.[15] The preceding discussion has touched upon some of the basics relating to these four topics. Additional legal detail on each is set out below.

---

[15] Other complaints involving one's personal rights, such as defamation and breach of confidence, are not considered as part of the realm of personality rights and are not considered here. Sometimes, a possible relationship between privacy rights and personality rights is considered, but usually rejected. See, for example, D. Gibson, "Common Law Protection of Privacy: What to Do Until the Legislators Arrive", in Klar, *Studies in Canadian Tort Law*, (Toronto: Butterworths, 1977), at p. 88, which rejects the idea that misappropriation of personality action, based on one's public reputation (which is a commercial asset), has anything to do with privacy law that protects a person's private life. Privacy seems more a part of criminal law rather than Canadian civil law. See Part VI of the *Criminal Code*, R.S.C. 1985, c. C-46, as amended. However, several provinces have privacy statutes providing a statutory basis for such right. See, for example, in B.C.'s *Privacy Act*, R.S.B.C. 1979, c. 336 s. 3; Manitoba's *Privacy Act*, R.S.M. 1987, c. P125; Newfoundland's *Newfoundland Privacy Act*, R.S.N. 1990, c. P-22; and Quebec's *An Act Respecting the Protection of Personal Information in the Private Sector*, S.Q. 1993, c. 17, articles 35-50 of the *Civil Code*, and *Charter of Human Rights and Freedoms*, ss. 4-6. Under the B.C. statute, for example, a tort is created where a person uses the name or portrait of another person for advertising and promotion, trading in property, or services without appropriate consent. See also Louise Potvin, "Protection Against the Use of One's Own Likeness in Quebec Civil Law, Canadian Common Law and Constitutional Law (Part I)", (1997) 11 I.P.J. 203.

(a) Name and Other Trade-marks

(i) General

A trade-mark is any name, word, phrase, symbol, logo or design or possibly other identifying attribute which is used by a person for the purpose of uniquely identifying that person as the source of specific products or services.[16] Thus, a musician's performing name is a trade-mark and, from the point of view of exploiting the name, should be treated as a very valuable trade-mark.

A trade-mark, including a name, may be registered or unregistered. As discussed in detail in section 4(a)(ii)E below, significant and substantial extra rights, protections and benefits are available to registered trade-marks over and above those of trade-marks left unregistered. It is for this reason that trade-mark registrations are always highly recommended, at least for all important trade-marks. However, unregistered trade-marks can give very effective protection, particularly if the renown and reputation of the mark is extensive.

(ii) Registered Trade-marks

A. Generally

Registration of a trade-mark means registration in the government trade-marks office of the relevant jurisdiction, usually a national trade-marks office. In Canada, the Trade-marks Office is presently a division of the Canadian Intellectual Property Office. The person in Canada who makes decisions as to the registration of trade-marks, with the assistance of a sizeable staff, is the "Registrar of Trade-marks". In Canada, there are no provincial trade-mark registrations.

In the United States, the national office is known as the United States Patent and Trademark Office, or USPTO. In the United States, it is possible to register trade-marks on a state-by-state basis, but given the availability and advantages of a national registration system, there is usually little rationale for considering such an approach, particularly in the context of the international music business.

Generally, words, phrases, names, designs and logos, which are distinctive and distinguish a musician's wares or services in the marketplace,[17] can be registered as trade-marks.[18]

---

[16] See the *Trade-marks Act*, R.S.C. 1985, c. T-13, s. 2, definition of "trade-mark".

[17] For example, the Rolling Stones' Tongue & Lip Design, *Musidor B.V. v. Jabuna Pty. Ltd.* (1987), 17 C.P.R. (3d) 148 (T.M.O.B.).

B. Business Name Registration Distinguished

Registration of a trade-mark in the Trade-marks Office is totally different from registering a business name in a provincial business name office[19] such as the Ministry of Consumer and Commercial Relations office in Ontario.

When carrying on business under a business name that is not one's personal name (or formal corporation name), many provinces require registration of that business name with the appropriate provincial office. This procedure is a legal requirement to be able to carry on business under such name in the province. Its purpose is simply to protect the public so that the public can identify who is the actual person or legal entity operating the business. For example, if Band X puts on a concert but the stage collapses and spectators are injured, the spectators must be able to find out who is involved in Band X so that they can identify whom to sue.

There are sanctions if a business name is used without being registered with the province. In Ontario, for example, a business name must be registered for the business to be able to initiate and maintain a lawsuit.[20] If a group needs to sue a promoter because the band has not been paid for a performance, it may not be able to do so unless its name is registered with the provincial office.

It is critical to realize that a provincial name registration does not give any legal rights to the name or add to or strengthen any rights in the name that might already exist. A provincial name registration does not avoid or diminish in the slightest the need or desirability of obtaining a Canadian trade-mark registration. In particular, none of the additional rights accruing to a registered trade-mark are provided by a provincial name registration. Moreover, the fact of having a provincial name registration does not guarantee that the name can be registered as a trade-mark.[21]

As noted, provincial registration of a name is merely a legal prerequisite to doing business in the province, and such a registration should be obtained to carry on business in the province legally. However, having registered a business name because it is necessary to do so, there will be one side benefit — the registration will give notice

---

[18] Section 2 of the *Trade-marks Act, ibid.* See also Daniel R. Bereskin, "Selection, Proper Use and Maintenance of Trade Marks", in *Fundamentals of Trade Mark Practice*, (Toronto: L.S.U.C., 1989), at pp. CA 1-29.

[19] See also Chapter 11, "Business", regarding business name registration. Although registration of a business name as a domain name on the Internet is highly desirable, it does not negate the need for trade-mark registration.

[20] See *Business Name Act*, R.S.O. 1990, c. B.17, s. 7.

[21] The proper criteria for trade-mark registration still must be met; see discussion in section 4(a)(ii) D below.

to anyone who searches the business names register and thus it may deter someone else from using the same or a similar name.

One additional word of caution about business name registrations is in order. Whatever information is recorded as to the names and identities of the owners, whether it is the names of the partners in a partnership situation or the identity of a sole proprietor or corporate owner, should be consistent with the partnership and employment agreements that are in place. If consistency is lacking, when or if it becomes necessary to enforce rights in the name (for example, if a third party infringer appears on the scene), the infringer almost certainly will point to that lack of consistency as indicating that the name does not uniquely distinguish or identify only one legal entity. They will try to argue therefore that the name is an invalid trade-mark and has fallen into the public domain, and thus is available to be used by the defendant. Even if it is not ultimately successful, if such a defence can be raised, then obtaining appropriate relief against the infringer can be significantly delayed, diminished or made more doubtful, all at increased damage, cost, uncertainty and inconvenience to the musician.

It is therefore very important to make sure that any provincial name registration is accurate and consistent with the other legal structures in place and that, if those structures change (for example, if band members come or go), then the provincial name registration is kept up to date.

C. The Trade-mark Registration System

In most countries (including Canada, the United States and other major music countries, such as Japan, Germany and the United Kingdom), registration can occur only if there has been use of the trade-mark in the marketplace. If there are two conflicting applications in one country, priority will usually be based on the date of first use in that country of the two trade-marks.

In some countries,[22] the priority of applications is based on a first-to-file system, regardless of who may have used the mark first.

In some countries (including Canada and the United States), applications can be based on future proposed use. For conflicting applications of this nature, priority will be based on the filing dates of the applications. Such proposed use applications (called "intent-to-use" or "ITU" applications in the United States) will not actually be registered until such time as suitable evidence of actual use in the marketplace is submitted to the Trade-marks Office.

---

[22] Costa Rica and Guatemala, for example.

D. Grounds for Registration in Canada

In Canada, the *Trade-marks Act* governs the registration of trade-marks. Generally, an application for registration is made on one or more of the following grounds:[23] (1) the trade-mark has been used in Canada in the ordinary course of trade and is associated with the musician's services or wares; (2) proposed use in Canada, although use must be commenced before final registration is actually granted; (3) the trade-mark has been registered and used in a foreign country; and (4) a foreign trade-mark, which has not been used in Canada, has become known in Canada through promotional exposure and has come to be associated in the minds of the Canadian public with the goods and services of the foreign source.[24] Most musicians who apply for trade-mark registration do so on the basis of the first ground above. Ideally, it would be preferable to file even earlier on the basis of the second ground; however, at the beginning of a musical career when funds are tight and success uncertain, frequently it is not feasible to do so.

E. Advantages of Trade-mark Registration

There are some very significant legal, procedural and practical advantages to registration.

(1) Legal/Procedural

Upon registration, the trade-mark owner is granted the exclusive[25] right to use the trade-mark in association with the wares and services for which it was registered, nationally, throughout Canada, for 15 years.[26] A registration can be renewed indefinitely, provided a payment of trade-mark renewal fees is made every 15 years.[27] Once a trade-mark is registered, the presumption is that it is valid, unless shown to be invalid.[28] Further, in an infringement action it is presumed that the registrant is the owner of the trade-mark.[29]

---

[23] The *Trade-marks Act*, s. 16 and see also s. 30 which concerns the contents of a trade-mark application.

[24] *Ibid.*, ss. 16(1) and (5).

[25] *Ibid.*, s. 19.

[26] *Ibid.*, s. 46.

[27] *Ibid.*, s. 46.

[28] *Ibid.*, s. 19.

[29] *Ibid.*, s. 54(3).

If a person refers to someone else's registered trade-mark in a way which causes losses to the owner of the mark, even if there is no infringement of the trade-mark, the owner may be able to sue for depreciating the value of the goodwill attaching to the mark.[30]

Unregistered trade-marks cannot be the subject matter of actions for trade-mark infringement or depreciating the value of the goodwill; they may only support an action known as passing off. See below in section 6(a)(ii). With registered trade-marks and an infringement action (in contrast to unregistered trade-marks and a passing off action), there is no need to prove reputation. In most infringement cases, such proof would be offered in any event but perhaps not as extensively as in a passing off action. Registered trade-marks may be preferable for licensing, because of possible constitutional law questions about the validity of licensing unregistered marks; see section 5(a)(i) below.

Trade-mark registrations are frequently preferred by investors or lenders, because the trade-mark asset appears more significant. A lender's security interest in a trade-mark may be publicly and nationally recorded against a registered trade-mark in a manner which is more likely to come to the attention of the public (more specifically, to someone who may be thinking of purchasing or investing in that particular mark). Registration of a security interest in an unregistered trade-mark may be done only under general provincial security registration systems, which are much less specific and convenient. The availability of this national protection feature for a lender may make it more attractive to a potential lender to lend the funds in the first place.

(2) Practical Advantages

A registration will give notice to those seeking to use a similar mark that someone else has a prior claim to the mark if it is registered. The mere fact of having a registration underscores (to the public, to potential investors or business associates, to infringers and to the courts) the seriousness with which the owner regards his/her trade-mark rights and the value placed in them. A certificate from the Trade-marks Office leaves more of an impression and can add to the gravity of any complaint that must be advanced. A registration is easier to sell or present as a valuable asset which may make certain business transactions easier or more attractive. It also provides the justification for having used the mark (although not necessarily a legal defence), if another person makes an infringement claim against the musician, and

---

[30] *Ibid.*, s. 22(1).

thus improves the musician's bargaining position for trying to dispose of the claim in a favourable manner.

F. Unregistrable and Prohibited Trade-marks

Some trade-marks are not registrable at all or, in some cases, unless special circumstances exist. These include: (1) words which are primarily merely a name or surname; (2) words which are clearly descriptive; (3) words which are really the generic word or description for the actual wares or services; (4) trade-marks which are confusing with another registered trade-mark; and (5) trade-marks otherwise prohibited.[31]

However, some trade-marks which at first blush might not be considered to meet the criteria outlined in circumstances (1)-(3) above may in fact be, or become, possible to register. For example, a trade-mark that is a surname may be registered, if: (a) the name also has a dictionary meaning that is not clearly descriptive or deceptively misdescriptive of wares or services, for example, BROWN; (b) it is the name of a person who has been dead for over 30 years;[32] or, (c) it is a foreign surname which would not be recognized by the Canadian public as a surname in Canada (to the Canadian public, such foreign surnames actually may appear to be real foreign words of unknown meaning or even coined words).[33] Fictional names, often very important in the music business, are generally registrable. In some cases, it may be possible to register a trade-mark which does not meet some of the above criteria if it can be proved by affidavit evidence that the trade-mark has acquired distinctiveness[34] — that is, notwithstanding what the word may have brought to mind at the outset, by virtue of the owner's activities in the marketplace, the Canadian public has come to recognize the word as a trade-mark indicating wares or services emanating from the owner. If the owner can only establish that the trade-mark has acquired distinctiveness in certain limited geographic areas, the effect of a trade-mark registration may likewise be limited to those same areas.[35]

Also, the Act prohibits the adoption and use as a trade-mark or otherwise of any mark which consists of, or so nearly resembles as to be

---

[31] *Ibid.*, s. 12(1)(a)-(e) and ss. 9, 10.

[32] *Ibid.*, s. 12(1)(a). The *Trade-marks Act* sets out additional requirements regarding registered Trade-marks.

[33] See *Standard Oil Co. v. Canada (Registrar of Trade-marks)* (1968), 55 C.P.R. 49 (Can. Ex. Ct.); *Galanos v. Canada (Registrar of Trade-marks)* (1982), 69 C.P.R. (3d) 144 (F.C.T.D.); *Nishi v. Robert Morse Appliances Ltd.* (1990), 34 C.P.R. (3d) 161 (F.C.T.D.).

[34] See the *Trade-marks Act*, s. 12(2).

[35] *Ibid.*, s. 32(2).

likely mistaken for, indicia falling into the following categories: (i) various crests, arms, emblems, flags and other indicia of various government bodies (including Canadian federal, provincial and municipal governments and foreign countries), non-government bodies (including the United Nations and the Red Cross) or British royalty;[36] (ii) any matter which may falsely suggest a connection to a living individual;[37] (iii) a portrait or signature of a living individual or a person who died within the past 30 years;[38] (iv) any scandalous, obscene or immoral word or device;[39] or, (v) the officially published marks of any public authority (for example, universities, the Canadian Olympic Association, sport governing bodies, certain non-profit organizations).[40] Note: some of these marks (for example, official marks, portraits or signatures) could be registered with the consent of the party involved.

G. Persons Entitled to Registrations

As noted previously, generally a person is entitled to register a trade-mark if he or she is the first to use the trade-mark or make it known in Canada. If someone else has been using the same trade-mark or a confusingly similar one since an earlier date, that person may be entitled to the trade-mark. The person with the earlier use could object to any application or registration by the person with the later use. Formal objection on this ground may be made during the application process in a procedure known as an opposition, which takes place in the Trade-marks Office. Once an application has matured to registration, the objection can be made only in an expungement action in the Federal Court of Canada which must be started within five years of the registration date. The five year limitation period does not apply if the person objecting can prove that the owner of the registration selected and used the trade-mark with knowledge of the earlier trade-

---

[36] *Ibid.*, s. 9(1)(a)-(i.3) and 9(1)(m)-(o).

[37] *Ibid.*, s. 9(1)(k). For example, an application for the registration of the trade-mark "Here's Johnny" was denied based in part on this section and supporting evidence indicating that the phrase was better known to be associated with Johnny Carson. As the trade-mark applicant had no consent from Mr. Carson to adopt such a mark, the trade-mark falsely suggested a connection to Mr. Carson. See *Carson v. Reynolds* (1980), 49 C.P.R. (2d) 57 (F.C.T.D.). See also the case of *Fawcett v. Linda Lingerie Manufacturing Inc.* (1984), 2 C.P.R. (3d) 198 (T.M. Opp. Bd.). Farrah Fawcett was not successful in preventing use of the name "FARA" for women's loungewear in a trade-mark opposition proceeding.

[38] The *Trade-marks Act*, s. 9(1)(l).

[39] *Ibid.*, s. 9(1)(j).

[40] *Ibid.*, s. 9(1)(n)(iii).

mark.[11] Also as noted, if the applications are based on proposed use, then the person entitled will be the person who filed first.

For a trade-mark application, it is important to identify who, i.e., what legal entity, in fact has been or will be using the trade-mark. That entity should be the same as the entity that the musician intends should be owner. If it is not, unless the proper steps are taken, problems with the validity of the trade-mark may arise. For example, a discrepancy on these points may indicate that the trade-mark should be transferred or assigned[12] or that a trade-mark licence should be in place.[13]

It is crucial that the message to the public concerning ownership and use of a trade-mark be consistent. Thus, the Trade-marks Office records of ownership and use, the notices on or implications from publicly distributed materials (for example, products, advertisements and other promotional materials), provincial name registrations, and agreements regarding ownership and use all should be consistent with each other. If there are inconsistencies, problems may arise.[14]

H. Notices

Although not legally required in Canada for Canadian trade-marks, use of a trade-mark designation (for example, the "TM" or "*" symbol and/or suitable footnotes) with registered and unregistered trade-marks is advisable to inform the public of a musician's rights, as discussed at section 3(c) above (and sections 5(a) and 5(c) below, regarding licensing) and in Chapter 8, "Recording" regarding labelling and notice for recordings.

As noted above, in the United States, use of the symbol ® for a trade-mark registered in the United States provides additional legal advantages to the trade-mark owner.

I. Expungement

A registered trade-mark must be used in the normal course of trade in Canada. If it is not so used for a period of three years or more and there are no acceptable grounds to explain its non-use, all or part of the registration may be expunged, or struck out, for lack of use. If an interested party believes that the trade-mark has been abandoned, at nominal cost, it can initiate expungement proceedings before the

---

[11] *Ibid.*, s. 17.
[12] See section 5(a)(iii) below.
[13] See section 5(a)(i) & 5(a)(ii) below.
[14] For example, as set out at section 3(c) of the text, above.

Trade-marks Office. If a trade-mark owner wishes to maintain its registration, it will be put to the inconvenience and cost of preparing and filing affidavit evidence to prove use of the mark or a suitable excuse for non-use.[45]

The Federal Court of Canada also has an exclusive jurisdiction, through an action or application, to order that any entry in the trade-mark records be struck out or amended if it appears that the entry does not express accurately or define the rights of the person who owns the trade-mark.[46]

(iii) Unregistered Trade-marks and Passing Off

Unregistered trade-marks are also known as common law trade-marks. They are trade-marks that an owner has developed and used to identify his or her wares or services, but which have not been registered with a government trade-marks office. The strength of the rights associated with unregistered trade-marks can vary significantly, according to the strength, scope and uniqueness of the reputation that can be proved.

If an unregistered trade-mark used by a musician in the marketplace is distinctive,[47] not easily confused with another and is used to distinguish the musician's wares or services from those of others, it will acquire common law rights as a trade-mark on the basis that it will be recognized by the public in a given geographic territory, i.e., it will acquire a certain reputation or goodwill which can be protected.

The means for establishing a reputation can be almost limitless, but today might commonly include: (1) live performances under the mark/name; (2) audio or video broadcasting in any medium (radio, TV, Internet, music videos) under the mark/name; (3) media interviews and print or broadcast reports associated with the mark/name; (4) promotional or advertising materials associated with the mark/name published, circulated or broadcast in any medium; (5) sales and promotion of recordings in any medium (audio, video, Internet, multi-media, movie soundtracks) under the mark/name; and (6) sales and promotion of other merchandise under the mark/name.

The territorial extent of the rights in an unregistered trade-mark will be limited to where the mark is known; this may not be on a national basis. For example, a group using a name/mark only in

---

[45] The Trade-marks Act, s. 45.

[46] Ibid., s. 57.

[47] As for trade-marks as generally discussed above, "the purchaser must associate the goods or service with one source and one source only". See Daniel R. Bereskin, "Trade Marks" Bar Admission Course Corporate and Commercial Law Lectures Notes, (Toronto: L.S.U.C. 1980), cited above at note 2 at p. 10-3.

Ontario and only enjoying a reputation in that province would be unable to prevent another group in British Columbia from using the same unregistered name/mark.

The owner of an unregistered trade-mark could apply at any time to register such trade-marks, but the registration process takes time, usually at least 9 to 12 months if an application progresses fairly smoothly.

Rights in an unregistered trade-mark are enforced in an action for passing off — either at common law or contrary to section 7(b) or (c) of the *Trade-marks Act*.[48]

Passing off occurs when the public is likely to be deceived by misrepresentations made by one person which suggest that another person is selling the product/service or is somehow associated with the product/service, when in fact that is not the case. For example, if Band X is a well known group in a certain area and three musicians start up a group they call Bandex in the same area, they are very likely committing passing off because their name is so confusing with the well established name.

Historically, the following elements had to be established to succeed in a common law passing off action:

(1) a trade-mark or other identifying attribute had a reputation as indicating goods or services emanating from the complainant;

(2) the complainant was in a common field of activity with the defendant (i.e., they were in competition);

(3) a misrepresentation had been made by the defendant in the course of trade to customers of his/her goods or services to the effect that the complainant's reputation was the defendant's (usually, the misrepresentation was the use of the complainant's trade-mark or other identifying attribute or something close to it); and

(4) this caused actual damage to the complainant.[49]

In 1992, the Supreme Court of Canada considered the general principles of passing off actions and stated that there are three necessary components in these actions: (1) the existence of goodwill;

---

[48] Section 7(b) of the *Trade-marks Act* has been characterized as a statutory codification of common law passing off. See *Asbjorn Horgard A/S v. Gibbs/Nortac Industries Ltd.* reversed (1987) 14 C.P.R. (3d) 314 (F.C.A.).

[49] *A.G. Spalding and Bros. v. A.W. Gamage* (1917), 34 R.P.C. 289 (Lord Diplock). Originally passing off required confusion about a source of goods which arose from misrepresentation, and therefore the doctrine of common field of activity arose. The concept of passing off now may not be so restrictive. See *Consumers Distributing Co. v. Seiko Time Canada Ltd.*, [1984] 1 S.C.R. 583; *Asbjorn Horgard A/S v. Gibbs/Nortac Industries* supra in note 48.

(2) deception of the public due to a misrepresentation; and (3) actual or potential damage to the plaintiff.[50]

Notwithstanding the above, the Federal Court of Appeal expressed it very succinctly when it described passing off as:

"... a misrepresentation to the effect that one's goods or services are someone else's, or sponsored by or associated with that other person. It is effectively a "piggybacking" by misrepresentation."[51]

At common law, the principles of passing off may apply, not just to identifiable trade-marks (for example, names, words, phrases, logos), but perhaps to any recognizable and distinctive qualities or attributes of a trader's business which are known to indicate that business, i.e., that have a reputation as identifying that business as the unique source for goods and services offered in association with such an attribute. For example, passing off and related actions have arisen in relation to titles of songs,[52] characters,[53] personalities[54] and performances.[55] As carefully

---

[50] See *Ciba-Geigy Canada Ltd. v. Apotex Inc.* (1992), 44 C.P.R. (3d) 289 (S.C.C.). See also *Paramount Pictures v. Howley* (1991), 39 C.P.R. (3d) 419 (Ont. Gen. Div.), where the court applied the test developed in *Erven Warnink BV v. J. Townend & Sons (Hull) Ltd.*, [1979] 2 All E.R. 927 (U.K. H.L.). See also *A.G. Spalding & Bros. v. A.W. Gamage Ltd.* in note 49; *Henderson and Another*, in note 55. See also *Children's Television Workshop Inc. v. Woolworths (N.S.W.) Limited*, [1981] R.P.C. 187 (N.S.W.C.); and *Institut national des appellations d'origine des vins et eaux de vie v. Andre Wines* [1987] 60 O.R. (2d) 316 (Ont. H.C.).

[51] *Asbjorn*, supra in note 48 at 327-328.

[52] *Francis Day and Hunter Ltd. v. Twentieth Century Fox Corporation*, [1938] 3 D.L.R. 375 (Ont. C.A.). Here, no copyright protection was available to a title of a song. The song title "The Man Who Broke the Bank at Monte Carlo" was used as a title for a film; it was decided the song and the film were too different. However, an action may be possible if "the thing said to be passed off resembles the thing for which it is passed off". Whether this case would continue to represent the law in the context of modern licensing and merchandising practices may be an open question. In this case, it appears that the fact that the phrase in question was more than a mere title was completely ignored. The phrase in fact is the last line of a repeated chorus. Notwithstanding this fact, it appears that infringement by the taking of a "substantial part" of the song was not argued or considered.

[53] *Hexagon Pty. Ltd. v. Australian Broadcasting Commission*, [1976] R.P.C. 628 (N.S.W. S. Ct.). This involved a fictional film character called "Alvin Purple". This case is cited for example purposes only; it may not necessarily be followed in Canada. This question was left open in *Productions O.P., Inc. v. Groupe Morrow Inc.* (1988), 26 C.P.R. (3d) 223 (Que. S.C.). Where a character in a work is sufficiently delineated, it may come within the scope of copyright protection. See *Preston v. 20th Century Fox Canada Ltd.* (1990), 33 C.P.R. (3d) 242 (F.C.T.D.) at 275, affirmed (1993), 53 C.P.R. (3d) 407 (F.C.A).

[54] See *Krouse* and *Athans* case below at notes 66 and 67, although neither of these cases was decided on the basis of passing off.

[55] See *Henderson v. Radio Corp. Pty. Ltd.* (1969), R.P.C. 218 (N.S.W. C.A.) where an injunction and damages were granted to a professional ballroom dancing team whose image was used on a dance instruction album without their consent. This case has not yet been followed in Canada. This tort in Australia has been extended even further to

reviewed by the Supreme Court of Canada in the *Seiko* case,[56] the scope of passing off may be extending in broader directions.

Under sections 7(b) and (c) of the *Trade-marks Act*, a person cannot "direct public attention to his wares, services or business in such a way as to cause or be likely to cause confusion in Canada, at the time he commenced so to direct attention to them, between his wares, services or business and the wares, services or business of another"[57] and cannot "pass off other wares or services as and for those ordered or requested".[58]

Due to issues under Canada's constitution, it is likely that section 7(b) of the *Trade-marks Act* is only applicable to trade-marks and certain other specific types of intellectual property. It is likely that other aspects of a trader's business or reputation, which are nevertheless recognizable and distinctive of that business, if taken by a third party, would have to be made the subject of an action for common law passing off.

Law suits based on a breach of s. 7(b) of the Act may be brought in the Federal Court of Canada or in the superior court of a province. Complaints based on common law passing off may be brought only in the superior court of a province.[59]

(iv) Trespass

This action is based on the principle that a person may have a property right in his or her professional reputation and name.[60] Case law considering this issue has been divided. It has been decided that in the absence of libel, a person does not have property rights in his or her name and damage must be shown even where the use of the name

---

incorporate a kind of misappropriation of personality aspect. See *Hogan v. Koala Dundee Pty. Ltd.* (1988), 83 Aust. L.R. 187 (Fed. Ct. Aust.), and specifically the case of *Dunlop Ltd. v. Hogan* (1989), 87 Aust. L.R. 14 (Fed. Ct. Aust.) See discussion in the Howell article, "Personality Rights: A Canadian Perspective", cited below note 67, and Andrew Terry, "Image Filching and Passing Off in Australia: Misrepresentation or Misappropriation? Hogan v. Koala Dundee Pty. Ltd.", [1990] 6 E.I.P.R. 219. For a recent discussion of the state of the law of passing off in England, see Ruben Stone, "Titles, Character Names and Catch-phrases in the Film and Television Industry: Protection under the Law of Passing off", [1996] 7 Ent. L.R. 263.

[56] *Consumers Distributing Co. Ltd. v. Seiko Time Canada Ltd.* (1984), 1 C.P.R. (3d) 1 at 17-21 (S.C.C.).

[57] The *Trade-marks Act*, s. 7(b).

[58] *Ibid.*, s. 7(c).

[59] For a general overview, see G. Ronald Bell and Heather Probert, "The Constitutionality of Canadian Trade Mark Law" (1985), 4 C.P.R. (3d) 395. See also *Asbjorn*, supra in note 48.

[60] *Dixon v. Holden* (1869), L.R. 7 Eq. 488 at 494. This line of cases began with *Routh v. Webster* (1847), 10 Beav. 561.

is unauthorized.[61] It may be still arguable that a trespass has occurred when there is a use of a person's name or personality which has caused, or will probably cause, injury to the reputation of a business or profession. Whether this argument would be successful is uncertain.[62]

(b) Copyrights

(i) Generally

Details on copyright concepts and principles were discussed in Chapters 1, 2 and 4. These concepts and principles also apply to copyrights related to merchandising. However, copyrights related to merchandising generally involve copyright in artistic works - for example, the artwork for T-shirts, posters, pamphlets, programs and logos and photographs. Artistic works under the *Copyright Act* include paintings, drawings, sculpture, engravings and photographs.[63] For instance, these are often used on album covers and in merchandising schemes that promote musicians.

(ii) Photographs

Photographs are treated slightly differently from other artistic works in the *Copyright Act*. The term of copyright in photographs is outlined in Chapter 1, "Copyright".[64] There is a presumption when the photograph is commissioned, if there is no agreement to the contrary, that the person who commissioned the photograph owns the

---

[61] *Dockrell v. Dougall* (1899), 80 L.T. 556 (C.A.).

[62] The trial court in *Krouse* per Mr. Justice Haines found that there was trespass. The injury to Krouse's property was the commercial right of his likeness being used for advertisement purposes without consent. *Krouse v. Chrysler Canada Ltd.* (1971), 25 D.L.R. (3d) 49 at 68. This was rejected in the Ontario Court of Appeal, by Estey, J.A. (as he then was) on the basis that there is no property right in a name, and that trespass was confined to isolated cases explainable on other grounds, although he gave no indication from this case what the other grounds were.

[63] S. 2 of the *Copyright Act*, R.S.C. 1985, c. C-42 as amended.

[64] *Ibid.*, s. 10(1). See also Chapter 1, "Copyright" section 2 c) (vi). Note that under s. 10(1), where the owner is a corporation, the term of copyright is the remainder of the year of the making of the initial negative or plate from which the photograph was made plus 50 years. If there is no negative or plate, then it is the remainder of the year of the making of the photograph plus 50 years. If the author is an individual, or if the corporation is owned by the photographer (and owns the copyright to the photograph), it is the life of the photographer plus the remainder of the year of death of the photographer plus 50 years.

copyright.[65] This situation is the opposite to that involving other works, such as graphic works or logos.

(iii) Ownership

When commissioning artistic works, as noted above, it should be specified in writing who owns the copyright so that disputes and confusion can be avoided. The implications of the moral rights surrounding such works should be considered and dealt with also. Moral rights were discussed in Chapter 1, "Copyright".

(c) Personality

(i) Generally

One has the right to use one's own name, likeness, voice and celebrated attributes, that is, one's "personality", for commercial purposes,[66] although the limits of this right are not precise. The right has developed from case law and is related to causes of action in tort.[67]

---

[65] *Ibid.*, s. 13(2).

[66] *Krouse v. Chrysler Canada Ltd.* (1974), 1 O.R. (2d) 225 (C.A.) per Estey J.A. (as he then was) at 237-238, also cited at 40 D.L.R. (3d) 15.

[67] In Canada, see *Athans v. Canadian Adventure Camps Ltd.* (1977), 17 O.R. (2d) 425 (Ont. H.C.). Dicta in this case refers to a property right. See also *Joseph v. Daniels* (1986), 4 B.C.L.R. (2d) 239 (B.C.S.C.), which cited *Athans* and referred to such a right as a property right. There, the court found no misappropriation but awarded $550 for breach of contract, the "going rate" for the sale of such rights. In *Gould Estate v. Stoddart Publishing Co.* (1996), 74 C.P.R. (3d) 206 (Ont. Gen. Div.), photographs of Mr. Gould were used by the publisher in a book. The estate brought an action against the publisher under two general grounds: misappropriation of personality and copyright infringement. In dismissing the action in *obiter* the court stated that the right of publicity was characterized as a form of intangible property under Ontario law. Subsequently, on appeal by the plaintiff the Court of Appeal dismissed the appeal, but applied copyright concepts to find that Gould provided his consent to the publication of the photographs. See *Gould Estate v. Stoddart Publishing Co.* (1998), 80 C.P.R. (3d) 161 (Ont. C.A.). The right to publicity was also recognized in these post-*Athans* cases: *Racine v. C.J.R.C. Radio Capitale Ltee.* (1977), 35 C.P.R (2d) 236 (Ont. Co. Ct.), and *Heath v. Weist-Barron School of Television* (1981), 62 C.P.R. (2d) 92 (Ont. H.C.). See also the statutory basis referred to above in note 15. See also *Bogajewicz v. Sony Music of Canada Ltd.* (1995), 63 C.P.R. (3d) 458 (Que. S.C.), where the court found that the defendant infringed the plaintiff's rights (safeguard of dignity, respect for private life and peaceful enjoyment of property) which are protected under the provisions of Quebec's *Charter of Human Rights and Freedoms* (ss. 4-6), when the defendant used a photograph of the plaintiff without consent. Damages were set at $5000. See also *Shaw v. Berman* (1997), 72 C.P.R. (3d) 9 (Ont. Gen. Div.), affirmed 84 C.P.R. (3d) 286 (Ont. C.A), where appropriation of personality was claimed, but the court found that consent was given. See Eric M. Singer, "The Development of the

It appears that several jurisdictions may recognize an inheritable[68] right of publicity.[69]

(ii) Misappropriation of Personality

The tort of misappropriation of personality has at least two elements: (1) an individual or possibly a group of individuals, i.e., a "personality", has a name, likeness or other qualities which enjoy a reputation uniquely identifying that personality; and (2) the defendant without permission uses that name, likeness or other quality.[70] It may be

---

Common Law Tort of Appropriation of Personality in Canada", (1998), 15 C.I.P.R. 65; Robert G. Howell, "Personality Rights: A Canadian Perspective", in *Conference on Intellectual Property v. Issues in Advertising*, (Ottawa: CBA/CLE: 1990); Robert G. Howell, "The Common Law Appropriation of Personality", (1986), 2 I.P.J. 149; and Robert W. Judge, "Celebrity Look-alikes and Sound-alikes or Imitation is Not the Highest Form of Flattery", (1988), 20 C.P.R. (3d) 97, for legal articles discussing the parameters of personality law. See also Brenda L. Pritchard, "Wanted: Personalities - Dead or Alive", at page B-1; and Brian W. Gray, "What Price of Fame? Personality Rights in Canada and Beyond", at page B-47, both in *Entertainment, Advertising and Media Law*, (Toronto: L.S.U.C., 1996); Daniel R. Bereskin, "Merchandising Rights: Identifying the Legal Business Protection", Chapter F, *Entertainment, Advertising and Media Law*, (Toronto: L.S.U.C., 1989); Samuel K. Murumba, *Commercial Exploitation of Personality*, (Sydney: Law Book Co., 1986); Elise Orenstein, untitled article, Third Annual Licensing Intellectual Property Conference, (April 17, 1997: The Canadian Institute); and Louise Potvin, "Protection Against the Use of One's Own Likeness in Quebec Civil Law, Canadian Common Law and Constitutional Law (Part I)", (1997), 11 I.P.J. 203. See also Peter Jones, "Manipulating the Law Against Misleading Imagery: Photo-montage and Appropriation of Well-known Personality", [1999] 28 E.I.P.R. 1.

[68] The concept of "inheritable" means that the right can survive the death of the person who created or owned the right, and be passed by will or otherwise to that person's estate and heirs. If the right were not "inheritable", it would cease to exist at the death of the person who created the right; thus, the heirs and estate would not receive any enforceable right. Other words used to describe the "inheritable" concept are "devisable", "bequeathable" and "descendible".

[69] In Ontario, the trial court in *Gould Estate*, supra at note 67, recognized in *obiter* an inheritable right of publicity. In the U.S., 13 states have recognized an inheritable right of publicity through common law or statute. California and Tennessee, two of the major entertainment states, have enacted statutes. Under the Tennessee law, a 10 year inheritable right of publicity is provided; if the right is exercised during the 10 year period, the term extends indefinitely until a 2 year period of non-use occurs. In New York, cases have interpreted its *Civil Rights Law*, ss. 50-51 to create a non-inheritable right of publicity. Section 43(a) of the *Lanham Act*, 15 U.S.C. s. 1125(a)(1)(A) have defined comparable rights. Generally, see Candice Kersh, "Right of Privacy/Publicity in the United States", *Entertainment, Advertising & Media Law*, (L.S.U.C. Dept. of Continuing Education), pp. B-27 - B-32; Joseph J. Beard, "Casting Call at Forest Lawn: The Digital Resurrection of Deceased Entertainers - A 21st Century Challenge for Intellectual Property Law", (1993), 8 High Tech. L.J. 101 at pp. 147-150.

[70] *Joseph v. Daniels*, cited above, note 67, at 244. Note that *Gould*, supra in note 67, suggests there is a "sales v. subject" distinction. Therein, the tort may apply when the

an open question whether the tort requires a third element — namely, (3) whether the use must imply, wrongly of course, that the personality endorses the products or activities of the defendant.[71]

If the tort is established, damages are recoverable from the misappropriating party. Damages have been awarded based on a market test of the commercial value of the unauthorized use of one's personality. The court can make an assessment of what could have been received in the market for permission to publish a drawing or photograph of the person, for example.[72] The amount may be increased as a premium for the loss of the ability to have refused permission.

5. Licensing and Merchandising Agreements

Transferring copyright, by licensing, assignment and devolution, was discussed in Chapters 1 and 2, and will not be discussed here. The transfer of names and other trade-mark and personality rights is discussed below.[73]

(a) Names and Trade-marks

(i) Licence

At common law, the licensing of trade-marks led to their invalidity. The theory was that licensing meant there were at least two possible sources of the goods and services — the licensor (who owned the mark) and the licensee (who actually made, owned and sold the goods or services). This confusion as to source was anathema to the

---

identity of the personality merely is being used in some fashion - for example, to promote sales of something. However, if the person is the subject of the work or enterprise in question, the tort may not apply. See the discussion at page 213.

[71] See the comments of Estey, J.A. in *Krouse*, 40 D.L.R. (3d) 15 (Ont. C.A.) at 19.

[72] In *Athans*, a royalty of 10% was applied: 10¢ per copy of the unauthorized brochure and advertisement, times the number of distributed copies, totalling $500. See also *Racine v. C.J.R.C. Radio Capitale Ltee.* (1977), 17 0.R. (2d) (Co. Ct.) where $850 was awarded in damages for misappropriation of personality. In *Krouse v. Chrysler*, cited above note 62, $500 was awarded. A case involving James Cagney was settled for an undisclosed amount. It was cited in (1988) Vol. 10, No. 2, E.L.R. 16 and is mentioned in David Himelfarb's article, "A Canadian Perspective on the Protection of an Individual's Personality from Commercial Exploitation", in *Entertainment Publishing and the Arts Handbook*, (New York: Clark, Boardman Co., 1985), at pp. 263-277.

[73] For reference, see Gregory J. Battersby and Clark W. Grimes, "A Practical Look at Merchandising Contracts", in *Merchandising Law*, (Toronto: L.S.U.C., 1988), at pp. C1-C22.

fundamental requirement of a trade-mark that it identify a single unique source of the goods and services.

This deficiency in the common law was overcome through the *Trade-marks Act* which in 1953 introduced an exception to the common law to allow licensing of trade-marks if certain criteria were met. The mark had to be registered and the licensee had to be registered in the Trade-marks Office as a "registered user" under a formal "registered user agreement". Registered user agreements had to include provisions relating to standards and quality controls of the licensed wares and marking controls. Failure to comply with the registered user provisions of the Act put the validity of the licensor's trade-mark at risk.[74] Thus, names and unregistered marks could not be licensed safely. Similarly, marks registered for certain wares and services could not be licensed safely in respect of other wares and services; in connection with those other wares or services, the mark was essentially considered to be unregistered.

In 1993, the registered user regime was repealed. In its place, a new and broader exception to the common law to allow licensing was introduced. Pursuant to section 50 of the *Trade-marks Act* which now governs the licensing of names and trade-marks, registered trade-marks can be licensed, provided that proper controls are maintained. Unregistered trade-marks and names also can be licensed, again provided that proper controls are maintained.[75] However, some practitioners have questioned whether s. 50 is constitutionally valid in respect of names and unregistered trade-marks.[76] Although it is believed that s. 50 would survive a constitutional attack of this nature, it may be prudent for a musician to: (1) register as a trade-mark any name he/she wishes to license; and (2) ensure that the registration for any trade-mark to be licensed covers the particular wares or services which are to be licensed. Of course, all the other benefits of trade-mark registration would also result; see section 4(a)(ii)E above.

---

[74] Section 50(1)-(3) of the *Trade-marks Act*, R.S.C. 1970, c. T-10. See also Harold G. Fox, "The Canadian Law of Trade Marks and Unfair Competition, Third Edition", (Toronto: Carswell, 1972), Chapter VI, "Assignment, License and Devolution".

[75] See Section 50(1) of the *Trade-marks Act*, as amended. For a general discussion on this matter, see Brian W. Gray, "Trade-mark Licensing", in *On Your Mark*, (L.S.U.C.: Sept. 29, 1993), page D-1; Elise Orenstein, supra at 67.

[76] This is because this is subject matter which arguably might be within the exclusive jurisdiction of the provinces as part of "property and civil rights". But, given the court's conclusions about the constitutionality of s. 7(b) for unregistered trade-marks (per *Asbjorn*, supra note 48) as necessary for rounding out trade-mark law generally, it is believed that s. 50 would be found to be valid legislation as well.

(ii) Licensing Provisions

For merchandising purposes, the musician as licensor will retain ownership of the trade-mark. The musician must also retain the right to control the licensee's use of the trade-mark and the character and quality of the licensed wares and services made and sold by the licensee. When structuring a merchandising licence and relationship, there should be an active connection between the licensor and the licensee's merchandising activities. The licensor should exercise actual control or supervision over the licensee's activities. Merely accepting royalty payments without other involvement may not be sufficient to rise to the level of exercising actual control and, in such circumstances, there may be a risk that the licence would be considered to be just an invalid "paper" licence.[77] More detail on the typical content of a licence agreement is set out below.

(iii) Assignment

Pursuant to the *Trade-marks Act*, trade-marks (whether registered or unregistered) and names can be transferred or assigned.[78] However, care must be taken that the trade-mark does not lose its distinctiveness as a result of an assignment. For example, when a trade-mark is assigned, the assignee should amend the advertisements, publicity and labelling characteristics of the trade-mark to indicate to the public that there has been a transfer. Without this, the trade-mark may be invalid because of a lack of distinctiveness.[79]

Common assignment situations include: (1) if use of a mark has been by one entity, but the musician would prefer that the owner be a different entity, then a formal transfer document, called an assignment, preferably should be executed; (2) if there are inconsistencies amongst

---

[77] For example, in s. 45 expungement proceedings, when an owner of a registered trade-mark licensed its use to a third party, and the licence did not contain control provisions, the owner could not rely on the licensee's use of the trade-mark for its benefit in those proceedings. See *Sara Lee Corp. v. Intellectual Property Holding Co.* (1997), 76 C.P.R. (3d) 71 (T.M.H.O.). See also Geoffrey Hobbs, "Passing Off and the Licensing of Merchandising Rights", Part 2, (1980), Vol. 2, E.I.P.R. 79 at 81, which refers to *Tavener Rutledge Limited v. Trexapalm Limited*, [1975] F.S.R. 479, a case involving licensing of merchandising rights. There, Walton J. stated at 485 that there must be the provision for quality and control in the licensing, and quality control must be exercised.

[78] S. 48 of the *Trade-marks Act*. See also ss. 48-50 of *Trade-marks Act Regulations* (1996), S.O.R. 96-195.

[79] Notwithstanding the transfer, the public still might believe the old owner still owns the mark. The result is confusion because there is a discrepancy between who the public thinks is the owner and who is the actual owner. See *Wilkinson Sword (Canada) Ltd. v. Arthur Juda*, [1968] 2 Ex. C.R. 137 (Can. Ex. Ct.).

any Trade-marks Office records as to ownership and use, any notices on or implications from publicly distributed materials, any provincial name registrations, or any agreements regarding ownership and use, remedial steps may include execution of an assignment; and (3) sale of a business to another entity.

Some assignment situations may also require a licence from one party to another. For example, if the musician wants the trade-mark rights to be owned by a holding company for the purpose of trying to isolate his/her intellectual property rights from creditors on the tour circuit, he/she may wish to assign the trade-mark to a holding company, but since the musician would be the one actually performing the musical service, the musician should have a licence back from the holding company.

(b) Personality

(i) Licence

Personality rights can produce significant income if they are licensed or assigned. The practice of licensing such rights for endorsements or to advertising or novelty companies is widespread. Licensing personality rights is a common way of transferring such rights. Care should be taken that there is no conflict between merchandising licensing rights and any publishing, recording and merchandising agreements which obtain rights to use personal rights to promote songbook folios and records respectively.

(ii) Assignment and Devolution

The right to assign one's personality rights, at least during a person's lifetime, is part of the right to exploit one's personality. An assignment may not be practical or viable, since an assignment may attempt to transfer all rights in the assignor's personality to the assignee, while precluding the assignor from using aspects of his or her own personality.

Different jurisdictions treat personality rights after death in different manners. Some jurisdictions allow devolution of personality rights after death to the person's estate. In Ontario, the court stated in *obiter*, in *Gould Estate v. Stoddart Publishing Co.*, that a right of publicity (another term for personality right) was akin to copyright and should devolve to the estate.[80] U.S. court decisions have split on this issue. In the Lugosi case, which considered whether the Lugosi estate had control over Bela Lugosi's right in the character Count Dracula,[81] the court decided the right to one's personality did not survive death. However, in other cases, including involving Elvis Presley's estate,[82] where the right to publicity was much more apparently recognized, the right to publicity was not only assignable (in this case through a corporation to market merchandising commodities), but also survived Elvis Presley's death. The duration and scope of the right to publicity in the U.S. varies from state to state. Some states have enacted statutes to clarify this issue.[83]

Unless specifically litigated or a specific statute addresses the issue, it remains open whether or not personality rights in Canada can devolve to one's estate. However, an estate planner for a musician of substantial stature and potential in terms of exploitation of personality rights should make specific reference in a will to these rights.

(c) Contractual Issues

(i) *Generally*

In addition to the legal aspects discussed above in section 5(a), there are numerous contractual issues that should be addressed in a

---

[80] See note 69.

[81] *Lugosi v. Universal Pictures*, 139 Cal. Rptr. 35 2nd Dist (1977) 603 P. 2nd 425 (1979).

[82] See *Presley v. Crowell*, cited below in note 83. For a U.S. case involving a copyright infringement claim against New Kids on the Block on the basis of exceeding the scope of licensed uses, see *Marshall v. New Kids on the Block Partnership*, 780 F.Supp. (S.D.N.Y. 1991).

[83] Since both *Lugosi v. Universal Pictures* and *Presley v. Crowell* (cited above in notes 81 and 82) were decided, both Tennessee and California have enacted statutes that would recognize the descendability of personality right; *California Civil Code*, s. 990, and *Tennessee Code*, s. 47-25-1101 to 1105. The U.S. law in this area seems to be based on the following four rights: (1) the right of publicity (common law); (2) the right of privacy (statutory); (3) passing off (see the (1982) *Lanham Act*, 15 § 1051 C22); and (4) copyright (statutory). There is an inconsistency regarding the inheritability of this right at state and federal levels. The federal courts are in the affirmative. New York common law does not recognize this right. See *Stephano v. News Group Publications* (1984), 64 N.Y. (2d) 174, 485 N.Y.S. (2d) 474 N.E. (2d) 580. However, this right is set out in the Statutory Invasion of Privacy tort or the *Lanham Act*. The *Lugosi* case was overruled by statute under the *California Civil Code*, para. 990. The rights in California now continue for fifty years after the death of a person. In Tennessee, the issue was resolved as follows: Elvis Presley's estate lost on post-death rights in *Memphis Development Foundation v. Factors, etc.*, 616 F. (2d) 956 (6 S.I.R. 1980). However, Elvis Presley's estate won in *Presley v. Crowell*, 14 M.E.D.L. Rptr. 1043.

merchandising licence agreement.[84] The comments below highlight key concerns only. In specific situations, detailed checklists and precedents as well as expert advice and specific source materials should be consulted.

Generally, critical terms will include the following:

a.   The licensor must have the right to set and enforce standards for the products and control use of the mark. This should include the right to receive specimens from time to time and to inspect licensee's premises and practices. It also means that all proposed uses of the mark (i.e., all products, graphics, packaging, advertising, etc.) must be approved by licensor in advance and, once approved, cannot be changed without further consent. It may also mean controlling the channels of trade (i.e., who can be authorized customers of licensee — either specifically or by general description). As part of the licensor's standards, it should be required that all labelling be in compliance with the *Consumer Packaging and Labelling Act* and other laws.[85]

b.   The licensor must have the right to require trade-mark notices to be used and to specify same. Under section 50(2) of the *Trade-marks Act*, the use of proper trade-mark notices will now provide substantive legal advantages to the use of trade-mark notices in licensing situations. More specifically, if a notice is used specifying the identity of the trade-mark owner and that the use is licensed, it will be presumed (unless the contrary is proved) that a proper licence with proper control provisions is in place. Accordingly, whether it is specified in the licence agreement or established after the licence has been executed, the licensor should be entitled to require a notice such as the following to be applied to the products covered by the licence:

---

[84] See checklist in Appendix 6. For a more detailed checklist and a sample merchandising licence, see *Merchandising Law* (cited above in note 73), at pp. B-13-190 Checklist and at pp. B-20 - B-29 (licence). See also Gregory J. Battersby, "A Practical Look at Merchandising Licence Agreements", in *Merchandising Law*, *ibid.*, at pp. C-1 - C-2, which includes an annotated merchandising licence agreement at pp. C-9 - C-22. For useful sample merchandising and endorsement agreements, see also Martin E. Silfen, Chairman, *Counselling Clients in the Entertainment Industry 1982*, (New York: Practicing Law Institute, 1982), at pp. 1429-1437 for merchandising, and at pp. 1439-1465 for endorsements. See also Donald C. Farber, General Ed., *Entertainment Industry Contracts Negotiating and Drafting Guide*, (New York: Matthew Bender, 1990), Volume 4, "Music", Samuel J. Fox, Ed., at Chapter 152, "Tour Merchandising Licensing" and Form 155-1, "Tour Merchandising Licence Agreement" with commentary; Chapter 157, "Product Endorsement"; Form 157-01, "Product Endorsement Agreement" with commentary; and Chapter 18, "Retail Merchandising".

[85] R.S.C. 1985, c. C-38. See Chapter 8, "Recording" concerning this issue in the context of recording.

Band X™   TM of Band X, used under licence

c. Indemnification and product liability insurance coverage must be provided by the licensee: how much per occurrence and in aggregate?

Key business terms to consider will include:

1. Clear identification of the channels of trade (i.e., who can be authorized customers of the licensee and how are they to be reached; for example, is the arrangement for mail order, concert or retail agreement? Are the customers to be limited to particular classes or retailers?) Other aspects of the agreement will depend on how this issue is decided.

2. Clear identification of names, marks or other identifying attributes to be licensed (including registration or application numbers, dates, titles, countries).

3. Clear identification of products to be licensed.

4. What is the territory – i.e., to what country(ies) or groups of countries or parts of countries does the licence extend?

5. Is the arrangement to be exclusive or non-exclusive?
    • How will this affect the royalty rate?
    • Is it intended to allow the licensor to operate under the marks too?

6. How long will the arrangement last — short or long term? Would it be appropriate to have a relatively short initial term, with a right for licensee to renew for one or more renewal terms? An initial term should be at least long enough to allow licensee a reasonable opportunity to recoup initial investments in launching the products. Renewal term(s) could be for as long as makes sense. A licensee may wish to have multiple short renewal terms so as to be able to terminate the relationship if warranted.

7. What is the royalty?
    • What products attract the royalty?
    • Is the royalty a fixed amount per unit/territory/use/occasion or a percentage of sales?
    • Should a sliding scale according to sales be considered? Should a licensee have to pay less (or more) as the quantities increase?
    • When & how payable? How frequently?
    • Calculated on what? (gross sales, net sales or some other base?) A definition of "gross sales" or "net sales" should be clearly set out.

- Who is responsible for taxes on royalty (and other) payments? Do withholding taxes come into play?
- Currency of payments

8. Should any other fees or advances be paid (for example, a lump sum up-front payment)? Should they be returnable and/or recoupable? As noted elsewhere, publishing and recording agreements almost always involve advances which are non-returnable but recoupable. This is not usually appropriate in a merchandising licence. Advances in the context of music, publishing and recording agreements are discussed in Chapter 3, "Music Publishing" and Chapter 8, "Recording", and the reader may find it useful to consult those chapters.

9. Are performance obligations appropriate? That is, should there be minimum standards for the licensee to meet to keep the licence? If so, what are they? If the agreement is to be short term, such obligations may not be necessary. However, if the agreement is longer term, performance obligations become very important. A musician would not want to sign a deal and then have his/her rights tied up in the hands of an unsuccessful licensee for any length of time. Accordingly, possible performance obligations to consider would include:
   - Should there be a "best efforts" clause?
   - Should there be minimum sales per year?
   - Should there be payment of guaranteed minimum royalties?

   The consequences of failure to meet such obligations — for example, right to terminate plus remedies for breach of contract — should be spelled out.

10. Will the licensee be obligated to make efforts to advertise and promote the licensed products and to spend additional amounts on same? If so, what efforts and how much? Will the amount be an annual lump sum or will it be an additional percentage of sales? Budgeting and advance planning and approval are usually required.

11. Is a non-competition provision appropriate? If so, define carefully.

12. How can the agreement be terminated? An indefinite or perpetual licence should not normally be considered. Possible conditions for termination:
    - On notice by either party? If so, how long should the notice be?
    - On bankruptcy or insolvency?
    - Automatically, if there is a major breach by licensee?

- Change in ownership or attempted transfer of licence to a third party
- If licensee does not exploit the licensed rights?
- If a breach is not or cannot be cured in a certain amount of time? How long should that time be?
- Breach of a related agreement?

13. Is there any right to sub-license? (Usually, no!) If there is, it must be subject to approval by the licensor and carefully controlled. Any sub-licence must have all of the terms necessary to protect the licensor and the trade-marks. There should also be a direct agreement put in place between the licensor and the sub-licensee so that privity of contract is established; in effect, the "sub-licensee" becomes a direct licensee.

14. Is there any right for licensee to assign the agreement? (Usually, no!) A licensor usually wants to know the people with whom he/she is dealing. Any right to assign should be carefully set out.

15. Will there be any special provisions regarding defective products ("seconds") or end-of-line products ("close-outs")? How sold? To/through whom? Any special, limited distribution channels? Any special reduced royalty rate?

16. Should an ethical behaviour provision be included? (for example, no slave labour or child labour used in the production of goods)

17. Will the licensee have any right to dispose of inventory after termination? How and for how long?

Other more conventional terms and legal issues will include: periodic royalty statements and payment of royalties, obligation to keep proper accounting records, right of access to accounting records, audit, third party infringement clause, remedies for breach of contract, currency for payments (and methods of currency conversion), the nature of the contractual relationship, grey marketing controls, governing law, entirety clauses and other boilerplate provisions; and all should be addressed as well. In addition, there may be GST or other tax implications, a topic discussed in Chapter 12, "Tax". Should there be an acknowledgement of title? Should there be an acknowledgement of validity or should an undertaking not to infringe after termination be included (in some countries, provisions like these may be unenforceable; is that fact relevant to the agreement?). Should there be an arbitration provision in the event of dispute? Do any specialized international or jurisdictional considerations come into play (for example, are any proposed clauses potentially invalid in view of price restrictions, restraint of trade, intellectual property misuse, U.S. anti-trust laws, European Union restrictions, acknowledgements of intellectual property validity, or grant back provisions)? Are there any specific currency issues? Withholding taxes?[86]

Here are some additional questions to consider:

1.   Whether, in light of the licence, any new trade-mark applications need to be filed? In what countries? At whose cost?

2.   The law of a particular province/state will govern the agreement. Will it be necessary to obtain a formal legal opinion from a qualified lawyer in the relevant jurisdiction as to the effectiveness of the proposed agreement under the law of that jurisdiction?

(ii) Endorsements

Many of the contractual issues set out above in the context of the licence agreement are also applicable to the endorsement agreement and should be consulted when reviewing this section of this chapter.

An endorsement agreement may also contain specific terms not included in the merchandising agreement. For example, terms may include: (i) the obligation to be available for a certain period of time (for instance, two business days a year) to promote the product being endorsed; and (ii) to be present for photographs and film or television commercials. Are extra fees to be paid or expenses to be reimbursed? If expenses are to be covered, what class will the musician be entitled to travel (first class or economy)?

Generally, the musician will want to minimize the time commitment involved, and the scheduling of such commitment should be based on the mutual availability of the musician and the sponsor and it should take into consideration the musician's other professional engagements.

Photographs should be consistent with and even enhance, but not be detrimental to, the musician's image. The musician should have some right to reject photographs that are to be used in the endorsement.

Some jurisdictions in the U.S. require that an affidavit of use be sworn by the person endorsing the product, stating that he or she actually uses it. This practice is done to protect the integrity of the company should the person endorsing the product be questioned as to

---

[86] See Alex S. Konigsberg, "Aspects of International Licence Agreements and Cross-Border Considerations Inherent Therein", Chapter F in *Merchandising Law*, cited above at note 73, at pp. F-1- F-13 for a more complete discussion of such issues.

the truthfulness of whether he or she actually uses the product which is apparently being endorsed.[87]

In addition, the company engaging the musician to endorse its products may insist on a morals clause. The intent of this clause is to allow the immediate termination of the agreement should the musician engage in questionable behaviour, such as drug abuse or criminal acts, for instance, that may impugn the company's reputation and devalue the endorsement rights obtained.[88]

A musician should also consider his or her potential for being sued for product liability when endorsing a product. The musician should be indemnified and public liability insurance should be in place. This is imperative for all merchandising and endorsement arrangements.

(iii) Particular Merchandising Licence Agreements

A. Concert Venue

Concerning a merchandising licence with respect to concert sales, two issues arise: (a) what will the licensor provide?; and (b) what will the merchandiser provide? Typically, a licensee will provide transportation, crew, merchandise, sales people at the venue, food and hotel. The merchandiser may provide a crew and a person for light duties that do not interfere with the actual merchandising. See also the discussion in section 5(a) above.

B. Retail Merchandising

With respect to retail merchandising, it may be more difficult than with tour merchandising to determine how many sales have taken place. The royalty is less than that in the tour merchandising agreement and can range from a low of 3% to 4% to a high of 7% to 8% with the norm being 5% or 6%.[89] See also the discussion in section 5(a) above.

---

[87] See note 84, *Entertainment Industry Contracts Negotiating and Drafting Guide*, at p. 157-1-21.

[88] *Ibid.*, at p. 157-24 contains a sample U.S. morals clause.

[89] *Entertainment Industry Contracts*, cited in note 84 at pp. 158-158-3.

6. Enforcing Licensing and Merchandising Rights

(a) Trade-marks

(i) Infringement Actions

A. Generally

Registered trade-marks have statutory rights under the *Trade-marks Act* that do not apply to unregistered trade-marks. The right to sue for "infringement" is one such right. Infringement of rights in a registered trade-mark occurs when a person who is not entitled to use a trade-mark "sells, distributes or advertises wares or services in association with a confusing trade-mark or trade name".[90] However, a specific exception to trade-mark infringement is any bona fide use of a personal name as a trade name, or the use of a geographical name for a place of business or description of character or quality of wares or services, which is not likely to depreciate the goodwill attached to a trade-mark.[91]

The usual remedies in trade-mark infringement cases are an injunction, delivery up of infringing products, and a recovery of damages, or alternatively at the court's discretion the infringer's profits.[92]

Like other actions such as copyright infringement actions, it is possible to seek interim and interlocutory injunctions, and Anton Piller orders. A "John Doe" order, where orders are effective against as yet unidentified defendants, is also available in extraordinary circumstances. This may occur, for example, when a street vendor sells counterfeit merchandise at a concert and it is impossible prior to the concert to identify the infringing party.

A case involving the group name the "Ink Spots," a registered trade-mark, was the subject of a Quebec infringement action[93] and is illustrative of issues relating to musical group names. There, two musical groups were simultaneously using the name in Montreal to provide "lounge" type entertainment. One group brought a motion for an interlocutory injunction against the second to prohibit the second from using the name. It was argued that, through simultaneous use by

---

[90] S. 20 of the *Trade-marks Act*.

[91] *Ibid.*, ss. 20(a),(b)(i)&(ii).

[92] See generally, for example, David J.A. Cairns, *Remedies For Trademark Infringement*, (Toronto: Carswell, 1988). See also Gregory A. Piasetzski, Chapter G, "Legal Remedies and Tactics for Enforcing Merchandising Rights Against Infringers", in *Merchandising Law*, cited above at note 73, at p. G-15.

[93] *Dower v. Boatner* (1963),41 C.P.R. 216 (Que. Sup. Ct.) per Broussard, J.

the two groups, the name had lost its distinctiveness and that one group could not prevent the other from using it. A modified injunction was allowed, preserving the status quo, and one group was allowed to continue performing under the name "The Joe Boatner Ink Spots."

B. Jurisdiction

A crucial consideration is the court in which one chooses to bring the action. The Federal Court of Canada, although having jurisdiction on a Canada-wide basis, can only consider matters involving federal statutes, including the *Trade-marks Act* and *Copyright Act*. As such, if only a trade-mark or artistic work is involved, one can bring the action in the Federal Court and seek an injunction or other remedies on a Canada-wide basis. If the action also must involve common law passing off (based not on a trade-mark), or personality rights, or contractual issues, the musician would have to start an action in one province, and either: (1) pursue corresponding but independent actions in each other province of concern; or (2) obtain a judgement in the first province and seek to have the courts of the other provinces enforce it as well.[94] The scope of damages and remedies of each provincial action may be limited to those damages and remedies occurring in just that province for that action. In certain fact situations, an action could or should be considered in the United States or other countries.[95]

(ii) Other Trade-mark Causes of Action

A. Generally

The *Trade-marks Act* sets out several other bases for actions, some of which may apply to unregistered trade-marks, including:

---

[94] See *Federal Court Act*, R.S.C. 1985, c. F-7, s. 20, as amended. Notable cases which considered the jurisdictional split between the federal and provincial courts include: *MacDonald v. Vapor Canada Ltd.*, [1977] S.C.R. 134; *Asbjorn*, supra note 48; and *Lawther v. 424470 B.C. Ltd.* (1995), 60 C.P.R. (3d) 510 (F.C.T.D.). For a general overview, see Bell and Probert, "The Constitutionality of Canadian Trade Mark Law", cited above in note 59.

[95] See *Bi Rite Enterprises, Inc. v. Bruce Miner Company, Inc.*, 757 F.2d 444 (1st Cir. 1985) for a situation in which it was considered whether to uphold a foreign court's decision. In this case, various U.S. state laws were applied to uphold a preliminary British injunction, which prevented unauthorized distribution of posters which had infringed the U.S. right of publicity by bearing a person's likeness. British law was not applied in this case. By analogy, in certain situations, Canadian performers in the U.S. can be afforded the same protection of U.S. law. Of course, enforcement in the U.S. courts of U.S. rights owned by foreign entities would be completely appropriate at any time.

(1) using a registered trade-mark "in a manner that is likely to have the effect of depreciating the value of the goodwill" of the trade-mark;[96]

(2) "making a false or misleading statement tending to discredit the business, wares or services of a competitor";[97]

(3) directing "public attention to his wares, services, or business in such a way as to cause or be likely to cause confusion in Canada ...";[98]

(4) "passing off other wares or services as and for those ordered or requested";[99]

(5) making certain false statements which mislead the public as to certain aspects of the goods or services;[100] and,

(6) adopting, in connection with a business, a trade-mark which may be likely to be mistaken for any living individual.[101]

Although the language of the statute regarding the above is apparently quite broad, the constitutional validity of this legislation is likely to be limited to matters involving valid heads of federal jurisdiction, for example, trade-marks and copyrights. Nevertheless, they all should be considered when appropriate fact situations arise.

B. Passing off

Unregistered trade-marks are generally protected at common law at least in a limited geographic area by the law of passing off. Since many trade-marks which a musician may acquire are not registered, the action of passing off is relevant when considering the enforcement of unregistered trade-marks. Passing off was discussed in section 4(a)(iii) and will not be dealt with in detail here again; it is highlighted only in relation to unregistered trade-marks.

Unregistered trade-marks also may be protected under section 7(b) of the *Trade-marks Act* (see preceding section), which has been characterized as a statutory codification of common law passing off.[102] The applicability and constitutional validity of s. 7(b) in respect of unregistered trade-marks have been confirmed by the court.[103]

---

[96] The *Trade-marks Act*, s. 22(1).

[97] S. 7(a) of the *Trade-marks Act*.

[98] *Ibid.*, s. 7(b). See *Asbjorn* as cited in note 48.

[99] *Ibid.*, s. 7(c).

[100] *Ibid.*, s. 7(d). Note s. 7(e), the "unfair competition" section, has been found to be unconstitutional in *MacDonald*, cited above in note 94, and was confirmed as having no residual constitutionality even in respect to trade-marks. See *Bousquet v. Barmish Inc.* (1991), 37 C.P.R. (3d) 516 (F.C.T.D.), affirmed 150 N.R. 234 (F.C.A.).

[101] *Ibid.*, s. 9(1)(k). See *Baroness Spencer-Churchill v. Cohen* (1968), 55 C.P.R. 276.

[102] See *Asbjorn*, supra and the passage quoted in section 4(a)(iii) above in note 48.

[103] *Ibid.*

The distinction between a trade-mark infringement action and a passing off action is important. As discussed in section 4(a)(ii)E above, a person who has registered a trade-mark can rely on such registration in a trade-mark infringement action as evidence of the ownership of the trade-mark nationally throughout Canada; distinctiveness does not have to be proved. In a passing off action, it must be proved by the person bringing the action that such trade-mark, by virtue of its distinctiveness or reputation, has come to indicate to the public in a given territory that wares or services under the trade-mark originate from that person. A person's remedies for passing off will be limited to the geographic area in which he/she can prove he/she has such a reputation.

C. Criminal Offences

Generally, anyone who disobeys a federal statute may be guilty of an offence and may be liable to a fine and imprisonment.[104] The *Trade-marks Act* and the *Copyright Act* are federal statutes.

Some legislation directly contains offence provisions, some of which can be quite severe. The *Copyright Act* in particular includes some very severe sanctions for offences.

In addition, the Canadian *Criminal Code* contains specific sections relating to trade-marks. Under the *Criminal Code*, relevant offences include:

(1) forging trade-marks;[105]
(2) passing off or making false descriptions of products;[106]
(3) incomplete disclosure regarding sales of used, reconditioned or rebuilt goods;[107]
(4) possessing or disposing of instruments used in forging trade-marks;[108]
(5) defacing or concealing another person's trade-marks;[109] and
(6) as a trader, filling bottles having another person's trade-mark, with liquids for the purpose of sale.[110]

The various offences listed above will not be discussed in detail here. They are mentioned simply to alert the reader to the possibility

---

[104] *Criminal Code*, R.S.C. 1985, c. C-46, s. 126, as amended. See also Chapter 4, "Copyright Infringement", regarding criminal remedies under the *Copyright Act*, R.S.C. 1985, c. 42, as amended.

[105] Ss. 406-407 of the *Criminal Code* cited in note 104.

[106] *Ibid.*, s. 408.

[107] *Ibid.*, s. 411.

[108] *Ibid.*, s. 409.

[109] *Ibid.*, s. 410(a).

[110] *Ibid.*, s. 410(b).

that criminal charges might be laid in appropriate cases. There may be other relevant offences that should be assessed in specific fact situations.

The above offences are punishable on summary conviction or by way of indictment.[111] They may not be brought by private persons but only by the Crown by way of prosecution; however, in recent years, police have been increasingly co-operative with the public in considering criminal prosecution in respect of copyright or trade-mark issues.

D. *Customs Act*

It has been argued also that the *Customs Act* can be helpful in enforcing trade-mark rights. Generally, however, customs officials have been reluctant to act unless a complainant already had a judgement from a court in his/her favour. As it can take quite some time to obtain a judgement, in Canada it becomes almost impossible to have effective seizure remedies to prevent importation of infringing products. In the United States, customs seizure remedies are substantially more effective for the owner of any intellectual property.

(b) Personality Rights

A person's personality rights are common law rights enforceable by court action in a province, not in the Federal Court of Canada. Generally, such actions claim damages against the infringing party for appropriation of personality, passing off and trespass. These causes of action were discussed in section 6 above.

(c) Other Causes of Action

Other personal causes of action such as defamation or breach of confidence may be available, but are very fact-specific and are outside the scope of this chapter. In addition, legal remedies for copyright infringement were specifically covered in Chapter 4, "Copyright Infringement" and are not further discussed here.

---

[111] *Ibid.*, s. 412.

7. Specific Issues: Imitators

There have been a number of issues raised particularly in U.S. litigation involving "look-alike and sound-alike" performers and performances.[112] The issue presents itself most graphically in the context of so-called "clone" acts. A clone act is one that imitates an original group, usually a rock group that has attained international stature. Numerous issues are raised here, some of which have been discussed above, in the context of merchandising rights, including trade-mark infringement, passing off, copyright infringement, appropriation of personality, and possibly breaches of privacy statutes (depending on the jurisdiction). They include the following: (1) is it actionable under the *Trade-marks Act?*; (2) is it passing off or some type of actionable misrepresentation?; (3) is there copyright infringement involved?; (4) is it a misappropriation of personality at common law?; and (5) is it a breach of a privacy statute? The resolution of these issues will depend on the province where they took place.

The application of the law in this area is still developing and only tentative conclusions, in addition to the analysis set out above, can be offered at this stage.[113] The facts of each situation must be examined closely, as they will determine the rights and remedies which are available.

---

[112] In the U.S., notable cases include: *White v. Samsung Electronics,* 971 F.2d. 1395 (9th Cir. 1992), cert. denied 113 S. Ct. 2443 (1993), where the court held that Vanna White's right of publicity was infringed in an advertisement for Samsung VCRs featuring a robot dressed and posed like Ms. White as she generally appears in "The Wheel of Fortune"; *Waits v. Frito-Lay, Inc.,* 978 F. 2d 1093 (9th Cir. 1992), where Frito-Lay infringed the rights of Tom Waits by using a television advertisement having a background singer using Waits' distinctive singing and song style; *Allen v. National Video, Inc.* (1985), 226 U.S.P.D. 483 (S.D.N.Y.), where Woody Allen was successful in restraining a look-alike. See also *Allan v. Men's World Outlast, Inc.,* 670 F. Supp. 260 (S.D.N.Y. 1988); *Nurmi v. Peterson,* case 10 U.S.P.Q. 2d 1775 (C.D. Ca. 1989). Here the applicant was unsuccessful: "Vampira" against "Elvira". *Midler v. Ford Motor Co.,* 849 F. 2d 461 (9th Cir. 1988). See Robert M. Callagy and Mario Aieto, *Intellectual Property Issues in Advertising,* (Ottawa: CBA, 1990), at pp. 4-44 which discusses this case in detail. In Quebec, a motion for an interlocutory injunction relating to copyright and property rights in fictitious characters relating to Canadian impressionist Andre Phillip Gagnon was denied. See *Productions O.P., Inc. v. Groupe Morrow Inc.* (1988), 26 C.P.R. (3d) 223 (Que. S. Ct.).

[113] See *Estate of Elvis Presley v. Russen,* 513 F. Supp. 1339 (D.N.J. 1981), where the plaintiff obtained an injunction against the producer of "The Big El Show", a recreation of an Elvis concert by Larry Seth, an Elvis impersonator, on the grounds that the show infringed the estate's common law right of publicity. See also *Joplin Enterprises v. Allen,* 795 F. Supp. 349 (W.D. Wash. 1992), where the plaintiff unsuccessfully claimed infringement of its rights of publicity by the defendant's execution of a stage play about Janis Joplin. In the second act of the play, there was a recreation of a Janis Joplin concert. The defendant successfully relied on the statutory exemption in the *California Civil Code,* s. 990.

10

PERSONAL SERVICE CONTRACTS

Contributing Author: Ronald N. Hier, B.A., LL.B., LL.M.

1. Nature

(a) Generally

Many, if not all, contracts that musicians make in the course of their professional lives are personal service contracts.[1] Often, and particularly where the artist is a newcomer to the music business, they are made without meaningful negotiation and terms are dictated on a "take it or leave it" basis. Increasingly, these contracts have come under judicial scrutiny and some courts have not hesitated to overturn them. This chapter considers the essential characteristics of personal service contracts, the remedies available on breach, and the legal and equitable doctrines that apply where a musician or artist seeks relief from a contract that is manifestly unfair.

(b) Defined

A "personal service contract" can be defined as an agreement under which one party agrees to supply his or her own personal services to another. "Personal services" are those of a "special, unique and intellectual character"[2] or those which require the use of the contractor's personal skill.[3]

---

[1] For example, live performance, management, and recording contracts are all personal service contracts. Although publishing contracts are sometimes structured as "buy/sell" agreements, they may be structured as personal service contracts as well.

[2] Cheshire & Fifoot, *The Law of Contract*, 8th ed., (London: Butterworths, 1972), p. 220 as quoted in George D. Finlayson, "Personal Service Contracts", (1975), L.S.U.C. Special Lecture Series, p. 355. This formulation is often seen in the "boilerplate"of personal service contracts used in the entertainment industry.

[3] *Emerald Resources Ltd. v. Sterling Oil Properties Management Ltd.* (1969), 3 D.L.R. (3d) 630 (Alta. C.A.), at 647, affirmed (1970), 15 D.L.R. (3d) 256 (S.C.C.).

(c) Characteristics

An essential aspect of such contracts is that the contractor may not assign to a third party his or her contractual obligation to perform, although the benefit of his/her performance may be assigned if the contract so provides.[4] Moreover, although confidential, trust or fiduciary characteristics may be present in the relationship,[5] there is apparently no duty on the parties to disclose all relevant information prior to formation of the contract.[6]

2. Important Legal Doctrines Applicable

Many of the contracts entered into by musicians require that they provide their services for extended, even open-ended periods of time.[7] Often, services are to be provided on an exclusive basis and restrictive covenants are insisted upon. Artists have attempted to resist such contracts by appealing to a number of legal doctrines which, in appropriate circumstances, can render them unenforceable. These doctrines are considered briefly below.

---

[4] *Sullivan v. Gray*, [1942] 3 D.L.R. 269 (Ont. H.C.); see also *Tolhurst v. Associated Portland Cement Manufacture Ltd.* (1900), [1902] 2 K.B. 660 (Eng. C.A.), affirmed [1903] A.C. 414 (U.K. H.L.), with regard to assignment of the benefit; see also *Griffith v. Tower Publishing Company Limited*, [1897] 1 Ch. 21. The right to assign the benefit, however, may not be unlimited; see the *Holly Johnson* and *Stone Roses* cases discussed infra.

[5] These characteristics become relevant where the employee seeks specific relief. Courts are reluctant to grant specific performance if the effect thereof is to mar the relationship of "trust and confidence" necessary to support the employee/employer relationship; see, for example, *Page One Records Ltd. v. Britton* (1967), [1968] 1 W.L.R. 157 (Eng. Ch. Div.).

[6] *Gabriel v. Hamilton Tiger-Cat Football Club Ltd.* (1975), 8 O.R. (2d) 285 (Ont. H.C.), in which the court held that the principle of *uberrimae fidei* does not apply to personal service contracts.

[7] For example, it is not uncommon for recording agreements to provide for extensions of the term in the event that the artist fails to deliver "commercially acceptable masters" in the time frame stipulated by the agreement. Such agreements may also give the record company the right to demand that the artist record more than one album in any option period of the agreement, the right being exercisable within a stipulated time frame (the "notice period") after the recording of the first album. The election may be made after termination of the option period, but within the notice period, thus effectively extending the term of the agreement. For a discussion of these clauses, see Moses Avalon, *Confessions of a Record Producer*, (San Francisco: Miller Freeman Books, 1998), at pp. 186-93.

(a) Restraint of Trade and Public Policy

(i) Public Policy: A Discussion

On occasion and in limited circumstances, courts will strike down contracts on the basis of public policy.[8] This doctrine, which is intended to safeguard the public good, will be invoked where a contract offends the fundamental principles upon which society is based. One such principle is the notion that people should be at liberty to make free and unfettered use of their skills, knowledge, and talents.[9] The doctrine of restraint of trade has evolved to give form to this principle.

(ii) Restraint of Trade and Restrictive Covenants

A contract in restraint of trade is one in which a party, for a present advantage, agrees with another party to restrict his or her liberty in the future to carry on trade with persons not party to the contract.[10] Such contracts, although not illegal, are contrary to public policy, and are void if they fail to meet the test of reasonableness first enunciated in *Nordenfelt v. Maxim Nordenfelt Guns and Ammunition Co.*[11] This test looks to: (1) whether the restraint is reasonable in the interests of the parties; and (2) whether it is reasonable in the public interest. To be reasonable in the interest of the parties, the restraint must afford adequate protection to the covenantee; to be reasonable in the public

---

[8] Contracts susceptible to the doctrine include contracts to commit illegal acts, contracts that interfere with the administration of justice, contracts injurious to the state, contracts which encourage immorality, contracts affecting marriage and contracts in restraint of trade. For a discussion of the doctrine, see G.H.L. Fridman, *The Law of Contracts*, 3rd ed., (Toronto: Carswell, 1994), at pp. 370-415.

[9] Thus, it is often stated that no one should work under an agreement which is a contract of "slavery," see for example, *Horwood v. Millar's Timber & Trading Co. Ltd.*, [1917] 1 K.B. 305 (Eng. K.B.); see also *Lumley v. Wagner* (1852), 42 E.R. 687 (Eng. Ch. Div.).

[10] *Petrofina Ltd. v. Martin*, [1966] Ch. 146 (Eng. C.A.), at p. 180.

[11] *Nordenfelt v. Maxim Nordenfelt Guns & Ammunition Co.*, [1894] A.C. 535 (U.K. H.L.) at p. 565; see also *Herbert Morris Ltd. v. Saxelby*, [1916] 1 A.C. 688 (U.K. H.L.), at pp. 706-707. In *Tank Lining Corp. v. Dunlop Industries Ltd.* (1982), 40 O.R. (2d) 219, 140 D.L.R. (3d) 659 (Ont. C.A.), at 223 [O.R.] and 663 [D.L.R.], the court outlined a four stage inquiry: (1) is the covenant a restraint of trade?; (2) is the restraint against public policy and therefore void?; (3) can the restraint be justified as reasonable in the parties' interest?; and (4) is it justified with reference to the public? The onus of establishing (3) is on the covenantee; the onus of establishing (4) is on the covenantor. Detailed discussion of the doctrine of restraint of trade is beyond the scope of this text. For more, see M. J. Trebilcock, *The Common Law of Restraint of Trade*, (Toronto: Carswell, 1986).

interest it must not be injurious to the public.[12] In determining what is reasonable, the Supreme Court of Canada has opined that "...[L]ess latitude is allowed in the enforcement of restrictions as between employer and employee than as between vendor and purchaser of goodwill."[13] Contracts involving musicians fall into the first class, thereby attracting a high degree of scrutiny.

What, then, is an adequate level of protection for the covenantee? In employment cases, courts have looked to the employer's proprietary interests, reasoning that a covenant is acceptable if it protects such things as trade connections, methods or processes, but is unacceptable if its only purpose is to prevent competition.[14] Clearly, the re-recording restrictions found in virtually all recording contracts (which protect the company's proprietary interest in the recordings) are capable of providing adequate protection so long as the duration of the restriction is not undue.[15] Similarly, provisions in live performance contracts which require performers not to play in the same geographical area for a period of time subsequent to an engagement should prove unobjectionable if their duration is not unreasonable.[16] And agreements whereby artists agree to provide their services to record companies or music publishers on an exclusive basis are not, without more, voidable restraints of trade.[17] They may become so, however, when the terms of the restriction, considered in conjunction with the contract taken as a whole, are so onerous that the musician is effectively denied the opportunity to pursue his or her calling either during or after the agreement expires.[18]

---

[12] *Nordenfelt*, supra note 11, p. 565.

[13] *Maguire v. Northland Drug Co.*, [1935] S.C.R. 412 (S.C.C.) at p. 416.

[14] *J.G. Collins Insurance Agencies v. Elsley* (1978), 83 D.L.R. (3d) 1 (S.C.C.).

[15] Re-recording restrictions are covenants that prevent the artist from re-recording songs recorded pursuant to the contract for a stipulated period of time after termination of the agreement; for more on these clauses, see Jeffrey Brabec & Todd Brabec, *Music, Money and Success*, (New York: Schirmer Books, 1994), at p. 95, and Donald S. Passman, *All You Need To Know About the Music Business*, (New York: Simon & Schuster, 1998), at pp. 148-9.

[16] Such restrictions, like the promise to provide exclusive services often found in live performance contracts and recording and publishing agreements, can be justified on the basis that it is in the interest of both parties that the covenantor be so bound during the life of the contract. Such promises maximize the economic value of the artist's talent to both parties; for judicial recognition of this view, see *Leather Cloth Co. v. Lorsont* (1869), L.R. 9 Eq. 345, referred to in *Herbert Morris, Limited v. Saxelby*, [1916] 1 A.C. 688 (U.K. H.L.), at p. 701. Of course, the restraint must not be unreasonable.

[17] *William Robinson & Co. v. Heuer*, [1898] 2 Ch. 451.

[18] The attempt to argue that the covenantor obtained independent legal advice prior to signing the agreement has not found favour with the courts; see the *Holly Johnson* case, discussed infra.

(b) Unconscionability

The equitable doctrine of unconscionability permits rescission of a legally binding contract where the bargain is unreasonable or one of the parties has obtained an unfair advantage by the use of unconscionable means.[19] The effect of rescission is to restore the parties to their pre-contractual positions.[20] Because rescission is an equitable remedy, courts may refuse to exercise their discretion in favour of the plaintiff where it would be inequitable to do so.[21] The onus is on the party seeking to uphold the contract to prove that the bargain was fair, just and reasonable.[22]

(c) Inequality of Bargaining Power

In *Lloyd's Bank v. Bundy*,[23] Lord Denning provided a new, enlarged basis upon which unconscionable bargains could be set aside: inequality of bargaining power. Such inequality might arise in connection with a transaction, substantially unconscionable, where the bargaining power of one party "is grievously impaired by reason of his own needs or desires, or by his own ignorance or infirmity, coupled with undue influences or pressures brought to bear upon him for the benefit of the other",[24] and where the contract is made without independent legal advice.

Lord Denning's formulation has found favour with Canadian courts[25] which have pointed to the following factors deemed to

---

[19] Some commentators therefore distinguish between substantive and procedural unconscionability; see A.A. Leff, "Unconscionability and the Code — The Emperor's New Clause" (1967), 115 U. Pa. L. Rev. 485. Canadian courts have not always been willing to provide relief where only the latter is shown; see Fridman, supra note 8, at pp. 327-328 and the cases discussed therein. For a useful discussion in the Australian context, see Geoffrey Adelstein, "The Review of Harsh or Unfair Contracts" in *Music: The Business and the Law*, (Sydney: The Law Book Company Limited, 1986), chap. 12.

[20] Thus, in *LeSueur v. Morang & Co.* (1911), 45 S.C.R. 95 (S.C.C.), the court ordered the return of a manuscript where, contrary to its agreement, the publisher had refused to publish it in its entirety and notwithstanding that title had passed.

[21] Grounds for refusal include the plaintiff's laches, and his or her acquiescence or affirmation of the contract; see Fridman, supra, note 8 at pp. 817-819.

[22] Fridman, supra, note 8 at p. 327.

[23] [1974] 3 All E.R. 757 (Eng. C.A.). See, generally, M.J. Trebilcock, "The Doctrine of Inequality of Bargaining Power: Post-Benthamite Economics in the House of Lords" (1976), 26 Univ. of Toronto L.J. 359; S. M. Waddams, "Unconscionability in Contracts" (1976), 39 Mod. L.R. 369; and Richard A. Epstein, "Unconscionability: A Critical Reappraisal" (1975), 18 Journal of Law & Economics 293.

[24] *Ibid.*, at p. 765.

[25] See for example, *Harry v. Kreutziger* (1978), B.C.L.R. 166 (B.C. C.A.); *Moore v. Federal Business Development Bank* (1981), 30 Nfld. & P.E.I.R. 91 (P.E.I. S.C.).

constitute inequality of bargaining power: (1) ignorance, need, or distress of the weaker leaving him or her in the power of the stronger, coupled with proof of substantial unfairness in the bargain; (2) lack of independent legal advice;[26] (3) lack of business experience; (4) limited education; and (5) ignorance of the true effect of the transaction.

(d) Undue Influence

A second doctrine of equity, the doctrine of undue influence, permits rescission of a contract where it can be shown that one of the parties has used any form of oppression, coercion, compulsion or abuse of power or authority to obtain the consent of the other contracting party or otherwise 'victimize' him or her.[27] The onus of proof is on the party alleging lack of consent; however, where the parties stand in certain relationships, there arises a presumption of undue influence discharging the initial burden of proof.[28] These relationships include the relation of parent and child, principal and agent, doctor and patient, solicitor and client, and any relationship partaking of a confidential or fiduciary nature.[29]

Because what is at issue in cases of undue influence is the sufficiency of the plaintiff's consent, the issue of independent legal advice assumes particular importance. If the defendant can show that the plaintiff, having been advised by a lawyer, entered into the transaction with full knowledge and understanding of its terms, the court may refuse to grant a remedy.[30]

The doctrine of undue influence is often linked with the doctrine of unconscionability, and indeed, the two doctrines share a common foundation. The cases applying these doctrines (and the common law doctrine of restraint of trade) are discussed below.

---

[26] However, even the provision of independent legal advice may not prevent a court from rescinding a bargain which in other respects is unconscionable; see *Schroeder Music Publishing Co. v. Macauley*, discussed infra.

[27] Fridman, supra, note 8 at p. 320.

[28] Fridman, supra, note 8 at p. 321.

[29] Fridman, supra, note 8, at pp. 321-22.

30 Fridman, supra, note 8, at p. 321 and the cases cited at footnote 51 therein. However, the transaction also will not be set aside if the plaintiff had full knowledge notwithstanding the lack of independent legal advice.

(e) Specific Cases Involving Musicians

(i) Schroeder v. Macauley

In *Schroeder v. Macauley*,[31] the first of a line of English cases dealing with music industry contracts, the House of Lords set aside a standard form music publishing agreement made between a U.S.-controlled music publisher and a young and unknown English songwriter. Under the contract, the composer agreed to provide his exclusive services to the publisher for a period of five years with the proviso that if, during the term, the royalties and advances thereon exceeded a stipulated amount, the term would be extended automatically for a second period of five years. In addition, the composer assigned all copyright in his compositions to the publisher for the territory of the world, the publisher (but not the composer) had the right to terminate the contract upon written notice, and the publisher (but not the composer) could freely assign its rights under the agreement. While the contract provided for a small recoupable advance with further advances to be made upon recoupment of any prior advance, the publisher had no obligation to publish any of the composer's music.

In holding that the agreement was unenforceable because it was in restraint of trade, Lord Reid fastened on several features of the contract: (1) the composer could be tied for a period of ten years if the royalties in the first five years achieved a "very modest success"; (2) the publisher was not obliged to do anything with the musical compositions and could "put them in a drawer" subject only to payment of a very modest initial advance;[32] and (3) the composer could not terminate the agreement in the event the publisher chose not to publish the compositions.[33] In Lord Reid's view, the above provisions were

---

[31] *Schroeder Music Publishing Co. v. Macauley*, [1974] 3 All E.R. 616 (U.K. H.L.) For a discussion of this case and others, see I. E. Yanover and Harvey G. Kotler, Q.C., "Artist/Management Agreements and the English Music Trilogy: Another British Invasion?" in *Entertainment, Publishing and the Arts Handbook*, (New York: Clark, Boardman & Company Limited, 1989), at p. 181. For a useful overview of publishing and recording contracts, see Jane Tatt, "Music Publishing and Recording Contracts in Perspective", Vol. 9, Issue 5 (1987), E.I.P.R., 132; J. H. Woollcombe, "Fairness versus Certainty and Pop Goes The Music Contract" (1987), 7 E.I.P.R. 187. Note, however, that these articles antedate the *Holly Johnson, Stone Roses*, and *George Michael* cases discussed infra.

[32] Lord Reid chose not to read into the agreement an obligation on the part of the publisher to act in good faith, stating quite rightly at pp. 621-22 that an undertaking to use "best efforts" would be of little value to the composer in the absence of a right to terminate.

[33] The following provisions were held unobjectionable by the court: (1) the composer's obligation to provide his services exclusively to the publisher; and (2) the (standard) royalties payable with respect to piano copies, mechanical, synchronization

unjustifiable and one-sided, and offended against the precept that if contractual restrictions "appear to be unnecessary or to be reasonably capable of enforcement in an oppressive manner, then they must be justified before they can be enforced."[34]

Whilst the decision of Lord Reid was ultimately founded upon the axiom that "everyone should be free so far as practicable to earn a livelihood", Lord Diplock advanced a second reason for overturning the agreement. In his view, the contract was offensive because it resulted from an inequality of bargaining power which empowered the publisher to extract terms that were "unfairly onerous" to the songwriter. The doctrine of restraint of trade, he argued, was fundamentally concerned with the prevention of unconscionable bargains. It was the duty of the court to ensure that parties in a position of superior bargaining power do not use that power to drive unconscionable bargains.[35] Lord Diplock's analysis leaves open the questions whether the contract would have been enforced if it had emerged from give-and-take of negotiations, or if offered on a "take it or leave it basis" the composer had received more (a larger advance, for example) in return for his agreement.

(ii) Fleetwood Mac

In *Clifford Davis v. WEA Records*,[36] the former manager of the pop group Fleetwood Mac sought to enjoin the distribution in England of the group's album 'Heroes are Hard to Find', on the basis that his company owned the copyright in works recorded on the album pursuant to a publishing agreement between the company and two writer-members of the group. Robert Welch and Christine McVie had entered into standard form contracts, the terms of which were reminiscent of those in the *Schroeder* case discussed above. The agreements provided, *inter alia*, that the writers assign copyright throughout the world in all compositions written during the initial five

---

and performance rights. Lord Reid suggested that the composer's indemnity and the publisher's right to withhold royalties in the event of breach by the composer could be "oppressive", but these provisions do not figure in the reasons for judgment.

[34] *Schroeder Music Publishing Co. v. Macauley*, supra note 31 at p. 622. Interestingly, Lord Reid left open the possibility that the contract might have stood if the composer had a right of termination in the event of non-publication.

[35] *Ibid.*, at pp. 623-24. Lord Diplock's formulation was independent of, though reminiscent of Lord Denning's approach to unconscionability in *Lloyd's Bank v. Bundy* decided that same year. According to Lord Diplock, a fair bargain is one in which the restrictions are reasonably necessary for the protection of the covenantee and commensurate with the benefit to the covenantor.

[36] *Clifford Davis Management Ltd. v. W.E.A. Records Ltd.*, [1975] 1 All E.R. 237 (Eng. C.A.).

year term, which term could be extended for another five years at the option of the publisher; the publisher was not bound to publish any of the works, although in the case of Mrs. McVie, it undertook to use its best efforts to do so; the publisher had the right for six months to reject any work without payment; if it chose to accept it, its sole obligation was to pay one shilling per work accepted; and the publisher had a unilateral right of assignment.

In deciding for the appellants,[37] Lord Denning did not rely on the doctrine of restraint of trade, which he claimed did apply in such cases, but looked instead to the doctrine of inequality of bargaining power enunciated by him in *Lloyd's Bank v. Bundy.* He pointed to the following factors in support of his decision: (1) the terms of the contract were manifestly unfair — the composers were potentially tied for a period of ten years without a retaining fee and the publisher was not obliged to do anything other than use his best efforts to promote the compositions; (2) the copyrights were transferred for a grossly inadequate consideration; (3) the bargaining power of the composers was "gravely impaired" because the publisher was also manager of the group;[38] (4) undue influences were brought to bear,[39] and the composers had no access to independent legal advice. He further suggested that if the publisher wished to exact such onerous terms or so unconscionable a bargain, it should ensure that such advice was provided.

(iii) Gilbert O'Sullivan

In *O'Sullivan v. Management Agency,*[40] singer/songwriter Gilbert O'Sullivan succeeded in overturning publishing, recording, management and employment agreements made in consequence of his relationship with Gordon Mills, an internationally known manager and producer. The facts are as follows: O'Sullivan entered into a management agreement with Mills, who then arranged for O'Sullivan to enter into recording and publishing contracts with companies in

---

[37] Before the court was the refusal of a judge in chambers to discharge an interlocutory injunction obtained by the plaintiff.

[38] With respect thereto, Lord Denning claimed that the composers were in a position of dependency vis-à-vis their manager who was their "ladder to success", and further, they lacked negotiating skills and business acumen; see p. 240 of the judgment.

[39] Although no evidence was led on this point, Lord Denning was content to make the inference as the forms were cyclostyled, signed in the presence of the same witness, were drafted by lawyers and taken from the company's stock of forms.

[40] *O'Sullivan v. Management Agency,* [1985] 3 All E.R. 351 (Eng. C.A.).

which Mills was substantially interested.[41] Additionally, O'Sullivan signed a letter of inducement in support of an agreement between one of the Mills companies and an American record company, pursuant to which it obtained North American rights with respect to certain of O'Sullivan's recordings. All of the agreements were prepared by an associate of Mills and were signed by O'Sullivan without independent legal advice at a time when Mills was acting as his manager. As in the previous cases, O'Sullivan was a young man of limited business experience on the threshold of a career.

Several grounds of relief were advanced at trial and in the Court of Appeal. In the lower court, the trial judge upheld the plaintiff's claim that the contracts were in unreasonable restraint of trade and void because obtained by undue influence. The latter was presumed because of the special relationship between the parties.[42] The trial judge also found that the inducement letter had never created any contractual obligation binding on O'Sullivan.

The finding of restraint of trade was not contested in the Court of Appeal. Nor was it denied that Mills and O'Sullivan stood in a fiduciary relationship; indeed, the defendants accepted that the doctrine of undue influence applied on the facts.[43] Their only objection was that the companies operated by Mills should not be fixed with liability for Mills' actionable conduct. The court quickly disposed of this contention on the grounds that the companies were under Mills' de facto control, and that Mills and his associate were acting throughout in the course of their employment with the companies. In the result, the contracts were set aside and the copyrights and master tapes returned to the plaintiff.[44] The defendants were further required to account for their profits subject to an allowance for reasonable remuneration (including an element of profit)[45] and taxes paid by them and not reclaimable.

---

[41] O'Sullivan also entered into an employment agreement with a third company in the Mills group for the purpose of capturing his off-shore income; this company subsequently entered into a recording agreement with the recording company.

[42] The trial judge characterized Mills' position vis-à-vis O'Sullivan as one giving rise to a fiduciary relationship. Interestingly, O'Sullivan himself testified that no actual pressure had been exerted on him to sign the agreements; see p. 357 of the judgment.

[43] The defendants also accepted that: (1) there had been inequality of bargaining power; (2) Mills was under a duty, as manager, to advise on the agreements and to obtain independent advice; (3) that given such advice, O'Sullivan might have negotiated terms more favourable to himself; and (4) that the agreements were voidable; see p. 369 of the judgment.

[44] Excepted from the above were master recordings acquired by EMI and CBS pursuant to contracts with Mills' companies. These tapes and the rights to exploit them had been acquired for valuable consideration without knowledge of the defendants' behaviour.

[45] The allowance for the profit element was justified on the basis that under Mills' tutelage, O'Sullivan attained a level of success he failed to reach either before or after the period of their association.

What is perhaps most remarkable about this case is the court's willingness to set aside an agreement not manifestly oppressive, unfair or the result of actual overreaching. Once it was established that the presumption of undue influence had application, the court did not hesitate to overturn the agreement on the chance that if the plaintiff had had access to independent legal advice, he may have secured a (more) favourable agreement than the agreement he actually obtained.[46]

(iv) Elton John

In *John v. James*,[47] a case involving singer-songwriter Elton John and lyricist Bernie Taupin, the propriety of certain licensing arrangements made by their music publisher and John's record company were successfully called into question. A summary of the facts follows below.

In 1967, Elton John and Bernie Taupin entered a publishing contract with Dick James Music ("DJM"), a company controlled by Dick James, a prominent English music publisher.[48] In addition, John signed a recording contract with This Record Company, also owned by Dick James.[49] At the time they executed the agreements, John and Taupin were minors. Although their parents reviewed the contracts and signed an addendum to the effect that the agreements were for the benefit of their children, the contracts were never fully explained to John and Taupin, nor was independent legal advice obtained.[50] Shortly

---

[46] Underscoring the decision, perhaps, is the fact that O'Sullivan had originally requested a co-publishing arrangement with Mills and was under the impression that he had or was to obtain same. The court held that he had been deceived by Mills.

[47] [1991] F.S.R. 397 (Ch.); see also [1986] S.T.C. 352. (H.C.).

[48] The contract, which provided for assignment of the copyright for the full term thereof throughout the world, was for a term of three years. The term could be extended for a further three years at the option of either party and John and Taupin were contractually bound to deliver a minimum of eighteen songs, acceptable to DJM, in each of the two terms. The agreement further provided that each term could be extended until the minimum contractual requirement was met. If DJM rejected a song, John and Taupin were free to offer it to other publishers. A small recoupable advance was provided and there was a standard royalty. DJM could freely assign the benefit of the agreement.

[49] This agreement was for a term of five years and required John to record at least four seven inch sides per year. This Record Company ("TRC") had the right to select the material subject to John's consent. John's royalty was 20% of net monies received net of production costs. John was to record exclusively for TRC. There was a five year re-recording restriction. To exploit the master recordings, TRC had the right to grant licences to any firm or company in any part of the world.

[50] Tatt, supra note 31 at p. 134. This case is also discussed in detail in Deborah Brice's article "Artists' Contracts: Elton John Case" (1986), Vol. 4 I.M.L. 2.

thereafter, DJM became John's manager.[51] In 1970, the recording contract was replaced by a new agreement under which John received a larger royalty. In 1970, as well, the management agreement was rewritten; the commission was lowered and it was made clear that John's recording activities were to be excluded from the provisions of the agreement.

In the early 1970's, DJM set up a group of wholly-owned foreign subsidiaries which were intended to act as sub-publishers with respect to the DJM catalogue of songs. The agreements generally provided that the sub-publishers would retain a percentage of receipts greater than had been the case when the rights had been administered by independent third parties. As well, in early 1969 DJM terminated an agreement it had with Philips and caused TRC to enter into a pressing and distribution agreement with Pye Records. Subsequently, a third company, DJM Records, was incorporated as a wholly-owned subsidiary of TRC and interposed between TRC and Pye. The effect of this transaction was to reduce the royalties available to Elton John under his agreement with TRC.

In 1972, following the decision in the *Schroeder* case, Elton John obtained legal advice that the publishing contract was unobjectionable; however, it was suggested to him that in view of the arrangements between DJM and its subsidiaries, an audit should be carried out. His advisers then attempted to uncover the relevant contracts, but the matter was not pursued seriously. By February of 1975, all of the agreements had expired. Although John continued to press for an explanation, no steps of consequence were taken until the issue of a writ in 1982.

In his statement of claim, John alleged that the contracts had been obtained by reason of undue influence. He also argued that there was a breach of a fiduciary relationship arising out of the publishing and recording agreements. The remedies he sought were: (1) an account of profits; (2) the setting aside of the agreements; and (3) delivery up of master recordings. The court agreed with John that the contracts had been procured by the undue influence of Dick James and that they were unconscionable.[52] However, in view of John's delay in instituting

---

[51] This agreement, executed in 1968, was for a term of five years, and entitled DJM to a 30% commission on all John's income from any branch of the entertainment industry. The agreement included "best endeavours" language requiring DJM to use its best endeavours to further Elton John's career.

[52] The court objected to the following features of the publishing contract: (1) its potential duration; and (2) the lack of any provision for early termination or return of copyrights if successful publication was not achieved. The court was unwilling to imply an obligation on the publisher to use its best efforts and stated that even if such an obligation existed, it would afford the writers little protection; see pp. 450-452 of the judgment. With respect to the recording contract, the court noted that while a five year

proceedings, the benefits he obtained under the contracts, and the work done by DJM, the court neither set aside the agreements nor returned the copyrights. The court did find a breach of fiduciary duty when Dick James Music negotiated with its sub-publishers, holding that Dick James Music had an obligation to negotiate so that the writers' and publisher's interests would not conflict under the sub-publishing arrangement.[53]

The court also found a breach of fiduciary obligation under the recording contract and ordered an account of profits. An allowance was made for expenses and for the skill and labour of promoting the artists' publishing rights and recordings. The defendants were also permitted a fair profit element.[54]

The Elton John case has not been appealed, and although its precedential value has been questioned,[55] it is clear that this case is consistent with the applicable legal doctrines and does provide certain guidelines that are useful in negotiating and drafting recording and publishing agreements.

(v) Frankie Goes to Hollywood

In *Zang Tumb Tuum Records Ltd. and Another v. Johnson* (the "*Holly Johnson*" case)[56], standard form recording and publishing agreements again were called into question. In 1983 and 1984 Holly Johnson and members of his band 'Frankie Goes To Hollywood' entered into recording and publishing agreements with ZTT Records (the recording contract) and Perfect Songs Publishing Ltd. (the publishing contract). Both companies were owned and directed by Trevor Horn, a well-known record producer, and his wife, Jill Sinclair. Johnson had the benefit of expert legal advice and was represented by a professional

---

term might not be unreasonable, as it afforded the record company a chance to recoup an investment laden with risk, it failed to provide for an improvement in the royalty rate, if the artist proved successful.

[53] *Ibid.*, at p. 135.

[54] *Ibid.*, at p. 135.

[55] Yanover, supra note 31at p. 197.

[56] Independent Law Reports, 2 August 1989. (C.A.). For a discussion of this case, see J. Stephen Stone and Dorothy Graham, "Deals You Can Refuse", (1992-93), 3 M.C.L.R. 265 at pp. 281-84; S. Greenfield & G. Osborne, "Unconscionability and Contract: The Creeping Roots of Bundy", (1992), The Denning L.J. 65 at p. 70-71; Kevin Garnett, Case Comment, "The Holly Johnson Case", [1990] 5 E.I.P.R. 175 and in particular p. 176 for a discussion of the terms of the agreements; see also David Lester, Artists' Contracts, "Setting Contracts Aside: A Reappraisal" (1988), 7 I.M.L. 650; Chapter D, "Frankie Goes to Court" , *Entertainment, Advertising and Media Law*, (Toronto: L.S.U.C., 1989); and John Swan, "Frankie Goes to Court: Drafting Entertainment Contracts", *Ibid.*, at D-19, D-45 at pp. D-30-31.

manager at the time the contracts were signed.[57] Two albums were released and proved enormously successful. Johnson decided to leave the band and attempted to terminate the contracts. When Horn refused, he brought an action, alleging the agreements were unenforceable as being in unreasonable restraint of trade. The Court of Appeal agreed. The following facts appear to have swayed the court: Horn was an experienced and influential producer of popular records; the plaintiff and his band mates were "young men in fairly humble circumstances and of little business experience";[58] Horn took the position that he would not enter into a recording contract unless the band signed a publishing agreement with him as well; and the two companies were wholly-owned and controlled by Horn and his wife. In addition, the contract contained several clauses that were objectionable to the court: the band was bound to the two companies for a potential period of eight to nine years;[59] a leaving members' clause gave the companies the right to contract with the leaving member on the same terms and conditions as under the first agreement; and any new members were to be bound by the terms of the contract.[60] These provisions alone were sufficient for the court to declare that the "recording agreement as a whole is unenforceable because it is an unreasonable restraint of trade."[61]

The court also fastened on certain terms of the recording and publishing agreements that were a potential cause of concern, including the following: the recording agreement gave the record company the absolute discretion to release the group's recordings, to choose the producer and songs to be recorded, to determine if the songs so recorded were commercially acceptable masters, and to control the recording budget.[62] With regard to the publishing agreement, the court was concerned that Johnson, as a result of his worldwide assignment of copyright, could not perform any of his own songs without the publisher's consent. The existence of "best efforts" language in the publishing contract could not operate so as to save the agreement.

---

[57] Stohn, supra, note 56 at p. 281.

[58] Dillon, L.J., as quoted by Stohn, Ibid., at p. 282.

[59] The contract provided for an initial term of seven months, but the artists irrevocably granted to the companies options to extend the term for two successive option periods and five successive contract periods each of which were defined to be the greater of twelve months or 120 days after the delivery of the minimum recording commitment.

[60] This clause, however, was declared unenforceable due to uncertainty.

[61] Court of Appeal transcript, 26 July, 1989, at p. 12 as quoted by Greenfield and Osborne, supra, note 56 at p. 70.

[62] A potential conflict of interest arose from the fact that the record company was financially interested in the recording studio where the masters were to be recorded; see Stohn, supra, note 56 at p. 283.

Although the *Holly Johnson* case was decided solely with reference to the doctrine of restraint of trade, the court was mindful of, and alluded to, the principles laid down in *Schroeder v. Macauley*. In the words of Dillon, L.J., "... the terms of the recording agreement and publishing agreement put forward by the recording company and the publishing company, even after such concessions as were made during the negotiations, were so one-sided and unfair that consistently with the principles applied... [in *Schroeder*]... they cannot stand...".[63] This suggests that even in the absence of undue influence, simple inequality of bargaining power may suffice to upset a contract made with full knowledge of all material facts.

(vi) The Stone Roses

In *Silvertone Records v. Mountfield & Ors*, and *Zomba Music v. Mountfield & Ors*,[64] the band 'Stone Roses' successfully challenged recording and publishing agreements on the ground that they were unenforceable as an unreasonable restraint of trade. Like the *Holly Johnson* and earlier cases, the judgment combined elements drawn from both the law of restraint of trade and inequality of bargaining power. A summary of the facts follows below.

The Stone Roses entered into agreements with Zomba Music Publishing Ltd. and Zomba Records.[65] At the time, they were young, inexperienced and unsuccessful. Their manager, equally inexperienced, negotiated improved financial terms for the band but failed to question the royalty calculations and several other provisions of the agreement. Subsequent to the decision in the *Holly Johnson* case, the record company became concerned that the agreement might not stand due to the lack of substantial negotiation and instituted a second round of negotiations. It was agreed, *inter alia*, that the band should be provided with more money for promotional expenses and wages and a larger advance was paid to the group, but the contract's essential terms were left unchanged.[66] Although the manager had retained a lawyer to advise with respect to the negotiations, the Court found that he was not "an experienced music lawyer".[67]

---

[63] *Ibid.*, p. 3, as quoted by Greenfield and Osborne at p. 71.

[64] Unreported, (May 20, 1991), Doc. S-6909, (Q.B.).

[65] Zomba Records subsequently assigned its rights to Silvertone Records Ltd.

[66] These negotiations were regarded essentially as a sham by the record company and were undertaken simply to secure the appearance that the contracts were negotiated freely.

[67] Page 33 of the judgment quoted by Greenfield & Osborne, supra, note 56 at p. 72. As in the *Holly Johnson* case, both agreements were offered to the band as a package deal.

In finding for the band, the court objected to a number of provisions in both agreements. First, under the recording agreement, the band was tied to the companies for a minimum of seven years. An alternative calculation provided that the term would expire nine months after a U.S. release, but as there was no obligation on the company to secure a U.S. release, the contract was potentially of unlimited duration. Second, the record company was granted exclusive rights to exploit, reproduce, distribute and release the band's recordings in perpetuity if they chose to do so. Third, the band was prevented for a period of ten years from re-recording any of the works recorded for the company, and they were not allowed to perform the works if there was a possibility they could be recorded for the purpose of making and releasing records. Fourth, the agreement applied to 'the world and its solar system', a territory which hardly could be more extensive.[68] These provisions, when taken together, were sufficient to render the agreement an unreasonable restraint of trade.

Since the publishing agreement was tied to the recording agreement, the court ruled it had to fail as well. Humphries, J. did, however, examine the agreement and concluded that although it was negotiated fairly, it contained several clauses of an objectionable nature. These included an irrevocable right to an assignment of rights, the unfettered right to exploit the compositions, but only a limited obligation on the publisher to exploit the rights assigned. Although there was a reversion clause, there was no guarantee that the compositions actually would be published, yet for the term of the agreement, the compositions remained exclusively with the publisher. The court found that the initial term of this agreement was tied to the term of the recording agreement, which was indefinite.[69] The unfettered right of the publisher to make adaptations and arrangements was also found to be unreasonable.

Despite the fact that there was a severability clause in the publishing agreement, the court would not take it upon itself to rewrite the agreement and stated "it is not right that parties should make an unfair agreement then go to the court and get the court to produce a

---

[68] Humphries, J. as quoted by Greenfield and Osborne, supra, note 56 at p. 71. In addition, the court objected to provisions which gave the record company the right to authorize product endorsements without the band's consent, a unilateral right of termination and assignment, the right to withhold royalties and advances in the event of any breach no matter how trivial, the right to control all aspects of the recording process resulting in an "unfair deprivation... of any right of artistic control", and the right to demand the recording of an unlimited number of promotional and music videos. Also problematic were the royalty calculations (which were based on 90% of records sold), the lack of a limit on free goods, and a clause permitting the company to limit payment for merchandising rights to a maximum of fifteen hundred pounds.

[69] Page 36 of the judgment.

maximum contract which they would have been entitled to ask for".[70] Nor did the court, consistent with the *Holly Johnson* case, accede to the argument that estoppel or waiver were applicable on the facts. As a result, the recording and publishing contracts were found to be an "unfair, unjustified, and unjustifiable restraint of trade".[71]

(vii) George Michael

The most recent case to consider the validity of recording contracts in the context of restraint of trade is the *George Michael* case.[72] This case arose as a result of the entertainer's dissatisfaction with Sony Music, and the way it handled his career, following its take-over of CBS, Michael's former record company. To extricate himself from the relationship, Michael brought an action claiming that his recording contract was void and unenforceable as being in unreasonable restraint of trade. In 1994, the High Court ruled against him. A summary of the facts on which the judgment turned follows below.

In early 1982, George Michael and Andrew Ridgley, who performed together as 'Wham!', entered into a recording contract with Inner Vision. The following year, their first album, 'Fantastic', was released and rose to number one on the British pop charts. A dispute arose between the group and their record company, and in October of 1983, the band took legal action, claiming that their contract was in unreasonable restraint of trade. The action was settled and a second recording agreement (the '1984 Agreement') was entered into between CBS, which had distributed the album under licence from Inner Vision, and the members of 'Wham!'. The agreement called for the band to deliver, at no less than yearly intervals, eight albums at the option of CBS. Two very successful albums were released. In 1986, the band broke up, but pursuant to a leaving members clause the 1984 agreement continued to apply to Michael. In November of 1987, Michael's first solo album, 'Faith', was released and sold fifteen million copies worldwide. Michael sought to renegotiate the 1984 agreement, CBS agreed, and in January 1988, a new agreement (the '1988

---

[70] *Ibid.*, p. 37.

[71] *Ibid.*, p. 38.

[72] *Panayiotou v. Sony Music Entertainment (UK) Ltd.*, [1994] E.M.L.R. 229. This case is discussed in Alan Coulthard, "George Michael v Sony Music — A Challenge to Artistic Freedom?", (1995), 58 Mod. L. Rev. 731; Michael A. Smith, "Restraint of Trade in the Music Industry", [1994] 5 Ent. L.R. 182; and Theresa E. Van Beveren, "The Demise of the Long-term Personal Services Contract in the Music Industry: Artistic Freedom Against Company Profit", (1996), 3 U.C.L.A. Ent. L. Rev. 377.

Agreement')[73] was made, containing substantially improved terms, but it required Michael to deliver two additional albums. Unlike the 1984 Agreement, the agreement had a fixed term of fifteen years. In 1990, a further renegotiation designed to place Michael on par with Sony's American superstars took place,[74] and a second solo album was released. This album sold only five million copies and Michael became concerned about the manner in which he was being marketed and promoted by Sony. In early 1992, he received legal advice that he could seek to overturn the contracts, but shortly thereafter requested an advance of one million dollars. The advance was paid. In August of 1992, Michael repaid the advance and brought suit in October of that year.

Michael claimed that the 1988 Agreement was void for two reasons: (1) it was in unreasonable restraint of trade; and (2) it ran afoul of Article 85(2) of the Treaty of Rome.[75] With respect to (1), the court held that since the 1988 Agreement was a renegotiation of the 1984 Agreement, which itself was the compromise of an earlier action, it would be contrary to public policy for the court to permit Michael to argue restraint of trade; to do so would violate the policy that settlements, made bona fide on the advice of solicitors, should not be challenged.[76] The court also held that Michael had affirmed the 1988 contract by requesting the advance in 1992 at a time when he knew that the contract could be challenged[77], and it disposed of his Treaty of Rome claim.

However, the court did go on to consider whether the 1988 Agreement was in unreasonable restraint of trade. It applied the test enunciated in *Nordenfelt* after first ascertaining that the contract was in

---

[73] This agreement contained many of the terms standard in recording contracts. In particular, Sony owned the master recordings and the copyrights therein, Sony exercised control over the artist, Sony had the right to assign its rights under the contract, and Sony was under no positive duty to exploit the master recordings. However, if an album were not released in the U.K., Michael had the right to terminate the agreement and also could require the release in certain major territories though third party licensees in defined circumstances; see Smith, supra note 72 at p.184 and 186.

[74] Sony had taken over CBS in 1988.

[75] This article prohibits agreements between 'undertakings' which may affect trade between 'member states' and which have as their object or effect the "prevention, restriction or distortion of competition within the common market." The court's comments on this aspect of the case are beyond the scope of this book.

[76] It has been suggested that the court incorrectly applied the law in this regard; see Coulthard, supra note 72 at p. 736, who argues that the 1984 Agreement was not a compromise of a suit between Michael and CBS, but rather, part of a settlement between Michael and Inner Vision.

[77] It has been suggested by Coulthard, supra note 72 at pp. 741-743, that the court was in error and that "as a matter of law... no defence of affirmation or acquiescence should be available to a restraint of trade claim."

restraint of trade,[78] and then reviewed the terms of the agreement. The court held that as between the parties, the restrictions were justified and fair, in large part resting this conclusion on the fact that Michael would be amply compensated for the contractual restrictions he had agreed to endure.[79]

The George Michael case would appear to be of limited precedential value. The case was not decided on the basis of restraint of trade doctrine, and therefore the court's opinion on the fairness or justification of the terms imposed on George Michael is obiter. Moreover, George Michael was not the victim of rampant inequality of bargaining power. Rather, throughout the negotiations and commensurate with his growing success, Michael continued to receive large and increasing advances. Perhaps the most startling aspect of the decision was the court's willingness to accept Sony's argument that the fifteen year term was necessary and reasonable to protect Sony's investment in Michael, when such a term most likely exceeds what is commercially necessary with respect to an artist of Michael's stature.[80]

(f) Personal Service Agreements in the Music Industry: Drafting Guidelines

There are a number of drafting guidelines that can be extracted from the cases discussed above. These are set out below.

1. Agreements, including management, recording, publishing and merchandising contracts, to be enforceable, should be fair and reasonable in view of all the facts relative to such agreements.

2. The reasonableness of exclusive recording, publishing, merchandising and management contracts depends on all of the terms of such agreements. Terms should be no more restrictive than is reasonable to protect the parties' legitimate interests. Case law suggests that covenantees may not be able to rely on standard industry practice as a justification for onerous contractual terms.

3. The term of any agreement cannot be too long or indeterminate; if the term is too long, the agreement may be set aside. What is too long?

---

[78] Here, the court relied on the judgment of Lord Wilberforce in *Esso Petroleum Co. v. Harper's Garage (Stourport) Ltd.*, [1967] 1 All E.R. 699 (U.K. H.L.), in holding that "once it is satisfied that the contract... is (in ordinary parlance) in restraint of trade... [it is necessary]... to consider whether... sufficient grounds exist for excluding the contract from the application of the doctrine..."; see p. 327 of the judgment.

[79] The second branch of the *Nordenfelt* test was not argued by Michael and was not considered by the judge.

[80] See Coulthard, supra, note 72 at pp. 737 and 740-741.

In the *Schroeder* and *Davis* cases, a five-year publishing agreement with an option to extend for five years was too long. In the *Gilbert O'Sullivan* case, a five-year term coupled with a right to extend the term for a further two years was too long. In the *Elton John* case, a three-year publishing agreement, with an option to either party to extend for three more years, was too long. In the *Holly Johnson* case, seven options for a minimum of one year each, to be extended for 120 days to complete the minimum recording commitment (if not yet fulfilled), was too long. In the *Stone Roses* case, a term of seven years (or one tied to a non-guaranteed U.S. release), was both indefinite and, even if for seven years, too long.[81] Therefore there is great uncertainty as to what is a reasonable or unreasonable length of time. Prudence suggests that the shorter the term, the more likely it will be held to be a reasonable and justifiable restraint of trade.

4. In the absence of language requiring the publisher or record company to use its 'best endeavours' to exploit the recordings and copyrights, the courts likely will not imply such an obligation.[82] Even if the contract does address the issue, the agreement will be unenforceable if it is otherwise invalid.[83] However, a 'best endeavours' clause, coupled with a right to terminate in the event of non-exploitation, may save the agreement.[84] Therefore it is suggested that all agreements should contain a right of termination, exercisable in the event of failure to exploit the compositions, or obtain a release within a particular time frame or particular territory.

5. If a publisher has a contractual right to restrict the artist from performing songs that he or she wrote, by refusing to grant a mechanical licence, this may render the agreement unenforceable and in restraint of trade.[85]

6. Advances should be commensurate with success.[86]

7. Under any recording or production agreement, there should be an obligation to record and release the minimum recording commitment. Failure to release should obligate the company to re-assign the rights to the masters, subject to a royalty override where the company has paid

---

[81] Only the *George Michael* case accepted a term in excess of ten years as reasonable.

[82] *Schroeder Music Publishing Co. v. Macauley*, discussed supra.

[83] The *Holly Johnson* and *Fleetwood Mac* cases, discussed supra.

[84] In *Schroeder Music Publishing Co. v. Macauley*, Lord Reid suggested that the inclusion of a right of termination would give the contract 'a very different appearance' even in the absence of a positive obligation to exploit the compositions.

[85] The *Holly Johnson* case.

[86] L.S.U.C. supra, note 56, p. D-16, paragraph 4. See also the comments of Lord Denning in the *Fleetwood Mac* case.

for the recordings. Presumably, the release should occur in at least one major territory.[87]

8. Publishing contracts should provide for a right of reversion, exercisable if the compositions are not exploited within a reasonable period of time. In the *Holly Johnson* case, the court objected to a five-year publishing agreement, which contained both a reversion and a right to extend the term for a further period of three years, on the basis that the duration of the total term, prior to the reversion, was too long.

9. The fact that a musician does not bring an action as soon as he or she is advised that a contract may be unenforceable because it is in restraint of trade will not necessarily give rise to a successful defence of waiver or estoppel.[88] However, where the action is based on a claim of undue influence, delay on the part of the plaintiff may limit the remedies available.[89]

10. The artist should have some control over all aspects of the recording process, and particularly with respect to the recording and video budget and choice of producer.[90]

11. The leaving members clause is very much suspect and cannot be too onerous. It was suggested in obiter by the court in the *Holly Johnson* case that the standard leaving members clause alone would have resulted in the court finding that the record agreement was void as being in restraint of trade.

12. A severability clause will not serve to uphold an agreement which is in restraint of trade.[91]

13. The right to assign should be restricted.[92] According to the *Holly Johnson* case, it would appear that a requirement to consult with or give notice to the artist would not be sufficient to save the agreement; it may be that a right of approval is also required. If approval is not required, the agreement should provide for a limited right to assign to: (1) a major record company or major publisher, whichever is applicable in a given case; or (2) a company of standing in the industry or equal to that of the assignor; or (3) a successor company or a related company.

---

[87] *Ibid.*, p. D-15. Note that the courts have not dealt with this issue specifically.

[88] See the *Stone Roses* and *Holly Johnson* cases, but see the *George Michael* case where such an argument was accepted on the facts.

[89] See the *Elton John* case.

[90] The *Holly Johnson* and *Stone Roses* cases, discussed, supra.

[91] The *Stone Roses* case.

[92] An unfettered right to assign was looked upon with particular disfavour in the *Schroeder* case.

14. Agreements should be drafted explicitly and with as much certainly as possible.[93]

15. The term of a recording agreement is critical, but it must be read in conjunction with the minimum recording commitment. What should be the minimum recording commitment? In the *Holly Johnson* case, one 'single' in each of the first three contract periods was insufficient. Arguably, the industry standard would be acceptable, that is, one album of masters per contract period.

16. According to the *Holly Johnson* case, the recording budget should not exceed what is commercially reasonable, and the musicians should be consulted and preferably should approve all recording and video budgets.

17. There is a fiduciary obligation on managers which the courts will enforce when managers enter into publishing and recording agreements with their clients.[94] Because the law presumes such agreements to be the result of undue influence, managers should ensure that their clients receive competent independent legal advice.[95]

18. With respect to publishing agreements, it has been suggested that an initial royalty of 10% to 12% of the retail selling price for sheet music and 50% of net receipts for the exploitation of other rights would be acceptable for an unknown writer.[96] Nonetheless, royalty rates and the provision of advances should be reviewed as the songwriter or recording artist gains success.[97] A clause providing for a

---

[93] The court in *Holly Johnson* refused to enforce the leaving members clause, primarily on the ground of vagueness.

[94] The *Gilbert O'Sullivan* and *Elton John* cases, discussed supra.

[95] Following the *Stone Roses* case, it would appear that not only must the advice be independent, but it must be given by a lawyer competent to advise, i.e., one who specializes in music law and the negotiation of music industry contracts.

[96] These fairly standard terms were not objected to by Lord Reid in the *Schroeder* case. However, it is standard practice to enter into a co-publishing agreement whereby the songwriter/co-publisher is entitled to 75% of net receipts. See Chapter 3, "Music Publishing". According to Tatt, supra, note 31, at p. 136, "there is no reason why the company should continue to pay low royalty rates once it has recouped its investment in the artist and . . . it would not harm record companies to include an obligation to review royalty rates in all their contracts". In future, Tatt suggests "we may be seeing a licensing type of situation which is more common in the book publishing industry whereby the artist holds onto rights and licenses them to the respective publishers". There is no indication the music business will adapt such a model; see for example, the contracts at issue in the *George Michael* case.

[97] The insufficient consideration received by artists who tie themselves to long-term restrictive contracts has been the focus of judicial comment and is an underlying theme of all the music industry cases. Indeed, the only reported case lost by an artist is the *George Michael* case, one in which the judge was satisfied with the level of remuneration attained by the artist.

periodic review and renegotiation of these matters, or one requiring a royalty escalation based on the attainment of specified sales plateaux, may be sufficient to allay any judicial concerns regarding artist remuneration. In this regard, it is standard practice to grant co-publishing contracts whereby the co-publishing songwriter achieves 75% of net receipts.

19. Any independent legal advice required to be given must be dispensed by one who is competent to advise with respect to music industry contracts.[98] However, the provision of competent legal advice will not save an agreement that is otherwise objectionable.[99]

20. It has been suggested that an indemnity provision too widely drafted could be in unreasonable restraint of trade.[100] What is too wide? The courts have yet to say.

21. In the event of a publisher's failure to exploit the compositions under a publishing agreement, the composer should have the right to terminate. Likewise, the musician should have a right to terminate if the recording company fails to record or release recordings.

22. Record companies should not be given an unfettered right to edit masters, nor should music publishers have an unfettered right to alter compositions and lyrics.

23. Record companies and music publishers should not be given an unfettered discretion with respect to copyright infringement actions. In particular, the writer or artist should not have to remunerate the company for its legal costs if the company successfully defends an infringement claim, or at the very least, the artist should have the right to approve any settlement over a specified amount.[101]

24. Language which permits the withholding of royalties and advances in the event of any breach by the artist may be oppressive.[102] The same may apply with respect to a breach of a re-recording restriction.

25. If there is some reasonable limit on the restrictive provisions discussed above, they may be justified and the contract may be enforceable.

---

[98] The *Stone Roses* case, discussed supra.

[99] The *Holly Johnson* case, discussed supra.

[100] In the *Schroeder* case, Lord Reid opined that such a clause "could be rather oppressive".

[101] For more drafting guidelines, see Brabec & Brabec, supra, note 15 at pp. 25-26.

[102] In the *Schroeder* case, Lord Reid opined that such a clause "could be rather oppressive".

3. Remedies for Breach

The primary remedy accorded an innocent party for breach of contract is an action for damages.[103] However, in certain circumstances, an aggrieved party may be entitled to an injunction, specific performance, equitable damages, or rescission. However, because of their nature, not all of these remedies are equally available with respect to the breach of a personal service contract. The remedies typically obtained are discussed below.

(a) Between the Parties

(i) Damages

In the absence of a stipulation providing for injunctive relief, damages are the remedy most preferred by the courts,[104] and damages will be awarded if the plaintiff's loss is capable of calculation.[105] The usual measure of the loss is the cost of purchasing substitute services,[106] although in principle, if they can be demonstrated, lost profits should be recoverable.[107] Alternatively, if profits are speculative, the plaintiff may be entitled to recover expenses incurred prior to the breach.[108]

(ii) Specific Performance

Courts are reluctant to enforce specific performance of a personal service contract.[109] This tendency appears to be a "strong reluctance

---

[103] Non-contractual remedies are also available; these include actions in tort, restitution, and the quasi-contractual remedies of quantum meruit and quantum valebat.

[104] See, for example, *Capitol Records-EMI of Canada Ltd. v. Gosewich* (1977), 36 C.P.R. (2d) 36 (Ont. H.C.), wherein the court noted at p. 39 that "the very nature of a contract of services puts serious limitations on the right of an employer to claim an injunction". However, where the services are of a "special, unique or intellectual character", an injunction may lie; see the *Bette Davis* case, discussed infra.

[105] *Ibid*, at p. 39.

[106] S.M. Waddams, *The Law of Damages*, 2nd Ed., (Aurora: Canada Law Book Ltd., 1998), at para. 2.20; see for example, *Detroit Football Club v. Dublinski* (1957), 7 D.L.R. (2d) 9 (Ont. C.A.).

[107] *Ibid.*, para. 2-2. However, as Waddams points out, the plaintiff is under a duty to mitigate. This normally entails that he or she replace the defaulting party, something that is not possible where the contract requires the performance of services which are unique to the defendant.

[108] *Anglia Television Ltd. v. Reed* (1971), [1972] 1 Q.B. 60 (Eng. C.A.).

[109] This line of authority can be traced from *Lumley v. Wagner* (1852), 42 E.R. 687 (Eng. Ch. Div.), followed in many other cases, including *Warner Brothers Pictures Inc. v.*

rather than a rule".[110] Despite this fact, no court has yet ordered specific performance for breach of a personal service contract by a performer.

The courts are reluctant to order specific performance for a variety of reasons: (1) they doubt their ability to supervise the adequacy of performance; (2) a decree of specific performance would result in involuntary servitude and be tantamount to a form of slavery; and (3) where the employee sues, the courts are unwilling to impose on employers relationships that may require a high degree of trust and confidence, qualities which, as a result of the breach, may be lacking between the parties.

However, the courts have been willing to enforce by injunction a negative covenant, if such covenant is reasonably in the interest of the party seeking it, and the injunction does not amount indirectly to a decree of specific performance.

(iii) Injunction

Many of the exclusive personal service contracts made by entertainers and composers contain stipulations whereby the artist covenants not to provide his or her services to third parties during the currency of the agreement. The negative covenant may be accompanied by an acknowledgment that, due to the 'unique intellectual character' of the services provided and the difficulty of estimating damages, in the event of breach by the artist, an injunction is the appropriate remedy. Such language may serve as the basis for the granting of an injunction.

In *Warner Brothers Pictures Inc. v. Nelson*,[111] a case involving film actress Bette Davis, a negative stipulation of this kind was given effect by the English Court of King's Bench. As a result of a salary dispute, the actress had refused to perform under her exclusive film contract with Warner Brothers, had gone to England, and entered into a contract with a third party. The company brought suit in the English courts, claiming an injunction not to compel her to honour her contract, but to forbid her from working for another film company. After deciding that Bette Davis' contract was not in restraint of trade, the court

---

Nelson (1936), [1937] 1 K.B. 209 (Eng. K.B.) (the *Bette Davis* case); *Page One Records Ltd. v. Britton*, [1967] 3 All E.R. 822 (Eng. Ch. Div.); *Kapp v. British Columbia Lions Football Club* (1967), 61 W.W.R. 31 (B.C. S.C.); *Nili Holdings Ltd. v. Rose* (1981), 123 D.L.R. (3d) 454 (B.C. S.C.). See also the *Holly Johnson* case cited above in note 41 in this regard.

[110] *C.H. Giles & Co. v. Morris*, [1972] 1 W.L.R. 307 (Eng. Ch. Div.) at p. 318 per Megary J., as quoted in Sharpe, *Injunctions and Specific Performance*, (Aurora: Canada Law Book, 1998), at para. 7.540.

[111] (1936), [1937] 1 K.B. 209 (Eng. K.B.).

considered whether an injunction would lie. In ruling that it would, the court agreed that to grant the injunction, was not, in effect, to grant specific performance of her contract because Davis, who could make her living otherwise than in the film industry, would not be compelled to remain idle or return to work for Warner Bros.[112] The court also supported its decision by noting that there was uncontradicted evidence of the difficulty of ascertaining damages and further, that in cases of this kind, the injury suffered was often out of all proportion to any money damages that could be assessed by a jury.[113]

Although the decision in *Warner Bros.* was made without reference to the doctrine of restraint of trade, it has been suggested that the granting of an injunction should be subject to the reasonableness requirement enunciated in the restraint of trade cases.[114] This approach was taken in *Detroit Football Co. v. Dublinski*,[115] wherein McRuer, C.J.H.C., held that in determining whether a negative covenant should be enforced, the court must examine: (1) whether the restriction is no more than is reasonably necessary to protect the covenantee; (2) what interest it is designed to protect; and (3) what interest an injunction, if granted, would protect.[116] The court concluded that an injunction should not be granted where the only interest protected by the injunction was the plaintiff's interest in having the positive obligations of the defendant fulfilled.[117]

Because they are scrutinized carefully by the courts, negative covenants should be drafted carefully; the restrictions should be reasonable and no greater than are required to protect the legitimate

---

[112] See p. 216-217 of the judgment and the cases cited therein which provide the judicial underpinning for the proposition accepted by the court that an injunction to enforce a negative covenant will not be granted if its effect is specifically to enforce the contract or to decree that the defendant either remain idle or perform the positive covenants of the contract.

[113] *Ibid.*, at pp. 220-221. The court was also swayed by the language of the contract, which provided, *inter alia*, that a breach may "cost the producer great and irreparable injury and damage" not "reasonably or adequately compensated in damages".

[114] See Sharpe, supra note 110, at paras. 9.290 - 9.300. In the *Bette Davis* case, the court held that because the covenant was concerned with what was to happen during the contract term, there was no room for the application of the doctrine of restraint of trade. Sharpe has argued, on the authority of *Petrofina (U.K.) Ltd. v. Martin*, [1966] Ch. 146 (Eng. C.A.) that the doctrine should so apply.

[115] Supra, note 106.

[116] *Ibid.*, p. 754.

[117] *Ibid.*, pp. 767-768. Note that not all positive covenants are suspect; if the obligation is in substance negative, the court may grant an injunction; see Sharpe, supra, note 110 at paras. 9.80 - 9.90. For a case in which the court refused to enforce a restrictive covenant against a musician because the covenantee bar-owner had no legitimate interest therein, see *Stardust Enterprises Ltd. v. Berube* (1989), 25 C.P.R. (3d) 98 (N.B. Q.B.).

interests of the covenantee.[118] If the above criteria are satisfied, the court will issue a permanent injunction almost as a matter of course; however, if an interlocutory injunction is sought, the court will apply the ordinary rules governing the issuance of such injunctions.[119]

(iv) Specific Cases Involving Musicians

A. Individuals

The first case involving a musician (an opera singer) was *Lumley v. Wagner*.[120] Wagner contracted with Lumley to sing at a theatre in London, and agreed not to perform in any other theatre, concert, or reunion, either publicly or in private, without Lumley's written authorization. The contract was breached when Wagner contracted with another party to sing for more money. The court refused to grant specific performance of the contract, but did enforce the negative covenant by granting an injunction. *Lumley v. Wagner* has been applied in Canada in *Nili Holdings Ltd. v. Rose*.[121]

In *Nili Holdings Ltd. v. Rose*, the defendant Rose, a jazz singer, contracted under the standard AFM contract to sing at Stuart's Restaurant, in the City of Victoria, B.C., for three years. There was an implied term, not denied by the defendant, that she would not perform in any hotels, lounges or restaurants in Victoria while the contract was in force. After 18 months, she advised the plaintiff that she wished to terminate the agreement. The plaintiff agreed to release her, subject to the condition that she not perform anywhere in Victoria other than at the plaintiff's restaurant, theatres, schools or park concerts during the remainder of the original term. Rose signed a memorandum acknowledging this condition. She then left Victoria, travelled to Ontario, Alberta and Vancouver, but returned to Victoria and sang at the Royal Oak Inn in Victoria for two weeks until an interim injunction was granted, preventing her from so doing until the date of trial.

At trial, Rose called into question the validity of the contract. No consent had been secured by the AFM executive as was required by the AFM local's by-laws.[122]. However, at the time the contract was made,

---

[118] See, for example, *Bassman v. Deloitte, Haskins & Sells of Canada* (1984), 44 O.R. (2d) 329 (Ont. H.C.), in which the court refused to sever the offending part of a restrictive covenant because of the way in which it was drafted.

[119] Sharpe, supra note 110 at para. 9.40.

[120] Supra, note 109.

[121] (1981), 123 D.L.R. (3d) 454 (B.C. S.C.).

[122] The by-laws provided that no contract for the rendition of musical services for a period longer than one year should become effective without approval of the International Executive Board.

neither Rose nor the plaintiff was aware of the by-laws. The court stated that Rose as a member of the AFM had an obligation to bring the by-laws to the attention of the plaintiff.

Several months into the contract, Rose did become aware of the by-laws but did nothing about renegotiating the agreement, nor did she submit it to the executive board for approval. In the result, the court held that neither party was aware of or intended to be bound by the union clauses and further, that since Rose continued into the second year of the contract, she had waived her right to rely on the AFM by-laws.

The defendant also argued that the memorandum had been made subject to a collateral oral agreement which permitted her to perform in lounges in Victoria. However, the alleged oral agreement was in conflict with the written memorandum, and the court applied the parole evidence rule and refused to vary the memorandum.

Ultimately, the restrictive covenant was upheld because it was found to be reasonable as to time and location and it protected the plaintiff's proprietary rights and interests. These interests were held to include the defendant's reputation, which had developed while she was performing for the plaintiff, and which was an asset that would be lost to the plaintiff and gained by any other restaurant that might employ her. Rather than assessing the market value of this asset, the court preferred to grant an injunction.

The court also considered the effect of an injunction on the public interest, holding that the public interest was not unduly injured since the only persons affected were a relatively small group of jazz listeners and not the community of Victoria taken as a whole. Moreover, Rose was an accomplished singer who intended to perform throughout Canada so that if the community were taken to be British Columbia or even all of Canada, the public would not be unduly affected if the covenant were enforced. In the result, the court granted judgment to the plaintiff, but directed that the injunction terminate as of the date of judgment lest it work too great a hardship on the defendant.

B. Groups

The leading case is *Page One Records v. Britton*.[123] In this case, the managers of the Troggs, a rock group popular in the late 1960's for their hit "Wild Thing", sought to obtain an interlocutory injunction to restrain the group from engaging a third party as their manager in breach of a management agreement they had made previously with the plaintiffs. That agreement was world-wide in scope and for a term of

---

[123] *Page One Records Ltd. v. Britton*, [1967] 3 All E.R. 822 (Eng. Ch. Div.).

five years. It contained a covenant that the band would not "engage any other person, firm or corporation to act as managers or agents"; the Troggs also undertook that they would not "act themselves in that capacity".

The court refused to grant an injunction for two reasons: (1) the totality of the obligations under the management agreement created obligations of trust and confidence which could not be enforced at the suit of the defendants, and this lack of mutuality precluded enforcement by the plaintiffs; and (2) taking judicial notice of the fact that rock groups need management to succeed, the court held that to enforce the negative covenant would be tantamount to ordering specific performance of a personal service contract. Finally, the court held that it was undesirable to put pressure on the band to employ as their manager a person in whom they had lost confidence, particularly where the manager was to act in a fiduciary capacity.[124]

(b) Third Parties

In addition to the covenantor, third parties may be liable when a personal service contract is breached. For example, if a third party induces a musician or performer to breach his or her contract by offering a contract on more favourable terms, this may result in an action for damages for inducing breach of contract.[125] Other actions, such as interference with contractual relations or conspiracy to injure in the course of business, should also be considered in appropriate situations.

---

[124] In *Denmark Productions Ltd. v. Boscobel Productions Ltd.* (1968), [1969] 1 Q.B. 699 (Eng. C.A.) discussed infra, Wynn, L.J. at p. 729 expressly adopted the views of the court in the *Troggs* case that the relationship of artist and manager requires a high degree of mutual confidence and went on to state at p. 734 that should a manager's actions cause that confidence to be lost, the artist is entitled to terminate the contract, but cf. the opinion of Salmon, L.J. at pp. 725-726.

[125] The seminal case is *Lumley v. Gye* (1853), 22 El. & Bl. 216, 118 E.R. 749 (Eng. Q.B.). Inducement to breach of contract is discussed in David F. Partlett, "From Victorian Opera to Rock and Rap: Inducement to Breach of Contract in the Music Industry", (1992), 66 Tulane L.R. 771. The elements of the tort are set out in *Posluns v. Toronto Stock Exchange and Gardiner* (1965), 53 D.L.R. (2d) 193 (Ont. C.A.) at 207, affirmed (1968), 67 D.L.R. (2d) 165 (S.C.C.), as follows: (1) a valid contract; (2) the defendant's actual or assumed awareness of the contract; (3) a breach procured by the defendant; (4) the breach was effected by the defendant's wrongful interference; and (5) damage suffered by the plaintiff.

4. Minors

It is common for performers in the music business to be minors. This is significant because under the law of contracts, certain contracts made by minors may not be binding. [126] The applicable rules are described briefly below.[127]

(a) Beneficial Test

Contracts made by minors may be placed in one of three classes: (1) enforceable contracts; (2) voidable contracts; and (3) void contracts. Enforceable contracts include contracts for necessaries, contracts of service, and contracts for the benefit of the minor. Essentially, a contract for the personal services of a minor will be binding if the contract as a whole is for the minor's benefit and it is in no way derogatory to his or her position.[128] The onus is on the person seeking to enforce the contract to establish that it was for the benefit of the minor.

What is beneficial? Here the courts have diverged. In *Toronto Marlboro Major Junior "A" Hockey Club v. Tonelli*,[129] the Ontario Court of Appeal refused to take the narrow view that "benefit" meant "pecuniary benefit", but stated that the economic aspects, even if of paramount

---

[126] Even though the word "infant" is used in older cases and articles, the word "minor" will be used herein because it is the current legal term. For a general review of the law concerning minors' contracts, see Chapter 10, "Minors' Contracts" in the *Ontario Law Reform Commission's Report on Amendment of the Law of Contracts*, (Toronto: Ministry of the Attorney General, 1987), pp. 177-214.

[127] Formerly governed by the common law, the determination of when minority ends and adulthood begins is controlled now by provincial statutes. See for example the *Age of Majority and Accountability Act*, R.S.O. 1990, c. A.7 which declares 18 to be the age of majority in Ontario; see also the *Age of Majority Act* for the following provinces: Alberta (R.S.A. 1980, c. A-4); Manitoba (C.C.S.M. c. A.7); P.E.I. (R.S.P.E.I. 1988, c. A-8); and Saskatchewan (R.S.S. 1978, c. A-6); and the *Quebec Civil Code*, Art. 153. The following provinces and territories have defined the age of majority as 19: British Columbia (R.S.B.C. 1996, c. 7); Newfoundland (S.N. 1995, c. A-4.2); New Brunswick (R.S.N.B. 1973, c. A-4); Northwest Territories (R.S.N.W.T. 1988, c. A-2); Nova Scotia (R.S.N.S. 1989, c. 4); and the Yukon (R.S.Y. 1986, c. 2). See articles 155-66, 1409, 1416, 1418, 1422, and 1423 of the *Quebec Civil Code*, with regard to a minor's capacity to contract in Quebec.

[128] Fridman, supra note 8 at p. 144.

[129] (1979), 96 D.L.R. (3d) 135 (Ont. C.A.) Here, the plaintiff sought to enforce a contract it entered with Tonelli at a time when he was 17 years old. The contract was for a three year period which term could be extended one year, and it further required Tonelli to pay 20% of his gross earnings to the plaintiff for the first three years of his professional career. Tonelli was given a minimal salary, and his room, board, medical and dental expenses and school tuition were paid by the team.

importance, should be counterbalanced by other factors.[130]   In the opinion of the majority, Tonelli's contract, taken as a whole, was one-sided and onerous, made between two parties in an unequal bargaining position and without the occurrence of any real negotiation. Tonelli was economically disadvantaged and the term of the contract exceeded what was needed to advance his hockey career. Being a minor's contract, the court chose to give it a special scrutiny and overturned it on the basis that the interests of the plaintiff were advanced at the expense of the defendant.

In *Chaplin v. Leslie Frewin (Publishers) Ltd.*,[131] the son of Charlie Chaplin, while a minor, contracted to write an autobiography, and later changed his mind when he learned that the book would contain material that was embarrassing and possibly libellous. A majority of the English Court of Appeal held that Chaplin's contract was beneficial given that money was to be paid and notwithstanding that publication of the book might affect his reputation detrimentally. In dissent, Lord Denning stated that discreditable conduct should not be exploited for money no matter how much the minor was paid.[132] The majority opinion was based on the premise that the publishing contract fell within the exception for contracts binding on minors because they enable them to earn a living and so are for their benefit.[133]

(b) Contract of Service

Many of the music industry contracts made by minors can be regarded as binding contracts of service. Such agreements include recording contracts,[134] management or agency contracts, and live performance or publishing contracts.[135] More problematic are licensing or distribution agreements which may, depending on their provisions, be considered trading contracts and hence not binding.[136]

---

[130] *Ibid.*, p. 151. Interestingly, the other factors were considered in the light of Lord Diplock's judgment in *Schroeder v. Macauley*.

[131] [1965] 3 All E.R. 764 (Eng. C.A.).

[132] Per Lord Denning M.R., cited in David R. Percy, "The Present Law of Infants Contracts" (1975), Vol. 53 Canadian Bar Review 1 at p. 10.

[133] *Ibid.*, p. 773.

[134] But cf. *A & M Records Inc. v. Joan Armatrading* (Dec. 8, 1978),(Unreported), in which an English Deputy High Court judge held that a recording contract was a contract to sell the product of the artist's labour and industry. This case is discussed in Harold Burnett, "Entertainment Contracts Injunctive Relief", (1985), 3 I.M.L. No. 2, p. 112 at p. 113; Burnett argues that it was wrongly decided.

[135] See *Chaplin v. Leslie Frewin (Publishers) Ltd.*, supra note 131, wherein the court held that a publishing contract was a valid contract of service.

[136] See Fridman, supra note 8 at p.143.

It may not always be easy to assess whether a contract is a binding contract of service or an unenforceable trading contract. The facts of each case and the specific wording of the agreement in question are relevant to this determination.

(c) Void and Voidable

Contracts that are not binding fall into two categories: (1) those which are voidable; and (2) those which are void. Voidable contracts include contracts which are valid unless repudiated, and those which are invalid unless ratified.[137] The former include contracts concerning land, shares, partnership agreements and marriage settlements. The latter include all other contracts made by a minor (other than contracts for necessaries or personal service and contracts which are void). Void contracts include those which are clearly prejudicial to the best interests of the minor.[138]

The distinction between a contract that is binding unless repudiated and a contract that is not binding unless ratified is uncertain and not always followed by the courts.[139] This uncertainty must be borne in mind when dealing with contracts involving minors. Another problem is that minors cannot be sued for fraudulent misrepresentation of their age. Moreover, minors may plead their minority in an action to enforce the contract notwithstanding their misrepresentation.[140]

(d) Other Relevant Issues

When dealing with minors, the practice is to have the minor's parent or guardian sign an agreement to secure the obligations of the minor under his or her contract. The agreement may take the form of a guarantee or indemnity. Some courts have held, however, that a

---

[137] Note that pursuant to the Statute of Frauds, if the contract is ratified during the minor's majority, no action may be brought upon the ratification unless it is made in writing by the minor or his or her duly authorized agent; R.S.O. 1990, c. S.19, s. 7.

[138] Fridman, supra, note 8 at pp. 150-51. Fridman states that there is some controversy as to whether there is such a category and suggests that if there is, it should be restricted to the class of contracts described in the text. Excluded therefrom are contracts simply lacking in any benefit to the minor.

[139] Percy, supra, note 132 at p. 15. See, for example, *Gretzky v. Ontario Minor Hockey Assn.* (1975), 64 D.L.R. (3d) 467 (Ont. H.C.), wherein a contract for services was held to be voidable because of Wayne Gretzky's age even though it was for his benefit.

[140] Fridman, supra note 8 at p. 155. However, Fridman also points out that in equity, a minor who engages in fraudulent misrepresentation may not be able to enforce the contract.

guarantee is not enforceable if the debt guaranteed arises in connection with a minor's contract that is void or voidable.[141] On the other hand, the courts have been willing to enforce indemnities given with respect to contracts held to be void.[142] Because of the technicalities of the law regarding the distinction between guarantees and indemnities, great care should be taken when drafting an agreement.[143]

Occasionally, a management agreement will provide for the execution of a power of attorney. Although minors cannot execute a valid power of attorney, they will be bound by a contract made by their agent on their authority if they themselves would have been bound had they made the contract in question.[144] Accordingly, powers of attorney should be removed from minors' contracts. However, minors can appoint an agent validly where they cannot earn their living without so doing.[145]

(e) The Kinks Case

There are few reported cases specifically involving the validity of minors' contracts in the music business. One such case involved the Kinks.[146] The Kinks contracted during their minority with Boscobel Productions Ltd., which was to act as their manager. This company subsequently appointed a second company, Denmark Productions Ltd., to act as co-manager. When Boscobel refused to comply with the obligations imposed on them under their contract with Denmark, the latter company sued. The defendants denied liability, *inter alia*, on the ground that since their contract with the Kinks was voidable, they were not bound under their contract with the plaintiff. The trial court held that since it was necessary for the Kinks to obtain the services of a manager in order to pursue their career successfully, the original management contract was analogous to a contract of service and therefore binding upon the group for its benefit.[147]

---

[141] See Fridman, supra note 8 at p. 156 and the cases cited therein.

[142] *Yeoman Credit Ltd. v. Latter*, [1961] 2 All E.R. 294 (Eng. C.A.).

[143] At least one province has provided a way through the morass. The *Infants Act*, R.S.B.C. 1996, c. 223, s. 23 makes the guarantor of a minor's contracts liable as if the minor was an adult at the time the contract was made.

[144] *Chitty on Contracts*, 27th ed., (London: Sweet & Maxwell), Vol. 1, p. 459.

[145] *Ibid.*, p. 459. This follows from the *Kinks* case, discussed infra.

[146] *Denmark Productions Ltd. v. Boscobel Productions Ltd.*, (Unreported). See case note, (1967), 111 S.J. 715 for a discussion of the trial judge's ruling.

[147] This finding of the trial judge, not appealed, was tacitly accepted by the Court of Appeal; see (1968), [1969] 1 Q.B. 699 (Eng. C.A.) at pp. 722 and 736. Note that in reversing the trial decision in favour of the plaintiff, the Court of Appeal applied the doctrine of unilateral repudiation, holding that because the plaintiff was engaged under its contract with the defendant to render personal services to the Kinks, the plaintiff

5. Note on Conflict of Laws

Contracts involving musicians are often national or international in scope. They may be formed in one jurisdiction and performed in another. Therefore there is a need for the contracting parties to consider the proper law of contract that is to apply to such transactions. The following is a brief discussion of some of the issues that may be relevant in such situations.

(a) Canada

Although the law of contract is uniform across the common law provinces, contracts made in the province of Quebec will be governed by civil law,[148] unless stipulated to the contrary. Moreover, as we have seen, the age of majority varies across the country, so that in certain cases it may be necessary to stipulate which provincial law is to apply in order to render a contract enforceable beyond question. Certainty can be achieved by designating the governing law and choosing the forum that will adjudicate in the event of a dispute.[149]

Where the contract is silent as to the choice of governing law, the courts will try either to infer what the parties would have intended, or if this is impossible, make a determination based on the system of law with which the transaction is connected most closely. Relevant factors include the place the contract was made, the place it is to be performed, the residence or place of business of the parties, and the subject matter of the contract.[150]

Assuming that the choice of law is not made simply to avoid the application of a particular local law, in which case it will be disregarded,

---

could not elect to keep the contract alive after the defendant's repudiation. This has been criticized and there has been a suggestion that subsequent cases have questioned the doctrine; see Harold Burnett, "Entertainment Contracts: 2 Injunctive Relief", (1986), 4 I.M.L., No. 2, p. 12 at pp. 12-13.

[148] In some circumstances this may prove advantageous. For example, pursuant to article 155 of the *Civil Code*, a minor who is older than fourteen is deemed to be of full age with respect to all acts pertaining to his or her employment or the practice of his or her craft or profession; contracts made with such persons are therefore enforceable.

[149] The validity of the parties' choice is recognized by the doctrine of "the proper law of contract". The doctrine, as formulated by Dicey and Morris, states that the proper law of contract is the system of law by which the parties intend the contract to be governed or if no clear intention is manifest, the system of law with which the transaction has the closest and most real connection; see *Dicey and Morris on the Conflict of Laws*, 11th Ed., (London: Stevens & Sons Ltd., 1987), Vol. 1 at p.1161-1162. The judicial forum, although not part of "the proper law of contract", can be specified also.

[150] J.G. Castel, *Canadian Conflict of Laws*, 4th Ed., (Toronto: Butterworths, 1997), at pp. 600-601.

the parties generally are free to choose the law that will govern.[151] The parties also can agree that different provisions of the contract will be governed by different laws, although most issues will be governed by the proper law.[152]

Finally, if the contract or one of its terms is invalid or void under the law of one of two systems of law that can apply, the courts may presume that the parties intended that the contract should be governed by the system of law under which the contract or the term is valid.[153]

(b) United States

Many Canadian artists contract with record companies based in the United States, particularly in the state of California. That state has enacted two laws which endeavour to protect recording artists who have signed long-term exclusive recording contracts. Section 3423 of the *California Civil Code* provides that a person may seek injunctive relief for a breach of a personal service contract "where the promised service is of a special, unique, unusual, extraordinary or intellectual character" if and only if he or she contractually guarantees certain minimum payments to the artist and actually makes the payments prior to seeking the injunction.[154] The second provision is section 2855 of the *California*

---

[151] Castel, supra note 150, at pp. 593-595. Other limitations require that the choice be "bona fide and legal" and that there be no reason for avoiding the choice on grounds of public policy. As well, courts may refuse to apply the law of a province unconnected with the transaction.

[152] *Ibid.*, p. 607.

[153] *Ibid.*, p. 598.

[154] Specifically, an injunction will not be granted unless the contract provides for the payment at a minimum of $9,000 in the first year of the contract, $12,000 in the second year, and $15,000 per annum in years three through six. After the third year, the record company actually must pay $15,000 per annum for the fourth and fifth year and $30,000 per annum before an injunction will be granted. The amounts are cumulative and may be paid any time prior to seeking an injunction: s. 3423(e)(2)(A)(i) and (ii). If the aggregate compensation received does not satisfy the above criteria, at least ten times that amount must be paid as a condition precedent to the granting of an injunction: s. 3423(e)(2)(B). For a detailed description of the provisions, see William I. Hochberg, "A Guide to the "9,000 Plus" Law: California's Statutory Insurance Policy Against Artists Defecting from Record Companies", *1995-96 Entertainment, Publishing and the Arts Handbook,* (New York: Clark, Boardman, Callaghan), p. 325. Articles that deal with pre-1994 law include Jeffrey B. Light, "The California Injunction Statute and the Music Industry: What Price Injunctive Relief?" (1982), Vol. 7 No. 2 *Art and the Law* 141; Tannenbaum "Enforcement of Personal Service Contracts in the Entertainment Industry" (1954), 42 Cal. L. Rev. 18, for an early review of personal services law, and note "Statutory Minimum Compensation and the Granting of Injunctive Relief to Enforce Personal Service Contracts in the Entertainment Industries: The Need for Legislative Reform" (1979), 52 Cal. L. Rev. 489, 491; "Enforcement of Negative Covenants in

Labor Code which provides that a contract for personal services may not be enforced beyond seven years from the date of commencement of service.[155] These laws may raise significant conflict of laws issues if a Canadian artist signs with a record company based in California. Often, the record company will seek to include choice of law and choice of forum clauses for jurisdictions outside of California (usually New York or Tennessee if it has offices in those states) to escape liability under these sections. However, if challenged, a California court may decide that the ouster of California law is contrary to public policy and California law may still apply.[156]

On the other hand, there are situations where it may be advantageous for a particular state law to apply. Both California and New York regulate talent agents.[157] These laws are important because U.S. courts have permitted artists to overturn contracts made with managers who, under the statutes, were acting as unlicensed talent agents.[158]

Consequently, Canadian musicians and their advisors should be familiar with and give careful consideration to the applicability of U.S. state law in situations where its application or non-application may prove advantageous or harmful to their interests.

Contracts with Performers of Distinction in their Field" (1985), 7 Whittier L. Rev. 1059; Mark Conrad and Wolf and Wilheim, "Giving Entertainers a Licence to Breach Their Contracts" (1987), 17 Golden Gate L. Rev. 1089.

[155] For a discussion of this section, see Gary A. Greenberg, " 'Seven Years to Life' : the Fight for Free Agency in the Record Business", *1995-96 Entertainment, Publishing and the Arts Handbook*, (New York: Clark, Boardman, Callaghan), p. 337. Also noteworthy is *California Labor Code* s. 3351.5 which provides that a person engaged to create specially commissioned work who agrees in his or her contract that the work is a "work[s] for hire" as defined in the U.S. copyright law is an "employee" for purposes of the Code. In Joseph B. Anderson, "The Work for Hire Doctrine and California Recording Contracts: A Recipe for Disaster", (1995), 17 Hastings Comm/Ent L.J. 587, the author argues that the effect of this definition and the terms of a typical recording contract are such as to render virtually all California record companies in breach of their obligations to pay unemployment insurance and worker's compensation premiums as well as minimum wages to their artists, thus making it possible for their artists to overturn these contracts, obtain the return of their recordings and sue, *inter alia*, for lost wages.

[156] *Boole v. Union Design*, 52 Cal. App. 207, 198 P. 416 (1921).

[157] *California Labor Code*, ss. 1700-1700.47; *New York General Business Law*, Article 11, para. 171.2.8. California exempts persons who attempt to obtain recording contracts and New York, while not excluding them, provides an exemption for persons who manage artists and who incidentally procure phonograph recordings. For a further discussion of these laws, see Chapter 6. California law also provides special rules with regard to contracts made between minors and talent agents. Thus, section 1700.36 of the *California Labor Code* provides that a minor cannot disaffirm a contract entered into with an employment agency if made on a blank form approved by the Labor Commissioner and the contract has been approved by the superior court of the county in which the minor resides.

[158] For more on this point, see Chapter 6, "Agents and Managers".

11
BUSINESS

Contributing Author: Ronald N. Hier, B.A., LL.B., LL.M.

1. Business Entities

(a) Types of Business Entities

There are three basic forms of business entity: (1) the sole proprietorship; (2) the partnership; and (3) the corporation. Most musicians carry on business in one of these forms.[1] The major characteristics of these entities are outlined below.

(b) Main Legal Characteristics

(i) Sole Proprietorship

A sole proprietorship is the simplest form of business entity. It occurs where an individual carries on a business personally. The business has no separate legal existence; all of its assets and liabilities belong to the proprietor and any profits or losses sustained by the business are taxed in the hands of its owner. Personal assets are not insulated from liability and are available to satisfy the debts of the

---

[1] Other forms include: (1) joint ventures; (2) limited partnerships; (3) franchise and licence arrangements; (4) non-profit corporations and associations. A joint venture is typically a single transaction or adventure in the nature of trade carried on by two or more parties. This form is used occasionally by record or publishing companies to carry on business in foreign territories. Limited partnerships are sometimes used to raise money for recordings, or to finance a musical group as is discussed below in sections 7(b)(ii)B and 7(c)(iii). A franchise or licence arrangement may be entered into to merchandise a group's name or record label. Non-profit organizations operate mainly in the field of classical music, where the possibility of profit is even less than in "pop" music. For a useful general reference on business entities and related tax and corporate issues, consult Gary S. Rossiter, *Business Legal Adviser*, (Toronto: Richard De Boo, 1991), 9th Supplement.

proprietorship. The sole proprietor cannot be employed by the sole proprietorship, but can employ others.

(ii) Partnership

A partnership exists where two or more persons carry on business in common with a view to profit. Partnerships can arise by express agreement or can be implied by law under the provincial statutes that regulate partnerships.[2] Musicians sometimes call this relationship a "co-op arrangement" not realizing that, in law, there can be a partnership where musicians, in the absence of any written agreement, form a group and carry on business in common.

Like the sole proprietorship, the partnership has no independent legal existence. Although profits and losses are calculated at the partnership level, each partner files his or her own tax return and no tax return is filed by the partnership. Partners are jointly and severally liable for all of the partnership's debts and they are at risk to the extent that they have personal assets available to satisfy such debts. Each partner is a trustee and agent of the other partners and the partnership assets.[3] Partners' obligations towards third parties are also shared jointly, unless the parties specify in writing to the contrary.[4] Finally, in the absence of a written agreement to the contrary, all partners are entitled to an equal share of partnership profits. The musical group partnership agreement is discussed in detail below.

(iii) Corporation

The corporation is the most sophisticated form of business entity. A separate entity in law, it has all the legal rights of a natural person[5] and exists in perpetuity. Profits (and losses) remain the property of the corporation and shareholders have no claim on profits until such time as dividends are declared or the corporation is wound up. Corporations are taxed independently of their shareholders. Perhaps the most important feature of the corporate form is the advantage of limited liability it confers on shareholders.[6] By reason of this feature, and

---

[2] See, for example, s. 2 of the *Partnerships Act*, R.S.O. 1990, c. P.5.

[3] A partnership is based on the principle of *uberrimae fidei* which means that partners must act in the utmost good faith towards each other; see ss. 6-19, 28-30 of the *Partnerships Act*, supra note 2.

[4] See s. 59 of the *Partnerships Act*, supra note 2.

[5] See for example, Ontario *Business Corporations Act*, R.S.O. 1990, c. B.16, s. 15. (hereafter "OBCA").

[6] OBCA s. 92.

subject to certain exceptions,[7] shareholders are not answerable for the debts and liabilities of the corporation and their personal assets remain free of any risk arising out of the corporation's business activities.

2. Factors in Choosing a Business Entity

(a) Generally

Numerous factors affect the determination of appropriate business entity. These factors are of two types: tax factors and business factors. Among the latter are: (1) the amount of debt incurred by the business and any corresponding need to obtain limited liability; (2) the costs associated with the various forms of organization; and (3) the ease of administration. Tax factors include: (1) the existence of profits or losses at a given stage of the musician or band's career which may affect his/her or their personal tax liabilities; (2) the musician's marginal tax rate and the possibility that a tax plan making use of a particular form of business organization can minimize the musician's tax burden; and (3) the possibility of using the tax rules to create a tax-minimizing estate plan.

In general, the most appropriate entity is the entity which provides the greatest flexibility in current and future business planning as well as the largest range of tax options. Most musicians carry on business as sole proprietors, or as members of a partnership. This is more often due to inadvertence than any conscious planning. However, such entities are often perfectly satisfactory, given that most musicians do not earn large sums of money, face little risk of incurring uninsurable liabilities, and have a recurring need to minimize costs.

(b) Need to Limit Liability

(i) Generally

Limited liability is one of the main reasons to incorporate, particularly where there is a real possibility of uninsurable risks. However, many of the risks arising in the music business are insurable.

---

[7] Exceptions are found in OBCA ss. 34(5), 108(5), and 243. These sections are respectively concerned with the improper reduction of stated capital, the receipt of corporate property on dissolution, both of which may prejudice creditors of the corporations, and the assumption of directorial powers under shareholder agreements which will expose shareholders to the liabilities faced by the directors of the corporation.

For example, a band can purchase liability insurance to cover the risk of certain lawsuits.[8] Other risks are uninsurable; these include the substantial financial risks involved in the acquisition of musical equipment, the production of demos, master recordings and videos. The music business is highly competitive and there is often a minimal chance of recouping these costs. In theory, to the extent that these costs are financed by outside sources, musician-borrowers may be able to shield themselves by structuring the loan so that the debtor is a corporation they control. However, in reality, a lender would not likely advance funds without first obtaining the musician's personal guarantee. Therefore, generally, unless there is some overriding factor, for the vast majority of musicians, the corporate form offers no particular advantages, at least with respect to the limiting of liability or the management of risk.

(ii) Corporate Aspects

The directors of a corporation are not completely isolated from liability. Liability may arise under corporate law or a host of statutes that seek to control the activities of corporations by fixing liability on directors for certain acts or omissions of the corporation. With respect to the former, directors will be liable if they engage in any of the following transactions: (1) the improper issuance of shares; (2) the improper authorization of financial assistance; (3) the improper purchase, acquisition, or redemption of shares; (4) the improper payment of commissions; (5) the improper payment of dividends; or (6) the making of an improper payment to shareholders.[9] Both directors and officers are liable to account to the corporation for any profits made in contravention of the statutory conflict of interest rules.[10]

With respect to the latter, directors may be liable, *inter alia*, for unpaid taxes[11], source deductions,[12] and arrears of contributions under

---

[8] For example, bands have been sued with respect to injuries sustained by spectators at live performances; see Chapter 7. Liability insurance can protect against these claims.

[9] See generally, OBCA s. 130; other grounds of liability under the OBCA include the provision of financial assistance to directors or shareholders while the corporation is insolvent (s. 20); the redemption of shares while the corporation is insolvent (s. 32); the declaration of dividends while the corporation is insolvent (s. 38); and the consenting to authorize the issuance of dividends for non-cash consideration (s. 130). Directors are also liable for unpaid wages (s. 131). Finally, directors must comply with all provisions of the Act and have a duty to act honestly and in good faith with a view to the best interests of the corporation (para. 134(1)(a)).

[10] OBCA s. 132.

[11] See for example, s. 323 of the *Excise Tax Act*, with respect to the collection of GST.

workers' compensation statutes. Pursuant to subsection 102(2) of the *Bankruptcy and Insolvency Act*, directors are absolutely liable if dividends are paid while the corporation is insolvent. Directors also may be liable under employment standards legislation; under occupational health and safety laws; under human rights codes; with respect to employee pension plans; and if they are insiders, under provincial securities laws and regulations.

Generally, the only liability a shareholder ordinarily incurs is to pay the stipulated consideration for the purchase of shares.[13]

(c) Persons Involved

(i) Number

Most musicians carry on business as individuals or as members of groups. Most groups have four or five members. Because the risk of incurring liability as a partner in a musical group is proportional to the size of the group, the risk can be reduced by utilization of the corporate form.

(ii) Formal Structure

Corporations are governed by complex statutory rules which govern the formation, organization, financial structure, ongoing operation and dissolution of the corporation. Changes cannot be effected simply; they generally require meetings of shareholders and approval of the board of directors. There is a requirement to provide timely information with respect to corporate changes under both the relevant corporations and corporate information statutes. All of the above entail legal and administrative costs. Partnerships are not subject to so extensive a set of rules. Consequently, it is often desirable to structure the relationship between members of a band as a partnership. In this way, the band can take advantage of the flexibility and economy that a partnership agreement provides.

---

[12] These include the source deductions and withholding taxes described in s. 227.1 of the *Income Tax Act*; s. 54(1) of the *Employment Insurance Act*; and s. 21.1 of the Canada Pension Plan.

[13] For exceptions, see footnote 7, supra.

(iii) Active or Passive Participation

Will musicians involved in the business have an active or a passive role? If their role is essentially passive they can be hired as employees. If the corporate form is chosen, employee/musicians can be given the opportunity to share in the growth and profits of the business without giving them any management rights.[14] If the musicians all wish to participate in the group's affairs, a partnership agreement or unanimous shareholders' agreement can address this issue.

Some groups are financed by passive investors ("silent partners") who will not be involved in the day-to-day management of the band's business affairs and who may wish to limit their exposure in the event of failure. In such cases, a limited partnership or corporation may be the appropriate entity.

(iv) Citizenship, Residence

The international character of the music business may affect the choice of business entity.

Often, British, American, or other non-Canadians carry on business with Canadian musicians. If the business is organized in corporate form, and if it is the intention of the band that all members serve on the board of directors, this will not be possible unless a majority of the band members/directors are "resident Canadians".[15]

The composition of the band could also have relevance under the *Investment Canada Act*,[16] which provides, *inter alia*, that investments by non-Canadians to establish a new Canadian business, or acquire control of a Canadian business, are subject to the notification requirements of the Act.[17] A "Canadian business" is defined as a business carried on in Canada that has a place of business in Canada, that has individuals who are employed or self-employed in connection with the business, and has assets in Canada used in the business.[18] Therefore, a band in a start-up position will be establishing a new Canadian business, which is

---

[14] Employees may share in profits by way of bonus, increased salary or the granting of stock options, for example.

[15] Subsection 118(3) OBCA. "Resident Canadians" are Canadian citizens or Canadian permanent residents ordinarily resident in Canada.

[16] R.S.C. 1985, c. 28 (1st Supp.), as amended (hereinafter the "ICA"). "Non-Canadian" is defined by reference to the definition of "Canadian" and would include persons who are neither Canadian citizens nor certain permanent residents ordinarily resident in Canada; see s. 3 of the Act.

[17] Section 11, ICA.

[18] *Ibid.*, s 3. A "business" is defined as any undertaking or enterprise capable of generating revenue and carried on in anticipation of profit.

subject to the Act, if the band is not a Canadian-controlled entity.[19] In this regard, partnerships are treated somewhat more favourably than corporations in that a corporation equally owned by two persons, at least one of whom is a non-Canadian, is deemed not to be a "Canadian-controlled entity".[20] No such rule applies to partnerships.

Where a majority of voting interests are owned by non-Canadians, or the group is controlled in fact by non-Canadians, the notification provisions of the Act will apply and the band will be subject to possible review by the Director of Investments.[21]

---

[19] Pursuant to ICA para. 26(1)(a), an entity is a "Canadian-controlled entity" where one Canadian owns (or two or more members of a voting group who are Canadians own) a majority of voting interests of the entity. Under para. 26(1)(b), if para. (a) does not apply, (i.e., no voting group of Canadians has a majority) and one non-Canadian or two or more non-Canadian members of a voting group have a majority, the entity is not a "Canadian-controlled entity". If neither (a) nor (b) applies, the Act looks to whether or not there is a voting group that controls the entity in fact, and if a majority of the voting interests of such a group are owned by non-Canadians, then the entity is deemed to be non-Canadian. If a majority of the voting interests are owned by non-Canadians, the entity is presumed to be non-Canadian unless there is control in fact by a Canadian or a voting group in which a majority of the voting interests are held by Canadians — see paras. 26(1)(c) and (d). Under these rules, a partnership equally owned by Canadians and non-Canadians will qualify as a "Canadian-controlled entity". If the entity is a corporation or limited partnership, it will also qualify as "Canadian-controlled" if the entity is not controlled in fact through the ownership of its voting interests, and if two-thirds of the members of its board of directors, or in the case of a limited partnership, two-thirds of its general partners, are Canadians. See also s. 26(2.1) for an exception to the above rules with respect to businesses related to Canada's cultural heritage.

[20] Subsection 26(6) ICA.

[21] The ICA sets out a system of notification and review which allows the federal government to prevent a proposed investment if it determines that the investment is not of net benefit to Canada. Relevant factors are enumerated in s. 20. Under the scheme, investors are required to notify the Director of Investments, who must then issue a certificate stating that the investment is not reviewable or will not be reviewable unless the investor receives a notice of review within a stated period of time; see ss. 11-13. The acquisition of control of a Canadian business is also reviewable if the value of the investment is over five million dollars; see s. 14. The thresholds increase for World Trade Organization investors. However, the acquisition of a "cultural business" is subject to the lower threshold; see s. 14.1 and specifically para. 14.1(5)(d). "Cultural business" includes, inter alia, the publication, distribution or sale of books, films, video recordings, audio or video music recordings, music in print or machine- readable form, radio communication, cable television, satellite programming and broadcast network services. Additionally, if the investment is for less than five million dollars but falls within a prescribed type of business activity related to Canada's cultural heritage or national identity, it is reviewable under s. 15. SOR/85-611 defines the publication, distribution or sale of books, films, video products, audio or video music recordings, music in print or machine-readable form as prescribed business activities; see s. 8 thereof and Schedule IV. For more information on the *Investment Canada Act*, see James M. Spence and Gabor J. G. Takach, *A Guide to the Investment Canada Act*, (Toronto: Butterworths, 1986).

(d) Financial

(i) Borrowing

The individual sole proprietor and members of a partnership are personally liable for monies borrowed in connection with their business activities. Shareholders of a borrowing corporation are not; liability rests with the corporation. Cognizant of this fact, banks and other lending institutions in most circumstances require personal guarantees from shareholders. This is particularly the case where the corporation is small or does not have a credit record, especially where the borrowers are musicians. Lending institutions tend to be conservative and lack understanding of the types of collateral, such as copyrights, available to musicians.[22]

Sometimes, it is possible for a musician to raise money through the sale of securities. Although securities may be sold by sole proprietors, partnerships or corporations, the corporate form lends itself to this type of financing and has greater flexibility than the partnership or sole proprietorship.

(ii) Ongoing Costs and Maintenance

Generally, the more sophisticated the business entity, the greater the costs. Ongoing costs include:

(1) government filing fees, which are typically greater for corporations than for partnerships or sole proprietorships;

(2) legal and accountancy fees, which also tend to be greater for corporations than for partnerships or sole proprietorships;

(3) the cost of amendments: while partners can make changes by simply re-writing the partnership agreement, in some cases, shareholders may need to amend the corporation's by-laws or articles of incorporation;[23] and

---

[22] This is one reason the Sound Recording Development Program and the Cultural Industries Development Fund, discussed below, have been created: specifically to assist the production of sound recordings. For a U.S. article on the use of copyright as collateral, see J. Kane Ditto, "Musical Copyright as Collateral in Secured Transactions" (1971), 19 ASCAP Symposium 219. This article was written prior to the 1976 *Copyright Act* and is somewhat dated, but still of interest.

[23] In most cases, however, shareholders will be able to effect changes through amendments to a unanimous shareholders' agreement.

(4) taxes. While all business profits are subject to the income tax, corporations are also subject to a tax on capital. Moreover, unlike partnerships and sole proprietorships, corporations are required to file their own tax returns.

(iii) Insurance

The cost of insuring a partnership can be less than the cost of incorporating and maintaining a corporation. Consequently, incorporation generally only makes sense where the business generates substantial income, is subject to substantial risk, or tax savings can be achieved by routing business income through a corporation.

(iv) Fluctuating Income

Due to the unpredictable nature of earnings in the music business, many musicians have incomes that fluctuate widely from year to year. Because the income tax is progressive, musicians who become successful may face a larger tax burden than individuals who earn the same total income, but whose income is constant from year to year. In recognition of this problem, the *Income Tax Act* formerly allowed musicians to average their income, thus reducing the effect of annual fluctuations in earnings. With the demise of income-averaging, one method of obtaining a similar result is to route the income through a corporation.[24] Where the corporation has a lower rate of tax than the musician's average rate, the corporation can, in theory, pay a non-fluctuating combination of salary and dividends, thus minimizing the effect of large fluctuations in the musician's income.

---

[24] Corporations are taxed at a flat rate. Therefore, to the extent that the corporation attains a sufficiently low rate of tax, savings may be realized. A sufficiently low rate is necessary because the gains accruing from the flat rate must be set against the tax that would have been paid had the musicians received the income directly. In the lean years, the combined effect of musicians' personal deductions and marginal rate may have resulted in less tax than would have been paid had the corporation received their pre-success income. These amounts must be recovered then in the fat years.

(e) Tax

(i) General Comments

Because of the variance in the taxation of business entities, tax is often an important factor in determining the choice of entity. However, it is not the only one. Business realities and the need to maintain flexibility should not be obscured by hypothetical tax advantages. Nonetheless, one should be mindful of the basic tax treatment afforded each form of entity.

A. Sole Proprietors and Partnerships

As noted above, the income and losses arising from the operation of a partnership or sole proprietorship belong to the partners or sole proprietor.[25] In any taxation year, this income is aggregated with income from all other sources, and losses are deductible therefrom. Sole proprietors and partners are taxed at the personal rates in effect in each taxation year. The amount of tax payable ultimately depends on the level of income attained.

Many groups operate in a loss position and most of them rarely last more than several years. In fact, it is common for many groups to disband within their first year of operation. Where it is anticipated that such losses will exist, it is often advisable to delay incorporation, so that the losses will be freely available to the members in the event the group disbands.[26] Similarly, where the band's income is low, it may be subject to a rate of tax in the hands of its members that is lower than the rate that would apply if the income had been earned by a corporation.[27]

---

[25] Sole proprietorships differ from partnerships in that partnership profits (and losses) are determined at the partnership level. Once determined, they are allocated to the partners who then bring them into income in the same manner as sole proprietors.

[26] If the band incorporates at the outset, such losses will be the property of the corporation and unavailable to the band. Moreover, if the corporation is wound up, any loss arising from the disposition of the members' shares is not treated as favourably as if the loss had been incurred directly by the band.

[27] This will depend on whether or not the corporation can access the small business deduction. If it can, there may be tax savings available with respect to undistributed corporate income.

B. Corporations

Where there is significant income, there are two main advantages available to the corporation: (1) the advantage of a potentially lower rate of tax; and (2) the advantage of deferral.[28] The low rate results from the small business deduction which may be claimed by Canadian-controlled private corporations. The deduction (which is actually a credit) permits a corporation to reduce the tax burden on the first $200,000 of active business income earned in Canada in each taxation year.[29] Corporations which can avail themselves of the deduction can achieve a rate approximately equal to 23%.[30] This low rate provides a powerful incentive for incorporation. As noted below, however, the *Income Tax Act* limits the circumstances in which the deduction will be made available to personal service corporations.

Corporations are also useful vehicles for income-splitting. In particular, the attribution rule contained in section 74.4 of the *Income Tax Act* does not apply with respect to the transfer of property to a "small business corporation" which carries on an active business primarily in Canada. Consequently, incorporation may offer the possibility of diverting income to a spouse or children whose marginal rate is lower than that of the musician.

(ii) Personal Service Corporations

Many athletes and entertainers have sought to take advantage of the small business deduction by incorporating and providing their services to third parties indirectly through their corporations.

This abuse has been eliminated by the enactment of detailed rules which deny the small business deduction to income earned by a "personal service business".[31] Generally, a "personal service business" is a business carried on by a corporation where: (1) an incorporated employee who performs services on behalf of the corporation or any person related to him or her owns at least 10% of any class of shares of the corporation; (2) the incorporated employee would be reasonably regarded as an officer or employee of the person or partnership to

---

[28] David I. Matheson, "The Star's Vehicle: Corporate and Tax Considerations" in *Supporting the Star (or the Prospect?)*, (Toronto: Canadian Bar Association—Ontario and Continuing Legal Education, 1978), at p. 6. This article is dated but still of some interest.

[29] See s. 125(1) of the *Income Tax Act* which provides for a deduction from the tax otherwise payable of an amount equal to 16% of net active business income in respect of businesses carried on in Canada in the taxation year.

[30] The actual rate will vary depending on provincial corporate tax rates.

[31] See ITA s. 125(7). A "personal service business" is excluded from the definition of "active business". Hence, no deduction is available.

whom the services were provided; and (3) the corporation employs less than six full-time employees.[32] Pursuant to these rules, musicians who cannot be reasonably regarded as 'officers' or 'employees' of the entity for which they are performing can avail themselves of the deduction.[33]

In determining its net income, a personal service corporation may deduct only: (1) an incorporated employee's remuneration for the year; (2) the cost of any benefit or allowance provided to the employee; (3) certain amounts expended in the year in connection with the negotiating of contracts or the sale of property; and (4) legal expenses paid to collect amounts owing for services rendered.[34] Despite these limitations, there will be circumstances in which the tax savings are greater than the disallowed expenses, and for some musicians, personal service corporations will prove an attractive way to minimize tax.

(iii) Family Members

In addition to splitting income in the manner described above, a taxpayer can shift income to family members by employing them in the business. However, care must be taken to ensure that any salary paid is reasonable lest Revenue Canada deny the deduction.[35]

(f) Other Factors

There are numerous other factors to be considered in choosing a business entity. These include: (1) the usefulness of the chosen entity in relation to the possibility of estate planning; (2) the prestige that may attach to the chosen entity (such as a corporation); and (3) the need for perpetual existence (which in the case of a group, may not exist since most groups do not last more than several years).

---

[32] ITA sub-para. 127(5)(d)(i). See also sub-para. (ii).

[33] See IT-73R4, para. 18. The test looks to whether there is a common law master/servant relationship, or whether the individuals performing the services are self-employed. Thus, players under contract to a symphony orchestra most likely would not qualify, but freelancers who provide their services to a variety of "employers" most likely will.

[34] See ITA para. 18(1)(p) and IT-73R4, para. 19.

[35] See ITA s. 67 which states that in computing income, no deduction shall be made in respect of an outlay or expense except to the extent that it was reasonable in the circumstances. See also s. 245, the general anti-avoidance rule.

3. Group Partnership Agreement: Key Provisions

For many groups, the partnership form is often the business form of choice because of its flexibility and low cost. It is important to have a written agreement to overcome the pitfalls which exist in partnership law, and specifically to deal with leaving members and dispute resolution.

The discussion below highlights considerations relevant to the drafting of a partnership agreement for a musical group.[36] It is assumed throughout that each member of the group is a partner.

(a) Purpose

The purposes and scope of the partnership should be set out clearly. The purposes of the partnership usually include: (1) recording and exploiting recordings; (2) performing and making personal appearances under the group name; (3) merchandising the names (both legal and professional), likeness, and personality of each musician and the group; (4) writing music and exploiting music publishing rights; (5) generally, furthering the activities of the musicians and their group in the entertainment field.[37]

(b) Responsibilities

(i) Musician

The musician members of the partnership should have their responsibilities set out clearly. These generally include: (a) using their best efforts, or their full time and effort to fulfil their obligations under the agreement; (b) refraining from activities that interfere with their obligations under the agreement, such as either working at a part-time job or "moonlighting" with another band; (c) participating in the management and direction of the group; and (d) more specific obligations such as banking or accounting.[38]

---

[36] For a partnership agreement checklist see Appendix 7; see also Robert Thorne, "Partnership Agreements for Recording Artists", in *Entertainment, Publishing and the Arts Handbook*, (New York: Clark Boardman, 1989), at pp. 225-228.

[37] "Partnership Agreement", *Counseling Clients in the Entertainment Industry 1982*, Volume 2, (New York: Practising Law Institute, 1982), at 1231. See Chapter 6, "Agents and Managers" for a discussion and definition of the term "entertainment field".

[38] *Ibid.*, p. 1233, 1235.

In addition, it should be made clear how the partnership agreement binds the partners.[39]

(ii) Manager

Although it is possible for the group's manager to be a partner, this is not the usual practice, nor is it desirable. However, if the manager is to be made a partner, the partnership agreement should address the issues that would otherwise form the subject of a separate management agreement.[40] The agreement also should address any potential conflicts of interest which may arise between the manager and members of the band.

(c) Contributions

(i) Money

All contributions of funds, whether in cash or by way of debt, and any repayment thereof, should be set out in the agreement. If a loan is to carry a specified rate of interest, this should be set out in writing.

(ii) Name

The group's name is probably its most important asset. It is therefore of paramount importance for the agreement to address the issue of who, if anyone, will have the right to use the name if the group disbands or a member leaves. Some agreements permit a former member to refer to himself/herself for a specified period of time as "formerly of ...[the band's name]". Other agreements prohibit this, as such use may devalue the exclusive rights the group acquires in the name as a trade name or trade mark. Typically a partnership agreement requires the leaving members to quitclaim rights to the group name and assign such rights to the remaining members of the partnership. Other arrangements are also possible.[41]

---

[39] See generally, Nina Stevenson, "Forming Groups", in Chapter 1, "Copyright"; and, Shane Simpson and Greg Stevens, *Music: The Business and the Law*, (Sydney: The Law Book Company Limited, 1986), at pp. 7-9.

[40] For a discussion of these issues, see Chapter 6.

[41] For a brief discussion of other possible solutions, see Donald S. Passman, *All You Need to Know About the Music Business*, (New York: Simon & Schuster, 1997), at pp. 314-315. These include: (1) an absolute ban on anyone using the name if the group breaks

(d) Assets

The partnership agreement should identify the partnership assets clearly. This can be done conveniently in a schedule to the agreement which can be reviewed and amended as needed. The key partnership assets are discussed below.

(i) Name

The name of the group, and the goodwill attached thereto (including trademarks), is usually stipulated to be an asset of the partnership.

(ii) Copyrights

Copyrights, including copyright in music and recordings, may be assets of the partnership if the parties so decide. Alternatively, copyright in music and the group's recordings may be excluded from partnership assets, and the copyright income may be brought directly into the income of each partner. This is an important consideration which has income tax implications.[42]

A key consideration to be addressed in the partnership agreement is how royalties and publishing income are to be divided. Generally, with regard to copyright income, an equal share, insofar as this is reasonable, is typical. In the alternative, where not all members of the group are songwriters, or do not participate in the writing of each song, an equal share of record royalties, but an unequal share of publishing income, may be most equitable.

(iii) Insurance

Any insurance held on group members, including life insurance, can be considered an asset of the partnership. This should be discussed

---

up; (2) a right in a majority of the members performing together to use the name; (3) restricting the right to use the name to a particular individual; or (4) restricting the right to use the name to a set of named individuals performing together. See also, with regard to the protection of the group's name, Helen L. Searle, "What's in a Name", *Copyright World*, Issue 72, August 1997, at p. 27; Barbara Singer, "A Rose by Any Other Name: Trademark Protection of the Names of Popular Music Groups", (1992), 14 Hastings Comm/Ent L.J. 331.

[42] See Chapter 12 for a discussion of the taxation of copyright.

and specified in the partnership agreement. Consideration should be given to insuring the lives of band members, with the partnership being named as beneficiary. One should be aware that insurance policies are subject to different accounting and tax treatment than other assets.

(iv) Equipment

Generally, musical equipment is owned by the members of the partnership and not by the partnership itself. However, if the group as a whole buys a sound system or other equipment, then such equipment will be a partnership asset.

(v) Other Assets

Other partnership assets might include stage sets, costumes or stage clothing, and should be dealt with in the partnership agreement.

(e) Share of Profits

(i) Determination of Profit

Partnership profits, which are commonly referred to as net profits, are computed by subtracting business expenses (incurred with respect to gross earnings) from the gross earnings of the partnership. Unless the partners agree to the contrary in writing, profits are divided equally among the partners. Gross earnings could include the following: (1) recording income; (2) publishing income, including writer and publisher shares; (3) income from personal appearances and live performances; and (4) merchandising and other subsidiary source income. The partnership must determine which revenue sources will be included in gross earnings and the allocation of expenses concerning such sources, because revenue that constitutes gross earnings and expenses in relation thereto will determine the allocation of profit among the partners.[43] This is clearly a key clause in this agreement.

---

[43] Assuming not all partners share equally in income from all sources.

(ii) *Ratio*

The net profits and losses of the partnership may be divided equally among all partners. Alternatively, partners may choose not to participate equally with respect to all sources of income providing for a variable allocation of profit and loss. For example, if one group member writes all of the songs, the agreement might provide that 100% of the profit from publishing should go to the songwriter. Alternatively, where a group collectively writes and arranges all of their music, the publishing income percentages may be: 30% to the lyricist; 40% to the composer of the music; and 30% divided equally among the remaining members of the group. Different ratios can be specified with respect to income from recording, merchandising and live performance. Typically, merchandising and live performance income is divided equally.[44]

(f) Members' Provisions

The volatile nature of most groups makes it imperative to stipulate what will happen if the following occurs: (1) a member leaves or a new member is added; (2) there is a temporary substitute member; (3) a member is bought out; (4) a member dies; (5) a member becomes disabled; (6) a member becomes mentally incapacitated; or (7) a member withdraws, voluntarily or involuntarily.

Before leaving, a partner should be required to give adequate notice. For example, if the group is on a national or world-wide tour and a member decides, without notice, to leave in the middle of the tour, contractual liabilities can arise. Finding a suitable replacement is often difficult as musicians can have unique abilities.

The agreement should also deal with the expulsion of members since if the agreement is silent and a member is expelled, an action for damages may result.[45] A buy-out provision may be the fairest solution to this problem. The usual practice is to have the former partner continue to share in net profit, in an agreed upon division, subject to the terms of the existing partnership, and recording, publishing, merchandising and management agreements, but only with respect to income sources

---

[44] This may not be the case with respect to live performance where one of the group members is an employee rather than a partner. Further, if the group intends to permit individual members to make personal endorsements for which they are solely entitled to the profits, this should be stated clearly in the agreement.

[45] See for example s. 25 of the *Partnership Act*, R.S.O. 1990, c. P.5, which states that no partner can be expelled by a majority of partners unless this power has been conferred by express agreement.

existing at the date on which the member leaves. However, sometimes when a member leaves, all group income may be reduced, and the leaving member, remaining members and new member will share in the reduced income on a *pro rata* basis.

The agreement also should provide for a right to substitute members in the event of illness or disability. Without such a provision, the death or removal of a member would cause the partnership to terminate, giving rise to bothersome and unnecessary tax complications. The agreement also should deal with the right to admit new members and provide for a buy-out in the event of the death or incapacity of a member.

(g) Dissolution

(i) Generally

A critical issue is what events will or will not trigger dissolution of the partnership. Unless otherwise agreed, general partnership law applies and the death or insolvency of a partner will result in dissolution of the partnership.[46] The agreement can also provide for termination on notice or termination after the expiration of an agreed term.[47]

(ii) Specific Issues

The partners should consider the effects of dissolution with respect to: (1) the group and third parties; (2) the group *inter se*.[48] Specific issues of importance are discussed briefly below.

A. Recording Contract

(1) Is the group in breach of the recording contract?

---

[46] *Ibid.*, s. 33(1). The partnership will also dissolve in the event of a happening which makes the carrying on of the business unlawful; see s. 34.

[47] *Ibid.*, s. 32(c).

[48] Walter Lorimer and Phalen G. Hurewitz, Eds., Section XI, "Break-up, Dissolution and Termination" in *Syllabus on Representing Musical Artists: Legal, Business and Practical Aspects,* (Los Angeles: Beverly Hills Bar Association and University of Southern California Law Center, 1975), at p. 466 and generally pp. 467-472. See also generally Thorne, supra note 36.

(2) What are the rights of the record company upon termination: (a) Can it substitute new members? (b) Are there any documents required such as contractual releases? (c) Are leaving members entitled to an accounting and should this be done separately or jointly? (d) Can the record company charge future advances against a departing member's royalties or does the departing member share in any future advances?

(3) Does the departing member have any rights in the master recordings?[49]

B. Publishing Contract

(1) Is the member protected adequately with respect to administration of copyright and a share of royalties?

(2) Is there a separate publishing company which should buy out the member?

(3) Is the member contractually bound to the management and/or agency contract?

C. Live Performance and Merchandising

(1) Is there a possibility of cancelled personal appearances and the need to mitigate damages?

(2) Is there a possibility of settling employment contracts with employees of the group?

(3) Are there any outstanding merchandising or endorsement contracts to be terminated?[50]

D. Assets

Who owns the group assets, including: (1) the group name; and (2) the musical equipment? How will this be determined and what documentation is needed to transfer ownership?[51] In the absence of an

---

[49] *Ibid.*, p. 467.

[50] The above list of issues set out in the text is not exhaustive. It is simply meant to highlight some of the issues which commonly arise on dissolution of a partnership. There are also tax implications beyond the scope of this book with regard to which skilled tax advice should be sought.

[51] Lorimer and Phelan, supra note 48 at pp. 467-472.

agreement to the contrary, net partnership assets will be divided
equally.

E. Post-dissolution Income

The distribution of post-dissolution income accruing to the
partnership should be dealt with.

(h) Term and Termination

The term of the agreement should be set out clearly. There should
be a requirement that adequate notice be given prior to termination.
This is to avoid some of the contingencies discussed above.

(i) General Provisions

There are other important matters to consider. A few of these
include: (1) accounting and audit rights; (2) representations and
warranties, including, for example, representations that: (a) the
member is free to enter into the agreement; (b) there are no
disabilities preventing the member from performing according to the
terms of the agreement; and (c) if required, the consent of a minor's
parents has been obtained; (3) the arbitration of disputes; (4) the
creation of a flexible procedure to amend the partnership agreement;
(5) the grant to the management committee of powers sufficient to
carry out the day-to-day activities of the partnership (such as
accounting, banking, and communication with personal
representatives), which powers may be exercised by one or more
partners;[52] (6) location of the head office; and (7) the impact of family
law legislation on the partnership.

The above list is not exhaustive. Other general provisions can and
should be added. As is evident, the partnership agreement can be an
extremely flexible tool in structuring the relationship between the
partners and the conduct of their business affairs.

---

[52] The agreement should also specify whether major management decisions require
either a majority or unanimous decision. For a checklist dealing with this agreement, see
Appendix 7.

4. Agreement with Musician for Services

(a) Generally

The agreement should state clearly that it is an agreement for personal services and that the legal relationship between the parties is that of independent contractors.[53] The responsibilities of the parties should be set out clearly. In what follows, it is assumed that an individual musician is contracting with a group.

(b) Services

What services is the musician providing? Services could consist of all entertainment services including performance, personal appearances and promotion, recording, film and television, all under a general agreement; alternatively, the musician may be hired to provide specific services with respect to a specific tour, for example. Where relevant, the right to exploit the musician's personality rights should be granted to the group so that the group in turn can grant the right to a record company. Such right should include the right to use the musician's name, likeness, and biographical material in connection with the group's business including any and all merchandising activities.

The agreement also should deal with such matters as rehearsals, provision of instruments, and stage costumes.[54] Generally, the musician should be obligated to take instructions from the manager or the management committee of the group partnership. In the normal case, the musician would not participate in banking arrangements or other financial aspects of the group's business and there would be no acquisition of rights in the group's name.

---

[53] It is important to bear in mind that there are significant tax implications hinging on the characterization of the relationship. If the agreement is structured as a contract of service (an employment agreement), the band will be required to deduct income taxes and (possibly) EHT, and to make contributions to the CPP, EI and workers' compensation plans. None of these costs are relevant to contracts for services.

[54] Whether or not the musician is obligated to dress in a particular fashion is relevant; for example, with respect to certain "show groups" that have specific dress requirements.

(c) Term

The term of the agreement may be co-extensive with any recording agreement, the length of a tour, or with the partnership's year end. The group should reserve the right to terminate the relationship, if the musician becomes unfit or unable to perform the services required under the agreement.

(d) Compensation

Ordinarily, the musician will be paid on a fee basis and will not participate in royalty income. However, if the musician is to be paid royalties, he or she should be paid on the same basis as members of the group, that is, subject to recoupment, and any other relevant provisions set out in any relevant agreement. Whether or not a share of advances is payable to the musician is a negotiable issue. A share of record advances, for example, typically would not include any money actually paid for record production, video or tour support. If the musician is entitled to a share of merchandising income, this should be a specified percentage of net income. Recording or television and movie union scales also may be payable to the musician. If the musician contributes controlled compositions under the songwriting agreement, then the musician should be asked to license them to the record company on the same terms as those binding the group. Alternatively, it may be specified that the group member is an employee-for-hire, and that any rights arising in connection with his or her contributions to the musical compositions or masters are the property of the group.

(e) General Provisions

The agreement should provide for injunctive relief in the event the musician fails to fulfill his or her obligations under the contract. The agreement also should contain the standard representations and warranties and an indemnity given with respect to any breach thereof. A non-competition clause (including a re-recording restriction) should be considered, if relevant.

The agreement should provide further for the placing of adequate insurance with respect to both the musician and the musician's equipment. If the musician is to share in the group's profits, the agreement should state that such profits will be determined in accordance with the partnership agreement.

Other provisions to be included are: (1) the entirety clause; (2) a default and cure clause; (3) a no partnership or joint venture clause; (4) a payment of legal and accounting fees clause; (5) a governing law clause; and (6) a morals clause. With respect to the latter, the group should contract for the right to terminate the agreement if the musician engages in any criminal activities, or significantly changes his or her personal habits or appearance such that the change materially affects the musician's performance of his or her obligations under this agreement.[55]

(f) Termination

The right to terminate should be contingent on any of the following: (1) force majeure; or (2) notice, with or without cause, subject to a time frame. During the notice period, the musician should be obliged to continue to perform pursuant to the terms of the agreement and upon termination, to return equipment belonging to the group.

5. Business Name Registration

Some musicians who are sole proprietors carry on business in their own names, while others use business names.[56] When a business is carried on under a name other than the proprietor's legal name, the business name must be registered.[57] Persons in a partnership must register the firm name and any other name under which the partnership does business.[58] Corporations must register trading names.[59] Failure to register a business name is an offence[60], and a person who has failed to register a business name may not maintain an action in court.[61]

---

[55] For useful precedents, consult Form 146-1, "Employment of Band Members Contract", and Form 152-1, "Short Form Side Management Contract", in Chapter IV "Music", Samuel J. Fox and Donald C. Farber, Eds., *Entertainment Industry Contracts* (New York: Matthew Bender, 1990).

[56] For example, Jane Musician may carry on business as Jane Musician Productions.

[57] See for example, s. 2(2), the *Business Names Act*, R.S.O. 1990, c. B.17 (the "BNA").

[58] *Ibid.*, ss. 2(3) and (3.1).

[59] *Ibid.*, s. 2(1).

[60] *Ibid.*, s.10. In the case of an individual, the penalty for failure to register is a fine of not more than $2,000. Corporations are liable for a fine of not more than $25,000, and a director or officer who authorizes or acquiesces in the offence is liable to a fine of not more than $2,000.

[61] *Ibid.*, s. 7, but see s. 7(2) under which the court may grant leave where there are mitigating factors.

The primary purpose of registration is to inform others of prior use of the name. Thus, no rights are acquired on registration of a business name.[62] However, where one name is the same or deceptively similar to another name previously registered, the prior registrant may be able to sue the subsequent registrant.[63] In such cases, a court can order cancellation of the registration, and by implication, the subsequent registrant would need to acquire and register a new business name.

Because each province has its own statutes concerning business name registration, the appropriate provincial statute should be consulted prior to registration of a name.

6. Family Law Issues [64]

(a) Generally

Ontario family law recognizes marriage as a form of partnership. Both spouses are treated equally and have mutual obligations with respect to support of the family and each other. Generally, on marriage breakdown or termination of a spousal relationship, each spouse is entitled to an equal share of assets accumulated during the marriage.[65] In the absence of an agreement to the contrary, all of the following can be considered net family property, and these items could be subject to an equalization order:[66] (1) business assets accumulated by a musician; (2) a partnership interest; or (3) a share in a corporation held by a musician.

While a discussion of the detailed calculation of equalization payments is beyond the scope of this chapter, it is important to note the circumstances in which a musician's business affairs will be affected by the *Family Law Act.* Under the Ontario family law regime, the right to an equalization payment will arise: (1) if the parties divorce; (2) if the marriage is declared a nullity; (3) where the spouses separate and there is no reasonable prospect that they will resume co-habitation; (4) where

---

[62] However, the use of a business name may result in the acquisition of rights under the *Trade-marks Act* or at common law. A detailed and specific name search should take place prior to registration. These issues are discussed in Chapter 9, "Merchandising".

[63] Section 6 of the BNA. Damages not exceeding $500 may be awarded.

[64] The following discussion is based on the Ontario *Family Law Act,* R.S.O. 1990, c. F.3. Because each province has its own unique and detailed family laws, they should be consulted as circumstances warrant.

[65] *Ibid.,* s. 5(1). For a useful general reference, see James F. Kennedy, J. Alex Langford, Eds., *The New Family Law Act For Solicitors,* (Toronto: L.S.U.C. - C.L.E., 1986).

[66] For a definition of "net family property" (the relevant concept), see s. 4(1) of the *Family Law Act.* See also the definition of "property", which includes "any interest, present or future, vested or contingent, in real or personal property".

one spouse dies and the surviving spouse owns net family property worth less than the net family property of the deceased; and (5) where the spouses are co-habiting, and there is a serious danger one spouse is depleting his or her net family property, then the other spouse may apply for equalization.[67]

Because of the broad powers given to the court, the making of an equalization order can have a significant impact on a musician's business activities and relations with third parties.[68] Moreover, the Act specifically recognizes that there may be situations in which the only reasonable method of satisfying an award is to order the sale of a business.[69] For these reasons, it is desirable for musicians who are married or who contemplate marriage to enter into a marriage contract.

(b) Structuring Agreements

The most common advice given by lawyers is to suggest that spouses enter into a marriage contract.[70] It has been suggested specifically that the agreement "limit or exempt the value of the share interest from the net family property equation and/or from enforcement under an equalization order... Such provisions may in fact be a requirement of third parties, lenders, or remaining shareholders in certain circumstances." [71] Where the musician is a shareholder or partner, it is also advisable that the musician's spouse become a party to any shareholder or partnership agreement.[72] Both the marriage

---

[67] *Ibid.*, ss. 5(1)-(3).

[68] Under para. 9(1)(d) of the Act, the court has the power to order the sale of property or transfer of property to a spouse. Under para. 9(1)(b), the court can place a charge on property to secure an obligation imposed by the order.

[69] *Ibid.*, s. 11(1). Also, under s. 11(2), the court may order a spouse to transfer shares or order a corporation to issue shares to the other spouse.

[70] Subsection 52(1) of the Act permits spouses or prospective spouses to enter into an agreement, in which they agree on their respective rights and obligations on separation or dissolution of the marriage, including ownership in or division of property. Thus, by agreement, spouses can exclude business assets from net family property. To render the contract and other agreements discussed in the text enforceable, independent legal advice should be obtained by the spouse.

[71] L. Michelle Mannering and Terry Wayne Hainsworth, "Private Corporations — Keeping Control in the Wake of the Family Law Act", (1986), (Ontario) 6 C.F.L.Q. 23 at p. 24. Subsection 2(10) of the Act specifically allows an opting out by a domestic agreement. Section 55 sets out the formalities.

[72] This will have the effect of binding the non-titled spouse to the agreement. It also has been suggested that the corporation or partnership become a party to the marriage contract; see Mannering, supra note 71 at p. 24, see also James C. MacDonald & Kenneth L. Boland, "Marriage Contracts and Corporations, Partnerships and Businesses", in David C. Simmonds & Evita M. Roch, eds, *Marriage Contracts*, (Toronto: Carswell, 1988), at pp.

MUSICIANS AND THE LAW

contract and shareholder/partnership agreement should include an appropriate method for valuation of the shares or partnership interest, and the latter should provide for a buy-out of the musician's interest in the event of death or an application by the non-titled spouse under the *Family Law Act*. The marriage contract should further provide that the non-titled spouse, in the event of an application, will not require the transfer, pledging or delivery of shares in execution.[73] If the spouse is not made a party to any shareholder agreement, a court may be willing to make an order awarding an ownership interest to the spouse.[74] A spouse who has a beneficial interest or security in a corporation may be able to bring an oppression remedy, thereby disrupting the operation of the business.

In many cases, a non-titled spouse may not wish to exempt the titled spouse's business assets from his or her net family property, nor will he or she sign a marriage contract or shareholders' or partnership agreement. In such cases, unilateral action may be the only possible course of action for partners or shareholders who wish to limit the effect of the *Family Law Act* on their business activities.[75]

199-213. However, it also has been suggested that in some cases, it may be preferable to have the spouse execute an adoption agreement so as to minimize any leverage the spouse may have in the event of marriage difficulties; see Stephen M. Grant, "Business Interest and Family Law", (1999), 17 C.F.L.Q. 67 at p. 81.

[73] See Lorne H. Wolfson, "The Family Law Act: How Planning For It May Ruin Your Marriage While Not Planning For It May Destroy Your Company", (1989), 4 C.F.L.Q. 223, at p. 235. Where no shareholders' or partnership agreement exists, various methods of insulating business assets have been suggested. According to Mannering and Hainsworth, supra note 71, at pp. 28-30, the titled spouse can: (1) subscribe for shares with excluded property; (2) use criss-cross insurance to fund the purchase of a deceased shareholder's shares, thus excluding them from net family property; and (3) freeze the value of his or her share interest. Where there is a shareholders' agreement, but no buy-out clause, the agreement at least should restrict the transfer, sale, issuance or encumbrance of shares, preferably by requiring the consent of all shareholders; see Wolfson, at pp. 234-235. Lastly, the Articles of Incorporation can restrict the issuance, transfer or encumbrance of shares or require that all shareholders be party to a shareholders' agreement. Precedents for some of the above clauses can be found in MacDonald and Boland, supra note 72, at Schedules A-C of chap. 8.

[74] For a discussion of cases in which Ontario courts have ordered the transfer or encumbrance of shares or corporate assets, see Grant, supra note 72, at pp. 74-75.

[75] As to which, see Mannering, supra note 71.

7. Financing

(a) Generally

A musical venture may involve a combination of recording,[76] live performance showcases and the production of one or more music videos. For the purpose of what follows, it is assumed that the investor will be investing in such a venture.[77]

Generally, a potential investor should ask the following questions: (1) Is the venture sound? (2) Is there a real chance of making a profit? (3) Does the investment offer any tax advantages? (4) Is there a risk of unlimited liability? (5) Is there a secondary market for the investment? (6) What is the liquidity of the investment? (7) How is the investment structured? (8) Is the investor investing in part of a project or all of a project (or indeed several projects)?

Typically, an investor will look for a short-term investment that yields deductions (losses) which can be taken against other sources of income in any given taxation year. As well, the investor will seek an investment which can be earned out of current funds to obviate the possibility that repayment will require further capitalization of the venture. In any investment, the definitions of "net income",[78] the return to the investor, and any restriction or "ceiling" on the return are crucial. However, there is no standard rate of return for investing in a music venture. The rate is negotiable and should reflect the degree of risk to which the investor's funds are put.

Although at least one rock star has turned to the capital markets as a way of realizing the value of his catalogue,[79] for the most part the public offering of shares is quite irrelevant to such projects.[80] Funds

---

[76] Several masters or an album's-worth may be recorded for presentation to third party record companies, or a record production company.

[77] Investors can invest also in management, recording, publishing or merchandising ventures. A typical project includes a video, record album and /or publishing interest.

[78] Note that merchandising and live performance income are not usually part of the revenue from which an investor is repaid, since the musician needs a source of income free and clear from the obligation to recoup in order to earn a living.

[79] In 1997, David Bowie launched a $55 million bond issue (the so-called "Bowie Bonds"). The ten-year bonds were collateralized by a fifteen-year licensing deal with EMI, pursuant to which the record company gained the right to release 25 albums made between 1969 and 1990; for details, see Official David Bowie Press Release, dated May 22, 1997 at http://www.bowiewonderworld.com. Bowie Bonds also have been issued by other artists, notably Holland/Dozier/Holland. For a general discussion of the advantages of such bond issues, see Andrew Wilkinson, "Securitization for the Music Industry", *Copyright World*, Issue 86, December 1998, p. 26.

[80] Even if the regulatory hurdles could be overcome, virtually all such ventures are simply too small and inexpensive to warrant such an issue. Indeed, most ventures of the kind discussed in the text require an investment in the range of $25,000 to $30,000.

typically come from friends, family, private investors (including managers), granting agencies and occasionally banks or other lending institutions.

Investment can be by way of debt or equity. Obvious sources of debt financing include: (1) loans from band members; (2) bank loans (in which case the loan is invariably secured by way of personal guarantee, collateral mortgage or both); (3) government programs; (4) friends or family; and (5) managers, record companies, music publishers or merchandising companies.[81] The debt itself may be secured, unsecured, or convertible. However, unless the lender is in some way related to the band, the fixed (and relatively low) yield obtainable on a note or under a loan agreement is simply too unattractive to induce conventional lenders to invest in such projects.

Equity investors obtain ownership of a share in either the venture or the assets created pursuant to the venture.[82] Equity can come from the following sources: (1) group members; (2) friends or family; and (3) sources of venture capital. Equity can take various forms: a share in a corporation, an interest in a partnership, or co-ownership interest in publishing, record masters or other property. Equity may entitle the investor to participate in the management of the enterprise, and may afford the right to vote. When an investor seeks equity participation, the problems that may arise are often substantial and complex. In many cases, resolution of the legal issues can be achieved only at a prohibitive cost.

Investing in the music business is not an insurable risk. Most ventures are designed as investments that have no stated market, with uncertain prospects and minimal liquidation value. Accordingly, such investments should be made carefully and only on receipt of competent legal and accounting advice.[83]

(b) Business Entities

The discussion below is intended to highlight some of the issues pertaining to the investment of funds in the entities discussed. Unless stated otherwise, it is assumed that the investment is an equity investment.

---

[81] Included in this category is the tour support provided by companies anxious to trade on the band's name and image. It is not unusual for the cost of a tour to be totally underwritten by a corporate sponsor.

[82] Such assets could include copyrights, master recordings and music videos.

[83] See Robert Garton-Smith, Chapter 14, "Financing Music Ventures", in *Music: The Business and the Law*, supra note 34, at pp. 182-90, for a general discussion of these issues. Although written from an Australian legal perspective, the material is still useful.

(i) Sole Proprietorship

Although it is legally possible for investors to make an equity investment in a sole proprietorship, there are a number of difficulties. If the investment calls for investors to receive a share of the profits of the business, the investors will be deemed to be partners of the proprietor.[84] It may be possible to avoid this result by granting the investors a share in the gross returns of the business or, if the proprietor has assets capable of yielding income (e.g. a record master), giving the investors an ownership interest in the property, but even here, it is possible that the investors may be regarded as partners of the sole proprietor.[85] While these structures carry the risk that investors may be liable for the debts of the business, there is one off-setting advantage: the investors will be able to access their *pro rata* share of any operating losses and, subject to the provisions of the *Income Tax Act*, use them to reduce their taxable income.

Alternatively, the investment can be structured as a loan.[86] While this structure carries the advantage that investors will not be at risk for the debts of the business, there is a corresponding disadvantage: the investors will not be able to access any operating losses; these will remain the property of the sole proprietor operating the business.

(ii) Partnership

A. Generally

As noted above, partners are jointly and severally liable for the firm's debts. Consequently, investors who purchase a partnership interest potentially face liability in excess of the cost of their investment. For this reason, it is often desirable to structure the investment as a limited partnership. Limited partnerships provide investors with the limited liability available to shareholders, but allow the tax advantages associated with general partnerships.

---

[84] See the *Partnerships Act*, R.S.O. 1990, c. P.5, s. 3.

[85] Sections 2 and 3 of the *Partnerships Act* state that such arrangements do not of themselves create a partnership, but they do no rule it out either.

[86] Section 4 of the *Partnerships Act* states that the receipt of a rate of interest varying with the profits or a share of the profits does not of itself make the lender a partner or liable as such if the contract is in writing.

B. Limited Partnership

Under the *Limited Partnerships Act*,[87] a limited partnership is formed upon filing a declaration.[88] There must be at least one limited partner and one general partner.[89] The limited partnership expires five years after the date of filing but can be renewed.[90] A person may be both a limited partner and a general partner[91] but limited liability can be lost if a limited partner engages in control of the limited partnership. A limited partner can contract to provide money and property to the limited partnership, but not services.[92] Where the surname of a limited partner, who is not a general partner, appears in the firm name, the limited partner is liable as a general partner to any creditor of the limited partnership who has advanced credit to the partnership without actual knowledge that the limited partner is not a general partner.[93] A general partner has no right to admit a person as a limited partner unless the right is granted under the partnership agreement.[94] A limited partner has the right to share in the profits and to have his or her contribution returned.[95] If the limited partner takes part in the control of the business, he or she will be liable as a general partner.[96] An interest in a limited partnership is assignable,[97] however, where the assignee is a substituted limited partner, the record of limited partners must be amended for the assignment to become effective.[98] Where a limited partnership changes its name, a new declaration signed by at least one of the general partners must be filed.[99]

A limited partnership will be dissolved on the death, retirement or mental incompetency of a general partner, unless the business is continued by the remaining general partners pursuant to the partnership agreement with the consent of all the remaining

---

[87] *Limited Partnerships Act*, R.S.O. 1990, c. L.16. Each province will have its own relevant statute which should be consulted.

[88] *Ibid.*, s. 3.

[89] *Ibid.*, s. 2(2).

[90] *Ibid.*, ss. 3(3) and (4).

[91] *Ibid.*, s. 5(1).

[92] *Ibid.*, s. 7(1).

[93] *Ibid.*, s. 6.

[94] *Ibid.*, para. 8(f). Where the agreement is silent, all of the limited partners must give their written consent or ratify the admission.

[95] *Ibid.*, s. 11(1).

[96] *Ibid.*, s. 13(1).

[97] *Ibid.*, s. 18(1).

[98] *Ibid.*, s. 18(5). A substituted limited partner has all the rights and powers of his/her assignor. An assignee who is not a substituted assignee only has the right to a share of profits and return of his/her contribution; see s. 18(3).

[99] *Ibid.*, s. 19(3).

partners.[100] A limited partnership may be dissolved by contract or consent.[101] No extra-provincial limited partnership may carry on business in Ontario unless it files a declaration.[102] All limited partnerships must keep at their principal place of business a copy of the limited partnership agreement, the declaration and any amendments thereto.[103] Any person who contravenes any provision of the Act or regulations commits an offence and is liable to a fine of not more than $2,000 or, if the person is a corporation, not more than $20,000.[104] Finally, a limited partnership that has unpaid fees or penalties or in respect of which a declaration has not been filed may not maintain an action in a court in Ontario without leave.[105]

The use of a limited partnership as an investment vehicle may give rise to concerns under the *Securities Act.* These concerns and possible exemptions are discussed below.

(iii) Corporation

Investments structured in corporate form give investors limited liability but deny them the use of any losses sustained by the corporation. Moreover, in order to comply with an exemption granted to issuers under the *Securities Act,* the articles of incorporation of virtually all private companies contain a restriction on the transfer of shares. Accordingly, they have little, if any, resale value.[106] As well, if the investors are parties to a unanimous shareholders' agreement, they may become liable to the extent the shareholders assume any of the powers of directors under the agreement.[107]

The use of a corporation as an investment vehicle may give rise to concerns under the *Securities Act.* These concerns and possible exemptions are discussed below.

---

[100] *Ibid.,* s. 21.

[101] If dissolved by agreement , s. 23 requires the filing of a declaration by at least one of the general partners.

[102] *Ibid.,* s. 25(1); see generally ss. 25-28 for rules concerning extra-provincial limited partnerships.

[103] *Ibid.,* paras. 33(1)(a)-(c); but see s. 33(2) for extra-provincial limited partnerships.

[104] *Ibid.,* s. 35(1).

[105] *Ibid.,* s. 20(1).

[106] Such restrictions are not exclusive to corporations; they also may be found in limited partnership agreements.

[107] See s. 108(5), Ontario *Business Corporations Act.*

(c) Securities Issues

(i) Generally

Complex issues arise under the *Securities Act*[108] with respect to investments in musical ventures. Three threshold questions exist: (1) Is the investment a security within the meaning of the *Securities Act*? (2) Is there a trade in the security? (3) Is there a distribution of the security? Only if the threshold questions are all answered in the negative can the transaction go forward free of the disclosure and licensing requirements found in the *Securities Act.*

The definition of a security[109] is extremely broad and includes, *inter alia*: (1) a document commonly known as a security; (2) a document constituting evidence of title to or interest in capital, assets, property, profits, earnings, or royalties of any person or company; (3) any bond, debenture, note or other evidence of indebtedness, shares, stock, unit, unit certificate, and participation certificate; (4) an investment contract;[110] (5) a profit sharing agreement; and (6) a document constituting evidence of an option in a security.

As a general rule, the Act requires a person who trades in a security to register as a dealer.[111] As well, where the trade is a distribution of a security, a preliminary prospectus and prospectus must be filed with the Director.[112] Both the registration and prospectus requirements are subject to specific exemptions, the most important of which are the private company exemption, the seed capital exemption, and the exemption for purchases of not less than $150,000.[113] Because

---

[108] R.S.O. 1990, c. S.5. Each province will have its own relevant statute which should be consulted. For useful general source material, consult Donald C. Ross, *Basic Securities Law*, (Toronto: L.S.U.C., 1989).

[109] *Ibid.*, paras. 1(1)(a)-(p).

[110] Investment contracts probably have given rise to more litigation than any other category of security. An investment contract can be defined as an instrument pursuant to which investors give their money to a third party in a common enterprise with others, and with respect to which they rely on the skill and ability of the third party for the success of the investment; see, for example, *Sunfour Estates N.V.*, January 24, 1992, O.S.C.B. 269, following *SEC v. W.J. Howey Co.*, 328 U.S. 293 (1946). More broadly, there is a transaction in securities where an investor's money is subject to the risks of "an enterprise over which he exercises no managerial control"; see Ross, supra note 107, at pp. 17-19.

[111] *Ibid.*, para. 25(1)(a).

[112] Subsection 53(1).

[113] There is also an exemption for purchasers recognized by the Commission as "exempt purchasers". The registration and prospectus exemptions operate in parallel as is shown below (the numbers refer to relevant sections of the *Securities Act*):

most investments in music ventures do not exceed this amount, the former exemptions are the most important. They are discussed briefly below.

(ii) Private Company

To obtain the benefit of this exemption, the company must qualify as a private company[114] under the *Securities Act* and the securities must not be offered to the public.[115] The advantage of this exemption is that no offering memorandum is required.

(iii) Limited Partnership/Seed Capital

A. Outlined

Units in a limited partnership fall within the definition of "security". Accordingly, any trade in partnership units, if they have not been issued previously, requires the filing of a prospectus and any person trading in such units will have to register as a dealer.

Type	Registration	Prospectus
Exempt purchaser	35(1)4.	72(1)(c)
$150,000 acquisition	35(1)5.	72(1)(d)
(Regulation 1015, s.27(1))		
Seed Capital	35(1)21.	72(1)(p)
Private Company	35(2)10.	73(1)(a)

[114] Under s. 1(1) of the *Securities Act*, a private company is a company in whose constating document the right to transfer shares is restricted, the number of shareholders is limited to not more than 50, and any invitation to the public to subscribe for securities is prohibited.

[115] According to one authority, the "determination of who is and who is not a member of the public is plagued with uncertainty"; see Victor P. Alboini, *1997 Ontario Securities Act*, (Toronto: Carswell, 1996), at p. 202. Alboini lists the following factors which are relevant to a determination of this issue: (1) the number of offerees; (2) the number of purchasers; (3) the sophistication of the purchasers; (4) their relationship to the vendor; (5) the manner in which the offer is made; (6) the purpose of the offering; and (7) circumstances related to the vendor. He states that "Canadian courts and securities administrators have expressed a preference for two tests": the "common bonds of interest" test employed in *R. v. Piepgrass* (1959), 29 W.W.R. 218 (Alta. C.A.); and the "need to know" test employed in *SEC v. Ralston Purina Co.*, 346 U.S. 119 (1953). Under the former, persons who were friends or associates of the vendor or who have a common bond of interest or association are not members of the public; under the latter, persons who can fend for themselves or who have access to prospectus-level disclosure are not members of the public.

Fortunately, the Act provides a pair of exemptions.[116] Briefly, a trade will be exempt if: (1) not more than 50 potential purchasers are solicited; (2) a sale is made to not more than 25 purchasers; (3) all sales are completed within a six month period; (4) the purchasers receive substantially the same information as would be found in a prospectus and are individuals who, by virtue of their net worth and investment experience or consultation with a registered adviser or dealer who is not the promoter, are able to evaluate the investment;[117] (5) the offer and sale of the security are not accompanied by advertising and there are no promotional or selling expenses made in connection therewith (other than professional expenses); and (6) the promoter has not acted as the promoter of another issuer relying on the exemption in the previous twelve months. Finally, an issuer which has relied on the exemption may not rely on it a second time.

Reliance on the exemption necessitates preparation of an offering memorandum.[118] The memorandum, which must provide prospectus-level disclosure, normally includes a description of the issuer, its business and management, particulars of the securities being issued, resale restrictions which apply to the purchasers of the securities, and the identification of any significant risks associated with the investment. Prospective purchasers usually expect to receive audited financial statements for the most recently completed fiscal year, as well as interim financial statements and financial projections.

The offering memorandum must include a contractual right of action available to the investor in the event of a misrepresentation[119] and must be filed with the Commission.[120] Within ten days of a trade, the issuer must file a Report of Trade in Form 20.[121]

The first trade in a security acquired pursuant to the exemption is a distribution unless the trade qualifies for an exemption under certain provisions of subsection 72(1) or the securities are held for at least eighteen months from the later of the date of the initial trade or the date the issuer became a reporting issuer, and the vendor files a report

---

[116] The so-called 'seed capital' exemption is found in paras. 35(1)21 and 72(1)(p) of the Act.

[117] These are class "A" purchasers. A second class, class "B" purchasers, includes directors and officers of the issuer and parents, siblings, children or spouses of such individuals; see items (B)(C)(D) of sub-para. 72(1)(p)(ii).

[118] See the definition of 'offering memorandum' in s. 32(1) of the General Regulation to the *Securities Act*, R.R.O. 1990, Reg. 1015. Pursuant to the definition, an offering memorandum is required in connection with any distribution exempt from the prospectus requirement under paras. 72(1)(c)(d) or (p).

[119] Regulation 1015, s.32(3).

[120] Regulation 1015, s. 32(4).

[121] Section 72(3) of the Act.

within ten days of the trade.[122] Where there is doubt as to whether a trade requires the issuance of a prospectus, or a distribution is in progress, a ruling can be obtained from the Commission.[123]

B. Problems

There are a number of problems with respect to the sale of limited partnership interests by way of offering memorandum. These include: (1) ambiguities in the relevant legal definitions;[124] (2) the potential liability arising from the contractual right of action; (3) the need to specify risk factors adequately, as some risks are inherent in the music business itself; (4) the lack of a minimum/maximum offering and the possibility that the funds invested will be insufficient to promote the recording and the project generally; and (5) the inability to advertise the offering.

In structuring the agreement, the following additional issues should be considered: (1) the overall budget for the project; (2) the definition of net profit; (3) the relative ranking of the funds contributed pursuant to the agreement and any later contribution vis-à-vis profit participation and the return of capital; (4) the closing date and any conditions on closing;[125] (5) the identity of the general partner;[126] (6) the desirability of granting a broad power of attorney to the general partner;[127] (7) rules for amendment of the limited partnership agreement; and (8) the use of language permitting the general partner to execute and file the declaration on behalf of the limited partners.

If the project includes a video, one should consider the possibility that it will qualify for an accelerated rate of capital cost allowance under the *Income Tax Act* and if so, certification should be obtained.

---

[122] Sub-paragraph 72(4)(b)(iv). Other trades are exempt as well; see sub-paras. (i) - (iii). Form 21 is used.

[123] Subsections 74(1) and (2) respectively.

[124] According to Alboini, supra note 115, it is often difficult to qualify and determine the net worth of investors. Moreover, the need to provide prospectus-level disclosure and ensure that each investor satisfies the test set out in the Act often makes it difficult to obtain an opinion letter from counsel.

[125] For example, the offering could be contingent on a minimum or maximum number of units being taken up within a defined period of time. It is also important to set up a realistic time frame during which the limited partners can recoup.

[126] Often, the general partner will be the artist. This may give rise to a potential or actual conflict of interest. Because of the duties partners owe to each other, this arrangement is legally problematic.

[127] Such a power might permit the general partner to enter into third party agreements potentially affecting the limited partnership's net income. For example, the partnership could enter into an agreement with the group's manager, entitling him or her to take a commission based on the project's gross earnings.

Finally, steps should be taken to avoid any potential or actual conflict of interest and it should be made clear to the investors that they are investing in a highly speculative venture with a high probability of loss.

The limited partnership agreement and offering memorandum should be supported by the following agreements where applicable: (1) a music video production contract; (2) an agreement with a producer for the production of recordings; (3) the recording contract; (4) the publishing contract; (5) the management contract; (6) the merchandising contract; and (7) any other contracts material to the investment.

For most musicians seeking to utilize the seed capital exemption, it is often difficult to meet the conditions of closing on which the offering ultimately depends. There are substantial legal, accounting and administrative costs associated with preparation of the offering memorandum and there are attendant risks of legal liability. For these reasons, unless there is some overriding tax advantage, it is often preferable to structure the investment as a share purchase, utilizing the private company exemption.

(iv) Summary

Because of the costs involved in making recordings and music videos, musicians often turn to third parties as a source of funds. Such investments can be structured in a variety of ways to accommodate the needs of both the musician and investor. However, the music business is inherently risky and in many cases the costs associated with structuring the investment and the high probability of loss make the investment unattractive to all but the most risk-averse or star-struck of investors. Fortunately, there are numerous government grants and loans available; these programs, discussed below, offer a viable alternative to the methods discussed above.

(d) Funding Programs

(i) Sound Recording Development Program

A. Generally

The Sound Recording Development Program ("SRDP"), a program of the Department of Canadian Heritage ("DOCH") represents a major commitment of the federal government with respect to Canadian cultural policy and the music business. The program currently consists of the following components: (1) audio and video; (2) marketing and touring; (3) business development; (4) specialized music production; (5) specialized music distribution; and (6) support to federal policy development. Items 1, 2, 3, and 5 are administered on behalf of the DOCH by FACTOR and Musicaction. Item 4 is administered by the Canada Council for the Arts.[128] Funding is by way of loans and grants.

B. FACTOR/ Musicaction

The Foundation To Assist Canadian Talent on Records ("FACTOR") and its francophone counterpart, Musicaction, which together are known as "FMC", assist the DOCH in administering SRDP funds. FACTOR was founded in 1982 by CHUM Limited, Moffat Communications, Rogers Broadcasting, the Canadian Independent Record Producers Association and the Canadian Music Publishers Association and subsequently amalgamated with the Canadian Talent Library. FACTOR continues to be supported by numerous Canadian broadcasters.

FACTOR's purpose is to stimulate the growth and development of the independent recording industry in Canada. It has a wide range of programs through which it provides grants or loans to artists, copyright owners, music publishers and songwriters.[129] As well, FACTOR provides a variety of loans to established record labels for the production, marketing and promotion of recordings and music videos.[130] FACTOR will fund up to fifty percent of the eligible budget of any project it approves.[131]

---

[128] The SRDP is administered through the Canada Council's program of grants for sound recordings, discussed infra.

[129] The current programs are: publisher and songwriter demo, professional demo award, professional songwriters' educational seminar and workshop program, independent artist recording loan, FACTOR loan, video grant, international show-casing, domestic show-casing, international tour support, international marketing, business development, specialized music distribution, domestic tour support, domestic marketing, and marketing and promotion for sound recording. Because these programs change, interested parties should consult FACTOR.

[130] These are the direct board approval loans. There are currently five programs, including DBA Level-1, DBA Level-2, DBA classical, DBA video grant and DBA master acquisition component.

[131] However, FACTOR's contribution when combined with any other government funding cannot exceed 75% of the eligible budget.

C. Loans and Grants

Because FACTOR's mandate is the promotion of the Canadian independent recording industry, applicants must reside in Canada and be Canadian citizens or landed immigrants. Companies must be Canadian-owned or Canadian-controlled. As a general rule, 50% of the material to be recorded must be 100% Canadian.[132] While it is possible to record outside of Canada or use the services of non-Canadians, such costs are not eligible expenses.[133]

The successful applicant is obligated to enter into a binding contract which sets out the terms and conditions of the loan or grant. Expenses must be supported by invoices, cancelled cheques, credit card receipts or money order receipts. Cash payments are not acceptable. Where the agreement calls for completion of, and/or release of the masters by a specified date, failure to comply is an event of default entitling FACTOR to enforce its remedies under the agreement. Budgets can be modified after approval in FACTOR's discretion if FACTOR is provided with a supplementary budget and the reason for the changes.

Where an applicant seeks a loan under the FACTOR loan program, FACTOR requires that the applicant have a fully-executed distribution agreement in place with a FACTOR-recognized distributor at the time the application is made. Pursuant to the loan agreement, FACTOR is entitled to a royalty on every record sold and not returned, but the borrower is entitled to retain 100% of all advances, minimum guarantee payments or other consideration received (other than publishing revenue and record royalties) until such time as it has recouped its share of production costs. After recoupment, FACTOR is entitled to 100% of such advances until the funds disbursed by FACTOR are fully repaid.[134]

The existence of a misrepresentation or material inaccuracy in any document supplied to FACTOR or any falsity in the application is an event of default under the agreement. A common pitfall to be avoided

---

[132] Material will be Canadian if the artist is Canadian, the music and lyrics are written by Canadians, and the recording is produced in Canada.

[133] Other ineligible costs include management and legal fees, manufacturing costs, hospitality expenses, local transport, equipment, musical instrument supplies, and GST. Non-qualifying expenses will vary depending on whether the project is a sound recording, video, tour or show-case, or a radio syndication. For specific details, consult FACTOR.

[134] See FACTOR Loan Agreement, Article 3.00. In general, FACTOR is entitled to a royalty of $1.00 per unit sold for a period of two years commencing with the domestic release. After two years, the outstanding balance of the loan, if any, will be forgiven. Where FACTOR provides additional funds for promotion and marketing, the two-year period will be extended from the date of such additional loan.

is to incur costs before an application has been made; such costs are excluded from the definition of 'production costs' under the agreement and will not be funded by FACTOR even if the application is approved. In certain cases, FACTOR will make loans to complete a partially finished master or to remix masters.

D. Jury System

FACTOR applications are reviewed by juries comprised of individuals drawn from the recording and broadcast industries.[135] Applicants are judged on the basis of the quality of the music, lyrics, vocals, musicianship, originality, production, sales potential, radio airplay potential and physical presentation of the project. Jury decisions must be unanimous. Depending on the program, an application will be evaluated by either a single jury or three juries.[136]

E. Eligibility Criteria

For purposes of the FACTOR loan agreement, an album is a cassette tape, CD or long-playing vinyl disc containing the equivalent of no fewer than eight masters or having an aggregate playing time of at least forty minutes. FACTOR's maximum contribution is 50% of an approved recording budget. The other 50% is to be made in cash by the applicant.

The requirement of national distribution acceptable to FACTOR will preclude musicians from being eligible unless a national distributor supports the application. However, some musicians will meet the criteria for FACTOR's grant programs and may qualify for the independent artist recording loan as well.

(ii) VideoFact

VideoFact, a program established in 1984 by the MuchMusic Network, provides financial assistance to Canadian companies and individuals involved in the production of music videos so as to "increase

---

[135] The jury system is used with respect to the following FACTOR programs: publisher and songwriter demo, professional demo award, independent artist recording loan and FACTOR loan.

[136] Independent artist recording loan and FACTOR loan applications are evaluated by a maximum of three juries, two of which must unanimously favour the application before it is approved. The demo awards are dealt with by a single jury.

the number and quality of music videos produced in Canada".[137] Although the majority of applicants are record companies with national distribution, VideoFact does not discourage applications by musicians who do not have record releases with nationally distributed record companies. VideoFact will award up to 50% of the production budget to a maximum of $15,000. Payment is made upon receipt of the completed video. The grant is for production of the video and does not include the cost of recording the musical soundtrack. Only costs directly related to the production of the video are eligible.[138] The award is open to Canadian-controlled record labels, video production companies and Canadian individuals.[139] To be eligible, the rights to the master recording and master video must be owned by a Canadian, the music must satisfy at least two of the 'MAPL' criteria defined by the CRTC,[140] and either (1) the video director or production company must be Canadian, or (2) the production facilities must be located in Canada. VideoFact grants are not determined by a particular genre of music.

(iii) Cultural Industries Development Fund

The Cultural Industries Development Fund, a program of the Department of Canadian Heritage, targets entrepreneurs working in the publishing, sound recording, film and video production and multimedia industries in Canada. The program provides financial services, including term loans, and is administered by the Business Development Bank of Canada. Loans range in size from $20,000 to $200,000. To qualify, applicants must be at least 75% Canadian-owned, or controlled and in business for at least two years. Gross revenues in the most recent financial year must equal or exceed $200,000;[141] record companies must have annual sales of at least $50,000, and applicants must possess the skill and financial resources to meet their financial obligations. Approximately 30% of these funds are allocated to francophone businesses.[142] Because access to the program is limited to

---

[137] VideoFact application form, p. 1.

[138] Ineligible expenses include management, legal and accounting fees, travel, accommodation, recording of the musical soundtrack and duplication costs.

[139] Such individuals must be Canadian citizens or landed immigrants and can include producers, managers and artists.

[140] MAPL is an acronym for (M)usic composed by a Canadian; (A)rtist who is the principal performer is Canadian; (P)erformance or production takes place in Canada; or (L)yrics are written by a Canadian.

[141] Such applicants can include music publishers. Funds available to the music industry are currently split equally between (1) the publishing sector and (2) the recording and film sector.

[142] CIRPA newsletter, August 1991, p. 5.

the production sector, individual musicians are ineligible for the program.

According to the CIRPA, the loan program was instituted for the following reasons: (1) "perception problems — cultural industries do not fit the typical profile of business firms"; (2) "risk problems — cultural businesses often pose too high a risk for prospective financiers"; and (3) "collateral problems — cultural firms have few hard assets that lenders will accept as collateral".[143]

(iv) Arts Council Funding

The Canada Council for Arts and the various provincial Arts Councils provide a wide array of programs designed to assist musicians and musical groups. For the most part, these programs target the field of classical music,[144] but there are several programs of interest to the non-classical performer or songwriter. These include the grants awarded by the Ontario Arts Council through its Popular Music Program[145] and by the Canada Council through its Sound Recording Program. The latter, a component of the SRDP, supports Canadian "specialized music"[146] with grants of up to $20,000 to qualifying Canadian artists, ensembles, bands, record companies and independent producers. Also available is the "demo option", a program intended to support emerging professional performers. Grants will cover up to 60% of eligible expenses, which include the costs of recording, post-production, manufacturing, and promotion. Eligible genres include contemporary Canadian composition or songwriting in the classical music of all world cultures, jazz, folk, world music, fusion of music, First People's music, spoken word, electro-acoustic and

---

[143] *Ibid.*, p. 5.

[144] The Canada Council, for example, currently makes grants or awards with respect to the following programs: choir, small ensembles, opera/musical theatre, professional orchestra, classical contemporary/new music, music touring grants, grants to individual musicians, residencies and commissioning of Canadian compositions, music festival programming, international performance assistance, project grants to artists and annual grants to managers or agents, the first people's program, the Jules Leger prize for chamber music, and grants for sound recordings.

[145] These grants are available to Ontario-based professional artists seeking assistance for projects taking place in Ontario. Projects may include composing, songwriting, sound recording up to the master tape stage, and self-presented live public performances. The OAC also has a recording program for classical music, and programs which support the composition of contemporary classical works and the presentation of live music.

[146] "Specialized music" is defined by the Canada Council as "any musical production whose intent and/or content places creativity, self-expression and/or experimentation above the current demands and format expectations of the mainstream recording industry"; see The Canada Council for the Arts, Program Information, Music Section, Grants for Sound Recording.

musique actuelle.[147] Where the project also qualifies for FACTOR funding, the Canada Council and FACTOR together will fund a maximum of 75% of the project costs.

(v) Ontario Sound Recording Tax Credit

The recently enacted Ontario Sound Recording Tax Credit[148] permits a corporation that is an "eligible sound recording company" to deduct from its tax otherwise payable for a taxation year under Part II of the *Corporations Tax Act* an amount equal to its Ontario sound recording tax credit. Where the credit is greater than the corporation's Part II tax liability, the balance may be applied against any capital or insurance taxes payable under the Act[149] and any excess remaining may be claimed as a refund.[150]

To qualify, a corporation must: (1) carry on a sound recording business, primarily;[151] (2) have carried on the business for at least 24 months before the beginning of the taxation year; (3) carry on the business primarily at a permanent establishment in Ontario; (4) earn at least 50 percent of its taxable income in Ontario; (5) bear the financial risk associated with the business; and (6) implement a plan for the distribution of at least one sound recording within twelve months prior to the start of the first taxation year for which it claims the credit.[152]

The credit is only available with respect to "eligible Canadian sound recordings" by "emerging Canadian artists or groups", i.e., Canadian resident musicians or vocalists who individually or as members of a group have not had a gold record in Canada, the U.S. or certain other major markets.[153]

To qualify as an eligible Canadian sound recording, the music or lyrics must be performed by an emerging Canadian artist or group, the music and lyrics must be written primarily by Canadian residents, substantially all of the activities carried out to produce the recording

---

[147] *Ibid.*

[148] *Corporations Tax Act*, R.S.O. 1990, c. C.39, s. 43.12, enacted by S.O. 1998, s. 43, in force January 1, 1999 (herein "the Act").

[149] *Ibid.*, s. 43.12(2).

[150] *Ibid.*, s. 43.12(13).

[151] Subsection 905(3) of Reg. 183 of R.R.O. 1990 (General Regulation under the *Corporations Tax Act*) as amended by Ont. Reg. 419/99, in force January 2, 1999 for the definition of "sound recording business" (herein "the Regulation").

[152] Additionally, the corporation must be a Canadian-controlled private corporation under ss. 26-28 of the *Investment Canada Act* and may not be a corporation to which the corporate minimum tax applied for a previous taxation year if in such year the corporation had assets greater than $10 million or revenues greater than $20 million; see s. 905(3) 6 of the Regulation.

[153] Subsection 905(4) of the Regulation.

must be performed in Ontario, the recording company must have exclusive contractual control of the master tape for at least five years, and must make plans for the distribution of the recording.[154]

The credit is limited to the lesser of (a) 20% of "qualifying expenditures" and (b) an amount calculated in accordance with the regulations.[155] "Qualifying expenditures" include, *inter alia*, expenditures incurred on account of property used primarily in Ontario for the production of the recording, including artists' royalties, session fees, graphics, software, the production of a music video, and marketing.[156]

To obtain the credit, the sound recording company first must apply to the Minister of Citizenship, Culture and Recreation for certification that the company is an eligible Canadian recording company[157] and that the recording is an eligible Canadian sound recording, and then deliver a copy of the certificate with its tax return.[158]

---

[154] The type of plan will depend on the company's gross revenues: companies with revenues of less than $500,000 in the prior taxation year must have a plan considered appropriate by the Minister of Citizenship, Culture and Recreation; other companies are required to enter into arrangements for national distribution of the sound recording; see s. 905(7) of the Regulation.

[155] Subsection 43.12(3) of the Act. For the "amount calculated", see s. 905(11) of the Regulation.

[156] See s. 905(9) of the Regulation for a complete list of qualifying expenditures.

[157] Subsection 43.12(6) of the Act.

[158] Subsection 43.12 (9) of the Act.

12

TAX

Contributing Author: Ronald N. Hier, B.A., LL.B., LL.M.

Introduction

This chapter briefly considers the taxation of musicians. The taxes discussed include the income tax, the goods and services tax, the retail sales tax, and the amusement tax, all of which potentially impact on a musician's business activities. Also described are the tax aspects of Canadian films and video productions and the effect of the Internal Revenue Code on the business income of Canadian musicians derived from U.S. sources. It should be noted that taxation is a complex, ever-changing area of law; accordingly, the reader is advised to seek competent professional advice with respect to the specifics of his or her tax situation.

1. Income Tax

(a) Income Sources

Canadian income tax law employs a source theory of taxation. Under this theory, the income (or losses) of a taxpayer are calculated on a source-by-source basis[1] and the aggregate of all sources forms the income on which the tax is calculated.[2] Because deductions can be taken only against income from a matching source, and different rules apply with respect to different sources, it becomes important to classify the potential sources of a musician's income.

Musicians have four main sources of income. These include income from: (1) copyright; (2) personal appearances and live performances; (3) record sales; and (4) merchandising and

---

[1] Paragraph 4(1)(a) *Income Tax Act* ("ITA").
[2] Section 3, ITA. Income first is reduced to taxable income by making the adjustments provided for in Division C of the Act; see s. 2(2).

endorsements. Additional sources include arts council grants, awards and prizes, income earned with respect to the management or booking of other musicians, insurance proceeds[3], and welfare or employment insurance.

(b) Basis for Taxation

Individuals resident in Canada at any time in a taxation year are subject to tax on their world-wide income from all sources in that taxation year.[4] The courts have held that an individual is resident in Canada if Canada is the place where he or she regularly or customarily lives.[5] Residence is ultimately a question of fact and where the individual has left Canada for all or part of a taxation year, Revenue Canada will look to such factors as the permanence and purpose of the stay abroad, his or her primary residential ties with Canada and elsewhere[6], and the regularity and length of visits to Canada. Any uncertainties attendant on the above definition would appear to be alleviated by the deeming provision found in subsection 250(1) of the Act. Pursuant to this subsection, a person will be deemed to be resident in Canada throughout a taxation year if he or she sojourned in Canada in the year for a period or periods in the aggregate equal to or exceeding 183 days.

(c) Legal Tests Related to Employee or Self-Employed Status

A key issue in the taxation of musicians is the characterization of their employment status. If musicians are self-employed, their income from a business for a taxation year is the profit therefrom;[7] if they are employees, their income is their salary or wages.[8] To determine their

---

[3] Proceeds of insurance might arise with respect to the theft or loss of musical instruments or the cancellation of an engagement. With respect to the former, para. 12(1)(g) requires the inclusion in income of insurance proceeds payable as compensation for damage to depreciable property of the taxpayer, to the extent the proceeds are used to repair the damage. Unused proceeds are treated as proceeds of disposition under sub-para. 13(21)(d)(iii) and potentially can give rise to a recapture of depreciation.

[4] Subsection 2(1), ITA. For Revenue Canada's view of what constitutes "residence", see IT-221R2.

[5] IT-221R2 , para. 2.

[6] Residential ties include such things as the location of the taxpayer's dwelling place, his/her spouse and dependants, his/her property and social ties; ibid., para. 6.

[7] Subsection 9(1), ITA.

[8] Subsection 5(1), ITA.

profit, taxpayers who are self-employed are entitled to deduct all expenses incurred in gaining or producing income.[9] Employees, on the other hand, are restricted in the amounts they may deduct.[10] Consequently, it is always desirable for musicians to structure a relationship so as to give rise to income from a business.

(i) Contract of Service or Contract for Services

The distinction between income from employment and income from a business is sometimes expressed in terms of whether musicians supply their services as employees under a contract of service, or as independent contractors under a contract for services. The test most commonly applied is the control test. Derived from the common law of master and servant, this test looks to the nature and degree of control exerted by the person alleged to be the employer. As one court has stated, "...the main measures to be considered must be the nature and the complexity of the task and the freedom of action given, i.e., the nature and degree of the detailed control over the person alleged to be the servant."[11] An alternative formulation asks whether the person alleged to be the employee is required to act under the direct supervision of another and is bound to conform to all reasonable orders given. If so, the taxpayer is an employee. However, where taxpayers undertake to produce a specified result employing their own means, free of any control or interference, they are independent contractors.[12]

The control test is not the only test employed by the courts. Other tests finding judicial favour include: (1) the integration test;[13] (2) the economic reality test;[14] and (3) the specific result test.[15] In *Wiebe Door*

---

[9] Generally, expenses are recognized in accordance with GAAP. However, ss. 18 and 67.1 of the Act provide specific limitations on the deductibility of certain expenses. See also s. 67, the general limitation on expenses.

[10] Allowable deductions are found in s. 8 of the Act.

[11] *Braive v. Minister of National Revenue* (1981), 81 D.T.C. 748 (T.R.B.), citing *Performing Rights Society Ltd. v. Mitchell & Booker (Palais de Danse) Ltd.*, [1924] 1 K.B. 762 (Eng. K.B.).

[12] *DiFrancesco v. Minister of National Revenue* (1964), 64 D.T.C. 106 (T.R.B.). Other indicia of control include a right to control the manner, place, time or amount of work to be done by the taxpayer.

[13] Under this test, the courts examine the extent to which the taxpayer's services are an integral part of the business; where they are ancillary or accessory, the taxpayer will be considered an independent contractor. For application of this test, see *Rosen v. R.* (1976), 76 D.T.C. 6274 (Fed. T.D.) and *Produce Processors v. Minister of National Revenue* (1980), 80 D.T.C. 1483 (T.R.B.).

[14] Under this test, the courts consider the extent to which the taxpayer is at risk of loss in the operation of the business. Business risks include the risks inherent in the supply and financing of equipment, the supply and payment of workers, and the supply

Services Ltd. v. Minister of National Revenue,[16] the Federal Court of Appeal eschewed the mechanistic application of the above tests, holding that no one test is determinative and that the court must strive to weigh all relevant factors so as to answer this question: "...is the person who has engaged himself to perform these services performing them in business on his own account?"[17] Ultimately, then, whether a musician is an employee or an independent contractor will depend on the facts and circumstances of each particular case.

The determination of whether musicians perform on their own account, however, is not always a simple exercise because contracts for the personal services of musicians are "hybrid in nature, incorporating elements of both contracts of service and contracts for service".[18] Cases involving musicians have, prior to *Wiebe*, and without exception, been decided on the basis of the control test; since *Wiebe*, however, the courts have employed the four-factor test described therein.[19]

Specific factors considered by the Tax Appeal Board in a series of often contradictory cases decided in the early to mid-1950's include: (1) whether the musicians have the right to select the material they perform;[20] (2) whether the musicians are required to attend rehearsals

---

of clients; see *Hauser v. Minister of National Revenue* (1978), 78 D.T.C 1532 (T.R.B.); *Alexander v. Minister of National Revenue* (1969), 70 D.T.C. 6006 (Can. Ex. Ct.).

[15] Under this test, the courts look to whether contractors engage to deliver a specific result which they are not required to procure personally; see Alexander, supra note 14.

[16] (1986) 87 D.T.C. 5025 (Fed. C.A.), reversed (October 29, 1986), Doc. 83-469 (UI) (T.C.C.).

[17] In *Wiebe*, the court considered the following factors relevant to the inquiry: (1) control; (2) entrepreneurship; and (3) organization. For yet another formulation which found favour with the Federal Court of Appeal, see *Montreal (City) v. Montreal Locomotive Works Ltd.*, [1947] 1 D.L.R. 161 (Can. P.C.), wherein the Privy Council adopted a four-fold test, looking at: (1) control; (2) ownership of tools; (3) chance of profit; and (4) risk of loss. In *Moose Jaw Kinsmen Flying Fins Inc. v. Minister of National Revenue* (1988), 88 D.T.C. 6099 (Fed. C.A.), the court, at p. 6100, called the decision in *Wiebe* "the definitive authority on this issue in the context of the Act." For recent applications of the test in non-musician cases, see *Bradford v. Minister of National Revenue* (1988), 88 D.T.C. 1661 (T.C.C.); *Floro v. Minister of National Revenue* (1988), 88 D.T.C. 1675 (T.C.C); *Campbell v. Minister of National Revenue* (1986), 87 D.T.C. 47 (T.C.C.).

[18] Russell Disney, *Federal Tax Issues of Concern to the Arts Community in Canada: An Analysis*, (Ottawa: Department of the Secretary of State, 1977), at p. 6.

[19] For the recent applications of the test in the context of unemployment insurance, see *Thunder Bay Symphony Orchestra Ass. Inc. v. Minister of National Revenue*, [1998] T.C.J. No. 955 (T.C.C.); *Pitaro v. Minister of National Revenue*, [1987] T.C.J. No. 11 (T.C.C.); *Les promotions C.G.S. Inc. v. Minister of National Revenue*, [1988] T.C.J. No. 414 (T.C.C.); and *Big Pond Publishing and Production Ltd. v. Minister of National Revenue*, [1998] T.C.J. No. 935 (T.C.C.).

[20] *Hanson v. Minister of National Revenue* (1952), 52 D.T.C. 261 (T.A.B.); *Cavazzi v. Minister of National Revenue* (1952), 52 D.T.C. 334 (T.A.B.).

or report at fixed hours;[21] (3) whether the musicians are in the steady employ of anyone, or work a variety of engagements;[22] (4) whether the musicians arrange their own bookings;[23] (5) whether the musicians provide their services on an exclusive basis for an extended period of time;[24] (6) whether the musicians' working hours, dress code and the type of music to be performed are controlled by a third party;[25] (7) whether the musicians work part-time;[26] and more generally (8) whether the musicians are subject to complete control of the services they are to render under the contract.[27]

Revenue Canada takes the position that musicians may be employees if the party with whom they contract has, *inter alia*, the right: (1) to make alterations in the size of the ensemble; (2) to choose unilaterally the style of music performed; and (3) to dictate the time and place of performance and rehearsal; and has the obligations (a) to pay for overtime; and (b) to provide or authorize transportation for the artists.[28] Revenue Canada further states that musicians may be self-

---

[21] *Ibid.* See also *Allard v. Minister of National Revenue* (1952), 52 D.T.C. 197 (T.A.B.) and *Cavazzi,* supra note 20.

[22] *No. 33 v. Minister of National Revenue* (1951), 51 D.T.C. 430 (T.A.B.); see also *Bradanovich v. Minister of National Revenue* (1959), 59 D.T.C. 453 (T.A.B.); *Hunter v. Minister of National Revenue* (1951), 51 D.T.C. 213 (T.A.B.); *No. 46 v. Minister of National Revenue* (1952), 52 D.T.C. 81 (T.A.B.); *Lewis v. Minister of National Revenue* (1952), 52 D.T.C. 92 (T.A.B.). In *Iosch v. Minister of National Revenue* (1952), 52 D.T.C. 94 (T.A.B.), the courts found the musicians to be self-employed, but in three other cases, the court took a contrary view: *MacPherson v. Minister of National Revenue* (1955), 55 D.T.C. 376 (T.A.B.); *Pepper v. Minister of National Revenue* (1954), 54 D.T.C. 104 (T.A.B); and *Houghton v. Minister of National Revenue* (1952), 52 D.T.C. 393 (T.A.B.). In *MacPherson,* the court found that the taxpayer was an employee, notwithstanding that he had numerous engagements, because at all times he was under the direction of a leader who controlled rehearsals, the time of arrival at engagements, and the manner in which the music was to be played.

[23] *No. 33 v. Minister of National Revenue* (1951), 51 D.T.C. 430 (T.A.B.).

[24] *Performing Rights Society Ltd. v. Mitchell & Booker (Palais de Danse) Ltd.,* [1924] 1 K.B. 762 (Eng. K.B.).

[25] *Kaczynski v. Minister of National Revenue* (1988), 88 D.T.C. 6095 (Fed. C.A.).

[26] *Harvey v. Minister of National Revenue* (1952), 52 D.T.C. 61 (T.A.B.); *Collins v. Minister of National Revenue* (1952), 52 D.T.C. 68 (T.A.B.).

[27] *Carrick v. Minister of National Revenue* (1955), 55 D.T.C 56 (T.A.B); *Grondin v. Minister of National Revenue* (1955), 55 D.T.C 167 (T.A.B.). See also *Chlumecky v. Minister of National Revenue* (1955), 55 D.T.C. 183 (T.A.B.); *Blunt v. Minister of National Revenue* (1956), 56 D.T.C. 73 (T.A.B.); *MacKay v. Minister of National Revenue* (1958), 58 D.T.C. 447 (T.A.B.).

[28] IT-525R, para. 6. See also *Vancouver Symphony Society v. Minister of National Revenue,* a decision of the Pension Appeals Board, Jan. 11, 1974, found at 1974 C.B. & P.G.R., p. 6179. Although not a tax case, the Board relied, *inter alia,* on the factors enumerated above to find that musicians who had contracted with the Symphony Society were in 'pensionable employment'. For a case reaching the opposite result, see the *Edmonton Symphony Society v. Minister of National Revenue,* a decision of the Pension Appeals Board, dated October 27, 1980, found at 1974 C.B. & P.G.R., p. 6545. The Board distinguished

employed if: (1) they have a chance of profit and a risk of loss; (2) they provide their own instruments and equipment; (3) they have a number of different engagements throughout the year; (4) they regularly audition or make applications for engagements; (5) they retain the services of an agent on a continuing basis; (6) they can select, pay, direct and dismiss helpers or employees; (7) they can arrange the time, place, and nature of their performance; and (8) they are entitled to remuneration directly related to rehearsals and performances.[29]

The courts have recognized that musicians can be employees with respect to one engagement and self-employed with respect to others in the course of a single taxation year,[30] but they may not be employees and self-employed under the same arrangement or contract.[31] In cases where application of the appropriate legal test will support either classification, the intentions of the parties will govern.[32] It is therefore advisable for the parties to make their intentions known in any written contract governing the terms of their relationship.

(ii) Reasonable Expectation of Profit

Although musicians may be self-employed under the above tests, they will be permitted to deduct expenses only to the extent that their business has a reasonable expectation of profit.[33] In *Moldowan v. R.*,[34] the Supreme Court of Canada held that whether there is a reasonable expectation of profit can be determined objectively by having regard to the "...profit and loss experience in past years, the taxpayer's training, the taxpayer's intended course of action... [and]... the capability of the

---

the former case by noting that the Edmonton Symphony had not entered into a collective agreement with the AFM as had been done by the Vancouver Symphony Society. See also *Thunder Bay Symphony Orchestra Ass. Inc.*, supra note 19, wherein core musicians of the Thunder Bay Symphony were held to be employees, in part on the basis that the master agreement dictated hours of work, provided for overtime pay, and subjected the musicians to the musical control of the orchestra's director.

[29] IT-525R, para. 7.

[30] *MacKay v. Minister of National Revenue*, supra note 27; *Chlumecky*, supra note 27; *Pepper v. Minister of National Revenue*, supra note 22. See also IT-525R, para. 2.

[31] IT-525R, para. 2.

[32] *Bradford v. Minister of National Revenue* (1988), 88 D.T.C. 1661 (T.C.C.). See also *Edmonton Symphony Society v. Minister of National Revenue*, supra note 28, where this principal was applied by the Pension Appeals Board in the face of ambiguity as to the proper classification of the contract.

[33] *Seymour v. Minister of National* Revenue (1982), 82 D.T.C. 1706 (T.R.B.). For a recent discussion of the reasonable expectation of profits test, see Brian S. Nichols, "Chants and Ritual Incantation: Rethinking the Reasonable Expectation of Profit Test", Report *of the Proceedings of the Forty-Eighth Tax Conference, 1996 Conference Report*, (Toronto: Canadian Tax Foundation, 1997), at p. 28:1.

[34] (1977), 77 D.T.C. 5213 (S.C.C.).

venture as capitalized to show a profit after charging capital cost allowance."[35] The court noted that the factors listed were not intended to be exhaustive, and further stated that "factors will differ with the nature and extent of the undertaking."[36]

The difficulty of applying this test to the arts is well illustrated by the case of *Schip v. Minister of National Revenue.*[37] Schip was a fine art photographer who had studied extensively and had received degrees in the subject. His work was exhibited in numerous photo exhibitions and art magazines. He received Canada Council and Ontario Arts Council grants given to 'professional artists', and was considered a professional by gallery owners. In refusing to allow the deduction of his business losses from his employment income, the court ruled that because he was operating in an immature business, one in which it was difficult to make a living, the appellant had no reasonable expectation of profit[38].

Many musicians and artists cannot be said to have a reasonable expectation of profit, nor can cultural and artistic pursuits always be measured in terms of profit.[39] Schip's situation parallels that of many musicians, particularly those who stray from the commercial mainstream, for whom there is little likelihood that their activities could ever give rise to a reasonable expectation of profit.[40] Where the test in *Moldowan* is not satisfied, a musician will have a 'hobby' loss not deductible from other sources of income.

Although Revenue Canada has seen fit to relax the test in connection with the activities of artists and writers, no such relief is afforded at present to musicians or performers.[41]

---

[35] *Ibid.*, p. 5217.

[36] *Ibid.*, p. 5217.

[37] (1983), 83 D.T.C. 190 (T.R.B.).

[38] The court recognized, however, that should the business prove profitable at some point in the future, the losses could be carried forward and deducted at that time. The unsatisfactory nature of this decision has been recognized by Revenue Canada, at least with respect to visual artists and writers; see IT-504R2 wherein it is stated in para. 7 that "it is possible that...[an artist or writer]... may not realize a profit during his or her lifetime but still have a reasonable expectation of profit" if the endeavour is carried in a manner that suggests it is a business. For the relevant factors, see footnote 41, infra.

[39] See Disney, supra note 18, and more recently, *Report of the Sub-Committee on the Taxation of Visual and Performing Artists and Writers*, (Ottawa: Supply and Services Canada, 1984), for recognition of these difficulties. Note that the ITA has been amended to address some of the concerns of visual artists. See ITA s. 10 (6)-(8) for inventory valuation, and ITA ss. 118.1(6) and (7) for charitable gifts of capital property and art.

[40] Many musicians, including rock, classical, and jazz performers, who reside outside the commercial mainstream, often do not make a living from their music. They rely on their spouses or parents, and work at full- or part-time jobs to finance their musical pursuits.

[41] In IT-504R2, para. 5, Revenue Canada states that the following factors will be considered in determining whether artists or writers have a reasonable expectation of profit: (1) the amount of time devoted to the endeavour; (2) the extent to which the

(d) Deductions

(i) Employees

Musicians who are employees are entitled to the deductions found in section 8 of the Act. The most important of these include the deduction for musical instrument costs,[42] artists' employment expenses,[43] union dues,[44] contributions to registered pension plans,[45] travelling and motor vehicle expenses,[46] and the cost of maintaining a work space in the home.[47]

Musical instrument costs will be deductible if musicians are required to provide a musical instrument under the terms of their employment contract. The deduction, which may not exceed the musician's income from the employment, is limited to the aggregate of all amounts expended on maintenance, rental, insurance in the taxation year, and any capital cost allowance claimed with respect to the instrument.[48]

Musicians who are employed to compose or perform music are entitled to deduct amounts actually paid before the end of the taxation year in respect of expenses incurred for the purpose of earning income from those activities. The deduction is limited to the lesser of $1,000 or 20% of the aggregate income from artistic activities net of any amounts deducted with respect to musical instrument and/or motor vehicle costs. Expenses in excess of this amount may be carried forward to the next taxation year and if not deductible therein, carried forward indefinitely.[49]

---

artists or writers have publicly presented their work; (3) representation by a dealer or agent; (4) the amount of revenue received from the endeavour; (5) the historical record of profit and losses; (6) a variation over time in the popularity of the artist's works; (7) the type of expenditures claimed and their relevance to the endeavour; (8) education and membership in professional organizations; (9) any growth in gross revenues from exploitation of the work over time; and (10) the nature of the work and its commercial potential. These tests may be helpful if applied by analogy to musicians. See generally, paras. 4-7.

[42] Paragraph 8(1)(p).

[43] Paragraph 8(1)(q).

[44] Paragraph 8(1)(i); see also *MacPherson v. Minister of National Revenue*, supra note 22, wherein the taxpayer was permitted to deduct union dues under s. 11 of the 1948 Act.

[45] Paragraph 8(1)(m).

[46] Paragraphs 8(1)(h) and (h.1). Note that where musicians are required to be away for a period of at least twelve hours from the municipality where they normally work, they may be entitled to deduct the cost of meals under s-s. 8(4).

[47] Paragraph 8(1)(m).

[48] Musical instruments are class 8 property and CCA may be taken at a rate of 20%.

[49] See IT-525R, para. 17. Note that pursuant to the wording of para. 8(1)(q) where an expense is deductible thereunder and under another provision as well, if no

Additional deductions available to musicians who are employees include the standard deductions for CPP and EI contributions[50] and a deduction for any amount paid on account of legal expenses incurred to collect or establish a right to salary or wages owed by the employer or a former employer.[51]

(ii) Self-Employment

Subject to the Act and generally accepted accounting principles, self-employed musicians can deduct all expenses reasonably incurred for the purpose of earning income from a business or property. Where musicians earn their income partly from employment and partly as independent contractors, the expenses will be allowed in proportion.[52]

A. Allowable Expenses[53]

(1) insurance premiums on musical instruments and equipment;[54]

(2) cost of repairs to instruments and equipment including the cost of new reeds, strings, pads, and accessories;[55]

(3) legal and accounting fees;[56]

---

deduction is taken under the latter, any excess cannot be carried forward since the expense was deductible in the prior taxation year.

[50] Paragraph 8(1)(l.1).

[51] Paragraph 8(1)(b).

[52] See *No. 124 v. Minister of National Revenue* (1953), 53 D.T.C. 426; *Pepper v. Minister of National Revenue* (1954), 54 D.T.C. 104; *Chlumecky v. Minister of National Revenue* (1955), 55 D.T.C. 183 (T.A.B.); *Blunt v. Minister of National Revenue* (1956), 56 D.T.C. 73 (T.A.B.).

[53] The list in the text is drawn from IT-525, para. 11. For digests of cases dealing with musicians' expenses, only some of which are documented here, see *Canadian Tax Reporter*, (Toronto: CCH Canadian Limited, 1993) at p. 4322, para. 4765.

[54] *Crawford v. Minister of National Revenue* (1954), 54 D.T.C. 478 (T.A.B.); *Avison v. Minister of National Revenue* (1952), 52 D.T.C. 284 (T.A.B.); *Harvey v. Minister of National Revenue* (1952), 52 D.T.C. 61 (T.A.B.).

[55] *Hunter v. Minister of National Revenue* (1951), 51 D.T.C. 213 (T.A.B.); *Yssellyn v. Minister of National Revenue* (1952), 52 D.T.C. 135 (T.A.B.); *Avison v. Minister of National Revenue* (1952), 52 D.T.C. 284 (T.A.B.); *Harvey v. Minister of National Revenue* (1952), 52 D.T.C. 61 (T.A.B.); *Iosch v. Minister of National Revenue* (1952), 52 D.T.C. 94 (T.A.B).

[56] *Iosch v. Minister of National Revenue* (1952), 52 D.T.C. 94 (T.A.B.); *Crawford v. Minister of National Revenue* (1954), 54 D.T.C. 478 (T.A.B.); but see *Blunt v. Minister of National Revenue* (1956), 56 D.T.C. 73 (T.A.B.) wherein fees for the preparation of income tax returns were held not to be deductible. As to legal fees, they will not be deductible if they are not incurred in the ordinary course of business and do not result in the creation of a "lasting benefit"; see *Madden v. Minister of National Revenue* (1956), 56 D.T.C. 256 (T.A.B.).

(4) union dues and professional membership dues;[57]

(5) agent's commissions;[58]

(6) remuneration paid to a substitute or assistant;[59]

(7) the costs of special make-up required for special appearances or hairstyling required for public appearances;[60]

(8) publicity expenses consisting generally of the cost of having photographs made and sent with a descriptive commentary to producers and the media, and including the cost of advertisements in talent magazines;[61]

(9) transportation expenses related to an engagement (including an audition) under one of the following conditions: (a) where the engagement is out of town (in which case board and lodging also would be allowable;[62] (b) a large instrument or equipment must be carried;[63] (c) dress clothes must be worn from a residence to the place of engagement; or (d) one engagement follows another so closely that a car or taxi is the only means by which the engagement can be fulfilled.[64]

---

[57] *No. 33 v. Minister of National Revenue* (1951), 51 D.T.C. 430 (T.A.B.); *Collins v. Minister of National Revenue* (1952), 52 D.T.C. 68 (T.A.B.); *Iosch v. Minister of National Revenue* (1952), 52 D.T.C. 94 (T.A.B.); *Piggott v. Minister of National Revenue* (1954), 54 D.T.C. 314 (T.A.B.); *Cavazzi v. Minister of National Revenue* (1954), 54 D.T.C. 484 (T.A.B.); *Morgan v. Minister of National Revenue* (1956), 56 D.T.C. 197 (T.A.B.).

[58] *No. 33 v. Minister of National Revenue* (1951), 51 D.T.C. 430 (T.A.B.).

[59] Substitutes: *Ysselstyn v. Minister of National Revenue* (1952), 52 D.T.C. 135 (T.A.B.); Assistants: *No. 165 v. Minister of National Revenue* (1954), 54 D.T.C. 240 (T.A.B.).

[60] *No. 91 v. Minister of National Revenue* (1953), 53 D.T.C. 146 (T.A.B.); *No. 93 v. Minister of National Revenue* (1953), 53 D.T.C. 154 (T.A.B.); *No. 94 v. Minister of National Revenue* (1953), 53 D.T.C. 157 (T.A.B.); *No. 122 v. Minister of National Revenue* (1953), 53 D.T.C. 399 (T.A.B.); see also *Avison v. Minister of National Revenue* (1952), 52 D.T.C. 284 (T.A.B.); *Piggott v. Minister of National Revenue* (1954), 54 D.T.C. 314 (T.A.B.). As to hairstyling expenses, they have been held to be non-deductible; see *No. 428 v. Minister of National Revenue* (1957), 57 D.T.C. 310 (T.A.B.); and *No. 33 v. Minister of National Revenue* (1951), 51 D.T.C. 430 (T.A.B.) also holding make-up not deductible.

[61] *Piggott v. Minister of National Revenue* (1954), 54 D.T.C. 314; *Wald v. Minister of National Revenue* (1954), 54 D.T.C. 485 (T.A.B.); *Ferbey v. Minister of National Revenue* (1954), 54 D.T.C. 486 (T.A.B.)

[62] *No . 46 v. Minister of National Revenue* (1952), 52 D.T.C. 81 (T.A.B.) but see *No. 47 v. Minister of National Revenue* (1952), 52 D.T.C. 90 (T.A.B.).

[63] *Cavazzi v. Minister of National Revenue* (1954), 54 D.T.C. 484 (T.A.B.); *Bradanovich v. Minister of National Revenue* (1959), 59 D.T.C. 453 (T.A.B.); *Collins v. Minister of National Revenue* (1952), 52 D.T.C. 68 (T.A.B.).

[64] *No. 482 v. Minister of National Revenue* (1958), 58 D.T.C. 83 (T.A.B.).However, travelling expenses to seek an engagement are not deductible: *Morgan v. Minister of National Revenue* (1956), 56 D.T.C. 197 (T.A.B.). In general, travelling expenses must exceed the expenses of normally travelling to and from work and must relate exclusively

(10) the costs of videotaping or recording performances where required for their preparation or presentation;

(11) telephone expenses, including an applicable portion of the cost of a telephone in a residence listed as a business phone;[65]

(12) capital cost allowance on instruments, sheet music, scores, scripts, transcriptions, arrangements, equipment,[66] and wardrobe (to qualify for capital cost allowance the wardrobe must be acquired by the artist specifically to earn self-employment income);[67]

(13) the cost of repairs, alterations, and cleaning of clothes for the purpose of their use in self-employment, or required as a result of such use;[68]

(14) maintenance costs of part of the artist's residence used for professional purposes;[69]

(15) the cost of music, acting, or other lessons incurred for a particular role or part or for the purpose of general self-improvement in the individual's artistic field.[70]

---

to the earning process. For Revenue Canada's views on the motor vehicle expenses of self-employed individuals, see IT-521R.

[65] *No. 46 v. Minister of National Revenue* (1952), 52 D.T.C. 81 (T.A.B.); *Lewis v. Minister of National Revenue* (1952), 52 D.T.C. 92 (T.A.B.).

[66] With regard to arrangements, in *Ambrose v. Minister of National Revenue* (1967), 67 D.T.C 42 (T.A.B.), the court allowed Tommy Ambrose to expense the cost of arrangements where it was shown that they could be used only once and therefore were not of enduring value.

[67] In *Giroux v. Minister of National Revenue* (1957), 57 D.T.C. 238 (T.A.B.), the court stated that expenditures for costumes which could be worn only on stage were capital outlays for depreciable property and therefore deductible under the Act.

[68] Revenue Canada's position is apparently more generous than the courts'; see *Avison v. Minister of National Revenue* (1952), 52 D.T.C. 284 (T.A.B.); *Crawford v. Minister of National Revenue* (1952), 52 D.T.C 331 (T.A.B.); *Collins v. Minister of National Revenue* (1952), 52 D.T.C. 68 (T.A.B.). However, because such expenses may be disallowed on the grounds that they are personal living expenses within para. 18(1)(h), they should be documented carefully.

[69] While numerous cases have disallowed a deduction for studio expenses where musicians use a room in their home exclusively for practising (see, for example, *Crawford v. Minister of National Revenue* (1952), 52 D.T.C. 331 (T.A.B.); *No. 46 v. Minister of National Revenue* (1952), 52 D.T.C. 81 (T.A.B.); *Iosch v. Minister of National Revenue* (1952), 52 D.T.C. 94 (T.A.B.)), the cost of renting a studio is deductible: *Piggott v. Minister of National Revenue* (1954), 54 D.T.C. 315 (T.A.B.); see also para. 12(1)(d). Musicians who use a room in their home as their principal place of business are entitled to the deduction contained in s. 18(12). For Revenue Canada's view as to what constitutes a principal place of business, see IT-514, para. 2. Amounts deducted may include a pro-rated portion of rent, CCA, property insurance and taxes, and operating costs not exceeding the income of the business; any excess may be carried forward indefinitely. Where CCA is claimed, the exemption from capital gains tax given with respect to the disposition of a principal residence will not apply.

(16) the cost of industry-related periodicals.[71]

B. Not Allowable

Generally, personal expenses and capital expenditures are not deductible.[72] With respect to the latter, however, the Act permits the deduction of capital cost allowance. Items of relevance to musicians qualifying for capital cost allowance include instruments, sheet music, scores, scripts, transcriptions, arrangements, equipment and, if used specifically to earn income from a business, wardrobe.[73] CCA may be taken at the rate of 20% per annum on the declining balance method.[74]

Videotaping and recording costs incurred specifically for the purpose of study and general self-improvement are not deductible.[75]

(e) Assessment Appeals

(i) Generally

A tax assessment is generally assumed to be correct and the onus of proof is on the taxpayer to prove that it is incorrect.[76] Where a taxpayer contests the disallowance of a business expense, the taxpayer will have to provide proof, *inter alia*, that (1) the expenses were made as claimed; (2) the expenses are deductible under some provision of the Act; (3) the taxpayer was self-employed; and (4) (if this is an issue) there was a reasonable expectation of profit at the time the expense was incurred.

---

[70] *No. 122 v. Minister of National Revenue* (1953), 53 D.T.C. 399; *No. 77 v. Minister of National Revenue* (1953), 53 D.T.C. 27 (T.A.B.); *Chlumecky v. Minister of National Revenue* (1955), 55 D.T.C. 183 (T.A.B.).

[71] Generally not allowable; see, for example, *Lewis v. Minister of National Revenue* (1952), 52 D.T.C. 97 (T.A.B.), but where the expense is necessary to earn income, it may be allowed: *No. 162 v. Minister of National Revenue* (1954), 54 D.T.C. 210 (T.A.B.); *No. 218 v. Minister of National Revenue* (1955), 55 D.T.C. 5 (T.A.B.); *Giroux v. Minister of National Revenue* (1957), 57 D.T.C. 238 (T.A.B.).

[72] Paras. 18(1)(h) and 18(1)(b). The former, however, does permit the deduction of travelling expenses incurred in the course of carrying on a business while away from home; see also s. 67.1 with respect to a limitation on deductions for food and entertainment.

[73] IT-525R; para. 10(l).

[74] The items enumerated fall under para. (i) of Class 8 of Sch. II to the Act. Computers fall under para. (f) of Class 10 for a 30% rate; software falls under para. (o) of Class 12 for a 100% rate.

[75] IT-525R, para. 11 (c). Such costs are deductible where the recording of a performance is required for its preparation or presentation; see para. 10(j).

[76] *Johnston v. Minister of National Revenue* (1948), 3 D.T.C. 1182 (S.C.C.).

(ii) Proving Assessments Incorrect

Numerous appeals brought by musicians have failed, not because the court questioned the legal validity of an impugned deduction, but simply due to an insufficiency of proof.[77] Therefore it is imperative that musicians keep accurate books and records; such records will include written contracts, bank statements and cancelled cheques, as well as receipts and vouchers for any expenses claimed. All books and records must be held for six years from the end of the taxation year to which they relate[78], and may be destroyed prior to expiration of this period only if written permission for their disposal is given by the Minister.[79]

Notes relating to specific engagements can be written on the invoices and receipts to which they relate. Separate business and personal credit cards are useful to record business costs and to segregate business and personal expenses. The use of such methods should enable musicians to ascertain their expenses accurately and (if challenged) to substantiate them as they relate to different sources of income.

---

[77] See, for example, *Allard v. Minister of National Revenue* (1952), 52 D.T.C. 197 (T.A.B.); *Crawford v. Minister of National Revenue* (1952), 52 D.T.C. 331 (T.A.B.). The lack of documentary evidence may frustrate also the taxpayer's argument that he/she is self-employed; see, for example, *Cavazzi v. Minister of National Revenue* (1952), 52 D.T.C 334 (T.A.B), where such a claim failed due to the absence of proof, and *Cavazzi v. Minister of National Revenue* (1954), 54 D.T.C. 484 (T.A.B.), wherein the same taxpayer succeeded where such proof was proffered. On occasion, however, the court will accept oral evidence; see *Morgan v. Minister of National Revenue* (1956), 56 D.TC. 197 (T.A.B.); *Piggott v. Minister of National Revenue* (1954), 54 D.T.C. 314 (T.A.B.); and *Valente v. Minister of National Revenue*, [1991] T.C.J. No. 487 (T.C.C.).

[78] Subsections 230(1) and (4) of the Act. Note that pursuant to para. 152(4)(c), the Minister at any time may assess tax for a taxation year and, within the normal reassessment period, may assess, reassess or make additional assessments of tax. Subsection 152(3.1) defines the normal reassessment period as three years for taxpayers other than mutual fund trusts and non-CCPCs. Under para. 152(4)(b), before the date that is three years after the expiration of the normal reassessment period for taxpayers, the Minister may reassess or assess tax on the grounds contained in sub-paras. (i)-(iv). Accordingly, there is the potential that taxpayers can be assessed or reassessed any time within six years following the date of the mailing of an original notice of assessment. As well, under sub-para. 152(4)(a)(i), taxpayers may be assessed at any time if they have committed fraud or made a willful misrepresentation in filing.

[79] Subsection 230(8).

2. Specific Types of Income and Property

(a) Arts Council Grants and Prizes

Musicians, particularly classical musicians, may receive arts council grants. If the musician is self-employed, the grant will be included in income under section 9 of the Act.[80] If the musician does not carry on a business, and if the grant can be characterized as a scholarship, fellowship, bursary or a prize that is to be used in the production of a musical work, it will be included in income under paragraph 56(1)(n) of the Act and the musician will be entitled to deduct the greater of $500 or the sum total of all expenses incurred by the taxpayer in the year for the purpose of fulfilling the conditions under which the grant was received.[81] If the musician receives the grant from an employer, unless it constitutes remuneration from an office or employment,[82] it will be included in income under paragraph 6(1)(a) of the Act; in either case no deduction will be available under paragraph 56(1)(n).[83]

Musicians who receive research grants which are intended for pure research, and are not intended to advance an academic career, will be required to include such amounts in income by virtue of paragraph 56(1)(o) of the Act.[84] The amount of the grant may be reduced by any expenses incurred in the year for the purpose of carrying out the research, but any excess expenses may not be used to reduce other income.

If musicians receive a 'prescribed prize' for achievement in a field of endeavour ordinarily carried on by them, such a prize will be tax-exempt. A prescribed prize is any prize recognized by the general public and that is awarded for meritorious achievement in the arts, sciences or service to the public.[85]

---

[80] IT-75R3, para. 18.

[81] Expenses, however, may not exceed the amount of the grant. Eligible expenses include all expenses in the year for the purpose of fulfilling the grant, other than reimbursed expenses, expenses otherwise deductible in computing the taxpayer's income, and with certain exceptions, personal or living expenses.

[82] Where the grant constitutes remuneration, it will be included in income under s. 5; see, for example, *Lafferty v. Minister of National Revenue* (1969), 69 D.T.C. 198 (T.A.B.), in which a taxpayer received a Canada Council grant as a subsidy to his ordinary salary paid by the centre which employed him. The court held that such amount was taxable under s. 5 of the Act.

[83] IT-75R3, para. 17.

[84] *R. v. Taylor* (1979), (sub nom. *Taylor v. Minister of National Revenue*), 79 D.T.C. 331 (T.R.B.).

[85] Reg. 7700. Such prizes do not include an amount that can be reasonably regarded as having been received as compensation for services rendered or to be rendered. For a recent case interpreting the exemption, see *Foulds v. R.*, [1997] 2 C.T.C. 2660 (T.C.C.).

(b) Copyright

(i) *Generally*

Musicians and composers who obtain compensation for services rendered in creating a copyrighted work normally will be required to treat such amounts as taxable income receipts, irrespective of the form of the transaction.[86] Thus, even where the composer assigns the copyright for a lump sum, the proceeds will be taxable as income from a business.[87] However, if musicians dispose of their copyrights for a lump sum at a time when they are no longer active in the music business, the courts may be inclined to treat the transaction as on capital account.[88] Similarly, the grant of a licence to republish a work for a lump sum, where the author is not required to do any additional work pursuant to the licence, may give rise to a capital receipt.[89]

If the consideration for the sale takes the form of a royalty dependent on use of the copyright, paragraph 12(1)(g) will require the royalty payments to be included in income notwithstanding that the transaction otherwise might be characterized as on capital account. This paragraph also will apply where the author retains the copyright and receives royalties dependent on the use of the copyright.

Where musicians carry on a business, costs of an ongoing nature incurred to develop intellectual property should be fully deductible as current business expenses.[90] Such costs could include those relating to demo recordings or the preparation of lead sheets.

---

[86] *No. 682 v. Minister of National Revenue* (1960), 60 D.T.C. 65 (T.A.B.); *Hobbs v. Hussey*, 24 T.C. 153; *Glasson v. Rougier*, 26 T.C. 86. For more on the taxation of copyright, see Neal Armstrong and David W. Smith, "Canadian Federal Tax Considerations", in *Hughes on Trade Marks*, (Toronto: Butterworths, 1984); see also, John M. Coyne, "Patents, Copyright and Know-How", in the *Report of Proceedings of the Twenty-First Tax Conference*, (Toronto: Canadian Tax Foundation, 1969), p. 390 at pp. 397-401; see also Harold Fox, *The Canadian Law of Copyright and Industrial Design*, (Toronto: Carswell, 1967).

[87] *LaRue v. Minister of National Revenue* (1963), 63 D.T.C. 553 (T.A.B.); *Glasson v. Rougier*, 26 T.C. 86. However, an outright sale for a lump sum, by a person whose usual activities do not include the creation of copyrighted works, is a disposition on capital account; see *No. 63 v. Minister of National Revenue* (1952), 52 D.T.C. 282 (T.A.B.); *Beare v. Carter*, [1940] 2 K.B. 187; *Withers v. Nethersole*, [1948] 1 All E.R. 400 (U.K. H.L.); *Trustees of Earl Haig v. C.I.R.* (1939), 22 T.C. 725 (C.S. (1st Div.)); *No. 486 v. Minister of National Revenue* (1958), 58 D.T.C. 67 (T.A.B.); see also *Mason v. Innes*, [1967] 2 All E.R. 926.

[88] *Withers v. Nethersole*, [1948] 1 All E.R. 400 (U.K. H.L.).

[89] *LaRue v. Minister of National Revenue* (1963), 63 D.T.C. 553 (T.A.B.). See also *Hould v. Minister of National Revenue* (1965), 65 D.T.C. 624 (T.A.B.), wherein it is suggested that the outright sale of a copyright for an agreed amount could give rise to a capital gain. See also *Crépeau v. Minister of National Revenue* (1965), 65 D.T.C. 99 (T.A.B.).

[90] James R. Wilson, *Tax Consequences of Transfers of Technology*, (Toronto: Insight Press, 1984), p. 26; see also Armstrong and Smith, supra note 86, at p. 803.

The sale of original manuscripts, sketches, notes or other materials relating to the creation of intellectual property is on capital account and will give rise to a capital gain.[91]

Damages for copyright infringement will be treated as on income account where the damages are compensation for profits,[92] but exemplary or punitive damages, which do not attempt to compensate for the loss of profits, have been held to be capital receipts.[93]

(ii) Foreign Copyright Royalties and Withholding Tax

The music business is international in scope and composers often receive copyright royalties from foreign sources. In the absence of relieving legislation, such royalties would be taxable both at the source of origin and in Canada. This issue of double taxation is dealt with partially under Canadian domestic tax law and partially by treaty. Thus, for example, under Article XII of the Canada-U.S. Income Tax Convention, copyright royalties in respect of the production or reproduction of a musical work arising in the U.S., and beneficially owned by a resident of Canada, are exempt from taxation in the U.S., so long as the beneficial owner of the copyright does not carry on business in the United States through a permanent establishment in the U.S. or does not provide personal services in the U.S. through a fixed base.[94] Apart from this treaty, or any other relevant treaty, Canada exempts the following from withholding tax: (1) royalties; or (2) similar payments made to non-residents regarding a copyright in respect of the production or reproduction of any literary, dramatic, musical or artistic work.[95]

(c) Record Masters and Videotapes

(i) Income Tax Aspects

Many musicians independently produce record masters or videotapes. They do so in the belief that record companies are more likely to sign a musician who has a following. Two ways to increase that

---

[91] *Schafer v. Minister of National Revenue* (1981), 81 D.T.C. 226 (T.A.B.).
[92] *Vaughan v. Archie Parnell and Alfred Zeitlin Ltd.* (1940), 23 T.C. 505 (K.B.); *Donald Hart Ltd. v. Minister of National Revenue* (1959), 59 D.T.C. 1134 (Can. Ex. Ct.).
[93] *Cartwright & Sons Ltd. v. Minister of National Revenue* (1961), 61 D.T.C. 499 (T.A.B.).
[94] The Canada-U.S. Income Tax Convention 1980, Article XII, Para. 3. et seq.
[95] Sub-paragraph 212(1)(d)(vi) of the Act.

following are to produce a record master from which records can be manufactured, and to produce videotapes which can be played in bars, clubs or on television. Independently-produced recordings can provide a source of income as well as a means of securing commitments from promoters and bar owners for live performances.

Since they are not destined for sale, record masters will normally constitute depreciable property in the hands of the producer, eligible for capital cost allowance at the rate of 20%.[96] The treatment of the cost of video tapes, if they are used for the purpose of earning income, will depend on the facts.[97] If the video is retained for further showing, it normally will be considered depreciable property subject to capital cost allowance at the rate of 30%. Video cassettes owned by the band used for the purpose of earning income fall under Class 8 and are subject to capital cost allowance at a rate of 20% per annum.[98]

The views of Revenue Canada with respect to master recordings are as follows:[99]

"15.The capital cost of a master recording medium (e.g., a tape or disk) used in the music industry for the making of records, tapes and compact disks is considered to include the costs related to the production of the master recording medium. Such costs would include applicable overhead plus expenditures for (a) scripts, musical arrangements and materials; (b) remuneration of writers, producers, directors, musicians, performers and technicians; and (c) the rental or other costs of a studio and sound recording and other equipment.

16. If a taxpayer is not in the business of making records, tapes or compact disks but has only invested therein, his investment will be considered a capital expenditure. Whether or not capital cost allowance will be permitted on this investment is dependent upon what has been acquired and whether or not it can be considered to have been acquired for the purpose of gaining or producing income.

18.Where acquired computer software or an acquired videotape, film, master recording tape or related assets is leased, it may represent a leasing properties to which the capital cost allowance restrictions in subsection 1100(15) of the Regulations apply. Subsection 1100(17) provides that these restrictions do not apply to a film or videotape certified by the Minister of Communications."

---

[96] Master recordings are included in Class 8.

[97] IT-283R2, para. 1.

[98] Unless they are rented out and are not expected to be rented to any one person for more than seven days in any 30 day period, in which case they fall into Class 12 (100%).

[99] IT-283R2.

(ii) Other Relevant Issues

Musicians who own and run record production companies or recording studios, and who purchase tangible personal property for resale, should consider applying for purchase exemption certificates which permit them to claim an exemption from retail sales with respect to such purchases.

Two other issues are raised with respect to film and videotapes and master recordings: (1) the advisability of seeking certification of a music video as a "Canadian film or video production"; (2) the requirement of a vendor's permit when musicians sell their independent recordings. These issues are discussed below.

(iii) Certification of Videotapes

A. Generally

To encourage the growth of the Canadian motion picture industry, the *Income Tax Act* contains two incentives targeted to Canadian-produced films and videos: (a) a write-off of the capital cost of a certified Canadian film or video production, available to investors and producers; and (b) a tax credit for certified Canadian film and video productions, available to producers.[100] Music videos may be certified under the relevant definitions; thus, the tax benefits associated with certification are potentially available with respect to any music project that includes a video.

B. Certification

Films and videos certified after March, 1996 are "Canadian film or video productions".[101] To qualify for certification, the producer must be a Canadian citizen or permanent resident; not less than 75% of the production and post-production costs[102] must be payable to Canadians; and the Minister of Canadian Heritage must allot not less than six

---

[100] A second tax credit, the film or video production services tax credit, which is available with respect to non-certified but accredited film or video productions under s. 125.5 of the Act, is not discussed herein as it is primarily of interest to foreign producers of films and television series who operate in Canada.

[101] For the definition of "Canadian film or video production", see Reg. 1106(3).

[102] Excluded from such costs are: above-the-line costs; costs determined by reference to the amount of income from the production; insurance, financing, brokerage, legal and accounting fees; and similar amounts.

points for individuals who provided services in respect of the film or tape (above-the-line costs), as follows:

(A) for the director	two points
(B) for the screenwriter	two points
(C) for the highest paid performer	one point
(D) for the second highest paid performer	one point
(E) for the art director	one point
(F) for the director of photography	one point
(G) for the music composer	one point
(H) for the picture editor	one point

The regulations require that at least two points be allotted from (A) or (B) and at least one point from (C) or (D).[103]

Productions which are "excluded productions" will not qualify as Canadian film or video productions. Excluded productions include: (1) productions for which no certificate of completion was issued within 30 months after the end of the taxation year in which principal photography commenced;[104] (2) productions with respect to which the producer-corporation does not hold the exclusive world-wide copyright for all commercial exploitation purposes for the twenty-five year period that begins at the time the production has been completed and is commercially exploitable;[105] and (3) productions with respect to which there is no distribution agreement with a Canadian distributor for consideration at fair market value or a corporation holding a broadcasting licence issued by the CRTC for television markets to have the production shown in Canada.[106]

Certified Canadian film and video productions are Class 10 assets entitled to capital cost allowance at the rate of 30% on the declining balance method.[107] Taxpayers may take an additional allowance not exceeding the lesser of: (a) the income for the year from the property; and (2) the undepreciated capital cost of the property as of the end of the year.[108]

---

[103] Note that animated productions are governed by the point system found in sub-para. 1106(4)(a)(ii).

[104] To qualify, production also must be completed within two years after the end of the year in which principal photography commenced.

[105] The corporation is also required to control the initial licensing of commercial exploitation and to retain a share of revenues from the exploitation of the production in non-Canadian markets acceptable to the Minister of Canadian Heritage.

[106] Also excluded are productions distributed in Canada within a two year period by non-Canadians, as well as various kinds of non-dramatic productions.

[107] Schedule II, Class 10, para.(x).

[108] Reg. 1100(1)(m). For additional rules regarding the computation of CCA, see Regs. 1100(21.1) and 1101(5k.1). Note that where an investor acquires an interest in a Canadian film or video production as a member of a limited partnership, the at-risk rules contained in s. 96(2.2) may apply to limit the deduction of losses under s. 96(2.1).

C. Canadian Film or Video Production Tax Credit

Pursuant to section 125.4 of the Act, a refundable tax credit may be claimed by qualified corporations with respect to the labour costs incurred in connection with Canadian film or video productions.[109] The credit is equal to 25% of the qualified labour expenditure incurred in a taxation year. Because a qualified labour expenditure cannot exceed 48% of the cost of production, the maximum credit is 12% of the cost of production, net of government assistance.

The credit is only available to qualified corporations. Essentially, these are taxable Canadian corporations primarily engaged in the taxation year in a Canadian film or video production business carried on in Canada through a permanent establishment.[110]

The credit, which is calculated with reference to labour expenditures only, is limited to the salary and wages of employees and the remuneration paid to independent contractors attributable to the production.[111]

The credit is not available for any Canadian film or video production for which investors, or partnerships in which investors have an interest, may deduct an amount for the production in computing their income in a taxation year.[112]

(iv) Retail Sales Tax

Musicians who sell their own cassettes or compact discs should be aware that such transactions are subject to the collection and payment of retail sales tax.[113] Vendors of recordings must apply for and receive a permit to transact business prior to making a sale of such recordings. Non-compliance is an offence and the offender is subject to a fine of not less than $100 per day for each day the offence continues.[114] Vendors are agents for the collection of the tax and are required to levy and collect it at the time of sale.[115] They are also required to make

---

[109] Subsection 125.4 (3) ITA.
[110] Subsection 125.4(1) ITA.
[111] Subsection 125.4(1) ITA.
[112] Subsection 125.4(4) ITA.
[113] The tax is exigible with respect to the sale of tangible personal property and certain services; see for example, *Retail Sales Tax Act*, R.S.O. 1990, c. R.31.
[114] *Ibid.*, ss. 5(1) and (7).
[115] *Ibid.*, ss. 10 and 12; see also s. 2(6).

returns and keep records.[116] However, in recognition of their efforts to collect the tax, vendors are entitled to compensation.[117]

In Ontario, promotional copies of recordings distributed by musicians, formerly exempt, are now subject to tax. Musicians who are promotional distributors must pay retail sales tax on the amount by which the full fair value of the property distributed exceeds any amount paid for the property by the recipients. The recipients, as well, are liable for tax on the amount they pay.[118]

(v) Amusement Tax

In some provinces, taxes are exigible with respect to admission to a place of amusement. In Ontario, for example, where the price of admission is greater than $4, a tax of 10% must be paid on the price of admission.[119] A 'place of amusement' includes, *inter alia*, a place where an entertainment is staged or where facilities for dancing are provided to the public with the service of liquor, beer or wine and to which admission is granted upon payment of a price of admission.[120] The obligation to collect and remit the tax extends to persons who own or operate a place of amusement; consequently, it generally will not apply to musicians. In addition to the other duties imposed on vendors under the Act, vendors who operate places of amusement are required to keep records of the charges made for entry.[121]

An exemption from the tax is provided if: (1) no performer receives any remuneration; (2) 90% of the performers who regularly participate in the cast of a musical performance are Canadian citizens, resident in Canada or permanent residents; or (3) the event is held under the auspices of a Canadian amateur athletic association or registered charity,[122] a labour organization, fraternal benefit society, an

---

[116] *Ibid.*, s. 15; see also s. 16. The form and substance of the records are prescribed by regulation. Records should not be destroyed without permission from the Retail Sales Tax Branch.

[117] *Ibid.*, s. 14. Vendors are currently entitled to a maximum of $1,500 per annum as an offset on taxes remitted. The compensation is determined according to a sliding scale.

[118] *Ibid.*, s. 2(22). See also Retail Sales Tax Interpretation Bulletin, No. 1-98, 4/98.

[119] *Ibid.*, s. 2(5). Amusement taxes are also exigible in Saskatchewan: the *Rural Municipality Act, 1989*, c. R-26.1, s. 337; the *Urban Municipality Act, 1984*, c. U-11, s. 310; in Manitoba: the *Municipal Act*, c. M225, ss. 329-33; in Nova Scotia: *Theatres and Amusements Act*, R.S.N.S. 1989, c. 466, s. 9(2); and in Newfoundland: *St. John's Assessment Act*, R.S.N. 1990, c. S-11, ss. 19-21.

[120] *Retail Sales Tax Act*, R.S.O. 1990, c. R.31, s. 1.

[121] *Ibid.*, s. 16(3). Note that operators are vendors within the Act; accordingly they are fixed with the same rights and duties as vendors who sell tangible personal property or who sell or render a taxable service.

[122] As these terms are defined in s. 248(1) of the *Income Tax Act* (Canada).

agricultural society during an agricultural fair, or a prescribed organization supported by the province of Ontario.[123]

(d) Trade Marks and Trade Names

Many successful musicians realize enormous sums from the licensing of their trademarks. Such receipts, if in the form of royalties, normally will be treated and taxed as income, either under principles generally applicable or under paragraph 12(1)(g) of the Act.[124] However, a lump sum payment for disposition of a trademark or trade name as part of an ongoing business will be treated as a capital receipt unless the taxpayer regularly disposes of such rights.[125] If a trademark is acquired on capital account, the acquisition cost will be treated as an eligible capital expenditure and the taxpayer will be entitled to the deduction found in paragraph 20(1)(b) of the Act.[126] If the taxpayer subsequently has a negative balance in his or her cumulative eligible capital account, this amount generally will be included in income; however, for individuals and certain partnerships, part of the amount may be deemed to be a capital gain.[127]

The costs of obtaining a trademark registration are deductible business expenses.[128]

(e) U.S. Tax

Many Canadian musicians perform in the U.S. and in certain cases, their U.S. earnings will be subject to U.S. tax. The following is a brief outline of the applicable rules.[129]

---

[123] The *Retail Sales Tax Act*, s. 9(2). For a list of prescribed organizations, see R.R.O. 1990, Regulation 1012, Schedule 1.

[124] See Armstrong and Smith, supra note 86, at p. 833.

[125] *Ibid.*, pp. 832-33. See also, *No. 63 v. Minister of National Revenue* (1952), 52 D.T.C. 282 (T.A.B.); *The Dixie Lee Co. Ltd. v. Minister of National Revenue* (1971), 71 D.T.C. 406 (T.A.B.).

[126] IT-143R2, para. 10. Under para. 20(1)(b), taxpayers are entitled to deduct 7% of their cumulative eligible capital in respect of their business at the end of the taxation year.

[127] Subparagraph 14(1)(a)(v) of the Act.

[128] IT-143R2, para. 9. Such costs include design, legal and registration costs, and any payments made to third parties to refrain from contesting the registration.

[129] For a description of the applicable rules, see Don Robert Spellmann, "United States Tax Rules for Nonresident Authors, Artists, Musicians and Other Creative Professionals", [1994] 27 Vanderbilt J. of Transnational L. 219; for entertainers contemplating a move to the U.S., see Sheri Jeffrey, "Pre-Residency Tax Planning for the Foreign Entertainer, Athlete or Other Talent", [1992] 12 Loyola of Los Angeles Ent. L.J. 311. For a general discussion of cross-border taxation, see Francois Chagnon, "Cross-

The United States taxes the income of nonresident aliens in either of two cases: (1) where the income derives from a U.S. source not effectively connected with a U.S. trade or business;[130] and (2) where the income derives from a U.S source and is effectively connected with a U.S. trade or business.[131] In the former case, the U.S. imposes a tax of 30% on gross income[132]; while in the latter case tax is imposed at the graduated rates applicable to U.S. residents. Nonresidents taxed under (2) are entitled to any appropriate deductions or credits and must file U.S. tax returns to claim them.[133]

Pursuant to the Internal Revenue Code, compensation for labour or services performed in the U.S. is deemed not to be income from a U.S. source if the nonresident individual is present in the United States for a total of not more than 90 days in the taxable year, his or her aggregate compensation does not exceed $3,000, and the services are performed for a nonresident alien not engaged in a trade or business in the U.S.[134] Canadian musicians who are active in the U.S., and who do not qualify for the exemption, will be subject to withholding tax at a rate of 30% on their gross U.S. income.[135] Such musicians also will have to file a U.S. tax return if additional taxes are due or they wish to seek a refund.[136]

A musician who spends any amount of time in the U.S. also should be aware of the U.S. substantial presence test. Under this test, a person will be a resident of the U.S. for tax purposes if he or she is present in the U.S. at least 31 days in the current year and has been present in the

---

Border Taxation of Artists, Entertainers and Athletes", *Report of the Proceedings of the Forty-Ninth Tax Conference, 1997 Conference Report*, (Toronto: Canadian Tax Foundation), at p. 24:1.

[130] I.R.C. para. 871(a)(1).

[131] I.R.C. para. 871(b).

[132] I.R.C. para. 871(a)(1). The tax is collected by means of a withholding system; under I.R.C. para. 1441(a), non-resident aliens and foreign partnerships generally are subject to a 30% withholding tax on gross income earned in the United States. Exempted are items of income (other than compensation for personal services) effectively connected with the conduct of a trade or business in the United States: IRC para. 1441(c)(1). Note that self-employed nonresidents who receive compensation income connected with a U.S trade or business are subject to both the withholding and filing regimes.

[133] I.R.C. para. 873(a).

[134] I.R.C. para. 861(a)(3).

[135] I.R.C. para. 1441(c)(1). The above result is modified, however, by the Canada-U.S. Income Tax Convention, discussed infra.

[136] Spellmann, supra, note 129 at p.228. Canadian musicians who receive compensation for the performance of labour or personal services in the U.S. also may be subject to U.S. tax under I.R.C. para. 864(b)(1) on the basis that the income is from a U.S. trade or business; see I.R.C. para 864(b)(1)(B) for a similar deeming provision where the services are performed for a nonresident not engaged in trade or business in the U.S.

U.S. for at least 183 days over the current and previous two years according to a weighted formula.[137] An exception is provided if the individual is present in the U.S. for less than 183 days in the current year and has a tax home in a foreign country; in such cases, he or she will not be treated as a nonresident alien in the current year.[138]

The above rules are somewhat mitigated by the Canada-U.S. Income Tax Convention which provides special rules for the taxation of the income earned in the U.S. by Canadian residents[139] and by Canadian artists in particular. With respect to the latter, Article XVI provides an exemption from U.S. tax unless the artist's income is equal to or greater than $15,000.[140] Further, where the artist is taxable in the U.S., withholding tax on the first $5,000 of U.S.-source income may not exceed 10%.[141]

In general, to minimize their U.S. tax liabilities, Canadian performers active in the U.S. should attempt to limit their compensation to the amount stipulated in the treaty. They should be careful not to be physically present in the U.S. for more than 182 days in any taxable year. If they are taxable in the U.S., they should attempt to structure their affairs so that the lowest rates will apply.[142]

---

[137] I.R.C. sub-para. 7701(b)(3)(A). Under the formula, the number of days the individual is present in the U.S. in the current year, plus 1/3 of the days in the previous year, and 1/6 of the days in the year previous to the previous year are aggregated. If they total at least 183 days, the individual is resident in the U.S.

[138] I.R.S. sub-para 7701(b)(3)(B).

[139] Thus, although the U.S., pursuant to Article XV, para. 1, is entitled to tax the employment income of a Canadian resident derived in the U.S., para. 2 exempts the first $10,000 so earned, and any amount earned in the U.S. if the Canadian resident is in the U.S. for less than 183 days and his or her pay is not borne by a U.S. employer or a permanent establishment or fixed bases of his or her employer in the U.S. Pursuant to Article XIV, the U.S. is only entitled to tax a Canadian resident in respect of independent personal services provided in the U.S. where the income is attributable to a fixed base in the U.S.

[140] Article XVI, para. 1. See para. 2 for an anti-avoidance rule.

[141] Article XVII.

[142] See Spellmann, supra note 129 for some planning ideas. With respect to withholding taxes, it has been suggested that Canadian performers can arrange with the IRS for the taxes to be withheld by a U.S. agent; this would permit the performer to earn interest on the taxes until such time as the taxes fall due: David I. Matheson in "The Star's Vehicle — Corporate and Tax Considerations", in *Supporting the Star (or a Prospect?)*, (Toronto: CBA-O, 1978), p. 1. at p. 30.

3. Tax Planning

(a) Generally

Tax planning is a concept that ranges from simple measures such as taking full advantage of all deductions available to a self-employed individual, to the establishment of residency in a low tax jurisdiction to escape the reach of Canada's tax laws. The following discussion highlights some of the ways a musician can benefit from tax planning.

(1) Wherever possible, musicians should attempt to structure their business relationships so as to be treated as independent contractors under the Act. As discussed above, independent contractors are entitled to deductions unavailable to individuals who are employees.

(2) If it is feasible in the circumstances and warranted, contracts should stipulate for the payment of compensation over time rather than in a lump sum. This may have the effect of reducing taxes where the lump sum payment would be taxed at a higher marginal rate than the periodic payments.

(3) If the musician's income is large enough, it may be possible to reduce taxes by setting up a personal service corporation able to take advantage of the small business deduction. As well, corporations can be used by high-earning individuals to reduce taxes by providing part of the owner's compensation in the form of dividends, qualifying for the dividend tax credit.

(4) If the musician has a family, it may be possible to reduce taxes by shifting income to family members. Subject to the attribution rules, this may be accomplished by the use of trusts or Canadian-controlled private corporations. Alternatively, family members who provide services to the musician can be put on the payroll.

(b) Some Trust, Estate, and Gift Suggestions

Under the provisions of the Act dealing with the taxation of trusts,[143] in certain limited circumstances, it is possible to settle property on a trust and shift the trust's income to family members by means of the preferred beneficiary election.[144] Where the beneficiaries are taxed at a rate lower than that applicable to the trust and settlor, this can

---

[143] ITA, ss. 104-108.

[144] ITA, s. 104(14). Such transfers, however, are subject to the attribution rules found in ss. 74.1 through 74.5.

result in significant tax savings. Taxes also can be deferred by the transfer of property to a spouse or spousal trust either *inter vivos*[145] or by will.[146] The making of charitable gifts, *inter vivos* or by will, also can serve to reduce a taxpayer's income.[147] Other possibilities include the implementation of an estate freeze or a gifting program in favour of adult children of the donor. Needless to say, whatever plan is contemplated, the taxpayer should seek the advice of competent tax professionals.

4. Goods and Services Tax

(a) Generally

The Goods and Services Tax (the GST) affects virtually every aspect of a musician's commercial activities. Musicians are affected as taxpayers and, if required to register, as tax collectors. The GST is levied on the recipient of any taxable supply of a property or service made in Canada.[148] Tax is payable at the rate of 7% on the value of the consideration for the supply.[149] Certain taxable supplies are zero-rated and taxed at the rate of 0%.[150] Other supplies are completely exempt.[151] As is the case with respect to provincial retail sales taxes, responsibility for collection of the tax rests with the supplier.[152]

---

[145] ITA, s. 73(1).

[146] ITA, s. 70(6).

[147] See ITA s. 118.1. In general, where a taxpayer gifts capital property to a designated institution, the gift will not give rise to a capital gain, but the taxpayer will be entitled to a tax credit based on the fair market value of the gifted property.

[148] GST is also payable with respect to goods imported into Canada. The tax must be paid at such time as any customs duties are paid; see generally ss. 212-216 of the *Excise Tax Act*, R.S.C. 1985, c. E-15. ("ETA").

[149] Subsection 165(1) ETA. However, if the supply is made in a 'participating province', the rate is 15%. Participating provinces currently include Nova Scotia, New Brunswick, Newfoundland and Prince Edward Island. Pursuant to s. 154 of the Act, the consideration for the supply included any tax imposed under an Act of Parliament in respect of the supply of property or services.

[150] Zero-rated supplies are listed in Schedule VI. They include such items as prescription drugs and basic groceries.

[151] Exempt supplies are listed in Schedule V. They include, *inter alia*, the health services listed in Part II of the Schedule. Residential leases for a period longer than one month are also exempt; see Schedule V, Part I, s. 6(a).

[152] Subsection 221(1) ETA.

(i) Taxable Supply/Commercial Activity

Taxable supplies are supplies made in the course of a commercial activity.[153] A commercial activity includes any business carried on with a reasonable expectation of profit.[154] Accordingly, any musician (other than an employee) who is engaged in a commercial activity will, unless exempt, be required to register under the Act and collect the tax.

Because most businesses will both collect and be liable for the tax, registrants are entitled to claim input tax credits for taxes paid which can be set off against the GST collected with respect to their own taxable supplies.[155] GST returns must be remitted periodically[156] and failure to remit GST can result in penalties [157] and/or fines and jail terms.[158]

Although the Act does not generally apply to nonresidents, a nonresident with a permanent establishment in Canada will be deemed a resident for purposes of the Act.[159] Moreover, where a nonresident makes a supply in the course of carrying on business in Canada, the supply will attract GST if it satisfies the statutory test for the making of supplies in Canada.[160]

(ii) Persons/Small Supplier

As a general rule, every person who makes a taxable supply in Canada in the course of a commercial activity engaged in by the person in Canada is required to register. However, the Act exempts small suppliers.[161] A person is a small supplier if the total consideration that

---

[153] A supply includes the provision of any property or a service in any manner including sale, transfer, barter, exchange, licence, rental, lease, gift or disposition; s. 123 ETA.

[154] A business includes any profession, trade or calling; s. 123 ETA.

[155] Subsection 169(1) ETA.

[156] Under s. 237(1), where the reporting period is a fiscal year, registrants are required to pay an installment within one month after the end of each fiscal quarter.

[157] Subsection 280(1) provides for a penalty equal to 6% per annum with interest at the prescribed rate; see generally, ss. 278-285 ETA.

[158] There are a variety of offences under the Act, including failure to make a return (s. 326(1)); making a false return (s. 326(2)); and failure to remit (s. 329(1)). Fines to a maximum of $1,000 plus 20% of the net tax and/or a jail term not exceeding six months are possible; see generally, ss. 326-332.

[159] Subsection 132(2) ETA. A permanent establishment includes any fixed place of business.

[160] As to which, see s. 142 ETA. According to Revenue Canada, a nonresident will carry on business in Canada if he or she has a significant presence in Canada; see GST New Memorandum, chap. 2.5, para. 19.

[161] Paragraph 240(1)(a) ETA.

came due or was paid for taxable supplies made by him or her in or out of Canada throughout the preceding four fiscal quarters does not exceed $30,000.[162] Although small suppliers are not required to collect the tax, they are not entitled to input tax credits.[163] Therefore, it is often advisable for small suppliers to register.

(iii) Invoices/Documentation

The following information is required on all sales invoices:

(1) the vendor's business or trading name; (2) the invoice date or the date the GST was paid or became payable; (3) the total amount paid or payable; (4) an indication of the items subject to GST at 7% or at 0%, or an indication that the items are exempt, and either the total GST charged or a statement indicating that the price includes GST; (5) the GST registration number; (6) the purchaser's name or trading name; (7) the terms of payment; and (8) a brief description of the goods and services.[164]

(iv) When Payable

GST is payable on the earlier of the day the consideration for the supply is paid and the day the consideration comes due.[165] The Act deems the consideration to become due on the earlier of: (1) the earlier of the invoice date or issue date; (2) the day the invoice would have been issued but for any undue delay; and (3) the date the recipient is required to pay the consideration.[166] In the absence of an invoice, appropriate documents may include contracts, credit card receipts, sales slips, and accounting statements.

(v) Business Expenses

As a general rule, registrants are entitled to an input tax credit with respect to all purchases and operating expenses related to their

---

[162] Subsection 148(1) ETA.

[163] Subsection 169(1) ETA.

[164] General Information for GST Registrants, March 1997. Items (4) and (5)are required only for sales of $30 and over; items (6), (7) and (8) are required only for sales over $150.

[165] Subsection 168(1) ETA.

[166] Subsection 152(1) ETA.

commercial activities.[167] Input tax credits cannot be claimed with respect to goods or services purchased for personal consumption.[168] Where property or a service (other than capital property) acquired in the course of commercial activities is subsequently used for personal consumption, the Act deems a supply to have been made and tax on the fair market value of the consideration for the supply will be payable by the registrant.[169]

(vi) Other General Aspects

With respect to passenger vehicles, no ITC may be claimed on the portion of the purchase price that currently exceeds $26,000.[170] With respect to leased vehicles, no ITC may be claimed on lease costs exceeding the maximum lease costs deductible under the *Income Tax Act* (currently $650 per month). ITC on any excess amount is recaptured at the end of the registrant's fiscal year.[171]

ITCs may be claimed with respect to 50% of all food, beverage and entertainment expenses to which subsection 67.1(1) of the *Income Tax Act* applies. Registrants who file quarterly can claim the credit on the full amount of all such expenditures incurred during the course of the year and remit GST on the 50% portion on their first return for the following taxation year. For annual filers, adjustments must be made on their return for the year.[172] Alternatively, registrants can limit their claim when initially claiming their ITCs.

As a general rule, GST is payable on lease payments.

(b) Specific Issues Concerning Musicians

(i) Employment Status

Musicians who are employees do not carry on business. Therefore, any supplies made by such musicians are not made in the course of a

---

[167] For limitations on the right to claim an input tax credit, see s. 170 ETA.

[168] See s. 199(1) with respect to personal property which is capital property not primarily used in commercial activities of the registrant; see s. 208(1) with respect to real property which is capital property used primarily for personal use and enjoyment. See also s. 200(2) and s. 206(4) which create tax liabilities where personal and real property which are capital property of the registrant are converted from a commercial to a non-commercial use.

[169] Subsection 172(1) ETA.

[170] Section 201 ETA.

[171] Section 235 ETA.

[172] Subsection 236(1) ETA.

commercial activity and there is no need to register, collect and remit GST. Likewise, if musicians are engaged in a business but there is no reasonable expectation of profit, they will not be engaging in a commercial activity and there will be no need to register.

Where a musician is a member of a group that is a partnership, the partnership (and not its individual members) is required to register.[173] If all the other band members are in the employ of one member, the employer/member will be required to register. If the band is carried on through a corporate entity, the corporation will be required to register.

(ii) Membership Fees

Certain supplies made by public sector bodies are exempt supplies pursuant to Part VI of Schedule V to the Act.[174] Thus, the supply of a membership in the AFM is normally exempt from GST. Under the relevant rules, a supply will be exempt only if the musician does not receive more than the following benefits:

"1) the right to vote or participate in meetings; 2) the right to receive or acquire goods and services supplied to members at full fair market value; 3) the right to receive nominal discounts for goods or services provided by the organization, such as a discount to a conference, when the total value of all discounts is insignificant in relation to the membership fee; 4) the right to receive periodic newsletters or other publications of insignificant value in relation to the membership fee or which provide information on the organization's activities or financial status (except for such publications which are of significant value in relation to the amount charged for the membership and for which a fee is ordinarily charged to non-members); 5) an indirect benefit intended to accrue to all members; 6) the investigation of a complaint or a service of a conciliator to settle a dispute involving members".[175]

(iii) Agency Relationships

Musicians often hire booking agents to provide them with engagements. In this situation, the musician will charge GST on the engagement fee, and pay GST on the agent's fee. For example, assuming an engagement fee of $1,000, the musician will collect $70. If the agency fee is 10% of the engagement fee, the musician will pay GST

---

[173] For special rules concerning partnerships, see s. 272.1 ETA.

[174] ETA Schedule V, Part VI, s. 17.

[175] *GST: Goods and Services Tax For the Arts and Entertainment Industry*, (Ottawa: Revenue Canada, 1990), p. 14.

on $100. Thus, the total amount owing to the agent, inclusive of GST, will be $107.[176]

If the agent supplies the services of a musician who is not registered and does not so inform the customer in writing; or if the musician is registered, but the agent does not disclose the musician's identity to the purchaser; or if the agent does not enter into a written agreement with the recipient or invoice the recipient in the name of the musician, then (1) the musician is considered to have supplied services to the agent and not to the recipient; and (2) the agent becomes responsible for collecting and remitting GST due from the recipient.[177]

(iv) Management Commissions

Management commissions are subject to GST on the same basis as described in paragraph (iii) above.

(v) Royalties/Advances/Reserves

Royalties and advances are a payment for rights. When rights are granted they are "supplied", and GST is generally payable in relation thereto.[178] The calculation of the GST applicable to royalty advances depends on whether the contract stipulates that the advance is inclusive or exclusive of GST. For example, if GST is excluded, 7% must be added to the fee paid for the specific right. However, if GST is included, the payment is calculated by multiplying the amount of the payment by 7/107. Because GST is payable with respect to the advance, the party making the advance will be entitled to claim an input tax credit. The unearned portion of the advance can be written off "with no GST consequences".[179] Where royalties are subject to reserves, GST is payable on the day the reserve is actually liquidated, or the date it should have been liquidated. GST is not collected or payable with respect to royalties or advances paid concerning rights exploited outside Canada.[180]

---

[176] *Ibid.*, p. 17.

[177] *Ibid.*, p. 18.

[178] See the definitions of "property" and "supply" in s. 123 ETA.

[179] *Ibid.*, p. 19. Note that options attract tax on the same basis as advances and royalties. See also Michael Mulholony, *GST Handbook for the Recording Industry*, (Toronto: FACTOR, 1990), at p.5.

[180] Paragraph 142(2)(c) ETA. See also Schedule VI, Part V, s. 10., and GST Memorandum 300-3-5, paras. 115-117.

(vi) Copyright Collectives

Copyright collectives such as SOCAN collect royalties in connection with the supply of intangible personal property on behalf of their members. Although GST is payable with respect to such transactions, the Act deems the supply to have been made by the collective with the result that the tax is collected and remitted not by its members, but by the copyright collective. Moreover, the Act deems any services supplied by the collective to its members with respect to its licensing activities not to be a supply so that no GST is payable by the members with respect thereto.[181] Revenue received from a collective, however, will be included in a musician's income and used to determine whether the musician is a small supplier.

(vii) Musical Instruments

Musicians who are in the employ of a registrant or who are members of a registered partnership, and who acquire a musical instrument on their own account, are entitled to a rebate of GST paid by them, if they are not entitled to claim an ITC with respect thereto. Unless the musicians reside in a participating province, the rebate is limited to 7/107 of any capital cost allowance or lease payments deducted by the musicians in computing their income for the year under the *Income Tax Act*, net of any amount received from the partnership or their employer as a reimbursement in respect of the amounts deducted.[182]

Musical instruments are also subject to a special rule for claiming ITCs. Where an individual who is a registrant uses a musical instrument that is capital property, in an employment of the individual or in a business carried on by a partnership of which he or she is a member, such use is deemed to be a use in a commercial activity.[183] If the deemed use, when combined with the actual use in commercial activities, reaches the threshold of use primarily in commercial activities, the registrant will be entitled to claim a full ITC with respect to the acquisition of the instrument.[184] By way of example, a registrant who uses an instrument 40% as an employee and 25% as an

---

[181] Subsection 177(2) ETA. A list of prescribed collectives may be found in (GST/HST) Regulations, P.C. 1990-2734, Dec. 18, 1990, SOR/91-25.

[182] Subsection 253(1) ETA. See s. 253(2) for a restriction on the amount of the rebate where the musician is a member of a registered partnership.

[183] Subsection 199(5) ETA. The effect of the subsection is to make musical instruments so used subject to the provisions for acquisition, change in use, ceasing to use and sale of capital property found in ss. 199(2)(3) and 200(2)(3) of the Act.

[184] GST Memorandum 400-3-9, Capital Personal Property, para. 24.

independent contractor will be entitled to a full ITC.[185] However, where the instrument is primarily used not in a commercial activity (i.e., more than 50%), no ITC will be available.[186]

(viii) Music Lessons

Because music lessons are, by regulation, the prescribed equivalents of music courses that follow a curriculum designated by a school authority, they are exempt from GST.[187] However, the supply of a membership in a music society is not an exempt supply.[188]

(ix) Record Production Transactions

Because the supply of financial services is exempt from GST,[189] no tax is payable with respect to the issue of a financial instrument or the payment of money as interest. Therefore, FACTOR loans are exempt from tax.[190] However, all production costs relating to recording (e.g. session fees, payments to producers and engineers, studio and equipment rentals, tape costs, etc.) are subject to the normal rules, and adequate documentation must be kept to support a claim to ITCs. Such documentation should include relevant invoices and contracts. Where records are manufactured pursuant to a distribution agreement, and assuming the distributor label is registered, GST is to be paid "on the net amount of the payment on account of sales after any deduction for manufacturing or direct promotional expenses which have already been paid, or are payable by distributor."[191] If there is no invoice, GST is payable when the ownership of records changes hands; otherwise it is payable on the date of the invoice.[192]

GST is payable with respect to all royalty payments made pursuant to the issue of a mechanical or performing rights licence, irrespective of whether the SOCAN member or the CMRRA-represented music publisher is a GST registrant.[193]

---

[185] *Ibid.*, para. 24.

[186] Paragraph 199(2)(a) ETA.

[187] The Equivalent Courses (GST) Regulations, P.C. 1990-2736, 18/12/90, SOR 91-27. See also Schedule V, Part III, s. 9 to the ETA.

[188] *Cosmopolitan Music Society v. R.*, (sub nom. *Cosmopolitan Music Society v. Canada*), [1995] G.S.T.C. 19 (T.C.C.).

[189] Schedule V, Part VII, s. 1 to the ETA; see also s. 123 ETA and the definition of "financial service" therein.

[190] *Goods and Services Tax for the Arts and Entertainment Industry*, supra note 175 at p. 6.

[191] *Ibid.*, p. 5.

[192] *Ibid.*, p. 5.

[193] *Ibid.*, p. 7.

INTRODUCTION TO APPENDICES

The forms and checklists in the following appendices are provided as samples but they are not intended for use without skilled legal advice to ensure their accuracy and applicability in specific contractual situations. They are meant to be used in conjunction with the comments concerning such agreements in the relevant chapters in the text. One should consult the general agreement checklist and general provisions checklist before drafting all specific agreements. It is also useful to consult the composer-publisher agreement checklist for contract provisions relevant to other agreements referred to in checklists included in Appendix 2, and the exclusive term recording agreement checklist for contract provisions relevant to other agreements referred to in checklists included in Appendix 5.

APPENDIX 1
COPYRIGHT ADMINISTRATION

Mechanical Licence

LICENSOR:
CONCÉDANT: **CMRRA**
Canadian Musical Reproduction Rights Agency Limited
56 Wellesley Street West, Suite 320, Toronto, Ontario Canada M5S 2S3
Phone: (416) 926-1966 Fax: (416) 926-7521 E-Mail: (416) 926-0912
Compuserve: 72355,411 AT&T Mail: !CMRRA
GST Registration Number R 0076696

LICENSEE:
CONCESSIONNAIRE:

APPLICATION No
N° DE LA DEMANDE
LICENSE No
N° DE LICENCE
LICENSE TYPE
TYPE DE LICENCE

DESCRIPTION OF MUSICAL WORK
DESCRIPTION DE L'OEUVRE MUSICALE
TITLE:
TITRE:
COMPOSER / AUTHOR:
AUTEUR /
COMPOSITEUR:

COPYRIGHT OWNER /
ADMINISTRATOR:
TITULAIRE /
ADMINISTRATEUR
DU DROIT D'AUTEUR:

PERCENTAGE:
POURCENTAGE:

ADDITIONAL
PUBLISHING
INFORMATION:
RENSEIGNEMENTS
SUPPLÉMENTAIRES:
DESCRIPTION OF RECORDING
DESCRIPTION DE L'ENREGISTREMENT PHONOGRAPHIQUE
ARTIST / GROUP:
ARTISTE / GROUPE:
PLAYING TIME OF MUSICAL WORK IN RECORDING:
DURÉE DE L'OEUVRE MUSICALE SUR L'ENREGISTREMENT PHONOGRAPHIQUE:
TOTAL PLAYING TIME OF RECORDING:
DURÉE DE L'ENREGISTREMENT PHONOGRAPHIQUE:

RELEASE DATE:
DATE DE MISE EN
CIRCULATION:

CATALOGUE No.:
No DE CATALOGUE:

CONTRIVANCE:
ORGANE:

ROYALTY RATE:
TAUX DE
REDEVANCE:

LABEL:
ÉTIQUETTE:

TERRITORY:
TERRITOIRE:

ADDITIONAL TERMS
DISPOSITIONS COMPLÉMENTAIRES

PLEASE

READ

LICENSE

TERMS

ON

REVERSE

SIDE

VEUILLEZ

LIRE AU

VERSO

LES

DISPOSITIONS

DE LA

PRÉSENTE

LICENCE

ISSUED BY CMRRA
DÉLIVRÉE PAR C.M.R.R.A

DAVID A. BASSKIN (GENERAL MANAGER)

DATE OF ISSUE
DATE DE DÉLIVRANCE _____

ACCEPTED BY LICENSEE
ACCEPTÉE PAR LE
CONCESSIONNAIRE

PLEASE SIGN HERE / SIGNATURE

DATE OF ACCEPTANCE
DATE D'ACCEPTATION

MANUFACTURER PLEASE SIGN AND RETURN TO CMRRA.
FABRIQUANT VEUILLEZ SIGNER ET RENVOYER À CMRRA.

LICENCE TERMS*

[* Please consult the original CMRRA Mechanical Licence Form for the French version of the Licence Terms.]

1.   GRANT OF LICENCE
           At the request of Licensee and in its capacity as agent for the Copyright Owner/Administrator, Licensor
           hereby grants to
Licensee a non-exclusive licence to reproduce the Musical Work described above on the Recording described above
and to distribute and sell such Recording in the Territory set out above for private use by the public, subject to the
terms and conditions which follow.

2.   ARRANGEMENT OR ALTERATION OF MUSICAL WORK
           Licensee may arrange the Musical Work for the limited purpose and to the limited extent necessary to
           conform it to the
style or manner of interpretation of the Artist/Group involved, but shall have no right to insert new words into the
existing lyrics, substitute or add new lyrics, alter the basic melody or otherwise arrange the music; or generally,
change the fundamental character and unity of the Musical Work. Licensee may not, subject to subsection 4(4) of the
Copyright Act R.S., c. 55, S. 1 claim any ownership or other interest in, or register, any arrangement permitted under
the paragraph, as a work under such Act.

3.   LABEL AND JACKET INFORMATION
           Licensee shall imprint the Title of the Musical Work followed by the name(s) of the Composer/Author
           and Copyright
Owner/Administrator on the label, jacket or tape container of every Recording made under this licence.

4.   LIMITATIONS ON USE
           All reproduction or other use of the Musical Work not specifically authorized by this licence, or by the
           written consent of
Licensor, is prohibited including, without limiting the generality of the foregoing, the following:
(a)   Any printing of the music and/or lyrics of the Musical Work.
(b)   Any parody or translation of the lyrics of the Musical Work.
(c)   Any rental of the Recording, or sale of the Recording for the purpose of rental.
(d)   Any commercial use of the Recording other than for distribution and sale in the Territory for private use
           by the public.
(e)   Any reproduction of the Musical Work in any audio-visual recording.
(f)   Any importation of copies of the Recording into the Territory or exportation of the Recording outside the
           Territory.
(g)   Any sale in bulk of the Recording.
(h)   Any reproduction of the Musical Work in any type of contrivance not set out above, or in a contrivance
           having a different
           catalogue number than is set out above.
(i)   Any reproduction, distribution or sale of the Musical Work under a label other than is set out above.

5.   ROYALTY PAYMENT
5.1   Licensee shall pay Licensor royalties at the Royalty Rate set out above for each reproduction of the
           Musical Work, in
whole or in part, in every Recording sold or otherwise distributed in the Territory under this licence.
5.2   Payments shall be made quarterly, no later than 45 days after the last day of March, June, September
           and December of each
year, for all sales and other distributions made during the quarter.
5.3   Licensee shall pay Licensor interest on all unpaid royalties, from the date when such royalties were due
until they are paid, at an annual rate equal to five per cent (5%) in excess of the prime rate established from time to
time by the Bank of Canada.

6.   ROYALTY STATEMENTS
6.1   Licensee shall deliver along with each royalty payment, an accurate statement of sales which sets out
clearly the number of units of the Recording that have been sold and otherwise distributed and which indicates
royalties due to each Copyright Owner/Administrator for each Musical Work embodied in the Recording.
6.2   Licensee shall in the quarterly statement itself, or separately, give Licensor written notification when the
Recording has been deleted from Licensee's catalogue and, at that time, shall give Licensor an accounting of
inventory, sales and other distributions to such date and unless otherwise specifically agreed with Licensor, shall pay
royalties as provided by the terms of this licence on all sales and other distributions of the Recording subsequent to
such date.

7.   RETENTION AND VERIFICATION OF BOOKS AND RECORDS
7.1   Licensee shall keep, in Canada, accurate and up to date books of account and supporting
documentation relating to the manufacture, stockage, delivery, sale or other distribution, return, destruction and all
other inventory movement of the Recording made, sold and otherwise distributed under this licence.
7.2   Licensee shall advise Licensor and Licensor's agents, upon request therefor, where such records,
books, supporting documentation, and inventory are kept and shall grant Licensor and Licensor's agents free and
unimpeded access thereto in the offices, working places, factories, warehouses, computer data banks and other
places where they are kept, for the purpose of conducting an examination thereof and verifying Licensee's
compliance with the terms of this licence and royalty payments made and due.
7.3   Licensor and Licensor's agents shall have the right to take hand written extracts and to make
photocopies and computer reports of such records, books and supporting documentation as Licensor and Licensor's
agents determine are reasonably necessary or convenient for the efficient conduct of the above examination.
7.4   Where Licensee is acting as the licensing and/or royalty administrator for a third party, Licensee shall
ensure through its agreements with such third party that Licensor shall have the same rights of examination and
verification in relation to such third party as are set out under paragraphs 7.1, 7.2 and 7.3 above.

8.   COPYRIGHT ACT
8.1   This licence shall be subject to the Copyright Act R.S., c. 55, S. 1 and any amendment thereto, or new
Act which may come into effect after the date of this licence, and the Royalty Rate set out above shall be
automatically amended to conform with any new higher rate resulting from such new or amended Copyright Act for all
units of the Recording distributed after such new Act or amendment comes into effect.

9.   TERMINATION

9.1   This licence shall terminate automatically upon Licensee's insolvency, assignment in bankruptcy, the appointment of a receiver or the breach of any of the provisions of paragraphs 2, 4 and 10.1 hereof. Licensee shall notify Licensor forthwith of such insolvency, assignment or appointment.

9.2   Licensor may terminate this licence upon Licensee's breach of any of the other terms hereof by giving notice in writing of such breach, by ordinary or registered mail, telegram or telex to Licensee at Licensee's address set out above. If Licensee fails to remedy the breach complained of within fourteen (14) days of the date of mailing of the notice, then this licence shall automatically terminate on the fifteenth day.

9.3   Upon termination, all Recordings in the possession, control or custody of Licensee upon which royalties have not been paid as required by the terms of this licence, shall be and remain the property of Licensor until such royalties have been paid.

9.4   Any manufacture, sale, distribution or other use of the Recording after termination of this licence, shall be actionable as an act of infringement of copyright in the Musical Work.

10.   ADDITIONAL TERMS

10.1   This licence is personal to the Licensee only and the rights and obligations under it may not be assigned or transferred without Licensor's prior consent in writing.

10.2   Any waiver by Licensor of any term of this licence, or any right or interest arising therefrom, shall only be effective if in writing signed by Licensor; any waiver shall not imply any waiver of any other term, right or interest waived; no waiver of a breach of this licence shall be deemed to be a waiver of any preceding, continuing or succeeding breach hereof.

10.3   This licence may not be modified, amended or altered except by written agreement signed by the parties hereto.

10.4   Licensor represents only the Copyright Owner/Administrator has advised Licensor that Copyright Owner/Administrator
owns and/or controls the mechanical recording rights in the Musical Work identified above and that Licensor has been authorized by Copyright Owner/Administrator to grant this licence. Licensor makes no other expressed or implied representation or warranty.

10.5   Licensor reserves all rights not expressly granted under this licence. Any use of the Musical Work and any manufacture, distribution or sale of the Recording outside of the terms of this licence shall be actionable as acts of copyright infringement in the Musical Work.

10.6   This licence shall grant no rights to Licensee and shall be of no effect whatsoever unless signed and dated by Licensee, and returned to Licensor within 15 days from the Date of Issue of this licence.

Synchronization Licence

LICENSOR

CMRRA
Canadian Musical Reproduction Rights Agency Limited
56 Wellesley Street West, Suite 320, Toronto, Ontario Canada M5S 2S3
Phone   (416) 926-1966   Fax: (416) 926-7521   E-Mail   (416) 926-0912
Compuserve 77331,611   AT&T Mail: !CMRRA
GST Registration Number R 100766696

LICENCE NO.
LICENCE TYPE

LICENSEE

WHEREAS: THE PUBLISHER HAS ADVISED LICENSOR THAT PUBLISHER OWNS AND/OR ADMINISTERS THE COPYRIGHT IN AND CONTROLS THE REPRODUCTION RIGHTS IN THE MUSICAL WORK IN THE SHARE INDICATED IN THE DESCRIPTION OF MUSICAL WORK BELOW AND HAS AUTHORIZED LICENSOR TO GRANT THIS LICENCE

1. **GRANT OF LICENCE**

AT LICENCEE'S REQUEST, IN ITS CAPACITY AS AGENT FOR PUBLISHER, IN CONSIDERATION OF THE FEE BELOW AND SUBJECT TO THE TERMS BELOW, LICENSOR HEREBY GRANTS TO LICENSEE A NON EXCLUSIVE LICENCE TO RECORD THE MUSICAL WORK IN SYNCHRONIZATION OR TIMED RELATION WITH THE VISUAL ELEMENTS OF THE PRODUCTION BELOW, TO MAKE, DISTRIBUTE AND TO AUTHORIZE OTHERS TO MAKE AND DISTRIBUTE COPIES THEREOF ONLY ACCORDING TO AND FOR THE USE(S) STIPULATED IN THE DESCRIPTION OF USE BELOW

2. **DESCRIPTION OF MUSICAL WORK**

A) TITLE

B) WRITER(S)

C) PUBLISHER   SHARE

3. **DESCRIPTION OF PRODUCTION**

A) PRODUCTION FORMAT :
B) LENGTH OF PRODUCTION:
C) DISTRIBUTION FORMAT :

D) PRODUCTION TYPE :
E) PRODUCER(S) NAME
F) PRODUCTION TITLE :

4. **DESCRIPTION OF USE**

A) DURATION OF MUSICAL WORK IN PRODUCTION:
B) NUMBER OF USES OF MUSICAL WORK IN PRODUCTION:

C) TYPES OF USE:
D) TERRITORY :

E) TERM:
COMMENCING ON   ENDING ON

F) NUMBER OF PLAYS DURING TERM :

G) MARKET:

5. **FEE (For Publisher's Share)**

A) SYNCHRONIZATION FEE
B) SALES FEE:

C) RENTAL FEE:

D) ADVANCE : NON RETURNABLE ADVANCE OF   AGAINST
E) PAYMENT CURRENCY :

6. **ADDITIONAL TERMS**

PLEASE READ LICENSE TERMS ON REVERSE SIDE

VEUILLEZ LIRE AU VERSO LES DISPOSI-TIONS DE LA PRÉSENTE LICENCE

DATE OF ISSUANCE OF LICENCE BY CMRRA

ACCEPTED FOR LICENSEE

BY _____

DATE _____

ACCEPTED FOR CMRRA

BY _____

DATE _____

STANDARD TERMS

1. PAYMENT OF FEE
    LICENSEE SHALL PAY THE SYNCHRONIZATION FEE AND ADVANCE (IF ANY) IN FULL TO LICENSOR
    UPON LICENSEES EXECUTION HEREOF WHERE SALES AND/OR RENTALS FOR HOME USE ARE
    AUTHORIZED BY THIS LICENCE. PAYMENT THEREFOR SHALL, UNLESS OTHERWISE PROVIDED
    HEREIN, BE MADE SEMI-ANNUALLY NO LATER THAN 45 DAYS AFTER THE LAST DAY OF JUNE AND
    DECEMBER OF EACH YEAR FOR ALL SALES AND/OR RENTALS MADE DURING THE SIX-MONTH
    PERIOD. PAYMENTS SHALL BE MADE IN THE CURRENCY INDICATED UNDER FEE ABOVE.

2. SALE / RENTAL STATEMENTS
    LICENSEE SHALL DELIVER ALONG WITH EACH RENTAL AND/OR SALE PAYMENT AN ACCURATE
    STATEMENT IN A FORM ACCEPTABLE TO LICENSOR SETTING OUT THE TOTAL NUMBER OF UNITS
    OF THE VIDEOCASSETTE/DISC THAT HAVE BEEN SOLD OR RENTED AND AMOUNTS DUE TO THE
    PUBLISHER FOR SUCH SALE AND/OR RENTALS.

3. TRAILERS
    PRODUCTION AS USED IN THIS LICENCE SHALL INCLUDE, WHERE APPLICABLE, THE TRAILERS
    THEREOF. RIGHTS GRANTED WITH RESPECT TO SUCH TRAILERS ARE HERBY LIMITED TO THE
    SOLE PURPOSE OF ADVERTISING AND PROMOTING THE PRODUCTION.

4. CUE SHEETS
    LICENSEE SHALL DELIVER TO LICENSOR CONCURRENTLY WITH PAYMENT OF THE
    SYNCHRONIZATION FEE AND ADVANCE (IF ANY), CUE SHEETS SIGNED BY THE PRODUCER AND IN
    A FORM ACCEPTABLE TO THE CANADIAN PERFORMING RIGHTS ORGANIZATIONS, LISTING ALL OF
    THE MUSIC RECORDED IN THE PRODUCTION.

5. PERFORMING RIGHTS
    THIS IS A LICENCE TO RECORD ONLY AND, UNLESS SPECIFICALLY OTHERWISE PROVIDED HEREIN,
    DOES NOT GRANT ANY RIGHT TO PERFORM THE MUSICAL WORK IN PUBLIC OR TO AUTHORIZE
    OTHERS TO DO SO.

6. SOUND RECORDINGS
    THIS IS A LICENCE TO RECORD THE MUSICAL WORK DESCRIBED ABOVE ONLY AND, UNLESS
    SPECIFICALLY OTHERWISE PROVIDED HEREIN, DOES NOT GRANT ANY RIGHT TO RECORD THE
    PERFORMANCE OF THE MUSICAL WORK FROM A COMMERCIALLY RELEASED SOUND RECORDING,
    OR TO AUTHORIZE OTHERS TO DO SO.

7. LICENCE RESTRICTIONS
    ANY USE OF THE MUSICAL WORK WHICH IS NOT SPECIFICALLY AUTHORIZED BY THIS LICENCE IS
    PROHIBITED AND, WITHOUT RESTRICTING THE GENERALITY OF THE FOREGOING, DOES NOT
    INCLUDE ANY RIGHT TO:
    A)   TRANSLATE, PARODY OR PRINT THE MUSIC OR LYRICS, OR BOTH, OR TO ALTER THE
         FUNDAMENTAL CHARACTER, OF THE MUSICAL WORK.
    B)   RECORD OR REPRODUCE THE MUSICAL WORK APART FROM THE SOUNDTRACK OF THE
         PRODUCTION OR TO REPRODUCE SUCH SOUNDTRACK OTHER THAN AS PART OF AND FOR
         USE IN THE PRODUCTION.
    C)   USE THE TITLE FOR SUBTITLE OF THE MUSICAL WORK AS THE TITLE OF THE PRODUCTION.

8. RETENTION AND VERIFICATION OF BOOKS AND RECORDS
    WHERE SALES AND/OR RENTALS ARE AUTHORIZED BY THIS LICENCE, LICENSEE SHALL KEEP IN
    CANADA ACCURATE AND UP-TO-DATE BOOKS OF ACCOUNT AND SUPPORTING DOCUMENTATION
    RELATING TO THE MANUFACTURE AND INVENTORY MOVEMENT OF VIDEOTAPES/DISCS UNDER
    THIS LICENCE AND LICENSOR SHALL HAVE THE RIGHT UPON REASONABLE NOTICE TO LICENSEE
    TO EXAMINE AND TAKE EXTRACTS THEREOF TO VERIFY LICENSEE'S COMPLIANCE WITH THE
    TERMS OF THE LICENCE AND THE PAYMENT OF SALE AND/OR RENTAL FEES DUE HEREUNDER.

9. TERMINATION
    LICENSOR MAY TERMINATE THIS LICENCE UPON LICENSEE'S BREACH THEREOF BY GIVING NOTICE
    IN WRITING OF SUCH BREACH BY REGISTERED MAIL, TELEGRAM OR TELEX TO LICENSEE AT
    LICENSEE'S ADDRESS. IF LICENSEE FAILS TO REMEDY THE BREACH COMPLAINED OF WITHIN
    THIRTY (30) DAYS OF THE DATE OF THE NOTICE, THEN THIS LICENCE SHALL TERMINATE ON THE
    THIRTY-FIRST DAY. UPON TERMINATION, ALL USE OF THE MUSICAL WORK AND ALL
    MANUFACTURE, DISTRIBUTION, SALE OR OFFERING FOR SALE OF VIDEOTAPES/DISCS
    AUTHORIZED TO HAVE BEEN MADE UNDER THIS LICENCE SHALL BE UNAUTHORIZED AND
    LICENSOR AND PUBLISHER SHALL BE ENTITLED TO ALL LEGAL AND EQUITABLE REMEDIES
    PROVIDED BY LAW AS WOULD HAVE BEEN AVAILABLE IF THIS LICENCE HAD NOT BEEN GRANTED.

10. ASSIGNMENT
     THIS LICENCE IS PERSONAL TO THE LICENSEE AND SUBJECT TO THE EXERCISE BY LICENSEE OF
     THE RIGHTS SET OUT UNDER THE GRANT OF LICENCE ABOVE. THE RIGHTS AND OBLIGATIONS
     UNDER IT MAY NOT BE ASSIGNED OR OTHERWISE TRANSFERRED WITHOUT LICENSOR'S PRIOR
     CONSENT IN WRITING.

11. WAIVER
     ANY WAIVER BY LICENSOR OF ANY RIGHTS OR INTEREST UNDER THIS LICENCE SHALL NOT IMPLY
     THE WAIVER OF ANY OTHER RIGHT OR INTEREST OR OF LICENSOR'S RIGHT TO SUBSEQUENTLY
     ENFORCE SUCH RIGHT OR INTEREST AND NO WAIVER OF A BREACH OF THIS LICENCE SHALL BE
     DEEMED TO BE A WAIVER OF ANY PRECEDING, CONTINUING OR SUCCEEDING BREACH THEREOF.

12. WARRANTY
     LICENSOR REPRESENTS ONLY THAT PUBLISHER HAS ADVISED LICENSOR THAT PUBLISHER OWNS
     AND/OR CONTROLS THE REPRODUCTION RIGHTS IN THE MUSICAL WORK AND HAS AUTHORIZED
     LICENSOR TO GRANT THIS LICENCE. LICENSOR MAKES NOT OTHER EXPRESS OR IMPLIED
     REPRESENTATION OR WARRANTY AS TO PUBLISHER'S RIGHTS LICENSED HEREUNDER. IN THE
     EVENT THIS REPRESENTATION IS BREACHED AND LICENSEE SUFFERS DAMAGES AS A RESULT,
     LICENSOR'S LIABILITY FOR SUCH BREACH SHALL NOT EXCEED THE LESSER OF SUCH DAMAGES
     OR AMOUNTS PAID PURSUANT TO PARAGRAPH 5 HEREIN.

13. GENERAL RESERVATIONS OF RIGHTS
     LICENSOR RESERVES ALL RIGHTS NOT EXPRESSLY GRANTED UNDER THIS LICENCE. ANY USE OF
     THE MUSICAL WORK OUTSIDE OF THE TERMS HEREOF OR AFTER THE EXPIRATION OF THE TERMS
     SHALL BE UNAUTHORIZED AND MAY BE ACTIONABLE AS AN ACT OF COPYRIGHT INFRINGEMENT IN
     THE MUSICAL WORK.

14. APPLICABLE LAW
     THIS LICENCE SHALL BE GOVERNED BY THE LAWS OF CANADA AND SHALL BE DEEMED TO HAVE
     BEEN MADE IN TORONTO, CANADA.

Writer - Membership Agreement and Assignment of Performing Rights

SOCAN

WRITER

MEMBERSHIP AGREEMENT AND ASSIGNMENT OF PERFORMING RIGHTS

AGREEMENT made this   day of   19   .

BETWEEN:

of

Referred to in this agreement as "MEMBER".

— and —

SOCIETY OF COMPOSERS, AUTHORS AND MUSIC PUBLISHERS OF CANADA, a company incorporated under Part II of the Canada Corporations Act, having its Head Office at 41 Valleybrook Drive, Don Mills, Ontario M3B 2S6 Canada referred to in this agreement as "SOCIETY".

In consideration of the mutual covenants and promises in this agreement and for other good and valuable consideration, SOCIETY and MEMBER agree as follows:

1. **TERM**

    The term of this agreement is two years from the date that the agreement is signed by MEMBER and SOCIETY and for extended terms of two years each as provided in paragraph 2, unless terminated by either party in accordance with paragraph 3.

2. **AUTOMATIC EXTENSION OF TERM**

    At the end of any two year term, this agreement will be automatically extended for an additional two year term unless terminated by notice as stated in paragraph 3.

3. **METHOD OF TERMINATION**

    This agreement may be terminated at the end of any two year term. Either MEMBER or SOCIETY may effect termination of this agreement, effective at the end of any two year term, by giving written notice to the other party by registered mail at least three months before the end of any two year term.

4. **DEFINITIONS**

    4.1 "MUSICAL WORK"

    means any musical work or any part of a musical work now existing or created after this agreement has been signed and any words that are associated with the musical work, and shall include (without limiting this definition) the vocal and instrumental music whether live or contained in any reproduction of the musical work on any medium used to reproduce sound (including but not limited to any audio-visual work whether on film, tape, disc or on any other medium and whether now known or later invented).

    4.2 "PERFORMING"

    The word "performing" means performing by any means and in any manner and without limiting this definition, includes communication by telecommunication and by any other means whether now known or later invented and "PERFORMANCE" and "PERFORM" shall have corresponding meanings.

4.3 "PERFORMING RIGHT"

The expression "performing right" includes any right that now exists or may exist in the future under the law applicable anywhere in the world, of performance of any musical work in public by any means whether now known or later invented and in any manner, and of communication of any musical work to the public by telecommunication or authorizing or prohibiting any public performance or any communication of any musical work by means of telecommunication but does not include any of the following:

(i) The performance of an opera, operetta, musical play, or similar work in its entirety insofar as it consists of words and music that were written expressly for it and when performed with the dramatic action, costumes or scenery of that work, except in cases where the performance is delivered as part of a pre-recorded audio-visual work (including but not limited to film and video).

(ii) The performance of a choreographic work in its entirety insofar as it consists of words and music or music alone written expressly for it and when performed with the live visual representation of that same choreographic work, except in cases where the performance is delivered as part of a pre-recorded audio-visual work (including but not limited to film and video).

5. ASSIGNMENT OF PERFORMING RIGHTS

MEMBER assigns to SOCIETY for the term of this agreement and in accordance with the By-laws and the Rules and Regulations of SOCIETY as amended from time to time, all performing rights in every part, share or interest in every musical work that was created by MEMBER alone, jointly or in collaboration with others before the date of this agreement and that is now owned, in whole or in part by MEMBER and all performing rights in every part, share, or interest in every musical work that may be created by MEMBER alone, jointly or in collaboration with others in whole or in part, during the term of this agreement. It is understood that the rights assigned by this agreement are exclusive to SOCIETY for the term of this agreement.

The assignment of all performing rights in musical works created during the term of this agreement shall be deemed to be assigned to SOCIETY by this agreement for the term stated, at the same time the work is created by MEMBER.

6. WARRANTY OF TITLE OF MUSICAL WORKS ASSIGNED

MEMBER warrants that member has the right and authority to assign the rights to SOCIETY in accordance with this agreement. MEMBER warrants that the musical works, the performing rights of which are assigned by this agreement, do not and will not infringe the copyright in any other work and that MEMBER will reimburse SOCIETY for any loss, costs or damages which SOCIETY may incur if a claim is made against SOCIETY which relates to the rights assigned by this agreement. Furthermore, MEMBER shall not enter into any other agreement under which MEMBER is required to create any musical work or part of any musical work, without inserting in the agreement a provision that makes that agreement subject to the assignment in this agreement.

7. OBLIGATIONS OF MEMBERS

7.1 NOTIFICATION OF WORKS

Upon signing this agreement, MEMBER shall notify SOCIETY in the manner prescribed by SOCIETY, of all those works that are assigned by this agreement, and MEMBER shall notify SOCIETY of any and all additional works at the time MEMBER creates those works and shall also, when requested by SOCIETY, provide SOCIETY with a copy or recording of each work. SOCIETY shall not be responsible for any loss or damage that may be caused by MEMBER's failure to comply with this provision.

7.2 CO-OPERATION IN INFRINGEMENT ACTIONS

If required, MEMBER agrees from time to time during the term of this agreement to execute any documents that are reasonably required by SOCIETY and to do those acts that are necessary to allow SOCIETY to enforce the rights assigned by this agreement.

7.3 INTERESTS OF THE SOCIETY

MEMBER shall not do anything that may prejudice the interests of SOCIETY and shall co-operate with SOCIETY and its officers and with fellow members in furthering the interests of SOCIETY and shall give to SOCIETY its officers and fellow members, all reasonable assistance in that behalf.

8. OBLIGATIONS OF SOCIETY

8.1 COLLECTION OF ROYALTIES

SOCIETY shall use its best efforts to collect all royalties that are properly payable to SOCIETY for the licensing in Canada of the rights that are assigned to it and for licensing of those rights in other territories throughout the world. It is understood that SOCIETY may enter into agreements with similar societies in other territories and that the licensing of the rights assigned or licensed by SOCIETY in respect of these territories and the distribution of the royalties collected from the licensing of those rights in those territories are subject to the laws and distribution rules of the societies in those territories.

8.2 DISTRIBUTION OF ROYALTIES

SOCIETY shall distribute to MEMBER, in accordance with the By-Laws, Rules and Regulations of SOCIETY as amended from time to time, those royalties, if any, that are earned on account of the licensing of the performing rights in those musical works assigned to SOCIETY by MEMBER by this agreement.

8.3 INFRINGEMENTS OF PERFORMING RIGHTS

SOCIETY and any Society with which SOCIETY has a reciprocal agreement shall have the right to institute or defend in its own name or in the name of the MEMBER, or otherwise, legal proceedings in respect of the rights assigned and MEMBER shall not be required to pay for any of the costs, charges and expenses of those proceedings.

9. ELECTION OF BOARD OF DIRECTORS

MEMBER'S right to vote in the election of the Board of Directors and the weight of that vote shall be determined according to the provisions of the By-Laws, Rules and Regulations of SOCIETY.

10. ASSIGNMENT

This agreement and the rights and obligations under this agreement are not transferable or assignable by MEMBER except in accordance with the Rules and Regulations of SOCIETY.

11. SUCCESSORS AND ASSIGNEES OF THIS AGREEMENT

This agreement shall be binding on the heirs, legal representatives or other successors in interest and assigns of MEMBER and SOCIETY.

12. NO IMPLIED TERMS

This agreement is the only and complete agreement between MEMBER and SOCIETY and no additional terms are or may be implied, nor can any terms be changed except in writing signed by both parties and expressly made part of this agreement. If part of this agreement is declared void by a court of competent jurisdiction, the remaining parts shall continue to be binding and shall have the same force and effect as if the void part were deleted from the agreement.

SIGNED

by MEMBER _____

in the presence of _____
                            (Signature of witness)

_____
                    (Print name and address of witness here)

this _____ day of _____, 19 ____.

SIGNED SEALED AND DELIVERED by

SOCIETY OF COMPOSERS, AUTHORS AND MUSIC PUBLISHERS OF CANADA

per _____

this _____ day of _____, 19 ____.

Publisher – Membership Agreement and Assignment of Performing Rights

PUBLISHER

MEMBERSHIP AGREEMENT AND ASSIGNMENT OF PERFORMING RIGHTS

AGREEMENT made this   day of   19   .

BETWEEN:

of

Referred to in this agreement as "MEMBER".

— and —

SOCIETY OF COMPOSERS, AUTHORS AND MUSIC PUBLISHERS OF CANADA, a company incorporated under Part II of the Canada Corporations Act, having its Head Office at 41 Valleybrook Drive, Don Mills, Ontario M3B 2S6 Canada referred to in this agreement as "SOCIETY".

In consideration of the mutual covenants and promises in this agreement and for other good and valuable consideration, SOCIETY and MEMBER agree as follows:

1. **TERM**

    The term of this agreement is two years from the date that the agreement is signed by MEMBER and SOCIETY and for extended terms of two years each as provided in paragraph 2, unless terminated by either party in accordance with paragraph 3.

2. **AUTOMATIC EXTENSION OF TERM**

    At the end of any two year term, this agreement will be automatically extended for an additional two year term unless terminated by notice as stated in paragraph 3.

3. **METHOD OF TERMINATION**

    This agreement may be terminated at the end of any two year term. Either MEMBER or SOCIETY may effect termination of this agreement, effective at the end of any two year term, by giving written notice to the other party by registered mail at least three months before the end of any two year term.

4. **DEFINITIONS**

    4.1 "MUSICAL WORK"

    means any musical work or any part of a musical work now existing or created after this agreement has been signed and any words that are associated with the musical work, and shall include, (without limiting this definition) the vocal and instrumental music whether live or contained in any reproduction of the musical work on any medium used to reproduce sound (including but not limited to any audio-visual work whether on film, tape, disc or on any other medium and whether now known or later invented).

    4.2 "PERFORMING"

    The word "performing" means performing by any means and in any manner and without limiting this definition, includes communication by telecommunication and by any other means whether now known or later invented and "PERFORMANCE" and "PER-FORM" shall have corresponding meanings.

4.3 "PERFORMING RIGHT"

The expression "performing right" includes any right that now exists or may exist in the future under the law applicable anywhere in the world, of performance of any musical work in public by any means whether now known or later invented and in any manner, and of communication of any musical work to the public by telecommunication or authorizing or prohibiting any public performance or any communication of any musical work by means of telecommunication but does not include any of the following:

(i) The performance of an opera, operetta, musical play, or similar work in its entirety insofar as it consists of words and music that were written expressly for it and when performed with the dramatic action, costumes or scenery of that work, except in cases where the performance is delivered as part of a pre-recorded audio-visual work (including but not limited to film and video).

(ii) The performance of a choreographic work in its entirety insofar as it consists of words and music or music alone written expressly for it and when performed with the live visual representation of that same choreographic work, except in cases where the performance is delivered as part of a pre-recorded audio-visual work (including but not limited to film and video).

5. ASSIGNMENT OF PERFORMING RIGHTS

MEMBER assigns to SOCIETY for the term of this agreement and in accordance with the By-laws and the Rules and Regulations of SOCIETY as amended from time to time, all performing rights in every part, share or interest in every musical work that is now owned or controlled in whole or in part by MEMBER and all performing rights in every part, share, or interest in every musical work that may be owned or controlled by MEMBER in whole or in part, during the term of this agreement. It is understood that the rights assigned by this agreement are exclusive to SOCIETY for the term of this agreement.

6. WARRANTY OF TITLE OF MUSICAL WORKS ASSIGNED

MEMBER warrants that member has the right and authority to assign the rights to SOCIETY in accordance with this agreement. MEMBER warrants that the musical works, the performing rights of which are assigned by this agreement, do not and will not infringe the copyright in any other work and that MEMBER will reimburse SOCIETY for any loss, costs or damages which SOCIETY may incur if a claim is made against SOCIETY which relates to the rights assigned by this agreement.

7. OBLIGATIONS OF MEMBERS

7.1 NOTIFICATION OF WORKS

Upon signing this agreement, MEMBER shall notify SOCIETY in the manner prescribed by SOCIETY, of all those works that are assigned by this agreement, and MEMBER shall notify SOCIETY of any and all additional works at the time MEMBER acquires those works and shall also, when requested by SOCIETY, provide SOCIETY with a copy or recording of each work. SOCIETY shall not be responsible for any loss or damage that may be caused by MEMBER's failure to comply with this provision.

7.2 CO-OPERATION IN INFRINGEMENT ACTIONS

If required, MEMBER agrees from time to time during the term of this agreement to execute any documents that are reasonably required by SOCIETY and to do those acts that are necessary to allow SOCIETY to enforce the rights assigned by this agreement.

7.3 INTERESTS OF THE SOCIETY

Member shall not do anything that may prejudice the interests of SOCIETY and shall co-operate with SOCIETY and its officers and with fellow members in furthering the interests of SOCIETY and shall give to SOCIETY its officers and fellow members, all reasonable assistance in that behalf.

8. OBLIGATIONS OF SOCIETY

8.1 COLLECTION OF ROYALTIES

SOCIETY shall use its best efforts to collect all royalties that are properly payable to SOCIETY for the licensing in Canada of the rights that are assigned to it and for licensing of those rights in other territories throughout the world. It is understood that SOCIETY may enter into agreements with similar societies in other territories and that the licensing of the rights assigned or licensed by SOCIETY in respect of these territories and the distribution of the royalties collected from the licensing of those rights in those territories are subject to the laws and distribution rules of the societies in those territories.

8.2 DISTRIBUTION OF ROYALTIES

SOCIETY shall distribute to MEMBER, in accordance with the By-Laws, Rules and Regulations of SOCIETY as amended from time to time, those royalties, if any, that are earned on account of the licensing of the performing rights in those musical works assigned to SOCIETY by MEMBER by this agreement.

8.3 INFRINGEMENTS OF PERFORMING RIGHTS

SOCIETY and any Society with which SOCIETY has a reciprocal agreement shall have the right to institute or defend in its own name or in the name of the MEMBER, or otherwise, legal proceedings in respect of the rights assigned and MEMBER shall not be required to pay for any of the costs, charges and expenses of those proceedings.

9. ELECTION OF BOARD OF DIRECTORS

Member's right to vote in the election of the Board of Directors and the weight of that vote shall be determined according to the provisions of the By-Laws, Rules and Regulations of SOCIETY.

10. ASSIGNMENT

This agreement and the rights and obligations under this agreement are not transferable or assignable by MEMBER except in accordance with the Rules and Regulations of SOCIETY.

11. SUCCESSORS AND ASSIGNEES OF THIS AGREEMENT

This agreement shall be binding on the heirs, legal representatives or other successors in interest and assigns of MEMBER and SOCIETY.

12. NO IMPLIED TERMS

This agreement is the only and complete agreement between MEMBER and SOCIETY and no additional terms are or may be implied, nor can any terms be changed except in writing signed by both parties and expressly made part of this agreement. If part of this agreement is declared void by a court of competent jurisdiction, the remaining parts shall continue to be binding and shall have the same force and effect as if the void part were deleted from the agreement.

SIGNED

by MEMBER _____
                    (authorized signature)   (if incorporated affix seal)

_____
                              (Print Name)

in the presence of _____
                                        (Signature of witness)

_____
                    (Print name and address of witness here)

this _____ day of _____ , 19_____.

SIGNED SEALED AND DELIVERED by

SOCIETY OF COMPOSERS, AUTHORS AND MUSIC PUBLISHERS OF CANADA

per _____

this _____ day of _____ , 19_____.

Author-Composer Agreement

SODRAC

AGREEMENT

BETWEEN: SOCIETY FOR REPRODUCTION RIGHTS OF AUTHORS, COMPOSERS AND PUBLISHERS IN CANADA (SODRAC) INC.

     Hereinafter called "SODRAC"

AND:

    ....
          (Name)

    ....

    ....
          (Address)

    Hereinafter called "AUTHOR-COMPOSER"

THE PARTIES HEREBY AGREE AS FOLLOWS:

1. The AUTHOR-COMPOSER assigns to SODRAC, for the world, the exclusive of reproduction of his Works.

2. For the purpose of the Agreement, the word "Work(s)" shall mean, as the case may be, any or all the musical or dramatico-musical works in which the AUTHOR-COMPOSER owns, exclusively or jointly, a part or the whole of the reproduction rights or an interest therein at the time of the execution of this contract and all those in which he shall hold such rights during the term of this contract.

3. The reproduction right under this contract contemplates any material fixation of the Work by any means now known or which may be invented, other than graphic reproduction, without restricting the generality of the foregoing, reproductions on phonogram, wire, tape, cassette and other similar contrivances; private copying; cinematographic reproductions; radio and television reproductions; reproductions on audiovisual contrivances of any kind; any use of these contrivances, such as: sale or rental for private use, public audition and broadcasting in all their forms, etc.

4. The rights assigned under paragraph 1 include the following rights as well as all those rights flowing therefrom:

   - To authorize the reproduction of the Work and to grant licenses to that effect;

PARTIES INITIALS

....

- To prohibit the reproduction of the Work and to take the necessary steps in order to do so;

- To collect and to distribute the royalties resulting from the reproduction right including remuneration for private copying;

- Generally to monitor the reproduction of the Work;

- To inspect the books and records of users;

- To institute legal proceedings for the recovery of amounts owing;

- To negotiate, compromise, and enter into settlements prior to or following the institution of legal proceedings.

5. Notwithstanding the assignment under paragraph 1 and subject to the provisions of paragraph 6, the AUTHOR-COMPOSER shall have the right to allow the participation of a publisher in the revenues to which the AUTHOR-COMPOSER is entitled pursuant to the exercise by SODRAC of the rights described herein respecting the reproduction of his Works.

6. The AUTHOR-COMPOSER undertakes to include the following provision in contracts into which he enters with any publisher:

"By reason of the original copyright owner's membership in the Society for Reproduction Rights of Authors, Composers and Publishers in Canada (SODRAC) Inc., royalties shall be collected directly from users by SODRAC in Canada or the local Societies entrusted with SODRAC's repertoire in foreign territories.

The royalties collected from abroad by the sister Societies shall be distributed by SODRAC for its members.

The present agreed clause will apply even in the case of an advance recoupable on reproduction rights."

7. The AUTHOR-COMPOSER undertakes to provide complete information regarding his Works using the prescribed forms provided by SODRAC upon execution of this contract and to keep his repertoire up to date, by filling a new declaration form for each Work added thereto. Furthermore, he shall submit and file a copy of any agreement affecting the exercise by SODRAC of the right herein assigned.

8. SODRAC shall remit to the AUTHOR-COMPOSER the amounts that it receives after deducting a commission of ten percent (10%) for amounts collected in Canada except on lump sums which derive from blanket licenses, a commission of fifteen percent (15%) will be deducted. With respect to amounts from other countries, SODRAC shall remit to the AUTHOR-COMPOSER, minus five percent (5%), any amount it receives from the collection societies with which it has agreements.

PARTIES INITIALS

....

9.   SODRAC shall remit the amounts owed to the AUTHOR-COMPOSER on March 15, June 15, September 15 and December 15 of each year.

10.   The AUTHOR-COMPOSER shall have access to his file upon forty-eight (48) hour notice.

11.   The AUTHOR-COMPOSER may not, subject to paragraphs 5 and 6 herein, enter into any agreement whatsoever in which the subject matter is the rights assigned to SODRAC under this agreement. Furthermore, the AUTHOR-COMPOSER may not collect directly from users any amount whatsoever which is payable to SODRAC and undertakes to remit immediately to SODRAC any amount which, for whatever reason, is paid to him directly.

12.   The AUTHOR-COMPOSER undertakes to cooperate and to participate in any legal proceeding instituted by SODRAC in the exercise of the rights assigned, entrusted or recognized to it herein or flowing therefrom.

13.   The AUTHOR-COMPOSER undertakes to sign, at the request of SODRAC, any document that SODRAC requires to exercise effectively the rights and obligations entrusted to it herein.

14.   SODRAC may at conditions it sees fit, assign or entrust the execution of the rights and obligations under this Agreement to any collection society to represent it throughout the world.

15.   This agreement shall remain in effect until March 31, 2001. It shall then automatically renew under the same terms, for periods of two (2) years, unless one of the parties, at least ninety days (90) days before the termination date, gives the other party notice of its intention to terminate the Agreement.

16.   SODRAC undertakes to carry out its functions with due diligence, skill and good faith on the understanding that its obligations herein are means rather than ends.

CONTRACT SIGNED IN .... **THIS** ..... **DAY OF** ...., **19** ...

Claudette Fortier   duly authorized
General Manager, SODRAC   **by Author-Composer**

APPENDIX 2
MUSIC PUBLISHING

I.   GENERAL CHECKLISTS

1.   GENERAL CONTRACT DRAFTING CHECKLIST*

1.   Proper parties

2.   Dates applicable
    a)   signing
    b)   the effective date
    c)   other

3.   Grant of rights
    a)   specified
    b)   limitations

4.   Term

5.   Territory

6.   Exclusive/non-exclusive

7.   Revocable/irrevocable

8.   Termination

9.   Representations/Warranties/Indemnity

10.   Accounting and Audit

11.   General Provisions (see General Contract Provisions checklist)

* Consider for each agreement.

2.　**GENERAL CONTRACT PROVISIONS CHECKLIST***

1.　Accounting and Audit

2.　Amendments

3.　Arbitration

4.　Assignment

5.　Bankruptcy

6.　Default and Cure

7.　Definitions

8.　Entity

9.　Force Majeure

10.　Governing Law

11.　Heirs and Assigns

12.　Indemnification

13.　Injunctive Relief

14.　Key Person

15.　Minors

16.　No Agency

17.　Notices

18.　Reference to Prior Agreement

19.　Representations and Warranties

20.　Severability

21.　Termination

22.　Union Compliance

*　**Consider for each agreement.**

II.   MUSIC PUBLISHING CHECKLISTS

1. **MECHANICAL LICENCE CHECKLIST**

1. Grant of rights
   a) title of musical composition
   b) copyright owner(s)
   c) administrator(s)
   d) label
   e) time
   f) writer
   g) artist
   h) usage
   i) record catalogue number
   j) release date
   k) record title

2. Territory
   a) Canada
   b) U.S.
   c) worldwide

3. Accounting
   a) royalty rate
   b) payment date
   c) statements - contents of
   d) timing - quarterly, semi-annual

4. Audit
   a) books and records
   b) statements
   c) right to take extracts, photocopy

5. Non-compliance
   a) revocation of licence
      (i) failure to pay royalties
      (ii) failure to allow audit
   b) interest penalty - for overdue payments

6. Limitations on grant of rights
   a) no adaptations without consent
   b) other - if applicable

7. Non-assignable/Non-exclusive

8. General Provisions

2.   <u>SYNCHRONIZATION LICENCE CHECKLIST</u>*

1.   Grant of rights
   a)   media - TV, film, video cassette, motion picture, disc, trailers, radio, film, other
   b)   programme type
   c)   type of use - all or part of the music
   d)   re-use rights - yes or no
   e)   term
   f)   territory

2.   Reservation of rights
   a)   no adaptation/translation of lyric
   b)   non-exclusive
   c)   no prior licence
   d)   use of title - yes or no
   e)   irrevocable vs. revocable
   f)   moral rights

3.   Payment to
   a)   who
   b)   when
   c)   how
   d)   how much

4.   Credit
   a)   songwriter(s)
   b)   music publisher(s)

5.   Union requirements
   a)   AFM
   b)   ACTRA

6.   Representations, Warranties and Indemnity
   a)   worldwide rights to grant

7.   Termination
   a)   breach of representation and warranties
   b)   non-compliance of terms

8.   General Provisions
   a)   audit and accounting
   b)   governing law
   c)   other

*   **Note:**   **U.S. requires theatrical performance licence to be obtained from music publisher.**

3.   SONGWRITER-PUBLISHER AGREEMENT CHECKLIST

I.   SONGWRITER'S OBLIGATIONS

1. Generally
   a)   exclusive agreement
   b)   entity
   c)   joint and several obligations of writers
   d)   employment relationship/work-made-for-hire

2. Assignment
   a)   copyright ownership of musical compositions assigned to publisher
   b)   songwriter cannot assign except
       (i)   to a corporation substantially owned by and under which songwriter carries on business
       (ii)   monies owing under the agreement to songwriter to a third party

3. Grant of rights
   a)   generally "all right, title and interest", legal and equitable, including all copyrights to:
       i)   title
       ii)   words
       iii)   music
   b)   territory
   c)   controlled compositions - defined
   d)   collaboration
   e)   right to secure copyright
   f)   exclusive (if long term agreement rather than single song agreement)

4. Reservation of rights
   a)   moral rights
   b)   first right to record - if songwriter is also a recording artist
   c)   grand performing rights

5. Prior contract
   a)   especially regarding performance rights with performing rights society - maintained in force
   b)   maintain membership in performing rights society
   c)   not modify pre-existing contract(s)
   d)   other - e.g., previous publishing agreement

6. Representations and Warranties
    a) exclusive contract
    b) musical compositions are original (within meaning of *Copyright Act*)
    c) right and capacity to make contract
    d) no adverse claims exist - particularly copyright infringement claims

7. Indemnity

II.   PUBLISHER'S OBLIGATIONS

1. Compensation to songwriter
    a) advances
        (i)   foreign
        (ii)   signing
        (iii) option
        (iv)   catalogue
        (v)   other
    b) royalties - net receipts
        i)   piano or vocal copies
               $10\text{-}12^1/_2\%$ retail (or wholesale) selling price
        ii) $10\text{-}12^1/_2\%$ of retail (or wholesale) selling price - folio and print income
        iii)   mechanical income - 50/50 - controlled composition rate
        iv)   performing rights income - 50/50
        v)   foreign income (see sub-publishing) - 50/50
        vi)   band/orchestration - on copies sold and paid for
        vii)   50/50 - any other usage (subsidiary rights)
        viii) 50/50 any licence by publisher/sub-publisher - use of song in whole or in part (includes: synchronization, phonograph, electrical transcriptions, any and all other "source, right, known or which may come into existence" - except performing rights
        ix)   50/50 unspecified uses royalties
        x)   collaboration - e.g., lyricist/composer/translator
        xi)   no royalties on professional copies - right to limit
        xii)   paid at source?

2. Accounting and Audit
    a) timing
        i)   quarterly or semi-annually - e.g., 45 days after January 1st and July 1st
        ii)   quarterly for mechanical royalties
    b) content of royalty statements

c)   time to object to royalty statements - typically 1-2 years

d)   public accountant, or other representative - on ____ days notice - examine books, records, take extracts, photocopy

e)   if fail to render statements or allow audit - terminate on __ days notice, subject to reversion of all rights

f)   is this a "tied deal"?

g)   is it cross-collateralized with another agreement?

3.   Professional copies

   a)   lead sheet, demo, or master recordings

   b)   what costs to be borne by publisher

   c)   control over selection of material

   d)   promotional material

4.   Obligation to exploit and promote

   a)   release record to general public "through normal commercial retail channels" within __ months

   b)   exploit performance of song and recordings

   c)   reversion, for example, if no demo or master recording or other performance obligation

   d)   term of agreement terminates if no exploitation as per paragraph 4(a) above.

5.   Alterations and adaptations

   a)   upon consent of composer

   b)   changes, editing, arrangements, title

   c)   moral rights

   d)   translation - effect on royalties

6.   Personality Rights

   a)   right to use name (including professional names), likeness, biographical material - in connection with exploiting songs

   b)   credit on recording, music, mechanical, electronic transcriptions etc.

   c)   no endorsement or merchandising rights granted without written consent

   d)   exclusive during the term, non-exclusive thereafter

   e)   not conflict with similar grant under other agreements

7.   Infringement actions

   a)   publisher pays costs of action

   b)   writer gets __ % of amount received less expenses

   c)   notice to writer of claim by publisher

   d)   pay songwriter royalties into trust - subject to songwriter posting bond

8.   Non-assignment
     a)   personal services - not assignable
     b)   restriction on publisher's right to assign

9.   Reversion
     a)   rights granted to revert by contract terms - for example, if not exploited
     b)   by statute

10.   First option clause
     a)   on future works
     b)   time to exercise

11.   Power of attorney
     a)   attorney in fact - limit to specific uses
     b)   copyright registrations

12.   Controlled compositions

13.   Remedies

14.   Withholding tax

15.   Recording contract
     a)   co-terminus with publishing contract, if with same entity, or
     b)   otherwise

16.   Cross-collateralization

17.   Definitions
     a)   net receipts - expenses
     b)   compositions governed under contract
     c)   other

III.   GENERAL PROVISIONS

1.   Notice
     a)   registered mail, courier, fax, personal delivery, other

2.   Governing law

3.   Heirs, administrators and assigns

4.   Bankruptcy - publisher
     a)   composer's right to terminate contract
     b)   reversion of all rights, or right of first refusal to acquire
     c)   re-assignment of rights

5.   Term and option periods
     a)   same as recording contract, or
     b)   specified term
     c)   depends if single song or long term exclusive contract

6. Termination
    a) recording contract - see term and option periods, 5 (a-c) above - co-terminus with this contract or otherwise
    b) termination of agreement – after 3-5 years, for example
    c) failure to account
    d) failure to allow audit
    e) failure to exploit
    f) bankruptcy

7. Indemnity
    a) by writer
    b) by publisher

8. Prior contracts

9. Default and Cure

10. Independent legal advice

4.   ADMINISTRATION AGREEMENT CHECKLIST*

1.   Administration rights
    a)   non-exclusive or exclusive
    b)   rights granted
    c)   audit, accounting and royalty statements
    d)   copyright infringement actions

2.   Compensation
    a)   typical range 10 - 25% of gross or net receipts - can be lower
    b)   initial and further advances
    c)   royalties for cover and original recordings secured by publisher
    d)   black box payments
    e)   pipeline income - after termination of the term

3.   Expenses
    a)   registration fees
    b)   promotional
    c)   lead sheets
    d)   demos
    e)   legal
    f)   travel
    g)   accounting

4.   Personality rights - extent of right to use

5.   Legal relationship
    a)   no - partnership, joint venture, etc.
    b)   no assignment
    c)   songwriter inducement letter

6.   Representations, warranties, indemnity

7.   Term and options

8.   Moral rights

9.   General Provisions

*   **See also Sub-publishing checklist.**

5.   <u>CO-PUBLISHING AGREEMENT CHECKLIST</u>

1.   Ownership of copyrights
    a)   usually 50/50 composer/publisher of all right, title, interest, including copyrights - to which musical compositions
    b)   for full term of copyright or a limited term
    c)   reversion of rights- specified
    d)   territory
        (i)   Canada
        (ii)   United States
        (iii) worldwide
    e)   reserve
        (i)   first right to record to composer-publisher if he or she is also a recording artist
        (ii)   grand performing rights

2.   Administration rights
    a)   exclusive right to administer and exploit
    b)   all or partial copyright
    c)   right to sub-publish
    d)   obligation to register copyrights
    e)   administration fees, if any, e.g. 10-15% of gross or net receipts, or lower
    f)   performing rights paid
        (i)   directly, or
        (ii)   through the administrator co-publisher

3.   Compensation
    a)   25% co-publisher, 75% composer/co-publisher of net receipts
    b)   songwriter paid "at source"?
    c)   advances on signing, options, other
    d)   cover versions, mechanical rates
    e)   lawsuits - % share of each party

4.   Expenses
    a)   equally split
    b)   define

5.   Representations, Warranties and Indemnity

6.   Assignment
    a)   rights to assign
    b)   right of first refusal or last refusal

7. Term and Options
    a) initial term and rights to extend the term
    b) performance obligations

8. Sub-publishing
    a) extent of such rights
    b) effect on royalties

9. Moral rights

10. Songwriter agreement and inducement letter

11. Termination rights

12. General Provisions

6. **SUB-PUBLISHING AGREEMENT CHECKLIST**

1. General considerations
    a) territory
    b) term
    c) grant of rights
    d) musical compositions governed by the contract
    e) residence of authors

2. Sub-Publisher's rights
    a) generally
        (i)   exclusive
        (ii) non-exclusive
    b) print, publish
    c) mechanical/synchronization
        (i)   generally-exclusive right to grant non-exclusive licences
        (ii) synchronization consent - when required
    d) adapt, translate, arrange - consent when required
    e) exclusive rights
        (i)   register copyrights in name of publisher
        (ii)   collect royalties, payments
        (iii) subject to agreement with performing rights society
        (iv)   other
    f) other obligations
        (i)   provide publisher with copies
        (ii) release dates - sub-publisher's obligations

3. Reservation of rights
    a) publisher exclusively reserves
        (i)   all rights, to adapt, arrange, translate
        (ii)   dramatization rights - grand performing rights
        (iii) other specified or unspecified uses
        (iv)   literary versions
        (v)   audio-visual rights - synchronization rights - worldwide right to grant
        (vi)   generally - any rights not granted to sub-publisher
    b) songwriter's moral rights

4. Payment
    a) advance
        (i)   signing
        (ii)   options
        (iii) other
    b) ___% - retail or wholesale selling price of print each
        (i)   except folios - not on professional copies

    c)   ___% of performance income

    d)   __% of mechanical on original recordings

    e)   __% for cover recordings

    f)   % ___ all unspecified uses

    g)   gross $ - deductions

    h)   black box payments

    i)   pipeline income - after the term

    j)   withholding tax/tax credit

5.   Statements of account

    a)   should be itemized

    b)   withholding tax

    c)   currency

    d)   quarterly or semi-annual

6.   Accounting and Audit rights

7.   Copyright registration

    a)   name of entity registering - power of attorney

8.   Copyright infringement actions

    a)   sub-publisher non-exclusive right to pursue

    b)   % split after legal costs

9.   Governing law

10.   Bankruptcy

11.   Songwriter inducement letter

12.   General Provisions

7. **SALE OF CATALOGUE AGREEMENT CHECKLIST**

1. Grant of rights
    a) all right, title and interest - to which musical compositions
    b) inventory, piano copies, orchestrations, plates, engravings, recordings, all rights, money, accounts, and benefits accruing under all agreements
    c) check renewal and reversion rights

2. Evaluation of purchase price
    a) unpaid royalties
    b) reversion of copyrights
    c) litigation and copyright infringement actions
    d) extent of rights in catalogue
    e) future plans for exploitation
    f) employee contracts
    g) examine chain of copyright title
    h) examine all assignments, licences
        and other agreements in force
    i) SOCAN
        (i)   accounting, unrecouped advances
        (ii) titles listed, etc.
    j) mortgages, liens, encumbrances
    k) advances - unrecouped
    l) key person
    m) other sale of business considerations, *Bulk Sales Act* etc.

3. Payment of purchase price

4. Tax implications
    a) share purchase
    b) asset purchase

5. Warranties and Representations
    a) true, lawful owner
    b) compositions not encumbered
    c) no lawsuit, claims or other liabilities
    d) capacity to contract - especially if minors
    e) survival of representations, warranties, indemnity - after sale

6. Indemnification

7. Notify
    a) SOCAN
    b) songwriters - is consent required?
    c) other - relevant parties

8. General Provisions

APPENDIX 3
AGENTS AND MANAGERS

I. AFM Forms

A.F.M. EXCLUSIVE AGENT-MUSICIAN AGREEMENT

(Three Years or Less)
NOT FOR USE IN STATE OF CALIFORNIA

Name of Agent	Legal Name of Musician
Address of Agent	Professional Name of Musician
A.F.M. Booking Agent Number	Name of Musician's Orchestra or Group
	Musician's A.F.M. Locals

This Agreement Begins on _____, 19____, and Ends on _____, 19____.

1. Scope of Agreement

Musician hereby employs Agent and Agent hereby accepts employment as Musician's exclusive booking agent, manager and representative throughout the world with respect to musician's services, appearances and endeavors as a musician. As used in this agreement "Musician" refers to the undersigned musician and to musicians performing with any orchestra or group which Musician leads or conducts and whom Musician shall make subject to the terms of this agreement; "A.F.M." refers to the American Federation of Musicians of the United States and Canada.

2. Duties of Agent

(a) Agent agrees to use reasonable efforts in the performance of the following duties: assist Musician in obtaining, obtain offers of, and negotiate, engagements for Musician; advise, aid, counsel and guide Musician with respect to Musician's professional career; promote and publicize Musician's name and talents; carry on business correspondence in Musician's behalf relating to Musician's professional career; cooperate with duly constituted and authorized representatives of Musician in the performance of such duties.

(b) Agent will maintain office, staff and facilities reasonably adequate for the rendition of such services.

(c) Agent will not accept any engagements for Musician without Musician's prior approval which shall not be unreasonably withheld.

(d) Agent shall fully comply with all applicable laws, rules and regulations of governmental authorities and secure such licenses as may be required for the rendition of services hereunder.

3. Rights of Agent

(a) Agent may render similar services to others and may engage in other businesses and ventures, subject, however, to the limitations imposed by 8 below.

(b) Musician will promptly refer to Agent all communications, written or oral, received by or on behalf of Musician relating to the services and appearances by Musician.

(c) Without Agent's written consent, Musician will not engage any other person, firm or corporation to perform the services to be performed by Agent hereunder (except that Musician may employ a personal manager) nor will Musician perform or appear professionally or offer so to do except through Agent.

(d) Agent may publicize the fact that Agent is the exclusive booking agent and representative for Musician.

(e) Agent shall have the right to use or to permit others to use Musician's name and likeness in advertising or publicity relating to Musician's services and appearances but without cost or expense to Musician unless Musician shall otherwise specifically agree in writing.

1

(f) In the event of Musician's breach of this agreement, Agent's sole right and remedy for such breach shall be the receipt from Musician of the commissions specified in this agreement, but only if, as, and when, Musician receives moneys or other consideration on which such commissions are payable hereunder.

4. Compensation of Agent

(a) In consideration of the services to be rendered by Agent hereunder, Musician agrees to pay to Agent commissions equal to the percentages, set forth below, of the gross moneys received by Musician, directly or indirectly, for each engagement on which commissions are payable hereunder:

(i) Fifteen per cent (15%) if the duration of the engagement is two (2) or more consecutive days per week.

(ii) Twenty per cent (20%) for Single Miscellaneous Engagements of one (1) day duration — each for a different employer in a different location.

(iii) In no event, however, shall the payment of any such commissions result in the retention by Musician for any engagement of net moneys or other consideration in an amount less than the applicable minimum scale of the A.F.M. or of any local thereof having jurisdiction over such engagement.

(iv) In no event shall the payment of any such commissions result in the receipt by Agent for any engagement of commissions, fees or other consideration, directly, or indirectly, from any person or persons, including the Musician, which in aggregate exceed the commissions provided for in this agreement. Any commission, fee, or other consideration received by Agent from any source other than Musician, directly or indirectly, on account of, as a result of, or in connection with supplying the services of Musician shall be reported to Musician and the amount thereof shall be deducted from the commissions payable by the Musician hereunder.

(b) Commissions shall become due and payable to Agent immediately following the receipt thereof by Musician or by anyone else in Musician's behalf.

(c) No commissions shall be payable on any engagement if Musician is not paid for such engagement irrespective of the reasons for such non-payment to Musician, including but not limited to non-payment by reason of the fault of Musician. This shall not preclude the awarding of damages by the International Executive Board to a booking agent to compensate him for actual expenses incurred as the direct result of the cancellation of an engagement when such cancellation was the fault of the member.

(d) Agent's commissions shall be payable on all moneys or other considerations received by Musician pursuant to contracts for engagements negotiated or entered into during the term of this agreement; if specifically agreed to by Musician by initialing the margin hereof, to contracts for engagements in existence at the commencement of the term hereof (excluding, however, any engagements as to which Musician is under prior obligation to pay commissions to another agent); and to any modifications, extensions and renewals thereof or substitutions therefor regardless of when Musician shall receive such moneys or other considerations.

(e) As used in this paragraph and elsewhere in this agreement the term "gross earnings" shall mean the gross amounts received by Musician for each engagement less costs and expenses incurred in collecting amounts due for any engagement, including costs of arbitration, litigation and attorney's fees.

(f) If specifically agreed to by Musician by initialing the margin hereof, the following shall apply:

(i) Musician shall advance to Agent against Agent's final commissions an amount not exceeding the following percentages of the gross amounts received for each engagement 15% on engagements of three (3) days or less; 10% on all other engagements.

(ii) If Musician shall so request and shall simultaneously furnish Agent with the data relating to deductions, the Agent within 45 days following the end of each 12 months period during the term of this agreement and within 45 days following the termination of this Agreement, shall account to and furnish Musician with a detailed statement itemizing the gross amounts received for all engagements during the period to which such accounting relates, the moneys or other considerations upon which Agent's commissions are based, and the amount of Agent's commissions resulting from such computations. Upon request, a copy of such statement shall be furnished promptly to the Office of the President of the A.F.M.

(iii) Any balances owed by or to the parties shall be paid as follows: by the Agent at the time of rendering such statement; by the Musician within 30 days after receipt of such statement.

5. Duration and Termination of Agreement

(a) The term of this agreement shall be as stated in the opening heading hereof, subject to termination as provided in 5 (b), 6 and 10 below.

(b) In addition to termination pursuant to other provisions of this agreement, this agreement may be terminated by either party, by notice as provided below, if Musician

(i) is unemployed for four (4) consecutive weeks at any time during the term hereof; or

(ii) does not obtain employment for at least twenty (20) cumulative weeks of engagements to be performed during each of the first and second six (6) months periods during the term hereof; or

(iii) does not obtain employment for at least forty (40) cumulative weeks of engagements to be performed during each subsequent year of the term hereof.

(c) Notice of such termination shall be given by certified mail addressed to the addressee at his last known address and a copy thereof shall be sent to the A.F.M. Such termination shall be effective as of the date of mailing of such notice if and when approved by the A.F.M. Such notice shall be mailed no later than two (2) weeks following the occurrence of any event described in (i) above: two (2) weeks following a period in excess of thirteen (13) of the cumulative weeks of unemployment specified in (ii) above; and two (2) weeks following a period in excess of twenty-six (26) of the cumulative weeks of unemployment specified in (iii) above. Failure to give notice as aforesaid shall constitute a waiver of the right to terminate based upon the happening of such prior events.

(d) Musician's disability resulting in failure to perform engagements and Musician's unreasonable refusal to accept and perform engagements shall not by themselves either deprive Agent of its right to or give Musician the right to terminate (as provided in (b) above).

(e) As used in this agreement, a "week" shall commence on Sunday and terminate on Saturday. A "week of engagements" shall mean any one of the following:

(i) a week during which Musician is to perform on at least four (4) days; or

(ii) a week during which Musician's gross earnings equals or exceeds the lowest such gross earnings obtained by Musician for performances rendered during any one of the immediately preceding six (6) weeks; or

(iii) a week during which Musician is to perform engagements on commercial television or radio or in concert for compensation equal at least to three (3) times the minimum scales of the A.F.M. or of any local thereof having jurisdiction applicable to such engagements.

6. Agent's Maintenance of A.F.M. Booking Agent Agreement

Agent represents that Agent is presently a party to an A.F.M. Booking Agent Agreement which is in full force and effect. If such A.F.M. Booking Agent Agreement shall terminate, the rights of the parties hereunder shall be governed by the terms and conditions of said Booking Agent Agreement relating to the effect of termination of such agreements which are incorporated herein by reference.

7. No other Agreements

This is the only and the complete agreement between the parties relating to all or any part of the subject matter covered by this agreement.* There is no other agreement, arrangement or participation between the parties, nor do the parties stand in any relationship to each other which is not created by this agreement,* whereby the terms and conditions of this agreement are avoided or evaded, directly or indirectly, such as, by way of example but not limitation, contracts, arrangements, relationships or participations relating to publicity services, business management, personal management, music publishing, or instruction.

* (A.F.M. Personal Management Agreement Excepted.)

8. Incorporation of A.F.M. Bylaws, etc.

There are incorporated into and made part of this agreement, as though fully set forth herein, the present and future provisions of the Bylaws, Rules, Regulations and Resolutions of the A.F.M. and those of its locals which do not conflict therewith. The parties acknowledge their responsibility to be fully acquainted, now and for the duration of this agreement, with the contents thereof.

9. Submission and Determination of Disputes

Every claim, dispute, controversy or difference arising out of, dealing with, relating to, or affecting the interpretation or application of this agreement, or the violation or breach, or the threatened violation or breach thereof shall be submitted, heard and determined by the International Executive Board of the A.F.M., in accordance with the rules of such Board (regardless of the termination or purported termination of this agreement or of the Agent's A.F.M. Booking Agent Agreement), and such determination shall be conclusive, final and binding on the parties.

10. No Assignment of this Agreement

This agreement shall be personal to the parties and shall not be transferable or assignable by operation of law or otherwise without the prior consent of the Musician and of the A.F.M. The obligations imposed by this agreement shall be binding upon the parties. The Musician may terminate this agreement at any time within ninety (90) days after the transfer of a controlling interest in the Agent.

11. Negotiation for Renewal

Neither party shall enter into negotiations for or agree to the renewal or extension of this agreement prior to the beginning of the final year of the term hereof.

12. Approval by A.F.M.

This agreement shall not become effective unless, within thirty (30) days following its execution, an executed copy thereof is filed with and is thereafter approved in writing by the A.F.M.

IN WITNESS WHEREOF, the parties hereto have executed this agreement the____day of_____, 19____.

By _____

Agent		Musician
Title or Capacity		Residence Address
		City State Zip Code

Agent Representing No More Than Two Clients

If specifically agreed to by the parties by signing below:

(a) Agent warrants and represents that Agent presently serves, and Agent agrees that during the term hereof Agent will restrict its activities to serving, as booking agent, or manager, or representative, no more than one other musical soloist, orchestra, band or performing group. If such warranty and representation is untrue, this agreement is null and void. If such agreement is broken, this agreement shall automatically terminate.

(b) In consideration thereof, the parties agree that the provisions of 4(a) (i) and (ii) and 4(f) above shall be inapplicable and that the compensation of Agent shall be as set forth in Schedule 1 attached. In no event, however, shall the payment of any commission result in the retention by Musician for any engagement of net moneys or other consideration in an amount less than the applicable minimum scale of the A.F.M. or of any local thereof.

By _____

Agent	Musician
Title or Capacity	

AMERICAN FEDERATION OF MUSICIANS OF THE UNITED STATES AND CANADA

Personal Management Agreement

This Agreement, made this _____ day of _____, 19____, by and between _____

hereinafter called "Personal Manager," and _____

_____

_____

_____

hereinafter called "Artists."

    WHEREAS, the Artists are engaged in the field of entertainment and are desirous of utilizing the services of a Personal Manager to aid them in furthering their careers; and

    WHEREAS, the Personal Manager is experienced and qualified to manage the business affairs of the Artists and assist them in the furtherence of their professional careers as entertainers;

    NOW, THEREFORE, be it resolved that in consideration of the covenants contained herein, the Artists both jointly and severally and the Personal Manager agree as follows:

1. The Personal Manager agrees to advise and counsel the Artists with respect to the following:
   - (a) The selection of literary, artistic and musical materials.
   - (b) Any and all matters relating to publicity, public relations and advertising.
   - (c) The adoption of proper format for the best presentation of the Artists' talents.
   - (d) The selection of Booking Agents to procure maximum employment for the Artists.
   - (e) The types of employment which the Artists should accept and which would prove most beneficial to their careers.
   - (f) Any and all other duties customarily performed by Personal Managers in the entertainment field.

2. The Artists expressly authorize the Personal Manager to approve and permit any and all publicity and advertising, including the use of the Artist's names, photographs and likeness.

3. It is specifically understood and agreed between the Parties hereto that the duties of the Personal Manager do not include the soliciting, procurement or negotiation for employment of the services of the Artists, which duties are normally performed by a Booking Agent.

4. In consideration of the services to be performed by the Personal Manager under the terms of this Agreement, the Artists agree to pay the Personal Manager a sum equal to _____% of any and all gross monies or other consideration received by the Artists as a result of their activities in the entertainment or related fields, said sums to be paid weekly, but only after the Artists have actually received the aforementioned monies or consideration.

5. It is expressly understood and agreed between the Parties that the Personal Manager is not restricted to render his services exclusively to the Artists and that he shall be permitted to represent other persons or groups or to engage in other business activities which do not interfere with the performance of his obligations under this Agreement.

6. The Parties agree that this Agreement shall be subject to the Constitution, By-laws and Regulations of the American Federation of Musicians and that any portion of this Agreement which is in conflict therewith shall be null and void and of no effect whatsoever.

7. The Parties agree that this Agreement cannot be assigned in whole or in part by either Party without the express consent in writing of the other.

8. This Agreement shall be in effect for _____* year(s) from the date hereof and shall not be extended except by written mutual consent.

9. In witness whereof, the Parties hereto have set their hands and seals this _____ day of _____, 19____.

WITNESS

_____   _____(SEAL)
                                                           Personal Manager

_____   _____(SEAL)
                                                           Artist

_____   _____(SEAL)
                                                           Artist

_____   _____(SEAL)
                                                            Artist

_____   _____(SEAL)
                                                            Artist

_____   _____(SEAL)
                                                           Artist

*The International Executive Board advises that these contracts should not exceed three years.

II.   MANAGEMENT

1.   MANAGEMENT AGREEMENT CHECKLIST

I.   GENERAL CONSIDERATIONS

    1.   General
        a)   trust
        b)   contacts
        c)   advice
        d)   money

    2.   Trial Basis

    3.   No Partnership

    4.   Independent legal advice

    5.   Conflicts of interest

    6.   Enforceability of agreement

    7.   Exclusivity

II.   NEGOTIABLE ISSUES

    1.   Power of attorney/manager's authority
        a)   limit:
            (i)   to short term agreements
            (ii)   no merchandising, endorsement, commercial tie-in agreements – without consent
            (iii)   live performance – short term (i.e. less than ___ days)
        b)   irrevocable – during the term
        c)   "coupled with an interest"

    2.   Compensation – gross vs. net income
        a)   commission rates: 10 – 25% commission of gross
        b)   exclusions
            (i)   advances applied to production, e.g., records, videos, interactive devices
            (ii)   independent radio promotion
            (iii)   tour support
            (iv)   other
        c)   continuing after term – "sunset" clause
            (i)   % in perpetuity – if so, what source(s), or
            (ii)   reduce overtime
        d)   time of payment
        e)   treatment of loans

III. OTHER

1. Key Person
   a) manager and artist – right to terminate

2. Management expenses
   a) limit to $___.00/monthly, or single expenditure – or consent required

3. Performance obligations/term/options
   a) obtain recording agreement
   b) other gross income
   c) other criteria, e.g., merchandising or film agreement

4. Term
   a) how many years
   b) subject to paragraph 3 above
   c) right to extend or suspend the term of the agreement for length of recording agreement

5. Group members clauses
   a) joint and several obligations
   b) leaving, joining, replacing, substituting members

6. Directions to third parties

7. Definitions
   (a) gross/net income
   (b) parties
   (c) scope of management services

8. Assignment
   a) manager – yes – subject to qualification and key person
   b) musician – yes – but
      (i) only to corporation carrying on business
      (ii) monies owing to artist under the contract

9. Name clause
   a) representation and warranties
   b) indemnity

10. Representations and Warranties
    (a) manager
    (b) musician

11. General Provisions
    (a) accounting and audit
    (b) arbitration
    (c) termination
    (d) notice
    (e) default and cure

APPENDIX 4

LIVE PERFORMANCE

I. AFM Forms

AMERICAN FEDERATION OF MUSICIANS
OF THE UNITED STATES AND CANADA

LIVE PERFORMANCE CONTRACT FOR CANADA
(CANADIAN ENGAGEMENTS ONLY)

Form LPCC
Side 1

Whereas this contract is entered into by the undersigned engager (herein referred to as the "Purchaser") for the personal services of the musician(s)/performer(s) named on the reverse (Side II) of this contract (herein referred to as the "Musicians") who are engaged severally through their representative, being the undersigned Leader. This contract confirms that, said Musician(s) will hold themselves available to perform according to the terms and conditions set out in herein

Name of Orchestra/Group: _____ consisting of _____ Musician(s).
(state number)

AND WHEREAS, it is acknowledged by all parties named herein, that the Musician(s) (including their representative Leader) are members of Local(s) (herein referred to as the "Local") of the American Federation of Musicians of the United States and Canada (herein referred to as the "AFM") and nothing in this contract shall ever be so construed as to interfere with any obligations which the Musicians may owe to their respective Local as provided under its rules, regulations, bylaws or constitution and those of the AFM which, under the circumstances, may be appropriate;

AND WHEREAS, said member Musician(s) (including the Leader) according to said rules, are bound to adhere to the professional standards (code of ethics) as established and maintained by the AFM and its Locals;

AND WHEREAS, the terms and conditions set out in (i) the recitals hereto and (ii) in SCHEDULE I on Side II hereof, as well as (iii) in part (b) (when initialed) all of which form an integral part of this contract in conjunction with the details specified in this SECTION A, and as in attached rider. Rider attached? Yes ☐ No ☐

NOW THEREFORE, for the good and valuable considerations set out herein, the parties expressly agree further as follows:

SECTION A - Particulars of Performance(s) - Purpose: _____
(Show, Dance, Concert, Tower, Club)

Venue: _____
(Name, Address, Telephone etc.)

Date(s) of performance(s): _____

Hours: _____
(Number of Performances etc, starting time, Fin-share total etc.)

Special requirements: _____

FEE AGREED UPON: $_____ + GST/HST (as applicable) _____ TOTAL $_____

Leader To Be Paid As Follows: (Please state: when payable and method of payment i.e. cash, certified cheque etc.)

DEPOSIT AMOUNT (non-refundable): $_____ to be included with signed copy of contract;

BALANCE AMOUNT: $_____ TO BE PAID: _____

Note: Unspecified overtime is subject to (i) availability of performing Musician(s) and, (ii) payment of additional fees on a pro rata amount of the Fee agree upon, calculated in half (½) hour units, or as otherwise agreed to between the Purchaser and the Leader.

Purchaser's Name: _____ (Or state proper corporate name)	**Leader's Name:** _____ (To state proper corporate name of band/orchestra)
Mailing Address: _____	**Mailing Address:** _____
City: _____	**City:** _____
Province: _____ **Postal Code:** _____	**Province:** _____ **Postal Code:** _____
Phone: ( ) _____ **Fax:** _____	**Phone:** ( ) _____ **Fax:** _____
E-Mail: _____	**E-Mail:** _____

The Signatory to this contract accepts personal liability for the fees payable herein, unless said Signatory is the authorized representative of a purchaser who is financially solvent and has the legal capacity to be bound by all provisions hereof

The Signatory/Leader in signing this contract acknowledges being the Musician(s)' representative who, on behalf of the Musician(s) named herein, agree to provide the performance(s) according to the terms set out above and in Schedule I (see Side II).

We, the signatory parties, confirm the terms detailed herein and in SCHEDULE I on the reverse or as attached:

_____ ___/___/___ Purchaser's Signature month day year	_____ ___/___/___ Leader's Signature month day year

Part (b): This Part (b) to be initialed only when applicable AFM/Local tariffs, agreements or authorizations stipulate contributions to:

"THE AMERICAN FEDERATION of MUSICIANS' and EMPLOYERS' PENSION WELFARE FUND (CANADA)".

The Purchaser (named herein), designates a portion of the 'Fee agreed upon' as individual 'pension credits' to the personal accounts of the Musicians performing herein pursuant to the terms and conditions detailed in the Appendix I, AFM-EPW-Fund Participation Agreement, attached hereto.

Purchaser's initials confirms this designation of funds: [____]   Leader's initials confirms agreement herein: [____]

NOTICE. This form of contract is protected by copyright. Its use to cover the services of any Musician(s) who are not members of the AFM is strictly prohibited and may subject the non-member user to legal sanctions.

Side II – Form LPCC   *Note: Pursuant to specific provisions of the Ontario Consumer Protection Act, the name and address of all musicians must be included in all duplicate copies of this executory form contract. Other Provinces and Territories may have similar statutes.*

Local No.	(For additional Musicians, attach a Continuation Sheet (or list)) Surname Given Name(s)		GST/HST Registration #	Fees	GST/HST As applicable
	(Leader)				
	(Address)				
	(Musician)				
	(Address)				
	(Musician)				
	(Address)				
	(Musician)				
	(Address)				
	(Musician)				
	(Address)				
	(Musician)				
	(Address)				
	(Musician)				
	(Address)				
	(Musician)				
	(Address)				
	(Musician)				
	(Address)				
	(Musician)				
	(Address)				
	(Musician)				
	(Address)				
	(Musician)				
	(Address)				

SCHEDULE 1 - AFM/LOCAL REQUIREMENTS (AS THEY RELATE TO THE PERFORMANCE(S) CONTRACTED HEREIN):

The parties to this contract: (i) shall not permit any performance(s) or rehearsal(s) related to the performance(s) to be recorded, reproduced, broadcast, transmitted or re-transmitted in any manner, or in any media, or by any means whatsoever, in the absence of a specific written agreement with the AFM, or the Local having jurisdiction over the performance(s) contracted herein, and; (ii) agree that the AFM and/or its Locals accept no liability, either express or implied, with respect to said performance(s) and/or rehearsal(s), and that, the AFM and its Locals are fully indemnified by the parties hereto for any and all claims, losses or liabilities resulting therefrom.

The Purchaser (i) shall provide performance facilities which are adequate for the health and safety of the Musicians and their equipment, and; (ii) agrees that the Business Representative of the Musician(s) Local in whose jurisdiction the Musician(s) are performing, shall have access to the venue in which the Musician(s) rehearse/perform for the purpose of conferring with the Musician(s), and; (iii) hereby authorizes the Leader to replace any Musician(s) who, by illness, absence, or for any other personal or professional reason, does not perform or can not perform any or all of the services contracted for herein without liability to the purchaser, and; (iv) represents and warrants that there does not exist against the Purchaser any outstanding claim in favour of any Musician(s), the AFM or its Local(s) and agrees that no Musician(s) of any Local will be required to perform any provisions of this contract or to render any services for the Purchaser, as long as any monetary judgement by a court against the Purchaser, in favour of the AFM, any Local or its Musician(s), remains unsatisfied or unpaid, in whole or in part. The Leader shall distribute the fees received from the Purchaser to the Musician(s) in the manner prescribed by the AFM's Bylaws and/or those of the Local having jurisdiction.

GOVERNING STATUTES AND OTHER LEGAL REQUIREMENTS:

The parties to this contract will submit every claim, dispute, controversy or difference involving the performance(s) and arising out of, or connected with this contract, to the Local having jurisdiction herein, or the Canadian Office of the AFM whichever may be appropriate in the circumstances. If such submission does not result in a mutually acceptable settlement of the matter(s) in dispute, either signatory party to this contract may initiate proceedings in a Canadian court of competent jurisdiction to have the disputed matters adjudicated. For purpose of adjudication and, unless otherwise agreed to by the parties in writing, this contract and all matters arising hereunder shall be governed by and construed in accordance with the laws of the Province or Territory in which the performance(s) occurs and the laws of Canada applicable therein. If any provision of this contract is determined at any time by a court of competent jurisdiction to be invalid, illegal or unenforceable, such provision or part thereof shall be severable from this contract and the remainder of this contract will remain in full force and effect and will be construed as if such invalid, illegal or unenforceable provision or part thereof had been deleted herefrom. This contract may be executed in one or more counterparts, all of which together will constitute one and the same contract, and one or more of such counterparts may be delivered by facsimile transmission. This contract including the recitals hereto, Section A, Schedule 1 and any addendum(s)/rider(s) authorized and/or, signed by the parties and attached hereto constitutes the entire agreement with respect to the matters described herein, and it supersedes any and all other oral or other written contracts or representations between the parties and it shall not be altered further, except by an amendment in writing signed by all the parties hereto.

In addition to the fees set out in Section A, the Purchaser shall obtain and pay any and all licenses, approvals, consents, permits, fees and royalties required to be obtained, including but not limited to public performing rights fees to be paid to SOCAN or to any other person, firm, corporation, organization, governmental authority, (or agent thereof) legally entitled to require licensing, payment of fees, approvals, permits and consents pursuant to the Copyright Act or otherwise concerning the performance(s) and shall fully indemnify and save harmless the Musician(s), the AFM and its Locals from any and all claims, losses and liabilities now or hereafter arising with respect to such liabilities concerning the performance(s) and is authorized or unauthorized recording, reproduction, broadcast, transmission or re-transmission of any kind.

No party hereto will be held liable for delay, loss damage or non-fulfillment of the terms of this contract if and to the extent that such delay, loss damage or non-fulfillment is caused by an occurrence beyond the reasonable control of such party, including but not limited to proven sickness or accident to any Musician(s), delay of transportation services or accident to means of transportation, riots, strikes, epidemics, acts of God, compliance with any act, regulation, order or request of any governmental authority or agency, or any other causes, whether direct or indirect, not within the reasonable control of such party, and which by the exercise of reasonable diligence such party is unable to prevent such delay, loss damage or non-fulfillment of the provisions of this contract or otherwise to be rendered by such party hereto. Exempt from these *force majeure* provisions are engagements contracted as open air performance(s) wherein the weather being unpredictable, the payments specified herein are payable by the Purchaser unless expressly provided for otherwise in writing, by all parties hereto. Furthermore, any Musician(s) who are parties to or affected by this contract, whose performance(s) and/or services are covered hereunder, who are prevented, suspended or stopped by reason of any strike, ban, unfair list or order or requirement of the AFM, shall be free to accept and engage in other performance(s) for other purchasers of music or other leaders without any restraint, hindrance, penalty, obligation or liability hereunder whatsoever, notwithstanding any other provisions of this contract to the contrary. All parties to this contract acknowledge that the performance(s) herein contracted are provided by self-employed/independent contractors and that fees paid herein are not subject to individual income tax deductions or *standard* employment related benefits. The method of distributing the fees contracted herein, or any other term(s) or condition(s) detailed within this contract, shall not imply, infer, or be construed in a manner so that the Musician(s) performing hereunder are deemed to be other than independent contractors in the absence of a written agreement to the contrary. GST or HST shall be calculated only on that portion of fees which represents payment to each individual Musician, provided the Musician(s) have made their GST/HST registration number available to the Leader and the Leader has listed this number on this contract. When said registration numbers are not detailed herein and in those individual circumstances wherein GST/HST is appropriate, it shall be deemed included as part of the fees paid by the Purchaser, received by the Leader and subsequently distributed to the individual Musician(s) performing hereunder.

Revised June 15, 1999 LPerf/lpcc.wpd

AMERICAN FEDERATION OF MUSICIANS
and
EMPLOYERS' PENSION WELFARE FUND (CANADA)
2255 Sheppard Avenue East, Suite A110
North York, Ontario M2J 4Y1
Tel: 416-497-4702 Fax: 416-497-4742
E-mail – afmepw.can@sympatico.ca
AFM-EPW Fund – Appendix I (Participation Agreement)   Side I

This Appendix I acknowledges that the Musician(s) named in the AFM (contract) Form LPCC and referenced herein is/are bonafide members of AFM Locals, thereby eligible to receive the amounts herein designated as 'pension credits'. Further, this Participation Agreement confirms that the pension contributions designated by Part (b) of AFM Form LPCC do not exceed an amount equivalent to 10% of the fees payable to each musician pursuant to AFM/Local tariffs, agreements or authorizations appropriate to the performances specified therein.

In particular, and upon acceptance/verification of the Local as provided below, this authorization is included as part of the terms/conditions for the purpose of Part (b) of AFM Form LPCC applicable to:

Purchaser (Employer) _____
(Please Print)

Leader _____
(Please Print)
Name of Orchestra/Group _____ Consisting of _____ Musician/Employee(s)
(Please Print)   (State number)

Date(s)/Time(s) of Performance(s) _____

Type: _____ Fee Agreed Upon: $ _____ Received by Leader: __/__/__
(i.e. concert, dance show, club etc)   (As per Form LPCC)   (Month Day Year)

Said engagement(s) subject to AFM-EPW Fund contributions as follows:
Name(s) of Leader and Musician(s)

Local No.	Surname	Given Name(s)	SIN No.	Base Amount for calculating Contributions	Percentage Rate @ %	AFM-EPW Credits
	(Leader)					

Please include additional names of musicians, etc., on the reverse Side II of this form. →   (Including subtotal from Side II) **TOTAL AMOUNT PAYABLE** $

With respect to the contributions payable herein, it is further acknowledged that Provincial statutes/regulations govern this multi-employer pension plan, pursuant to the 'Agreement and Declaration of Trust' dated April 9, 1962.

THEREFORE, for purposes of pension credits only, the Purchaser named herein is referenced as the 'Employer' and the Musician(s) listed herein is/are referenced the 'Employees'. *Note: These designations of Employer/Employee(s) are for the exclusive purpose of eligibility/acceptance of the 'pension credits' as provided herein. Said designations are not to be considered for any other purpose whatsoever as the applicable terms of SCHEDULE I of the above referenced contract (Form LPCC) prevail.*

FURTHER, The Leader (named herein) confirms the following:
(i) The Purchaser (Employer) authorized the individual 'pension credits' as prescribed herein, and;
(ii) Said amounts have been included in the 'Fee agreed upon', which have been paid to myself as Leader and as stipulated by AFM Form LPCC, therefore, the Purchaser (Employer) is absolved from any further obligation herein, and;
(iii) The amount included herein is forwarded in conformity with the rules of the AFM and/or its Local and the entitlements afforded all Local members thereof.

Total amount payable to 'AFM/EPW Fund Canada': $ _____ Confirmed by: _____ __/__/__
(specify amount)   (Leader's Signature)   (Month Day Year)

This part to be completed by a designated representative of AFM Local having jurisdiction.   AFM Local No. _____

Form of Remittance: Leader's cheque ☐   Other ☐
(Please Specify)

THIS WILL confirm that the amount of $ _____ represents individual 'pension credits' which have been negotiated and received in conformity with the requirements of Local tariffs or agreements, or as otherwise stipulated and agreed to herein.

By: _____   _____   __/__/__
(Signature of Local Representative)   (Title)   (Month Day Year)

Names of Musician(s)

Local No.	Surname	Given Name(s)	SIN No.	Base Amount for calculating Credits	Percentage Rate	AFM-EPW Credits
					SUBTOTAL (add to page 1)	$

Revised June 17/99, 1999 (per appendix)

II.   Rider Checklist

1.   LIVE PERFORMANCE AGREEMENT RIDER CHECKLIST

1.   Parties Involved
   a)   musician - by booking agent on musician's behalf
   b)   promoter
   c)   venue
   d)   sponsor
      i)   local radio station or newspaper
      ii)   tour sponsor
   e)   record companies
      i)   right to record album, video
      ii)   tour support

2.   Production Agreement
   a)   basic contract terms
      i)   time and place
         A.   obligations to play
         B.   producer to supply venue
      ii)   duration of concert
      iii)   artist to have control over production, presentation and performance
      iv)   capacity of hall
      v)   manner and amount of compensation
         A.   flat fee plus % of net after expenses
         B.   flat fee plus % of gross over fixed amount
         C.   flat fee only
         D.   how payable
            (i)   % or all up front
            (ii)   certified cheque or otherwise
         E.   personal guarantee (if any) other
      vi)   access to books, ticket manifest
      vii)   advertising
         A.   obligation to advertise
         B.   who bears expense
         C.   how concert to be billed
         D.   quality control over ads
         E.   supply of press kits
         F.   act to supply own designs and recordings for ads
         G.   producer do other ads

      vii)   place and time of musicians' rehearsals and access to hall

      viii)   payment of travel costs

      ix)   option for further concerts

      x)   restrictive covenant

             A.   geographic area

             B.   time

      xi)   necessary services

             A.   equipment

             B.   technicians

             C.   ushers, etc.

             D.   security: what requirements

             E.   insurance

      xii)   no-show clause

             A.   on specified events

             B.   return of deposit - yes or no

             C.   arrangements for new concert, if any

      xiii)   musician's right to cancel - failure of producer to fulfil obligations or musician can perform and sue for damages

      xiv)   producer's right to cancel - if tickets sold are less than specified number within a given time, not usually included, but artist may allow

      xv)   musician reserves: right to restrict photos, videos, recording, other

      xvi)   ensure performance rights licence paid

      xvii)   producer to obtain liability insurance

      xviii)   arrangements for merchandising sales

      xix)   producer to comply with local laws, fire regulation, etc. and obtain permits and visas

      xx)   producer to comply with union requirements, e.g. IATSE, AFM, etc.

      xxi)   right to approve opening act

             A.   submission of demo if unknown

             B.   length of band's appearance

             C.   billing compared to star's billing (% of star's billing)

    b)   Additional terms of rider

      i)   special props and lighting

      ii)   limit on complimentary tickets

      iii)   producer to supply notarized ticket manifest

      iv)   no liability of musician for counterfeit tickets

      v)   special services

             A.   stage manager

             B.   power

          C.   stagehands for loading

          D.   sound technicians

          E.   backup musicians

          F.   rental equipment

     vi)   security for band

          A.   before, during and after concert

          B.   backstage

     vii)   band comforts (perks)

          A.   transportation

          B.   food and drink

          C.   dressing rooms

          D.   other

     viii)   arrangements for interviews

     ix)   restrictions on musician's behaviour for example, no smoking, drinking, obscenities, drugs

     x)   promoter not employee of backing musicians hired by artist

  c)   boilerplate

     i)   producer cannot assign rights to the contract

     ii)   not a partnership or joint venture, etc.

     iii)   no liability on artist for failure of producer to fulfill obligations (with agreement to indemnify)

     iv)   withholding tax

     v)   entirety clause

     vi)   requirement that performance not involve

          A.   illegal acts

          B.   contrary to union rules, regulations, by-laws

          C.   contract to be read down to comply with all laws

     vii)   choice of governing law

     viii)   riders are incorporated as part of agreement

3.   Promotion agreement

  a)   if applicable

4.   Outdoor concert/festival

  a)   injunction - "no illegal performance" clause - protect promoter from having to pay if concert enjoined

  b)   Other:

     (i)   insurance

     (ii)   third party liability

     (iii)   cancellations

     (iv)   equipment

APPENDIX 5

RECORDING

1. EXCLUSIVE TERM RECORDING AGREEMENT CHECKLIST*

I. MUSICIAN'S RIGHTS AND OBLIGATIONS

1. Obligations
   a) exclusive recording services
      (i) creation of masters
      (ii) no other contract
      (iii) work-made-for-hire
   b) personality rights
      (i) exclusive during term – but only re: record sales
      (ii) non-exclusive thereafter
      (iii) merchandising rights?
   c) film and video device
      (i) relate to production, manufacturing, distribution, exploitation of recordings
      (ii) minimum commitment - minimum budget
   d) other master recordings
      (i) submit to record company
      (ii) record company to acquire all rights, licences, to use other recordings, videos, etc. recorded prior to the date of the record agreement
   e) re-recording: restriction
      (i) masters
      (ii) permitted uses

2. Options
   a) irrevocable
   b) subject to same terms, or variable per year
   c) automatic - unless notice - 30 days prior to commencement of option date
   d) number
   e) subject to performance obligations of record company, e.g. release commitments

* **Can also be used as a checklist for a record production agreement**

3.   Recordings
    a)   minimum commitment
        (i)   generally 1 LP per contract period
        (ii)   other - e.g., EP's, 12", dance mixes
    b)   prior
        (i)   if company acquires - right to use such recording(s), film, video
    c)   delivery date
        (i)   approvals, consents, licences, permission, sample clearance
        (ii)   ___ months from beginning of contract period
    d)   additional recordings
        (i)   overcall beyond minimum in contract period
        (ii)   on ___ days' notice
    e)   "pay or play"
        (i)   record company final say
        (ii)   complete recording
        (iii) union scale or other advance
    f)   release guarantees
    g)   artistic control
        (i)   choice of producer
        (ii)   material to be recorded
        (iii) quality of recordings
        (iv)   artwork
        (v)   marketing
        (vi)   video
        (vii) choice of singles
        (viii) studio
        (ix)   other

4.   Recording Sessions
    a)   time, place
        (i)   designated by company, or artist, or mutually
        (ii)   who has final decision
    b)   material
        (i)   record company or artist final say re: material to be recorded, producers, support staff, session players, etc. See 3(g), above.
    c)   best efforts
        (i)   musician, e.g., rehearse, take record company's instructions, devote time to promote career, live performance
        (ii)   record company to exploit recordings
    d)   costs - minimum recording budget

i)　　record company pays:
- advances
- under recording contract and publishing contract, if applicable

ii)　delay:
- musician to reimburse company or record company deducts from royalties

5.　Masters
- a)　creation
  - (i)　artist sole featured performer
  - (ii)　quality recording studio
  - (iii)　songs not previously recorded
  - (iv)　company can elect not to accept songs/masters
  - (v)　not > 5 min. = 1 master - subject to definition of master
  - (vi)　no unauthorized dubbing
  - (vii)　moral rights
- b)　quality
  - (i)　technically, artistically, and commercially satisfactory
- c)　multiple LP
  - (i)　not required to accept delivery of all - if do so = 1 LP
- d)　other recordings - not in compliance
- e)　outtakes - who controls release?

6.　Royalties/Advances
- a)　subject to complete performance by musician of all provisions of agreement
- b)　basic Canadian rate
- c)　paid when
- d)　basic U.S. rate
- e)　basic foreign rate
- f)　club rate
- g)　CD rates
- h)　advances: foreign, signing, option, label, tour support, other
- i)　institutional (educational, military) rate
- j)　promotional rate
- k)　special merchandise rate
- l)　flat fee rate
- m)　EP rate
- n)　royalty rate application
- o)　net earned royalty receipts
- p)　wholesale rate
- q)　internet / digital transmissions
- r)　budget, premium, mid-price
- s)　change of royalty calculation method

t) controlled compositions
u) off stage sales
v) other configurations
w) copyright: neighbouring rights, blank levies, mechanicals, synchronizations
x) producer "in" or "out"

7. Computation of Royalties
   a) royalty base
      (i)   retail list price / wholesale / P.P.D. / net receipts
      (ii) royalties on 90% or 100% of records sold
   b) records sold
      (i)   company must be paid
      (ii)   minus returns, credit and exchanges
      (iii) reserves - % - when liquidated?
   c) records not sold
      (i)   bonus, free records, record club
      (ii)   deletes, discontinued recordings
      (iii) promotion - samples, criticism - not for resale, e.g., DJ's, radio, TV, film company, record reviews
      (iv)   records sold as scrap
      (v)   use in transportation carriers
      (vi)   rights to limit
   d) timing
      (i)   generally, semi-annual, or
      (ii) quarterly, regarding mechanicals
   e) packaging deductions, for example, 15% - in record disc form - 20% - reel to reel, tapes, cassettes - 25% - CD's, DAT, other
   f) taxes
   g) recoupment of:
      (i)   recording costs
      (ii)   what % of video costs?
      (iii) other recoupable costs and advances
   h) coupling royalties
      -   royalty rate x $\dfrac{\text{number of masters recorded by Artist}}{\text{total number of masters on LP}}$
   i) joint performance royalties
      -   royalty = $\dfrac{1}{\text{total number of royalty artists}}$ x royalty
   j) foreign
      (i)   computed in foreign currency
      (ii)   paid - receipt by company in Canadian currency minus cost of exchange
      (iii) reduced - subject to royalty payments

        (iv)   blocked currency - deposit into an interest bearing trust deposit

        (v)   notify artist of release

   k)   change to other method

       -     not to reduce artists' share of royalties or times for payment

   l)   videos

   m)   other special recordings

   n)   cross-collateralization

   o)   recoupment

   p)   controlled compositions

   q)   off stage sales

8.   Accounting/Payment/Audit

   a)   generally

        (i)   semi-annual statements

        (ii)   quarterly statement for mechanicals

   b)   content - statement + payment net amount <u>less</u>

        (i)   unrecouped advance and chargeable costs, union, guild payments

        (ii)   royalties in foreign banks

        (iii) packaging deductions

        (iv)   taxes

        (v)   subject to reserves

        (vi)   controlled compositions

   c)   statements binding

        (i)   unless object within specified time

        (ii)   court action - within 1 - 3 years of delivery

   d)   audit

        (i)   who? e.g.- lawyer/accountant

        (ii)   entity not then auditing books of record company

        (iii) extent of rights - timing, right to take extracts, photocopy

9.   Record company's rights in masters

   a)   all intellectual property rights in masters

   b)   outtakes – right to exploit

   c)   use of name and likeness of artist to exploit recordings

   d)   registration - copyright

        (i)   in recordings/masters

        (ii)   deemed employment relationship

        (iii) contract of service - work-made-for-hire

   e)   power of attorney

        (i)   revocable / irrevocable

        (ii)   coupled with an interest

        (iii) lawful attorney-in-fact

          (iv)   limitations - during and after term

    f)   rights - exclusive - worldwide

          (i)   produce, manufacture, distribute, exploit, sell

          (ii)   lease, license, convey, any manner

          (iii)   release under trademark, trade name, label names

          (iv)   authorize performance in public, broadcast

          (vi)   use artist's name - include professional and legal name(s), - exclusive during term, non-exclusive after

          (vi)   coupling - other recordings

          (vii) flat fee, or cent rate basis

          (viii) broadcast, communicate by telecommunication, Internet, digital transmissions

          (ix)   refrain from or permit all of foregoing

    g)   merchandise

          (i)   exclusive during term, non-exclusive thereafter

          (ii)   for full term of contract

          (iii)   engage in or authorize merchandising

          (iv)   % - net receipts

10.   Mechanical and synchronization licences

    a)   company pays copyright owners

    b)   all compositions - not just controlled compositions

    c)   CMRRA/Harry Fox - company as licensee

    d)   controlled composition rate

11.   Neighbouring rights / blank tape levies

    a)   paid directly

    b)   cross-collateralized?

12.   Representations and Warranties

    a)   musician free and clear to perform and execute contract, no disabilities, restrictions, grant all rights

    b)   musician shall do no acts inconsistent with company's rights

    c)   no copyright claims - statutory rights

    d)   no prior unreleased recordings, no contract

    e)   no payment to gain exposure (payola $)

    f)   member of AFM or ACTRA (for example)

    g)   name rights

II.   RECORD COMPANY RIGHTS AND OBLIGATIONS

1.   Term and options
    a)   how many
    b)   suspension
        A.   late masters
        B.   fulfil by delivery
        C.   force majeure
        D.   default and cure
        E.   effect of regarding accounting and royalties
    c)   effect of default
    d)   extension rights
    e)   additional recording obligations
    f)   release and other commitments, e.g. advance payments

2.   Leaving member(s)
    a)   Generally
        (i)   add/replace
        (ii)   notice
        (iii)   designate replacement
        (iv)   right of approval
        (v)   individuals contractually bound
        (vi)   what terms are the same or not
    b)   If group disbands
        (i)   right to terminate contract
        (ii)   right to terminate
        (iii)   options joint and several
        (iv)   substitute contract
        (v)   re-negotiate

3.   Record and video - record and release obligations
    a)   option(s) - subject to minimum release commitments in guaranteed territory or territories
    b)   remain in effect during contract - no waiver
        (i)   audio-visual rights - films, video
        (ii)   union scale applicable
        (iv)   advance or other fees payable

4.   Indemnification
    a)   payment - by artist
    b)   withhold royalties - subject to bond
    c)   notice of claim

5.   Miscellaneous
    a)   (i)   interviews, promo
        (ii)   interviews not to interfere unreasonably with professional commitments of artist

      (iii) personal appearances, radio, TV, etc., promote, publicize, exploit masters

      (iv) no payment unless company receives payment

      (v)   minimum budgets for recordings and video

- b) musician to maintain professional act, live engagements
- c) billing, exclusive recording artist of "XYZ Record Company"
- d) life insurance - paid by company - not recoupable
- e) union - annual payment, compliance
- f) tour support - recoupable
- g) credits

6. Remedies
   - a) cumulative
   - b) restitution - if void - separate contract
   - c) injunction
     - (i) interlocutory
     - (ii) permanent
   - d) any damages
   - e) term - obligations - if violate
   - f) take action in musician's or company's name

7. Breach of contract
   - a) default and cure
   - b) injunctive relief
   - c) waiver

8. General Provisions
   - a) remedies
   - b) breach
   - c) notice
   - d) entirety
   - e) governing law
   - f) confidentiality
   - g) captions/headings
   - h) heirs, assigns
   - i) no partnership
   - j) incorporate by reference other contracts
   - k) definitions
   - l) independent legal advice
   - m) joint/several obligations
   - n) force majeure
   - o) assignment rights
   - p) contracting entities

2. PRODUCER AGREEMENT WITH RECORD COMPANY CHECKLIST

1. Nature of services
   (a) non-exclusive
   (b) independent contractor

2. Functions - subject to record company's approval
   (a) select personnel
   (b) select material to be recorded
   (c) supervise recording sessions
   (d) budget the recording
   (e) take care of all paperwork including union contracts
   (f) control the artistic, technical and commercial standards of the record production
   (g) be responsible for re-recording, re-mixing - if record company is unsatisfied
   (h) edit the recording
   (i) supervise mastering and test pressing
   (j) other: engineer, mix or re-mix
   (k) generally – oversee all aspects of the recording

3. Payment
   (a) lump sum fee, advance
   (b) plus royalty (typically 1-3% of suggested retail list price)
   (c) directly by record company?
   (d) effect of over budget penalty
   (e) when is producer to be paid - after what recoupable costs are recouped? At what rate? e.g. artist's net royalty rate
   (f) *pro rata* formula if producer has not produced all masters on release, subject to "A-Side" protection
   (g) are there royalty escalations?
   (h) Share of advances?:
       (i) upon artist signing record contract
       (ii) foreign
       (iii) other
   (i) off stage sales

4. Credit may be as follows: "producer shall be accorded credit on all album covers, album liners, single labels and in trade ads 1/2 page or greater":
   (a) produced (or co-produced) by —.
   (b) mixed by ———.
   (c) engineered by ———.

5.   Name and likeness -   to promote recordings

6.   Mechanical royalties - record company's responsibility

7.   Representations and Warranties - similar to those in the exclusive recording agreement.

8.   Indemnity

9.   Notice

10.   Delivery dates of masters

11.   Moral rights

12.   Inducement letter

13.   Right to participate in performing or mechanical rights of composer, or neighbouring rights

14.   Video royalties
      (a)   same as master royalties; or
      (b)   otherwise

15.   Definitions

16.   Accounting and audit rights

17.   General Provisions

3.   DISTRIBUTION AGREEMENT CHECKLIST

1.   Other relevant agreements

    a)   security agreement - letter of credit
    b)   trade mark licence agreement - if applicable

2.   Term
    a)   ___ years
    b)   options

3.   Territory

4.   Grant of rights
    a)   usually right to distribute through normal commercial retail channels
    b)   television sales - reserved to record production company
    c)   motion picture uses - reserved to record production company
    d)   consent - other uses
    e)   sound track - lower %
    f)   audio visual rights - pricing programmes
    g)   distributor's right to reject libellous, obscene recordings
    h)   no right to export outside territory, or sell to exporters in territory
    i)   records only, or records and videos
    j)   off stage and Internet sales
    k)   other rights reserved by record production company

5.   Check representations/warranties in recording agreement

6.   No right to alter masters

7.   Advance
    a)   mechanicals
    b)   manufacturing
    c)   other

8.   Trade mark rights - reserved to record production company

9.   Fees
    a)   % charged for distribution
    b)   other chargeable costs, promotion, artwork

10.   Free goods
    a)   limit - usually 10-20% of records shipped

11.   Budget/Economy/Cut outs/Deletes

12. Previous distribution
    a)   record label – cost of honouring returns

13. Record production company responsible for:
    a)   taxes/AFM payments/royalties
    b)   production/manufacture records, videos

14. Name/likeness rights of artist(s) and/or record producer(s) - right to use

15. Termination
    a)   on what grounds
    b)   right to sell off inventory on hand after term

16. Key person
    a)   record production company
    b)   distributor

17. Cross-collateralization of acts on label

18. Reserves
    a)   specify
    b)   typical reserve - 25%

19. General provisions
    a)   accounting and audit
    b)   notice
    c)   other

4.   LICENCE OF RECORD MASTERS CHECKLIST

1.   Grant of rights
   a)   all masters in catalogue vs. specified masters
   b)   exclusive/non-exclusive
   c)   what rights are excluded?
   d)   manufacture, distribute, sell, advertise, perform, broadcast
   e)   use of personality rights of the musician
   f)   cover records
   g)   no t.v. rights
   h)   no export rights
   i)   no edit rights
   j)   other rights reserved

2.   Payment
   a)   advance
   b)   royalties
      (i)   12-16% of suggested retail list price for LPs - range can be higher
      (ii)   singles, other configurations
   c)   currency
   d)   union payments - who pays?
   e)   neighbouring rights
   f)   blank tape levies

3.   Territory

4.   Trade Marks
   a)   quality control
   b)   quality of sample pressings - supply free of charge
   c)   ownership by licensor - licensee no ownership
   d)   supply label information
   e)   reproduction - supervise quality
   f)   approval of artist - if required

5.   Coupling/joint performances
   a)   allowed? - if so specify how paid and exercised

6.   Copyright clearances
   a)   mechanical and synchronization or other licences – who pays? – generally licensee
   b)   % of copies of records sold; industry or statutory note – basis for payment

7.   Term/Option(s)
   a)   3 - 7 years - could be longer
   b)   subject to minimum release commitment(s)
   c)   right of first refusal for further recordings

      d)   sell off rights regarding inventory post term - usually 6 months

8.   Accounting/Audit
      a)   usually every 3 - 6 months
      b)   reserves
          (i)   specify
          (ii) liquidate
      c)   extent of audit rights
      d)   content and timing of statements

9.   Customs/Taxes
      a)   duty
      b)   shipment
      c)   tax
      d)   deduct
      e)   withhold

10.   Termination of rights:
      a)   failure to pay royalties
      b)   failure to pay advance
      c)   failure to meet contract requirements - e.g. release commitment
      d)   bankruptcy
      e)   fail to account or allow an audit
      f)   default and cure

11.   Representations/Warranties/Indemnity
      a)   licensor
      b)   licensee

12.   General Provisions
      a)   governing law
      b)   non-assignment
      c)   notice
      d)   other

5. LABELLING, CREDIT AND NOTICES ON RECORDINGS CHECKLIST

1. Surface Areas:
   a) outside cover
   b) inside cover
   c) actual record label

2. Copyright Notices
   a) Generally, the sound recording(s) and all works which are part of the sound recording(s) such as:
      (i) artwork;
      (ii) record cover;
      (iii) record label;
      (iv) photographs;
      (v) lyrics;
      (vi) title;
   b) Legal basis
      (i) *Berne Convention* - copyright notice advisable, but not required.
      (ii) *Universal Copyright Convention* - copyright notice advisable, but not required.
      (iii) *Buenos Aires Convention* - "All Rights Reserved".
   (c) Contents of notice:
      (i) "P" - sound recordings
      "C" – artistic works, plus
      (ii) copyright owner's name;
      (iii) year of first publication.

3. Trademarks and trade names:
   a) Generally
   Numerous trademark and trade names are included on recordings.
   b) Legal basis
      (i) For Canada, notice is not required, but advisable.
      (ii) For the U.S., notice is not required, but advisable.
   c) Contents
      (i) If registered in the U.S. Patents Office - 'R' with a circle in the middle,
      (ii) or in the case of a trademark which is not yet registered, the letters T.M., plus
      (iii) trademark owner's name
      (iv) year of publication

4. Credit
    a)   Generally, the legal requirement to give credit for recordings arises these ways:
        (i)   by contract – especially record producer agreements;
        (ii)   by implied contractual rights;
        (iii) moral rights;
        (iv) by custom;
        (v)   by case law.
    b)   Contents
        (i)   Generally
        (ii)   determined by 3 a) (i-v), above

5. *Consumer Packaging & Labelling Act* requirements
For labels on recordings, the information required is as follows:
    a)   Identity
        (i)   the identity and address of the entity by or for whom the recording was manufactured.
        (ii)   must be 1/16 of an inch high and legible.
    b)   Language
        (i)   only one official language is required (English or French).
        (ii)   to be placed on the cover of the recording
        (iii) in ordinarily legible manner of writing.
    c)   Foreign records
        •   The cover of a foreign recording must indicate it was only imported for a named distributor if:
        (i)   the Canadian distributor is named on the cover;
        (ii)   if the geographic origin of the album is stated on the cover; otherwise, it is not necessary to use the wording "imported for";
        (iii) if the record cover was made in a place different from the actual recording then this must be stated as well.

6. Industry notices:
Various other notices which are not legally required, include:
    a)   (i)   Juno Awards sticker or
        (ii)   other stickers which include notice of hit single or featured artist
    b)   The RPM MAPL logo:
        (i)   Consists of - a circle with the letters MAPL in the four sectors in the circle.

(ii)   MAPL logo indicates:

      M -   music composed by a Canadian;

      A -   the music or lyrics are principally performed by a Canadian;

      P -   production: (A)   is wholly recorded in Canada or

                     (B)   is performed wholly in Canada and broadcast live in Canada;

      L -   lyrics were written by a Canadian.

(iii)   Use - this logo is to be used in its original size and only with record titles.

c)   Bar coding and digital, stereo or mono codings.

d)   Warning stickers - for potentially obscene recordings - CRIA's Guideline - "Explicit Lyrics - Parental Advisory"

e)   SOCAN, NRCC, or other performing or collective rights society

6.   MASTER PURCHASE/SALE AGREEMENT CHECKLIST*

1.   Grant of rights
   a)   all right/title/interest to which master(s), inventory, agreements, rights and benefits accruing
   b)   deliver all reproduction rights, privileges, assignments
   c)   is musician's consent required?
   d)   renewal and reversion rights

2.   Evaluation
   a)   unrecouped advance(s)
   b)   agreements in force – effect of restrictive covenants
   c)   unpaid royalties
   d)   reversion of copyrights
   e)   litigation and copyright infringement actions
   f)   future plans for exploitation
   g)   employee contracts
   h)   examine chain of copyright title
   i)   examine all assignments, licences
        and other agreements in force
   j)   accounting
   k)   mortgages, liens, encumbrances
   l)   advances - unrecouped
   m)   key person
   n)   other sale of business considerations (*Bulk Sales Act*, etc.)

3.   Payment
   a)   royalty - % override and/or
   b)   periodic vs. lump sum payment(s)
   c)   union payments
   d)   other

4.   Seller's representations/warranties/indemnity
   a)   exclusive owner - entire right, title, interest
   b)   of all or specified masters
   c)   compliance with rules, regulations of AFM and other unions
   d)   right to authorize to enter into and perform contract
   e)   no claims, liens, encumbrances outstanding
   f)   musicians, producers and other parties paid
   g)   cost, expenses, legal
   h)   withhold royalties
   i)   no lawsuit, claims or other liabilities

*   **See also Sale of Music Publishing Catalogue Checklist and Master Use Licence Agreement Checklist.**

    j)   capacity to contract - especially if minors

    k)   survival - after sale

5.   Tax implications

    a)   share purchase, or

    b)   asset purchase

6.   Notify

    a)   artists - is consent required?

    b)   other - relevant parties

    c)   re: agreements in force

7.   General Provisions

    a)   governing law

    b)   entirety

    c)   other

7.   MUSIC VIDEO PRODUCTION AGREEMENT CHECKLIST

1.   Video producer's obligations
   a)   delivery of script, story board prior to photography
   b)   delivery date of finished video
   c)   video to be broadcast quality
   d)   obtain clearances, releases, licenses and all rights required to make the video including copyrights and moral rights except those supplied by record company
   e)   to comply with insurance and AFM and other union obligations
   f)   responsible for all costs, taxes, insurance, union payments, etc.

2.   Main aspects of the agreement
   a)   specify length of video
   b)   song performed - which version
   c)   musician performing
   d)   producer
   e)   director
   f)   date photography is to begin and end
   g)   format (16mm/35mm/video)
   h)   location of filming/video taping

3.   Grant of rights
   a)   usually a work-for-hire or deemed assignment
   b)   definition of video, includes all elements of finished product and all work in progress including negatives and prints, etc.

4.   Record company rights
   a)   to approve script, story board
   b)   to approve all aspects of pre and post production
   c)   to approve the final video
   d)   to edit, change video - subject to rights of director or video producer, if any, to make first changes of video producer.
   e)   right to use name and likeness of the video producer
   f)   consultation rights with director and producer
   g)   to be paid damages in order to ensure timely delivery

5.   Fee
   a)   usually flat fee for services as follows:
      (i)   % on signing agreement
      (ii)   % on delivery of script
      (iii)   % on acceptance of final video
      (iv)   % on completed video
   b)   whether or not director or producer participates in video or record sales or other royalties - subject to negotiation

6. Insurance
    a)   minimum insurance obligations
    b)   video producer to obtain

7. General Provisions
    a)   representations and warranties
    b)   indemnity
    c)   no partnership
    d)   injunctive relief
    e)   union requirements
    f)   accounting and audit

8.   MASTER USE LICENCE CHECKLIST

1. Grant of rights
   a) all right/title/interest
      (i) exhibit, distribute, exploit
      (ii) worldwide
      (iii) usually non-exclusive
   b) reproduction – extent of rights, privileges
   c) notice to and consent of artist - moral rights
   d) sound track rights - yes or no
   e) use in trailers, ads, promotion
   f) name, likeness and biographical material of artist
   g) uses: free TV, cable, pay TV, C.A.T.V., home use, video cassettes.
   h) term:
      (i) specified, or
      (ii) perpetual

2. Payment
   a) royalty - % of recordings sold and paid for
   b) lump sum
   c) re-use fees
   d) timing – usually semi-annual

3. Credit
   a) recording musician
   b) recording company

4. Representations and Warranties
   a) Licensor
      (i) exclusive owner - all masters
      (ii) all right, title, interest
   b) Licensee
      (i) comply with rules, regulations of AFM and other unions, obtain clearances, union and publisher
      (ii) right to enter into and perform contract
      (iii) re: title usage
      (iv) no claims
      (v) artists paid

5. Indemnification

6. General Provisions
   a) governing law
   b) accounting and audit
   c) other

APPENDIX 6

MERCHANDISING

1.   ENDORSEMENT AGREEMENT CHECKLIST

1.   Grant of rights
   a)   extent of use of name, likeness, etc.
   b)   revocable/irrevocable
   c)   exclusive/non-exclusive
   d)   term
   e)   territory
   f)   promotional commitment
   g)   affidavit of use

2.   Payment
   a)   advance
       (i)   on signing
       (ii)   other
   b)   % royalty, or
   c)   fee - union scale, or above

3.   Quality control
   a)   labelling
   b)   standards
   c)   approval
       (i)   musician
       (ii)   where advertised
       (iii)   credit and billing
   d)   right to approve or reject promotional material, photographs, etc.
   e)   samples

4.   Termination
   a)   dispose of inventory
   b)   sell off period for remaining merchandise

5.   Accounting/Audit
   a)   statements
       (i)   quarterly/semi-annual, other

(ii)   contents - returns, bad debts
(iii) time to object
b)   examine books
c)   take extracts, photocopy
d)   extent of audit rights

6.   Indemnification of musician
a)   product liability insurance
b)   for what breaches

7.   Morals Clause
a)   right to terminate if breached

8.   General Provisions
a)   governing law
b)   entirety
c)   non-assignment of rights
d)   other

2.　**MERCHANDISING LICENCE CHECKLIST**

1.　Grant of Rights
　　a)　no assignment or sub-licence rights
　　b)　what is granted - restrictions on use(s)
　　c)　term, time, territory
　　d)　limitations, for example, no resale
　　e)　exclusive/non-exclusive
　　f)　definition of licensed property, products - depends on whether mail order, concert venue or retail agreement
　　g)　reserved rights
　　h)　subject to licensee's obligations regarding:
　　　　(i)　advertising
　　　　(ii)　marketing
　　　　(iii)　trade mark and copyright protection

2.　Term/Extensions
　　a)　initial term
　　b)　renewals
　　c)　options

3.　Compensation
　　a)　royalty rate
　　　　(i)　% net or gross sales - depends on type of sale
　　　　(ii)　% - escalate based on increased sales
　　b)　minimum advance
　　c)　statements
　　d)　currency

4.　Indemnification
　　a)　product liability insurance - specify amount
　　b)　licensee indemnify licensor against any claims
　　c)　release of licensor liability

5.　Goodwill / Trademarks
　　a)　quality control - "high standard" - define sample submission
　　b)　subject to periodic examination of merchandise by licensor
　　c)　trademark protection rights

6.　Labelling
　　a)　trademarks and copyright notice(s)
　　b)　comply with *Consumer Labelling and Packaging Act*
　　c)　other

7.　Promotional material
　　a)　product subject to licensor's approval in writing
　　b)　is the property of licensor
　　c)　limitation on free goods

8. Distribution
    a) no competitive product
    b) obligation to distribute - where, how, etc.

9. Accounting and Audit
    a) inspection
    b) statements - contents - time to object
    c) right to take extracts, photocopy
    d) extent of audit rights

10. Concert Sales
    a) What will licensor provide?
        (i)   transportation crew, merchandise
        (ii)   sales people at venues with merchandise
        (iii) food, hotel?
    b) What will merchandiser provide?
        (i)   e.g., crew person for light duties - not to interfere with merchandising

11. General Provisions
    a) bankruptcy - n.b. - right to return of goods immediately
    b) on termination
        (i)   dispose of merchandise on hand, or
        (ii)   right to purchase
    c) legal remedies
    d) relationship - no joint venture, agency, partnership
    e) entirety
    f) governing law
    g) representations and warranties
    h) arbitration
    i) blocked currency

APPENDIX 7

BUSINESS

1. **MUSICAL GROUP PARTNERSHIP AGREEMENT CHECKLIST**

1. Purpose
   Should be defined clearly and may include:
   a) recording and exploiting recordings
   b) performances, personal appearances
   c) merchandising
   d) publishing

2. Responsibilities
   a) refrain from moonlighting
   b) non-competition
   c) participating in the management direction of the group
   d) fulfilling obligations under the partnership agreement

3. Contributions
   a) Monetary contributions - how recouped?
   b) assets - specify
      (i) Rights to the group name - what happens when: leaving member, dissolution of the partnership, death or incapacity of a group member.
      (ii) Copyrights to be an asset of the partnership? If so, a separate publishing agreement governing this should be set up.
      (iii) Insurance
   c) Insurance
      (i) disability insurance,
      (ii) musical equipment insurance,
      (iii) third party liability insurance,
      (iv) other
   d) Equipment
      (i) What equipment is owned by the partnership? e.g., a sound system may be owned by the partnership.
      (ii) What is owned by the individuals?
   e) Share of Profits
      (i) determination of net profits or net income
      (ii) ordinarily profits - split equally and *pro rata*
      (iii) depending on the source of income and agreement,

profit sharing may vary.

4.   Group Member Provisions
      a)   leaving members
      b)   adding new members
      c)   temporarily substituting new members for old members
      d)   buying out members
      e)   death
      f)   disability of members
      g)   mental incapacity
      h)   an order under family law legislation

      In view of the above:
      (i)   notice of expulsion, termination or buy-out
             mechanism should be expressly set out.
      (ii)   impact of family law - whether or not members are
             required to enter into a domestic agreement.

5.   Dissolution
      a)   events triggering dissolution.
      b)   ordinarily death, insolvency, charged on a partner's share
            could not dissolve the partnership.

6.   Liabilities
      a)   third party liabilities should be considered and addressed in
            the agreement.

7.   Termination
      a)   how can the agreement be terminated?
      b)   effect of termination concerning:
            (i)   the partnership name
            (ii)   existing agreements such as record, music publishing,
                   merchandising and live performance agreements
            (iii) assets of the partnership

8.   General Provisions
      a)   accounting and audit
      b)   representations and warranties
      c)   minors
      d)   arbitration
      e)   amendment of the agreement
      f)   adequate powers for management committee
      g)   location of head office
      h)   other

2.   AGREEMENT FOR MUSICIAN'S SERVICES CHECKLIST*

1.   Parties
   a)   sole proprietor, partnership, corporation
   b)   independent contractors vs. employee tax deductions
   c)   subject to management direction of the group

2.   Services - could include:
   a)   live performance only
   b)   recording
   c)   merchandising - extent of use of personality rights
   d)   songwriting - who owns copyright to songs written?
   e)   personal appearances in videos, films
   f)   exclusive or non-exclusive

3.   Term
   a)   fixed term, or
   b)   co-terminus with recording agreement

4.   Compensation
   a)   payment
       (i)   weekly
       (ii)   monthly
       (iii)   other
   b)   royalties - same basis as group
   c)   accumulation of fees and royalties
   d)   share of advances?
   e)   what sources of revenue - depends on services performed as outlined in 2., above
   f)   union scale or otherwise

5.   Termination
   a)   grounds for termination
       (i)   with cause
       (ii)   without cause

6.   General Provisions
   a)   injunctive relief
       (i)   morals clause
       (ii)   breach of agreement
   b)   indemnity
   c)   restrictive covenants
   d)   insurance
   e)   accounting/audit rights
   f)   assignment rights to corporation
   g)   GST and other tax implications

*   **See also partnership agreement checklist for other considerations that may be relevant to this agreement.**

INDEX